955
WE

Wells, Tim

444 days

444 DAYS

444 DAYS

The Hostages Remember

Tim Wells

HARCOURT BRACE JOVANOVICH, PUBLISHERS
San Diego   New York   London

Requests for permission to make copies of any part of the work should be
mailed to: Permissions, Harcourt Brace Jovanovich, Publishers,
Orlando, Florida 32887.

Library of Congress Cataloging in Publication Data

Wells, Tim.
  444 days.

  Includes index.
  1. Iran Hostage Crisis, 1979–1981—Personal
narratives. I. Title. II. Title: Four hundred forty-four days.
E183.8.I7W45 1985   955.054   85–10038
ISBN 0-15-132803-X

Designed by Francesca M. Smith
Printed in the United States of America

First edition
A B C D E

For Mom, Dad, and Jen

Contents

Map   viii

Foreword   ix

Part One: Iran   1

Part Two: November 4, 1979   31

Part Three: The First Month   97

Part Four: December 1979   177

Part Five: In Hiding with the Canadians   217

Part Six: Waiting   241

Part Seven: Dispersal   299

Part Eight: Prison   355

Part Nine: Liberation   405

Index   457

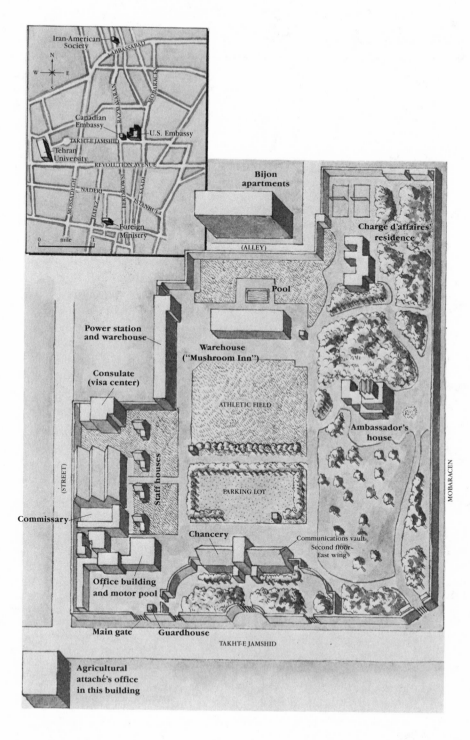

Iran-American Society

ABBASSABAD

N
W · E
S

RAZM ARARAN

MOBARACEN

Canadian Embassy

U.S. Embassy

TAKHT-E JAMSHID

Tehran University

REVOLUTION AVENUE

MOSSADEGH

NADERI

HAFEZ

FERDOWSI

SAADI

ISTANBUL

Foreign Ministry

0   mile   1

Bijon apartments

(ALLEY)

Charge d'affaires' residence

Pool

Power station and warehouse

Warehouse ("Mushroom Inn")

Consulate (visa center)

ATHLETIC FIELD

Ambassador's house

Staff houses

PARKING LOT

Commissary

Chancery

Communications vault
Second floor—
East wing

Office building and motor pool

Main gate   Guardhouse

TAKHT-E JAMSHID

MOBARACEN

Agricultural attaché's office in this building

Foreword

THE IRANIAN HOSTAGE crisis was probably the most publicized and yet unknown event in American history. For the entire time the hostages were held, news from Tehran dominated headlines and images from Iran flickered across our television screens. Those images remain vivid today: armed terrorists parading blindfolded Americans across the embassy compound; huge mobs chanting anti-American slogans in front of the embassy; President Carter and the shah of Iran being burned in effigy; Ayatollah Khomeini addressing the multitudes from his balcony in Qöm; Sadegh Ghotbzadeh briefing the press; the wreckage from the rescue mission at Desert One. In spite of the steady stream of publicity, precious little was known about the actual circumstances of the hostages' captivity. Most of the information received by the American public was based on speculation, rumor, and the militants' own propaganda. Hard facts simply did not exist. After the failure of the rescue mission in April, we didn't even know where the hostages were being kept.

When they were finally released in January of 1981, the hostages returned to a whirlwind of publicity that was followed by relative silence. As a consequence, popular perceptions about the treatment of the hostages are based almost entirely on journalistic accounts that have done as much to distort as to reveal the actual conditions of their captivity. As a group, the hostages feel that much of what has been written about them in the popular press is neither accurate nor truthful, and many resent the way they have been treated by the news media. One hostage explained, "It didn't take me long to learn that the media have no soul. All they wanted were the most sensational aspects of the story. That led to a lot of exaggerated commentary when we were released."

This oral history is an attempt to redress that grievance. In order to obtain accurate first-person accounts of the captivity, I have spent the past 2½ years talking with the former hostages. In the process I traveled over twenty thousand miles and gathered in excess of five thousand pages of interview transcript. Throughout every step of the endeavor my guiding concept has been to provide an opportunity for the hostages to describe their experiences and to have those experiences transcribed into a narrative framework. What follows is the result of that effort.

I am deeply indebted to numerous individuals without whose assistance this book could not have been written. First and foremost are the people whose memories appear in this volume. They willingly invited a stranger into their homes, opened their hearts, and patiently spent hour after hour answering questions. It should be noted that they gave freely of their time and have not received any financial compensation. In recognition of their efforts a charitable contribution is being made to a nonprofit organization designed to benefit families of Americans who died in the course of public service, including persons who died in the 1980 Iranian rescue mission and persons who died in the 1983 bombing of the American embassy in Beirut, Lebanon.

I would also like to thank those former hostages and members of their families who allowed themselves to be interviewed but whose stories do not appear in this book. Their insights and experiences have not been lost. All of the interviews were recorded on cassette tape, and in order to insure that the entire record remains complete, all of the recordings, along with verbatim transcripts, are being housed at Perkins Library on the campus of Duke University, where they will be made available to scholars, historians, and interested persons.

I was blessed with two readers, Chris Riggall and Michael Riggall, who offered suggestions for improvement while the manuscript was in progress. They gave generously of their time whenever it was requested—usually on extremely short notice a few days before a rapidly approaching deadline. In the early stages of the project, Sharon Gray assisted with typing and organizational chores, while David Pursiano helped with logistics, transportation, enthusiasm, and goodwill. Winnie Kelly Holbrooke offered much needed professional advice and was a source of morale and support.

Those who provided me with food and shelter during my many months on the road include Col. Charles Scott and his wife, Katherine, Joe and Cheri Hall, Bill and Angela Belk, Maggie and Clyde McClellan, Kevin Hermening, Cort Barnes, Tram Turner, Jim Perry, Andrea Sanford, Charles Ingebretson, David Pursiano, Terry Reagan, Chris Riggall, Butch Smith; Melanie, Alex, and Laurel; and Sarah, Tom, Peter, Teresa, and little Timothy Wilson, whose birth coincided with a research trip to the West Coast.

A special word of thanks is owed to Dr. Ole R. Holsti of Duke University, whose encouragement, advice, and assistance were extremely helpful, and to Doris Betts of the University of North Carolina for pointing me down the road.

Last but not least is my editor, Donald Knox, who is undoubtedly the best editor any writer has ever had the pleasure of working with. His extremely capable assistant, Naomi Grady, has also earned a special place in my heart.

Tim Wells
Asheville, North Carolina
April 1985

Part One

Iran

1 Revolution

ALL AMERICAN PRESIDENTS, dating from the administration of President Truman, considered Mohammed Reza Pahlavi, the shah of Iran, to be a strong ally whose friendship was vital to American interests in the Persian Gulf. In order to reaffirm America's traditionally close relations with Iran, President Carter received the shah at the White House on November 15, 1977. That morning, several hundred Iranian demonstrators gathered near the White House, where they waved placards and shouted antishah slogans. A few scuffles erupted, and the police used tear gas to disperse the mob. President Carter later recalled: "On the south lawn of the White House, I stood and wept. . . . Unfortunately, an ill wind seemed to have been blowing directly toward us as we greeted the leader of Iran, and the gas fumes engulfed us all."*

Forty-six days later, on December 31, 1977, President Carter met with the shah at Niyavaran Palace in Tehran. No demonstrators were present, and the shah appeared to be in complete control. He commanded an army of more than 400,000 men, had loyal secret police and gendarmerie organizations, and his government exercised strict control over the press. At a dinner banquet in the shah's palace, President Carter toasted the Iranian monarch, saying: "Iran, because of the great leadership of the Shah, is an island of stability in one of the most troubled areas of the world. This is a great tribute to you, Your Majesty, and to your leadership and to the respect and the admiration and love which your people give you."†

At the time President Carter was toasting the shah, Ayatollah Ruhollah Khomeini was living in Najaf, Iraq. He had been exiled by the shah in 1964 for his participation in antigovernment demonstrations, and had not set foot in Iran during the intervening thirteen years. In spite of his exile, Khomeini managed to maintain contact with a network of Iranian religious leaders, students, and political activists. He frequently lectured clerics and students visiting Najaf on the need for revolution. Many of his lectures were recorded on cassette tapes, and these tapes, along with the ayatollah's writings, were surreptitiously distributed throughout Iran. In 1977, Khomeini's son was killed, presumably by the shah's secret police (SAVAK), for his participation in

---

* James Earl Carter, *Keeping Faith: Memoirs of a President* (New York: Bantam Books, 1982), p. 433.
† Pierre Salinger, *America Held Hostage* (New York: Doubleday & Co., Inc., 1981), p. 4.

revolutionary activity. Khomeini publicly blamed the shah for the murder of his son and vowed revenge. His call to revolution was strident and unyielding. He accused the shah of being "a traitor to Islam," and charged that the sons of God were being imprisoned and murdered by SAVAK while the shah engaged in the "animal pleasures of the West." It was the duty of all Moslems, Khomeini preached, to see that this "germ of corruption" was stamped out. The monarchy must be smashed.

One week after President Carter's New Year's Eve visit to Tehran, the first revolutionary demonstrations broke out in Iran. On January 7, 1978, an article entitled "Iran and the Red and Black Imperialism" appeared in the newspaper *Etteláat*. It accused Khomeini of engaging in homosexual activity and of conspiring with foreign communist powers to destroy Iran. The article had been drafted by the shah's former prime minister and was published at the shah's insistence. In Qöm, seminary students reacted to the accusations against Khomeini's character by taking to the streets in protest. Two days later, in an attempt to quell this unrest, government troops fired into a crowd. Six demonstrators fell dead. In the weeks that followed a series of mourning ceremonies were held throughout Iran. These public mournings frequently developed into massive demonstrations and riots.

As the cycle of revolutionary violence began to unfold, none of the Americans who tell their stories in the pages that follow had any inkling that the events taking place in Iran would interrupt and forever alter the course of their lives.

COL. LELAND HOLLAND (*army attaché*): There's an interesting story about Khomeini. Back in the early 1960s he was nothing more than a backwoods mullah, a back-street padre, and he achieved his first notoriety when the United States sent our first military advisory group over to Iran in 1964. At this time, our military personnel wanted diplomatic immunity, so that American military advisors would not be subject to Iranian law, but to American law. This is a common practice all over the world, and was something that the shah agreed to do. But the Moslem clergy was opposed to granting immunity for American personnel, and Khomeini was in the forefront of the protests that surrounded this issue. He led several demonstrations, and in his speeches he told the Iranian people that this law meant that if an American colonel was to drive over someone's wife, nothing would be done to the colonel. Conversely, if an Iranian ran over the colonel's dog, then the Iranian would be prosecuted. There were several demonstrations and protests in which Khomeini was involved, and finally the shah cracked down and had the religious leaders locked up. They threw a whole calaboose full of ayatollahs and mullahs in prison. Khomeini was a mullah at this time, and the word was that he was going to be shot for his part in all of these disturbances. The only thing that saved him is that there was an unwritten law in Iran that an ayatollah is never executed. The shah would lock them up, but would never have one shot. In this prison with Khomeini there were four or five ayatollahs, and they held a secret conclave and elevated Khomeini to ayatollah status. That was how he became an ayatollah. Subsequently, the shah had him exiled instead of shot. The shah didn't have the guts to go ahead and shoot Khomeini back in 1964 when he had the chance. That was a decision that would come back to haunt him.

JOHN LIMBERT (*political officer*): I first went to Iran in 1964 with the Peace Corps. I was in a small town, and found a great deal of personal warmth and friendship. The people were always very friendly, in spite of the fact that on a political level many Iranians were hostile to the United States. In the summer of 1965 I can remember listening to the radio in Iran and hearing President Johnson talk about his decision to send troops to Vietnam. Many Iranians were upset by what we were doing in Vietnam. In general, I remember that a lot of Iranians were hostile toward American policy in the Third World.

Then in 1968 I went back to Iran. I taught at a university in Shiraz, and I noticed a tangible current of uneasiness among the university students. It wasn't anything that was expressed openly, but it was very much there. On the surface everything was very orderly and peaceful, certainly the monarchy seemed secure, but if you talked to the students you got a very different impression. There was this confused and smoldering resentment.

Most of the students I had contact with were from small towns. Many of them were from the little provincial cities around Shiraz. These were very conservative towns. The students came to the university and found that the rather humanistic set of values the university taught clashed with their own hometown, family, and religious values. They reacted in a number of different ways, sometimes violently. For example, there was an arts festival in Shiraz, and a modern dance performance was put on for the queen. The next evening the same dances were performed for the university students, and this precipitated a full-scale riot. To the students, modern dance was a manifestation of something alien. They didn't know much about it, but whatever it was, they didn't like it. They were going to stop it. The fact that it had been performed the night before in front of the queen increased the resentment—a resentment that only expressed itself in indirect and unusual ways. But it was very much there. It was a resentment that was not visible to most outside observers, and it was manifesting itself at a time when Iran was considered very secure politically, and very peaceful.

I can remember talking about it with a fellow by the name of Malcolm Butler, who was then the American vice-consul in Khorramshahr. We had dinner together one night and I mentioned some of these things to him. What I was talking about seemed to be beyond the scope of any kind of information that he had received. His terms of information were more along the lines of: the shah's regime is very strong, it has the army, it has tanks and machine guns, and it has SAVAK. Given the amount of unnoticed resentment that existed, it just didn't seem to me that the possession of machine guns was necessarily going to be an insurance policy for the Pahlavi regime. The only thing I could think of to say was, "Yes, but what happens when the man with the machine gun refuses to fire?"

COL. LELAND HOLLAND (*army attaché*): In November of 1978, there were demonstrations and riots all over Iran. The British embassy was attacked, and the revolutionaries burned 353 branches of the Iranian National Bank. Martial law was declared. That night Ambassador Sullivan* and the British ambassador went to see the shah. In essence, the shah told them: "Now the revolutionaries have played into my hands. They've given me an excuse to declare martial law, and we'll flood the city with tanks. We will force the situation on them." The Iranian military had 1,000 Chieftain tanks in their inventory and 400 American M-47s. Those tanks are awesome in combat, but they're not designed for revolutionary street fighting. That night I made the remark: "Sooner or later the militants will figure out those tanks are vulnerable. They'll crack a bottle of gasoline over the engine and set them on fire. Once the militants figure out how to do that, it will be time for Act III."

BARRY ROSEN (*press attaché*): When I arrived in Iran, I could see that four of the five banks on Takht-e Jamshid† had been destroyed. The street was strewn with glass, and the entire area looked like an absolute wreck. Everywhere on the avenue I heard, "*Marg bar Shah! Marg bar Shah!* (Death to the Shah! Death to the Shah!)" And I saw antishah slogans painted on the buildings. It was all very odd, because the buildings and businesses on Takht-e Jamshid were all new—but at the same time they looked tawdry and bleak.

---

* William Sullivan was the American ambassador to Iran from June 1977 through April 1979.
† Takht-e Jamshid is a major avenue in Tehran that passed directly in front of the American embassy.

The next morning I walked out of my hotel. I could hear shots being fired in the city and see tanks moving around in the street. This was only a few days after the November 4, 1978, student riot and the November 5 student bombing. It was obvious that the revolution was on its way. There had been riots in Iran prior to this with Mossadeq* in 1953, and with Khomeini in 1963, but there had never been anything as long and difficult as this. I knew that the shah was finished. He was already going, going, gone. It was only a question of time.

COL. THOMAS SCHAEFER (*defense attaché*): By November of 1978 there was no way that revolution was going to be turned around. I don't think there was anything that the United States or the Iranian military could have done. Events had progressed too far down the road, and there was dissent within the Iranian military. Some of the enlisted troops would not obey their commanders, and we knew there was sabotage going on in the air force. Disgruntled *homofars*† were purposely cutting hydraulic lines on aircraft, and things of that nature. Soldiers would disobey their officers, or run off to join the demonstrators. So there was very little that the Iranian military could have done.

BARRY ROSEN (*press attaché*): The entire country was falling apart. The shah had absolutely no support. There were demonstrations all over Tehran. Everyone in Iran had one desire, and that was to see the end of the Pahlavi dynasty. A lot of people didn't know what they wanted after the Pahlavi dynasty, but they sure did want to see it end. It was a revolution that included every political and religious spectrum in the entire country—the left, the right, and the center all wanted to see the shah go.

Even though martial law had been declared, one could hear *"Marg bar Shah! Marg bar Shah!"* throughout the evening and on into the night. Martial law was totally ineffective.

---

* Mohammed Mossadeq served as Iran's prime minister in 1953. His government was overthrown in a CIA-backed coup that returned the shah to the throne after a brief period of exile.
† Iranian air force technicians responsible for the maintenance of Iranian aircraft.

2 February 14, 1979

ON JANUARY 16, 1979, the shah left Iran and went into permanent exile. One of his final acts as chief of state was to appoint Shapour Bakhtiar prime minister. In the days that followed, Bakhtiar tried to establish a government capable of functioning in the absence of the monarchy, but met with little success. The new prime minister had virtually no popular support, and thousands of desertions continued to plague Iran's armed forces. On January 31, 1979, Ayatollah Khomeini returned to Iran, and enormous crowds pledged their support to him. Shortly thereafter Khomeini appointed his own revolutionary government. However, certain factions within the Iranian military remained loyal to Bakhtiar. The situation came to a head on February 9, 1979, at Doshen Tappeh Air Force Base. Inside the base, a group of air force technicians began an antigovernment uprising. Reinforcements were called in to restore order, and a firefight ensued. Armed revolutionaries rushed to the air force base to aid the pro-Khomeini technicians. After three days of fighting at two military bases, the Iranian army withdrew its support from the Bakhtiar government. Bakhtiar went into immediate hiding, and all of Iran's military troops were recalled from the various positions they had been protecting in Tehran, including the American embassy.

The collapse of the military represented the end of formal authority in Iran. Total chaos followed. Street fighting broke out in all the major cities as a massive wave of killing engulfed the entire country. Revolutionaries yearning for blood justice went to work settling old scores. Former government officials, SAVAK agents, policemen, members of the military, and civilians accused of "crimes against the revolution" were massacred. Armed revolutionary *komiteh*s (committees) patrolled the streets and arrested people at will. In the name of the revolution these neighborhood gangs confiscated property, organized show trials, carried out executions, and proclaimed their loyalty to a variety of religious leaders and political factions. The death toll reached well into the thousands. It was in this hysterical atmosphere that Khomeini's Provisional Government of Iran, headed by Prime Minister Mehdi Bazargan, seized the offices of state and tried to establish some semblance of order.

COL. LELAND HOLLAND (*army attaché*): Under the shah, nobody had a gun. You were forbidden to own one. Only the military and the police had guns. But when the revolution came, the Iranian armories were cracked open and guns and bullets were passed out to the population at large. Under the shah the Iranians had a great war-making machine. They legally reproduced the G-3, the German army rifle, and they made copies of Russian PRG SA-7 bazooka-type missiles. They were very good at weapons production. So when the armories were cracked, a huge number of guns and lots of ammunition hit the street in a hurry.

COL. THOMAS SCHAEFER (*defense attaché*): There were many harrowing experiences. Just driving to work could be an adventure. As a security precaution I varied the routes I took to the embassy, and the time of day I left my house. But there were still three or four incidents that took place. Once I came up the road and saw that it was blocked by a bunch of Iranians who had big clubs and hunks of wood in their hands. The driver did a quick 180 to get out of there. Then on another occasion somebody threw a firebomb at my car. A big woof of flame hit the trunk, but the bomb didn't detonate. Fortunately, it was just a fast burn instead of an explosion. So it got to be a very tough environment to live in.

COL. LELAND HOLLAND (*army attaché*): My family had been evacuated out of the country. In early February I started to camp at the embassy. It wasn't safe to walk up the streets to my house. There was a curfew that began at eight or nine o'clock in the evening. So I slept on the couch in my office. Occasionally I would send an embassy driver up to my house with my dirty uniforms and have him bring back some clean ones. Iran had become a very chaotic place. Armed bands of *komitehs* and revolutionary guards were roaming the streets. There was no law, no order, and no respect for authority. It just kept getting rougher and rougher. I was shot at near the embassy gate, which is a hell of a thing to happen to you. Every day it was getting more and more like Vietnam.

After the military units were recalled, the embassy went without protection for several days. We didn't have any Iranian security forces on duty. So the embassy was a fat target. We had a feeling that we were going to be tested.

I knew we might need help, so I started calling a bunch of old numbers, trying to find somebody who could give me an idea of what to do if we had trouble. You know, if we had a fire, I wanted to know how to get a fireman. Finally I managed to get hold of this guy who had been a general in the Iranian police force. He refused to converse in a normal manner. He would answer my questions with either "yes" or "no." That was it. I explained the situation to him, and he gave me four phone numbers. He said, "If you call, we'll be there to help."

Then he warned, "You must be very careful." So it was a damn dangerous time.

I wrote a memo on this, and I passed it around to the principal people on the embassy staff. The next morning—the morning of February 14—one of the political officers came into the office and began to ride the hell out of me over my memo. He said, "We don't need to worry about emergency phone numbers. The ayatollah broadcast an appeal this morning for everyone to turn in their guns. The ayatollah says that the revolution is over." Well, the ayatollah did tell everybody to turn in their guns, but he might as well have told them to quit eating ice cream.

BARRY ROSEN (*press attaché*): We had been told to stay at home during this period, and not to come into the embassy. I stayed away for a few days; then on February 14, I went back to the embassy with Jack Schellenberger. At that time I was trying to extricate the body of Joe Alex Morris, a *Los Angeles Times* correspondent, who had been killed in the firefight at Doshen Tappeh Air Force Base. Two other reporters had come in, and we were trying to figure out how we could get the body away from the air force base. I went upstairs to the second floor and into Ambassador Sullivan's office. About ten seconds later automatic weapons fire started to rip through the upper floors of the building. The windows were shattered, and the walls were riveted with bullets. We all hit the floor.

COL. THOMAS SCHAEFER (*defense attaché*): All of a sudden we heard some shots fired on the compound, which wasn't unusual, because we had heard gunfire on numerous occasions. But this time there were a great many shots. Harry Johnson* was standing at the window looking out, and I said, "Harry, get down! Those shots are coming in at us!" So we both got down on the floor. People were coming over the walls shooting. I can honestly say that attack sounded worse than any firefight I ever heard in Vietnam.

COL. LELAND HOLLAND (*army attaché*): Everybody was on the floor in the ambassador's office. The windows were blown out and lead was flying in. It was obvious that these guys were zeroing in on Sullivan's office. Whoever was staging the attack knew where the ambassador was, and they were doing a wingding job. I was scared shitless. We were all hunkered down, and I looked over at the political officer who had been riding me about my memo and said, "Hey, George, do you think that maybe these guys didn't get the word from the ayatollah?"

* Major Harold Johnson was the assistant air attaché.

Immediately, I got on the phone and started calling the numbers the police general had given me. On the third try I was finally able to reach the guy, and I told him, "Man, we need help right away!" I was assured that help would be on the way.

I remember General Stone* wanted to start spitting lead back at these guys who were shooting in at us, but the order from Ambassador Sullivan was not to fire back. That order went out over the radio. The marines were told not to fire unless it was absolutely necessary to defend their own lives. That was the right thing to do, because there was no way we could have won that fight. There were Iranians firing down on us from the tops of buildings with all kinds of weapons, and Sullivan didn't want to have any American-inflicted casualties out there, because once that started there was no way we could have won.

BARRY ROSEN (*press attaché*): Eventually, we were all able to crawl out of the ambassador's office and into the communications vault, where we went to work shredding cables. Ambassador Sullivan was commanding everything. We developed a bucket brigade to shred cables. This whole time, we were receiving tremendously heavy arms fire. The wall on that side of the embassy was literally shaking. I'm sure many of us had started to pray. Our marine security guards were trying to hold the attackers off with tear gas as they tried to break into the building.

COL. LELAND HOLLAND (*army attaché*): The militants were shooting their way through the metal door at the east end of the building, and lead was flying straight into that corridor. The marines teargassed the hell out of the place, but the Iranians managed to breach the building. We were all up on the second floor when the terrorists got in. Ambassador Sullivan had everyone in the vault, but he put me outside in the main corridor to surrender the building when these guys made their way up to the second floor. We still didn't know who the hell the attackers were. From the shouting and yelling going on, we determined that some of them had Turkish accents. We had an old Iranian over there by the name of Jordan, who spoke Farsi with that same kind of accent, so he was put at the door with me to act as an interpreter. He was an old fellow who had worked over in the consulate. Our instructions were to tell these guys that we were going to surrender the building to them, and that they would not be met by return fire. I thought we were going to be killed. There wasn't any other thought in

* General Harold Stone was the chief of the army section of the Military Assistance and Advisory Group.

my mind. I figured they'd blow us away as soon as I opened the door.
We stood there and heard them coming up the steps. When the militants
started coming up, old Jordan broke down and started to cry. He was
going to pieces. He had tears coming down his face. I said, "Damn,
man, don't break down on me now. I need you."

He said, "I'm a Jew. When they figure that out, they're going to kill
me."

"Hey, we're both in this together," I said. Then I opened the door.

These guys came bursting in and fanned out immediately. We were
slapped around and put up against the wall.

BARRY ROSEN (*press attaché*): When the attackers made their way onto
the second floor, it looked like that was the end. There was nothing
we could do but surrender. There were about twenty Americans in the
vault, and because I could speak Farsi the ambassador asked me to go
out and tell the attackers that we were all coming out of the vault. We
were surrendering ourselves to them. So we all lined up to march out.
As I was walking out the vault door I thought that I would probably
be shot on sight. I thought we were all going to be shot. But there was
nothing else we could do.

Outside the vault, the entire hallway was filled with tear gas. There
were a bunch of Iranians standing there in green khakis with automatic
weapons trained on us. They ordered us to move, and I translated their
orders. We all marched into the outer room of the ambassador's office,
which was strewn with glass and debris. They ordered us to take everything out of our pockets, and they lined us up and searched us. I was
still translating, and was telling everybody not to get upset, but to do
whatever the militants told us to do.

COL. LELAND HOLLAND (*army attaché*): When Ambassador Sullivan came
out of the vault, the militants immediately recognized him. He is an
extremely distinguished-looking fellow, and he had that shock of white
hair. He didn't speak a word of Farsi, but there was a young rotational
officer there by the name of Boyce, and his Farsi was pretty good, so
he interpreted for the ambassador. Sullivan was talking with a guy that
was supposedly one of the militant chiefs. They were demanding all
sorts of things, and said that they were going to take everybody down
to some revolutionary headquarters. They were obviously trying to
intimidate the ambassador, but Sullivan maintained a very cool outward
appearance. He is a real leader. In a crisis his feathers didn't ruffle.

COL. THOMAS SCHAEFER (*defense attaché*): When we surrendered, I was
in the back of the communications vault breaking up equipment. I was

the last American to leave the vault. Everyone was being gathered in the ambassador's office. They must have had about twenty of us there. As I was being escorted down the hall by a militant, another militant came up the stairwell right in front of us. As soon as he got to the window, a shot rang out and he was killed instantly. It was a militant shot by one of his own. He was hit in the head and fell back.

COL. LELAND HOLLAND (*army attaché*): I don't know how many Iranians were killed in that attack, but I do know that two or three of the militants were killed by their own bullets. The marine security desk on the first floor of the chancery was behind bulletproof glass, and one guy came running up and fired a submachine gun blast at it. The bullets ricocheted, and he was hit and killed by his own fire.

BARRY ROSEN (*press attaché*): After we were all gathered in the ambassador's office, a couple of the militants grabbed me and started to push me from office to office. They wanted me to open some safes for them, but I honestly didn't know any of the combinations except for those in my office downstairs. I was useless to them.

COL. LELAND HOLLAND (*army attaché*): There was a lot of pushing and shoving going on. In the ambassador's office they were searching and frisking us and lining us up against the wall. I remember there were a few blacks in there. One of them was a young marine, who had been dabbling around and looking into becoming a Moslem. They asked him, "Are you a Moslem?" He said, "Yes."

They said, "Have a seat. Sit down in this chair." And they pretty much left him alone.

Then they asked another young black kid, "Are you a Moslem?" He said, "Hell no!"

The militants beat him up and kicked him in the shins. They worked him over good.

BARRY ROSEN (*press attaché*): They brought me back to the ambassador's office. I was standing near the doorway when a bullet fired from outside the building came flying in the window and hit the picture of Secretary of State Vance that was on the wall. The picture fell to the floor. It just dropped straight down. That was how the counterattack started. I immediately closed the door on myself so that I would have some protection from the incoming fire, and ducked down on the floor. Once again, the building was riveted with bullets.

COL. LELAND HOLLAND (*army attaché*): We were all standing there, when there was some more shooting from the outside. It sounded just like the Fourth of July. *Bang! Bang! Bang! Brrrrp-brrrrp! Bang! Brrrp! Bang!* Another Iranian group, led by Ibrahim Yazdi,* got the word about the attack on the embassy, and they rushed down to take care of it. They were shooting the hell out of the place. Within a minute or two it was obvious to the militants who were holding us that they were now surrounded. So there was a parley held between the militant leaders and the leaders of the counterattack. There were some mullahs who came into the embassy, and they were walking around. The mullahs weren't running the show, but it was obvious that they were being listened to. The attackers claimed there was a SAVAK-e† in the embassy and that we were holding SAVAK spies. This was their excuse for staging the attack. The chiefs of these two Iranian groups talked, and the attackers basically negotiated their safe conduct out of the building in return for our safety. That was the trade-off. So they were all allowed to leave, and we were left in the hands of the Mujihadin group that staged the counter-attack.

BARRY ROSEN (*press attaché*): It was a very confusing situation. No one knew what was going on or what had happened. Within a matter of minutes the militants that had attacked us were no longer in power. They just left, and another Iranian group dressed in similar attire but wearing different arm bands appeared to be in charge. They said they had come from the imam's headquarters at Tehran University and that they were sorry for what had happened. They led us downstairs and outside the chancery, over to the area near the motor pool. I didn't know what was going on. I thought maybe they were going to shoot us. For all I knew, it could have been the same group attempting to calm us before an execution.

COL. THOMAS SCHAEFER (*defense attaché*): We were all taken out of the chancery and marched in front of a wall outside the building. At that time I wondered if this was the end of my life, because the militants had weapons and there didn't seem to be any control over what was going on. I thought it was possible that one of them might start firing at us.

---

* Ibrahim Yazdi was a member of Ayatollah Khomeini's Revolutionary Council. In April 1979 he was appointed foreign minister of Iran.
† An Iranian police informer who worked for the shah's secret police.

BARRY ROSEN (*press attaché*): Even though the revolutionary groups looked similar, the atmosphere had changed. These new people were friendly toward us, and they were upset by what had happened. They thought the attack was inexcusable, and a couple of them stood with me and told me so. They said that the imam's messenger would be there soon. Then Ibrahim Yazdi came over and talked to us. To paraphrase him, he pretty much said: "In times of revolution mistakes occur. Right now it is impossible for the government to control every group in Iran. But the Provisional Government of Iran did not want this to happen. We will try to insure your safety."

After Yazdi spoke, we were marched over to the ambassador's residence and some Iranian guards were put around the building. All of us were terribly shaken. We were sitting in the residence trying to piece all of this together, when some more automatic weapons fire came blasting in the window. I remember I landed on the floor underneath the ambassador's piano.

Apparently there was another sniper out there, but the group Yazdi had brought over was able to get whoever was doing the shooting, and that was the end of it. After that one burst of incoming fire, there wasn't any more shooting.

I went over to Charlie Nass's house, which was on the compound next to the ambassador's residence. He was the deputy chief of mission. We had a couple of glasses of Scotch over there. There was an Iranian guard with us who did not drink, but he was very friendly. He laid his rifle down and sat in the living room with us. I remember he took a liking to Lee Holland. Lee had a handgun, and this Iranian guard was very interested in that. I think Lee ended up giving it to him as a present. Jack Schellenberger was with this group, and he and I didn't want to stay on the compound any longer than we had to. We figured that was the most dangerous place to be. So we got permission to leave, and left by the rear gate of the embassy. I bought a newspaper on the street, and we hailed a taxi. I remember the headline in the newspaper was: "American Embassy Falls!" Then in the taxi, there was this little old lady sitting there, and she went on and on telling us how rotten America was, and how great it was that the embassy had been attacked. That sentiment was not uncommon in Iran. A lot of people seemed quite pleased by the attack.

Anyway, the taxi finally got us to Jack Schellenberger's house, and he and I sat up and drank ourselves silly that night.

3 A New Beginning

VICTOR TOMSETH (*chief political officer*): I arrived in Iran in April of 1976, as consul in one of our constituent posts in Shiraz. It was to have been a three-year assignment ending in 1979. But by the fall of 1978, Ambassador Sullivan recognized that the Pahlavi regime was not going to make it. He also recognized that in the post-Pahlavi period there would be a need for people who had some understanding of Iran. I think he assumed that the people who had questioned the Pahlavi regime and had been skeptical about its stability would somehow be better able to identify with the new crowd. For these reasons he asked me if I would be willing to stay in Iran for an extra year and come to Tehran to head the political section in the embassy. That was a very good job, and from my point of view it looked to be a very exciting one. It was obviously a period of great political ferment, which is what political officers tend to be interested in. So I jumped at the opportunity, and arrived in Tehran in February of 1979.

RICHARD QUEEN (*consular officer*): At the time of the February 14 attack, I was enrolled in Farsi language school at the Foreign Service Institute in Washington, D.C. I had been assigned to Tehran and was scheduled to arrive there in June. When I first heard the news about the attack, I remember thinking: "Well, it looks like Tehran is going to be an exciting place." I really wasn't very apprehensive. I simply thought it was going to be an exciting tour.

VICTOR TOMSETH (*chief political officer*): When I arrived in Tehran, my first job was to put the political section back together. Everything had been trashed. The building was full of tear gas. All of our communications equipment had been destroyed. We were without secretaries, and most of our American personnel had been evacuated. Only a relatively small group of us stayed on in February and March. It was a holding operation. In the political section we started to have some contacts with the Provisional Revolutionary Government that Mehdi Bazargan headed. We were attempting to develop a relationship with that government.

COL. CHARLES SCOTT (*chief of the Defense Liaison Office*): Iran was important to the United States because of its geographic location. It's a major oil-producing nation that sits on the Strait of Hormuz, through which a large portion of the West's oil must pass. In addition, it has an eleven-hundred-mile border with the Soviet Union, where we had listening posts that were very valuable in our intelligence collection efforts vis-à-vis the Soviet Union. So it was important for the United States to establish a new relationship with the postrevolutionary government, and this was exactly what the Carter administration wanted to do. In the months that followed the revolution, we made a concerted effort to get along with Iran. In this endeavor the Carter administration was very honest. We told the Iranians, "We are not going to interfere in Iran's internal affairs. We understand that Iran has a new government." So our national goals and objectives were right.

VICTOR TOMSETH (*chief political officer*): In May, we had a rather difficult time due to the Sense of the Senate resolution sponsored by Jacob Javits. The Javits resolution was critical of all the executions and the activities of the revolutionary courts.

This triggered large demonstrations in the street outside the embassy. The deputy prime minister called Charlie Nass and me in to tell us that we should delay the arrival of our newly appointed ambassador. A few days later, he called us in again and told us not to send the ambassador at all.

About that time, Charlie Nass convened a kind of bull session with half-a-dozen people who had been in Iran for quite a while. We hashed over the problem of whether or not circumstances were such that we had any hope at all of succeeding in our goal to build a new relationship with the new Iran. The conclusion was that the odds were very long. But there was also a consensus that no matter how long those odds, the stakes were so high that we had to try. We had to take the risk. In spite of this very real risk and the small likelihood of success, we had an obligation to do our best.

BARRY ROSEN (*press attaché*): In the interim between the February attack and the takeover of the embassy in November, our goal was to come to terms with the revolution and establish relations with the new government. But during this time we had some bad signals. The Iranian press was very, very bitter in its treatment of the United States. A lot of anti-American statements and articles were published that accused us of some of the wildest schemes in the world. America was accused of blowing up Iranian railways, of murdering people in villages, and of aiding the Kurdish rebellion—all of which was absolutely insane. At one point some documents were published which purported to describe an American scheme within the Iranian military to stage a countercoup against the revolution. It was preposterous because the documents were total fabrications. Yet these sorts of stories would just go on and on.

Of course, Iranians are great believers in the myth of American omnipotence, and there was a readiness on the part of a large segment of the population to accept such fabrications as fact. So that was not a good sign. Even though we did manage to establish some contacts with the Provisional Government and some of the more moderate elements within the clergy, on balance I'd have to say that we were holding on to the thinnest threads and saying that there was reason to hope.

4 New Arrivals

THROUGHOUT THE SUMMER of 1979, the United States continued to try to normalize relations with the Provisional Government of Iran, and the embassy staff gradually increased in size. By late 1979 approximately 75 Americans were assigned to the embassy in Tehran, a number that was still only a fraction of the pre-February staff. Many of the new arrivals were flown in on temporary duty assignments to help keep the embassy functioning until permanent party personnel could be trained and dispatched to Iran.

JOE HALL (*warrant officer*): In February of 1979, I was working at the American embassy in Athens, Greece. We were very aware of what was going on in Iran, and we followed the events there very closely.

After the Valentine's Day attack, almost all of the American personnel were evacuated out of Iran, and the defense attaché's office in Athens, where I was working, was instrumental in the evacuation of the military personnel. I talked to a lot of the evacuees as they came out, and what I remember the most is the obvious and visible sense of relief that the people felt at being able to get out of Iran. There was a navy captain who had worked for the defense attaché's office in Tehran, and when he came out he was assigned to our office in Geece for about three months. At one point during this time, there was some discussion about the possibility of having him reassigned to Tehran. One day he and his wife came into the embassy to check on his status, and they were told about the possibility of his being sent back to Tehran. When that happened his wife became hysterical. I remember seeing the two of them standing in the hall, and this lady was just a bundle of nerves. She was crying, and she looked at her husband and said, "You are not going back in there!" The navy captain looked pretty distraught himself. He was worn out and gray. His tour in Tehran had obviously aged him beyond his due. I remember seeing the two of them cling to each other in the hall, and I thought, "My God, that man is actually afraid to go back into the American embassy in Tehran."

That was before I had any idea that I was going to be assigned to Iran. I didn't even think it was possible.

SGT. PAUL LEWIS (*marine security guard*): The embassy in Iran was looking for volunteers, and I wanted to go to a hot spot. I've always been interested in politics and foreign affairs, and I wanted to be close to a sensitive situation. I thought Tehran was a unique opportunity. It was a chance to be close to a revolution that was still in progress. I didn't want some fantastic liberty post. I wanted to get a feel for foreign affairs where things were happening. So I volunteered for Tehran.

BILL BELK (*communications officer*): I was stationed in Brussels, Belgium, when a message came around from the State Department requesting communications volunteers for the American embassy in Iran. This must've been three or four months after the February attack. By this time, Iran had pretty much dropped out of the news and I assumed that the political situation had stabilized. This impression was confirmed by the State Department. They assured me that Tehran was a safe post. They said they were trying to rebuild the embassy staff after the February evacuation, and that everything was returning to normal. As a matter of fact, I was told that dependents would be allowed to return to Tehran in the not too distant future. Of course, nothing was said about the shah. He was living in exile somewhere, and I didn't even have the vaguest thought as to his whereabouts. That was something I didn't even think about. I went ahead and volunteered primarily because I was sick of the weather in Brussels. I'd always heard that Tehran was the jewel of the Middle East, and I figured it would be a nice change of pace.

JOE HALL (*warrant officer*): When my tour was up in Greece, I reported to the Attaché Affairs Section in the Pentagon, and they told me that they needed someone to go to Iran, and that I was the someone they had chosen. Well, I didn't want to have anything to do with that. After assisting in the evacuation of embassy personnel following the February attack, I knew too much about what Iran was like. I protested, but they told me that I had been selected because I didn't have any children, and because my wife was a government employee who was capable of taking care of herself. In spite of my objections, I was given a one-year unaccompanied tour.

My wife and I had an extremely close marriage, and being separated like that seemed like a tragedy to both of us. I was absolutely heart-broken. Tehran was the last place in the world that I wanted to go. But I also had a premonition that something was going to happen. The situation was so unstable that I had a feeling the embassy was going to be overrun. I remember thinking, "This tour will never last a full year. Those people hate Americans so much that something is going to happen. The embassy is going to be closed down, and we'll be evacuated out."

DON HOHMAN (*army medic*): When I flew into Iran I was the only American on the plane, which was a strange feeling. At the airport, I remember, the women were all wearing chadors. Black chadors. It was an amazing thing to see. Every woman in Iran was wearing the exact same clothes. They looked sort of like medieval nuns. It was kind of funny for me to be standing in the middle of this revolutionary situation—I was the only guy with a tennis racquet in hand. The embassy driver didn't have any trouble picking me out.

BILL BELK (*communications officer*): I caught the Pan Am flight from Frankfurt to Tehran. Shortly before my plane landed, I noticed that a lot of the Iranian women changed their clothes. When we boarded in Germany almost all of the women were wearing Western clothes, but about thirty minutes outside of Tehran a lot of the women got up to go to the bathroom, and then they came back out wearing chadors. They had their faces and their Western garments covered by long brown robes. That was quite a transition. I could tell that a lot of these people were apprehensive about landing in Tehran. They were afraid of what was happening in their own country.

As soon as I got off the airplane I knew the country was in turmoil. There were revolutionaries with guns all over the airport. Lots and lots of these guys standing around with G-3s and M-16s—but no one in uniform. They were all wearing grubby jeans and green fatigue jackets, with about three days' growth of beard on their faces. It was mass confusion inside that terminal. Beyond the customs counter there were about sixteen or seventeen of these *komiteh* members checking people's bags after they passed through customs. They were Khomeini's "Soldiers of God," and they were there to make sure that no one brought any newspapers or alcohol into Iran. Of course, I had my diplomatic passport and I thought this would clear me, but there wasn't any such thing as diplomatic immunity as far as those guys were concerned. A French diplomat was walking along beside me, and I stood in line behind him and watched as these guys tore through his bags. They were being very rough. They confiscated a small bottle of alcohol, one of those little 1.5-ounce bottles that are served on airplanes. I didn't have anything to hide, so I went ahead and let them run their grubby hands through my bags. When I walked outside, there were armed revolutionaries all over the street. Tehran was nothing but guns, guns, guns.

SGT. KEVIN HERMENING (*marine security guard*): When we flew into Iran, some of the marines from the embassy drove out to the airport to pick us up and take us back to the compound. It was getting dark when we left the terminal, and outside on the curb it was a total mob scene. People were pushing and shoving like you wouldn't believe, and all of these revolutionaries were running around with guns. I was scared. I didn't even want to look around. I just wanted to get in the marine van and get to the embassy. But I'll tell you, the physical elements of the van did not lend themselves to making me feel at ease. There were thick iron plates inside the doors and the windows were made of bulletproof glass. It was obvious that the van had been prepared to protect its occupants from any sniper fire or the possibility of a street ambush along the way. I remember sitting in there and thinking, "Welcome to Tehran."

CHARLES JONES (*communications officer*): I'd passed through Tehran in January of 1978, and when I arrived in the summer of 1979, I was immediately struck by how dark the city was. That seemed very strange to me. It was about nine o'clock at night when I got in, and there should have been millions of people out on the streets. But there was a total absence of nightlife, and most of the streetlights were out. It was a very dark city. There was none of the normal hustle and bustle. I remember riding from the airport to the embassy and thinking, "My goodness, this is a total transformation. Everything has come to a standstill."

JOE HALL (*warrant officer*): On my first night in Tehran, I heard gunfire out in the streets. Everyone at the embassy just kind of laughed it off. All of the cool heads who had been there for a while said, "Aw, this is nothing. It goes on every night. Don't worry about it. You'll get used to it."

I thought, "Yeah, sure I will." Lying in bed that night I was just heartsick. I'd never wanted the assignment to begin with, and I hated being separated from my wife.

BILL BELK (*communications officer*): I spent my first night at Bert Moore's*
house. I was staying with him until my apartment was ready. We got
up the next morning, and Bert took me over to the embassy. That was
the first time I saw the grounds, which were comprised of twenty-six
acres surrounded by a big, high wall. We went through a back gate.
There was an empty swimming pool to our left. Stacked all around this
empty pool was a huge amount of household furniture. There were
beds, sofas, mirrors, tables, easy chairs, rocking chairs, bookcases—all
kinds of stuff. It was odd to see all this furniture outdoors. There was
probably enough stuff sitting out there to furnish 200 homes. Out
behind the furniture was an area where there were about 150 abandoned
automobiles. They were parked on a recreation field. Then over to our
right was a big warehouse. I looked inside one of the warehouse rooms
and saw hundreds and hundreds of musical instruments—tubas, trum-
pets, drums, violins, flutes, saxophones—everything you'd need for a
symphony orchestra. The instruments were just stacked on the shelves
collecting dust.

Seeing all of this furniture and the automobiles and the instruments
was the first impression I had of how sudden the February evacuation
had been. When the revolution came and the embassy was attacked, a
huge number of people left Tehran in a very, very big hurry, and they
left with nothing more than what they could carry in a couple of suitcases. The country was in such total chaos that it was impossible for
them to have their household items shipped out. The freight companies
had all closed down. So all of this furniture was gathered up from various
apartments and private homes all over Tehran that had been occupied
by Americans, and the musical instruments were brought in from the
American School in Tehran. Bert explained that all of this stuff had
been brought over to the embassy so that the American government
could sell it at a public auction to try and liquidate the claims of the
people who had been evacuated out.

That made quite an impression on me. I thought that the revolution
was over and that things were returning to normal, but the remnants
of what had happened in February were everywhere. It made me feel
I had walked into a dangerous situation.

The main embassy building was across the compound. When I got
there, I looked up at the chancery and couldn't believe what I was
seeing. I remember my first thought was, "My God, that building looks
just like a prison." All of the windows were barred, and metal sand
bunkers had been put into the windows so that no one could shoot
down into the building from nearby rooftops like they had done in

* Bert Moore was the administrative officer at the embassy.

February. The walls were still scarred with bullet holes. The chancery looked like it was standing in the middle of a combat zone. I should've turned around and walked away. I never should have set a foot inside that building.

SGT. JAMES LOPEZ (*marine security guard*): I walked through town twice. Tehran was a desolate city. There was garbage in the streets and everything was closed. Most of the storefronts were locked up. The only stores open were music shops selling pirated tapes and grocery stores where the shelves were empty. There wasn't much of anything going on.

BRUCE GERMAN (*budget officer*): If you went walking at night, walking was an adventure, because you'd come across gun emplacements on street corners—machine guns surrounded by sandbags. So at night you had to be very careful. I always walked in groups, and we gave those gun emplacements a very wide berth.

BILL BELK (*communications officer*): During my first week in Tehran I had an opportunity to go into town with Rick Kupke.* It was really amazing because we'd walk into a bar and there wouldn't be any booze, not any beer. No alcohol of any kind, and no music. All you could order was a Coke. I remember we walked into this one place and a barfly came slinking up and wanted me to buy her a Coke. It was just like in Saigon, where the bar girls sit on your lap and want you to buy them a drink. It cost five dollars for a Coke, which turned me off immediately.

It was all very strange. You'd see a lot of people on the street, but very few of them would go into the bars. Before the revolution, when there was a whole slew of military and embassy personnel assigned to Tehran, the nightlife was very active. But after the revolution very few of the night spots were still open. A lot of old places were boarded up. I understand many of the restaurant and bar owners were shot in the first few months after Khomeini returned to Iran. I'm surprised that one place was even open. Looking back on it, that was a mighty dangerous thing to do. I didn't go out much after that. I pretty much stayed on the embassy compound and played chess or penny poker with some of the other embassy employees.

JOE HALL (*warrant officer*): One night six of us were sitting in my apartment complex playing poker, when all of a sudden we heard a very

* Frederick L. Kupke was a communications officer.

loud explosion, immediately followed by another explosion. Those explosions literally rocked the entire apartment complex, which was right outside the back gate of the embassy. It was obvious that the embassy was under some kind of fire. There was a guy with us who had been through the February 14 attack, and he was scheduled to fly out the next morning. He was a basket case. He was convinced that he was never going to get out of Iran alive. He was just sure of it, and then all of a sudden we start hearing these explosions. What happened was some militants fired a couple of RPGs* onto the compound. They hit the consulate and caused some damage to the building, but we were lucky that no one was killed. That's how vulnerable the embassy was. If somebody wanted to fire RPGs onto the compound, there was absolutely nothing we could do to stop them.

BILL BELK (*communications officer*): The thing that amazed me the most about Iran was how the government had absolutely no control over what was happening. There were big, highly publicized show trials— many of them on TV—where former officials in the shah's government or officers in the military were accused of all sorts of crimes. Then after the trial, these people were immediately taken up onto the roof and put in front of a firing squad. Armed bands of revolutionary zealots were roaming the streets and taking the law into their own hands. The police were powerless to stop them, because the worst thing you could possibly be in Iran was a policeman. That identified you with the shah's government. Most of the people who had been policemen were in hiding. The streets were literally turned over to these armed *komitehs*. Khomeini had appointed a Provisional Government, but they didn't have any real authority. The traditional institutions through which a government administers and functions were the very same institutions that were being attacked by the revolutionaries and the vigilante groups. A lot of the people within the Provisional Government were frightened. The last thing they wanted to do was engender the ill will of some two-bit mullah who controlled a revolutionary guard unit. That was the sort of thing that could get you shot, or send you into a very abrupt exile. So dealing with the Provisional Government was like trying to deal with a shadow—you could see it, but talking to it was pointless. In reality, there was no substance there.

* Rocket-propelled grenades.

5 Admitting the Shah

WHEN THE SHAH left Iran in January of 1979, he settled in Morocco for two months before being asked to leave, and then traveled to the Bahamas and Cuernavaca, Mexico, in search of a permanent place to reside. David Rockefeller and Henry Kissinger, two of his long-time associates, lobbied the Carter administration to have him admitted to the United States. All their overtures were rejected. President Carter felt that to bring the deposed Iranian monarch into the United States would endanger the safety of American embassy personnel in Tehran.

The shah had been suffering from chronic lymph cancer for several years, and throughout his period of exile his health steadily deteriorated. At the recommendation of David Rockefeller, Dr. Benjamin Kean flew to Mexico to examine the shah on two separate occasions. On October 18, 1979, Dr. Kean was informed of the shah's history of lymphoma. His examination revealed that the shah's condition was further complicated by obstructive jaundice and that surgery was required to remove the obstruction. That evening, Dr. Kean briefed a State Department physician on the shah's health. Through the State Department, President Carter was informed that the shah's condition was potentially fatal, and was told that diagnostic facilities available in Mexico were not adequate to meet the needs of his complicated illness. After consulting with Secretary of State Cyrus Vance, President Carter approved a recommendation to admit the shah into the United States for medical treatment.

In Tehran, Chargé d'Affaires Bruce Laingen, was instructed to inform the Provisional Government of Iran that the shah was going to be admitted to the United States. The following day, October 22, 1979, the shah boarded a Gulfstream jet for the United States and was admitted to New York Hospital late that evening.

VICTOR TOMSETH (*chief political officer*): During the summer, Bruce Laingen was asked in a very closely held cable for his assessment of what the consequences would be if the shah were admitted to the United States. His instructions were not to share the message with anyone else. But he thought it was unreasonable that he should make that assessment by himself, because he had only recently arrived in

Iran. So he turned to Phil Gast* and myself. We both agreed that as long as there was not a government in place able to enforce law and order, it would be the height of folly to admit the shah to the United States. Bruce was easily convinced of this, based upon what he had seen in the brief time that he had been in Iran. So a message to that effect was cabled to Washington.

In September there was another inquiry, asking if the situation had changed. Bruce said that the situation had not changed, and he reiterated that until there was a government in place that was capable of functioning, it would be very risky to admit the shah.

BRUCE LAINGEN (*chargé d'affaires*): I was instructed to inform Prime Minister Bazargan that the shah was to be admitted, and I did so. Of course, I was specifically instructed to ask him that security for the embassy be maintained against the possibility of public reaction. The response on the Iranian side of the table varied depending on the personalities involved. But the essential point was that Bazargan, as prime minister, assured me that the provisional Iranian government would do its best to provide security for the American embassy. It was that assurance I then conveyed to Washington.

BARRY ROSEN (*press attaché*): I was sitting right next to Bruce Laingen when he told us that the shah was going to be admitted to the United States, and I couldn't believe what I was hearing. The administration in Washington had made a decision that was totally contrary to all of the advice we had cabled from the embassy in Iran. I very strongly felt that the decision was at variance with all of the objectives we were working toward in Iran, and was at variance with our national interest. In addition, it jeopardized our personal safety. It was the sort of decision that signaled to the Iranians that we were attempting to overthrow the regime and return the shah to his throne.

I can remember walking out of that meeting and informing our USIA† personnel about the new turn of events. I knew there would be massive demonstrations, with the possibility of people coming over the wall and shooting at us as they had done on February 14. If that happened, I knew some of us might get killed. I told our personnel, "It's going to be very, very difficult around here for the next few weeks. I don't know if we'll be able to survive it."

---

* General Philip C. Gast was chief of the Military Assistance and Advisory Group.
† United States Information Agency.

BRUCE GERMAN (*budget officer*): I felt betrayed. The embassy had been firing off numerous telegrams to the States explaining that the situation was not good. All of those telegrams went unheeded. In Tehran, we had a series of hurry-up meetings, and the security officers pretty much said: "Keep a low profile, and perhaps the cloud will blow over." But I was frightened, and I'm not ashamed to admit it. I knew our lives were hanging by a thread.

We should have begun to depart in small groups of maybe three or five people at a time. The situation was very tense and very dangerous, and the State Department should have done something to filter non-essential personnel out, leaving only a skeleton crew in Tehran until the situation had a chance to stabilize.

CHARLES JONES (*communications officer*): I don't want to say that I felt safe, because I didn't. But I did think that the Khomeini government would do what it could to protect the embassy if anything happened. That's just standard diplomatic protocol. Every embassy everywhere in the world is dependent on the host country for protection. When the shah was admitted to the United States, I thought our position at the embassy was somewhat analogous to a previous situation I'd been in at the American embassy in Cairo during the Six-Day War. At that time, Gamal Nasser was the president of Egypt, and he was going on Egyptian radio and television yelling and screaming about America's support for Israel. He was making all kinds of accusations and saying that we had assisted in the surprise attacks on Egypt. He had the masses stirred up against the United States, much as Khomeini was doing in Iran. Then, on the night Nasser resigned, there were over a million Egyptians in the streets. They had torches, and they converged on the American embassy hollering, "Nasser! Nasser!" Yet the Egyptian police beat these people back. In spite of their dissatisfaction with the United States and the frantic hysteria of the people, the Egyptian government of Gamal Nasser did protect us. It was their responsibility to do so.

I felt the Khomeini regime and the Provisional Government of Iran would recognize the same international protocol. Throughout history, no matter what disagreements have existed between two nations, a legitimate government always does everything it can to protect the diplomatic community living in its midst. That's just basic civilized behavior. If you are extremely upset with another country, then you might break off diplomatic relations and tell all of the diplomats to pack their bags and leave. Which is something that I thought Khomeini might ask us to do, and which we would have gladly done. But never in my wildest dreams did I think that the Iranian government would sanction an out-and-out act of terrorism.

BARRY ROSEN (*press attaché*): It was my job to monitor the Iranian press, and in the beginning, I remember, the local press was just as shocked at the arrival of the shah in the United States as everyone else. Their reaction was total surprise. At the embassy, we made some statements that we thought were very clear. We explained that the shah had been admitted to the United States for treatment of lymphoma, and that he was being admitted for medical purposes only. We took pains to explain that the shah would not engage in any political activity while he was on American soil.

It was only after four or five days that press attacks on the United States started to avalanche, which was very disconcerting. It would have been preferable to see the avalanche come immediately and then level off. But things started slowly and then hit with a *bang*! That made the reaction hard to gauge. For a few days, we thought maybe we had begun to weather the storm, when in truth it was only beginning to get stormy. There were marches on the embassy in late October and early November, and the Iranian press was printing some hysterical diatribes against both the United States and the Provisional Government. There was obviously a great deal of disbelief about the illness of the shah. I remember one newspaper ran a story that said Iranians never get lymphoma; it was just not an Iranian disease. Next to the article there was a picture of the shah in Cuernavaca, dressed in his bright Mexican shirt, looking very healthy. So this was obviously an evil American lie. There had to be something behind it. Another coup was coming!

COL. CHARLES SCOTT (*military attaché*): It was a situation where truth didn't matter. Perceptions were much more important. A large portion of the Iranian people believed that the United States had the ability to pull strings and return the shah to power. Iranians believed that we were about 1,000 times more powerful in directing their internal affairs than we ever were. The truth was that at this time we had practically no influence in Iran. Our only purpose for being there was to try and establish a relationship with the new regime. But when the shah was admitted to the United States, we opened Pandora's box for the hardline revolutionaries. They could say, "Look what America did in 1953! They're getting ready to do it again! Another coup is in the wind! They're going to return the shah to power!" That accusation held a lot of water with a lot of people. Most Iranians believed it. It's hard for many Americans to understand that the entire Iranian population felt wronged by the shah, and by America's support of the shah. After he was admitted to the United States, they wanted to strike out at something American. You could search the entire country over, and there was only one target they could attack. That was the American embassy in Tehran.

SGT. ROCKY SICKMANN (*marine security guard*): Demonstrations became an everyday occurrence. We had television monitors in the embassy, and I used to sit there and watch all of these people out in the street chanting, *"Marg bar Amrika! Marg bar Amrika!"* It was kind of scary. Here I was, after the embassy had already been attacked in February, and most of our American personnel had been evacuated out for their own safety. It seemed like everybody in the country was screaming, "Death to America! Death to America!" That's the kind of thing that makes you wonder. We didn't know if they were going to come over the walls or not. But the demonstrations went on day after day, and nothing happened. After a while we got used to them.

CPL. WILLIAM GALLEGOS (*marine security guard*): The Iranians had some demonstrations that were pretty big, and we tightened our security at the embassy. The marines spent a couple of nights inside the chancery building so that we would be ready if anything did happen. I remember watching those demonstrations. There were masses and masses of people out in the street. Thousands of people were standing out there chanting, "Death to America!" But that's all there was to it. There wasn't any violence, and they didn't try to jump over the walls or anything.

After those demonstrations died down, we just went on with our regular duties.

Part Two

November 4, 1979

1 Under Siege

THE ENORMOUS SIZE of the American embassy compound in Tehran rendered it virtually indefensible. The grounds covered twenty-
seven acres near the downtown business district, which represented
the approximate equivalent of twenty-five city blocks. An eight-foot
wall surrounded the compound, which bordered on public avenues at
all points. The compound housed the main chancery building, the consulate, a large warehouse, the ambassador's residence, the deputy chief
of mission's residence, four small staff houses, several auxiliary buildings, two tennis courts, a swimming pool, a recreation field, and ex-
tensive lawns and gardens. Beyond the north wall was the Bijon Apartment
Building, where many of the embassy employees lived. In front of the
chancery, the main gates opened on Takht-e Jamshid, a four-lane boulevard that was one of Tehran's major east-west thoroughfares.

Thirteen marine security guards were stationed at the embassy to
provide internal security. The marines managed posts at the chancery,
the consulate, and the ambassador's residence. The host government
was responsible for external security, and a small detachment of Iranian
national police patrolled the perimeter of the compound and stood
guard at the embassy gates.

More than 200 Iranians were employed in secretarial and general
service positions at the American embassy, and hundreds of visitors
entered the compound every day on routine business. Consequently,
a large number of civilians had regular access to the compound.
Throughout the week of October 28, at least three Iranian college
students planning an attack on the embassy were able to enter and leave
the compound at will. These visits gave them ample opportunity to
study the physical layout of the grounds and to talk with local employees
and Iranian security personnel. On November 2 and 3, large numbers
of college students were bused into Tehran from outlying areas to
participate in a demonstration that was to take place on the fourth.
Many of the students were told that "something big" was going to
happen, but only a select group knew that the embassy was going to
be attacked.

CHARLES JONES (*communications officer*): On the night of November 3,
I had some Iranian friends over to my apartment, and they said that
there were going to be some demonstrations at the embassy the next
day. November 4 was the anniversary of an antishah demonstration in

which some students had been killed the previous year. On the third Khomeini went on the radio and made some inflammatory statements in which he referred to these students, who he said had been "martyred." My Iranian friends mentioned this in our conversation, but they didn't seem to think that the demonstration was going to be anything serious. In fact, we even made some plans for later in the week.

As a matter of course, I reported this conversation to our security people. They already knew that some demonstrations were coming down. But there had been so many demonstrations that we simply took it for granted that this one was just going to be like all of the others, and no extra security precautions were taken.

SGT. PAUL LEWIS (*marine security guard*): I flew into Iran on November 3. It was already dark when I got to the embassy, and the gunnery sergeant gave me a quick tour of the post. We walked around the compound and he showed me where the RPG rounds had hit in August. Then, at the chancery, I could see there were still rounds suspended in the bulletproof glass at the marine security guard post from the February attack. If you kicked the carpet you could stir up tear gas. It looked like the embassy had been attacked about a week before and not several months before. In looking at the security setup, I wasn't reassured at all. There was too much area for too few marines to cover. The gunny said he was having trouble getting appropriations to make all of the necessary improvements.

He took me by the Mushroom Inn,* where there was a VCR set up. Some of the other marines were in there watching TV. While we were there, the ambassador's cook came in and said he had been out in town and had heard there was going to be a large demonstration the next day. It gave me an uneasy feeling to see the locals coming in and telling the Americans what was happening. But the other marines didn't seem to be bothered by this news. They said that demonstrations were a routine occurrence and that it wasn't anything to worry about. But when I went to bed that night—my first night in Iran—I was feeling a little uneasy.

BILL BELK (*communications officer*): I'm an early riser, and on Sunday morning, November 4, I woke up at about 4:00 A.M. At the time I was living in Bert Moore's house, which was a beautiful place. I went down

---

* The Mushroom Inn was a large warehouse located in the center of the embassy compound, where a group of the hostages were held after the takeover of the embassy. The building's windowless concrete walls and dark, damp atmosphere inspired them to name it the Mushroom Inn.

to the kitchen and put on the transoceanic radio to get either the BBC or some shortwave radio news from the States. I got a cup of coffee and listened to the broadcast. It was so early that I had time to play a game of computer chess.

At about 7:00 A.M. Bert came down for breakfast. We talked over recent events. This must've been about twelve or thirteen days after the shah had been admitted to the United States. Bert told me that State Department people had been concerned about our situation, and after Friday's demonstration they were even more concerned. During the night he had received several phone calls from Washington. Henry Precht* had called. Security people had called. NEA† people had called. They all voiced their concern about what was going on in Tehran. Of course, they were much more worried than we were. We just didn't realize the seriousness of our own situation. We thought the Iranians had accepted the fact that the shah was in the United States. I don't think anyone thought they were ready to come over the embassy walls.

Before we walked over to the embassy compound, we looked out the window and checked to make sure there wasn't a gang of people waiting at the gate. There were only two uniformed policemen and a young fourteen- or fifteen-year-old kid. I noticed that there was some writing on the back wall, some Persian writing that had been done with a spray can. I hadn't seen any of that before.

CHARLES JONES (*communications officer*): November 4, I can remember that day just like it was yesterday. Normally I wear a suit to work, but on that morning I got up and thought, "Oh, what the heck. I'll dress casual." I put on a tie, a blue pullover sweater, and blue slacks. My apartment was on the sixth floor, and as I was moving about I could look out over the embassy compound. I remember looking out and saying to myself, "What a glorious morning. What a nice day to be alive." Then I walked to work, enjoying the fresh air. I remember thinking: "This compound is absolutely beautiful. It would be terrible if something were to happen and this place was attacked."

I walked upstairs to the communications center. Bill Belk and Rick Kupke were there. The three of us talked. I was in charge of the section, because our supervisor was out of the country. He was due back later that day, and he was going to bring his wife into Iran. Dependents had just been given the okay to return. In the course of our conversation I said, "That guy is crazy to be bringing his wife in here." But Bill Belk said that he didn't have any problems with it and that he was going to

---

* Henry Precht was head of the Iran Working Group at the State Department.
† Near Eastern Affairs.

bring his wife over, too. Well, I didn't say too much about that, because my plans were to stay in Iran for two years myself. I had a nice apartment and I really liked the people who were working in the communications section. I was thinking that Iran would probably turn out to be one of my better posts. As a matter of fact, all three of us agreed that we were having a lot of fun in Iran.

LEE SCHATZ (*agricultural attaché*): That day started off no different from any other. In the morning we had a nine o'clock staff meeting, as we always did. It was a short meeting, because Bruce Laingen and Victor Tomseth were going to go over to the Foreign Ministry. It was pretty much business as usual.

VICTOR TOMSETH (*chief political officer*): That day was a double anniversary. I think it was the anniversary of the day that Khomeini had gone off into exile in Turkey back in 1964, and also the first anniversary of a major riot in Tehran during which people had been killed at Tehran University. So there was a demonstration scheduled for that day. We had our staff meeting the first thing in the morning, and I remember the main debate was whether we should lower our flag to half-mast in recognition of the anniversary on which these three or four people had been killed at Tehran University. It was decided that we would not lower the flag.

SGT. ROCKY SICKMANN (*marine security guard*): At about nine o'clock that morning I was walking across the compound toward the chancery. On Takht-e Jamshid, the main street that passed in front of the embassy compound, I could hear a demonstration in progress. A big group of people was coming down the street toward the embassy, chanting their usual slogans. "Death to America! Death to the shah!" That kind of thing. I called the marine at Post One on my radio and reported that there was a demonstration in progress. That was routine procedure. We would monitor the demonstrations just to keep alert, while we carried on with our normal duties. The marine at Post One took my message and said, "Okay, I'll tell the security officer."

VICTOR TOMSETH (*chief political officer*): That morning Bruce Laingen had a meeting scheduled at the Foreign Ministry, ironically enough, on the subject of diplomatic immunity for military personnel at the embassy. Ann Swift* was the person who had the background information on that particular issue, and she was going to attend that meeting with

_____
* Elizabeth Ann Swift was in charge of the political section.

Bruce. However, she called me that morning to say that she was going to be late getting into the embassy. She asked if I could cover for her and attend the meeting at the Foreign Ministry. So I gathered up the papers on her desk concerning this matter and went off with Bruce.

JOHN LIMBERT (*political officer*): November 4 had been proclaimed Student Day, and there was going to be a march and rally at the University of Tehran. The university is in the western part of the city. The routes of march for people going to the rally from the east or northeast of the city would lead in front of the embassy. It was quite normal for marchers to pass the embassy on their way to some kind of gathering at the university and, as they went by, to shout some anti-American slogans. That morning groups started going by, and occasionally we would hear their anti-American slogans. There was not anything unusual about this.

LEE SCHATZ (*agricultural attaché*): My office was a block and a half away from the chancery. I had to walk out the front gate and down the wall to the right. After the morning staff meeting, I picked up my mail and was about to walk out, but there was a huge crowd of people passing in front of the gate. They were hollering and chanting and everything else. I couldn't go out just then. Whenever there was a demonstration in Tehran, it was the norm for people to pass the embassy in groups. So I just paced myself. As one group of people was moving past the embassy and down the street, another group was coming up the street. I went out the gate in the quiet space between the two groups, and walked over to my office.

RICHARD QUEEN (*consular officer*): I ate breakfast in a little trailer we used as a restaurant: sausage, eggs, and toast. Then I walked over to the consulate. That weekend there had been demonstrations outside the compound and the demonstrators had painted slogans all over the wall of the consulate. "Death to America! Down with the shah!" The usual stuff. So Dick Morefield, the consul general, closed the consulate to the general public. He told us to cull the files, and that's what we were doing. It was very tedious. I was with two other consular officers when we heard that there was a demonstration outside. Well, there was nothing unusual about that. We just kept on working.

JOE HALL (*warrant officer*): I was in my office when the demonstrations started outside. It got noisier and noisier, but my thought at the time was, "Big deal. They'll go away sooner or later, and then they'll be back this afternoon."

DON HOHMAN (*army medic*): That morning, after I made my rounds, I went into the clinic and I noticed something strange. Some of the local Iranian employees were grabbing their coats and leaving. At the time I couldn't figure out why, but in retrospect I can see they knew something was going on. There's no doubt in my mind that some of our locals knew the embassy was going to be hit. I called Al Golacinski, the security officer, and said, "Hey, what's going on? Some of the locals are walking out the door!"

Al said, "We've picked up some information that there is going to be a demonstration today. But don't worry about it. It's nothing unusual. Why don't you go back to your apartment and wait it out? We'll call you when it's over." So I closed up the medical unit and went back to my apartment. That was right before the attack began.

SGT. KEVIN HERMENING (*marine security guard*): I was walking through the lobby of the chancery when I happened to glance up at one of our closed-circuit TV monitors. I could see that a large crowd of demonstrators was forming up at the southeast corner of the embassy compound.

Al Golacinski, our security officer, had been trying to raise Constantine on the radio. Constantine was in charge of all of our Iranian security guards, and Al wanted to talk to him, but he couldn't get him on the radio. So Al told me to find Constantine and tell him to call. Which I did. It turned out Constantine was right in front of the main gate. I delivered the message, and as I was standing there I could see the demonstrators at the front gate. They were really loud, screaming and hollering and shaking their fists, chanting: *"Marg bar Amrika! Marg bar Amrika!"* I didn't like standing in front of the gate where I was totally exposed to them. They were so loud and so hyped up that being that close felt threatening. So I hurried back to the chancery.

JOE HALL (*warrant officer, at the chancery*): We had a radio in our office so we could hear what the marines and security officers were saying to one another. That way we could keep up with what the hell was going on. "Bulldog" was the code name for the security officer, Al Golacinski. Suddenly I heard on the radio, "Bulldog, someone's cut the chain on the gate and there are two or three Iranians inside." It was said in a very relaxed manner. So I stood up on the air conditioning unit in my office to look out over the big metal sandbox in the window. I looked toward the front of the embassy, but I couldn't see anybody. All I could see were a few heads back down there toward the gate. That was it.

CORT BARNES (*communications officer*): There was a big chain looped through the front gate. In retrospect, it was kind of dumb to have the chain accessible from the outside. The militants just came up with bolt cutters and cut it.

JOHN GRAVES (*public affairs officer*): I was in the press office with Barry Rosen. I'd lost a cap on a tooth and was just about to go to the dentist when there was this demonstration. We had seen many, and this one didn't look particularly bad. We knew that it was students and not some wild bunch from South Tehran, or gangsters, or something like that. They were students from the university, and we assumed that they wanted to get their yell in and this was their day to do it. So we had no great apprehension.

I happened to be at the window of the press office where I could actually see the gate, the main gate. I don't know quite how it opened; normally there's a big chain around it. But all of a sudden the gates opened and the first flood of students came in. They were mostly women carrying signs like: "Don't be afraid. We just want to set in." Set, not sit. No sign of weapons or anything like that. It didn't look at all serious. The main thing I remember is that one of the students' leaders embraced, in very profuse Persian style, the head of the Iranian security group that had been assigned to protect us. Which would indicate some collusion. Of course, Ali* had cased the place and had been inside the embassy compound several times during the preceding week. Anyway, I guess that's when I should've gone out the back gate to the dentist, but I was curious. I thought I'd hang around for another five or ten minutes and see what was going on. Which was a big mistake. I should've gone to the dentist.

SGT. ROCKY SICKMANN (*marine security guard*): I was in the motor pool area in front of the main gate when the students went over the wall. I was taking a box over there for shipment to Germany when I heard on my radio: "Recall! Recall! All marines to Post One!" So I turned and ran toward the chancery building. The militants were already coming through the gate and over the walls. We had two large steel doors at the front entrance of the main building, and those doors were being closed as I was running toward them. I screamed at the top of my lungs, "Hey, let me in! Don't close the doors yet! Let me in!" Bill Gallegos, one of the marine security guards, was there and he left the door open so that I could squeeze in. Immediately we locked up tight and put the bar down.

* Ali was a medical student involved in the planning of the takeover.

JOHN LIMBERT (*political officer*): I was down on the ground floor of the embassy near the marine station right at the front door. It must've been about 10:30, perhaps 10:40, when the students started coming over the wall. There were some closed-circuit television cameras around the embassy, and I could see it on the television monitor.

We had very heavy iron doors at the south and main entrances, which were immediately shut. They were very heavy doors. They could resist almost anything short of a bazooka. I can't remember there being any panic. The marines clearly knew what they were doing.

LEE SCHATZ (*agricultural attaché, at his office across the street from the embassy compound*): My secretary, Sorroyo, told me that there was some mail over at the chancery that had to be signed for. So I said, "Well, why don't you go over and get it, and while you're there get some coffee or something."

I was in my office reading through the cable traffic. The building I was in had huge picture windows, and there was a lot of street noise. It got very loud. I glanced out the window and saw Sorroyo running back across the intersection. I couldn't figure out why she was running. It puzzled me. She came hustling into my office and said, "Those people have gone over the wall!" So I jumped up and looked. I couldn't see much from my office, but was able to get a better view from an office up front. From there I could see the embassy gate, the motor pool area, and the driveway in front of the chancery. I saw people running around where they should not have been running. I thought, "Oh boy, here it goes."

SGT. ROCKY SICKMANN (*marine security guard, at the chancery*): Whenever there's trouble, we have a set security procedure that we follow. After we bolted the doors, we got our combat gear out. The time that I was the most frightened was when we were putting on our gear. I got my shotgun out, and my pistol. As I put bullets in my pistol, my hands shook because I was scared. But that fear only lasted a couple of minutes. I just followed the security procedure and did what I was supposed to do. Then the fear vanished.

BILL BELK (*communications officer, at the chancery*): One of the marine guards came bursting into the ambassador's office with his shotgun. He was sprawled out in front of the window like John Wayne in a war movie. I didn't see any need for that. Nobody was shooting. They weren't even throwing rocks. Primarily, we heard female voices. *"Marg bar Amrika! Marg bar Amrika!"* I looked out the window and didn't feel that it was anything real serious. I thought they were just going to march around the building and then be off. I noticed that there was someone directing them with a megaphone, which was normal. Initially, almost all of them were women. The black chadors were very dominant.

And this marine, he's spread-eagled on the floor, locked and loaded. I thought he was overreacting. You don't cock a weapon at unarmed women.

Outside, I saw a few men, but not a great many. They passed in full view of the window, chanting, *"Marg bar Amirka! Marg bar Amrika!"* There must've been two or three hundred of them. They were making a lot of noise. It just didn't look like anything serious.

LEE SCHATZ (*agricultural attaché, at his office across the street from the embassy compound*): It wasn't as if the gates were opened and everybody on the street flooded onto the compound. Instead, key people went in; I'd say maybe 150 or 200. I could see the front of the embassy building, and the first surge of demonstrators wasn't that large of a group.

When they entered the compound, they split and went off in two different directions. Which seemed odd. You'd think that if a crowd was hyped up and ready to the take the embassy, the normal impulse would have been for everyone to rush straight up to the chancery. But they took off in two different directions, with one group heading back toward the consulate. Instead of a mad rush at the chancery, it appeared that some people were stationed at strategic observation points, where they were close enough to holler from one person to the other. You know, someone would stop and stand by the corner of a building where he had a clear view of the courtyard or the motor pool. It had the appearance of something that was well planned.

SGT. WILLIAM QUARLES (*marine security guard, at the Bijon Apartments*): If you want to know the truth about it, I was asleep. I slept late that morning. My radio was charging, so I didn't have it turned on. Even though you always carry a radio with you, I didn't turn mine on when I was in the apartment because there was a telephone. If something happened, Post One could call.

I woke up and everything seemed normal to me. So I decided to go downstairs and have some breakfast. I went down to the kitchen and there was nobody there. So I decided to cook my own breakfast. I was going to whip up some bacon and eggs, and was standing there waiting for the bacon to cook when all of a sudden I heard a burst of chatter on the base station radio in the kitchen. I thought, "What the hell is going on?" Then I heard a couple of marines talking to each other about a demonstration. They were just talking about the status of the situation. I didn't think much of it, because those things happen every day. They were happening all the time. If they needed the marines they would call. So I kept the bacon frying.

Then I saw one of the marines, J. D. McKeel, darting across the street toward the embassy with his duty belt hanging over his neck. I thought, "Damn, what the hell is going on?" I went out into the hall and saw Corporal Kirtley. He explained that there was a demonstration in progress.

The marines had an apartment on the top floor, where we were to go when things got really sticky. Corporal Kirtley said he was going upstairs to sit by the radio and wait for further instructions. I went back to my apartment and put on my artillery uniform and my bulletproof vest. By that time I had forgotten all about the bacon. I just left it there on the stove.

When I had my gear on, I saw Sergeant Maples in the hall and told him I was going up to apartment 4. So he went to get his gear. Upstairs, Corporal Kirtley was standing there, staring out the window. I looked out and saw all these Iranians running around all over the compound. They looked like little ants, running around with big pictures of Khomeini on their chests. I said, "What the hell is going on?"

Kirtley said, "They went over the fence, man. The Iranian guards just stood there and let 'em through the gate."

GARY LEE (*general services officer*): I could hear the crowd chanting outside my office. My office was facing toward the rear, and I couldn't see what was going on in the front streets, but I could hear the noise. I knew they were having a demonstration, and it sounded like it was getting pretty rowdy. I heard the roar of the crowd getting louder and louder. I thought it was getting bigger. But it wasn't that the crowd was getting bigger. They were getting closer.

One of the Iranian locals that worked for me was up at the warehouse. He could see what was going on in front of the embassy. He called me on the phone and said, "Mr. Lee, you'd better leave your office. The students have come over the walls and are attacking the main building." I thought that was an eminently bright idea, and I threw a couple packs of cigarettes in my briefcase and walked out of the office.

It was kind of a misty day. A lousy day. I was looking around to see what was going on. By this time the crowds had already gotten in. They were over the walls. I could see these kids running around with armbands and pictures of Khomeini pinned to the front of their shirts. They were running up past the main building, through the compound toward the back. I was in the middle of them. They were young, rather scruffy-looking college-age kids. I didn't see any guns at that point, but I did see a few bicycle chains and a lot of sticks.

I knew I was supposed to head for the consulate if something like that happened, because the consulate was a safe haven. I was walking up the same direction they were all going, and they didn't pay any attention to me. I had a beard and longish hair. I think the reason they didn't bother me is that they didn't know if I was an American or an Iranian or what.

So I walked over to the consulate and knocked on the door. Jimmy Lopez, the marine security guard, let me in. There were about sixty people inside the consulate, mostly Iranian visa applicants and local employees. We put all of the civilians in the processing room up on the second floor where they couldn't be seen. We told them to sit down and stay low. The idea at that time was to get out of view.

COL. CHARLES SCOTT (*chief of the Defense Liaison Office, at the chancery*): There was nothing spontaneous about that attack. When the first mob stormed the main gate, other large groups started coming through our auxiliary gates as well. Demonstrators were rushing onto the compound and coming over the walls from all directions. Within a matter of minutes there were close to 1,000 demonstrators on the embassy grounds. It was a well-planned, well-executed attack.

BILL BELK (*communications officer, at the chancery*): There was a lot of radio traffic going in and out, and I could hear most of it. I knew that we were in contact with Bruce Laingen and Victor Tomseth over at the Foreign Ministry. In fact, one of the first things our security officer did was call them to brief them about the situation. I thought it was a stroke of good fortune that Laingen and Tomseth were at the Foreign Ministry. They had already started to return to the embassy when the Iranians crashed the main gate. Our security officer told them to turn around and go back to the Foreign Ministry. I think he was concerned about their safety. He didn't want the chargé d'affaires driving up with all of those demonstrators running wild, because it would have put them in a very vulnerable position.

VICTOR TOMSETH (*chief political officer, at the Iranian Foreign Ministry*): Our meeting at the Foreign Ministry went very well. Mike Howland, one of our security officers, had remained in the car while we attended the meeting. Just as we were coming out, Mike got the first word over the car radio that there was some sort of problem at the embassy. We had only gone a block or so when Al Golacinski came on the radio and said that we should not try to come back, because at that very moment there were hundreds of people pouring onto the compound. Immediately we turned around and went back to the Foreign Ministry with the aim of getting the Iranian government to do what governments are obliged to do in this type of situation—provide protection.

JOE HALL (*warrant officer, at the chancery*): We had some Iranian security personnel at the embassy, but they weren't very interested in trying to protect us. In fact, I understand that they were actually welcoming the militants as they came into the compound—shaking their hands and hugging them as they came through the gates. But I didn't pay a whole lot of attention to what those guys were doing. I knew they couldn't have kept that mob out if they'd wanted to. Thousands of Iranians were coming over the walls, and there was nothing a small detail of policemen could do about it.

My thought at the time was that the Iranian government would get involved. They were obligated to protect us, and I assumed they would do so. I pretty much figured someone would come over with a rescue force, as Yazdi had done during the February attack, and take care of the situation. That's just standard practice. Whenever an embassy is under siege, the diplomatic personnel are totally dependent on the host government for security. I knew the Provisional Government wasn't much of a government and that authority in Iran was very fragmented, but I still figured that someone would muster a relief force and take the necessary steps to ensure our safety. So it was only a matter of buttoning the building up tight and waiting the thing out.

COL. CHARLES SCOTT (*chief of the Defense Liaison Office, at the chancery*): From the second floor, I went downstairs to the marine guard station on the main floor and monitored the situation on the closed-circuit television screens. We had cameras located outside the main embassy building so that our security personnel could keep an eye on what was going on. But the militants ripped the cameras off the walls, and all of our screens went dead.

SGT. WILLIAM QUARLES (*marine security guard, at the Bijon Apartments*): I was just trying to be cool. I said, "I can't believe this. I don't believe these little knuckleheads think they're going to take over the embassy." You know, I was really pissed. I kept saying, "What in the hell do they think they're doing? They can't do this. They think they're going to take over the American embassy with all these marines around?" I was really eager to go over there and kick somebody's ass. I really was. I just wanted to bang a few heads.

Maples, Lewis, Kirtley, and myself were waiting for Post One to tell us to come across. See, we had to come out of our apartment building and race across the embassy grounds and into the emergency entrance. There had to be somebody there to open that thing up so we could get in. Post One said, "No, don't come across yet. There are too many people on the grounds. We don't want you to come through yet. Just stay where you are." So that's what we did.

GARY LEE (*general services officer, at the consulate*): Jimmy Lopez went back downstairs to look out the door window. There were swarms of students out there. Some of them spoke good English, and they kept hollering in to Jim: "Open up. We will not harm you. This is only a demonstration." Well, there was no way Lopez was going to open that fucking door!

2 On the Periphery

AT THE TIME of the attack, forty-eight Americans were in the main chancery building and eleven others were in the consulate. Both buildings were equipped with emergency security devices, including thick metal doors and barred windows. In both locations marine guards put security procedures into effect, so that the fifty-nine Americans in the two buildings were in safe areas. However, fifteen other Americans were in vulnerable positions, which could be penetrated easily. They included six people at the Bijon Apartments and nine others in auxiliary buildings on the compound.

BARRY ROSEN (*press attaché, at the press office*): The press office was located in the low two-story building near the motor pool area. We weren't in the main chancery, so we didn't have a marine security guard contingent or any of the security devices they had over there. I told my staff to lock the door and pull the shades down so we could wait this thing out. I could hear the students going from one office to another. They were making a lot of noise, and our local staff was very frightened. The students started to bang on the press office door, and I said, "Just keep quiet. Maybe they'll go away." But my secretary was absolutely terrified, and she opened the door. In came this swarming group of militants. I remember all of the girls were wearing chadors or had their faces covered with handkerchiefs. I told them, "You can't come in here! This is United States property! You are violating diplomatic immunity!"

The militants just scoffed at this. One of the men said, "We are now in control of this den of spies! You leave immediately!"

I continued to tell them that they had no business being there, but it didn't do any good. They just started to trash the office. They were very excited, and they threw newspapers, teletypes, and office files all over the place.

DON HOHMAN (*army medic, at the Bijon Apartments*): I went home and sat in my apartment. As the attack progressed, I listened to my hand-held radio trying to figure out what was going on. A lot of the radio traffic was garbled, because so many people were speaking at one time. But I could get the basic gist of what was happening. I thought, "Holy shit, something bad is coming down!"

Joe Hall and I shared the apartment, and we had a little black mongrel dog named Old Tom. That dog very seldom barked. But all of sudden Old Tom started barking like crazy. I could hear the militants inside the apartment building. It was a big building with an open stairwell, and my apartment was on the third floor. The Iranians were making a lot of noise, and I didn't know what the hell to do. They came right up to my apartment and started banging on the door—*bang! bang! bang!* I didn't answer. I just kept quiet. They were shouting at each other and pounding on doors up and down the hall. When I didn't answer, they moved on and went upstairs. My first thought was: "They're just looking for whatever they can find. They won't break into any of the apartments." But pretty soon they started coming back, and this time I could hear doors cracking. They were kicking the doors in. I heard the wood split. I got on the radio and told our security officer, Al Golacinski, that the Iranians were breaking into apartments. He told me to do whatever I could to escape and evade. My radio call name was Band-Aid, and the last thing Al said to me was, "You're on your own, Band-Aid."

I went onto the balcony at the back of my apartment, crawled over the banister, and dropped down to a balcony below me. Then I jumped to the ground. I had my radio and my aid pack with me. There was a wall behind the apartment building, and I figured I could climb over the wall and run down the street—make my way to a friendly embassy or something. Well, when I got to the top of the wall, one of the Iranian national policemen, whose job it was to provide embassy security, saw me and pointed me out to a bunch of militants. He was getting all excited, pointing his finger at me and jabbering away in Farsi. God, that made me angry! If he hadn't pointed me out, I could have slipped down the street without ever being noticed. But when he started screaming I was immediately surrounded by a bunch of terrorists. A couple of them had handguns, and the others were carrying large sticks and iron pipes. Ten or twelve of those assholes grabbed me and took me over to the embassy compound. They were getting pretty rough about it, too. There was a lot of pushing and shoving as we moved along. They stole my radio, and shouted at me: "You Americans! You Satans! You steal billions of dollars from Iran!"

As they dragged me across the compound, I saw Iranians running crazy all over the place. A great big mob had completely ringed the chancery. They were chanting slogans and shaking banners. I didn't know what was going on inside the building, but from the outside I could see that the Iranians were going to make as much trouble as they could. I also saw some more handguns. So there were plenty of weapons in that group that stormed the embassy.

Those assholes took me over to the commercial library. They had Barry Rosen and John Graves in there, along with a whole bunch of our Iranian employees. Everybody was just kind of huddled up in that one room. The militants put me in there and told me not to speak.

BARRY ROSEN (*press attaché*): The militants took us down to the commercial library, and gathered a big group in there. They must have captured fifty or sixty of us. Almost all of the people in this group were Iranians who worked at the embassy. There were only three or four Americans. The militants guarding us had automatic weapons, and I remember that most of our Iranian employees were very frightened. They were unbelievably excited and upset. I tried to calm some of these people down. I was walking around saying, "Look, this will all be over soon. Everything will be all right. Don't worry, you'll be able to go home when this is over."

DON HOHMAN (*army medic, at the commercial library*): The terrorists were in the room watching over us with guns, and that's a strange damn feeling, to be held at gunpoint like that. I guess John Graves, Barry Rosen, and I were among the first people to be taken hostage. From where I was sitting, I could look out the window and see the chancery building. I remember watching all of the Iranians out there and thinking, "This can't be real. It's got to be a dream."

3 Inside the Chancery

CORT BARNES (*communications officer, at the chancery*): In the communications center we were trying to figure out what to do with our classified stuff. We knew how to destroy it, but we hadn't received approval from the chargé. Our big destruction wasn't paperwork; our big destruction was equipment.

We were in radio contact with Laingen, and we asked him, "When can we begin?" He wanted to wait, and he said, "Don't do it yet."

CHARLES JONES (*communications officer, at the chancery*): There was so much confusion going on that I went ahead and began my destruction program early. Previous experience had taught me how rushed things can become in a crisis. I had been in Cairo during the Six-Day War and in Saigon during the fall of South Vietnam. I knew the tremendous amount of work that was involved in getting all of the necessary material and equipment destroyed. In Cairo the situation had become very tense, and we were incredibly rushed. After that experience I said to myself, "Never again. I don't ever want to be forced into that kind of situation again." At the embassy in Tehran we had a lot of documents that were superfluous to our needs, so even though the order to begin destruction hadn't come through, I went to work destroying all those nonessential documents. This was very early on. I remember one of the people in the section told me that I was panicking. He didn't think I should be doing it. I said, "No, I'm not panicking. I know what it's like to be in a situation when things really get down, so I'm getting ready in case anything like that happens here."

JOHN LIMBERT (*political officer, at the chancery*): A high precedence went off to Washington. At about 2:00 or 3:00 A.M. (Washington time) a watch officer in Washington received our message, and I talked to him until Ann Swift could get to the phone. She came to the desk of the chargé's secretary and took the call. We were in a big anteroom, in front of Mr. Laingen's office, that had about four or five telephone lines. I was trying to make contact with people in the Iranian government. First, I wanted to tell them what was going on. Second, I wanted to make sure that they would get some help to us.

I called the foreign minister's office, but he was not there. I called the prime minister's office and talked to one of the secretaries. I identified myself, told her where I was calling from, and started to explain the problem. After a few seconds she cut me off. She interrupted and said, "Oh, Mr. Metrinko!* It's so nice to hear from you, Mr. Metrinko! Tell me, are those visas ready that we sent over?" So I had to explain to her that no, I was not Mr. Metrinko, and that if they didn't do something she'd probably never get her visas.

In any case, after I explained what the problem was, she said, "Oh well, don't worry about it. We have a relief force of revolutionary guards and police which is on the way, and you have nothing to worry about. In twenty minutes or so they should be there."

I said, "Well, I'm happy to hear that. And I hope what you say is true."

"All the students want to do is read a declaration and leave," she said.

"Fine. If they want to read their declaration and leave, we have no argument with that. Our concern is that no blood be shed. That no one get hurt. We're very glad you have a group on the way. They should get these people out of here as soon as possible. If something should happen, we feel you will be responsible."

I reported all this back to Ann Swift, who was talking to Hal Saunders† in Washington.

BILL BELK (*communications officer, at the chancery*): Outside, hundreds of demonstrators were chanting anti-American slogans and banging on the doors trying to get in, but on the second floor of the chancery everyone remained calm. There was no great panic or undue anxiety. I don't think anyone thought that this situation would last more than an hour or two. The radio traffic back and forth between the security officer and our people at the Iranian Foreign Ministry was constant. We could hear Al Golacinski talking to Mike Howland, and we knew that Bruce Laingen and Vic Tomseth were inside the Foreign Ministry trying to make arrangements to have a relief force sent to the embassy. So we figured it was only a matter of time. The Iranian nationals were obligated to protect us, and everyone assumed that they would. As a matter of fact, at one point I heard Mike Howland say that a relief force was actually on its way.

---

* Michael Metrinko was a political officer at the embassy.
† Harold Saunders was assistant secretary of state for Near Eastern Affairs.

4 At the Foreign Ministry

BRUCE LAINGEN (*chargé d'affaires, at the Iranian Foreign Ministry*): We got to the chief of protocol rather quickly. I knew he couldn't make any decisions, but that he would be helpful to me in getting to the people who could. He had been very helpful to us throughout that summer. My effort was to get through him to the acting foreign minister.

The chief of protocol appeared to take some action within his means, but it was a very frustrating time, because it was apparent that the necessary people were not being reached. We had a lot of oral assurances that help was on the way, but they could not confirm to me that help was forthcoming. To what extent their assurances were wishful thinking, or based on actual information, I cannot say.

VICTOR TOMSETH (*chief political officer, at the Iranian Foreign Ministry*): Yazdi* and Bazargan† had gone to Algiers for some kind of anniversary celebration. They were expected back. In fact, I think they had already arrived in Tehran, but were not in the office when Bruce and I returned to the Foreign Ministry.

We went to the chief of protocol first. He was a very nice man and he wrung his hands a lot, but he was in no position to do anything. He took us to an undersecretary who was a protégé of Yazdi's. The undersecretary was not totally without understanding. He wouldn't do much himself, but at least he responded to our pleas for help. For example, Bruce would say, "How can I get in touch with the prime minister?" The undersecretary said, "You can't get the prime minister now, but you can talk to his brother."

5 Inside the Consulate

MARK LIJEK (*consular officer, at the consulate*): From time to time I'd peer out the window. I remember watching the demonstrators break into the commissary. They knocked through the door with some steel bars, got in, and started rampaging through there.

---

* Foreign Minister Ibrahim Yazdi.
† Prime Minister Mehdi Bazargan.

SGT. JAMES LOPEZ (*marine security guard, at the consulate*): I didn't think too much about what was going to happen next. I was too busy keeping everybody calm and trying to keep the place secured. We had bars on the windows, but the Iranians were breaking glass and reaching through the windows, grabbing filing cabinet drawers and things off of desk tops. Stuff like that. I hit a couple of them with a nightstick, and that pretty much stopped that.

GARY LEE (*general services officer, at the consulate*): Some of the locals were getting panicky. They heard people on the roof and they said, "They're on the roof! They're going to burn us out!" Well, there were some people on the roof, but the damn building was all concrete. There was no way they were going to burn it down. But the locals were getting upset. It was hot, you know, miserable conditions. It was stifling in there, because when we button up that building, she buttons up tight. These civilians could hear the guys on the roof pounding away, and they weren't very happy. Some were very, very frightened. Shahvastari* was extremely worried. I thought he was going to have a heart attack. He turned as white as a Caucasian. He'd gone through Tehran One, and had some bad memories. Now he was going through Tehran Two.

RICHARD QUEEN (*consular officer, at the consulate*): They tried smashing in the doors at the consulate from inside the compound. But these were massive metal doors that were electronically controlled. We heard footsteps on the roof above our heads. They were trying to burn down the building. It was raining, and they were trying to burn down the building. Then the lights went out. I remember a couple of the Iranian employees screamed. Some of the them got down under their desks. Then we heard glass breaking. There was one unprotected window. Everything else had bars on it, and all the windows facing the street had been bricked over. But for some reason this window had not been barred. It was the bathroom window on the second floor. Someone was in the process of climbing through it.

SGT. JAMES LOPEZ (*marine security guard, at the consulate*): We had one guy try and come in through the bathroom window on the second floor. I was down in the stairwell, just standing by, trying to listen on the radio, when someone came and told me that they heard the glass break. I ran into the bathroom, and some guy was climbing through the window. Gary Lee covered me with a shotgun. I went in with a gas grenade,

* Shahvastari was a local Iranian employee.

and the guy backed down out of the window. I had already popped the spoon, so I tossed the grenade out. Then we secured the door.

RICHARD QUEEN (*consular officer, at the consulate*): After that guy got a mouthful of tear gas and Lopez rolled the canister outside the window, we closed the door. Of course, you couldn't lock the bathroom door from the outside, so Mark Lijek and I got some clothes hangers and we tried to wire the door shut. Although I'm sure if someone pushed against it, the door would have opened.

CPL. STEVEN KIRTLEY (*marine security guard, at the Bijon Apartments*): We were listening to the radio. I heard when Jim Lopez popped a tear gas grenade in one of the bathrooms at the consulate. When that came over the radio, the security officer nearly went crazy. He was over at the chancery, and we could hear him say, "No! No! No! Don't do anything to antagonize these people!"

Then we heard Jim Lopez come on the radio and say, "Too late."

GARY LEE (*general services officer, at the consulate*): That one burst of tear gas that Lopez tossed out the window stopped them cold. Fifteen, twenty minutes later they were gone. The militants all went back down to the main building. We were completely forgotten at the consulate. Nobody cared about us anymore. They just left.

6 Inside the Chancery

SGT. KEVIN HERMENING (*marine security guard, at the chancery*): There were different rooms in the embassy building where the marine guards were stationed. My post was in the Defense Attaché Office vault, so I went in there. I remember Colonel Holland was there. He had a flak jacket on and he was very cool. At that point, he didn't think it was anything real serious. I took up my position and got some tear gas canisters ready, and attached my tear gas grenade launcher to my shotgun, in case we needed to use it.

My post was in the front of the building, and by climbing up on a desk I could look out over the metal sandboxes in the window. When I looked out I saw Iranians throughout the entire compound. They were coming over the walls and running around all over the place. Some of them were in the bushes right next to the chancery building.

They were young kids, and when they saw me with a helmet on and with a weapon in my hand it frightened them.

I thought, "Hey, this is really exciting. We're finally getting some action around here."

SGT. ROCKY SICKMANN (*marine security guard, at the chancery*): All of the marines had walkie-talkies, and we were monitoring the situation from our various positions and reporting back and forth to each other what was going on. My area was in a room that overlooked the front of the embassy and I was watching what was going on outside, when all of a sudden there was a message from the basement. Bill Gallegos was down there, and he said that the demonstrators had broken through one of the windows and they were climbing into the basement.

BILL BELK (*communications officer, at the chancery*): The most amazing thing about that attack was how quickly the students were able to breach the chancery. They got in through the only window in the entire embassy that was accessible by way of breaking it. They knew exactly which window to go to and what to have with them in order to get in. There's no doubt in my mind that someone tipped them off. They definitely had some inside information. It was simple. That particular window had sliding bars that were locked with a padlock.* The students walked up to the window with a pair of bolt cutters, cut the padlock, and pulled the bars back. Then they started climbing in. We learned from the marine guards that only women came in first.

CPL. WILLIAM GALLEGOS (*marine security guard, at the chancery*): There weren't enough marines to cover all the posts, and nobody was in the basement. I heard some noise down there and went running down to see what was going on. I saw that some of the Iranians had already come in through the window, and they were moving up from the back of the building. There must've been at least forty or fifty people down there. In front of this group was nothing but women. They were all wearing black chadors, and they had big pictures of Khomeini pinned to the front of them. All of the men were in the back behind the women. They moved forward up the hall. I had my shotgun and yelled, "*Est! Est!* (Stop! Stop!)" They didn't want to stop. I mean, they were radical. They had violent-looking faces, and they were chanting, "*Marg bar Amrika! Marg bar Amrika!*" I pumped a round into my shotgun,

---

* The students entered a basement window at the northwest end of the chancery. It was one of two basement windows equipped with sliding bars, designed to serve as emergency fire exits.

put it to my shoulder, and took aim. I was trying to back them off. Then the next thing I know, some tear gas canisters started popping behind me. I don't know what made them go off. We had lined canisters along the stairwells, and they just started popping, so the place filled up with tear gas. Which made the Iranians uncomfortable. The gas hit me, but it didn't really affect me. I put my gas mask on and I was okay. I just remember pumping rounds into my shotgun and moving the Iranians back.

I was the only American down in the basement. Right away Al Golacinski came running down the stairs. He had his gun out, and he came right over and started talking to the Iranians. He was the security officer, and he told them to move, that they were going to have to leave the building. Stuff like that. It was sort of strange, because in the group of militants Al recognized a couple of guys that he had dealt with before during a previous incident at the embassy. They were familiar faces, and Al talked to them. After a few minutes, he went back upstairs to use the phone, and he took one of these Iranians upstairs with him.

I took cover behind a safe and held the Iranians off with my shotgun. I made sure that all of them were kept in the back section of the basement so that none of them could get up the stairs and onto the main floor of the embassy.

JOE HALL (*warrant officer, at the chancery*): The Iranians got into the basement real quick. At the time, I was in the defense attaché office on the main floor, and we were wondering what the hell to do with our classified stuff. We'd actually been pulling documents out of the files in order to destroy them, when the word came through that the militants had managed to get into the basement. Everybody was immediately ordered upstairs to the second floor. We thought, well shit, we can't carry our classified stuff with us. If the militants did get through, we'd meet them in the hallway with our hands full. So Colonel Schaefer said, "Let's lock it up." We put all the classified documents in the safes and spun the dials.

BILL BELK (*communications officer, at the chancery*): Some of the tear gas was beginning to drift upstairs from the basement. Our marines had temporarily sealed off the section of the embassy where the students had come through the window. They were all very excited, and we could hear them screaming into their radios: "They're in the basement! They're in the basement!" Then Al Golacinski came on the radio. He was talking to someone, and he said it looked like the students were only going to stage a sit-in. I remember he said, "I'm going out to talk to them and see what they want."

CPL. WILLIAM GALLEGOS: Al went upstairs to use the phone, and then he came back down with the Iranian who had gone up there with him. He told me, "I'm going outside to talk with these people."

I said, "Don't do it, Al. Don't go out there."

"I know what I'm doing. I've got to talk to these people."

"Don't go out there. Don't do it."

Al said, "I'll be all right. I know what's going on." Then he handed me his gun and went out the window. Damn, I never saw him after that.

The Iranians who had come through the window were still in the embassy. They never left the building. Now I can't tell you everything I did to keep the militants from advancing, because some of our marine security procedures are classified. But I can tell you that delaying tactics were used. I kept them sealed off in that back section, and remained barricaded behind my safe holding them off with my shotgun for over an hour.

COL. CHARLES SCOTT (*chief of the Defense Liaison Office, at the chancery*): I got the word that Al Golacinski was outside talking to the demonstrators, and I thought, "My God, what's he doing out there?" He couldn't speak a word of Farsi, and there was no need for anyone to be out there talking with them. It's pointless to try and reason with a mob. One of the fundamental rules of security is that you never make yourself available as a hostage.

BILL BELK (*communications officer, at the chancery*): I wanted to see what was going on, so I turned left out of the communications center and went into an office where I could look out the window. We could see Al shaking his finger at the demonstrators, as if he was going to clear all of these people off of the compound by himself. He was giving them a hell of a sermon. But that didn't last long. The militants just knocked his hands away and led him off. The next time any of us saw him his hands were tied with nylon rope. He was already a hostage. That was a sad thing to see.

MALCOLM KALP (*economics officer, at the chancery*): Gradually everybody filtered upstairs. We cleaned out the basement* and the first floor, and got everybody up there—the Americans as well as the Iranian workers.

* When the attackers first came over the walls, all the Iranian embassy employees were evacuated to a secure area in the basement. As soon as the building was breached, they were led upstairs to the second floor.

Everybody sat along the walls on either side of the hall. The marines came around and started giving out gas masks.

Kathy Gross was the commercial section secretary. She was a young kid on her first tour. The poor girl had a Persian boyfriend. That was the reason she had come to Iran. I don't know what happened to the romance, but at the time, she was sitting there absolutely terrified. I sat beside her and tried to console her.

JOE HALL (*warrant officer, at the chancery*): As we were evacuating upstairs, we could hear the Iranians pounding on the big steel front doors with boards and things. They were hollering in and trying to get us to open up. A couple of us detoured into the marines' equipment room and started getting gas masks and weapons and carrying them upstairs. All of the civilian employees, which included Iranian embassy employees, had been evacuated upstairs. We passed out gas masks to everyone and taught them how to use them. We had to get the Iranians settled down. We got them along the wall and told them to keep their heads down and to stay calm. Some of the women were crying and carrying on.

I recall we came up short on gas masks. Kevin Hermening and I went without, and we paid dearly for not having gas masks.

7   At the Bijon Apartments

SGT. WILLIAM QUARLES (*marine security guard, at the Bijon Apartments*): Four of us marines were sitting in that top floor apartment. We also had an American woman in there with us. She was married to an Iranian and worked in the embassy library. She was seven, eight months pregnant, and sat there with her eyeballs popping out of her head. She was scared to death. She'd been through the February 14 thing and remembered when the bullets were flying around.

We knew there were Iranians in the apartment building. We could hear them busting down doors looking for Americans. We saw them drag a couple of people out from the apartments below us. I said, "Aw shit, man, they're gonna work their way up and come into this apartment." So we decided to barricade the door. We took furniture and a bookshelf and everything, and we packed it up against the door in anticipation of them trying to get in. Then we looked around and said, "Naw, we can't resist these guys." We wanted to fight, but we had this woman with us, and she was pregnant. We couldn't put her in a situation where she might get hurt because of something we did. So we said, we can't resist, because we might jeopardize her, and get her hurt. So we took all that stuff down.

SGT. PAUL LEWIS (*marine security guard, at the Bijon Apartments*): There was a lot of talk on the radio and it was hard to get an open net. But we did tell someone on the second floor of the chancery that we could hear the militants breaking into the apartments below us, and that it was just a matter of time they got up to us. We were told just to sit tight and not to resist. The Iranian Foreign Ministry had promised that there were government troops on the way, and it was just a matter of time before all of this was taken care of. So we weren't that worried. We thought it was just another big demonstration—the Iranians would air their demands and that would be it.

SGT. WILLIAM QUARLES (*marine security guard, at the Bijon Apartments*): We decided to hide our radios and just sit there and wait for 'em. Another marine and I hid our radios under the furniture, because we knew the Iranians wanted those walkie-talkies. Then we put a table down in the middle of the floor and all of us sat around it with our legs crossed, looking right at the door. And sure enough, these students busted in the door. The guy who was the leader had on camouflage fatigues. He had a beard and glasses, and he wore some funny kind of hat. He pointed a pistol at us and said, "Put your hands up. One by one."

He searched each of us and then led us out the door. There were about a dozen militants in the hall, waiting to escort us downstairs and over to the embassy. First he searched Kirtley, and they took him downstairs. Then he grabbed this woman's purse. She flipped out. She spoke perfect Farsi, and was furious because he took her purse from her. She wanted it back, but he wouldn't give it to her until he'd looked through it. She got very upset, and yelled and screamed and cried. I think the guy finally gave her her purse back, and they took her downstairs.

Then it was my turn. I had my hands over my head, and I also had on my bulletproof vest. He patted my chest and he said, "Oooh, you wear a bulletproof vest? What's the matter, you afraid of sticks?" I didn't say anything. He said, "You got a radio?" I said, "No, don't have no radio!" So he handed me out the door, and some other dude, with a big old picture of Khomeini on his chest, had me by the arm. He started taking me down the stairs.

As I was going down, the Iranian police were coming up the stairs. They were against all this stuff that was going on. One police officer, some young guy, came over and grabbed my hands and told me to put them down. So I put my hands down. He winked and gave me a sign like, "Everything's going to be okay. Everything's okay." A gentle smile, too. Made me relax. I thought, "Thank God! The rescue forces have arrived!"

SGT. PAUL LEWIS (*marine security guard*): As we were being taken down, a squad of policemen met us on about the fourth floor. I thought these guys were the reinforcements the Foreign Ministry had promised. So I put my hands down and leaned up against the wall. The radicals were trying to get us to put our hands back up, and we were pushing them away. I was laughing at them because the police were there, and the police had automatic weapons. But this one little twerp kept slapping my arms and telling me to put my hands up. I hit him with an open palm to the chest to keep him away from me. I thought the militants were finished, and I rocked that guy pretty good.

SGT. WILLIAM QUARLES (*marine security guard*): The police and the students were arguing in Farsi, so I couldn't understand a thing. I was watching the police officer in charge, and it was the most amazing thing, because he just backed down. He put his head to his chest and walked aside. Just backed down. Then, pop, my hands went back up over my head again.

SGT. PAUL LEWIS (*marine security guard*): The police and the radicals argued for about five minutes. Then one of the policemen pointed his rifle at me and told me to get my hands up. That worried me. I didn't feel like walking off with those guys after I'd just hit one of them.

They took us outside and over to the compound. As we were being led across the compound, we saw Al Golacinski walking toward us. I couldn't see that his hands were tied, and it looked like he was just walking down the sidewalk. Once again, I thought, "Okay, this is all over." I thought that Al had the Iranian security people with him, and that they would take care of the situation. But as it turned out, his hands were tied and he was being escorted the other way.

SGT. WILLIAM QUARLES (*marine security guard*): They took us all the way across the compound to the front of the embassy, near the main gate. There was a whole big mess of people there. Mobs of people. They were standing there chanting: *"Marg bar Amrika! Marg bar Amrika!"*

We were in the motor pool area. There were a bunch of Iranians swarming all over. They didn't know what in the hell they were doing.

They were going bananas, having a good old time, and the mobs kept on chanting: *"Marg bar Amrika! Marg bar Carter!"*

I was standing there with my hands on my head. This one guy tried to blindfold me, but I was too tall. He couldn't reach up that high. Iranians are little fellows, anyway. I'm six feet two and I looked like a giant to them. They made me get on my knees just so they could blindfold me. Then they took this big thick yellow nylon rope and tied my hands behind my back. One of them saw that I had on my bulletproof vest, and he decided that he wanted it. He tried to take it off me without untying my hands. He started ripping off my clothes—unbuttoned my shirt and started pulling. Then one guy chattered something in Farsi, and they untied my hands, took my shirt off, and took the vest.

Then they stripped me of my rank. That pissed me off. That really did.

8   Inside the Chancery

JOE HALL (*warrant officer, at the chancery*): I remember we'd peek out the windows and we'd see all these people down there. They had big banners that said, "We do not wish to harm you. We just wish to set in." They were getting more and more rowdy, and we could see there was getting to be more of them. I don't know how many were actually on the compound, but estimates run upwards of 3,000 or 4,000 people. I mean, there was a sea of people.

CHARLES JONES (*communications officer, at the chancery*): In the communications center we were in radio contact with Bruce Laingen, and I was in communication with Washington, D.C. We had a radio relay going with Kate Koob, who was talking to Washington on the telephone from the Iran-America Society.* At one point, Kate told us that Washington wanted to know if any of the students had any weapons. I couldn't see anything from the communications center, so I went up on the roof through a little trapdoor. I watched the demonstrators to see if I could determine whether or not any of these people were carrying weapons. From what I could see, there were no visible weapons. No rifles were being brandished or anything like that. While I was up there watching,

---

* The Iran-America Society was responsible for the administration of education and cultural exchange programs. It was located two miles west of the embassy, near Tehran University.

somebody downstairs came along and closed the trapdoor, so I couldn't get back in. I was stuck on the roof. I started banging on the trapdoor, trying to get someone to open it, and it was sort of humorous, because some of the people down below heard my banging and thought some of the terrorists had actually gotten up on the roof. They didn't want to let me back in. So I was hollering and screaming, "Hey, it's me. It's Charles Jones up here! Let me back in!" Finally, somebody heard me and opened the door. He wanted to know, "Hey, what were you doing on the roof?"

CORT BARNES (*communications officer, at the chancery*): We told Laingen that we had about two hours of destruction to do, and he said, "Okay, go ahead and begin." There were ten of us in the communications vault, and initially it was very hectic. Some of us were shredding documents, some of us were destroying the equipment, and a couple of people were maintaining communications with the outside.

In the vault, we had teletype equipment that was sensitive equipment. You don't destroy it, you disassemble it. We have methods for making the communications equipment either unrecognizable or unusable; unrecognizable being the first priority, unusable being the second. You can't just take a hammer to a teletype machine. It's useless. There are several integral parts that need to be taken out. So Phil Ward* and I began dismantling the equipment. We knew that we needed to destroy almost everything, except for the very last items that were necessary to remain in communication with Washington.

JOE HALL (*warrant officer, at the chancery*): I spent the better part of the remaining time shredding classified documents. I was down in the SRF† section, which (I don't suppose it's any secret now) was the CIA office. I had a .38 pistol with me. We got everything shredded that we thought we could shred.

Later, I found out that the people down in Laingen's office hadn't done a damn thing. I remember some of the secretaries and people down there were just sitting around on couches, acting like *c'est la vie*. Whatever was going to happen was going to happen. They didn't make any effort to destroy their classified stuff, and of course, as the world now knows, the Iranians eventually got into his safe.

BILL BELK (*communications officer, at the chancery*): After all our political section stuff had been destroyed, I walked into Laingen's office and

---

* Phil Ward was a communications officer.
† Station Reporting Facility.

talked to his secretary, Elizabeth Montagne, to see if Laingen had any documents to go to destruction. Laingen was at the Foreign Ministry and his safe was locked. Liz didn't know the combination and couldn't get into his safe. Every bit of our political section stuff had been destroyed, but we couldn't get Laingen's papers.

SGT. ROCKY SICKMANN (*marine security guard, at the chancery*): When the students first got into the basement, the marines all changed our guard posts to keep them from advancing. They were trying to move forward, and more and more of them kept coming through the window and into the embassy. We were under strict orders from Chargé Laingen not to fire our weapons. It wasn't up to us marines to start gunning people down just because there was trouble at the embassy. If we had started killing Iranians, that would've only made a bad situation much worse, so all we could do was try to delay them as best we could.

CPL. WILLIAM GALLEGOS (*marine security guard, at the chancery*): I was down in the basement, and had one section in the back of the embassy sealed off with my shotgun. I didn't know what the hell was going on upstairs. I radioed for help, but nobody came back to where I was. I was down there for a long time, too, just holding those people off. At one point, I heard a loud crash in the operators' room, and I had to run back to see what was going on. The militants had started moving up through the operators' section from another direction. So I grabbed a tear gas canister and threw it at them. Then I backed out of there.

SGT. ROCKY SICKMANN (*marine security guard, at the chancery*): I was up on the main floor guarding a stairwell. I couldn't see any of the Iranians, but I could see a couple of our marines down there with their shotguns. The militants kept on moving forward, and our guys were constantly backing up. As they came forward, the Iranians had nothing but women in the front, and our marines were pointing shotguns at these women. All of the Iranian men were behind the women. As they advanced, we laid down a little tear gas, and that slowed the militants down some. Then the order came over the radio for all of the marines to retreat up to the second floor where everyone else was holding out. When that happened, we destroyed the radio monitor at Post One and evacuated upstairs with the other marines. We took our weapons and a whole bunch of tear gas canisters up with us. We were ready in case we needed to use any of that stuff from the second floor.

BILL BELK (*communications officer, at the chancery*): All of a sudden six or eight marine security guards came running up the stairs to the second floor. I thought that was a mistake. In my opinion, the marines should not have been ordered to turn and run. They should have stood their ground and filled the basement up with tear gas. I don't mean just a couple of canisters; I mean laying it on 'em thick. The marines had gas masks on, and they should have just kept popping more tear gas every couple of minutes so that the Iranians could choke on it. But, of course, the chargé's order was for them to get upstairs with everybody else. So they came running up.

MALCOLM KALP (*economics officer, at the chancery*): Several of the marines and I took a big table and put it against the steel door, which was the only entrance onto the second floor. Then we picked up a refrigerator, which we put on top of the table, and pushed a couch against all of that. I wedged some secretarial boxes into the little space between the legs of the table and the door. That door was impregnable. Nothing was coming through that door.

A lot of weapons had been distributed. I picked up a shotgun and twenty-five rounds of ammunition. Then I just sat there. Basically, everybody was calm. There were a few people who were frightened, but mostly everybody was calm. Most people believed that the Iranian government would come over and rescue us like they did before. That is what was relayed to us over the phone.

I remembered what happened in February. I've often thought it was amazing that no Americans were killed when that group attacked the embassy. I had no idea what was going to happen to us. I thought surrender was possible, because in my opinion the United States hasn't shown any backbone in a long time. So I thought, "Well, surrender's possible, but I certainly hope not. I'd rather go the other way, and let's go down fighting if we have to."

Then the word came from Chargé Laingen. His quote was simply, "Don't do anything that will increase the level of violence. Don't even use tear gas."

SGT. KEVIN HERMENING (*marine security guard, at the chancery*): We had the heavy metal doors shut at the top of the stairs, and eventually the students made their way up there. We could hear them pounding on the doors and hollering into us, *"Dato boscom! Dato boscom!* (Open the door! Open the door!)" And some of them were hollering things like, "We don't want to hurt you. We only want to stage a political sit-in."

MALCOLM KALP (*economics officer, at the chancery*): The Iranians came up to the second floor and tried to burn the door down. Now how you burn down a steel door, I don't know. But they tried to burn it down. A couple of the marines got excited and started yelling, "They're burning the door! They're burning the door!" They kept feeling the back of it with their hands, and spraying with fire extinguishers. I felt the door and couldn't feel any heat, but figured if it made the marines happy to spray, let them spray.

After a while I crawled underneath the table and sat with my back against the wall and my shotgun across my lap, waiting.

BILL BELK (*communications officer, at the chancery*): As the takeover progressed, Mike Moeller, the NCOIC,* desperately wanted to take some decisive action. He wanted to make a stand. He was yelling at his troops in disgust, "What in the hell is the use of having a gun if you can't shoot?"

He had been ordered not to shoot and not to throw tear gas, and he was irritated, to say the least. There was a mob outside screaming for our blood, and Sergeant Moeller had his hands tied by orders from outside the embassy. He didn't know how to react to the situation. He had his Marine Corps training, which was very good. Unfortunately for him, he couldn't react in the way that he felt was proper. We were in a sanctuary, and the marines had all the weapons and ammunition they needed to protect us.

If I had been the NCOIC, I would've fired a few shots over the students' heads. That would have given warning. Based on my experience as a marine, I think that would've stopped them from advancing into the embassy. They didn't have many weapons themselves, and I don't think the Foreign Ministry would've allowed the takeover to continue if we had fired a few shots over their heads, just to warn them that, look, we're not playing games here.

COL. CHARLES SCOTT (*chief of the Defense Liaison Office, at the chancery*): If any shots had been fired, we would have all been killed. The Iranians came over the wall looking for martyrs. The reason they wore cloth silhouettes of Khomeini over their chests was because they knew that if there was violence, they could get a picture of an Iranian who had been shot with blood staining the silhouette of Khomeini. They were experts at propaganda, and that's the sort of news photo they wanted. When they came over the wall, they knew that some people might be killed, and it didn't bother them in the least. So when Laingen gave the order not to do anything that would increase the level of violence, he did the right thing.

---

* Noncommissioned officer in charge.

JOHN LIMBERT (*political officer, at the chancery*): The promised help was not coming, and the students were obviously doing more than just reading a declaration and leaving.

I got back on the telephone and spoke to the secretary in the prime minister's office. Once again, I was reassured that there was nothing to worry about, that everything was under control. I pressed, and I said, "I'm sorry, but the situation is much more serious than you realize. There's a possibility of bloodshed, and we don't want that to happen. This will be your responsibility."

She said, "Well, let me find out. Hold on just a second."

I ended up talking to any number of people. I finally ended up talking to one of the deputy prime ministers. I once again explained what was going on, and I explained the seriousness of the situation. I told him that I wanted to know specifically what was being done. I was told not to worry. I was told that everything was under control. I pressed, to say, "Well, yes, but what is being done? Or, what are you going to do?" He said, "What we are going to do is this: we are going to have a meeting this afternoon to decide what to do about this problem."

At that point I figured we were pretty much on our own. No immediate help was going to come.

I think at that point our aim was to protect our own people and the seventy-five to a hundred Iranian employees we were responsible for. Many of them were women—secretaries, technicians, and telephone people. With due respect to those who have suggested firing a few warning shots, I think if there had been bloodshed, these people were all just as vulnerable as we were.

SGT. ROCKY SICKMANN (*marine security guard*): From the second floor I looked out the windows. The Iranians had the whole building surrounded. They were all excited, and ran around like little kids in an amusement park or something. They were flipping us off, and I was standing there flipping them off in return, and saying, "Get out of here, you raspberries!"

SGT. KEVIN HERMENING (*marine security guard, at the chancery*): We could see that the militants had Al Golacinski's hands tied behind his back, and they were parading him around. There were a lot of people around him, and one of them had a pistol pointed right at Al. It was sort of misting out, and Al's hair was damp and all messed up, and his clothes were wrinkled. It was a pathetic thing to see someone being subjected to that kind of treatment. I really felt for Al. He's someone I have the greatest respect for. In the preceding months, he'd been able to calm down a few other disturbances that we'd had just by going out and negotiating with people. That's what he tried to do this time. I'm sure he knew he was subjecting himself to some risk when he went out. So you can't fault him for a lack of courage.

COL. CHARLES SCOTT (*chief of the Defense Liaison Office, at the chancery*): From the second floor, I could see Al outside the building. Several of the militants were parading him around. He was yelling up to us, "All they want to do is stage a sit-in. There's no sense in trying to keep them out of the building. It's futile. All they want to do is stage a sit-in."

He was already a hostage, and it was obvious that things were being yelled under duress.

BRUCE GERMAN (*budget officer, at the chancery*): The goons had set fires at various doors around the chancery, trying to smoke us out. The situation was tense. Very tense. The marines were scurrying around. At first they were carrying weapons; then they were told to put the weapons in the vault area out of sight. We didn't want to start something we couldn't finish.

I was in a feeling of terror. Panic. I didn't know what to do. So I just sat there with my gas mask, along with everyone else. We could hear the crowd chanting. They were throwing rocks and banging on the doors. Then there was the fire and the smoke. It was very scary. Very frightening. I believe it took its toll on all of us.

BILL BELK (*communications officer, at the chancery*): The marines were ordered to disarm, and a couple of them ran around saying, "Hide the guns! Hide the guns!" In the communications center we had a small room, a little booth used for privacy when we made long-distance calls to the States. We didn't have anywhere else to put the guns, so I stacked them all in this little booth. The marines were handing me .38s and shotguns. It felt very defeating. Here our guards were handing me the weapons they were supposed to use to protect us. They gathered all the weapons that had been distributed in the hall and handed them to me. I locked them in that little booth to keep the Iranians from getting them. We didn't want to be held at gunpoint with our own weapons.

MALCOLM KALP (*economics officer, at the chancery*): It was a concerted attack. The militants raided the bachelor officers' quarters, the ambassador's residence, the administrative offices, and all of the satellite buildings. They captured several Americans. After we barricaded the door and had done everything we could, I went over to one of the windows and looked out. There was Al Golacinski. They had him blindfolded and tied and led him around the building.

BILL BELK (*communications officer, at the chancery*): The militants were pounding on the steel doors at the top of the stairs and telling us to open the door up. They were screaming and hollering and kicking on the thing, and there was a lot of tear gas and smoke in the building, so it was a very tense time. But there was no way the Iranians could get through the door. It was a two-inch steel door, tungsten steel, barricaded with a couch and a refrigerator. They'd've had to burn the damn place down to get in where we were. Then they brought Al Golacinski upstairs and stood him outside the door.

COL. LELAND HOLLAND (*army attaché, at the chancery*): One of the militants put a gun up to Al Golacinski's head, and they told him to yell in and tell us to surrender or they were going to blow his brains out. Al was outside the door screaming in: "Open the fucking door! Goddammit! Open the door!" They had him out there with a gun to his head, and he was scared senseless, screaming in telling us to surrender.

MALCOLM KALP (*economics officer, at the chancery*): After they couldn't burn us out, they had Golacinski yell into us. He hollered, "Open the door! Open the door! They only want to read their demands and leave." So we decided to send one of our Americans who could speak fluent Persian out there. We pushed the table and refrigerator back, and he moved out.

JOHN LIMBERT (*political officer, at the chancery*): We knew the students had stolen Al Golacinski's radio, so we tried to contact them on the radio. They were outside the door leading onto the second floor. Finally, we were able to raise them on the radio. They didn't quite understand how to use the radios, but we were able to tell them that I was coming out to talk with them.

I volunteered to go out because I could speak fluent Persian. The idea was to try to delay them, if not talk them down. And also to find someone who was responsible, either from the government or the Revolutionary Council. Someone I could talk to, who they would listen to.

When I went outside there were maybe fifty or sixty of these fellows on the stairway. There was gas, there was smoke. One way you dissipate tear gas is to light a smoky fire. Apparently they had some pretty good practice during the revolution. So there was a lot of smoke, there was a lot of gas, and these fellows were clearly very, very excited, and very nervous. Most of them had clubs or sticks. One had a pistol pointed at Al Golacinski's head. Golacinski was standing about four or five rows deep. He was blindfolded, and his hands were tied behind his back. He was very clearly unhappy.

I tried to talk as calmly as I could, to find out who they were and what they wanted. To see if there was someone around that they would listen to. From inside Mike Metrinko yelled out through the door, saying, "We just heard on the radio that Khomeini has ordered the revolutionary guards to come and clear the embassy." Metrinko hollered this, but the students weren't having any of it. It was a nice try, but clearly it wasn't going to work.

They were arguing among themselves a lot, and I couldn't catch a lot of the details. What I remember most vividly is this one fellow who had the thickest Isfahani accent I have ever heard. He was terribly excited; his nerves were just jumping. I remember thinking, "This guy is capable of doing anything."

He asked, "Are you armed in there?"

I said, "That's no business of yours. What do you care?"

"We want to get in."

"Well, where is someone from the government?"

"We don't care about the government."

"What about the Revolutionary Council?"

"We don't care about the Revolutionary Council."

While this type of discussion was going on, they were arguing among themselves a lot. It wasn't clear if they had a leader or not. They kept referring to a five-man council that they had agreed would make the decisions. They were arguing about that. There was an impression of disorder and disorganization. One would say, "Let's go in now." Another would say, "No, we've got to let the council make this decision." Another would say, "Let's knock down the door." And another said, "No, we've got to do what the council says." So on and so forth.

Finally the fellow with the Isfahani accent said to me, "Tell them if they don't come out we are going to kill everyone. We're going to kill both of you." They put a blindfold on me and hollered through the door, "We'll give you ten minutes. If you guys don't come out in ten minutes we're going to shoot both of these guys."

BILL BELK (*communications officer, at the chancery*): When they said they were going to kill the two men outside, that was a rude awakening for me. I thought it was just a demonstration. I never dreamed that they were going to take over the embassy. It was an eerie feeling to know that someone might get blown away.

Captain Robinson* said, "Hold on. We've got Laingen on the phone. We're talking."

JOE HALL (*warrant officer, at the chancery*): Ann Swift was on the phone talking to Bruce Laingen, who finally gave us the order to let them in. There was nothing else we could do. They might've actually killed Golacinski or Limbert.

COL. CHARLES SCOTT (*chief of the Defense Liaison Office, at the chancery*): When the time came to surrender, everyone conducted themselves in an exemplary manner. There was a feeling of genuine fear among all of us, but there wasn't any panic. No one was yelling or screaming or falling apart. A couple of our Iranian employees were hysterical, but all of the Americans took it calmly, and did what they were supposed to do in order to avoid any unnecessary violence.

JOE HALL (*warrant officer, at the chancery*): I was standing right beside Ann Swift when the marines pulled the table and sofa away from the door. The marines hollered out, "Do not shoot. We are not armed, and we are letting you in."

JOHN LIMBERT (*political officer, in the stairwell*): Finally, after seven or eight minutes, someone yelled down from inside, saying, "We're coming out."
    The militants took me downstairs and out the front door. I was very relieved to get out of that gas and smoke. It was rainy and cold. It was good to be in the fresh air. I was feeling relieved to be alive. At that point, I remember thinking, being alive was a pretty good thing.

BILL BELK (*communications officer, at the chancery*): When we opened that door we were taken over immediately. The Iranians swarmed in. One guy looked at me and said, "Walk out the door." So I walked out the door. Two guys grabbed me, one on either side, put my hands behind my back, and tied my hands. They had a long nylon rope that they used to tie us up. After my hands were tied, this guy tried to cut the rope with a knife. The rope slipped and he gouged me, stabbed me in the back. I said, "Ouch!" And he said, "Oh, I'm sorry. I'm sorry. I didn't mean to hurt you." Which amazed me. They were much more gentle than I'd expected.
    They blindfolded me, and I didn't know what to do. I'd never ex-

* Captain Neal Robinson was an administrative officer.

perienced a blindfold before. I thought maybe they were going to take us out and shoot us. I just didn't know what to expect.

BRUCE GERMAN (*budget officer, at the chancery*): The first thing I saw was a mob of these bearded, dirty, screaming, fanatical types, with headbands and pictures of Khomeini pinned to their shirts. They came rushing in and looked in every possible room. They ran around looking for people, weapons, or whatever they could find.

We were given instructions to line up in the hall, women first. They told us they were going to escort us out of the building one at a time. As soon as we got to the checkpoint they had set up, they frisked us, blindfolded us, and tied our hands behind our backs.

I was escorted by two of them. As we were going out, they asked me to make some kind of a statement. They wanted me to condemn Carter and the United States government. I said, "I won't say anything. I'll give you my name and my position in the embassy. That's all you're going to get from me."

I was escorted down the steps and out onto the grounds, toward the screaming mob. I thought we were going to go in front of a firing squad.

JOE HALL (*warrant officer, at the chancery*): The said they did not have weapons, but the first guy I saw walk through the door had a pistol in his hand. Another guy had a holstered pistol. So they did have weapons. They had chains and sticks, and rakes and stuff.

They came in, in a mad rush, and took the phone out of Ann Swift's hand. She had been talking to someone at the State Department, giving them a blow by blow description. They said, "Line up. Line up. Do not talk. Do not for to speak." One by one they were tying our hands behind us and putting blindfolds over us.

COL. CHARLES SCOTT (*chief of the Defense Liaison Office, at the chancery*): As I was being dragged down the hall, I saw the militants pushing people around. They were questioning a couple of marines, who were dressed in battle fatigue uniforms. These Iranians were very agitated, and they kept asking the marines, "Where are the weapons? Where did you put your weapons?" The marines told them that there weren't any weapons. One of the militants got very, very nasty. He said, "I know there were weapons! I saw them! What did you do with them?"

"There aren't any weapons!"

"This is a lie!" He threatened, "If you don't tell us where the weapons are you will be taken out and shot! Right now! Right now!"

The marines just stood their ground and refused to tell him anything.

BILL BELK (*communications officer, at the chancery*): Two of them took me and started to lead me out. The stairs were crowded with Iranians, absolutely mobbed, and the crowd outside was chanting, "*Allah Akbar! Allah Akbar!* (God is great! God is great!)" Over and over again. "*Allah Akbar! Allah Akbar!*" It was continuous, as though God had delivered us to them.

As they were leading me down the stairs, these two guys were saying, "Don't be afraid. Don't be scared. We won't hurt you. We just want to teach you. We will bring you Khomeini's thoughts. We will teach you about God. We will teach the CIA not to do these terrible things to our country."

They led me out the front door, and that's when the picture of me was taken, the one that appeared on the cover of *Newsweek*. I can recall the thoughts I had at that moment. I wasn't really frightened. I guess I was more caught up with the excitement of events. But I do remember thinking that they might shoot me. I thought, "My God, if they are going to get rid of me, then I'll die with my head up." I could hear the constant chanting, "*Allah Akbar! Allah Akbar!*" In the face of all that ranting and raving, I raised up and stood at military attention. I could hear the cameras clicking. I thought, "To hell with them! I'm not going to let them think they have me at an advantage." So I stood straight and tall.

JOE HALL (*warrant officer, at the chancery*): After I was tied and blind-folded, I felt someone go through my pockets. Then they walked me down the steps and out of the embassy. I walked with my head held back so I could see underneath my blindfold. I was trying to see the ground to keep these fools from tripping me down the steps or some-thing. Outside, they turned me around in a circle two or three times, trying to confuse me, but I knew exactly where I was going because I could see out of the bottom of my blindfold. They walked me over to the ambassador's residence.

It had begun to rain, which was the first rain we'd had that year. I remember feeling the drizzle on my face. You know how you think the strangest thoughts at the damndest times? I thought, "I wish to hell this would get over with, so I could enjoy a little bit of this rainfall." Actually, I wasn't frightened. I remember how calm I was. I was think-ing, "Well, they're treating me gently. They're not manhandling me or slapping me around or anything." There was a person on each arm and they had a very gentle hold of me. I thought, "This is all going to be over soon. I'm going to get evacuated out of this damn place. I'm going to be home for Thanksgiving." It was almost a feeling of joy. I thought,

"This is the shortest damn assignment I'm ever going to have. It's all going to be over shortly."

CAPT. PAUL NEEDHAM (*air force supply officer, at the chancery*): At the time the decision was made to surrender, ten of us locked ourselves in the communications vault. I remember that when the *Pueblo* was taken a lot of cryptographic equipment and codes fell into the hands of the North Koreans, and I didn't want to be party to anything that allowed that to happen. So even though it wasn't my job, I went back to help make sure that everything in the vault was destroyed.

COL. LELAND HOLLAND (*army attaché, at the chancery*): They took me and plunked me down at a desk. I was wearing a pair of wash-and-wear slacks and a short-sleeve shirt. Even though I was dressed as a civilian, they knew exactly who I was.

This one guy came over and said, "Stand up!" I stood up, and I felt something sharp in my side. I looked down and could see that he didn't have a knife or anything, but he had a sharpened fingernail, and he pointed it in my side.

I was mad at them. Goddammit, they were a bunch of bastards.

He said, "Where are the guns?"

"What guns?"

"You know where the guns are."

"We haven't got any goddamn guns."

"They are here. You will be punished. Where are the guns?"

I said, "Look, I don't have any goddamn guns. Do you see anything on me? Do I have a gun? I'm a diplomat."

And he said, "You're a colonel in intelligence." So he knew who I was.

A couple of them took me over to the vault door. Inside, our personnel were frantically destroying documents, and they were still in the process of doing this. This guy said, "Open the door."

"I don't know how."

"You know! Open it!"

I said, "Look, you are wrong. You know when you go to the bank, and they've got a special door with a clock on it. This door operates the same way. Any time there's trouble they turn the lock and it cannot be opened for twenty-four hours. This door can't be opened until tomorrow morning."

A couple of them jabbered at each other for a minute. Finally, they decided to take me out. At least I bought a little bit of time for them in the vault.

CORT BARNES (*communications officer, in the communications vault*): When the door was opened to the second floor and everybody surrendered, there were ten of us in the vault area. We shut the door to the vault and remained locked in there for the next two hours or so. We were still destroying stuff. The Iranians knew we were in there, because we were making a lot of noise. It was unavoidable. We were chopping stuff up and cutting stuff up.

I remember Kevin Hermening looked out the fish-eye lens on the vault door. He could see the Iranians trashing the second floor. Then they put a piece of tape over the fish-eye lens so he couldn't see outside. We also had a closed-circuit TV system. The camera was outside the door, but they threw a towel over the camera, so our monitor wasn't showing anything but black.

They started a fire right outside the door. I don't know whether they did that to counteract the tear gas or whether they did it to frighten us. In any event, I could smell the smoke. It didn't affect us too much, though, and we continued with our destruction. It was pretty hectic up until about 2:00 or 2:30. At that point we had destroyed almost everything.

9 Abandoning the Consulate

As THE ATTACK on the chancery progressed, eleven Americans and a large group of Iranian embassy employees remained barricaded inside the consulate for approximately two hours. Their safety was not seriously threatened after the militants' unsuccessful attempt to crawl through the bathroom window, and the building was never penetrated. The Americans inside were able to monitor the events taking place at the chancery on their radios, and a decision was made to evacuate the consulate when the main embassy building was surrendered.

RICHARD QUEEN (*consular officer, at the consulate*): When we heard that the chancery was falling, Dick Morefield, the consul general, decided that we'd better abandon ship. We had direct access to a street that bordered the embassy compound. We couldn't really see the street very well, because the windows facing outside the compound had been bricked over to prevent rocket grenades from being fired in. There were a couple little window slits you could look out, but our view was limited.

We had a big sliding door, where the visa applicants entered, that opened onto the street. I went down with one of our Iranian guards. He unlocked it, and I opened the sliding door. I was rather nervous, because I didn't know what was on the other side of the door. There were just two or three policemen—well, revolutionary guards dressed as policemen. They knew me. So I talked to them in my halting Farsi and explained that we were leaving. Then I told Dick Morefield that we could leave. Dick had said to file out in groups of ten, but as it turned out a steady stream of people filed out. The Iranian policemen had little charts, and they just checked the IDs of people as they left.

ROBERT ODE (*consular officer, at the consulate*): When we lost radio contact with the chancery, Consul General Morefield decided to evacuate our building. We were going to go out the rear of the building, which actually served as the entrance for the visa applicants, and opened onto one of the back streets. I don't know how the selection was made, but I was asked to be the first in line, and everyone followed single file after me.

There was an elderly Iranian gentleman in the building, who was not an employee, but had been admitted due to special considerations. The poor man had very bad eyesight. He was almost blind, and he was absolutely terrified. I was asked to help him out of the building. He clung to me as we went down the stairs, and he kept patting my arm, saying, "God bless you, my son. God bless you. Oh, God bless you." Of course, I'm not so sure God was blessing me on that particular day.

When we went out of the building everything was quiet on the back street. There was a car there with a relative waiting for this elderly man. If I'd realized what was going on, I would've gotten in the car and said, "Take me too, and get me out of here." I would have asked them to take me to my apartment or to a friendly embassy. But I wasn't too concerned. It was quiet on the street, and I didn't think we were going to be taken as hostages. I thought it was a demonstration, just a sit-in or something of that nature. So I helped the elderly gentleman into the car, and was joined by Consul General Morefield, Richard Queen, Don Cooke, Gary Lee, and Jimmy Lopez.

MARK LIJEK (*consular officer, at the consulate*): Before we left the consulate, Jim Lopez told us that we should break up into small groups of five or six people, and that each group should have someone in it who knew the location of the British embassy. The idea was to walk out the door and try to get away, try to walk over to the British embassy.

When we got outside it was raining, and everything was kind of confused. After walking out the door we broke off into groups. Cora and I were with Joe and Kathy Stafford, Bob Anders, and another

American woman who had been at the consulate to get an immigrant visa for her Iranian husband. We were being guided by one of the consulate's Iranian employees, who knew how to get us to the British embassy.

Taking a left turn would have been the most direct way to get to the British embassy. But we didn't want to do that, because it would have taken us straight into all of the demonstrators. So we went straight, and essentially paralleled the main road in front of the embassy. I guess we walked about four blocks in a straight line. We only had to make one turn to get to the British embassy. When we were out of the immediate vicinity of our embassy, we turned left. When we got to the street the British embassy was on, some of the Iranian locals separated from our group.

The rest of us kept plodding along, following an Iranian woman who was leading us. It was still raining, and I was beginning to feel a little self-conscious walking around in a three-piece suit without either a raincoat or an umbrella. I was getting pretty wet. After we had gone another couple of blocks, this woman sort of pushed us off onto a side street. There were demonstrators up ahead in Ferdowsi Square, which we had to go through to get to the British embassy. It didn't look like a good idea to keep heading in that direction. This Iranian woman offered to take us to her house, but we were afraid that might put her and her family into some danger. About every two minutes, Bob Anders suggested that we should all go to his place. After it became apparent that it wasn't a good idea to continue on toward the British embassy, we all agreed with Bob and decided to go to his place.

CORA LIJEK (*consular officer*): We were all beginning to feel a little conspicuous—a group of five Americans standing around on this side street. I had the feeling that people were looking at us. It was not important where we went, so much as it was important to get off the street.

MARK LIJEK (*consular officer*): Unfortunately, Bob's apartment was fairly close to the American embassy, and in the opposite direction from which we had been heading. So we had to turn around and head back a few blocks. We took the most circuitous route we could. The last major street we had to cross was about four lanes wide, and it was a crucial point. There was a *komiteh* headquarters right there, and we didn't know what involvement, if any, they might have had with what was going on at the embassy. We certainly didn't want them to see us, so each of us crossed the street individually. We'd peer around the corner, and when it looked as if no one was watching, one of us would run across. Fortunately, there wasn't much traffic, and we were all able to cross the street pretty quickly, and get to Bob's apartment without incident.

GARY LEE (*general services officer, at the consulate*): We cleared everybody out of the consulate and out onto the back street. The Lijeks and Staffords took off in one group, and I saw Bob Anders walk up a back street. They were already gone. The basic idea was to get the Lijeks and Staffords out first because they were married couples. That left six of us at the building: Richard Queen, Don Cooke, Jimmy Lopez, Dick Morefield, Bob Ode, and myself. I helped Dick Morefield and Jim Lopez lock up. By this time the students were coming back. They were starting to gather around the consulate again, and we knew they could get in through that bathroom window. I went back in and made one last sweep of the building. I was downstairs when I heard Lopez, or Morefield, or someone holler, "They're coming in the window again!" And I said, "All right, let's go!" Lopez came down and we closed the doors behind us, just to slow the students down a little bit. That's when we left the building.

ROBERT ODE (*consular officer, at the consulate*): As we evacuated the building, a funny thing happened. One of the young consular officers handed me a briefcase and asked me to carry it out. I had no idea what was in it, but I said, "Yes, I'll take it." After leaving the elderly gentleman at the car, I was joined by the others. There was a young Iranian guard at the door, and he tried to take the briefcase from me. He was armed and I wasn't, but I struggled with him anyway. I protested and hassled him and managed to hang on to it. I refused to give him the briefcase, and pushed him to one side. He was probably as confused as I was. He could have shot me, if he'd wanted to.

RICHARD QUEEN (*consular officer, at the consulate*): Finally, after everybody had filed out, Dick Morefield shut the door and locked it. We started slowly walking along. I think our feeling was, we'll go to Dick's place, have some beers, play bridge, and wait this thing out. Tomorrow we'd be back at work. We had a day off. A free day off. So we were walking up the street at a rather leisurely pace. I remember an Iranian pulled up in a car and said, "Would you like a lift?" There wasn't enough room for all six of us, so we said, "No, thank you." And he drove on.

GARY LEE (*general services officer*): When we got to Iranshar Avenue, we all stood there like a bunch of tourists. We couldn't decide whether to go right or to go left or what. Morefield said, "Let's go to my house."

I said, "No, there's an embassy down around the corner. Let's go to the embassy." I didn't know if it was the Swiss embassy, or one of the others. We couldn't decide whether it was open or closed, because it was a Sunday.

Morefield said, "I've got a radio. We can keep in contact from my house and wait this thing out." It was a fairly long walk. I knew exactly where he lived. I said, "All right. What the hell?"

So we straggled out, a string of guys walking up the street. I was the last guy, bringing up the rear. I turned and I saw Manage, my secretary, walking up a side street to her apartment. I thought, "Shit, why don't I follow her? It isn't going to get me anywhere following these guys." Then I thought, "Aw, what the hell? Morefield is probably right. It'll be all over in a few hours. We can play chess and drink beer. You know, it'll be another Tehran One."

ROBERT ODE (*consular officer*): A light rain was falling as we proceeded up the street. I remember we got to the corner and someone said, "Let's go to the Swedish embassy." Someone else said, "It's closed today. This is Sunday." I don't know why he thought it would be closed, because Sunday is a regular workday in Tehran. Anyway, Morefield indicated that we should go to his house and just wait the thing out. So we turned right, and we were about half a block up the street when we were suddenly surrounded by these Iranian guards. I don't know if they were militia, or *pasdaran,** or *komiteh,* or what faction they belonged to. We were just suddenly surrounded by them. They shouted at us in English, "Go back! Go back!" We weren't about to put up with them, and started pushing our way forward. One of them fired his weapon over our heads. Then we knew they meant business, and we turned around.

GARY LEE (*general services officer*): I heard a shot fired up ahead. I looked up and saw Morefield being accosted by a bunch of Iranian military types wearing camouflage fatigues. They were brandishing their G-3s or AK-47s or whatever they had.

RICHARD QUEEN (*consular officer*): One of the policemen who was outside the consulate when we filed out joined forces with the militants. When we were about two, two and a half blocks away from the embassy they started chasing us. The policeman was armed, and he fired a shot over our heads. So we stopped. They surrounded us, yelling, "CIA! CIA! SAVAK!"

---

* Armed militants loyal to the revolutionary government.

ROBERT ODE (*consular officer*): They pushed us back down the street. I remember the street was jammed with cars. The traffic was unbelievable. We were walking against the traffic, and these *komiteh* guards, or militia, or whatever they were, dressed in camouflage uniforms, were shoving us back down the street. The general public didn't do anything about it. Whether they were as confused as we were, or frightened, or what, I don't know, but no one intervened on our behalf.

GARY LEE (*general services officer*): We were marched back at gunpoint. The street was busy. There were cars driving by, but the people weren't interested in us. I guess guns in Iran were so common that nobody paid any attention.

We were marched in the side gate, right beside the building we had just evacuated. There were militants all around. Some of these guys were really pissed off, because they had taken tear gas. And they knew it was us, because we'd just left the building. They were brandishing sticks and shoving guns in our backs.

RICHARD QUEEN (*consular officer*): At a side gate I remember seeing the lieutenant in charge of the police, who I'd initially told that we were leaving. He was talking to the militants and said something like, "What do you want these people for? They're really nothing important." They just brushed him aside.

ROBERT ODE (*consular officer*): We were brought into an open courtyard beside the co-op store. Of course, all this time I still had the briefcase the young consular officer had given me as we evacuated the building. I stood back, over by the store, because it had a corrugated iron roof that slanted down. I didn't see any point in standing in the rain, so I stepped under this little bit of protection. The terrorists didn't like that at all. They pulled me out from under the roof and told me to put my hands over my head. Since I had the briefcase, I had to put it on top of my head and fold my arms around it. One of the terrorists tried to take the briefcase from me. I said, "No! No! This is my briefcase!" I clung tenaciously to it. Well, he took it from me and opened it. All I could see in there were a few copies of the *ICA News Bulletin*—that is, press releases. Now why that young consular officer troubled me with that briefcase, I have no idea. To this day I have no idea. He didn't even have any personal items in it, just those press releases.

SGT. JAMES LOPEZ (*marine security guard*): They brought us back to the compound. When we were coming through the gate they started saying something about CIA to me, and I told them they were full of crap.

They separated me from the others for a while, and hit me a couple of times. Then they just walked us over to the ambassador's residence, where they were keeping everybody else.

10 At the Foreign Ministry

VICTOR TOMSETH (*chief political officer, at the Iranian Foreign Ministry*): When Foreign Minister Yazdi showed up, we moved into his office. It was our great hope that he would do what he had done in February: go to the compound, preferably with an armed force, and get the people to give it up to us. I think his unwillingness to do so was probably the best testimony of just how low the Provisional Revolutionary Government had fallen during the intervening eight months. They just had no credibility with anyone at all. Yazdi recognized that; hence his refusal to get involved.

BRUCE LAINGEN (*chargé d'affaires, at the Iranian Foreign Ministry*): I really don't know what time Yazdi arrived at the Foreign Ministry. Looking back on it, I have some feeling that he was in the Foreign Ministry longer than I appreciated. I think he was genuinely concerned about doing what he could to alleviate the situation, and he may have been trying to do something before I got to see him. But how long he had been there, I just don't know. He may well have been there when I first got into the Foreign Ministry. I was told he wasn't, but I just don't know. I'll never know.

It became increasingly clear that those officials with whom I was then dealing no longer had effective power. They were still in office, but as the hours wore on and the political focus centered on the streets of Tehran, and around our embassy, it was clear, I think to Yazdi as well, that his own capacity to affect that scene was rapidly being diminished by events.

11 In Hiding

LEE SCHATZ (*agricultural attaché, at his office across the street from the embassy compound*): I was watching the takeover without even thinking that someone could just as easily come walking into my office. Finally,

I got a phone call and was told to leave. I received instructions from Washington on what I was to do. I told my local Iranian employees that if someone did come to the office, they were to admit that I had been in the office at the time of the takeover, and that I was aware of the fact that the embassy had been taken over. But they didn't know where I was going. I made arrangements to have the Iranian driver take the embassy vehicle to his residence in north Tehran, which I knew the location of, and I got a couple of phone numbers so I could contact a local employee if the need arose. I wished them all good luck, and they wished me the same. Then I walked out the door and went into hiding.

MARK LIJEK (*consular officer, in hiding at a private apartment in Tehran with four other Americans*): Inside the apartment, Bob Anders handed out some sweaters and defrosted some chicken curry. We all felt good that we were dry and warm, and had gotten to a relatively safe place where we could wait things out.

CORA LIJEK (*consular officer, in hiding at a private apartment in Tehran with four other Americans*): We had an embassy network radio, which was on the same frequency as that being used by the marines. We could hear Mike Howland, who was over at the Foreign Ministry, and the people in the communications vault, who were still holding out. At about 4:30 we heard Charlie Jones sign off. He said that there was smoke coming in under the door, and that they were going to surrender the vault. That was really depressing. After that, we only heard Iranian voices on the radio.

12 Surrendering the Vault

SGT. KEVIN HERMENING (*marine security guard, inside the communications vault*): We figured we could stay locked in the vault for ten or twelve hours. In fact, we even broke out the C-ration case and a couple of extra tanks of water. We could hear the militants beating on the door trying to get in, but we figured there was no way. The vault was secure. We must've been in there destroying things for about two hours, when the militants brought Al Golacinski right outside the vault door. Tom Ahearn, who was in the vault with us, talked to them, and they started threatening to kill Al if we didn't open up.

CORT BARNES (*communications officer, inside the communications vault*):
Around three o'clock things got heavy. That's when they started saying
they wanted to come in right now, and that they had Golacinski outside
the door. Tom Ahearn was the ranking embassy officer in the vault at
that time, and he said that he was going to open the door. He didn't
have any choice. We asked him to stall for about five minutes.

Earlier the Defense Liaison Office had brought in a bunch of weapons.
When the decision was made to surrender the vault, we had to hide
the weapons. Initially, we were going to leave all the safe drawers open,
to show that we had destroyed everything and there was nothing there
that we were trying to hide. But then we had the dilemma of having
all these weapons and a big box of ammunition. We took some of the
weapons and put them in the safe drawers and locked them, and we
put the box of ammunition in one of the safes and locked it. That was
all that was in the safes. All of the papers had been destroyed. We had
some shotguns that wouldn't fit into the safes. In between our destruction area and equipment room there was a little utility room with a
small spiral staircase that led to the roof. It wasn't an emergency exit
or anything like that, but was just a way to get on the roof for maintenance. We had some antennas up there, and stuff like that. Rick
Kupke grabbed the shotguns and took them up on the roof. That's
where he was when the vault door was opened. He came downstairs
and walked right into a swarm of Iranians. He was the last one to
surrender.

CAPT. PAUL NEEDHAM (*air force logistics officer, in the communications
vault*): When the militants came through the door they had guns and
they had knives. They came in swinging—slapping and hitting us. Immediately I went into the classic POW position—my fingers locked
behind my head and my elbows locked in front of my nose—so I
couldn't be severely hit in any soft spots.

CORT BARNES (*communications officer, inside the communications vault*):
I decided I was going to play it cool, and I lit a cigarette. I looked
across the narrow space between the two sides of the communications
vault. There was a guy standing there with a shotgun. He was a little
guy, about five feet two, and it looked like he was carrying a cannon.
He just kind of waved it at me. I saw that and decided that these guys
were not playing games. I threw my cigarette down on the carpet and
bellied up right behind Phil Ward so that there would be no space for
them to hit us. I figured the closer together we were the less damage
they could do.

CHARLES JONES (*communications officer, inside the communications vault*): When the Iranians came in the vault, I was standing near Kevin Hermening. One of the militants came running toward us. He didn't know whether to point his gun at me or at Kevin. After a second's hesitation, he focused on Kevin. As soon as he did that, I ducked into a little side room and made sure all of the safes in there were closed and locked. I hurried over and spun the dials on all of the safes, and then I walked back into the main area. By this time, a whole slew of Iranians had come pouring in. There were militants all over the place. It was ludicrous. It almost looked funny to these guys running wild in this secure area of the American embassy, and I started laughing. The whole thing was just ridiculous. One of the Iranians trained his weapon on me and said, "What are you laughing at, motherfucker? I'll put your eyes out!"

Well, I thought that was funny, coming from this little punk, so I laughed at him. A bunch of them grabbed me and started beating and kicking me. Then it wasn't funny anymore.

SGT. KEVIN HERMENING (*marine security guard, inside the communications vault*): The Iranians were being real rough. They were hitting people, and I got whacked across the face a few times. That really made me angry. My arms were being held and I couldn't hit them back. There was no way for me to defend myself. So I just looked those guys straight in the eye. As they hit me, my eyes would bore right into theirs, really fierce and angry. That probably made it worse, too, because they'd just haul off and hit me again.

They jerked me out into the hallway, and I saw some of the other hostages kneeling against the wall, blindfolded, with their hands tied behind their backs. Some of them had burn bags* over their heads. When I saw that, my heart sank.

CHARLES JONES (*communications officer*): We were blindfolded and taken out in the hallway. Our hands were tied behind our backs and our heads were up against the wall. Beside me, I heard Tom Ahearn whisper, "Hey, who's next to me?"

I whispered, "It's me, Charles."

There was an Iranian guard right behind me, and when he heard me whisper, he pulled my head back and slammed it against the wall—*bang!* A couple of them roughed me up. One guy snatched a silver chain that I was wearing around my neck, and yanked it so hard that it broke. I was kicked in the ribs, and my hands were stepped on. After

---

* A bag used for the destruction of sensitive documents in emergency situations.

that, I shut up. I didn't answer any more whispers. I just knelt there against the wall with the others and kept my mouth shut.

SGT. KEVIN HERMENING (*marine security guard*): They took me back into the vault, and that was a very scary time, because they were trying to get me to open the safes. I didn't know any of the combinations, so there wasn't anything I could do to help them. I couldn't have helped them even if I'd wanted to. They had me in front of a safe and screamed and shouted, "Open the safe! Open the safe!"

"I don't know the combination!"

"Open the safe!"

"I can't! I don't know the combination!"

They kept shouting at me and threatening me, and I kept telling them there was nothing I could do. In the room behind me, I could hear them beating up an American. I think it might have been Regis Ragan.* They were really working him over.

It wasn't long before one of the Iranians pulled out a gun. He put it right up to my temple, rubbed it against my eye, and said, "Open the safe! Do it! Right now!"

"I don't know the combination!"

He pushed the gun in my temple and kept shouting, "Open the safe! Open it!" But there was nothing I could do. If they were going to kill me, they were going to kill me, and there wasn't anything I could do to stop them. They kept threatening and pushing the gun against my forehead and temple. It must've gone on for about fifteen or twenty minutes. Which is a very long time. I was incredibly frightened. Finally, the guy pulled the hammer back and said, "Open the safe right now!" When that hammer went back, I sat very, very still. I wasn't about to make any sudden moves.

CORT BARNES (*communications officer*): The militants were walking up and down the hall with guns. I could hear people getting hit and being threatened. I was very apprehensive, because I didn't know when one of these guys might go ahead and shoot somebody just as an example.

In times like that it's difficult to know what being courageous is. You know that the military or the government define courageous as someone who resists all the way. In my case, I just didn't know if I could pass the test. They wanted somebody to open the safes, and I was getting frightened. I was asking myself, "What am I going to do if they hold a gun to my head and say, 'Open the safe.' Will I do it?"

When you are in a hostile situation, and someone comes up to you

---

* Master Sergeant Regis Ragan was assigned to the Defense Attaché Office.

and puts a gun to your head, are you going to do what they want you to do? Or are you going to try to be a hero? It's one of those questions you can't answer. You have to be there. Until then, you just have to wonder, are you the person you think you are? Or would you discover you're not the person you always thought you were?

The idea of no longer living is something people wonder about. When you think about not living any longer, you look around yourself and say, "This is all going to be gone." It's very frightening, but the thought is fleeting, because you remain in the world, and you can't imagine what it would be like not to be here. I just can't imagine anybody really knowing what it is going to be like *not to be*.

In my situation, I was afraid that if somebody grabbed me and put a gun to my head and said, "Open that safe!" I might be tempted to open it. Or I might open it. I was afraid, and I was afraid of my fear. I didn't want to prove myself to be a coward. I just didn't want to be questioned at all. So I was trying to make myself as inconspicuous as possible. For some reason that is still unknown to me, I was never questioned. They never grabbed me, and I'll never understand why.

CHARLES JONES (*communications officer*): At about six or seven o'clock that evening I was taken out of the chancery. A couple of terrorists grabbed me, led me downstairs, and out the front doors. From under my blindfold I could see that I was being led across a field. This one guy had me by the arm, and as we were walking he had his gun pointed in toward me. That scared me. I thought, "Oh God, he's taking me out to shoot me! He's going to shoot me in this field!" My heart was pounding so hard that I thought I was on the verge of having a heart attack. And I remember this guy asking me, "Why are you shaking? Are you cold?" Then he said, "Don't be afraid. We're not going to harm you. There's no need to be afraid."

I thought, "Now why is he playing this game? Why is he saying these things just before he shoots me?"

He was jerking and pulling me, and I thought he was going to turn and shoot me at any moment. Then, finally, he led me into a building, and when we walked through the doors I heaved a sigh of relief that was probably heard in Detroit.

13 Captivity

SGT. JAMES LOPEZ (*marine security guard*): At the ambassador's residence they had us tied up and blindfolded in chairs in front of the windows. Which is a common terrorist tactic. That way if anybody comes in to rescue you, and they shoot through the windows, they take out the hostages.

BRUCE GERMAN (*budget officer, at the ambassador's residence*): I was tied to a chair with my hands behind my back, still blindfolded, facing a wall. I knew it was a wall because I inched forward with my foot and felt the wall with my toe. I wanted to find out where I was, and I couldn't feel anything to the side or behind me, and I couldn't raise the blindfold because my hands were tied behind my back. After a while I lifted my head back. I'd taken my glasses off, so my vision was blurred, but I could sort of look underneath the blindfold and see feet and furniture. I recognized the furniture and knew where I was. I was in the ambassador's residence. So that made me feel a little bit better. I was alive, and I knew where I was. Apparently I wasn't going to come to any immediate harm, which was a big comfort.

I heard all these people scurrying around, shouting orders in Farsi. Somebody came up to me and spoke in very broken English. He asked me if I was hungry. I said, "Yeah, I could use something to eat." He opened a candy bar and shoved a piece in my mouth. I remember it was stale, very stale, but it was lunch.

I heard them asking the other guys in the room if they were hungry, and I tried to do a head count. There were at least eight or ten Americans in the room with me. Which again provided a feeling of some security. I didn't want to be alone with that mob.

ROBERT ODE (*consular officer, at the ambassador's residence*): They were like a bunch of children who had cornered an animal of some sort. They didn't know what to do, except either to plague us, or do a small kindness of some sort. Some of them tried to give me dates. They pressed them to my lips. Since I was blindfolded at the time, with my hands tied tightly behind my back with a nylon cord, I said, "I refuse to eat anything I can't see." And I held my mouth tight.

One of the guards reached in my pocket for my embassy ID card. I said, "I am a diplomat. You are not even permitted to touch me! You keep your hands off me!" Of course, he ignored that completely. His

English wasn't very good, and he asked me if I spoke French. I said, "No, I don't," even though I do.

I was alone in the bedroom, and I heard one of the girls in another bedroom. She sounded very frightened. She was screaming, "No, no! Keep your hands off me! Keep your hands off me!" She was saying the same thing I was saying, but I was doing so on the basis that I was a diplomat. I think she was frightened that they were going to harm her in some way.

MALCOLM KALP (*economics officer, at the ambassador's residence*): As soon as the terrorists were in the house, they started writing everywhere— over the walls, on the ceiling, on the lamp shades; they'd open a drawer and write in the drawers. Everywhere. "Death to the shah!" "Death to Carter!" "Long live Khomeini!" I thought, "Boy, this is going to cost the American government a good bit of money to get this crock cleaned up."

RICHARD QUEEN (*consular officer, at the ambassador's residence*): They put Gary Lee and myself in one of the upstairs bedrooms. I remember we faced the mountains in the distance. The first snows had come on those mountains, and it was a very beautiful sight.

The Iranian militants seemed like a bunch of kids who had just had their day. They had defied authority and were bouncing around. We had been taken prisoner by a bunch of children. I was still sure that it was going to be over in a short time. I was sure that the Iranian government would come in and clean them out. It was just an interesting experience, something I could write friends and parents about. In a letter home I could say, "We were captured today. . . ." I remember Gary Lee said he was sure that an American plane was on the way over, and that it would pick us up when it arrived. I agreed with him. We were sitting in the bedroom having a calm, quiet conversation.

One of the Iranian militants went in to one of the back rooms and got some cigars. He smoked a cigar and was joking around. A couple of them tried to start political discussions. Stupidly, I got involved in one or two. They were incredibly naive and said the most ridiculous things. I remember one guy said something to the effect that Americans built Iranian roads poorly so they could get Iranians killed. I said, "No, Iranians are just lousy drivers. They're crazy. They've got to show everybody how fast they can drive." But he insisted that Americans built Iranian roads poorly to get Iranians killed. The conversations were actually on that level. Over and over again they came back to the idea that the shah had ruined their country, and America was responsible for the shah. Every evil that had ever befallen Iran was America's fault, and they were convinced that they were going to get the shah back. There was no doubt about that.

I'd speak to them in my blundering Farsi, but wasn't sure that I was being properly understood. Then, as evening rolled around, I remember watching the sunset. With the mountains it was nice, real beautiful.

JOE HALL (*warrant officer, at the ambassador's residence*): They took me down to the TV room in Laingen's residence and tied me to a chair. I sat there for an hour, blindfolded, my hands tied behind me. I could hear them scurrying around, in and out. I was near a door that led to the basement storage room where they stored a lot of canned goods, sodas, glassware, candles, and stuff like that, used for ambassadorial parties. There was a lot of candy in there. These guys were having a great time going in there and pilfering this stuff.

After about an hour, they came and took the blindfold off me. There must've been about six or eight Iranians in the room with me, but there was always a lot of coming and going. There were even women, Iranian women, going past. I thought, "Well, if they've got the women involved in this thing, it can't be too serious." They were smiling and laughing and sharing candy. Some guy came up to me, and with his old grubby hand, put some candy in my mouth. So I was sitting there tied to a chair chewing candy.

One little smart-alecky guy came up and took my shoe off. He reached under the television and pulled the cord out of the wall, doubled the cord up, and slapped me across the bottom of my foot with the cord. He said, "This is the way the shah's army tortured innocent Iranians." That first day or two there was a lot of horseshit going on. They knew we were powerless, and they were enjoying it to the fullest.

COL. LELAND HOLLAND (*army attaché, at the ambassador's residence*): The first group of kids that hit the embassy went through the building like a bunch of thieves. They climbed over everything, knocked over half the stuff, put some of it in their pockets, broke other stuff, and started writing all over the wall. If ever there was a bunch of horses' asses, that had to be them.

The girls in the group came in wearing chadors and no makeup. Some of them had zits all over their noses. I mean, they were a grungy-looking bunch of women. Iranian women can be quite ravishing, but not these animals. They had the uglies. They were females and that's where it ended.

BARRY ROSEN (*press attaché, at the ambassador's residence*): I was sitting in the cook's quarters, when an Iranian woman came in to interrogate me. She was wearing her revolutionary garb, which was not a chador, but was sort of the Mujihadin outfit for women: brown pants, a baggy shirt, and a handkerchief covering her face so that all I could see were her eyes. Her attitude suggested that I was some sort of evil character, and immediately she annoyed the hell out of me. She made all kinds of ridiculous accusations about the United States, and asked me what my job was.

I said, "I'm the press officer in the embassy."

She said, "No, this is a lie. You are CIA!" Then she went into a tirade about how the CIA had destroyed Iran, and how I had destroyed Iran. You know—I did it. I was personally responsible for all of the evil in the world. She got really worked up, and went on and on with her radical rhetoric and ridiculous accusations.

Well, there was a great big bottle of Scotch in the room, and without even thinking about what I was doing, I reached into the bureau and pulled out this gallon of Scotch. I told her that she needed to calm down and, holding the bottle toward her, asked if she would like a drink. To a devout Moslem that was an extreme insult. She became very incensed. All of a sudden a bunch of men came storming into the room. One of them pushed me against the wall. They roughed me up, berated me, and accused me of insulting Iranian womanhood.

JOHN LIMBERT (*political officer, at the ambassador's residence*): I ended up in a back room at the ambassador's residence. I guess it was one of the servants' rooms. There were a whole bunch of people in that room, and there was no attempt to keep us from talking or listening to the radio. The students brought a radio in, and we all sat around listening to the radio together. That first day no one had any idea of what was ahead. Among the students the feeling was: "Okay, we've done this. Now what do we do?" Our attitude was: "Okay, you've got us. So what? You've taken the building. You have all these people. But what are you going to do now?"

I don't think they had any idea. For one thing, they might have figured that there would be fighting. I think of lot of them expected bloodshed and shooting. When it happened the way it did, they didn't quite know what to do.

Most of them were curious. They were curious about me. I was curious about them. I asked them the same questions I might ask any young Iranian. I would ask where they were from, what university they attended, and what they were studying. And they'd ask me where I learned my Persian. We talked some about Islam, and we talked some about Christianity. They were very interested in the Biblical idea of turning the other cheek—if someone strikes one cheek, you should turn the other cheek. They wanted me to explain that.

They seemed to be kids about twenty years old, very much like many of the students I had in Shiraz, kids from small towns with rather strict upbringings. Many of them had probably never seen an American before. I think a lot of them were surprised to find out that we didn't have horns. They didn't know what an American was like, and some probably didn't even know where America is. They expected us to be some kind of monsters. It was a bit surprising for them to discover that we could speak to them in their own tongue. I got into some discussions of Persian literature that afternoon.

JOE HALL (*warrant officer, at the ambassador's residence*): Later that afternoon they took me upstairs. Earlier in the week there had been a Halloween party at the ambassador's residence that Joe Subic* had organized. A bunch of Halloween junk was still on the walls. You know, skeletons, big pumpkins, witches, and goblins pasted all over the walls and chimney in this big room where they'd had the party.

I remember one of the guards asked me in his thick Iranian accent, "What is dis? What is dis stuff?"

I said, "It's just for children."

He pointed at a skeleton. "Dis is for children? You do dis for children?"

"Yeah, it's an old German custom that the Americans latched onto. You know, you give candy to the children."

He couldn't understand how all these spooks and goblins and skeletons associated with children. And he wanted to know where all the children were. I said, "Well, you've got them all tied up right here in this room."

SGT. PAUL LEWIS (*marine security guard*): I was put in one of the prefab houses behind the chancery. Bill Quarles was in the room with me, and we were both tied and blindfolded. Our hands were tied behind our backs and our feet were tied to the chairs. Since I'd only arrived in Tehran the night before, I hadn't had a chance to meet Bill. I'd only known him for those thirty minutes or so that we were sitting in the apartment watching the takeover progress. But Bill impressed me, and he made me feel awfully good after we were captured. We were taken into this house and I could hear Quarles close to me. Almost immediately the Iranians tried to exploit the fact that he was black. They were talking to him about racism in the United States, and told him

---

* Sgt. Joseph Subic was assigned to the Defense Attaché Office.

that Iranians were more sympathetic with the cause of black people than most Americans were. That sort of thing. The only thing Bill would say was, "Where's my friend? Where's Lewis?" He wouldn't answer any of their questions or talk to them. The only thing he wanted was to make sure that I was still okay. From the way they were talking about whites and racism, maybe he had inferred that I was in trouble or something. All he would say was, "Where's Lewis? Where's my friend?" Hearing that made me feel good.

CHARLES JONES (*communications officer, at the ambassador's residence*): Inside the ambassador's residence, they sat me down at a big long table in the dining room. When they took my blindfold off, the first person I saw was Sergeant Walker, one of the black marines. They had TV cameras and lights in there, and they were interrogating Sergeant Walker. They were trying to get him to make some kind of statement that was critical of President Carter and critical of the American government. Sergeant Walker kept telling them, "I'm a marine. I'm an American. I'm not going to say anything against my government."

I was at the other end of the table, and they started interrogating me. They were asking me about what we had destroyed in the communications vault, and they kept saying, "Those documents belong to the people."

I said, "What people? The documents we destroyed belonged to the United States government. You have no claim to them. What I destroyed is none of your business."

But they kept asking, "What was destroyed? Why did you destroy it?"

I wasn't at all cooperative. I let them know that what I had done was none of their business.

This sort of thing went on and on. They'd say, "What are the combinations to the safes?"

"I don't know the combinations."

"Who does?"

"The officer in charge of the communications section. He's the only person who knows the combinations."

"Who is he?"

"He's not at the embassy today. He's in the United States on vacation."

"Who's in charge when he's gone?"

"I am."

"So you know the combinations!"

"No, I don't know the combinations. The officer in charge of the section is the only person who knows that, and he's not here."

We just went around and around in circles like that. It was obvious that those guys had no idea of what they were looking for. They thought we were all "spies," and that our wristwatches were really radios, and all sorts of ridiculous crap. They had these silly preconceived notions in their heads, and in interrogating us they were looking for someone to stand up and say, "Hey, I'm James Bond! I'm Agent 007! I'm a master spy!"

I tried to explain a little bit to them about international diplomacy and what the functions of an embassy were. But it was hopeless. They were absolutely convinced that everyone in the embassy was a spy. It was almost funny, in a pathetic sort of way.

I wasn't being at all sympathetic, and this seemed to disappoint them. They asked me, "Why aren't any of the blacks sympathetic to the cause of the Iranian people?" I guess they figured that if you were black, you should be sympathetic to them.

I kept telling them over and over, "Look, I'm an American. I'm a foreign service officer. What you guys are doing is illegal. There is no way I could ever be sympathetic to a terrorist action. The color of my skin doesn't change the fact that you are a terrorist."

BRUCE LAINGEN (*chargé d'affaires, at the Iranian Foreign Ministry with Michael Howland and Victor Tomseth*): Late in the evening Yazdi, in effect, suggested that I leave the Foreign Ministry. But I had no interest in doing that. I couldn't have gone back to the embassy with any effectiveness at that point, because the necessary help wasn't forthcoming. I suppose I could have gone out and sought refuge in a foreign embassy, but that would have shifted necessary responsibilities onto the shoulders of others. I decided to stay where I was and do what I could. The position I took with Yazdi was that I could not leave unless he could guarantee my security somewhere else, and that as long as I remained in the Foreign Ministry I had at least some reason to believe that my security would remain intact.

The day ended with Yazdi taking us down to the diplomatic reception rooms late in the evening. He told us that he had a cabinet meeting to go to, and assured us that the issue would be resolved that evening, or by the next morning at the latest. Whether he actually believed that or was simply trying to reassure us, I can't know. But I doubt that he could have been as confident as he suggested he was.

BILL BELK (*communications officer, at a staff house on the embassy compound*): It was very uncomfortable to have to sit in a chair with your hands tied behind your back. That first day they didn't untie my hands or take the blindfold off. I just sat in that chair wondering what the hell they were doing. I was in pain. The ropes they used were nylon, and it really hurt because they tied my hands too tight. My wrists were raw from the friction of the rope.

I had some cigarettes in my top shirt pocket, and after a few hours I spoke up and said, "Will you give me a cigarette?" One of the militants, who was hovering right in front of me, said, "Don'ta speak! Don'ta speak!" A minute or two later I felt someone reach into my pocket for a cigarette. He put it in my mouth and lit it. I damn near choked to death. I couldn't keep a cigarette in my mouth like that. But I tried to smoke it. After I'd gotten through with what little I wanted I spit it out on the floor.

RICHARD QUEEN (*consular officer, at the ambassador's residence*): After a while they took us downstairs to the kitchen. There were a couple of Iranian women down there, dressed in their chadors. The militants told them to make some food for us. So the Iranian women took some frozen steaks out of the freezer and threw them on the grill. They didn't realize that although the steak might look well done on the outside, the inside was still frozen unless you cook it for a long time. They untied our wrists and gave us forks, but no knives. We gnawed at the frozen steaks like Conan the Barbarian.

BILL BELK (*communications officer, at a staff house on the embassy compound*): They didn't give me anything to eat at all, until late at night. It must've been about 11:00 P.M. when I felt somebody with something cold at my lips. It was ice cream. They were trying to feed me a spoonful of ice cream. Just a spoonful. I think they used the same spoon for everybody. You know how you get dry and parched when you get excited. I had that one spoonful of ice cream, and that was all. That was dinner.

GARY LEE (*general services officer, at the ambassador's residence*): That evening was total chaos. The Iranians were shit-scared. They didn't know what was going to happen next. I was pretty much resigned to the fact that I was a dead man. I figured I was either going to get blown away by our stuff coming in, incoming rounds, or I was going to get blown away by the turkeys who had taken over the embassy. One way or the other, I was going to end up dead.

I sat there tied up. The students rolled in a television set. They were typical kids. They watched themselves take the embassy on TV. They were elated. The students figured this was the way to handle international affairs.

There were some guys with guns running around. Most of the guns were our own. You know, the guns that the marines had left behind in the main building. The Iranians opened the safes and got the guns. So we were being held with our own guns.

BRUCE GERMAN (*budget officer, at the ambassador's residence*): After several hours they took the blindfolds off for a short time. We all clicked our eyeballs around to see who was there. There were eight or ten of us, and in each case there was a goon with a club seated right in front of us. My guy spoke in very broken English, and claimed to be my protector. I said, "Who or what are you protecting me from?" Of course, he couldn't answer the question. He just said that he was my protector.

SGT. PAUL LEWIS (*marine security guard, at a staff house on the embassy compound*): Late that night the Iranians started collecting identification. Well, when I first heard about the attack, I put on my battle fatigues in a real hurry, and didn't take the time to pick up any identification. So I didn't have any. No wallet, no passport, no military ID. Nothing. So they took me away from the rest of the group and isolated me in a bedroom. They tied my hands and feet together and left me on the bed with a couple of guards in the room to watch me. Because I didn't have any identification, these guys accused me of being a CIA agent. I was sitting there on the bed with a very short haircut, wearing camouflage utilities, and obviously very young, and the Iranians were making up all sorts of stories as if I were some sort of master spy. They kept accusing me of working for the CIA, and of being in Iran to set up subversive cells and of torturing innocent Iranians.

COL. CHARLES SCOTT (*chief of the Defense Liaison Office, at the ambassador's residence*): Thanks to Joe Subic, my interrogation started on the night of November 4. Subic made a list for the Iranians, telling them who we were and what our jobs were. He did that on the first afternoon. I was sitting there blindfolded and I heard Subic tell them, "This is Colonel Chuck Scott. He's been in Iran many times before and he speaks fluent Persian. He was an attaché here in the sixties."

I could've punched his lights out for that. The Iranians branded me CIA right then and there. That night I was taken over to the chancery and sat down on a stool in one of the administrative offices. One of the militants, who the others referred to as Hossein,* began the interrogation. He started out by accusing me of being the CIA station chief,

---

* Hossein Sheikholislam was one of the militant leaders responsible for planning the attack on the embassy. He was present at numerous hostage interrogations. Currently he is deputy minister of foreign affairs in Iran.

which I denied. I said, "I'm Colonel Charles Scott, an officer in the United States Army."

He said, "Your name is not Charles Scott. You're George Lambrikis.* You weren't even born in the United States. You were born in Greece, and for many, many years you have been helping the shah with SAVAK. We know all about you, Mr. Lambrikis. You're not a colonel in the army. You are the CIA station chief. The sooner you admit that, the better off you'll be."

Immediately, this line of questioning became repetitious as hell. They kept accusing me of being the CIA station chief, and I denied it. While this was going on, the militants were playing the good guy/bad guy bit. There was one terrorist in there who I called Pig Face. Whenever I'd deny their allegations about being the CIA station chief, or denied that I was in Iran on a mission to overthrow the Khomeini government, Pig Face would get very agitated. He'd say, "This guy is lying to us! It's time to get the blood flowing! Let's get the blood flowing!" He was the bad guy who was ready to beat me to a pulp, while the main interrogator was playing the nice guy. Hossein repeatedly told me that the sooner I confessed the easier it would be on me. He would calm Pig Face down and tell me how much easier it would be if I cooperated with him.

As time went by, the interrogation became physical. Every now and then Pig Face would come up to me, slap me across the face, and say, "He's lying. Let's get the blood flowing!" Of course, my hands were tied, so there was nothing I could do except sit there and take it. They kept making the same accusations over and over again. I continued to deny that I was the CIA station chief and that I was plotting to overthrow the Khomeini regime and return the shah to Iran. None of that was true, and I told them so. I was punched in the stomach and kicked in the groin. They knocked me off the stool and kicked me while I was lying on the floor. That's an old SAVAK trick that the Iranians used under the shah to soften people up—knock someone down and play soccer with them, just to let you know they can do it. After that, they got their rubber hose, and they would shout their accusations and strike me with the hose. By this time, I had written myself off. I thought, "I haven't got a prayer of getting out of here alive."

SGT. WILLIAM QUARLES (*marine security guard, at a staff house in the embassy compound*): That night they moved me to another little house that was two doors down. While we were walking one guy said, "Don't

---

* George Lambrikis is a State Department political officer who served a tour of duty in Iran and was evacuated out after the February 14, 1979, attack.

worry. We aren't going to hurt you. We're your friends. Don't be afraid." He kept telling me stuff like that, trying to reassure me that I wasn't going to be taken out and shot. When we got into this other house, they sat me down and took my blindfold off. They tied my hands in front instead of behind me, and let me sit at a table. Four or five Iranians were crowding all around me, and all of them wanted to talk. A lot of Iranians spoke very good English; some of them had studied in the States. This one guy wanted to hold a regular conversation. They were asking me questions about what I thought of the shah, and what I thought of Bakhtiar, and what I thought of this and that. I would tell them, "I don't really know too much about what was going on then. I haven't been in Iran for very long."

One guy brought me a Coke. It was frozen, so he had to shake it up, which didn't help much. I just sat there sucking this giant ice cube, which was the only thing I had to eat all day. These Iranian students and I sat up real late that night. They kept asking questions and talking away. Corporal Kirtley was in the den, lying down on the couch. I knew he was listening, because at one point he sat up and said, "Yeah, just wait till the marines get here." There was an aircraft carrier out in the Persian Gulf, and he was waiting for the marines to show up. So was I. Everybody was anticipating big old CA-53s landing in the middle of this mess, with a whole attachment of marines jumping out and starting to get all this shit organized.

BILL BELK (*communications officer, at a staff house in the embassy compound*): Late that night I had to make a toilet run. We'd been tied up for several hours, and I was hurting. So I spoke up and said that I had to go to the toilet. A couple of them led me to the bathroom. One of them stayed right there with me. He untied my hands, but he wouldn't take the blindfold off. He just said, "It's in front of you. The toilet is in front of you." So I had to take a shot in the dark. When I was finished he immediately tied my hands back up and took me back to my chair. We sat in those chairs all night long. Somehow I managed to fall asleep.

JOE HALL (*warrant officer, at the ambassador's residence*): Around midnight I thought, "This is really getting old." I felt dirty, sweaty, and uncomfortable. I wanted to brush my teeth and go to bed. I was thinking about sleep. Some of the other hostages started falling asleep in their chairs. Finally, they came and untied me and took me to the bathroom. Then they brought me back to the dining room, gave me a blanket, and pointing at the floor said, "Sleep here." Thankfully, there was a carpet there, and I managed to get hold of a little throw pillow. So I got down on the floor and covered my head. I couldn't go to sleep because my hands were tied. It was very uncomfortable. So I played around under the blanket until I had loosened the knot. I remember waking up at five o'clock in the morning and thinking, "My God, is this still going on? I thought this was just a nightmare."

Part Three

The First Month

1 November 5, 1979

In tehran, news of the American embassy seizure was greeted with huge displays of public support. Massive crowds gathered in front of the embassy and several religious leaders endorsed the takeover. Revolutionary banners and posters of Khomeini were strung up on the compound walls, and a small podium was erected in front of the main gate. At a press conference, the student militants issued a statement in which they proclaimed themselves to be the "Student Followers of the Imam's Line." They demanded that the shah be returned to Iran to stand trial before a revolutionary court, and warned the United States that the hostages would be killed immediately if an attempt was made to rescue them. As an endless parade of speakers stepped forward to condemn the United States, American government officials repeatedly petitioned the Provisional Government of Iran to intervene on the hostages' behalf. In an atmosphere of near hysteria, a tense waiting game began.

Inside the embassy compound, the hostages were scattered throughout the ambassador's residence and the four staff houses. At the Iranian Foreign Ministry, Bruce Laingen and Victor Tomseth continued to negotiate with Provisional Government officials, knowing full well that political power in Iran was extremely fragmented, and that the Provisional Government's authority was tenuous at best.

Elsewhere in Tehran, nine American diplomats were hiding at four different locations, including two private apartments and the library of the Iran-America Society. Lee Schatz, the agricultural attaché, took refuge in an office building across the street from the embassy, where he had a clear view of the front portion of the compound. He was the only American diplomat in Iran who was able to monitor the activity at the American embassy.

LEE SCHATZ (*agricultural attaché, in hiding across the street from the embassy compound*): The crowds stayed in front of that embassy all night long. It was really an all-night show, with kind of a street fair atmosphere. Then, at daybreak, everything slowed down. By daylight, there was no real activity on the compound and the crowds were all gone. Everything was quiet.

GARY LEE (*general services officer, at the ambassador's residence*): I woke up the next morning, and the atmosphere was still sort of like a big college demonstration that had somehow succeeded. The students didn't really know what they were doing. It was all a big joke. I had the feeling that everyone expected the whole thing would end soon.

I remember waking up and thinking: "All right, these kids have done what they're going to do. They've made their point. The mob took us over, and the Iranian government didn't do anything. Okay, fair enough— they let them make their point. The next step is to proceed with normal protocol. The government is going to step in and do its duty. We're all diplomats and they'll kick us all out of the country. The end result will be a break in diplomatic relations."

Of course, at that point I was still giving the Iranians credit for being human beings.

JOHN LIMBERT (*political officer, at the ambassador's residence*): Outside my room all of the students were lining up to use the Iranian toilet.* It was one of the few Iranian toilets on the entire compound. Most of them were Western toilets, which the students didn't like to use. So they were all standing in line. At that point, they still weren't trying to stop me from moving around, and eventually I shoved my way into the line.

After using the toilet, I tried to get a glass of tea out of them. I'm something of an addict for tea, and if I don't get a glass in the morning I just don't feel quite right. They were making some for themselves, and I managed to get a glass.

JOE HALL (*warrant officer, at the ambassador's residence*): When I woke up they fed me some bread and jam and some hot tea. I remember how good it tasted. It really tasted great.

Then they led me down and tied me to a chair in the dining room of the ambassador's residence. They had about twelve or fourteen Americans tied up around this huge dining room table. We weren't allowed to speak, so we just sat there and looked at each other.

SGT. ROCKY SICKMANN (*marine security guard, at the ambassador's residence*): After giving us something to eat, they took me down and tied me up in the dining room of the ambassador's residence. The guards didn't allow us to talk. We couldn't even say anything to the person next to us. I remember thinking that it was the sort of situation that couldn't continue for a very long time, because the Iranians were using so many people. They had at least two or three guards for every hostage,

---

* An Iranian toilet is a basin implanted in the floor. Instead of sitting down on an upright bowl, one simply squats above an Iranian toilet without ever touching it.

plus they had the guards outside, and the girls in the kitchen who were cooking. Sooner or later, you'd think, these people would have to go to work or to school or something.

While we were sitting there, I saw that the whole house was being ripped apart. The students thought that the ambassador's residence was a big "spy center," and they were ripping stuff off the walls and looking for all kinds of secret devices. After the February 14 attack, our government had installed some pretty tight security at the ambassador's residence. Some sensor devices had been installed throughout the house that could be monitored from the marine position on the second floor. Well, the Iranians got their hands on these little sensors and thought they were "spy speakers." They just ripped them out of the walls. They also confiscated our watches, thinking they were miniature walkie-talkies. It was obvious that they didn't know what was going on.

SGT. PAUL LEWIS (*marine security guard, at a staff house in the embassy compound*): I was isolated in the bedroom of this house. That morning two guys came in. One of them didn't speak English very well, but the other did. The English speaker wanted to talk politics, and I argued with them for a little while. We talked about Vietnam, Mossadeq, and Central America. This guy talked about wars of imperialism, exploitation of the masses, exploitation of Third World countries—that sort of thing. There was a lot of Marxist influence in his theories, but he was very sensitive about being called a communist or a Marxist.

After these two guys left, I asked the guards in the room if I could be untied long enough to exercise. This request caused them to have a little conference, and after their conference they said yes, they would let me do that. But then they called so many guards into the room that it wasn't even worth it. They lined people up along the wall by the window, and they packed guards in around the doorway. I don't know what they thought I was going to do. I started stretching a little bit, and one of them asked if I knew martial arts. I said, "Oh, hell yes!" Then they brought in even more guards, and there wasn't any room left for me to exercise. It was just ridiculous. I had to tell them to scoot back just so I could have enough room to try and do a push-up. I thought, "To hell with this." I didn't even bother. I just lay back down on the bed and went back to the handcuffs.

LEE SCHATZ (*agricultural attaché, in hiding across the street from the embassy compound*): That morning, a big truck and several cars drove onto the compound. They pulled up, and the cars parked in such a manner that when they had their trunk lids up, it obscured the back of the truck from view. The people who were unloading the truck were obviously concerned about who might be watching them from inside the compound. They were unloading big pots for cooking, and huge piles of bread. They kept unloading this bread, and then they started unloading automatic weapons. Some of these rifles had folding metal stocks. They were probably G-3s, and there were lots of them. The people unloading these guns appeared to be concerned that there were others at the embassy who would not approve of what they were doing. It was as if there were various factions involved in the takeover, and some groups were more revolutionary than others. At any rate, a large number of guns came off that truck.

JOE HALL (*warrant officer, at the ambassador's residence*): That morning was the first time all of the guards were armed. They'd gotten the marine weapons they'd found in the safes, and they were armed to the teeth. Some of them were also wearing marine fatigues that they'd pilfered from personal quarters.

I remember looking over my shoulder and seeing a guard sitting there with one of the marine shotguns. He had that gun pointed right at my head, and his finger was resting on the trigger. He wasn't trying to intimidate me, he was just sitting there talking to one of the other guards. In the midst of all that chaos, I thought the chance for a fatal accident was pretty high. Those guys had no idea of what they were doing with those weapons. I thought, "Holy cow! This guy is going to blow my head off just because of some stupid accident." So I looked at one of the other guards who was standing near me, and sort of whispered to get his attention, "Hey, hey."

He said, "What do you want?"

"Could you ask that guy to point his gun somewhere else?"

So he walked over to the guard with the shotgun and said something to him. When the guy realized what he was doing, he looked at me with sort of a stupid sheepish grin on his face, and pointed his gun at the ceiling.

JOHN LIMBERT (*political officer, at the ambassador's residence*): It must've been about eleven o'clock in the morning when they came and pulled me out of my room. I remember going through the dining room, seeing the people tied up and blindfolded, and I thought, "Okay, things are going to take a turn for the worse."

I was led to a chair in the living room, tied to the chair, blindfolded, and warned not to talk. I was sitting next to a window, which was open, and I could hear the crowds outside. Behind us, the students were walking around cocking their guns.

We didn't know who the students were or what their purpose was.

Some of them didn't know, either. The unfamiliarity of the situation was terrifying. There was always the feeling that they might be capable of killing us.

When you can't see what's going on around you, you tend to imagine things going on around you—and it's easy for your imagination to get the best of you. As I sat there, I heard a rustling of paper, which was very frightening. I thought, "Maybe they're writing something down." I remembered having seen pictures of people who had been executed. Handwritten signs had been left on the bodies that identified the person as being guilty of this or that crime. So that rustling of paper frightened me. I was able to sneak a look out from underneath my blindfold, and saw it was just a student reading a newspaper.

LEE SCHATZ (*agricultural attaché, in hiding across the street from the embassy compound*): The Iranians called for people to come down to the embassy. I guess they issued a call over the radio, saying that there would be a rally in front of the embassy that afternoon.

I remember a mullah came in before they had their public prayers. The students escorted him onto the compound, and it was kind of like show and tell. They took him on a tour. After they paraded him around, he came back and led the masses in prayer from the tarmac in front of the motor pool. The mullah wasn't on the podium or anything. He was down on the ground, in the middle of the courtyard, with all the others. After their prayers, they had some speeches, and of course there was a lot of violent chanting.

That was a big crowd. The street was six lanes wide and had wide sidewalks, and that entire area in front of the embassy was mobbed. The street was solid with people for several blocks.

BILL BELK (*communications officer, at a staff house on the embassy compound*): I sat tied to my chair for the entire day. Outside I could hear shots being fired in the street, and there was a crowd out front. It sounded like there were millions of people in front of that embassy, and all of them were calling for our blood. Their screaming was causing the house to vibrate. I could actually feel the walls vibrate to the rhythm of their chants. *"Marg bar Amrika! Marg bar Amrika!"* Over and over again. *"Marg bar Amrika!"* Or, *"Allah Akbar! Allah Akbar!"*

CAPT. PAUL NEEDHAM (*air force logistics officer, at the ambassador's residence*): Around eleven o'clock that morning I heard Don Sharer being moved. As they were taking him out, he said, "If anyone gets out of here alive, tell my wife and my daughter that I love them." He thought he was going to be taken out and shot. So did I. I wasn't even free to make a move on any of the Iranians because I was tied to the chair. That was a frustrating feeling. So I just sat there and thought, "Oh boy, here we go."

They had tied us to chairs in a circle in one of the main rooms of the ambassador's residence, so that we were all facing outward toward the wall. I thought, "This is so that if someone does come in and try to rescue us, the Iranians can execute us very easily. They only have to keep a couple of people in the middle of the room with all of us tied up in a circle like this." I fully expected to be killed.

JOHN LIMBERT (*political officer, at the ambassador's residence*): I thought we were all going to get shot, and if we weren't shot, then the crowds would eventually come in and kill us. I knew Iranian history, and there are numerous instances of mobs being stirred up into extremely violent acts. I knew that if that mob outside was stirred up enough, and got into the building, they'd find us sitting there tied up in chairs. We would be helpless. I remember thinking that I was either going to get shot, or I was going to be killed by the mob outside. Either way, there was nothing I could do about it, and at least I could be thankful for having had a good life so far.

COL. LELAND HOLLAND (*army attaché, at the ambassador's residence*): I'd been through this damn routine in February of 1979. After that, I very honestly felt lucky to be alive. And here I am, blindfolded and tied to my chair, going through it again. Only this time it was a tougher thing. I was thinking: "Son of a bitch! How did I let myself get into this?"

BILL BELK (*communications officer, at a staff house on the embassy compound*): Outside the mob was just raving, but inside the Iranians were sort of relaxed. You know, they were students, and they would talk with us. This one guy, Seyyed, sat down beside me and talked to me about the Moslem faith. He told me about the teachings of Khomeini and the teachings of Ali Shariati.* I think he was trying to convince me that the students were right in taking over the embassy and right in demanding the return of the shah. He talked and talked, which made me feel a little bit better. He obviously wasn't going to take me out and shoot me. But still, with that crowd out there, I didn't know what to expect.

---

* Dr. Ali Shariati was an Iranian scholar whose writings made him a patron saint of the revolution.

2 At the Iranian Foreign Ministry

CHARGÉ D'AFFAIRES Bruce Laingen, political officer Victor Tomseth, and security officer Michael Howland spent the night of November 4 in the diplomatic reception room at the Iranian Foreign Ministry. They were not held under duress, but were free to leave at any time. However, Laingen and his colleagues chose to remain at the Foreign Ministry, where they could continue to exert pressure on Iranian government officials. The three Americans were able to maintain long-distance telephone communications with the State Department in Washington, D.C. From Tehran, Laingen kept American government officials apprised of his efforts at the Foreign Ministry, and he was able to pass along recommendations on how best to deal with the crisis at hand.

BRUCE LAINGEN (*chargé d'affaires, at the Iranian Foreign Ministry*): We were deeply concerned at the temperature of the passion on the streets, and we were mindful of that in every step we took. So we certainly did counsel caution and patience. Of course, it was difficult to recommend anything very sensitive from the Foreign Ministry in view of the limitations on our communications, but we did convey the impressions we had of the local scene and the ideas we had on how best to proceed. I became celebrated, I suppose, for counseling caution and patience. I felt strongly at the time that that was fundamental to any plan or action required.

From the outset, I had confidence that the situation could be resolved peacefully. If I had known then what I know now about the treatment that was accorded my colleagues, I think my sense of confidence would have been diminished somewhat, simply out of concern for accidents. But I did not believe that the Iranians would ever deliberately kill or harm us. I just didn't think that they sensed it would serve their purposes to do so.

VICTOR TOMSETH (*chief political officer, at the Iranian Foreign Ministry*): At the Foreign Ministry we were trying to do two things. First, we were trying to serve as a communications conduit between Washington and the various forums of power in Tehran, which included the Revolutionary Council, the Provisional Government, and officials at the Foreign Ministry. We had regular access to the senior people in the Foreign Ministry, and by telephone we were able to talk to others. During those first forty-eight hours, my assumption was that we could find a way to negotiate a resolution to the situation at the embassy. As confused as things were in Tehran, I felt that we would somehow manage to communicate with the key people necessary to resolve the problem. Second, by sheer presence and continued insistence, we were trying to impress upon the Iranians that they had a moral and legal obligation to do something. In essence, we were trying to hold them hostage by refusing to leave, and by bringing whatever pressure we could to bear upon these authorities.

3   At the Embassy

LEE SCHATZ (*agricultural attaché, in hiding across the street from the embassy compound*): Apparently the Iranians up front knew that they were going to be able to whip that crowd into a frenzy, yet still be able to control them. Some of the things I've read tend to make me believe that Iranians can be very violent in their verbal actions—you know, chanting, raising fists, throwing insults—yet never rise to action. I remember a quote from a book about an Iranian that said, "Haji Baba was all for the glory of war, except for the dying of men."

And that's sort of the way that crowd was. They were all for the beating of chests and getting whipped up into a frenzy. But they weren't going to take that additional step to violent action. If you had a crowd in the United States that whipped up, they'd rip apart anything that was close by just to get it out of their system. But out there, the mullahs seemed to have a very good understanding of the crowd and how to manipulate it. They knew what they were doing, and they used it to the hilt.

COL. THOMAS SCHAEFER (*defense attaché, at the ambassador's residence*): I remember being tied to a chair in the ambassador's house and blindfolded. I don't know how long that lasted. At first I was kept in a room near the kitchen. The militants didn't really know what to do with us. They kept looking in on us, wandering around like an uncontrolled mob of idiots. They stunk. They smelled. Now that they had completed this portion of the act, they were wondering, "What's the next step?"

As far as I could tell, there was very little leadership in those first couple of days—but of course, I didn't have the opportunity to see much.

For me, one thing that was very comforting was that I wasn't alone. You feel a certain safety in numbers. At some point I was moved upstairs and kept in the ambassador's bedroom. There were probably six or eight of us in that one room. That was very comforting to me. When everyone is getting the same treatment, you don't mind things quite as much. It's when you are put off by yourself that it becomes a tougher challenge.

Obviously, you sit there and wonder, "How long will this go on? Will some of us be singled out for special treatment? What are you going to do if they start beating on you?" Those kinds of things go through your mind. Then you think, "I wonder if my wife realizes that I'm okay." And I'd say to myself, "I've been through this before, and managed to come out alive." I'm sure I also thought about the fact that we had advised Washington not to let the shah into the United States. Now, I have a great admiration for President Carter, but at that time I'd sit there and think, "Damn it, Jimmy, what kind of a decision was that?" I had my moments of anger. But then, you have no choice but to accept it. And acceptance is a difficult thing. You have to say, "Hey, it happened. You might not like it, but baby, you are here."

JOHN LIMBERT (*political officer, at the ambassador's residence*): At about three or four o'clock in the afternoon there was one hopeful sign. They untied us and took us to the kitchen two at a time to feed us. The students stood around while we ate and made sure we didn't talk to one another. I remember thinking that if they were going to shoot us, they wouldn't bother to feed us.

SGT. PAUL LEWIS (*marine security guard, at a staff house on the embassy compound*): Later that afternoon, the guy who had been talking to me about wars of imperialism brought some other people into the room. He said they were from some sort of central committee, and that they had some questions to ask me. These people weren't nearly as friendly as the first guy. They wanted to know the combinations to safes, and they wanted to know the combinations to doors in the embassy. They also wanted to know who worked where. Of course, I knew absolutely nothing. I'd only been in Tehran fourteen hours before I was captured. So by this time I'd been in captivity longer than I'd been at the embassy. I didn't know who the administrative officer was, and I didn't know who the political officers were. I'd never checked in. I didn't even know how to get in the front door.

Of course, these guys didn't believe that. They yelled and grilled and warned and threatened. They'd say, "It's going to be very rough on you if we don't get into those safes! Now tell us the combinations! If you don't cooperate you're going to be here for a very long time!" I told them that I didn't know anything. But they kept on grilling and threatening. They said, "We know you're CIA. We've found documents in the embassy, and we know you're a spy. We also found the torture room. We know about that. We know that you participated in torturing innocent Iranians, and helped train SAVAK to torture."

Now I don't know if they actually believed what they were saying or not, but there wasn't anything that I could tell them. I knew there wasn't a "torture room" at the embassy, and I thought maybe they were talking about what we called the "bubble." The bubble was a secure, soundproof room for conferences. You can go in there to eliminate hostile electronic surveillance while discussing sensitive topics. It's a room that can't be bugged. And it is soundproof; if someone was standing out in the hallway, it would be impossible for them to hear any sounds coming out of that room. Maybe the Iranians thought it was there so no one could hear the screams. Maybe they did think it was a torture room.

CPL. WILLIAM GALLEGOS (*marine security guard, at the ambassador's residence*): Some of the militants came and got me in the afternoon and took me over to the marine office in the chancery. They wanted me to open the safes. I refused to do anything. I wouldn't say anything to them. They kept asking me my name, and I wouldn't tell them that. I just sat there. They blindfolded me. Some other guy came in who spoke good English. I don't think he was one of the regular students. That's probably why they blindfolded me. Anyway, he started asking me stuff like: "How do you open the safes? What are the combinations? Where are the weapons?"

I just sat there. I didn't say nothing. So they got a little rough. They pushed me around and slapped me a few times while I was sitting in the chair. I don't think they were trying to hurt me. It was more like they were trying to intimidate me. Still, I wouldn't say anything. I mean nothing.

They were asking me about people in the embassy. "Who is CIA? Who does this? Who does that?" They wanted to know the job functions of people on the embassy staff. They wanted to know what certain equipment was for. I wouldn't talk to them. I didn't say anything to anybody.

They put a gun to my head, and I still refused to answer them. I just sat there. I could hear this guy cock the gun. He pulled the hammer back, and I didn't know if he was going to shoot me or not. I didn't know what they were going to do. They kept asking: "What is the combination to the safe? How do you get in there? What do you have in there?" At the time, we probably had some weapons in there, and some radios. Maybe a bulletproof vest or something like that. Not much. We didn't keep anything important in there. But I wasn't about to help these guys. He pulled the trigger and dry-fired an empty chamber. Just like that—*click!* By this time, I was ready for anything. I mean, I was ready to be tortured. I figured that physical torture would be the easiest part of it. The psychological torture—the waiting, the seclusion, not knowing what was going on—was much worse. If they were roughing me up, I knew what I had to do. They could do whatever they wanted to me, and I wasn't going to give them the satisfaction of doing anything for them. That was my job. I was a marine. That's what I was trained for. I'm a firm believer in the armed forces, and I'm a firm believer in America. If those guys wanted to play games, they weren't going to get anything from me. I just sat there and didn't say nothing.

After a while, they took me back over to the ambassador's residence and tied me up in a chair. I could look under my blindfold and tell that everybody was sitting in a circle facing the walls in this one large room; it was the ballroom of the ambassador's residence. I was waiting for somebody to come in and get us out.

BILL BELK (*communications officer, at a staff house in the embassy compound*): You can't imagine what it's like to sit there tied up and listen to that chanting hour after hour. Those people were rabid. I was getting sick of it. I wanted it to stop. It just went on and on, hour after hour. All the while, this kid Seyyed was sitting there giving his religious lectures. He was telling me about Ali, the first imam, and said he was going to teach me about all of their prophets. He was sincere, too. There was a lot of coming and going and confusion among the students, but the chanting outside was the one thing that was constant.

SGT. PAUL LEWIS (*marine security guard, at a staff house in the embassy compound*): That chanting went on all afternoon and on into the night. It sounded like hundreds of thousands of people in the street—and they weren't that far away, either. They were just on the other side of the wall. Those people could really make some noise. Over and over again, "*Marg bar Amrika! Marg bar Amrika!*" It was so loud the sound almost became physical. The noise would just kind of throb through me.

I was worried that things might get out of hand and those people would come over the wall. I couldn't understand Farsi, and I didn't know what the speakers on the other side of the wall were telling those people. Finally, I asked one of the guards, "Hey, what is this *marg bar shit?*"

JOHN LIMBERT (*political officer, at the ambassador's residence*): At about ten or eleven o'clock that night, we just got out of our chairs and lay down on the floor. One of the students had the brilliant idea that they could tie our feet together to keep us from running away in the night. So I spent that night stretched out on the floor with my feet tied together. Fortunately, there were carpets on the floor. It certainly wasn't deluxe accommodations, but it was good to have gotten through the day alive.

ROBERT ODE (*consular officer, at the ambassador's residence*): That night I crawled under the dining room table to sleep. Instead of giving me a blanket, they took a piece of drapery and gave that to me. I just slept on the floor under the dining room table using this piece of drapery as a blanket.

JOE HALL (*warrant officer, at the ambassador's residence*): I remember there were several of us underneath the dining room table. That's where we spent the night. They kept our hands tied while we slept. I've had arthritic shoulders for years, and it was very uncomfortable for me to have my wrists tied like they were, all day and all night. My shoulders were sore, and it was especially uncomfortable at night to lie there with my hands tied. Fortunately, they tied our hands in front of us, and I discovered that it was easy to slip the knot. On that second night I was able to get my hands free. I just slipped the knot and pulled one hand free. I kept that hand hidden underneath my blanket so none of the Iranians could see what I'd done. If any of them came toward me, it would have been easy for me to put my hand back through the loop and tighten the slack.

BRUCE GERMAN (*budget officer, at the ambassador's residence*): I was asleep on the floor. I still had my blindfold on, and my hands were tied in front of me. At about three o'clock in the morning someone nudged me and asked my name.
   I said, "German."
   He said, "Up!"
   And I was taken outside.

CDR. ROBERT ENGELMANN (*naval supply corps officer*): On the second night, they took myself and a couple of others out of the embassy.

They woke me in the middle of the night, threw a blanket over my head, and stuck me in the trunk of a car.

BRUCE GERMAN (*budget officer*): I was put into a van with two or three other Americans. Not only was I still wearing my blindfold, but they pulled a heavy canvas money bag over my head. Then we were driven off the compound to a residence located somewhere in Tehran. I don't know what part of the city we were taken to. I never did find out. But five Americans were taken to this residence. So by the second night, the night of November 5, I was being kept off the compound.

CDR. ROBERT ENGELMANN (*naval supply corps officer*): They drove us up to northern Tehran and stuck us in a safe house. They had five of us Easter-egged up there. That way if the Americans came in and staged an Entebbe-style raid, they wouldn't be able to rescue everybody. Five of us would still be sitting in this house.

COL. CHARLES SCOTT (*military attaché, at the chancery*): At the embassy, my interrogation continued on into the night of November 5. Those guys didn't let up. It went on both day and night. There were threats, and veiled threats, and more physical abuse. I was kicked in the groin, punched in the stomach, and knocked off my stool. They continued to accuse me of being the CIA station chief, and they wanted a confession. They told me that I was never going to get out of there alive unless I sat down and wrote out a confession. I figured, "If they're going to kill me, they're going to kill me, and there's nothing I can do about it." My main objective was to protect my own integrity. I thought, "All I've got left is me. If I'm going to go out now, I'm going to go out in style."

Years and years ago, I'd read a book that proved to be helpful throughout the course of my interrogations. It was called *Brainwashing*, by a writer named Richardson. In his research, Richardson interviewed a number of prisoners from the Bamboo Curtain days when the communists took over in China. He wanted to know how some of these prisoners managed to survive the Chinese attempts to brainwash them, and do so while keeping their sanity and mental well-being intact. He discovered that those who survived had certain techniques in common, and among those techniques was that before the brainwashing actually started, before the physical and mental pressure began, these men set goals and objectives for themselves. These goals became their salvation when they were being tortured, or denied sleep, or kept in isolation. So when I was dragged over for interrogation on the first night, I knew I had to set some goals and objectives, because it would be very easy for me to become so exhausted or so frightened that I'd say, "Sure, I'll sign that confession for you. The American people will understand. They'll know it was done under duress." But as a soldier in the United States Army, I had certain loyalties to my country that I was obligated to uphold. There was no way around it. So I had to set goals, and they had to be realistic. You have to set limits beyond which you're not willing to go in order to save your life. And that's what I did.

My first goal was, no matter what the militants did, I wouldn't write a thing down for them. I knew they were looking for a written confession that they could take and wave before the TV cameras and the crowds. I wasn't about to let them have that. My second goal, right out of our military code of conduct, was that I wouldn't say anything that could be embarrassing to the United States. If they had the interrogation on tape and I said something that was contrary to U.S. policy, even if it was something that I believed, then that was the kind of thing that could have been broadcast over the news media and broadcast in the United States. That was also the kind of propaganda they were looking for, and if I ever came home I didn't want to have to hang my head. Third, also from the code of conduct, I wouldn't say anything that could bring any additional pressure or danger to my fellow hostages. And last, as a way of clarifying the situation in my own mind, I told myself, "The Iranians are the enemy. Even though we are not at war with Iran, they are the enemy in every sense of the word." In my simple soldier's mind, I had to keep that very clear.

During the first interrogation session the militants played the good guy/bad guy bit. But on the second night they were all bad guys. Like I said, I'd written myself off. I didn't think that I was going to get out of Iran alive. My only objective was to maintain my integrity.

They wanted me to confess to being the CIA station chief. They would say, "We know you were working on a military coup against our government." I'd deny it, and they would say, "We know otherwise! You were working on a military coup against Khomeini!" They tried everything they could to get me to sign a confession—threats, veiled threats, and physical abuse.

I'd been knocked off my stool and kicked so many times that I was pretty sure I had some serious internal injuries. They would threaten to burn my eyes out with cigarettes, and they'd threaten me with my life. There was one guy in there with a big knife like a machete. They would put my arm up on the table, and this guy would raise the knife like he was going to lop my arm off. And what can you do about it? All I could do was sit there. When they failed to follow through on their threats, that was an important signal. I knew that if they ever started cutting off limbs or fingers, not only would I not get out of there alive, but my body would never be found. Nobody would ever have heard from Chuck Scott again. But when they failed to follow through on some of their threats, it was my first indication that they weren't going to do anything that would put a permanent scar on me, which gave me an immediate edge. I knew I still had a chance of getting out of there alive. So that gave me hope, and it was an extremely important signal. I began to realize that there was only a certain level of violence they were going to carry out, and that they wouldn't proceed beyond that point.

They got out their rubber hose and beat on me with that, and they continued to knock me off the stool and kick me around until I thought I had a hernia. But I also became aware of the fact that they were being very careful not to mark my face. They weren't going to put any permanent scars on me. Finally, late at night on the fifth, they told me that if I did not sit down and write out a confession right then, they were going to take me outside and turn me over to the Iranian people. I was sitting in a chair with my elbows and wrists wired together. I was blindfolded. They stood me up and led me outside. I could feel the cold air against my face, and I could hear the mob. I couldn't see them, but I could feel and hear that there were huge mobs out there. They walked me over to the front gate to parade me in front of the mobs. They stood me so close to the gate that people could take punches at me and kick at me. If they'd left me there long enough, those people would have torn me apart. They really would have. The women were the worst—I could hear them, and feel them kicking and clawing away. As I stood there, I thought, "Sooner or later you're going to feel warm blood flowing. Somebody is going to slip a shiv in you." Those people were volatile. There's just no other way to describe it. They were extremely volatile. But the clowns who dragged me out to the gate stayed right there, and I could hear them shouting commands in Persian, saying, "Don't hit him in the head! Don't hit him in the head!" They were making sure that nobody put any permanent marks on me. There was a certain solace in hearing those commands. "Bear up under this," I said to myself. "It's not going to get any worse." And of course it never did. After a few minutes they took me back to the chancery, where the interrogation continued.

4 On the Outside

DURING THE FIRST twenty-four hours of the embassy siege, nine Americans managed to avoid capture. This group included the five people who had escaped from the consulate (Kathy Stafford, Joe Stafford, Cora Lijek, Mark Lijek, and Robert Anders), and Lee Schatz, the agricultural attaché. In addition, Lillian Johnson, an administrative secretary, spent the day of the attack hiding in the Bijon Apartments. Two other Americans, Katherine Koob and William Royer, maintained offices at the Iran-America Society, located near Tehran University, approximately two miles to the northwest of the embassy compound. Throughout the night of the fourth, William Royer and Katherine Koob maintained long-distance telephone communications with the State Department from the library of the Iran-America Society. Late that night, they were joined by Mark and Cora Lijek and Joe and Kathy Stafford, who assisted them in maintaining the direct communications link to Washington. Throughout this period, the American diplomats at the Iran-America Society were also in telephone contact with Bruce Laingen and Victor Tomseth at the Iranian Foreign Ministry.

WILLIAM ROYER (*director of academic courses, at the Iran-America Society*): We spent the night of the fourth in the library of the Iran-America Society, and I managed to get a couple hours of sleep. At about 5:30 on the morning of the fifth, the Lijeks and Staffords woke us up so they could leave. At that point, Kate and I continued our vigil on the telephone. In the morning everything was pretty quiet, and I'd banter with the State Department about the weather or football scores, that sort of thing. As time went on, we got a few calls coming in. Lee Schatz gave us a report. A couple of Iranians from our staff had gone over to the embassy to observe the situation, and they called to tell us what they could see. We passed this information on to the State Department.

MARK LIJEK (*consular officer*): That morning, when we left the Iran-America Society, Cora and I didn't want to go over to our apartment, because our landlady was crazy. She had been very concerned about having us there to begin with. She had never let me park my car inside her little compound, because she was afraid someone would see the diplomatic tags and blow the car up with a car bomb. We thought she might turn us in. So we went over to Joe and Kathy's, because their landlord was a reasonably good sort.

VICTOR TOMSETH (*chief political officer, at the Iranian Foreign Ministry*):
Lillian Johnson spent that whole first night in Gary Lee's apartment,
which was in the building right behind the embassy. The Iranians didn't
find her. We knew she was there, and we were talking to her over the
phone. Needless to say, by the second day Lillian was getting very
antsy. She wanted to get out of that apartment. Some Iranian friends
of Mike Howland were willing to go over and pick her up, and we
urged her to go into hiding with them, because that would be the safest
thing. But she wanted to join Kate Koob and Bill Royer at the Iran-
America Society, which is where she ended up.

MARK LIJEK (*consular officer, in hiding at an apartment in Tehran*): At
the Staffords' apartment, we got some sleep and some breakfast. Then
we all called our parents. Despite being somewhat backward, Iran had
a pretty good telephone system. Sometimes you could direct-dial the
States more easily than you could call across town. So each of us called
our parents for a few minutes to tell them that we were okay. After
that we just sat around and waited.

WILLIAM ROYER (*director of academic courses, at the Iran-America Society*):
I called my cook, who was Thai, and told him to bring me a change of
clothing and to get Mr. Graves's cook to bring a change of clothing for
Kate. When they arrived with our stuff, they said they thought they
should go over to the Thai embassy and let them know what the situation was just in case anything should happen. Well, we had one little
bug of a car that belonged to the center, which didn't have any special
license tags on it. That was important, because it didn't identify you as
a foreigner. The car I normally used did have diplomatic tags, which
immediately identified the occupants. We told Kate's driver to take our
domestic help over to the Thai embassy in the little Citroen that didn't
have the special tags. Then they were to come back and pick us up. Of
course, this temporarily left us without transportation. It looked like
this whole thing was going to drag on, and we had decided that it would
be advisable for us to get away from the Iran-America Society. We also
had an inkling that our long-distance telephone call to the State Department was being monitored. So things began to take on the guise
of an adventure, and timing became very important.

All of a sudden, three Iranian students showed up in the reception
area of the library. One of the assistant librarians, who was a local
Iranian employee, went out to talk to these students while Kate and I
snuck out the side door. We hurried over to the Goethe Institute,*

* A German cultural institute.

which was only a couple of blocks away. At the Goethe Institute we were very well received. The director and his assistant were most hospitable and helpful. After about an hour the two of them walked over to the Iran-America Society to see what the status of things was over there. They came back to report that the students had left. The coast was clear. So Kate and I went back to the center. I wanted to go home as quickly as possible, but there was still no car. Our driver had not returned. So I decided to wait for him.

In that short span of time, maybe fifteen or twenty minutes, a lot of students showed up. Once again I headed for the side door. I remember the janitor looked out the door and motioned me—it's clear! Come on! But there was a partitioned wall, around which the janitor could not see. When I rounded the wall to go down the steps, there were about fifteen students looking up at me. The janitor had locked the door to save his own skin, and he looked sort of bug-eyed at me through the glass. I was standing there with this stupid two-way radio, my briefcase, and a plastic bag with a change of underwear under my arm. What flashed through my mind was: "Well, do I drop everything and start slugging?" But I knew that would have been foolhardy. So I just tried to appear nonchalant, and started down the stairs with a tight-lipped grimace on my face, as if I was just going to stroll past them as though nothing were happening. They blocked my path and demanded to see my ID. I didn't respond. I just stood there and refused to give them anything. So it was a stalemate. I couldn't go anywhere. I had no way out.

LEE SCHATZ (*agricultural attaché, in hiding across the street fom the embassy compound*): I was on the phone talking to Kate Koob when the students returned to the Iran-America Society. I was reporting to her what I could see from my location, which she was repeating verbatim back to Washington. I remember she said that some students had come by once that morning. I thought that it was quite foolish for her to have gone back to that location. Then, as I was talking to her, the students came back again to pick them up.

VICTOR TOMSETH (*chief political officer, at the Iranian Foreign Ministry*): After the first false alarm I got on the phone. I was going to tell Kate to get out as soon as Lillian got there. You know, just to go someplace away from there. Hide out. I called her back, and Kate came on the line to tell me that the students had just arrived. Lillian Johnson was there with them, and all three of them—Kate, Lillian, and Bill Royer— were being taken down to the embassy. I felt very badly about that.

WILLIAM ROYER (*director of academic courses*): With one person on either side of me, I was escorted to a car. One of the students took my radio and my briefcase. Then the car backed up to the front door, and in a few minutes Kate and another young lady* were brought out, and we were all crammed into this car. The three of us were in the back seat, and there were three Iranians in the front seat. One of them brandished a gun, just to show us that he had plenty of authority. Then we tore off rather rapidly through the Tehran traffic to the embassy.

When we arrived at the gate, there was a crowd outside the embassy, chanting and ranting and raving. There was some discussion at the gate as to whether or not the car would get through. It was agreed that it could not. So we were taken out of the car, and with a guard on each flank to protect us from the jeering crowd, we were escorted through the gate. That stupid two-way radio that I had when I was captured was now being carried by one of the students as clear evidence that I was CIA or something ridiculous like that.

Kate and I were taken over to one of the small frame houses behind the motor pool. We were quickly ushered through the living room, and I remember seeing some Americans sitting in there. There were a couple of familiar faces, but most of them were people I hadn't met yet. They were just sitting there and looking at us as we came through. No attempt was made to greet us or make any gesture of recognition. I thought that was strange. It was obvious that they had been told not to make any kind of communicative act.

I was taken to one of the bedrooms, where I was thoroughly searched. Everything was taken out of my pockets, and my personal items were placed in a little plastic sandwich bag. I was told that I would get everything back. An effort was made to impress upon me the honesty and Islamic integrity that the students were working under, and I was repeatedly assured that everything would be returned.

They inspected everything in a rather curious manner. They went through my briefcase, obviously expecting to find some sort of spy equipment. I had a set of Cross pens, which were 14-karat gold, and they took them apart very carefully. They took the tops off, and twisted and turned and shook and felt and twisted, to see if these Cross pens were some sort of James Bond gadget—you know, some kind of intelligence instrument. Then when they looked at my shoes, they checked for a false sole, and tapped and pulled and tugged and flexed, and did all sorts of things to the shoe to see if it would fall apart and reveal a transmitter.

* Lillian Johnson.

They seemed to be very disappointed when nothing like that happened.

VICTOR TOMSETH (*chief political officer, at the Iranian Foreign Ministry*): As soon as we knew that Kate, Lillian, and Bill had been picked up, we knew we had to do something about Bob Anders, the Lijeks, and the Staffords. They just couldn't stay in their apartments. So I called the chargé d'affaires at the British embassy and asked him if he would take them in. He agreed to do so rather reluctantly.

CORA LIJEK (*consular officer, in hiding at a private apartment in Tehran*): We talked with Vic Tomseth, who was at the Foreign Ministry. He told us that some people from the British embassy were going to pick us up and take us to their residential compound in northern Tehran. They were supposed to pick us up at 5:30, but they didn't arrive as scheduled. After a while, Joe Stafford called the British embassy and spoke to the chargé d'affaires. I remember the British chargé told him: "The bastards are coming over the walls!" And he hung up.*

MARK LIJEK (*consular officer, in hiding at a private apartment in Tehran*): Now the British embassy was also under attack. Fortunately, the two guys who were supposed to pick us up had already left the embassy. They'd gotten lost on their way over to the apartment and arrived about forty-five minutes late, but they did arrive.

We got in the car and we headed up north. It was a bit strange, because the traffic was incredibly heavy. Tehran had huge traffic jams, and we were stuck in traffic, sitting in this car, being seen by other people. It made me a bit nervous. Bob had given me a bright yellow sweater, and I felt I was lit up like a Christmas tree. Fortunately, nobody paid any attention to us, and we arrived at the British residential compound without incident. We were all feeling pretty good about that. We had reached a relatively safe place, and we had a nice dinner.

---

* That evening the British embassy was attacked by a large mob of Iranian militants. They occupied the building for several hours, and voluntarily withdrew later that night. The British embassy was located in the downtown business district of Tehran and should not be confused with the residential compound, which was in a residential section of northern Tehran several miles from the embassy.

5 On the Inside: November 6–8, 1979

THE UNITED STATES government rejected the students' demand that the shah be returned to Iran, and continued to call upon the Provisional Government of Iran to honor its assurances that the embassy would be protected. In the briefing room of the State Department, spokesman Hodding Carter downplayed the possibility of a resort to military force, and focused on the responsibilities of the host government in Iran. Outlining the United States position, he simply stated: "We expect the Iranian government to secure the release of the Americans held and the return of the embassy compound to American authorities."

The Provisional Government repeatedly offered vague assurances that efforts were being made to deal with the crisis. But the precise nature of initiatives undertaken in Tehran were not known in Washington. Prime Minister Mehdi Bazargan was disturbed by the attack, and he desperately wanted to bring an end to the embassy siege. On Monday afternoon Bazargan appealed to Ayatollah Khomeini to support his attempts to resolve the crisis. Khomeini listened quietly, and then chose to ignore Bazargan's demands.

Inside the embassy compound, fifty-eight Americans were bound and not permitted to speak, as they entered their third day of captivity. Five others were sequestered at a residence in northern Tehran. Bruce Laingen, Victor Tomseth, and Michael Howland continued their vigil at the Foreign Ministry. Early Tuesday morning a large group of student militants gathered inside the embassy's front gate. Several rows deep, the militants knelt on small rugs, faced in the direction of Mecca, and recited their prayers. Worldwide attention was now focused on the American embassy in Tehran, yet the students responsible for the takeover still did not know what the reaction of their own government would be.

JOE HALL (*warrant officer, at the ambassador's residence*): We woke up and they fed us some bread and jam. I was really getting dirty and feeling very uncomfortable. I'd been wearing the same clothes for over forty-eight hours, and I hadn't been able to brush my teeth or anything like that. It was impossible to sleep well, and I woke up tired. Very tired.

These Iranians were running around just as chaotic as ever. They were sacking the place. Lots of people were coming and going. I was really getting apprehensive, and remember thinking, "What's going on here? When is this going to end?"

After breakfast they tied me to a chair at the dining room table and left a bunch of us sitting there just like they'd done the day before. That morning a couple of the guards came in and took Greg Persinger* out. After a little while they brought him back. Of course, any coming or going interested me. After Greg sat back down, he looked at me and our eyes met. Silently, I mouthed the word "What?" One of the guards saw me, and he slammed his hand down on the table. It scared the hell out of us. He jumped up and yelled, "No 'es talk! No 'es talk!" He rushed over, threw a blindfold on me, and jerked me up. I thought, "My God, these bastards are going to take me out and shoot me!" I thought that maybe they wanted to shoot someone as an example, and they just decided to use me.

They stood me in the hallway of the ambassador's residence for a little while. I was really nervous. "My God," I thought, "are they going to shoot me for that?" After a few minutes, a couple of guards took me outside and led me over to the chancery. They sat me down in the main foyer, right by the front door. I was blindfolded and my hands were tied. Behind me, I could hear all kinds of noise and confusion. The Iranians were using the radios that they had taken from us the first day, and telephones were ringing, and there was a crowd outside the front gate that was all hyped up and excited. People were coming and going, and some of the guards were opening and closing the bolts of their rifles. Those guys were real bad about that. They were always locking and loading their guns. I was still thinking they might shoot me.

I sat there for a couple of hours, but nothing happened. I guess it was a little show of force to scare the hell out of me.

Later, I found out from Greg Parsinger that they had taken him out and given him an English newspaper to read. They wanted to show him that they had made the news, and that what they had done was a big deal.

GARY LEE (*general services officer, at the ambassador's residence*): It was during this period that the Iranians came around with television cameras. These guys weren't with any of the international networks, but were from local Iranian TV, and they were inteviewing and filming us.

---

* Greg Persinger was a marine security guard.

I can remember them coming over with the camera and asking me, "What do you think of the shah?"

I said, "I don't know much about the shah."

This guy spoke very good English. He said, "You are going to be released very soon. How have you been treated by the students?"

I said, "Certainly not as a diplomat. But an effort has been made to feed me." Then I added, "I'll be very glad when this is over."

"Yes, I will too," he said.

JOHN LIMBERT (*political officer, at the ambassador's residence*): I spent November 6 tied to a chair flipping through a magazine. From the time we were taken, the question in my mind was: "Will Khomeini back the Provisional Government?" Up to the time of the takeover he had done so, at least verbally. He was always saying, "We should obey the government. Bazargan is my choice to be prime minister." So my hope was that Khomeini would back the Provisional Government in an attempt to reach a negotiated settlement.

CORT BARNES (*communications officer, at the ambassador's residence*): I was tied to a chair in the ambassador's residence, and I saw Ahmed Khomeini when he came through. He was wearing a gray, floor-length mullah's tunic and a black headband. He was guarded by two *pasdaran* revolutionaries with Uzi submachine guns. At first I didn't know who he was, but after he passed through somebody told me that he was Khomeini's son. That was the first indication I had that the takeover had the tacit approval of the Khomeini regime. The sight of those Uzis told me that there were either government troops or revolutionary guards involved. They never captured any Uzis from us. Those were regular-issue Iranian army weapons.

SGT. WILLIAM QUARLES (*marine security guard, at a staff house on the embassy compound*): I was sitting on the sofa with my hands tied. The students had a little tiny radio about the size of a six-transistor. They'd turn the thing all the way up, and seven or eight Iranians would all get around this one little radio and stick their ears right to it. They looked like a bunch of mice around a piece of cheese. I'd just look at them and laugh. When something really interesting was on the radio, everybody from the back room would come up and listen in. If the ayatollah was talking, everyone would be in there listening.

BILL BELK (*communications officer, at a staff house on the embassy compound*): Those students had to listen to the radio. They were dead certain of that. They had that radio on all the time. On November 6, I was being kept in the living room of that little prefab house, and I remember Bill Quarles was in the chair next to me. We could hear the crowd outside. They were screaming so much that I could still feel the house vibrating. In a situation like that you never know what to expect.

The men were off to the side of the room, squatting around this washtub, eating some kind of rice with peas mixture with their hands and listening to the radio, when all of a sudden a wild cheer went up. Seyyed was so happy that he rolled over on the floor and did a wild back flip. Not knowing what was going on, I asked what had happened. I was told that Khomeini had announced that he was pleased with what the students had done. He was pleased about the takeover.

CPL. STEVEN KIRTLEY (*marine security guard, at a staff house on the embassy compound*): All of a sudden this guy started jumping up and down, screaming, "Yea-yea-yea!" I asked one of them, "What happened?"

He said, "The imam has just come on the radio and blessed our action against the den of spies. What we are doing is a great thing! We are blessed by Allah!"

I thought, "Oh shit!" Up until that time I'd been expecting some sort of positive development. I'd been thinking that we'd get out of there soon. But when he said they had the imam's approval, there was no telling what would happen. It was then that I started feeling threatened.

SGT. WILLIAM QUARLES (*marine security guard, at a staff house on the embassy compound*): One guy came up to me and told me that the imam had said that what they were doing was right. Then he gave out some guidelines that Khomeini said the students were to follow. He said the hostages were to sleep in the beds while the students slept on the floor, and the hostages were to eat first and the students second. He said they were not going to treat us the way they had been treated under the shah, because they were Moslem and above that kind of thing.

JOHN LIMBERT (*political officer, at the ambassador's residence*): No one came up to me and told me that Khomeini had approved of the students' action. I learned by overhearing a snippet of news. I was sitting in the ambassador's residence. There was a loudspeaker on outside, over which the hourly news was broadcast. When the news came on, I heard one of the students say to another one, "Go out and tell them to turn that down." Then the loudspeaker was turned down so that I couldn't hear it. It was obvious that this particular student knew that some of the Americans could speak Persian, and he didn't want us to hear any news.

In the minute and a half or so before the radio was turned down, I heard that Bazargan and Yazdi had resigned.* Obviously, this was not a good thing to hear. It meant that it was probably going to be more difficult to get us out, as it was very clear to me that Bazargan and Yazdi had not received any backing from Khomeini. In other words, the hostage taking had forced a showdown between the government and its opponents, and Khomeini had refused to back the government against what he considered a popular street movement. Of course, this meant that the Provisional Government was not going to be able to get us out. If we were to be released, now it was only Khomeini's word that would get us out.

You see, at this time there were many different political currents competing for power and influence within Iran. What the students represented was a radical current with an Islamic guise. They did have many supporters, but it's important to remember that they also had opponents. This action was by no means unanimously supported by either the clergy or the population at large.

This explains why Khomeini's endorsement was not immediate. He didn't endorse the action until the sixth of November. In hindsight, what appears to have happened in the first couple of days is that various groups and large numbers of people came to the embassy in response to calls for them to do so. There was a well-orchestrated campaign of support that took many forms—demonstrations, letters of support, messages of support, telegrams, petitions, all kinds of things—all of which were designed to give the impression that the takeover was a "popular" action. I think this had an influence on Khomeini's eventual decision to endorse the students, rather than to back the government.

In doing what he did, I think Khomeini believed that he was responding to the popular will. His style of leadership has always been to lead from the rear. Khomeini is inclined to look and see which way the winds are blowing, and then endorse the strongest current, or what

---

* The resignation of Prime Minister Mehdi Bazargan was announced at 1:30 P.M. (Tehran time) on Tuesday, November 6, 1979. Bazargan had actually handed his letter of resignation to Khomeini on Monday evening, but Khomeini hesitated for several hours before accepting it and publicly endorsing the takeover of the American embassy.

At a press conference in front of the embassy, a student militant named Akbar said: "We were waiting to see if [the government] would expel us [from the embassy] or make problems, and immediately we gave speeches to explain why we had done what we did, saying that the reason was to protest against America's letting the shah in. We saw there was nothing from the government. We saw people coming, crowds coming. They were calling by telephone and sending messages of support. We realized our action was something great! Yes, something really great! It was like a bomb burst, and we realized then that we had to keep going." See John Kifner, "How a Sit-in Turned into a Siege," in *No Hiding Place* (New York: Times Books, 1981), p. 178.

appears to be the strongest current. I think the people who organized the attack on the embassy and who orchestrated the subsequent campaign of support understood Khomeini's way of thinking. They knew what types of actions he would be willing to respond to. I remember the first night we were there, I was able to listen to the news on the radio, and the students read the text of "Announcement Number One." God knows how many announcements they issued outside of the embassy, but the very first one began with a quotation from Khomeini. It was something to the effect of: "America is the source of all of our troubles." Then they went on to read the statement. They also referred to themselves as "Student Followers of the Imam's Line." So in the very beginning, prior to Khomeini's endorsement, the students were doing things to identify themselves with his policy. In hindsight, I'd probably say that this was done in a calculated attempt to attract his support. There's no question that those demonstrations in front of the embassy were very well organized. No question of that at all.

Of course, on November 6 I wasn't looking at the situation quite so analytically. I just knew that it was not a good sign that Yazdi and Bazargan had resigned. Their resignation did not bode well for our future.

ROBERT ODE (*consular officer, at the ambassador's residence*): The terrorists had about fifteen of us tied to hard straight-back chairs around the dining room table. They had the drapes pulled, so it was sort of semi-dark in the room. They came in and said that everyone had to surrender our jewelry, watches, and personal items for "security purposes." Then they began to collect these things from those of us they had tied up around this table. I tried to hide my wedding ring and a gold cameo ring that my parents had given me on my twenty-first birthday by sitting on my hands, but that didn't do any good. The terrorists pulled my hands out from underneath me. I recall one of the marine security guards, Rocky Sickmann, who was also tied up to one of the dining room chairs, saying: "Leave him alone! He's just an old man!" Since I don't like to regard myself as being old, I could have resented Rocky's remark, but I realized he was trying to help me.*

I was extremely angry, and I let the terrorists know they had no right to take my rings. They untied me, went through all my pockets, and took all of my personal items, including my rings, my watch, a ballpoint pen, and about eighty dollars in Iranian currency I had in my pocket. I was so angry that I stood up and shouted at them, "You're nothing but a bunch of goddamn thieves!" Some of the other hostages tried to

---

* At sixty-six Robert Ode was the oldest hostage.

hush me up a little bit. Perhaps they thought I was being a little fool-hardy, but I wasn't frightened. I was angry. The terrorists were trying to convince me that they were going to give these things back to me, and showed me an envelope they were putting them in. They had tried to write my name on the envelope, but it was misspelled and barely legible. I said, "You don't even have my name spelled correctly! How in the hell do you think I'm going to get these things back again?" I continued to call them "goddamn thieves," which is what they were. I got a ballpoint pen from one of them, and I printed my name on the envelope so that it could be read easily in case we ever got these things back.

DON HOHMAN (*army medic, at a staff house on the embassy compound*): Those first few days were crazy. Those Iranians were running all over the place, and they obviously didn't know what they were doing. They were moving people around and shuffling Americans in and out. Some of the Americans I'd never even seen before. I remember they brought Jerry Plotkin through and sat him down in the room with me, and I was wondering, "Now who in the hell is this guy?" Jerry was a civilian who just happened to be at the embassy when all this chaos went down. I'd never seen him before.

I was being bounced around like a rubber ball in those prefabs. They'd take me into one house, sit me down, and then the next thing I knew some guy would want to move over to the next house. So they'd take me over there, sit me down for a while, then some guy would come along and decide he wanted to move me from the front room to the back room. I was bouncing around just like a rubber ball. And they didn't even know how to feed us. They were giving us dates and rice and stuff like that—Iranian food. They didn't know how to care for us at all.

One of our guys had an attack of malaria, and the Iranians took me over to look at him. I took his blood pressure and was able to talk to him for a couple of minutes. He told me that the rag heads had taken his medication away from him, so I told them, "Give him his medication back, and he'll be okay." Then they took me next door. There was a Korean businessman sitting in there who had been taken hostage along with the rest of us.* He had high blood pressure, and once again the rag heads had taken his medication. The guy couldn't tell me the American name for his blood pressure medicine, so I couldn't get any from

---

* Five non-American hostages were captured on November 4, and were released by the students on November 22, 1979. They included two individuals from the Philippines, one from Bangladesh, one from Pakistan, and one from South Korea.

the medical unit. I didn't know what he had been using. But I told the guards, "Look, you've got to find this guy's medicine and give it back to him."

Among the Iranians there seemed to be some semblance of an organization, but at the same time they were very disorganized. I don't think they ever believed that they were going to get as far as they did. I think some of them had even envisioned the attack on the embassy as a kamikaze-type thing. They thought that when they went over the walls the marines would open fire—you know, it was a demonstration organized to show U.S. Marines killing Iranian students. In fact, a couple of them that spoke English even told me that they had signed their last will and testament on the night before the attack. They knew there was a chance that they were going to die when they went over the wall.

JOHN LIMBERT (*political officer, at the ambassador's residence*): News was very deliberately kept from us. Inside the embassy, the students' organization was very stratified, and the leadership was remote from us. The hostages rarely saw the actual leaders. The privates and the corporals were responsible for taking care of us.

I think that a lot of the Iranians who organized and planned this thing had spent time in prison themselves. I say this because there was a feeling of techniques half-learned and half-mastered in all of the blindfolding and constant movement of the hostages. I suspect that one of the things they had learned in the shah's prisons was that you don't tell anybody anything. You keep them blindfolded and deprive them of news and contact as much as you can. The more you do this, the more malleable your prisoners will become.

SGT. PAUL LEWIS (*marine security guard, at a staff house on the embassy compound*): I spent three days isolated in the bedroom, handcuffed and tied to the bed. The students from the central committee or whatever kept coming in to grill me, trying to get combinations and asking me who worked where at the embassy. When I told them that I didn't know anything they'd slap me around and threaten me. One of the things I noticed throughout these interrogation sessions was that if these guys smelled blood, or if they felt they were getting to you, they'd keep on coming at you. They wouldn't let up. There would be bunches of them in there trying to get in on the act. But if you stood your ground, they didn't push quite as hard.

They wanted to know what I did at the embassy, and they kept telling me that I was a CIA agent.

I kept saying, "No, I'm a marine."

Well, evidently marine was not a word in their vocabulary. They understood army and navy, but they couldn't figure out what a marine was. One guy asked me if I was a ranger.

I said, "No, not quite. It's different from that."

"Are you a commando?"

"No." I tried to explain that we were an amphibious force that was attached to the navy. So somebody asked, "Then you're a navy commando?"

I said, "Yeah, that's good enough. That's close enough."

So after that I was a "navy commando," but I still couldn't give them any combinations or tell them what anyone else did in the embassy. Finally, on the third day, this one guy came back into the room with a Uzi. He jerked that thing back and said, "You're going to tell us what we want to know, or we're going to execute you."

In POW training they tell you not to die in situations like that. To take what you can and work with it. But I was in a position where they could do whatever they wanted to me and I still couldn't give anything up, because I didn't know anything. Once again I told this guy, "I was here fourteen hours before the embassy was captured. I don't know a thing. My ID and my passport are in the room at the Bijon Apartments. You can go over there and look at them."

The guy just turned and walked out, and I never saw him again after that.

COL. LELAND HOLLAND (*army attaché, at the ambassador's residence*): There was a feeling of frustration and uncertainty. No doggone news. The embassy was captured, Carter was accused of something, and then the line went dead. To me the lack of news was one of the really grating and unnerving things. It added to the overriding sense of helplessness and frustration. I wanted someone to tell me what was going on, and the Iranians sure as hell weren't going to do it.

There was a lot of confusion. Here we are, a whole bunch of Americans who are stuck. We're in a big goddamn bind, and there was no set of rules. Little clusters of these guys would come around asking questions. They wanted to know who the defense attaché was and who the CIA agents were. Then one group came around with a questionnaire. They wanted to know all of our background data. They also asked for our "code word," when what they really wanted to know was our radio call sign. Anyway, I took their questionnaire and put down my name, rank, and serial number. That's all. Then I drew a line through the rest of it to obliterate it so they couldn't add anything to it later. They got hot about that, but they really didn't do anything.

Another time, a group of them came around with a tape recorder and asked me, "What is your name?"

I didn't know what they were up to, so I refused to talk.

They kept asking, "Where did you work? What is the number of your room?"

Well, it just so happened that the wing my office was in had recently been painted, and there were no numbers on the doors. I said, "My office doesn't have a number."

"They all have numbers."

"Mine doesn't. Mine is different."

They got a little testy with me, and once again asked, "What is the number of your office?"

I said, "Okay, it's 8-1-2 Green." Which, of course, is a little ditty: "I think I'm going to be sick because I ate one too green." These guys wrote that down and went away.

JOE HALL (*warrant officer, at the ambassador's residence*): I was being kept in Laingen's bedroom, and when I asked to go to the toilet, they took me into the bathroom just off his bedroom. There was a window in there, and I opened the thing and looked out. I could see all these Iranians taking candelabras, Persian carpets, furniture, and all sorts of stuff right out the front door. It was obvious that they were pilfering all this stuff.

When I was sitting there tied up in the bedroom, one guy after another would come in and go through Laingen's closet and chest of drawers. A guy would come in, take a shirt off the hanger, and if he didn't like it he'd throw it on the floor. When he found one or two that he liked, he'd walk off with them. Then another guy would come in. He'd go through the shirts on the hangers, and maybe go through the shirts that had been tossed on the floor. He'd find a few things that he liked and walked away. Pretty soon, everything had disappeared. I knew that everything that was in my house I could just kiss good-bye. I never thought of it any other way. I knew that all of my personal belongings had already been stolen.

DON HOHMAN (*army medic, at a staff house in the embassy compound*): Those first few days the rag heads were trying to feed us without untying our hands. Some guy would come up to you and try to put a date in your mouth or something. They weren't feeding us any American food at all, and we weren't used to the Iranian food. A couple of us said, "Hey, the commissary is full of food. Why don't you go over there, get us some American food, and feed us that?" But they said, "Oh no, that's stealing. We don't steal. We never steal." Which was total bullshit.

They were a bunch of thieves, and I used to tell them so. Anyway, they kept coming around with this stuff, and I'd say, "Get it away from me! Either I'll eat with my own hands, or I won't eat at all." I just refused to eat. Pretty soon they started untying our hands to let us eat.

BILL BELK (*communications officer, at a staff house in the embassy compound*): Don Hohman had to be the meanest, orneriest cuss these students had ever come across. He was just beautiful. Nothing they did could please him. They'd give him food, and he'd say, "I don't want your goddamn food!" They'd give him water, and he'd say, "I don't want your goddamn water!" He'd just tell them to go piss off.

I figured he was going to say something once too often, and they were going to take him out and blow him away.

DON HOHMAN (*army medic, at a staff house in the embassy compound*): They had their Red Lion Society come through. Apparently these people are similar to our Red Cross. They came through with a camera and a tape recorder. They were asking questions and taking pictures. This guy from the Red Lion Society said they would deliver a message to our families. Sister Mary* was there with them. That was the first time I'd ever seen her. I think she was there to translate and keep an eye on us. The guy with the tape recorder didn't speak very good English, but one of the questions they asked was: "What do you think about the action of the students?"

That really got me going. I just spouted off. I read them the riot act and told them that they were all a bunch of goddamn thieves. They were always talking about human rights and the shah and stuff, and I said, "Are you giving us any human rights? Here you are keeping us as prisoners. I have never done any wrong to any Iranian person—yet you've got me and you've got all of these other people here tied up as prisoners. And not only that, you've stolen everything out of my apartment!"

The rag heads used to get really angry when I called them thieves. One of them said, "Oh no! We never steal! We never steal!"

I said, "That's bullshit! I watched you take things out of my apartment. I sat there and watched two of my suitcases disappear. I know you stole things out of my apartment." Which was true. On the day of the takeover I saw one guy walk off with two suitcases from my apartment.

---

* Mary was one of the student leaders. She was frequently present at hostage interrogations and also at several press conferences held by the militants. She had spent four years in the United States and claimed to have received an undergraduate degree from the University of Pennsylvania. The hostages had a variety of nicknames for her, including Sister Philadelphia and Mary the Terrorist.

This rag head said, "You will get everything back. Every little penny will be given back to you." That was always their story whenever we asked about their stealing. They always said that everything would be returned.

Anyway, I just kept spouting off, calling them thieves and liars and reading them the riot act. Sister Philadelphia just kind of stood there and watched. She was keeping an eye on me, but she didn't say much of anything. After they'd heard enough, they walked away and took their tape recorder over to the next guy.

GARY LEE (*general services officer, at the ambassador's residence*): On the afternoon of the seventh, I was sitting in my chair reading the *Ladies' Home Journal*. We were all facing the wall so that none of us could see each other, and my hands were tied to the chair, but loosely, so I could flip through the pages of this magazine. All of a sudden, a couple of these guys came up and put a blindfold on me. When they approached, I could see a guy with a semiautomatic out of the corner of my eye, which made me a bit nervous. They bound my hands very tightly, took my boots off, and tied my feet to the legs of the chair. Then they stuffed some cotton under the blindfold so I couldn't sneak a peek from underneath it. In spite of the blindfold, I could tell when the light changed, which meant that the curtains had been drawn open. Then they opened the windows, and I heard this guy with the AK-47 lock and load above my left ear. I figured I was going to be shot and thrown out the window. I was sure I was dead. I waited for the bullets. My only thought was: "I wonder how my wife and daughter are going to take this?"

But nothing happened. After a while these guys took my blindfold off and left. They didn't say a word. They just walked off. If they were trying to scare me they sure as hell succeeded. I said to myself, "Hey, this son of a bitch is going to end bad."

DON HOHMAN (*army medic, at a staff house in the embassy compound*): The chanting was constant. I mean, those walls would tremble. On the third day I was just sitting there doing nothing, when the militants came up and put a blindfold on me. My hands were already tied. They put the blindfold on me, stood me up, and said, "We go."

I asked, "Where are we going?"

"You will see." And they led me outside.

I knew they were taking me toward the front gate, and I couldn't figure out why. I didn't know what they were going to do. I could hear the crowd, and they were all whipped up—ranting and raving. When we finally stopped, we were about three feet from the front gate. I thought, "They're going to give me to that crowd. This is it. This is the end. These people are going to tear me limb from limb." That scared me. It really did.

While I was standing there, they ripped my blindfold off, and all of a sudden I could see people screaming and chanting and reaching through the gate trying to claw at me. I was close enough that if somebody lunged, they could have stuck a knife in me. The gate only had a chain on it with a little padlock, and it would have been easy for the crowd to just fold that gate. I could see the street was totally packed with people. There were more people there than I'd ever seen at any other demonstration, and they were making so much noise from their chanting that I could feel the rumble. There were vibrations in the ground. It was like an earthquake beneath my feet. And I could see the hatred in their eyes. I figured I was going to get killed for no good reason. I'd never harmed anybody in Iran. You know, I'd just come through on a temporary duty assignment, and I didn't know anything about their politics. I didn't know what had them so whipped up and angry. I had just been sitting there when those guys brought me out and stood me in front of the gate. That was a mighty naked feeling.

They stood me there for a couple of minutes, and then they took me back. I guess they were trying to put some fear into me. Maybe they took me out there because I'd spouted off when the Red Lion Society came through. I don't know. They never told any of us why they did anything. But I was shaking when we got back to the house.

CAPT. PAUL NEEDHAM (*air force logistics officer, at a staff house in the embassy compound*): When I was being kept in the yellow staff house with Neal Robinson, I started doing exercises. Even though I had handcuffs on, I got down on my knuckles and did push-ups. I'd do fifty push-ups on my knuckles, while looking the guard right in the eye. I'd stare right at him the whole time. I wanted him to know that if I were loose, and he and I were one on one, I'd kill him. I wanted him to know that I had the power to do that in my hands.

BILL BELK (*communications officer, at a staff house in the embassy compound*): I have a severe allergic reaction to insect bites. If not properly treated, an insect bite can be fatal. On the night of the seventh, I was bitten by a red ant and suffered an allergic reaction. Don Hohman saved my life. I was sitting in a chair, and my hands were tied with strips of bedsheet. We were not allowed to talk to one another. At first I didn't even know I'd been bitten; then all of a sudden I could feel the swelling from the bite and my throat started to close off. I couldn't breathe. I mean, I couldn't breathe at all, and within two minutes I was fading in and out of consciousness.

SGT. WILLIAM QUARLES (*marine security guard, at a staff house in the embassy compound*): Bill Belk passed out. He just flat out fainted. The Iranians went absolutely berserk. They jabbed at each other in Farsi and didn't know what to think. They didn't know if Bill had died, or if he was joking around, or had just gone to sleep, or what. They didn't want anyone to die on them, so they went absolutely berserk.

They brought in one guy who was a medical student, and this guy came over and looked at Bill. But he didn't know what in the hell to do. Don Hohman was the medic. He told this guy that Bill needed a shot and he told him where to get it. But the Iranians couldn't find it. They were tearing the dispensary apart, but they didn't know where to look.

DON HOHMAN (*army medic, at a staff house in the embassy compound*): Bill started having edema, and he couldn't breathe. He was getting hives—the whole works. His throat was closing off, and that scared me. His breathing was causing a snoring sort of choking sound. I was screaming and yelling at this rag head. I said, "You either do something or he's going to die! I mean it! He's going to die!"

BILL BELK (*communications officer, at a staff house in the embassy compound*): I was fading in and out of consciousness. The last thing I remember was that Don Hohman was screaming at these guys to get me a shot of epinephrine. He was the medic and he knew exactly what was wrong with me. At the risk of his own life, he stood up, charged out the door, and headed for the dispensary to get the medication. He could have easily been shot.

DON HOHMAN (*army medic, at a staff house in the embassy compound*): When you're medically trained, you just don't stand there and let somebody go down the tubes. It's as simple as that. I took off like a crazy fool, and two of these guys followed me. When I went out the hallway, one of the guards hit me with the butt of his rifle. He didn't know who the hell I was, and I didn't know who the hell he was. All I knew was that I needed to get to the medical unit. The guard butt-stroked me with his rifle in order to knock me down. Then he locked and loaded on me. These other two guys caught up, and they didn't have their little identification tags on. So that caused some more confusion. It's amazing that guard didn't shoot all three of us. I got back on my feet, and I was sputtering and steaming. I had to get to the medical unit in order to help Bill. One of the militants who had followed behind me finally explained to the guard what was going on, and then he led me over to the medical unit. I grabbed some epinephrine, some oxygen, and a cardioverter, so that if Bill's heart stopped I could do something about it.

I took all of that back and hit Bill with an injection of .3 milliliters of epinephrine. He seemed to clear pretty quickly. When his throat started to close, that scared me. If he wasn't able to breathe, the only thing I could have done was a tracheotomy, which meant I'd have to go right through his throat, and I didn't want to have to do something like that there on the floor. Epinephrine is the front line of defense for anaphylaxis, so I gave Bill a shot of that. Fortunately, his throat cleared pretty quickly, and he resumed his normal pattern of breathing.

BILL BELK (*communications officer, at a staff house in the embassy compound*): Don Hohman gave me an injection, and I was out for some time after that. When I regained consciousness I was completely blind. I couldn't see. One of the Iranians asked me if I wanted to go to the hospital. I was frightened, and I thought, "There is no way they are going to get me to go to an Iranian hospital. If the United States comes in with a rescue team, I want to be right here. I want to be with my friends, and not lying on my back in some hospital." I didn't want to be like the woman who disappeared at Entebbe.

DON HOHMAN (*army medic, at a staff house in the embassy compound*): That night they didn't tie me up, and I was able to monitor Bill. They allowed me to do that. Through most of the night, I was checking his blood pressure and his pulse, and I made sure his breathing was okay. At first his blood pressure was kind of flaky, and his pulse was a little unsteady. But fortunately he settled down, and I knew he was going to be all right.

6 The Clark-Miller Mission

WHEN PRIME MINISTER Mehdi Bazargan resigned on November 6, 1979, the entire cabinet resigned with him, and the Provisional Government ceased to exist. Ayatollah Khomeini instructed the Revolutionary Council to assume the functions of government. The Revolutionary Council was comprised of fifteen religious and revolutionary leaders who met with Khomeini on a regular basis and advised him on matters of state. For nine months the Revolutionary Council had coexisted alongside the Provisional Government. Its membership was dominated by clerics and radicals who frequently engaged in policy disputes with Bazargan.

In Washington, President Carter felt that it was important to establish contact with the Revolutionary Council as soon as possible. Ramsey Clark was immediately dispatched to Tehran as a presidential envoy. Clark was chosen for the mission because he had been an extremely vocal critic of United States support for the shah's regime, and in 1979 he had interviewed Ayatollah Khomeini in Paris. William Miller, a fluent Farsi speaker and staff director of the Senate Intelligence Committee, was chosen to accompany Clark. The two men were authorized to negotiate on behalf of the United States, and administration officials hoped that they would be able to establish a framework for negotiations with the Revolutionary Council. Clark and Miller flew out of Washington on board an Air Force 707, which was large enough to bring the hostages back from Tehran in the event that their mission achieved a dramatic breakthrough.

VICTOR TOMSETH (*chief political officer, at the Iranian Foreign Ministry with Bruce Laingen and Mike Howland*): When the Bazargan government collapsed, I didn't necessarily conclude that the chances for a resolution to the problem had been significantly diminished. The Provisional Government didn't count for that much, anyway. We recognized that the Revolutionary Council counted for a lot more than the Provisional Government, and from the Foreign Ministry we were able to speak to Ayatollah Behesti, who was a key figure on the Revolutionary Council.

After the first day, one of the main things that Bruce Laingen and I were involved in at the Foreign Ministry was trying to clear the way for Ramsey Clark and Bill Miller to come out to Tehran. We cleared this through the Foreign Ministry people we had seen, and Bruce also spoke to Ayatollah Behesti on the telephone. In this conversation, Bruce received an indication from Behesti that he would be prepared to see Ramsey Clark and Bill Miller when they arrived.

Clark and Miller were in Turkey and actually en route to Tehran when Khomeini took to the airwaves and said that if these two people arrived no one was to talk to them. When that happened, I began to think that the situation we were dealing with was now qualitatively different, in the sense that there wasn't any coordinated decision-making process at all. Prior to this, I had assumed that we would be able to negotiate a resolution to the situation, but after Khomeini's remarks on Ramsey Clark and Bill Miller my conclusion shifted rather dramatically. I now realized that this was going to be a very difficult negotiation that would take a considerable amount of time. I also concluded that there was no longer any meaningful role the three of us could play at the Foreign Ministry. There was nothing more that we were going to be able to do. If Khomeini wasn't prepared to have anyone talk to Clark and Miller, then it wouldn't make any difference who we talked to. So we settled in for a long wait. As a matter of fact, we were able to talk to our families on the telephone, and I remember telling my wife that we were probably going to be in Tehran for a while—but I didn't have any idea that it was going to be for more than a year. I was thinking that it might extend beyond the first of 1980, that it could be a month or two.

7   On the Inside: November 7–9, 1979

BILL BELK (*communications officer, at a staff house in the embassy compound*): I was kept in this little yellow house for about five days. Don Hohman and I were put in a back bedroom. Our hands were still tied, but the guards were no longer using the nylon ropes. They took the ropes off and tied us up with strips of bedsheet, which was easier on our hands. We were tied, but very loosely. It was sort of silly that the students even considered us as being tied up.

The chanting outside was constant. Seyyed persisted in giving me his religious lectures. He would sit there beside me and talk and talk. Their religion saddened me. Their religious beliefs were strange. They believed that after death they would go to paradise where they would have sweet water—which is wine—beautiful women, and good food. Of course, this was everything that they had renounced in this life. It was very, very sad to see all of these young people who felt that they should give up all that is beautiful in the world for the maybe of a religious tomorrow. Those kids were brainwashed something terrible. The loudspeakers were going all the time, calling them to prayer. It was a very sad thing to see.

In one of his little lectures, Seyyed told me the story of Haagar. Haagar was a black maid who was the mother of Ismael, and there is a stone attributed to her at the site of Mecca. After telling me this story, Seyyed said, "We will free all of the slave blacks of America! They will rise up and follow Khomeini!" He was so naive that he actually believed this. So did some of the other students. Most of them weren't very sophisticated. They believed that the blacks in the United States were ready to revolt, and that they would rise up in revolution when given guidance from Khomeini. It was sad to see that they believed their own propaganda.

SGT. PAUL LEWIS (*marine security guard, at a staff house in the embassy compound*): I think the students were sort of divided into groups by college subject, because for a while I had a bunch of medical students guarding me. I remember one guy by the name of Ali. He was the leader of the group, and he always looked out of place because he was a slick dresser. His hair was always blow-dried and his beard was trimmed. He managed to get out and get clean clothes, while these other guys wore the same dirty clothes day after day.

Ali wasn't too bad of a guy. He'd let us take our handcuffs off in the evening before we went to bed, just so we could realx a little bit. I don't think he was authorized to do it, either, because if someone came by he'd tell us to put them back on.

He was one of the few guards you could almost have an intelligent conversation with. When it was quiet and there weren't too many people around, Ali and another big tall guy would sit and talk. In order to keep them away from the confrontation points between Iran and the United States, I would usually try to draw them out about their experiences in the revolution. That was like asking them to talk about the homecoming football game in which they were the heroes. When they talked about the revolution, their eyes just sparkled. They really believed that Iran was on the road to success. They thought that now they had gotten rid of the shah, there was going to be some sort of democratic theocracy. They would talk about elections and getting the economy going, self-sufficiency and becoming truly nonaligned. They seemed to have some pretty good ideals, but they were also blind to many of the abuses that were going on in the revolution.

JOHN GRAVES (*public affairs officer*): After the takeover I had several discussions with a medical student by the name of Ali. He told me that the students were not interested in the shah at all. Their concern was that the revolution was running down, perhaps similar to the way that Mao Tse-tung had had the impression that his revolution was running down in China, and then had the Cultural Revolution to galvanize the public, regain the impetus, and peak the revolution. The students felt that Bazargan wasn't capable of wrenching Iran out of the previous patterns, and they were afraid the country would fall back into its traditional position of being dominated by the West. So the students were very much interested in galvanizing the public and regaining the revolutionary momentum.

In the early fall of 1979 they conjured up a program where they tried to get poor people to move into the houses and hotels that had been vacated as a result of the revolution. Many of the wealthy people, the so-called *taghuti*, "the tainted people," who owned property and were associated with the shah, felt that the situation had become dangerous and left the country. The students thought it would be a brilliant idea to get poor people to move into these houses, because they needed better places to live. There were a few sit-ins, or squat-ins, but the squatters didn't stay long. I guess they went back to their hovels in south Tehran. So the idea didn't generate any real enthusiasm among the masses, and the students were perplexed as to what they could possibly do.

Then along came this golden opportunity when the United States let the shah into America. The students felt that this was an issue that would inflame the crowds. They did not want to get the shah back. Ali said several times that the shah was "washed up." They didn't care about the shah. Initially, the students intended to stay only two or three days. Then they got stuck with their own slogan. The masses took the slogan very seriously. I didn't see them, but I sure could hear them. It sounded like hundreds of thousands of people out there chanting, "Death to the shah! Death to the shah!"

The last time I saw Ali he was very discouraged. He felt the whole thing was turning into a mess. I guess he threw in the towel and went back to the hospital or something. As far as I know, many of the medical students, perhaps all of them, threw in the towel fairly early on. That left us in the hands of the more fanatical and less sophisticated guards.

BILL BELK (*communications officer, at a staff house in the embassy compound*): As time went by, there seemed to be a sorting out of the students. A lot of them just disappeared. The first couple of days it seemed that the medical students were in control; then, as time went by, it seemed to be mostly engineering students, or militants who weren't students at all. Some of those guys were pretty old. One of them was even bald. But I remember, to begin with, most of the people who were guarding us were very proud of the fact that they were medical students. Then they seemed to disappear. Which was too bad, because they were nicer than the other crew. I remember one medical student came in and remarked about how poorly dressed he was, which was kind of funny, because he had on a coat that was ripped and torn in every direction. His coat looked like it had been passed on from father to son for at least three or four generations. The guy was really a character, and not unpleasant at all. Then there was another fellow in the medical student group who untied my hands so I could play chess with him. One of the militant leaders came around and got very upset.

He thoroughly chewed this medical student out. Then the militant leader tied me back up, and I never saw the medical student again. He disappeared after that incident.

SGT. ROCKY SICKMANN (*marine security guard, at the ambassador's residence*): When the takeover first happened, some of the students were trying to be nice. But some of the others were assholes. They had things that they held against us. A big hang-up with them was Black Friday, when a lot of students and demonstrators had been killed in the street. During that year, President Carter had come on television and given the shah a vote of confidence. He said the United States would continue to back the shah. These students didn't like that. Supposedly, a lot of the demonstrators that had been killed on Black Friday were friends or brothers and sisters of the students that were holding us. They saw us as being part of President Carter's policy. As far as they were concerned all Americans were wrong, and they held everything that had happened to their friends and their family against us. They were using us to get back at President Carter and to get back at America.

Some of them would do things just to be mean. They would tie somebody's hands real tight. Or when you were blindfolded and they were guiding you to the bathroom they would purposely push you into a door or a wall, so you'd hit your head. They'd do that and laugh. And there wasn't anything you could do, except maybe curse at them.

JOHN GRAVES (*public affairs officer*): At first the students didn't know who I was. When they asked me, I said that I was an English teacher and that I was involved in development programs and scholarships. That sort of thing. On the fourth day they found a protocol list, and my name was number two on the protocol list. They also found some ridiculous book that has been published for years by the East Germans, which purports to list all of America's CIA agents. My picture was in this ridiculous book.

I was awakened by a whole group of armed students standing over me, with one very tough-looking student I'd never seen before. I was told to get up. They had the protocol list. One of them put his finger on my chest and said: "You not English teacher. You big boss." Another student showed me this damn book, with my picture in it. I kept saying that it wasn't me, that it wasn't my picture. But that didn't get me anywhere.

They hauled me outside. At that point I thought I was going to be shot. It was very cold, and I could feel the vibrations of the chanting crowd. I was thrown in the back of a station wagon and taken off the compound. I was isolated and kept off the compound for the next three weeks.

GARY LEE (*general service officer, at the ambassador's residence*): I was tied up in the ambassador's residence, and I had no idea what had happened to the five who had gotten out of the consulate. I didn't know where they had gone. I was hoping they were out on the loose somewhere. I was hoping that they had gotten away.

8 On the Outside: November 6–10, 1979

FOLLOWING THE SEIZURE of the embassy, news accounts indicated some confusion over the actual number of Americans who had been taken hostage. Published reports estimated that between forty-five and seventy-five hostages were being held by the Iranian militants.* The State Department refused to confirm or deny any numbers. Meanwhile, American journalists pressed the Carter administration for an accurate count of all embassy personnel stationed in Tehran at the time of the attack, and for a list of names. Administration officials steadfastly refused to release this information, because it would have alerted the militants to the fact that six American diplomats remained unaccounted for. In Washington, the whereabouts of these six people was a highly classified piece of information.

On the evening of November 5, the five Americans who had fled from the consulate arrived at the British residential compound, which was located in a residential section of Tehran several miles from the British embassy. That same evening, a group of armed Iranian militants attacked the British embassy and occupied it for five hours before they voluntarily withdrew.

A sixth American, Lee Schatz, left the office building across the street from the American embassy, where he had been hiding, and took up residence in a private apartment in Tehran. Throughout this period, all six Americans remained in telephone contact with Bruce Laingen, Victor Tomseth, and Michael Howland at the Foreign Ministry.

* The actual number was sixty-three, which with the three men at the Foreign Ministry made a total of sixty-six.

CORA LIJEK (*consular officer, in hiding at the British residential compound in Tehran*): The British put us in an empty house on the residential compound. We were told to be very careful and not to turn any lights on in the house, because they were afraid that some of their local Iranian employees, who knew that the house wasn't supposed to be occupied, would get suspicious if they saw lights. The one thing that was not so good about the British residential compound was that they had a gardener who was a very ardent revolutionary, and who belonged to a *komiteh*. Once before, he had brought a bunch of mullahs onto the compound, so the British were a little worried about him. Consequently, we had to keep all the curtains shut and try to be very quiet. The idea was to make it seem as though we weren't really there. During the day we could hear the gardener working outside. That was a little disconcerting.

MARK LIJEK (*consular officer, in hiding at the British residential compound in Tehran*): Even though we knew that the British embassy had been attacked, we didn't think there would be trouble at the residential compound. Considering the circumstances, we were fairly comfortable. At night we kept all the lights off. There was a Pakistani gate guard who thought that this was a good idea. In case anyone did show up, he wanted to be able to tell them there was no one there.

We weren't aware of it at the time, but apparently a crowd did appear at the gates. They saw that all the lights were out, and the guard got them to go away.

VICTOR TOMSETH (*chief political officer, at the Iranian Foreign Ministry*): We were in contact with the British by phone, and the British chargé d'affaires was getting increasingly nervous. Finally, after a couple of days, he said: "You've got to find some other place to hide these people. We are just in too tenuous a position."

CORA LIJEK (*consular officer, in hiding at the British residential compound in Tehran*): That afternoon we got a call from Vic Tomseth, and we were told that we were going to have to leave. We weren't given any reason, and we didn't feel too good about the situation. If we had known about the mob that had appeared during the night we probably would have felt better about leaving, because it was just as dangerous for the British as it was for us. But not knowing what had transpired, we felt like we were being kicked out. We thought we had found a safe place, and now we were being asked to leave. We were not very happy.

VICTOR TOMSETH (*chief political officer, at the Iranian Foreign Ministry*):
We were convinced that our phone at the Foreign Ministry was being
monitored by the Iranians. So we had a double problem. We had to
find a place to hide these people, and we needed to do it in a way that
would not compromise their security. This meant we couldn't speak in
English, French, German, or any other widely spoken language. Fortunately, I do speak Thai, and there was a Thai who had worked for
our American ICA* people. I had spoken to him on the first afternoon
and had gotten a number where he would be. I called him, and speaking
in Thai, asked him if he would be willing to try and hide these five
Americans. He had access to a house way up in northern Tehran, quite
a way away from the embassy, where some Americans had lived. I
thought that if he could just hide them up there for a few days, that
would take care of it. Of course, at the time, I was still thinking that
things at the embassy could be resolved fairly quickly.

MARK LIJEK (*consular officer, in hiding at the British residential compound
in Tehran*): We felt a bit insecure because the place we were going to
was an American embassy house. But it was reasonably far from the
embassy, and was about the best that could be arranged. Of course, we
didn't have much choice in the matter, and didn't have any better
alternatives ourselves, so we agreed to go.

   That evening our British hosts had us over for dinner again, and after
dark we were taken over to this house in northern Tehran where we
were dropped off. Sam, the Thai, told us that there was an old man in
the neighborhood who belonged to a *komiteh*. As we were driving by
we saw someone on the street, and he looked us over. We assumed
that this was the guy Sam told us about, so that got things off on a
nervous footing as far as that house was concerned.

LEE SCHATZ (*agricultural attaché, in hiding at a private apartment in
Tehran*): When I finally left the office building where I had been hiding,
I went to a private residence and spent the next several days in a high-
rise apartment building. There was a cleaning lady who came in, and I
felt a bit of paranoia over the fact that anyone knew of my existence.
I spoke to her as if I knew very little English. She knew who was
supposed to be in the apartment, so I figured I would play the role of
a European guest who was not fluent in English, and I tried to stay out
of the way while she did her work.

   It was a typical Western apartment, which had two bedrooms, so I
had a room of my own. The person I was staying with went to work

* International Communications Agency.

every morning, so I'd sleep late and spend most of the day reading. Then in the evening we'd have dinner, and I'd talk with the person who was keeping me in hiding. Other than my concern over the cleaning lady, there were no real problems for me. I knew how lucky I was compared to what I imagined was going on downtown at the embassy.

I knew that the other five Americans were on the road and were free. But I lost track of them. I didn't worry about it, because I didn't see any reason why I needed to know where they were and vice versa. There was no need for any unnecessary phone calls.

MARK LIJEK (*consular officer, in hiding at the Tehran residence of an American hostage*): Once we got settled in this house we found that there was nothing to read. All of the books were in French.

To pass the time we played poker using matches and screws. We'd arrived on Tuesday night, and we were really beginning to wonder what was going on. Nothing had happened. We were getting some news reports, and events in Iran were not encouraging. There had been no strong reaction from the American government, and Bazargan had resigned on grounds that his attempts to end the occupation of the embassy had failed. This clearly indicated to us that Khomeini was now 100 percent behind the takeover. It was no longer just the work of a student group. That was not encouraging.

LEE SCHATZ (*agricultural attaché, in hiding at a private apartment in Tehran*): I had access to both the international press and the *Tehran Times*. In reading these news reports it very quickly became obvious that the Iranians and the Americans were not negotiating on a continuum that would lead to a meeting of the minds. There was just no common ground to negotiate toward. The Iranian hatred of the shah was so intense that the kinds of solutions the Iranians were asking for were not the kinds of solutions that the United States would pursue in order to resolve the problem. I mean, the issue revolved around one person: the shah. It was a situation which could have been resolved if we were a society which would have thrown the shah to the lions in order to save a number of our people. But we're not that kind of a society, and I had the feeling that this was going to evolve into a long-drawn-out affair.

MARK LIJEK (*consular officer, in hiding at the Tehran residence of an American hostage*): I was always concerned that once the students established themselves at the embassy, they would find the office that had a record of the embassy houses. Then I assumed that they would go out and search those houses, either looking for people like us, or for evidence of spying. So that concerned us. I remember the house we were in had some movies of a shah-oriented cultural event, which we hid in a hole in the ceiling. If we were caught, we didn't want those films lying around.

We stayed in that house for four days, and I felt that we had to move somewhere else fairly quickly. I thought it was only a matter of time before the students came looking for us.

LEE SCHATZ (*agricultural attaché, in hiding at a private apartment in Tehran*): During the time I was hiding in that apartment, there were nights when I didn't sleep. I could hear people on rooftops all over town screaming, "*Allah Akbar! Allah Akbar!*" That would go on for hours and hours. I'd also hear automatic weapons fire at all hours of the night. Then at dawn a dog would bark, and a car would backfire. There were times when I was so tuned in to what was going on all around me that I couldn't sleep. The "what ifs?" had settled in. There were some Iranian employees who brought me to the residence I was staying in, and I'd worry: what if they slipped up and said something to someone? What if the cleaning lady did something that was inopportune? What if the students really came looking for other Americans?

CORA LIJEK (*consular officer, in hiding at the Tehran residence of an American hostage*): One night we all slept in our clothes. For some reason Sam, the Thai, was convinced that the *komiteh* was going to arrive that night and arrest all of us. So he devised an elaborate escape plan, where we would sneak out the back door, climb over the wall, and walk three blocks down the street to another embassy house if we needed to. That made us all the more nervous. I remember there was a guard in the neighborhood who would blow his whistle every hour on the hour as a signal that everything was all right. It was a spooky thing to hear. Since we were all tense to begin with, it woke us up constantly. That was a very bad night.

To make matters worse, there was an old Thai housekeeper in the house, and she started acting very strangely. She kept muttering that we drank all the liquor in the house, which consisted of a six-pack of beer and a bottle of Chianti, and that we were eating all the food. She wanted to know, what would her master say when he got home?

MARK LIJEK (*consular officer, in hiding at the Tehran residence of an American hostage*): Of course, we didn't think it would improve the situation to tell her that her master wasn't likely to come home anytime soon. She kept getting progressively worse, and we were afraid she might turn us in or do something totally crazy. We talked about various schemes to control her, like locking her up in the basement, but decided that it just wasn't practical.

On Thursday, Bob Anders called John Sheardown. John was in charge of immigration at the Canadian embassy, which was the same capacity Bob had worked in at the American embassy. I guess they were reasonably good friends. John Sheardown was very forthcoming. As soon as Bob introduced himself, John said, "Why didn't you call sooner? Come on over to my house." That was very encouraging. Then Bob went on to say, "Well, there are a few others with me, and we all might need a place to stay." John said that of course we were all welcome.

Then we had to decide whether or not to take the Canadians up on their offer. The reason we didn't jump at it right away was the same reason we had turned down other invitations: we didn't want to involve other people. We just didn't feel it was right to endanger others. So we were a little bit hesitant about imposing ourselves on them. But the situation was getting out of hand.

VICTOR TOMSETH (*chief political officer, at the Iranian Foreign Ministry*): Within a few days the students began searching the houses where Americans had lived. The gardener at one of these houses tipped off the Thai who was taking care of the Americans, and this news was carried back to the five who were holed up in one of those houses.

MARK LIJEK (*consular officer, in hiding at the Tehran residence of an American hostage*): On Saturday morning, Sam came in and said we had to go. We had to leave immediately. So we walked about three blocks down to Kate Koob's old house, which was on the same street. We went out in such a hurry that we left our laundry behind. I lost half my shirts and some of my underwear.

As soon as we got to Kate's, we realized that her house would not be an acceptable place for us to hide. The house we'd just left was set back from the street and had a wall in front of it. But Kate's house was right on the road. You could stand on the sidewalk and see right into the kitchen. There was just no way that we could hide in there.

At Kate's, the first thing Bob Anders did was call John Sheardown. John arranged to have two British fellows come over and pick us up so he could take us in. We did all of this in broad daylight. We didn't want to stay at Kate's for one moment longer than was necessary.

When we got to the Sheardowns', we were served drinks and made to feel very welcome. I remember Ken Taylor* was there, and I didn't recognize him. He looked much too young to be an ambassador, but

* Ken Taylor was the Canadian ambassador to Iran.

John was talking as though the ambassador was in our presence. Finally, I asked him where the ambassador was. At that point we were introduced all the way around.

LEE SCHATZ (*agricultural attaché, in hiding at a private apartment in Tehran*): At the end of two weeks, the person I was staying with came home from work and said, "You're going to leave. A man is going to come by and pick you up in half an hour, and you're going to go with him." That was it. No explanation as to what was going on. It just came out of the blue. I wasn't even told where I was going. This person simply apologized, and said that a decision had been made to move me.

Pretty soon a fellow came in and introduced himself as John. I had packed all of my things into a knapsack, and as we went downstairs we made small talk. He wasn't giving me any explanation as to what was going on. I figured he was CIA. I was sure of it. I mean, this guy was too cool for words. When we got outside, it was like some kind of cops and robbers show. We got into a real dark midnight-blue Mercedes, and I saw two guys sitting in a trail car at the other end of the parking lot.

As soon as I sat down on the front seat, this guy turned to me, stuck his hand out, and said, "I'm John Sheardown. I'm the consular officer at the Canadian embassy." Then he made a comment about going by the embassy to pick up some things for my friends.

I said, "What do you mean?"

The last I'd heard, the other five were with the British, and I assumed they were still there. This was the first indication I'd had that they were with the Canadians. We drove over to the Canadian embassy and picked up some clothes for Mark Lijek and some other odds and ends. Then we drove over to John Sheardown's personal residence, where I had a reunion with the others.

9 On the Inside: November 7–16, 1979

AT THE AMERICAN embassy, the militants continued to conduct a seemingly endless series of rallies and demonstrations in front of the main gate. Inside the embassy buildings, the hostages remained bound both night and day. Many of the hostages knew that American residences were being broken into, because they saw some of the militants guarding them wearing military fatigues, sweaters, and coats that had been stolen from them and their colleagues.

During the first week of captivity, approximately twenty-five hostages were moved out of the ambassador's residence and taken to the basement of the embassy warehouse. The warehouse was a particularly depressing place to be held, because prior to the revolution it had housed sensitive communications equipment and was designed for secure radio and other communications. The windowless concrete walls made an atmosphere that was dark, clammy, and damp. The hostages soon dubbed their new home the Mushroom Inn. A second group of hostages was temporarily relocated in the large waiting room of the consulate, while others remained at the ambassador's residence.

ROBERT ODE (*consular officer*): On the third night, shortly after I had crawled under the dining room table to get some sleep, I was handcuffed and blindfolded with a blanket over my head and taken from the ambassador's residence. They took me over to the Mushroom Inn. There were probably twenty-five or thirty hostages sitting or lying on the floor over there. It had no windows at all, and by the time we were put in there the air conditioning had ceased to function. I think it got its name because it was more suited to growing mushrooms than it was to keeping hostages. I was in one corner of this large room, sandwiched in between Al Golacinski and Steve Lauterbach. Every once in a while one of the guards would decide that my hands weren't tied quite tightly enough, so he'd come over and tie them up again. I was just lying on the hard floor along with everybody else.

CAPT. PAUL NEEDHAM (*air force logistics officer*): On Wednesday I was moved over to the Mushroom Inn. A bunch of us were kept over there in very unsanitary conditions. Most of the hostages were lined up against the wall. We were able to see people, but we couldn't communicate. That was something the Iranians were very paranoid about. If we were just drumming our fingers on the floor out of nervousness, or if we made eye contact, one of the guards would run over and say: "Do not communicate! Do not talk!" Every once in a while I'd feel my oats and would shout right back, "I'm not talking to anybody! I'm not sending any messages!"

Even though we couldn't communicate it was helpful to see other people. In looking around, the reaction of others varied. Some people were dazed. They were sitting with an expression like: "I can't believe this is happening to me." Some of the others appeared to be sharp. You could tell they were plotting: "How are we going to get out of this alive? How do we not give them any information? How do we refuse to cooperate?" You could sense that people were thinking about these types of things.

BARRY ROSEN (*press attaché*): In the middle of the night, the students took me over to the Mushroom Inn. It was a very weird place to be. The atmosphere down there was disgusting. The thing I remember the most is the abominable heat and the darkness of the place. It was intolerable. It was abominably hot. I also remember that there were mounds of books in there from the American high school in Tehran. There were thousands of books just lying in piles.

There must've been fifteen or twenty of us down there, and by this time we all looked shoddy. It's hard to wear your suit clothes every day, day in and day out, and then sleep in them, too. We looked rumpled and exhausted. Many people were not able to sleep. No matter how you moved, the floor was hard and it was difficult to sleep. It was hot and uncomfortable. Of course, you couldn't talk. The Iranians were paranoid about any form of communication. Hand signals or gestures upset them. It was as if we were spying by using hand signals to wave at a fellow hostage.

You'd lie there and think, "When am I going to get out of here? How am I going to get out of here?" And I'd wonder about whether or not I was really there. It was very strange. At times it seemed as if it was just a very, very bad movie. I'd wonder: why? Why me? Why us? Why had we been selected for this honor? In essence, I felt like I'd been raped by the Iranians, and the oppressiveness of it was almost intolerable. But what could I do? Scream out? Yell? Shout "I want out of here!" What good would that do? Right then, everybody else wanted out too.

SGT. ROCKY SICKMANN (*marine security guard, at the Mushroom Inn*): We were all situated in this one large room with pillars in the middle of it, and one time the lights went out. We were in this basement with no windows, so when that happened it was totally dark. You should have heard those Iranians. They went berserk! We couldn't see them, but we sure could hear them running all over the place. They were scrambling around, very excited, talking in Farsi. All of us started yelling and screaming just to make them think something was going on. When the lights finally came back on, the students had eyes that were as big as silver dollars. We were all cracking up. That really upset them. They wanted us to think that they were in total control. So when we started screaming in the dark and laughing, they got upset.

ROBERT ODE (*consular officer, at the Mushroom Inn*): One night, I was lying on the floor of the Mushroom trying to get some sleep when I realized that there were some bright lights shining on me. I rolled over to see what was going on. The Iranians had these bright television lights focused on me and they were filming me with TV cameras. I was so annoyed that I gave them the finger.

In English, one of them said, "This is for television."

I shoved my finger right in front of the camera. "Yes, and this is for you."

BARRY ROSEN (*press attaché, at the Mushroom Inn*): I very vividly remember them coming around with a movie camera and filming us. They tried to interview some of us, but most of us told them to leave us alone or refused to answer. I also remember one Iranian down there who was more or less the spokesman, and one day he said, "Don't think there will be any Entebbe here." Everybody just kind of sat there, stoic. We were all trying to preserve our dignity, to the extent that was possible.

BILL BELK (*communications officer, at the Mushroom Inn*): I was dead certain that the United States would come in and get us. There was just no way they'd leave us there for that long. You can't drive a truck through four million people, so I figured the plan would call for dropping troops in with helicopters and using our firepower to get us out of there.

Well, when they put me in the Mushroom Inn, I was near a ventilator and I could hear a few outside noises. The first time the heater came on, I thought it was a helicopter. It sounded exactly like a helicopter. When that ventilator went off, I thought, "Oh man, this is a regular invasion!" I sat up, and I was ready to get to the first Iranian as quick as I could. I was ready to knock one of those guys from here to kingdom come, and grab a weapon. I was alert and ready to go. I was listening for the first sounds of any commotion. They always had a few guys walking around with guns, and I was ready to grab one and bust through the door.

That happened a few times. Every time that ventilator came on, I thought, "Christ, this might be it!" Then I heard it a couple more times, and realized that it was only the stupid heater. Nobody was coming in to get us. No way.

ROBERT ODE (*consular officer, at the Mushroom Inn*): On the day we were captured, I had on a brand-new pair of loafers. Because they were so new, they were stiff, and I found it very difficult to get them on without a shoehorn. On our second night in captivity, I took them off when I crawled under the table to go to sleep, but in the morning I had such a difficult time getting them back on that I didn't take them off at all for the next ten days or so. I was confident that a rescue attempt was going to be made. I would even picture it in my mind—how the U.S. Army or Marines were going to come in and rescue us. At night, when I'd lie down to go to sleep, I'd take my shirt off and sleep in my trousers, but I didn't dare take my shoes off, because when the rescue forces arrived, I wasn't about to get caught trying to run out of the Mushroom in my bare feet. I was afraid that I wouldn't be able to run fast enough. So I kept those shoes on all the time.

BRUCE GERMAN (*budget officer, at a house in northern Tehran*): I didn't expect a rescue mission simply because no one would know where to find us. We were in some house somewhere in Tehran. A rescue team just couldn't have found us. If the United States had come in and had tried a rescue at an early date, some of us would not have been there.

Since a rescue attempt didn't seem feasible, my only hope was that there were negotiations going on and that a meeting of the minds would be reached. I kept hoping that someone would come through the door and say, "Okay, you guys can go home now." That was the one hope I was holding on to.

JOE HALL (*warrant officer, at the ambassador's residence*): I was in the middle of the best sleep I'd had. We'd been tied up and sleeping on the floor, which was very uncomfortable and made it very difficult to get any sleep at night. After a few nights of this, I finally managed to fall asleep from sheer exhaustion. I mean, I was really sawing logs for the first time in the entire ordeal. Then these guys came in and woke all of us up at three o'clock in the morning. They put army blankets over our heads and tied the blankets about our necks so we couldn't see. Then they put all of us into a car. They had about six of us crammed into this sedan with two or three guards, and they drove all over the compound like they were trying to confuse us as to where we were going. There were some speed bumps we bounced over, and I remember they'd go around the corners awfully damn fast. But as tight as we were packed in there, nobody was getting thrown around or hurt. I knew we were just driving around in circles, and when we pulled up in front of the consular section I knew exactly where we were. They took us into the big reception area and sat me down on a bench. When they got us out of the car they were being real gentle with us. There were a bunch of hostages inside the consular section. I was thinking,

"Hey, maybe they're going to let us go. Maybe they are getting us all together for a release."

I sat there on the bench for about an hour. Then they took the blanket off my head, and I could see all these other Americans. I think there were nineteen of us in there. On the floor we each had a little pallet that consisted of one blanket and a pillow. It was a hard concrete floor, and we just slept on the floor.

GARY LEE (*general services officer, at the consulate*): It was really uncomfortable inside the consulate. This was November, and it was getting colder every day. There was no heat, and it was colder than hell. We were all lying around in there, reading whatever we could. The Iranians had passed out some books and old magazines. Of course, at this time reading wasn't very important to us. It was hard to concentrate on anything, and we were still hoping this fiasco was going to end fairly quickly. We wanted to get the hell out of there. That's all that was on our minds.

It was while we were in the consulate that the Swiss ambassador and a couple of other ambassadors came walking through. There was a whole mob of us being kept in the same room. We were sleeping in our clothes, and we hadn't had a bath in about a week or ten days. The smell must have been overwhelming to those guys coming in from the outside. But this little entourage walked through and saw that we were all lying there trussed up like a bunch of turkeys.

JOE HALL (*warrant officer, at the consulate*): I saw the foreign ambassadors when they came in. It was just a quick walk through to make sure that no one was broken or bleeding. I guess it was a diplomatic mission to make sure that we were all still alive. We were all lying around, and I remember one of those guys said, "Well, you all look like you're doing pretty well."

I thought, "Oh yeah, it's just a picnic in here."

Another one of them leaned over and asked one of the hostages, "How are you doing?"

He looked up and said, "Fine."

Well, we weren't dead, and we were healthy. So I guess maybe we were doing fine.

We slept on those hard concrete floors for three nights in a row, and I had bruises on the sides of my hips and on my shoulders. I was just as tender as could be from continually lying on that concrete floor with nothing but a blanket underneath me. Day and night we were on the concrete floor, and it was impossible to rest my weight on a part of my body that wasn't sore.

I knew that there were some mattresses in the embassy warehouse, and on our third day inside the consulate I said to the guard who seemed to be the group leader, "You know, the embassy warehouse is full of mattresses. There must be hundreds of mattresses over there. If we're going to stay here for a long time, couldn't you bring us some mattresses to lie on?"

All he said was, "We will see."

Well, a little later I went to the bathroom, and I tried to scrub out my underwear and my socks with a bar of soap. When I came out, there were mattresses on the floor. Each of us had a mattress. My God, that was like heaven. To me that mattress was like a little safe haven—my little ship in the sea. Besides being comfortable, it was a real boost for morale.

Then the next day we were given toothbrushes. That was nice. We didn't have any toothpaste, and we had to use hand soap to clean our teeth, but still that toothbrush was nice.

JOHN LIMBERT (*political officer, at the consulate*): It was while we were in the consulate that some of the interrogations started. Every now and then we could see some of the students come in and take somebody out. We wouldn't know where they had gone. I remember once they took Jerry Miele out, and when they brought him back he was being sort of shoved and pushed a bit. It was obvious that he had not been treated very well.

COL. LELAND HOLLAND (*army attaché, at the consulate*): While I was in the consular section, there were a couple of these guys who knew who I was. They'd take me out two or three times a day and try an intimidation routine. They'd say things like, "We know you're a big man in this embassy. You're a colonel in intelligence. And we're going to have a lot to do with you." It was kind of like having the neighborhood bully stop me on the street and tell me that he was going to kick my ass on Tuesday. I was supposed to sit there and worry about Tuesday.

If they had talked nice to me, I would have returned the favor. But when they started to bark, I was arrogant in return. Finally, I said to them, "I want to see your leader." I just sat there and demanded to see their leader.

They took me into a room where there were two Iranians. One of them spoke flawless English, and the other one didn't speak English at all. I said, "Your people keep telling me that I'm a very important person here. I want to inform you of something. The American people think just as much of one American as they do of one thousand Americans. If you want your shah back, you don't need an embassy full of us. All you need is one American. Since I'm so important, I'll volunteer to stay here. You can let the rest of them go, and I'll stay behind."

Of course, these guys said no, that wasn't necessary. Then the one guy who spoke fluent English explained to me that the Bazargan government had fallen and the revolutionary government was now in charge. They expected the shah back within ten days, and we would all be free within two weeks. So a deal wasn't necessary.

Now this little episode accomplished two things. First, we hadn't had any news. I didn't know the Bazargan government had collapsed. So I got some news from them. Second, by meeting them head on, instead of cowering in front of their intimidation game, these two rattle-heads dropped the bit about how I was a very important man at the embassy. They dropped the intimidation bit and didn't take me out for my daily dose. They never brought that up again. When they took me back to the consulate, I wasn't sure of what I'd accomplished, but through incidents like this, and in watching them relate to others, I was beginning to develop a strategy for dealing with them. Due to the fact that they weren't coming back to give me my daily dose of intimidation, I knew that something had worked. I was beginning to see a pattern develop, and I could see that it was best to meet them head on. You don't ask them for anything. You demand things. You stand up to them, because if you don't they'll walk all over you.

JOHN LIMBERT (*political officer, at the consulate*): My first interrogation took place during the day. At about four o'clock in the afternoon I was taken from the consulate over to the chancery and into what had been my own office. It was a rather strange feeling to be sitting there in my own office. There was a demonstration going on outside, which I could hear, and a fellow walked in with an embassy burn bag over his head. He had a couple of holes punched out for the eyes so he could see. In his very courteous Persian manner, he apologized for the way he appeared, and said, "I'm sorry I have to talk to you in this way."

I said, "Oh, that's all right. Don't worry about it." I tried to keep up the façade of Iranian courtesy as much as I could. The Persian language is beautiful, because you can talk for five minutes and say absolutely nothing, which can be very useful in many cases.

I remember this guy with the burn bag spoke very good English. He was clearly a cut above the average twenty-year-olds that we were dealing with most of the time. He was much more sophisticated than those kids.

My interrogation was actually very formal. In addition to this fellow with the burn bag, there was a young Iranian note taker in there to write down what I said. The basic question was: "What Iranians have you seen in the last two months?" They were very concerned about any Iranian I knew or had met. Of course, I was concerned about the safety of innocent people, who could have been endangered if their names came up in an interrogation or showed up on embassy documents. I had to presume that they had the documents that were not destroyed in some of the safes. All of that was innocuous stuff. It certainly did not support their claims of plots against the revolution, or counterrevolutions, or anything like that. But given the right cast of mind and a manipulative mentality, a routine meeting with an Iranian official could be blown up into anything. They could make anything they wanted to out of a normal diplomatic contact. So I was concerned about the safety of some of these people. I figured the best way to deal with that question was to give them a whole long series of names that had no particular rhyme or reason, and out of which they could make nothing. I just figured I'd deluge them with names—everybody from the clerk at the corner drugstore to Ayatollah Montazari.* I gave them names like the minister of the interior, and somebody in the Foreign Ministry that I'd seen officially. I just threw all these names at them, figuring that it was better to give them fifty names than to give them five. What were they going to do with Ayatollah Montazari's name? Or the minister of the interior? When I was asked, "What did you talk about with so and so?" I would simply answer, "Normal business." Or, "Official business."

Of course, the situation was a bit worrisome, because they could have simply looked in my desk and found my telephone address book. I don't know why they didn't take that from my desk and go down the list of names I had written in there and ask: "Who is he? Who is she? Who is he?" To my mind that would have been a much more fruitful way of going about the interrogation, and it wouldn't have given me the chance to be as evasive. But there didn't seem to be much rhyme or reason to what this guy was doing. There was no real follow-up.

I remember he asked me about the 1953 coup. I said, "I don't know anything about that. I was ten years old at the time. I only know what I've read, and I did read Richard Cottam's book."

He said, "Oh, you mean *Nationalism in Iran?*"

That surprised me. I was very surprised by the fact that he knew the name of the book. It had never been allowed to appear in Iran, and the only Iranians who had ever heard of it were people who had studied abroad and tended to be politically active. But he didn't really follow up on the 1953 coup. He just wandered off into another blind alley.

* Ayatollah Montazari was the Friday prayer leader in Tehran. He is often referred to as Khomeini's most likely successor.

He would say things like: "What about the vault?"

I said, "I don't know anything about the vault. I can't get into it. Only certain people are allowed in, and I don't have any permission to go in there."

"What about your agents in Kurdistan? How do you communicate with them?"

"I don't know what you're talking about. We don't have any agents in Kurdistan."

"When was the last time you saw Ezz al-Din Hoseini?"*

"I don't know anything about Ezz al-Din Hoseini."

"Where is your radio equipment?"

"There isn't any kind of radio equipment."

This kind of thing went on for a while. I don't know what they wanted. I guess they were fishing. At this time they had some serious trouble in Kurdistan, and a lot of their propaganda claimed that their trouble with the Kurds was somehow the fault of the United States. Of course, that was patently false. But it didn't keep them from trying to manufacture something. Maybe that's what this guy was trying to do.

At any rate, the tone of that first interrogation was not hostile. It was friendly.

JOHN GRAVES (*public affairs officer*): In their interrogations, they were out to prove that the embassy wasn't a normal embassy, but that it was a center for spying and subversion. Their big obsession was that the United States was plotting to overthrow the Khomeini regime and reinstall the shah. I guess they had reason to suppose that, since we'd already done it once before with the ouster of Mossadeq in the early fifties. Kermit Roosevelt bragged about it in a damn book, so we couldn't very well deny our intervention.

They found no proof of a coup against Khomeini or anything like that. As a matter of fact, that was not our policy. We had decided that once Khomeini was in power, it was in our long-term interest to try and work out some kind of relationship with him and his regime. Which is not to say that we agreed with what he was doing, but that we were not actively opposing.

That they found no evidence of what they were looking for gave them great problems, because in terms of their own psychology they had to find such evidence in order to justify what they were doing. They had to believe that they had taken over a den of spies and subversives. They worked very hard at that. The documents that they

* Ezz al-Din Hoseini is a Kurdish rebel leader.

confiscated didn't show what they wanted at all. But then, they misread many of them.

COL. CHARLES SCOTT (*military attaché, at the chancery*): Every embassy in every country in the world collects intelligence. That's part of the reason they are there. All of what we were doing in Iran was strictly overt intelligence collection; you know, the gathering of information to assist us in decision making. We'd go out, talk to people, and write reports on it. This was all very straightforward.

Yet the Iranians were so paranoid that they believed that anything that was classified had to be something bad. Otherwise, they reasoned, why would it be classified? Of course, any Iranian who was mentioned in any secret document was automatically in trouble. In spite of this, the militants didn't understand anything about protection of sources. They didn't understand that there are a lot of simple bureaucratic reasons for classifying material. But to the Iranians, if something was classified it was automatically bad, and there is just no way you can defend against that kind of thinking. The Iranian perception that we were all a nest of spies was a bum rap. But the way the Islamic mind worked, they needed a justification for taking over the embassy, and that justification was, "They are all spies."

JOHN LIMBERT (*political officer, at the consulate*): A few days after my first interrogation, I underwent a second interrogation. This one wasn't done in the daytime, but took place in the middle of the night. I think many of these people spent some time in a SAVAK prison, or else they had read a book on interrogations, because there was this feeling of a technique only half-mastered. They came over to the consulate to get me in the middle of the night, but somehow they weren't quite capable of managing to get the frightening atmosphere they wanted.

They took me out of the consulate and down into the basement of the chancery. This time the interrogator was not wearing a burn bag over his head. Instead, I was blindfolded. Even though I was blindfolded, I could see out from under the bottom of my blindfold. There was a sheet of glass covering the table, and I could see the interrogator's reflection in the glass. So I knew who he was, and I could see how he was reacting. In spite of the blindfold, I wasn't totally deprived of sight. I'd recognize that interrogator today if I were to see him.

Basically, we went through the same questions as in the previous interrogation, but this time it was no longer Mr. Nice Guy asking the questions. Now the same questions were being asked by Mr. Threat.

They started in again by asking things like: "How do you communicate with Kurdistan?"

"I don't."

"Where is your radio equipment?"

"There isn't any."

Then they mentioned this train that had been blown up down in southern Tehran a few weeks before, and they tried to use that to threaten me. They said, "We think the CIA blew that train up. And we think you know who the people are that were involved."

I said, "You're free to think what you want."

They went on and accused me of having contacts with all sorts of groups that I had no knowledge of, and they threatened me by saying, "You know what we do with people who are spies."

I'd just say, "Do what you want." Sitting there blindfolded, I wasn't in much of a position to argue with them. They could make any kind of wild accusation they wanted to make. In that situation, I realized how perceptive Solzhenitsyn is. The only way to respond to that kind of interrogation was to be as dumb as possible. To simply say, "There isn't any." Or, "I don't know what you're talking about."

Once again they wanted to know about any Iranians I'd been in contact with, and they said: "Name all of the Iranians you have met with in the past two months." So once again, the names I gave them were basically the names of public figures. I didn't give them the names of other less well-known people, people I might have known socially, or people they could have gone after for family reasons. Instead, I tried to stick to the names of people I dealt with at the embassy. If they wanted to go after these public figures that was their business. Once again, I just deluged them with those sorts of names.

JOHN GRAVES (*public affairs officer*): I had considerable knowledge of the kind of interrogation they were trying to do. When I was in Vietnam, I served as a stand-in for the provisional governor of a Vietnamese province. One of our programs was the Chu Hoi, the prisoner interrogation program. One of the things that I learned from that experience was that the rigid personality, the rigid mentality, was the easiest by far to crack. The prisoners we had the most trouble with were the ones who agreed with almost anything we said. We didn't learn anything from them, because they agreed to everything. They would simply play back to you what you told them. So you got nowhere. You couldn't get any real leverage or psychological pressure on them, because they weren't fighting back. They weren't opposing; they weren't rigid; they weren't tough. They were bending. I thought that was an interesting phenomenon, and my intention was to see whether it would work. But my interrogators never got enough pressure on me, so I couldn't find out whether it would work or not.

They seemed to be following some kind of manual. Maybe the PLO gave them a manual or something on how to interrogate prisoners. The chief reason they didn't do well is that instead of hammering away at me, they would go off on long diatribes, fifteen, twenty-minute dissertations justifying what they were doing. Justifying the takeover. Which gave me a chance to rest. They tried to keep me awake all around the clock. They didn't understand that very well. They kept me awake all night, but they let me sleep during the day. They certainly were incompetent as interrogators. But I guess that's good that they weren't very competent.

In fact, I remember this one little fellow who was terribly short, maybe four foot nine. We called him the Dwarf. At one point, when I was cold and hungry and had been without sleep, I remember this little guy coming to me and patting me on the side, saying, "You be all right. Don't worry. You be all right." Which gave my morale a tremendous boost.

COL. CHARLES SCOTT (*military attaché, at the chancery*): My interrogations went on daily and nightly. I don't know how many sessions I had. I lost count. I wasn't trying to count them. I just didn't think it was going to last that long. But it went on for about three weeks.

One of the funnier things occurred on the second day. They cut my safe open because I refused to open it for them. In the safe, they found a one-pound box of tobacco—but they didn't know what it was. They spent four or five hours quizzing me and asking me what was in the box. I refused to tell them, and they were afraid to open it because they thought it might be a booby trap or something. They wet this box of tobacco down to make sure that it wasn't a bomb, and of course, when they finally did manage to get it open they found there was nothing in there but tobacco. I thoroughly enjoyed that.

At first, the big area they concentrated on in the interrogations was trying to make me the bad guy, the CIA station chief. They never really dropped that, but after a few days a different team came in and tried a different tack. They'd ask, "What were you doing in the embassy?" I'd tell them, and they'd say, "No! We know otherwise. You were here working on a military coup against Khomeini!" I'd deny it, and we'd go over it again and again and again.

One of the things they found in my safe were some personal letters from people I had worked with at Force Command in Atlanta. During my interrogation, they got bogged down on these letters, and wasted hours and hours and hours getting into things that were neither classified nor critical. When they got off on a tangent like that, I'd try to kill as much time as I could. That way they weren't beating me around.

They were especially big on acronyms. I remember this one guy wanted to know what MOBEX was. When he first asked me about that, I thought, "What is this guy talking about?" And I asked, "What's a MOBEX? What do you mean, MOBEX?"

"You got a letter from someone that said you were the director of MOBEX."

Then I realized that he was talking about a mobilization exercise in America. There's nothing classified about it at all. We have newspaper reporters who write about it all the time. So I went into a big long dissertation about the strength of our National Guard and reserve forces. They spent hours and hours listening to that and writing all this stuff down. It was as if I was giving them a brand-new order of battle. I just kept going. I figured, "Hey, as long as they're wasting time with this, they're not beating me about the head and shoulders and asking who the CIA station chief is."

Then they spent about three days on my Vietnam record. They had my bio, which informed them that I'd been decorated for valor in Vietnam. Well, my having served in Vietnam automatically made me a war criminal in their eyes. They wanted to know: "How many Vietnamese did you kill? How many babies did you kill?"

My answer was that while I was in Vietnam I was involved with a project called *Edap-Anang* where I was not tearing things down but was building them up. We did have a lot of civic action projects going on in the areas that we were trying to pacify. So I concentrated on those. That's all I would talk about. Of course, the truth was that I saw plenty of combat and was there as a warrior. But I didn't want to let them know that.

They went on and on about Vietnam and made all kinds of ludicrous threats. I understand that Dave Roeder* got the same kind of threats. They kept telling me that I was a war criminal, and that when they were through with me, they were going to bundle me up and ship me to North Vietnam.

JOHN LIMBERT (*political officer*): In talking about the interrogations or the embassy documents, it's important to remember that the students had no doubt that the United States was out to overthrow Khomeini in a coup, or was out to overthrow the revolution. That was an article of faith with them. They believed that everything that was wrong with

---

* Lt. Col. Dave Roeder was the assistant air force attaché. He flew numerous combat missions over Vietnam.

Iran was the fault of the United States. When you believe that, evidence doesn't make much difference. Their evidence consisted of things like the existence of a paper shredder, or a car radio, or the receipts from the embassy cashier's funds. All of these things became "evidence."

In front of the embassy, they knew their audience and they knew how to manipulate them. They were dealing in an atmosphere that was already very hysterical. In that kind of atmosphere, reason and evidence are not the kinds of things that talk. The audience they were playing to had no knowledge of diplomacy or international relations. So there was a cynical kind of manipulation of a very unsophisticated public opinion taking place outside the embassy. The students didn't have what they would have liked to have had in the way of evidence, but they were perfectly capable of using what they did have as the basis for the most hysterical and outrageous accusations against the United States. Out of this absolute faith that the United States was somehow plotting to overthrow the revolution, these various objects became "evidence." Their audience out there chanting in front of the embassy didn't know what a paper shredder was used for. They didn't know that a hospital had a paper shredder and a bank had a paper shredder. So the students could triumphantly hold up their prizes and say, "Look what we found! We found evidence that the United States is plotting to overthrow Khomeini and bring back the shah! We found evidence that the United States is plotting against us in Kurdistan!" And that "evidence" had its desired effect.

10 November 17–19, 1979

On NOVEMBER 17, 1979, Ayatollah Khomeini ordered the students at the embassy to release all the female and black hostages who "had not committed acts of espionage" against Iran. In a public statement, Khomeini said that these hostages should be released because "Islam has a special respect toward women," and that blacks had spent ages living "under American pressure and tyranny." His order to release them was intended as a gesture of Iran's solidarity with the struggle of all the oppressed minorities in America.

CHARLES JONES (*communications officer, at a staff house in the embassy compound*): From the consular section, I was moved over to one of the prefab houses on the compound. The Iranians were keeping four or five hostages in this particular house, including one of the black marines, one of the women, a civilian businessman, and a Korean businessman that had been picked up with the rest of us.

Now the interesting thing about that prefab was it was used as a meeting place for the terrorists. In the evening, twenty or thirty of the "students" would converge on the house, and they would pray together in the living room and have long political discussions that lasted very late into the night. It was almost like a picnic-type atmosphere, because they would bring dates and snacks and would drink tea and talk. They would tell us hostages to join them in their discussions. We couldn't talk to the other Americans, but we could talk to the guards. They would say, "Sit with us. Take some dates." So I'd eat some darn dates, and they would start off on their anti-American rhetoric. They were very sincere in trying to convince me that what they had done by taking us hostage was right, and of course I was trying to convince them of the wrongness of their act. I told them that I thought they were a bunch of animals, and said all kinds of things that didn't endear me to them at all.

SGT. WILLIAM QUARLES (*marine security guard, at a staff house in the embassy compound*): I used to watch the students a lot because I wanted to know what they were doing. One day I was sitting in there with my hands tied when this Iranian came in the room. He was talking with the guard who was in charge, but he was looking over in the direction where I was sitting. Then he talked to another little group of students, and as soon as he started talking to them, they started looking over toward me. The head student kept looking at me and smiling and winking. I knew something was going on.

Then later that day one of the students came up to me and said, "Perhaps you should go free soon."

I said, "Oh yeah? When?"

"I don't know," he said. "Maybe one week. Maybe two weeks."

CHARLES JONES (*communications officer, at a staff house in the embassy compound*): One night things seemed a little strange. I noticed that a couple of the guards were talking, and while they were talking they'd look over at me. So I knew they were talking about me. Then one of the honcho guards waved his hand in a dismissive gesture, like, "Never mind him. He's of no consequence. Forget about him." I didn't think anything of it at the time, but in retrospect I know that was the night they were getting ready to release the eight blacks and the five women. I suppose I was a candidate for release, but because they didn't like me I was separated from the others. They moved me into a back bedroom and left me there. I had no idea what was going on. I just knew that there was a lot of activity and things seemed a little strange.

SGT. WILLIAM QUARLES (*marine security guard, at a staff house in the embassy compound*): In the morning I woke up and the students untied my hands for breakfast. When I got through eating, they didn't tie my hands back up. I was so used to being tied up by then, I said, "Hey, aren't you gonna—?" And I held up my hands.

The guard said, "Naw." And he waved his hand like, "Don't worry about it." So I sat there with my hands untied. I was wondering, "What the fuck is going on now?" They had moved all the white guys out of there the night before, and I was sitting in the living room by myself. Then they moved me to a bedroom, and as I went down the hall I saw Sergeant Maples* sitting in the middle room of this house. They had moved him in. Everything felt like it was getting kind of loose. A little while later, they brought Kathy Gross† in the house and put her in another room. There was a lot of movement going on, and I said to myself, "Shit, something is happening here." I wasn't thinking about going home or being released, I was just wondering what the hell they were up to.

One of the students came in, and he started talking to me about politics and the revolution. Then another came in, and he started talking to me about the same kind of stuff. Then another student after that. All day long these guys were coming in and talking to me. I mean one right after the other. That Iranian woman, Mary, came in there too. She talked my ear off about the revolution, about the ayatollah, about politics, about the shah, and about SAVAK, the shah's secret police—she went on and on. I said to myself, "They're trying to pump my head full of ideology. They're trying to brainwash me and turn me to their way of thinking. I got to keep my name, rank, and serial number in my head. That's all I want to keep in my head."

So I sat there and kept saying, "Yeah. Yeah, I understand." But all that stuff they were telling me went in one ear and out the other. Two minutes later, if they'd asked me what they'd said, I couldn't have told them.

Later that afternoon they put me in the same room with Sergeant Maples. Man, we were happy to see each other. It was really good to see him. The Iranians had somebody sitting in there with us, but maybe for thirty seconds they'd leave us alone when they'd change students

---

* Sgt. Ladell Maples, a marine security guard, was one of nine black Americans taken hostage.
† Kathy Gross, an embassy secretary, was one of seven female hostages.

or somebody would get up and do something. Whenever that happened, Maples and I would start whispering. We were saying things like: "God-damn, do you think we're getting out of here?"

"I don't know, man. We just might get out of here. I don't know what the hell is going on."

"Do you think anybody else is going to get out?"

"I don't know. I hope so."

We carried on that type of conversation whenever we could. The students kept on talking about the shah, the ayatollah, and politics. But like I said, I didn't give a shit what they were thinking. Although one guy did come in there, and what he said touched me. He was an older guy, and he was talking to us about the shah's regime, and how bad people had it under the shah. While he was talking to us, he broke down and cried. He was upset because SAVAK had killed his brother, his sister, and his father. He said they were tortured, and he was telling Maples and me about that and broke down in tears. I felt for him. You know, what he had to say touched me. It touched me a lot.

Anyway, that evening the students came in with some dinner for us. They gave us American hamburgers, potato chips, and pickles. Then that same night, they took Kathy Gross, Sgt. Maples, and myself over to a big press conference. They didn't tell us what was going on; all they said was that there was somebody outside who wanted to see us. They took us out to the courtyard area between the commissary and the consulate building. A bunch of Iranians were standing around with guns, and they had big floodlights and cameras set up everywhere. They led us right up onto a stage, and there was a great big picture of the ayatollah behind us with some crazy little writing underneath it. In front of us, there must've been 200 or 250 reporters from dozens of different countries. As soon as we walked out, the cameras went crazy. *Click-click! Whirr-click-click!* Flashbulbs were popping, and those cameras were going a mile a minute. You talk about shock! I had no idea this was coming. It took me totally by surprise. I was scared to death. I didn't know what the hell to say, and I didn't know what the hell to do. But all of a sudden I realized why the students had been feeding me their ideology about the shah and the ayatollah all day long. They knew there was going to be this press conference, and they wanted me to say some of the things they had been telling me.

I sat down on a little chair. It was cold out there. I was shaking and shivering because it was so cold. Up on the stage with the three of us there was an Iranian, and he was trying to keep the reporters organized. They were all jumping up and shouting questions at us, and this guy wanted them to ask one question at a time. He was finally able to get a little bit of order. The reporters were asking Ladell, Kathy, and myself questions. They wanted to know how we felt about the shah, how we had been treated, and how the other hostages were doing. To tell you the truth, I really can't remember anything I said, not specifically. I was in a state of shock. I didn't feel like I was free to say what I wanted, either, because I didn't know I was going to be released soon. I thought I was going to have to go back and keep on living with the students. The Iranians weren't directing me or telling me what I had to say, but I felt very restrained by their presence. I didn't want to say anything that would cause any harm to me or any of the other hostages. So I kept my answers short and said I hadn't been beaten up or anything like that. I wanted to get the hell away from there. I was hoping one of the militants would grab me and take me away, but it seemed like that press conference went on forever.

When that interview was finally over, we were all taken back to the little house on the compound. People were running in and out of the house, and cameras were still clicking. There was a whole lot of excitement. In the living room, I did another interview for Iranian TV with an Iranian woman asking questions. In the middle of all this excitement, one little guy came over to me and said, "You know, you are going to be a very big man when you go back to America."

"Oh yeah?"

"Yes. You will be very famous. Very famous."

I didn't think anything of it. All I wanted was to get the hell out of Iran.

That night, they took Kathy and put her in a back bedroom, and they put Maples and me in the den. We slept there on the floor.

CHARLES JONES (*communications officer, at a staff house in the embassy compound*): The next morning I woke up at about seven o'clock, and there was a lot of commotion. I looked around, and strange, strange— I realized that I was the only person in the house, with the exception of one female guard. Normally there were about twenty-five or thirty guards around, but on this morning she was the only guard and I was the only hostage. She kept going over to the window and looking out. It was obvious that something was going on outside, because I could hear a lot of rushing around and coming and going. People were hollering in Farsi, and everything seemed very busy. This girl kept looking out the window, and I tried to raise myself up on the bed so I could see what was going on, but she didn't like that at all. She let me know she didn't want me looking out the window. I remember thinking, "Boy, if I wanted to escape, it would be easy to overpower her and get the hell out of here." But then, where would I go? It sounded like there were hundreds of Iranians running around outside, so that ended that.

SGT. WILLIAM QUARLES (*marine security guard*): Early that morning they took Kathy Gross, Ladell Maples, and myself out, and put the three of us in a Land-Rover. They told us we were going home. Before we left this one guy shook my hand and acted like we were best friends, saying, "Good luck. Have a safe trip." Stuff like that. There were a couple of Iranians in the Land-Rover with us, and they had guns. The guy sitting right behind me had an Uzi submachine gun. We drove out the gate; it was so early that the streets in front of the embassy were clear. There weren't any demonstrations going on at that hour. The only people out there were media people. ABC and CBS had camera crews filming us, and the Germans and the French had camera crews. It was sort of funny, because all of these media people followed us all the way to the airport. They were pulling up beside our Land-Rover shooting pictures. As we were driving through Tehran, I remember, the city itself was real quiet. Nobody was in the streets and nobody was bothering us. It was like a normal day in a normal city.

At the airport they drove us right up to the ramp of the plane and put us on a commercial flight to Copenhagen. I couldn't believe it. We were actually going home! The three of us flew right out of Iran. What a great feeling that was! The plane was full of passengers, and once we were in the air, some of the passengers would come up to us and shake our hands and tell us how happy they were that we got out. Even the Iranian passengers were coming up and shaking our hands. Maples, Kathy, and I were sitting together, and we were really happy. We were the first ones out, and we were smiling and talking to the other passengers that came up to us.

When we landed in Copenhagen, we were immediately transferred from that commercial flight to a military hospital plane. There were some doctors and nurses on board, and they were real nice and took care of us. We took off for Germany, and while we were flying along, we were eating and talking with the doctors. There was a psychiatrist there with us, but I couldn't say much about my own feelings right then. I couldn't just blurt out and tell him how bad I felt for all of the other people who were still being held hostage. Even though I was happy to be out, there was a deeper part of me that was real, real sad. This psychiatrist looked at me and said, "Quarles, I can tell right now that you want to cry. You have a very strong personality that won't allow you to break down and cry, but on the inside you feel bad and want to cry." Which was true. Even though I didn't break down, I was thinking about everybody still at the embassy. A lot of those people were my friends, and I felt for them. I was sitting on board that hospital plane feeling tired, depressed, and filthy. All I wanted was to be left alone. I had so many emotions going on inside me that I needed some time to get my head on. I was thinking, "Damn, man, I'm on an airplane flying home, and all my friends are still living under a gun."

11 On the Inside: November 20–30, 1979

KATHY GROSS, Sgt. Ladell Maples, and Sgt. William Quarles were flown out of Tehran on November 19, 1979. That evening ten more hostages were paraded in front of the television cameras for a press conference at the embassy. Behind them, a large banner read: "Oppressed blacks!! The United States Government is our common enemy." The next day, these ten were also released. Two women and one black male remained in captivity. The student militants accused all three of being "American spies," and threatened that all the remaining hostages would be put on trial in front of a revolutionary tribunal unless the shah was returned to Iran.

Inside the embassy buildings, most of the hostages remained unaware of the fact that thirteen of their colleagues had been released. For them, the grim routine of captivity continued with no immediate end in sight.

CHARLES JONES (*communications officer, at a staff house in the embassy compound*): I was the only black the terrorists didn't release. I think the main reason for that was because the Iranians thought I was a CIA agent. On the day of the takeover, I was caught in the communications vault destroying documents. They considered that to be a very, very unfriendly act, and they thought we were all spies. I was also the head of the communications section, and they figured that covered CIA operations, which it didn't. I didn't have anything to do with the CIA, but the Iranians didn't believe that. It's sort of ironic that they kept me, because some of the people they let go had much more sensitive jobs than me. But the Iranians didn't know what the hell they were doing. They didn't like me from day one, and I didn't like them. So they decided to keep me when they let the others go. Of course, at the time I wasn't aware of that. I didn't realize that they had let any of us go.

JOE HALL (*warrant officer*): In mid-November I was moved again. In the middle of the night they came over and got me and took me back over to the ambassador's residence. I was put in the upstairs sitting room with Gary Lee and Tom Ahearn. Those were some extremely long days. The Iranians would get us up at seven o'clock in the morning and tie us to our chairs. Then they'd keep us sitting all day long on hard straight-back chairs. They wouldn't untie us until late at night, when they'd tell us to lie down and go to sleep. Boy, my ass was as sore as could be from sitting all day long in those hard chairs. That was incredibly uncomfortable, especially being tied up the way we were. That was rough.

While we were in there, the Iranians gave us some books that they let us read. I guess Ambassador Sullivan must've had an older daughter with him during his time in Iran, because the residence was full of gothic love stories. The Iranians found those things in the house and gave them to us. They were terrible—the kind of book with a woman on the cover running away from some castle against a stormy sky. I sat there and tried to read those damn things. With my hands tied, it was difficult to manipulate the pages, because I could only hold the book in one hand. I kept dropping the damn thing, and one of the guards would come over and stick it back in my hand—upside down or right side up, it didn't much matter.

DON HOHMAN (*army medic*): I was moved from that little prefab house over to the ambassador's residence, where Mr. Laingen had been quartered. I was put into a pale blue room on the second floor with Bill Belk, Kevin Hermening, and another guy named Bob Blucker. I'd never seen Blucker before. He'd just come in from East Germany, and he had a little goatee beard. I had no idea who he was. He was sitting in there with us, and I was thinking, "Boy, this is getting stranger and stranger. There are people in here that I don't even know." I couldn't help but wonder if he was an Iranian plant.

While we were there, the Iranians gave us some little pocket books that they had found in Mr. Laingen's residence. The one they gave to me was written in French. I can't read French and I told the guards so, but they wouldn't get me another book. So I just sat there and looked at these foreign words. God, it was boring!

COL. THOMAS SCHAEFER (*defense attaché, at the ambassador's residence*): In a situation like that boredom can become very acute. So it's important that you keep your mind occupied. I remember I'd sit there and play mind games. I took statistics as part of my master's program, so I'd try to work out statistical problems in my head. I also remember doing a lot of constructive daydreaming. One of the first books I was given was a travel book of the States. It had a map and listed various things you could see and do in each state. So I used that to plan and visualize a trip that I was going to take around the United States. I'd also sing songs in my mind, and would make up lyrics to tunes that I already knew. When you are sitting there with your arms tied, and your body is sore from sitting so long, boredom is your greatest challenge.

SGT. ROCKY SICKMANN (*marine security guard, at the ambassador's residence*): I was put in a room in the ambassador's residence with Staff Sergeant Moeller and Jim Lopez. Our hands were still bound, and we had to sit there and face the corner. During this time, Jim Lopez became very sick. He had chicken pox, and we could hear him telling them that he was very ill, but the guards didn't believe him. We weren't able to look at Jim or talk to him, because if we turned our heads the guards would jump right at us and shout, "Don't look! Keep your head facing straight! Don't look at anyone!"

As the days went by, Jim kept on talking to them about being ill. Finally the militants brought somebody in to look at him. This guy was supposed to be a doctor, but I don't know who he was. Anyway, he said that Jim would have to be moved, and they took him out. That was the last time I saw Jim.

SGT. JAMES LOPEZ (*marine security guard, at the ambassador's residence*): I was sick. I came down with chicken pox and was bedridden. I was in bad shape. It lasted about a month or so. I lost forty pounds. I couldn't keep any food down. I was real sick. They had me isolated in one of the bedrooms at the ambassador's residence. There was no sun, and I was lying in that one little room.

The thing was, I had my own private bath. I had all these sores from my chicken pox, and the guards were getting pissed because I was taking two showers a day. The bathroom was right there, and all I had to do was walk in and take a shower. The guards would get pissed off because I wouldn't ask permission to do it. Then they cut me down to one shower a day, and some of the sores started getting infected. But that was how they got their jollies. They were friggin' chicken shit.

BILL BELK (*communications officer, at the ambassador's residence*): You can't imagine what it's like to sit there tied up day after day. It was much, much worse than just having to deal with a few days of boredom. None of us knew if we were going to live through this thing, so the anxiety was constant. That was the worst of it. Outside on the compound we'd hear occasional gunshots, and we didn't know if they were out there executing hostages, or just accidentally discharging their weapons. Everywhere you moved, somebody had a gun pointed at you. Those guys were into a big intimidation game. Some of the terrorists were rabid. They wanted you looking straight into the corner, and if you turned your head right or left they'd jump up and smack you.

JOE HALL (*warrant officer, at the ambassador's residence*): Sitting there tied up to those chairs, I was really getting desperate, but I didn't want to act like I was concerned. I didn't want the Iranians to know how desperate I was. Finally I said to one of the guards, "Can you tell me what's going on? Can't you tell us what's going to happen?"

He said, "Wait one minute."

Then he went off, and came back with one of his comrades. I heard the door open and looked back over my shoulder, and this Iranian was pointing at me. His comrade was standing there with him kind of growling at me. I thought, "Oh geez, I'm really in trouble now just for asking a simple question."

But nothing happened. The strange thing was, later that night, November 21, I had the best meal I'd had in Tehran. It was even better than most of the meals I'd had prior to being taken hostage. They brought each of us a tenderloin tip, a baked potato, and some greens. It was hot and it tasted great. They also served a big cup of tea with it. I looked at that meal and I thought, "Good Lord, this is great!"

12 Northern Tehran: November 20–30, 1979

ON NOVEMBER 20, 1979, President Carter ordered a naval task force stationed in the Philippines, which included the aircraft carrier *Kitty Hawk*, to set sail for the Arabian Sea south of Iran. The militants holding the hostages were afraid that the United States might launch a rescue mission, and they wanted to make sure that some of the hostages would not be found if a rescue attempt was made. Five hostages had been removed from the compound on November 5, and were being held in a residential suburb of northern Tehran [see p. 110]. As the naval task force sailed toward the Arabian Sea, at least fifteen additional hostages were removed from the compound and taken to three or four different locations in northern Tehran, where they were held in homes of wealthy Iranians who had fled during the revolution.

JOE HALL (*warrant officer*): On the night of November 21 a bunch of us got moved. They came in the middle of the night, put handcuffs on me, and blindfolded me very securely. Those handcuffs scared me. I'd always been tied before, and I didn't like the feel of those handcuffs one bit. Then they put six or eight of us in a van, and we went bombing around Tehran for what seemed like hours. It was probably an hour and a half later when we finally got to where we were going. And it was cold, too. This was in the middle of November, and I wasn't dressed very warmly.

JOHN LIMBERT (*political officer*): That move was not very pleasant. When I was put into the van it was my first experience with handcuffs—which was extremely unpleasant. All of my life I had worked either as an academic or as a foreign service officer, and firsthand encounters with violence had never been part of my life. I'd been sheltered from it. When I was moved in the middle of the night, those handcuffs really upset me. It brought to mind an observation that Solzhenitsyn made during his time as a Soviet prisoner. Solzhenitsyn observed that some people can be broken down just by cursing at them. Some of the prisoners that were in the Russian camps with him had backgrounds that were so genteel, and their standards of behavior were so high, that all the Soviet police had to do was come in and call them some bad names and that would upset them. It was the worst thing you could do to them. I suppose handcuffs were like that with me. I felt absolutely helpless. I remember thinking, "Oh my God, this isn't supposed to be happening to me." I felt just like a prisoner. Later on I was handcuffed and it didn't bother me at all, but by then I was a veteran hostage. That first experience was very unpleasant.

COL. LELAND HOLLAND (*army attaché*): When they took us up to this house on the hill in northern Tehran I really got down in the dumps. I knew that if there was a rescue attempt and we were off the embassy compound sitting out in the middle of a city of five million people, there was no way in hell a rescue team would find us. As soon as that van went out the gate, I thought, "Oh shit!"

BARRY ROSEN (*press attaché*): We were taken out of the van and shoved into a room that had carpeting on the floor. My blindfold was slightly ajar, and I was able to see. There were big chandeliers, French doors, white walls, and a thick brownish carpet. The decoration was sort of a French Louis XIV style, or a gaudy Iranian version of that. This was obviously the home of a *taghut*, a wealthy Iranian who had fled because of the revolution.

It was freezing cold in there, and we were left tied up in this room until the morning.

CDR. ROBERT ENGELMANN (*naval supply corps officer, at a house in northern Tehran*): I had been taken off the embassy compound on the second night and stuck in northern Tehran [see p. 110]. I guess the Iranians had a couple of other safe houses up there too, where people were hidden away in case of a rescue attempt.

I spent a month up there on a bed with my hands and feet tied. What the militants did was they tore off lengths of sheet and tied both our hands and feet with these sheets. We were tied both day and night. Don Sharer and Morehead Kennedy were on the bed with me. And that's all there was to it. I mean that literally—three guys tied up on a bed. We weren't allowed to talk, and there wasn't anything we could do. So we just sat there. The Iranians took our clothes, and we were sitting on the bed in our skivvies. These guys figured that we wouldn't go anywhere in our skivvies because Persians are extremely modest, and *they* wouldn't go anywhere in their skivvies. Of course, Americans aren't quite as shy.

Downstairs, we could hear the guards watching television. They liked to see themselves on the news. We always had a guard in the room with us, but there was one guy who would get up and leave the room when he heard something on television that was associated with the takeover. He'd leave his gun or his knife there on the chair. So we had to call to another guard and tell him his friend forgot his knife. It was there on the chair.

There were a couple of times when we talked about making a break for it. We'd whisper to each other under the sheets—you know, pillow talk. In a sense, it would have been easy to try, but I wasn't eager to do it just because there was nowhere to go. It was November in north Tehran, and we were sitting up on the side of a mountain in a city of four million Iranians. We didn't know where we were, and we didn't know Tehran. If we were to go running around in our skivvies, we would have stuck out. And where would we go? If I'd had a place to go, maybe I would have wanted to try and make a break for it. But up there I just wasn't eager to try. There was no place to go.

BRUCE GERMAN (*budget officer, at a house in northern Tehran with Dick Morefield*): We'd ask for books, and the goons used to bring us textbooks—elementary biology books and geometry books. Just terrible! Finally, I got fed up and said, "Bring me a Bible!"

This goon said, "Oh, we have to check with the student council on that."

"What? All I want is a Bible. It's my holy book. You read the Koran, and I read the Bible."

Finally, after a couple of days the goons relented and brought me a pocket-size edition of the New Testament. They thought that was a big concession on their part.

COL. LELAND HOLLAND (*army attaché, at a house in northern Tehran*): The first book they gave me was a goddamn geometry textbook. This guy came in and said, "Here is book." He dropped it down and walked out. Geometry isn't thrilling to me to begin with. I've never liked math. That was sort of like trying to get me to read the Koran.

BRUCE GERMAN (*budget officer, at a house in northern Tehran with Dick Morefield*): Not being able to talk was terribly depressing. People have an intrinsic desire to speak, to say "good morning" or "how are you?" Not to be able to do any of that was very frustrating, and it became even more difficult as time passed. I didn't understand what was happening. Obviously I knew I'd been taken hostage, but I didn't know why. I couldn't ask questions.

The goons didn't want to hear a thing. "Don'ta speak!" That was it. Period. You couldn't appeal to them on any level. All they'd say was, "Don'ta speak!" or, "No speak! No speak!"

Even though Dick Morefield and I were not allowed to talk, we managed to communicate whenever the guard turned his back or went to the toilet. We'd use eye signals, hand signals, nods and gestures. They wouldn't give us any pencils or paper, so we couldn't pass notes. But whatever little communication we managed was a big help, a definite boost to morale.

CAPT. PAUL NEEDHAM (*air force logistics officer, at a house in northern Tehran with four other hostages*): One time the guard in our room fell asleep, and Tom Schaefer looked out the window to see if he could figure out where we were. He'd been in Tehran for a couple of years, so he got up and looked, but he wasn't sure exactly where we were. However, he did verify that there was a guard with a gun outside, which helped us decide that we didn't want to jump out of the window right then.

JOE HALL (*warrant officer, at a house in northern Tehran*): It was colder than hell in this house. I ended up in a bedroom with Lee Holland. This room had one big double bed in it that was hard as a rock. There were two pillows, a blanket, and one strange piece of cloth that was about six feet wide and twelve feet long. We used that piece of cloth as a blanket because it was very, very cold in there. Lee Holland and I stayed on this bed for twelve days.

All they fed us were canned goods—canned ravioli, canned chili, canned soup. When they made soup, they'd take the can and stick it on the burner for a while, then serve it to us kind of lukewarm with a spoon in the can. That stuff was concentrated, and it gave us some real gastrointestinal problems. Colonel Holland and I had some very ripe farting contests. But there was no way we could help it, and no way we could get away from each other.

Strangely enough, Colonel Holland and I were allowed to talk. This was the first time I'd been able to talk to anybody at all. The two of us carried on some of the damnedest conversations in the world. We became pretty good friends just from living together on that huge bed in that little tiny room. We sat there, and we must have told each other everything that had ever happened to us in our entire lives.

JOHN LIMBERT (*political officer, at a house in northern Tehran with three other hostages*): Occasionally we were able to convince one of the guards to open the window a little so we could get some fresh air. Outside, we could hear traffic and we could hear birds singing. We could also hear kids and freedom. All the normal sounds of life and freedom were taking place just beyond our window. Yet I suppose it was a relief that we didn't hear the demonstrations that were going on in front of the embassy. That was the one benefit of being tucked away off the embassy compound.

While we were being held in this house up in northern Tehran, I started asking the students for reading material that was written in Persian. They gave me a lot of books on religious and political subjects. They gave me books by one of their patron saints, Ali Shariati, and I used that as a basis for talking to them. I would try to draw them out in conversation by asking them the meaning of words or ideas. I would say things like, "Explain martyrdom to me. Why is this something that people would want to do?"

Most of the students who were guarding us were not so sophisticated as to simply say, "Oh, shut up!" Instead, they were young enough and naive enough to really want to explain these things to me. So this was a way of drawing them out. It was a way of getting them to talk, which did two things for me. First of all, it helped to relieve the boredom. The days were passing awfully slowly—very, very slowly—and this was a way of bringing some variety to the endless hours of waiting. Second, it was a way of establishing my own individuality. I could see them as individuals, and hoped they would see me as an individual and not just some Yankee imperialist. I wanted them to see me as a person with a name, with ideas, and with a personality. I thought that maybe it would do me some good. It was something that could even go so far as to save my life. If there had been a rescue raid, for example, and the person sitting across from me knew my name and had talked to me, then perhaps he would hesitate before shooting me. Or if someone was sick and needed something, it is very difficult to turn down medical attention to someone you know.

BARRY ROSEN (*press attaché, at a house in northern Tehran*): Some of the militants were like caricatures out of Woody Allen's movie *Bananas*, with their revolutionary costumes, their swaggering, and their guns. In fact, I even had a *Bananas* scene while we were in this place in northern Tehran.

One day a guard came into our room with a questionnaire, and he told us that we were to write down our address in Tehran and to give directions on how to get there. Jerry Miele started to explain something about how he had moved to a new address. According to the rules of their little game, I wasn't supposed to open my mouth unless I was directly spoken to. But I spoke up anyway and said, "We don't have to, you know. We are diplomats. According to the Geneva Convention we do not need to provide private information. You're not supposed to have us here. So why should we give you any kind of answer?"

In all of this, I was talking to Jerry as well as to the guard, and at that point Jerry refused to cooperate any further as well.

The guard was kind of stumped. This surprised him. He thought we would just sit there and fill that little questionnaire out. When I told him we didn't have to and refused to cooperate, he didn't know what to do. He said, "Okay, I'll find out."

He left, and for about half an hour all was fine and dandy. Then a couple of militants came in, pointed at me, and said, "You! Come with us!"

I said to myself, "Why did I have to open my big mouth? So I give them my address, big deal. What am I doing?"

They blindfolded me, took me downstairs, and through some big huge doors. When they took the blindfold off I was standing in this velveteen-walled hall, with big huge chandeliers. This home had a raunchy Louis XIV style of decoration. In the corner was a short little Iranian sitting behind a big French desk. He was so small that when he sat in the desk chair his legs didn't even reach the floor. His feet dangled an inch or two above the carpet. On either side of him were several Iranians dressed in various sorts of grubby revolutionary outfits. It was as if they were waiting for some kind of military inspection, because they all had their rifles pointing straight up toward the ceiling. It was like a scene out of a Woody Allen movie—except it was true. I was placed in front of the little wimp at the desk, and sat down across from him. He said, "If you don't fill this questionnaire out accurately in every detail, we will kill you. I am going to count from ten to one, and if you don't answer by then you will be shot." One of them came up behind me and stuck an automatic rifle to the back of my head, while this other guy started to count: "Ten, nine, eight, . . ."

Underneath it all, I knew they weren't going to shoot me. I knew that this was just part of their grand act. They were trying to intimidate me. But I could feel the gun at the back of my head, and it wasn't a time to be brave. I didn't think it was wise to test them on the off chance that they would actually pull the trigger.

A few more seconds clicked off, with this guy counting, ". . . five, four, three, . . ."

Finally, I said, "Okay, I'll do it."

Then, the funny part of it was that they were all relieved. They were as relieved as I was. To cap this whole episode off, I wrote down the wrong address on the questionnaire. I gave them an old address where I was no longer living. I wrote that all out for them and gave it to the little wimp, who seemed very satisfied. Then a couple of guards took me upstairs, and I was never questioned again. It was back to my chair and my book, with nothing to do but sit in this ridiculously absurd environment.

13 George Hansen Visit

As the diplomatic stalemate between the United States and Iran continued, Congressman George Hansen of Idaho ignored the Carter administration's request that he remain in the United States, and flew to Iran at his own expense. He described himself as a "do-it-yourself ambassador," and told reporters in Tehran that he had arrived to try to "build some bridges and open some doors." Although he was not empowered to negotiate on behalf of the United States, Mr. Hansen did meet with Iran's newly appointed foreign minister, Abol-Hasan Bani-Sadr, to suggest that a congressional investigation of Iran's grievances against the shah might be arranged.*

* In Washington, Congressman Hansen came under sharp criticism from numerous sources. White House Press Secretary Jody Powell said that Mr. Hansen's trip was "counterproductive" and that he was giving the Iranians a false impression "as to what either Congress or the administration believes." Speaker of the House Tip O'Neill joined several other congressmen in characterizing Hansen's trip as being "self-serving" and said that his attempt to negotiate with the Iranians was "totally out of bounds."

On November 25, 1979, Mr. Hansen was permitted to visit some of the hostages who were being held at the embassy.

DON HOHMAN (*army medic, at the ambassador's residence*): The Iranians made us sit in these chairs all day long. We couldn't get up and stretch out on the floor, or anything like that. We had to stay in the chairs. Well, you can only sit like that for about four or five hours at a time. After that, it's impossible to get in a comfortable position. You can wiggle and squirm, but you can't get comfortable. So I was getting pissed off—pissed off at the Iranians, and doubly pissed at our government for not doing anything. I'm a military person, and I felt that the United States government should react to what had happened. If somebody stomps on your foot, then you should stomp right back. Then in walks this congressman from Idaho, George Hansen. Out of the blue, he comes walking through the door.

BILL BELK (*communications officer, at the ambassador's residence*): I was in a room with Bill Royer and Don Hohman when a bunch of militants came rushing through the door. They were carrying G-3s and Uzis and shotguns. I didn't realize they had so many weapons. We were told that someone was coming in who would talk to us. Then they brought in this congressman from Idaho. He was a big, big guy. He must've been about six-four. Of course, the militants were all around him. There must've been at least fifty militants in there. I've never seen so many Uzis and shotguns in one room in all my life. This congressman came over and introduced himself. He saw that my hands were tied, and he said, "I want to assure you that I will contact your family. Is there anyone you want me to call?"

I said, "Yes, I'd like you to call my wife. Please tell her that I'm alive and well."

He said, "I certainly will." Then he moved on. He didn't know my name or anything. He didn't even ask who the hell I was. He went over to see Bill Royer, and Royer said that he was awfully glad to see him there. I was thinking to myself, "What good is it going to do if he doesn't even know my name? How can he get in touch with my family if he doesn't know who I am?" Of course, he never called Angela. He never called anybody. He was there just to get a bunch of publicity and make a big splash for himself.

GARY LEE (*general services officer, at the ambassador's residence*): That was the weirdest situation. Here we are, a group of diplomats all tied up, with those crowds out there chanting day after day, making all kinds of noise. Then in strolls George Hansen with his entourage of Iranians and the television cameras rolling. He handled it sort of like it was election day. He was walking up to the Americans saying, "Hi, I'm Congressman Hansen from Idaho. Who are you? And where are you from?" Then he came around to me and asked basically the same questions, and said something like, "I want you to know we're all thinking about you. We're doing all we can to end this quickly."

SGT. PAUL LEWIS (*marine security guard, at the ambassador's residence*): I was asleep. Sound asleep. An Iranian kicked me, and when I woke up there was this big guy standing there. He looked like an American. I stood up, and he introduced himself as Congressman George Hansen, and said he was there to talk to the Iranians. Of course, I wanted to ask him a couple of questions. I wanted to know if he had come to negotiate with an entire delegation, and what his status was. I wanted to know what was going on. But *wooosh!* He shook my hand and was gone.

GARY LEE (*general services officer, at the ambassador's residence*): That left me totally nonplussed. I didn't have a clue as to what was going on in the outside world. Then here comes this guy from the States, wanders in and goes around talking to people, and wanders out. Here I am sitting in this goddamn building, all tied up and pissed off as hell, and this guy just wanders off. I couldn't believe it.

SGT. PAUL LEWIS (*marine security guard, at the ambassador's residence*): George Hansen came and went so fast it didn't even seem real. The students were always telling us that there were American reporters outside the embassy who were dying to talk to us. Hamid would always laugh about how if he went out for a walk, all of the reporters wanted to talk to him. And he'd brag about how much he could get if he taped a conversation with one of us—you know, how much the American press was willing to pay for a statement from a hostage. So we knew the reporters were out there. Then the next thing I know, there's an American congressman walking around. All the while, we're captive. We're prisoners. It seemed like Americans were free to walk all over the place, but we had to remain tied up. That didn't make any sense.*

---

* When he emerged from the embassy after his visit with the hostages, Congressman Hansen told reporters: "They were happy people. It brought tears to your eyes, for one of them to see one of their countrymen again who grabbed their hand and said, 'Hi.' If that doesn't make every dime and every sacrifice worthwhile."

Part Four

December 1979

1 December 1–10, 1979

THE COLLAPSE OF the Provisional Government and the failure of the Clark-Miller mission in early November had resulted in a total breakdown of face-to-face dialogue between the United States and Iran. During the first two weeks of the crisis, President Carter invoked a series of economic sanctions against Iran, including the cancellation of a military spare parts shipment and the discontinuation of all Iranian oil imports to the United States. He also froze approximately twelve billion dollars of Iranian assets in American banks. President Carter frequently reiterated his concern for the safety of the hostages. As long as they remained unharmed, he said, he would refrain from military action that might result in unnecessary bloodshed.

Throughout the first week of December, a series of confusing and contradictory signals emanated from Tehran. At a press conference on December 7, Foreign Minister Sadegh Ghotbzadeh promised a major development within twenty-four hours. He said, "Those hostages who can be proven not to have consciously engaged in espionage will be freed." From the embassy, the militants countered by saying that Ghotbzadeh had no authority over them, and that they were responsible only to Ayatollah Khomeini. Later in the day, a communiqué was issued in which the militants proudly proclaimed: "We will release nobody, nobody at all. . . . To reveal the treacherous plots of the United States, and to punish the criminal United States, the American spies will definitely be tried."

In the meantime, the hostages who had been tucked away in various locations throughout northern Tehran were returned to the embassy compound in a series of late-night moves.

CAPT. PAUL NEEDHAM (*air force logistics officer*): In early December they brought me back to the compound and put me in the ambassador's residence. I slept on the hard floor for a couple of nights. On the sixth of December they moved me upstairs, and I finally got a mattress. I was sleeping when they came in at about two o'clock in the morning and woke me up. Then they hauled me out for an interrogation.

There were three Iranians down there in the basement. One guy was about five foot nine, and he must've weighed 250 pounds. He wore an army field jacket, and he had a ski mask over his head. He could speak some English, but not fluently. He was the main interrogator. They had another guy in there who was the interpreter, and then there was a slimy, short little guy who was the enforcer. He would sit there drumming his fingers on the table.

They were asking me all kinds of questions. They were asking about Chile, the CIA, and Vietnam, saying how bad it all was. If they wanted to talk about how bad the United States was, I was more than happy to talk to them and discuss these things. I figured it kept them off other matters. I'd agree with some things they said, disagree with others, and sometimes would not take any stand. I'd just let them talk. Then at one point they asked about some of the people in the embassy and what their job functions were. Of course I wasn't going to talk about anyone in the embassy. I just kept talking and talking about other things, and they never followed up on their questions. After about three hours, the guy with the ski mask said, "Well, it's been very nice talking with you. Now I want you to go back and think about what you can tell us. And I want you to know that what you tell us will be used to help make some future decisions."

I thought, "Oh, right, like whether I go home or whether I get killed. That's what my mind is supposed to wander to—future decisions."

They put me in solitary confinement, and after I was in solitary for a while, the guy with the ski mask came in and said, "Have you thought about anything yet?"

I said, "Yeah, here's a list of the things that I can talk about." On that list was every foreign military sales case we'd had with Iran that I could think of. It was all public information. I said, "I can talk about all of these things."

He threw the paper back at me and said, "This is not what I want to talk about!"

"Well, that's all I know."

JOE HALL (*warrant officer*): On the night of December 3, I was taken back over to the embassy compound and separated from Colonel Holland. At about three o'clock in the morning I was thrown into the basement of the embassy warehouse, the Mushroom Inn. That same night, they started my interrogation.

That interrogation was one of the most intense things I've ever gone through. They put me into a room down in the basement of the Mushroom Inn, and it was as cold as could be in there. I was wearing a pair of slacks and a short-sleeve shirt. I had shoes on, but no socks. When they came and got me, they didn't give me any time to put my socks on. And I was cold. Extremely cold.

There were three Iranians in this room. One guy was wearing a green army field jacket, and he was a real ringleader. There was that woman, Mary. Only I didn't call her Mary at the time. I didn't know who the hell she was. And there was another guy dressed in a business suit, and he had a paper bag over his head.

They were asking me all these questions about Colonel Holland and Colonel Schaefer, and they were asking me about embassy documents that they had found. They kept making all kinds of accusations, and asked who was CIA, who did this or that. They accused the United States of being involved in all kinds of things that I had never heard of. I'd deny knowing anything about it, and they'd think I was lying. They kept coming at me and coming at me. It went on and on. I kept lying and denying and refusing to answer. I was cold. As cold as could be. And I was sweating profusely. I just broke into a cold sweat. I guess that was from fear. God, it was scary! I was exhausted, and they just kept going at me and going at me. They'd ask me about Colonel Holland or Colonel Schaefer, and they'd accuse me of being CIA. They'd make some accusations about the United States trying to destroy Iranian agriculture and how the CIA was trying to wreck the economy. It was becoming more and more difficult for me, because I was so exhausted and my state of mind was deteriorating. It's difficult to be in a position where you don't know what your interrogators are talking about, because you don't know how to prepare a story. If you know what they're talking about, then at least you know how to lie. But those guys were talking about all kinds of nonsense that I'd honestly never heard of, and then were expecting me to give them information on it.

There was an enforcer type who would come in and stare at me. He had an Uzi submachine gun. If they didn't like what I was saying, he would shove that gun in the back of my head. They'd threaten to blow my head off, and all I could do was sit there. Then a couple of times, he slapped the hell out of me. With an open hand he'd slap my head, or he'd punch me in the face. I was tied up, and I couldn't defend myself. I felt like I could beat this guy's ass to pieces if I could get my hands on him—but I couldn't. That was frustrating. It was incredibly frustrating not to be able to retaliate. More than anything, it made me angry—very, very angry. In fact, it made me so angry that my anger overcame my fear. I started to shout right back at these guys. When that happened, they started backing off on me.

They decided to leave me sitting in there alone for about eight hours. When they returned, they'd obviously gone back over to the chancery, and had riffled around in stuff to see what else they could find. They started asking me questions about my passport. They wanted to know, "Why do you have two passports?"

"I don't have two passports," I said. "I only have one passport."

"No, this is a lie! You have two passports! Why do you have two passports?"

"I don't have two passports."

"You have a red passport and a black passport."

"I only have one passport."

Well, what had happened was that I had gone to Iran on an official red passport. After I arrived, I requested a diplomatic passport because the embassy wanted us to have diplomatic passports. A day or two before the embassy was taken I called Mark Lijek and said, "Hey, has my diplomatic passport come in yet?" He said, "No, it's not in." So I'd forgotten about it. Obviously, it had arrived during the two intervening days, and the Iranians found it in the passport office. Of course, there was nothing shady about it. Both passports had the same picture and the same information, but those dumbshits didn't know the first thing about diplomatic protocol or procedure. They pulled out these passports, and suddenly I had two passports when I'd just finished telling them I only had one. So I'm sitting there thinking, "How in the hell do I beat this rap?"

The guy persisted, "Why do you have two passports?"

"Ask Mark Lijek," I said. "He'll explain it to you."

"Who is Mark Lijek?"

"He's one of the Americans."

Of course, the Iranians didn't have Mark Lijek. He was in hiding with the Canadians. But I didn't know that. I didn't know who was where. Fortunately, they didn't have the sense to follow up on Mark Lijek, and I just sat there and listened to their crap.

After a while, they said, "We have some questions we want you to answer. You are going to stay here until you answer them." They gave me a note pad and a list of eight questions. They wanted me to tell them all I knew about Colonel Holland and Colonel Schaefer. They also had a question on there about the airplane that belonged to the Defense Attaché's Office, and they wanted me to tell them about this "spy airplane." I tried to answer them as innocuously as I could. I just started writing, "Colonel Shaefer is a career air force colonel. He's a career pilot, handsome and debonair. He's married and has three children." You know, I wrote pages of this kind of stuff. Eventually they came in and took it, and took me back to my room in the Mushroom.

I pulled the blanket over my head and went to sleep. All total, my interrogation went on for thirty-six continuous hours. Then that was the end of it. I was only called in for that one session. But when they took me back they said, "We will be talking to you some more. We have some more questions we want to ask you." For months I feared a continuation of that interrogation. I just dreaded it. Especially when I saw others being taken out and interrogated repeatedly. I was sure they were going to come and get me again.

CAPT. PAUL NEEDHAM (*air force logistics officer*): They moved me over to the Mushroom, and they kept pulling me out at night and taking me down to be interrogated. At this point, all of us had our hands tied. But during my interrogation period, when they brought me back out into the room where some of the other hostages were, they would untie my hands to make it appear that I was cooperating with them and giving them all kinds of information. They were trying to set me apart from everybody else by leaving my hands untied.

But the guards were kind of funny. One group didn't know what the other was doing. A new shift would come on, and one of them would see my hands were untied so he'd come over and tie me up. Then another guy would come through, who was in charge of the interrogation, and he'd say, "No, no! He's supposed to be untied!" And he would untie me. Then somebody else would come in and tie my hands back up. They really didn't know what they were doing.

In the interrogations, their questions seemed to center around who my points of contact were in the Iranian air force. They just naturally assumed I was a spy, and that there were Iranians who were giving me information. What they wanted to do was finger those people in the Iranian air force. So they kept asking me who my points of contact were.

I'd say, "I didn't have any. I was only here on temporary duty. You know that. You've got the records. The person who had all those points of contact left on the twenty-second of October. I took him to the airport. That was Colonel Rinker, and he took all of that back so he could give it to the guy who is supposed to replace me. You guys took over the embassy too soon! I don't know any of these people."

They would just keep hammering away at me, demanding to know who my points of contact were. I'd get the same questions over and over and over. The enforcer was always there to imply that if I didn't answer the questions, it would become physical. He'd get up and move around, and the interrogators would kind of play the good guy/bad guy routine. The interpreter would let me know, "Hey, I really ought to tell him things because he's the good guy," and the enforcer was the bad guy who wanted to beat the living daylights out of me. This little game was almost comical. It became so predictable that I could've written the script.

Of course, they could have beaten me any time they wanted to. So they did have physical leverage. But I didn't pay too much attention to it, because I couldn't divulge anything anyway. I honestly didn't know anything. So I just kept talking about the things that I wanted to talk about, hoping that would put them off and they'd get tired of dealing with me. That strategy seemed to work. After about six sessions they finally realized that I wasn't going to give them anything that would be of value to them and they left me alone.

COL. LELAND HOLLAND (*army attaché, at the Mushroom Inn*): Down in the Mushroom they yanked one guy from our office in for an interrogation. They took him down into that cold room and asked him all sorts of questions. He said, "Look, I've only been here a month. I don't know nothing from nothing. I just push paper." Apparently he conned the Iranians into believing it.

The next day this guy was put into a room with Sam Gillette. He said, "Have they talked to you yet?"

Sam said, "No."

"Well, I think they're going to. This looked like it worked for me. Play the dumb clerk routine."

Well, the Iranians took Sam Gillette out for his interrogation, and Sam told them the same thing. He played the dumb clerk. The Iranians never bothered Sam any more after that.

COL. THOMAS SCHAEFER (*defense attaché, at the Mushroom Inn*): The Iranians interrogated quite a few people, and I knew that sooner or later they were going to come and get me. I told myself, "You know you are going to be interrogated, so you'd better start to prepare your answers right now." And I began to ask myself every question that I thought the militants would, or could, ask me. I knew that they probably had my military biography, which was an unclassified document that was left in my desk, so I had to assume that there were going to be certain things they knew about me. That part of it, I figured, I would go ahead and talk to them about. But there were other questions I knew that I would want to evade or become very dumb about. I didn't want to talk about anything that was classified, and I didn't want to talk to them about any of my Iranian contacts. Because I could see them taking other Americans out, I had plenty of time to prepare myself and to think about what they might ask, and how I would answer. I knew that sooner or later they were going to come and get me.

2 The Mushroom Inn: December 1979

BILL BELK (*communications officer*): The students had a thing about moving people. My God, you'd stay in a room three or four days, and then you'd be moved somewhere else. They'd come in the middle of the night, when you were sound asleep and disoriented. To blindfold you,

they'd throw a blanket over your head. It would be freezing cold outside, and you'd have to walk out in the cold. I hated it. Everybody
hated it. I cussed 'em out every time they did it.

GARY LEE (*general services officer*): Shortly after Congressman Hansen's
visit, the Iranians threw a blanket over my head, led me outside, and
put me in a car. We drove around the compound for a while; then they
took me out and led me down a long series of steps. This confused
me. I didn't know where we were. I thought I knew every inch of that
compound, but those stairs puzzled me. I was being led deeper and
deeper into the ground. When we came to the bottom, they took me
through a whole long series of turns and deposited me in what was to
be my home for the next few months. They pulled the blanket off my
head, and I realized that I was down in the Mushroom Inn.

CPL. WILLIAM GALLEGOS (*marine security guard*): When they moved us,
they played games with us. Like the night when they moved me from
the ambassador's residence down into the Mushroom Inn. I was with
Bert Moore when they took us down into the basement of that place.
They took Bert down some stairs, and I couldn't figure out what was
going on. It seemed like it took them forever. Several minutes later
they came back and got me, and took me down the back stairs of the
Mushroom Inn. I remember going down all these stairs, and then at
the bottom they put me up against a wall. I smelled gunpowder, and I
thought, "Oh shit, they're killing everybody down here!" I didn't know
what was going on. While I was standing there they put a rifle to my
head. I could hear the action of the bolt as this guy locked and loaded.
All I said was, "Make room for me, God. Here I come." There was
nothing I could do except stand there. If these guys were going to
shoot me, they were going to shoot me.

The next thing I heard was this guy snicker a little. He thought this
was funny. Then there was some whispering in Farsi, and they moved
me on into a room and put me into a little cubicle. That was the
Mushroom.

BILL BELK (*communications officer, at the Mushroom Inn*): The Mushroom
Inn was a depressing damn place. It was dark, dreary, cold, and damp.
Absolutely no sunlight, and absolutely no fresh air. This was a particularly depressing time, because I was counting the days. Every day was
an eternity—an absolute eternity. One day would slowly pass after the
other, and then the days would pass into weeks. I was really depressed.
My clothes were dirty, my hair was dirty, I was dirty, and I must've
smelled awful.

There were about twenty other Americans down there. The Iranians had taken bookcases and shelves, and things like that, and used them as barricades to make small cubicles along the walls of the Mushroom Inn. I was put in one of those small cubicles. I had a chair in there, but they wouldn't let me sit in that chair and look at any of the other hostages, and I couldn't stand up. The only time I was allowed to sit in the chair was when I was eating. When I wasn't eating, I had to lie down on the mattress. I don't think I was off that mattress for more than an hour a day. The only time was when I was eating or going to the bathroom, and then when I was finished I had to lie right back down. You just can't imagine how that makes your bones feel. My entire body was aching from lying down so much. It was just awful. I was really getting depressed.

To make matters worse, the toilets were stopped up. When I first went to the bathroom in the Mushroom Inn, I couldn't believe it. It was sickening. In Iran people don't normally use American toilets. An Iranian toilet is a hole at floor level that you squat over, as if you were going out in the woods. We used to call them "Iranian bomb sites." Of course, in the embassy buildings we had American toilets, but the students weren't used to using them, and they wouldn't sit on the seat when they had to take a crap. Instead, they'd stand on the seat and squat above the bowl like they were squatting over a hole in the ground. When I walked into the bathroom, I saw that the students had defecated on the backs of all three toilets at the base of the seat. It was unbelievable how filthy they were. They'd just take a crap and leave the mess there without making any effort to clean it up. I thought, "My God, this is a terrible thing!" It smelled awful, and it got progressively worse. As time passed it became more and more filthy. I thought, "My God, these people just live and breathe filth."

SGT. PAUL LEWIS (*marine security guard, at the Mushroom Inn*): Emotionally, I think I was doing okay during the time I spent down in the Mushroom Inn. The physical abuse was pretty much finished by then. In the first couple of weeks there were a few guards who would come up and harass you or mess with you if they felt like it. But in the Mushroom the guards weren't walking up to you and giving you a slap while you were tied up anymore. They would pretty much just sit at their desks and watch you, which was annoying in itself. I think my major emotion at the time was anger. I was still wearing handcuffs, and I was angry about that.

Those were some incredibly long days. After the interrogations and the abuse were over there wasn't anything left to focus on, and the boredom became even more tedious. I'm not saying it was better when they were asking questions and slapping and kicking you around, but at least that gave you something to focus on. It kept your adrenaline up. You were constantly thinking of defenses, and your mind was alert and active. But when they just left you alone, there was all that time stretching out in front of you day after day, and nothing to occupy it with. I found that I couldn't sleep enough. A lot of times I got my schedule screwed up. I slept during the day, and then couldn't sleep at night. I just lay there in the dark and twiddled my thumbs.

CPL. WILLIAM GALLEGOS (*marine security guard, at the Mushroom Inn*): Nothing happened down in the Mushroom Inn. Every day was just like the next. At first I was getting depressed, but then I adjusted to my surroundings. I just kind of blanked out everything, and quit worrying about when we were going to go home. I kept my mind occupied by doing mathematics problems in my head, or by thinking about facts and dates I'd learned in history. Stuff like that. But I never thought about going home. I just said to myself, "Forget it. Unless you want to be depressed all the time you can't think about home." I just blocked all that stuff out. If you dwell on whether or not you're ever going home again, or start thinking about your family or your girlfriend, then you are going to get depressed. I could see it happening to people around me. The best thing is to forget about your family and your friends. Don't think about them. Forget about going home, and live in your surroundings. That was the way I felt.

JOHN LIMBERT (*political officer, at the Mushroom Inn*): The living conditions in the Mushroom were a little bit better, because we had some access to books. The students had also moved some armchairs in, and we were allowed to sit in our cubicle and read. That was the first time they had done anything like that. They also brought in a few board games, and I started playing chess with Gary Lee. They allowed the two of us to play chess, but we were still not permitted to talk to each other.

There was a toilet and a shower at the end of the hall, and it got pretty raunchy. We would nag the students and try to shame them. We'd say, "That place is awful. It's filthy. Somebody is going to get sick. If somebody gets sick they could die. You don't want a sick hostage on your hands, and you don't want a dead hostage on your hands." We kept after them about that. We'd say, "We'll clean it up. Just give us the soap powder and the mops." By nagging at them, we eventually shamed them into cleaning it up themselves. They finally went in there and cleaned the bathroom. It gave us a great deal of satisfaction to have them go mucking around in that place.

SGT. PAUL LEWIS (*marine security guard, at the Mushroom Inn*): When I was in the Mushroom, the scar from my appendectomy started to run. It was oozing pus. I didn't know what was wrong. I finally managed to get it across to one of the Iranians that I'd had a recent operation and the scar was open. They brought in a medical student, but I didn't want him messing with me. I told them I either wanted a real doctor to look at it, or let it run. This medical student put a Band-Aid on the scar, and a little while later they did bring a doctor in. He was an older gentleman, and he saw that a stitch had been left in there from when they'd sewed me up. He plucked that stitch out, and within a couple of days it healed right up. That almost broke my heart. I had been hoping that I'd get real sick, so they'd have to move me out of there.

BILL BELK (*communications officer, at the Mushroom Inn*): I remember the guy in the cubicle across from me would go for long periods of time without eating. He'd hold his trousers out in front of his stomach to show the Iranians how much weight he'd lost. He must've lost thirty or forty pounds. It was amazing. I've never seen a guy drop so much weight in such a short time. Of course, I didn't realize that the same thing was happening to me. We were all losing weight because of the constant stress. I think the stress had as much do with weight loss as diet did. We were a pretty tired and haggard-looking crew. None of us knew if we were going to make it through this thing alive, and that took its toll on all of us.

RICHARD QUEEN (*consular officer, at the Mushroom Inn*): Actually, the food wasn't too bad. For breakfast we usually had Iranian bread and tea. I remember they brought around three different types of bread. There was one kind that we called "wallpaper bread." It was supposed to be eaten when it was warm, and you'd put food inside it, roll it up and eat it like a crepe. But the students always gave it to us in flat, brittle shingles. If you tried to put butter on it, it would just crumble, and all you'd have would be a handful of crumbs for breakfast.

Then we had one Western meal a day, which was given to us at lunchtime. And it wasn't bad. Often it was something like lasagna or hamburgers. Things like that. There was a Pakistani at the embassy who had worked for Chargé Laingen, and after the takeover he volunteered to remain behind and do all of the cooking for us. He wasn't accustomed to cooking for so many people, and he was working under difficult circumstances, to say the least. But he did the best he could with what he was given. His meals usually tasted like souped-up college dorm food.

SGT. PAUL LEWIS (*marine security guard, at the Mushroom Inn*): The militants must have found a million cans of Campbell's chicken noodle soup over in the commissary. Every night we had chicken noodle soup, and it never filled you up. I used to hate to see them come and get my damn bowl, because I knew what was coming—chicken noodle soup. I got to the point where I quit eating it.

BILL BELK (*communications officer, at the Mushroom Inn*): The routine was that the Iranians would come around and collect our plates, then give us our food. One time I saw that the guards were coming around giving everybody cans of soda pop along with the evening meal. When they came into my cubicle, they put two beers down on my table. I looked up and couldn't believe it. Two beers! That really cracked me up. I knew they hadn't done it on purpose, and I could see that everybody else had soda pop. Of course, any kind of alcohol is against their religion. Alcohol has been against the law in Iran ever since Khomeini came into power. Well, I didn't say a word to them. I drank my two beers and didn't say a word.

JOE HALL (*warrant officer, at the Mushroom Inn*): The students lived their religion to a much greater extent than we did. Very few of the Americans in Iran were all that zealous about religion. In fact, the Iranians used to mock us about our lack of religious faith, and they made a very obvious show of praying in front of us. On several occasions they made statements about our not being as religious as they were, and they suggested that we did not believe in our God to the extent that they believed in theirs. I think some of them were confused as to why we didn't have any deeper religious convictions. I remember one of them asking me why I didn't pray, and I told him, "Perhaps I pray in private, rather than going through all the motions like you do in front of me." However, there were a couple of Americans who were very devout, and I think the Iranians respected those individuals a little bit more.

BRUCE GERMAN (*budget officer*): In their religious beliefs the goons were fanatical. It was the kind of thing that came up all the time in their conversations. I've always believed that God is a benevolent God, but the goons seemed to think that God was one for vengeance.

At one point, I asked for an English version of the Koran. Of course they were more than happy to bring it to me, because they thought they might convert me or something. But I just wanted to use it as a tool. I wanted to see what kind of people I was dealing with, and get a little understanding of them. I'll tell you, reading the Koran opened my eyes. Their religion does in fact believe in vengeance. It's kind of frightening when you realize they don't value their own lives, and that their greatest joy would be to go out and be a martyr. So how could they value our lives when they don't treasure their own?

CAPT. PAUL NEEDHAM (*air force logistics officer, at the Mushroom Inn*): I don't discuss religion very easily, but I can say that it definitely helped. I've always considered myself to be somewhat religious, and I turned to God as I have for most of my life. God and Jesus definitely helped see me through captivity. Without that I don't know how I would have handled it. I had a lot of help in making it through.

JOE HALL (*warrant officer, at the Mushroom Inn*): I think of myself as an agnostic. When I was in the Mushroom Inn, I saw some of the other hostages praying, and I was becoming more and more desperate myself, so I tried to turn to religion. Every morning I would read two or three chapters of the Bible. Unfortunately, it was kind of a superficial reading, and I didn't get much out of it. I just figured that if it would bring me closer to God, and help get me out of Iran, then I would do it.

After watching some of the other hostages pray, I got on my knees and tried to communicate with God. But I didn't get anything out of it. I do believe in God—in a Supreme Being—but I don't believe in the hocus-pocus that goes along with organized religion. A favorite author of mine once said that organized religion is like being forced to watch a sunset, and that's the way I've always felt. So I quit trying to pray. One night I just said, "God, if you exist, please take care of my wife and my family, and I won't ask for anything for myself. I'll take care of myself if you'll take care of them."

SGT. PAUL LEWIS (*marine security guard, at the Mushroom Inn*): While I was down there, some guard walked up to my mattress on the floor and said, "Do you want to see a movie?"

I was bored to death. Of course I wanted to see a movie. Two guards came and got me and took me into this large room where books from the American school library were stored. The Iranians had cleaned out a corner, and they showed us a BBC film that had clips of the confrontations between the shah's troops and the demonstrators. Then they wanted to talk about the revolution. They had a little table there with a lot of revolutionary literature on it. I think they were trying to indoctrinate us, or make us sympathetic to their cause, because they were really playing Mr. Nice Guy in there.

CPL. STEVEN KIRTLEY (*marine security guard, at the Mushroom Inn*): They'd take two or three of us in and show us a film about the revolution and how people revolted against the shah. The guards would bring us tea and talk to us about all the bad things that the shah supposedly did. Then they'd try to encourage us to write home about these things. They wanted us to write letters about the shah and how terrible he was. We never did.

SGT. PAUL LEWIS (*marine security guard, at the Mushroom Inn*): When they took me in to see that film, they dangled some mail in front of us. That was the first time I saw any mail. In a situation like that, you can't imagine how the sight of an envelope will almost drive you nuts. Then they let me look at a letter from my parents. They didn't let me keep it; they just let me read it and took it right back. Of course, it was good to hear from home and to know that my folks knew I was there, and that people cared. But at the same time reading that letter was almost disappointing. All my family could write was small talk. They told me about what my brother and sisters were doing. That kind of stuff. There wasn't anything in it that had any real substance, and I wanted some news. I wanted to know if there were any negotiations in progress, and what the terms were. I wanted to know where the Sixth Fleet was. Of course, my family couldn't write anything like that, because if they did the letter would have been thrown away. The censor would have pitched it.

CPL. WILLIAM GALLEGOS (*marine security guard, at the Mushroom Inn*): The militants were always trying to indoctrinate us. They used to take us into this little room where they had a slide projector and a screen, and they would flash pictures of dead bodies in front of us. Or they would show us Algerian psychological warfare films. They'd sit a couple of us in there and they'd flash pictures of dead bodies on the screen. They'd tell us, "This is what the shah did. This is what SAVAK did. This is what the CIA did."

Pretty soon we started laughing at the films. We'd do it to make the Iranians mad. They'd flash a picture of a dead body on the screen and we'd say, "Hey, that was good! Can we see that again? Can we see that picture again?" We'd laugh and laugh. But these guys got mad, and they wouldn't show them to us any more. After that, they stopped taking us in there.

CAPT. PAUL NEEDHAM (*air force logistics officer, at the Mushroom Inn*): Occasionally they would show me a picture of a starving baby in Biafra. Of course, they would try to blame starvation in Biafra on the United States. They would blame all of the evil in the world on America. America was the Great Satan.

I would look at the picture and say, "Yes, it is terrible." Then I'd say, "You know, you guys are getting $40 a barrel for oil right now. You could buy all the grain in the world. What are you doing about it? What are you doing for world hunger? You're holding us hostage, aren't you? That's really doing a lot of good for the world, isn't it?" I just turned the tables on them. They didn't spend too much time trying to talk to me.

JOHN LIMBERT (*political officer, at the Mushroom Inn*): We were in constant proximity to the guards. There were perhaps five or six guards in the room at any one time, and there were a lot of contradictions and paradoxes in our relationships with them. During my time in the Mushroom, I started to establish my own area that I was in control of. If a student came into my cubicle, I would treat him as I would treat a guest who was visiting me in my office or my home. Many of them were still in school, and they would bring their lessons around and ask for help. I guess they were getting on toward exam time, and a few of them were panicking about that. They would come around with all kinds of lessons: English, physics, history, political science. Basically, they were doing a lot of work in English, and they wanted help with some of the terms. So I started to tutor them. I did so with the idea that this was a way for me to establish my own identity. It was also a way for me to establish some dominance over them. They became indebted to me. I was in a position to give or not to give something that they wanted.

There were many different personalities among the students. Some of them would bring me books about religion or about their patron saints, and they were willing to sit and talk with me. In these conversations there would be a tacit agreement that we would not talk about the conditions we were living in. We would carry on conversations about religion or schoolwork as though the prison situation didn't exist. But in this way I was able to establish myself as a teacher, as someone who was older than they were, who could assist them in their studies. Now, not all of the students reacted to me in this way, but some of them did.

I can remember several of those that were down there in the Mushroom with us. There were a couple that we called Mutt and Jeff. One of them was a very tall, thin fellow. He was sort of a goofy character, but he was very good-natured. He was always smiling. He used to bring the tea around for us, and he had a smile for each of us. He would pour the tea and say, "This is really good tea. It's just terrific tea." I don't think he was being insincere, either. One time he was pouring my tea and he said, "Boy, this is great tea. You're really going to like this tea." And I quoted a Persian proverb to him which says: "A daughter

that is praised by her own mother is not going to make a good bride."
I suppose the American equivalent would be: "A face that only a mother
could love." But he understood my joke in regard to his praise of the
tea, and he thought that was hilarious. He went off and told the other
students that this joke had been made about the tea. That's how par-
adoxical the situation was. Here we were in this damn jail, where it
was presumably possible that they might shoot us tomorrow, yet in
spite of these conditions this fellow could smile at each of us. He could
laugh at my joke and say, "You know, that's one of the funniest things
I've ever heard." That was one of the paradoxes of captivity.

Then there was another little fellow in there by the name of Mehdi.
He was very small and he talked all the time. Just yak, yak, yak, yak.
He loved to argue and he loved to complain. A group of students would
get together at the end of the room, and they'd talk at all hours of the
night. There were times when that would make it difficult to sleep,
because it was nothing but chatter. Constant chatter. That was Mehdi.
However, he did say a few things that caught my ear. At one point, he
was complaining to the other students, and I very vividly remember
him saying: "Well, you know I was against taking hostages from the
very beginning. We never should have done it." He was speaking in
Persian, and I didn't do anything to indicate that I had overheard this.
But it was a nice thing to hear. It was indicative of the fact that there
were many different views among the students. They had different
opinions on what should be done with us, and how we should be treated.
This comment, in particular, was nice to hear.

JOE HALL (*warrant officer, at the Mushroom Inn*): I didn't speak a word
of Farsi, but I was with Rich Queen down in the Mushroom. Richard's
Farsi was only negligible, but he did pick up key words, and he was
obviously overhearing a few things. He would whisper to me, and he
was the catalyst for any news I heard. At one point, he thought he
heard the students talking about our release, and he heard them say
that they were voting on whether or not to let us go, or whether to
kill us. We never knew what was going on. But it was obvious that they
were having power struggles among themselves, and some dissension
among the troops.

RICHARD QUEEN (*consular officer, at the Mushroom Inn*): There was one
time in early December when I was sure that the militants were talking
about releasing us. At the time, I was in the Mushroom, an underground
tomb. And my little cubicle was right next to the phone. I was sure I
heard them talking about making plane reservations. I heard them
mention Alitalia, and was sure that they were talking about getting

plane tickets for all of us. I remember those conversations quite well. They even mentioned the next day as the time we were to leave. Needless to say, I was absolutely jumping with excitement.

That night as the hours drew closer and closer to the next day—the day of our release—I got more and more excited. On the night before I got all ready to go, thinking that we would be released that day. I laundered my one or two shirts and hung them up to dry, so I could put them on in the morning. Then the morning arrived and I washed and shaved, thinking, "This is it! This is the day!" When I came out of the bathroom, I said to the guard, "What time will they take us out?"

"Take you? What do you mean, take you?"

"When are we going to be released?"

He said, "You're not. You're not going to be released."

That crushed me. I came back to my cubicle with tears swelling in my eyes and threw my towel against the wall. My morale just plummeted. I lay down on my mattress absolutely devastated. That was the one time I really thought about doing myself in. I was so devastated that I tested the vault door to see if it was locked. I was in this tomb, and there was only one way out. If that door had been open, I would have kept on moving. I knew there was a guard out there, and I thought maybe he would shoot me. It was sort of like attempting suicide without the mess of cutting one's wrists.

During one of my most depressed periods, I was told that Bruce Laingen and Colonel Schaefer were on trial in front of a revolutionary court. I could hear periodic shots being fired on the compound, and I was sure they were taking us out and shooting us one at a time.

GARY LEE (*general services officer, at the Mushroom Inn*): I thought that Bruce Laingen, Vic Tomseth, and Mike Howland were dead. The rumor was that they had been driving back from the Foreign Ministry and got into a firefight, and were blown away. For months and months several of us thought that those three had been shot.

3 More Interrogations

JOE HALL (*warrant officer*): While I was down in the Mushroom, I saw that the Iranians were interrogating Colonel Holland and Colonel Schaefer. Colonel Holland was first, and his interrogation went on for several days. They would take him out and bring him back, take him out and bring him back. And you could see the poor guy wasn't having any fun.

Then they started in on Colonel Schaefer. They'd take him out at four o'clock in the morning and bring him back at eight o'clock at night to use the toilet. Then they'd take him back. After a few days he looked pretty gray and distraught. One time, I went into the bathroom and saw that he had taken a bar of soap and written on the wall: "Wear warm clothes for interrogations." God, I felt for him. My heart just went out to the man. I knew exactly what he was going through. As poorly as he was being treated, every time they would lead him by my space he would wink at me. That's the kind of guy he is. He's a great man, and I respect the hell out of him.

Well, this went on for a couple of weeks, then suddenly Colonel Schaefer just disappeared. We never saw him again. We didn't know where he had gone. We were all very concerned about him.

COL. THOMAS SCHAEFER (*defense attaché*): I refer to the interrogations as my period of "cold storage." This is because the interrogations took place in a room without any heat. I could see my breath for the entire time I was in there. They'd bring me a cup of hot tea, and it would be cold in a matter of minutes. All I had in there was one thin blanket and a folding metal chair. The food was brought in at irregular intervals so I couldn't bank on that to know what time it was.

During the interrogation period, I only left that cold room to go to the bathroom. This was important because it meant I had access to toilet paper. In order to stay warm, I wrapped myself in toilet paper from neck to toe and then pulled my clothes back on over the toilet paper. I would also walk ten, twelve, or fourteen miles a day. I had a belt that I made into a yardstick, and I measured the room so that I knew how many yards I was walking. I would walk back and forth across the room to stay warm. Then I would usually only get an hour or two of sleep at a time.

COL. LELAND HOLLAND (*army attaché*): Their routine for the interrogations was to take me down to this room that was as cold as the weather outside, and this was December—the dead of winter. I mean, it was colder than a bear in there. The militants took me down to this room and left me sitting there in my bare feet and a T-shirt for two or three hours. That was the routine. Then at about the time I was good and blue, they came in all dressed up warmly and started asking questions. By this time, I was one nervous guy. I was jumping and moving just to keep warm. This went on for several days, and I was really afraid that I was going to get pneumonia or something like that. I figured they would purposely let me die rather than give me any kind of medical treatment.

They'd leave me sitting in that room and go away. I knew damn well they'd gone off to bed. Every now and then one guy would come into the room and look at me. They didn't want me sleeping. He'd look at me and then back out. Once I started dozing, and he hit me with a rifle butt. It was obvious that they were trying to wear me down both emotionally and physically.

It became very obvious to me that somebody they had previously questioned had done some talking, because they were telling me things that were not in the files. They had information they should not have had. But how were they getting this information? Was it being extracted, or was it being freely volunteered? That was something I didn't know. But it was a goddamn startling fact when they came in and started telling me what it was that I knew. They were hitting poop that was accurate, and they knew it. I thought, "Goddamn, they're coming in with something, and there's no way I can mislead them. They have got the file plus supplementary information." That was a nerve-racking session. All I could do was sit there and wonder, "What's going to happen next?" They would ask the same questions over and over and over and over again. It was like: "You're going to stay here until you get it right." I guess they were looking for me to make a mistake and trip over my own words.

Specifically, they were interested in a number of things. One of the big things they wanted was to know about any Iranians we had been working with or had been in contact with. The key to their thinking seemed to be that if an American had been in Iran for a reasonable length of time, then that American was automatically a CIA spy. Second, any Iranians that any Americans dealt with were automatically as guilty as the "CIA spies." The militants who took over the embassy believed that an Iranian who gave us any kind of help or information had done a horrible thing. It was obvious that they were going to go after these people. If you named names or gave them identities, then you could really get some of the Iranians in trouble, because the hard-core militants considered them collaborators, and they wanted to get them. Of course, I had been in contact with a lot of Iranians. Since I was a representative of the army, there were a lot of things about the Iranian army that we were interested in—officially, legally, and legitimately so. One thing of interest was that the Iranians did purchase some Russian equipment, so we were interested in any sort of Iranian army equipment, particularly if it was a Russian brand of mousetrap. But the militants didn't understand this sort of thing. They were convinced that everything we did was done to undermine the revolution. So I felt it was important not to give them the identities of any Iranians I had dealt with, because they considered those people to be collaborators and traitors.

COL. THOMAS SCHAEFER (*defense attaché*): One of the primary things they were interested in was my Iranian contacts. They'd ask me about certain Iranians, but I would become evasive. I'd say things like, "I have a hard time remembering American names. How can you expect me to remember Iranian names?" That was one of the major things I didn't want to talk about, because I was afraid the militants would go after these people and make life very difficult for them. I was afraid they might be picked up, interrogated, and tortured for having had contact with me or with the Defense Attaché's office. There were a lot of Iranians they asked about that I honestly did not know. But in other cases there might have been people I did know, and it was important to deny any contact with them. Then there were some who I could be sure that the militants knew I'd had contact with. I knew the militants had read a lot of documents, and it would have been foolish for me to deny contact with someone like the chief of the air force or the head of J-2. They were obviously people I had met. In dealing with questions about them I could tell limited truths, because a lot of those meetings were normal protocol events. If they were asking about someone that I knew they were aware I had been in contact with, I would go ahead and admit to it. I would say, "Of course I was in contact with him. It was part of my duty as an attaché. If I was going to discuss problems the Iranian air force was having in introducing a new aircraft into the inventory, who do I think I should contact? Who would you contact to discuss such a matter?"

I would say that the interrogators were semiprofessional. Most of them were Iranians. Although there was one fellow in there who I wasn't sure about. He wore the PLO headgear, and he never let me see his face. The only thing I ever saw were his eyebrows and the top of his nose. It appeared to me that he was something other than Iranian. His features were not sharp at all. I had the feeling that he was some type of an outsider, possibly Syrian. I would suspect that he was PLO but it is only a suspicion. I can't be certain. Then the fellow Hossein was also there. He was involved in most of my interrogations.

In questioning me, the militants were interested in some classified things that I didn't want to get into. There were things that I either refused to talk about, or about which I made myself very dumb. One of the things you learn in survival school is to become very dumb during your interrogations. Loss of memory can be a big help.

They certainly didn't understand anything about the job of a defense attaché. For instance, they had a hard time believing that a routine part of my job was to visit Iranian air force headquarters, or to visit the joint military headquarters, or intelligence headquarters. We might have had routine protocol meetings or discussed things like inventory or spare parts contracts, but to the militants there was something very suspicious about these sorts of meetings. They automatically assumed you were always plotting against the revolution. They couldn't believe that we were working with the Khomeini government and were trying to establish good cross-talks between the military. When the militants found documents in the files that demonstrated this sort of objective, they either misread them or refused to believe them. In fact, one of the militants told me that this was all disinformation that had been put into the files, and that it was purposely done to confuse them. They also couldn't believe that a routine part of my job was to entertain Iranians in my home. I tried to educate them to the fact that part of my job was to have social engagements with members of the host country. But they couldn't understand that. They felt that there was something terrible about an Iranian coming into my home. So I felt that it was important to deny as many contacts as I could, and to refute or deny many of the accusations they were making.

COL. LELAND HOLLAND (*army attaché*): One time they were really giving me the business in one of those long twenty-four-hour or thirty-two-hour interrogations. They were being pretty tough about it—they were putting guns to my head and threatening to pull the trigger. They wanted to know about my Vietnam experience, and they wanted to know everything I had done while I was there. Vietnam was a big thing with them. They tried to tell us that we were all war criminals. They gave me some sheets of paper and left me alone in the room with some questions. I took the ballpoint pen and I started writing. I wrote all about how I was born on a farm in northeastern Illinois, and by page 37 I was just beginning my sophomore year of high school. That's how far I had gotten when they came in and discovered what I was doing. Oh God, they got upset about that.

COL. THOMAS SCHAEFER (*defense attaché*): One of the techniques I used throughout the course of the interrogations was to go off on tangents whenever I could. At one point, the militants were very interested in a trip I had taken to India, Afghanistan, and Pakistan. They had my passport, so they knew that I had been to all of these countries, and they wanted to know why. I said, "I was on a boondoggle." Then it took me nearly an hour to explain what "boondoggle" meant. I told them that my wife and I were on a shopping spree, and that we wanted to buy jewelry and wooden things in Islamabad and Kabul. I went on and on about that trip, and they took copious notes. I couldn't believe it. I found that they would listen to almost any kind of garbage. So I figured, if they're going to let me get off on tangents like this and write it all down, then I'm going to give them one hell of a good story. I found that was a good technique. In that sense, they were not very good interrogators. They shouldn't have let me get off on tangents like that, but when they did I would keep going and keep talking about the things I wanted to talk about. That kept them off the more sensitive areas that I refused to discuss. I had prepared myself well enough in advance so that I knew what things I felt I could discuss, and that helped. In my mind, I'd already answered most of their questions before they ever came and interrogated me.

COL. LELAND HOLLAND (*army attaché*): During the interrogations, I wasn't at the point where I wanted to commit suicide. But if fingernails started getting yanked, or they started smashing testicles or something like that, I was going to end it. That's one thing I would have done.

Every place I was kept in, there was some way I could have killed myself. In one room I was in, there was a big old heavy piece of wire that came down out of the wall. I think it was from an intercom that they had ripped out. So I went over and tugged on it real hard, to make sure it was anchored solidly. If I'd had to, I could have hung myself. I was bound and determined that I was not going to let them have what they wanted to know. And every place I was in you could have done something. You could have garroted yourself, or there was enough broken glass lying around so that you could have slashed your wrists. I was surprised that the Iranians weren't tidier about things like that. Because it was always possible to end it if you needed to.

There were a couple of times when they came in with guns and put them to my head. After a while I was numb. I was beat. I was tired. I was exhausted. I said, "Bullshit! Pull the fuckin' trigger!" I was almost at the point of wishing they would. You know, it would have got the goddamn thing over with. I'd seen Mashala* pull a few tricks when he was bringing people in. He'd have a guy sitting there blindfolded, put the gun up to his head, point it toward the sky, and pull the trigger. Well, they hadn't gotten what they wanted out of me, and I thought that was what they were probably going to do. I thought, "They're not

* Mashala Kashani was a Mujihadin guerrilla in charge of a revolutionary *komiteh*. At the time of the February 14, 1979, attack, he arrived with Foreign Minister Ibrahim Yazdi to help liberate the embassy. He remained encamped on the embassy grounds through June 1979 for the self-proclaimed purpose of providing embassy protection.

going to kill me. They're going to bust my eardrums." And I said, "Pull the fuckin' trigger!"

But they didn't do anything. When they didn't, I thought, "Aha! There's something going on here." It was sort of like catching a second wind. I had challenged them on it, and they didn't follow through. My battery was charged up again. I felt renewed. I was ready to tap dance along, and spar and fence with them a while longer.

COL. THOMAS SCHAEFER (*defense attaché*): They never did start beating up on me. As far as I'm concerned, there was very little physical abuse. The physical thing was that the room was very cold, and it was difficult to get any sleep. There was a lot of mental strain, and they were making the physical environment as uncomfortable as they could. For the first time in my life, I could feel myself losing control of my thinking and my body functions, just from the fatigue and the cold. That was a frightening feeling. It almost became overwhelming. As a matter of fact, the interrogations ended after two weeks when I said, "Hey, take me and shoot me. I've had enough. Just take me out and shoot me." Within twenty minutes I was taken into a warm room, and there were no more interrogations. It was the sort of thing that made me wonder, "You dummy, why did you wait fourteen days to say that?"

4 Escape

BILL BELK (*communications officer, at the ambassador's residence*): In mid-December they threw a blanket over my head and moved me out of the Mushroom Inn. I was put in the maid's quarters on the second floor of the ambassador's residence. It was a very small room—about six by nine—and Malcolm Kalp was in there with me. Our only luxury was that we had an adjoining bathroom that we could use.

Malcolm loved to pass notes. We had confiscated a couple of pencils, and every time I went into the bathroom I'd find a note from Malcolm. He would hide them up over the top of the door frame in the bathroom, and I'd always do the same and leave a note for him. By passing notes, we decided that we would try to make an escape attempt. I figured that if we could get out of the building and over the compound wall, then we could commandeer a vehicle and make our way to a friendly embassy where we could seek asylum. Either that, or we could hide out and try to make telephone contact with a friendly embassy, and try to arrange for some sort of assistance. I figured if we could get to Bert Moore's old residence, then we could have a place to hide for a few hours, and hopefully would have access to a telephone. I was thinking primarily of the British embassy, the Swiss embassy, or the Australian embassy. I had some friends at the Australian embassy who might have been able to provide shelter, or who might have been able to provide transportation to get us out of Tehran and down to the Persian Gulf, where we could be smuggled out of the country. I wasn't exactly sure what the best strategy would be, but I felt that if we could get over the wall and hot-wire a vehicle, then we would be on our way.

To prepare for our escape, I stole the drain plug from the sink. It was a hard piece of metal that fit nicely in my hand. If we needed to knock someone out, that drain plug would definitely have done the job. If I'd used it to hit somebody in the temple, it would have knocked them cold.

Well, in one of his notes Malcolm let me know that he didn't want to hurt anyone. That was something I couldn't agree with at all. That worried me. I didn't know who Malcolm was. He was new at the embassy, and I didn't know anything about him or his training. When I read his note I thought, "Oh no, that's no way to feel! If we get out there and it comes down to hurting someone, and Malcolm won't go along with me, then it'll be more dangerous for the two of us to be out there together than if I go alone." If it was necessary to hit somebody or kill somebody, I was ready to do it. I couldn't see going out there with someone who didn't want to hurt an Iranian standing in our way. So I decided to go alone.

We had a guard in the room with us twenty-four hours a day. There was a guard in there all day and all night. But there was this one guy who would come on the late shift and sack out almost immediately. He'd go right to sleep. This guy would really saw some logs, and I figured I could slip out unnoticed while he was snoozing. So on the night of December 23, I watched this particular guard and waited until he went to sleep. Then I fixed my mattress with a rolled-up blanket so it looked like there was somebody in the bed, and I went out the door.

Just to the right of our room was a stairway that led down to the kitchen. I figured if I could get through the kitchen and out onto the compound, I could just keep on walking. I didn't have any reason to suspect that there would be people in the kitchen at that hour. I thought that if I could make it out that door, then I could sneak across the compound to the rear wall and be gone. I crept down the stairs and discovered that this was not a good idea. I could hear lots of people in the kitchen area, and when I peeked around the corner there were militants all over the damn place. So I crept back up the stairs to a landing where there was a window that looked out over the kitchen roof. I had a razor blade hidden in my shoe, and I cut the screen out of the window and crawled out onto the roof. The thing I remember the most is that all of the outdoor lights in the entire compound were turned on. That shocked me. For the entire time that we had been held hostage, there had never been any outside lights on. But on that particular night, every damn light on the compound was on. From where I was sitting on the roof, I could see the guards as plain as day down below. There were students walking around all over the damn place. And it was cold as hell outside. I was shivering up on that damn roof.

At the back of the house, just outside the kitchen window, there was a little wooden alcove. I managed to crawl down into that alcove by stepping onto an air conditioning unit and then climbing onto a cluster of gas bottles. These bottles were inside the alcove. I wanted to get across the courtyard at the back of the house, but there was an armed guard standing at the back gate, and I didn't know what the hell to do about him. The only way out was for me to go right past that guard. These students kept coming and going out the back gate. I hid in the little alcove for about an hour, watching the students come in and out of the residence, and in and out of the courtyard behind the house. Finally, I said to myself, "Well, hell, there's only one way that I'm going to get out of here, and that's to follow some of these students out." I decided that the best thing to do was to pretend I was a student.

After a while, a group of about six students came out of the house and headed across the courtyard toward the back gate. They were making a bunch of noise. You know, yak, yak, yak, yak. Just jabbering away. So I pulled my sweater up over my head, as if I was coming out of the house and was putting it on for the first time. I kept it over my face as if I was trying to adjust it and stepped in behind these students. Believe it or not, I walked right past the gate guard. No problem. He didn't even flinch. He just stood there holding his damn gun as if it was a little toy, and I strolled on past him.

Beyond the courtyard, there was a chain-link fence between the back of the ambassador's residence and the Mushroom Inn, that divided the work areas on the compound from the residence areas. I knew there was a small gap in the divider fence. That gap had been rusted out and kicked over. It wasn't there purposely. I was going to go through that break in the fence, then keep moving past the DCM's residence to the rear of the compound. When I ducked through the gap I heard someone say, "*Est! Est!* (Stop! Stop!)" I turned and saw a female guard standing right there on a little platform by the Mushroom. She had her weapon trained on me. When I went through the fence she was about three feet from me. Immediately, I grabbed her by the leg and reached for her weapon. I put my left hand on the stacking swivel and forced her gun straight up so that she couldn't shoot me. She was screaming and hollering and tugging and everything else. I mean, she was in an absolute panic. With my right hand I reached for the release clip on the magazine of her gun. She pulled the trigger and got off one wild shot before I managed to press the release clip and pull the magazine out of her rifle. I knew that meant she had one more round in the chamber, because when you fire a G-3 it automatically chambers another round. She kept struggling and hollering, and another wild shot went off. When that happened I knew she couldn't shoot me, and I took off running. I heard her pull the trigger a couple more times, and I tossed her magazine in the bushes as I went.

Because of all the noise, another guard was coming up from around the Mushroom. I could hear him running toward us, but I was moving out as fast as my feet could carry me. I was headed toward the rear of the compound when this guy came around and got off a couple of shots. He didn't miss me by much, either. I kept running and managed to get beyond the tennis courts and over into the area where all the reclaimed automobiles were parked. I must've covered about 100 yards. I cut down and weaved my way through all of these parked cars. Apparently, the one guard lost sight of me, because I didn't hear any more shots. I was trying to make it to the compound wall. Just beyond the wall, there was an alleyway. I figured if I could get on the other side of that wall and out to the street, I could commandeer a vehicle and get the hell away. There was a place along the wall where there were six or seven steps on the inside of the compound, so that someone could go up and look out over the wall. I knew that from those steps I could get up on top of the wall. So that's the point I was heading for. I managed to get over there, and ran up the steps, and I was ready to jump over the wall, when I saw two Iranian police officers running up the street. They saw me on the wall, and they both let go with rifle fire. I could hear the bullets snap right by my head. When a bullet flies past your head like that, you can hear it real loud. There was a real quick *snap! snap!* When those bullets went zinging past my head, I lost my balance and fell back into the compound. When I fell, I hurt my knee and couldn't run.

Well, there was a big portable ice cooler right near there, the kind you take out on a picnic. That thing was just lying there from an old softball game or something. I knew I couldn't run anywhere else, so I crawled inside the ice cooler. That thing must've been about two feet by four feet, and it was full of water. I wiggled down inside the thing and sat in the ice water. It was cold as hell, and I was frightened. When those bullets went flying by my head, I knew those guys were trying to kill me. I could hear Iranians running around all over the damn compound. They were all excited and screaming and hollering. I just huddled up inside the ice cooler. "Oh shit," I thought, "here comes the bad news!"

SGT. PAUL LEWIS (*marine security guard, at the ambassador's residence*): Rocky Sickmann, J. D. McKeel, and I were lying on the floor of the ambassador's residence. It was late, and everything had quieted down for the night. Then we heard a single shot, which wasn't unusual, because those guys were always accidentally discharging their weapons. But then, right after that, we heard two or three more shots, followed by a couple more. Then there was all sorts of screaming and yelling. We could hear the guards running around all over the place. A couple of guys came bursting into our room, and we had some extra guards standing over us. We didn't know what had happened, but we sure could hear the commotion. There was a lot of racket, and it was obvious that these guys were excited.

BILL BELK (*communications officer*): I could see Iranians searching around all over the place. They were going like hell trying to find me, all of them carrying guns and lights and stuff. A whole big group of them came up near the area where I was hiding. One guy even walked right past me. They were searching all around, and I was sitting inside the ice cooler. I could see out through a little slit, and saw about fifteen or twenty Iranians converged within ten feet of me. They were all excited—just running their mouths a mile a minute. They searched this whole area. I crouched down and kept as quiet and still as I could. When they didn't see me right away, I started hoping they were going to go converge on another area, and a bunch of guys did go running off in other directions. Then, just on a lark, this one guy started walking over to the ice cooler. I saw him coming over, and there was nowhere for me to go. He was coming right toward me. All I could do was sit there and wait. He came over and looked down into that ice cooler, and when he saw me he gasped and jumped about a mile—he was startled. Real startled. He trained his gun on me and said something in Farsi. I crawled out and was immediately surrounded. About a dozen guns were cocked and ready.

I put my hands up, and one guy grabbed me and put my hands behind my head. Then he took my sweater and pulled it over my head. They slapped me around with the sweater over my head, so I couldn't see where the punches were coming from. One guy slugged me in the belly, and another guy hit me in the head. They turned me around and threw me on the ground. They kicked me several times and picked me up, and hit me and slapped me. They might have been using a stick and they might have pistol-whipped me, I don't know. One guy came up from behind me and put me into a full nelson,* so I had to walk with my neck forced way down. They blindfolded me and put me into a car.

I was taken over to the chancery. They threw me onto the floor of this room with a blanket on top of me. A couple of them were smacking and kicking me. This one guy was just a sadistic ass; he was very thoroughly enjoying the whole thing. There must've been a heater in the room, because I remember it was very hot in there. I'd had the wind knocked out of me and I couldn't breathe, so I was trying to pull the blanket off. But they didn't want me to move. They were standing over me shouting, "Don't move! Don't move!"

A little bit later four or five militants came in and questioned me. They wanted to know about Malcolm Kalp, who I'd been in the room with. They accused me of being in the CIA. They kept saying, "You're CIA! You were taking a message for Malcolm Kalp! Who were you going to see? Where were you going? You were taking a message out for Kalp! You're CIA!"

I kept saying, "No way, man. I just wanted to get home for Christmas."

There were four or five of these assholes shouting at me and roughing me up. I'd hurt my leg, and they kicked me in the leg. This one guy said, "You know what happens to people who try to escape? We shoot them." Then they put a gun to my head, right against the bone behind my ear, where I could feel it, and they pulled the hammer back and snapped it. That was their idea of fun. I thought they were going to blow my head off, and I'll tell you, when that hammer snaps it's a shocking event. Your butt really puckers up.

They kept shouting at me and browbeating me. They said, "Malcolm Kalp has already told us that you were delivering a message for him! We know you're CIA! What is your code name? Who is your contact?" Everything they were saying was absolutely ridiculous.

When they said these ridiculous things, I'd say, "You're out of your goddamn mind." And even though my hands were tied, I flipped them the bird.

They went crazy. They were shouting, "Allah is against you! There is no escape! Allah is against you!" All sorts of crazy things.

This sort of thing went on for about two hours. Then the thing that hurt me the most happened when they were getting ready to move me to another room. This one guy came in with handcuffs, and he was a real sadistic mother. He tightened the steels on the handcuffs so that they hurt like hell. He tightened those steels down as far as he could

---

* A wrestling hold in which two hands are placed behind the neck to press the head forward.

get them. I've never experienced anything that put me in so much pain. He hit me in the head a couple of times just for kicks. My hands were turning blue, and I told him that the handcuffs were hurting me. He said, "It doesn't matter! It doesn't matter!" That's all he knew how to say. "It doesn't matter!"

With my hands still handcuffed, they bound my arms and legs to a straight-back chair with nylon rope, and left me sitting there. I remember thinking, "This is going to be one hell of a way to spend Christmas."

5   Christmas in Captivity

JOE HALL (*warrant officer, at the Mushroom Inn*): Three or four days prior to Christmas, I noticed that the guards were eating little candy canes and Christmas candies. I knew damn well that stuff had been sent for us. I mean, it had to have come from the United States. The Iranians don't even celebrate Christmas. But the students were eating all of this Christmas candy, and even though it had been sent for us we weren't getting any of it. I figured that something was going to be done for Christmas. I just had a feeling that they were going to do something.

JOHN LIMBERT (*political officer, at the Mushroom Inn*): As the holidays approached, I had this vague hope that we would be released. I kept thinking, "Wouldn't it be nice if they released us on Christmas as some kind of religious or symbolic gesture?" I made a few discreet inquiries among the students, and it was obvious that a release was not in the cards. Then they brought around a photocopy of a little newspaper clip that said that Khomeini had approved the visit of American clergymen for Christmas, and that he had specified black clergymen.* Well, that was not very good news, because it meant that we would still be around for Christmas.

SGT. PAUL LEWIS (*marine security guard, at the ambassador's residence*): The Iranians were always making a big deal about being religious people, and when they were getting ready for their big Christmas push, they kept telling us that they respected our religion. They came into

---

* A delegation of three American clergymen and the Roman Catholic Archbishop of Algiers were invited to visit the hostages. The three Americans included Rev. William Sloan Coffin, of the United Church of Christ, Rev. William Howard, president of the National Council of the Churches of Christ, and Msgr. Thomas Gumbleton, auxiliary bishop of the Roman Catholic Archdiocese of Detroit.

our room four or five times and asked us what kind of Christmas services we would like to have. We told them that we would like something very quiet, and said that a dignified service with all of the other Americans would be nice. They wrote all of our suggestions down and said, "Yeah, yeah. We will do that."

SGT. ROCKY SICKMANN (*marine security guard, at the ambassador's residence*): They told us that we were going to be able to go to confession and take communion. I was looking forward to going to confession. I wanted to confess all of my sins, and all of the hatred I felt toward the Iranians. In my religion, I've always been taught that it's wrong to have so much hatred for somebody. But with what they were doing to us and the way they were constantly lying, I couldn't help it. I hated them. My hatred was like a disease. If something had happened where we would have had to kill one of them, I wouldn't have hesitated to do so. I've never had a feeling like that before, where I so badly wanted to kill somebody for what they were doing—what they were doing to me, my friends, our families, and our country. It was just so humiliating. There was the constant lying. They put people through mock executions, threatened to kill us, and supposedly played Russian roulette with a couple of the secretaries. It's inhuman to do things like that. I hated them for doing these things. I was hoping that confession and a religious service would release some of the hatred I felt.

That Christmas Eve, before they took us into the service, they gathered four or five of us and took us down into the basement of the ambassador's residence, where they showed us some more revolutionary films. They showed us films of the shah's army shooting people, and they showed us pictures of people who had been shot when they were nude. We'd seen all these gruesome things before, and I was starting to wonder what the hell was going on. They loved to show us pictures of people who were dead or had been tortured. I guess they wanted us to get on television and make some derogatory statements about the shah and President Carter.

WILLIAM ROYER (*director of academic courses, at the ambassador's residence*): I was being kept in the ambassador's residence, and my roommates and I were told that there was going to be a Christmas celebration. Downstairs, I could hear someone practicing the piano. Hymns and Christmas carols were being played in the ballroom of the residence.

At about two o'clock in the morning, we were rousted out of bed to go downstairs. Six of us went in one group. When we entered the ballroom there was a big Christmas tree and party lights were hanging from the ceiling. The dining table was laid out with a buffet of sweets and fruits. It all looked very festive. Then, lined up on one side of the room were a bunch of fatigue-clad students, who were there to watch us.

The six of us met with Sloan Coffin. I found him to be a very fine person, and I was touched by the occasion. It was a very meaningful service. Very personal. We sang a couple of hymns and had a few words with the chaplain. He assured us that we were being thought of back home, and that measures were being taken to resolve the situation.

ROBERT ODE (*consular officer, at the ambassador's residence*): We went down in various small groups. First one group of hostages was taken down, then a little bit later another group would go. A terrorist came in and told us that we were going to go down to the Christmas service. At the time, I was in a room with Bruce German and Robert Blucker. Blucker refused to attend the Christmas services, so Bruce and I proceeded to wait and wait and wait. A couple of hours passed, and they never came back to get us. We kept waiting and waiting, until finally both Bruce and I gave up. We crawled onto our mattresses and went to bed. I'd given up on the idea. Then at about 2:30 in the morning, these terrorists came into the room and got us. We were blindfolded and taken down to the living room of the ambassador's residence. Just before the door was opened, they took our blindfolds off so the American clergy wouldn't see that we had been blindfolded.

We were brought into the room and seated on the sofa for this service. They sandwiched a terrorist in between each one of us on the sofa. Sloan Coffin, the American clergyman, played the piano, and we sort of joined in halfheartedly and sang some Christmas carols. Then Sloan Coffin said a prayer, and after that we were permitted to go to the table and fill a plate with some of the goodies. I took an apple, an orange, some of the nutmeats, and some cookies.

The whole thing was a farce as far as I was concerned. It was pure propaganda. I remember Sloan Coffin, in attempting to give us some comfort, wasn't very comforting, because his whole attitude seemed to be more sympathetic to the terrorists than to any of the hostages.

SGT. PAUL LEWIS (*marine security guard, at the ambassador's residence*): I was a little upset with Reverend Coffin. As a sign of brotherhood, he wanted us to sing Christmas carols and hold hands with the Iranians sitting beside us. I refused to have anything to do with that. I wasn't about to hold hands with those guys, and I wouldn't sing. I just sat there. Before we left, Sloan Coffin hugged each of us, and I told him, "This is all bullshit. Total bullshit." In those words.

SGT. ROCKY SICKMANN: (*marine security guard, at the ambassador's residence*): Cookies and candy and pastries were all spread out for the TV cameras, like we were having a great time. The Iranians had said that we were going to be able to take communion and go to confession, but all we did was sing a song and say a prayer. That was all. When we got up to leave, Sloan Coffin came over to us and very softly said that everyone at home was praying for us, and to stay strong. Right away, the Iranians came over and broke us up, because they didn't want any messages being passed. Still, Reverend Coffin's message helped me. It was an indication that people back home were concerned.

CAPT. PAUL NEEDHAM (*air force logistics officer*): I saw the minister from the National Council of Churches. I asked him what bowl game Nebraska was playing in, but he didn't know. The last football score I'd heard was that Nebraska had beaten Missouri 21–20 on the third of November. That came over the line just before we were taken. Since it was obvious that this guy had been invited in by the Iranians and couldn't do anything to help us get released, the only thing I cared to find out about was how Nebraska's football team was doing. He couldn't answer that, so he wasn't much help to me.

BRUCE GERMAN (*budget officer*): I asked Sloan Coffin if he could deliver a message to my wife and family and let them know that I was doing okay. Later, I learned that my wife did get in touch with him, and she asked about me. She wanted to know how I looked and if I had anything to say. Was there any message? He told her that he couldn't remember, that we all looked the same. And, of course, she had sent a message with him for me, which I never received.

JOE HALL (*warrant officer*): I thought we were going to have a nice little service. I thought it would be nice for us to have a chance to share some sort of Christmas spirit with each other—but those asshole Iranians destroyed that with all their cameras and their hype.

I went in thinking we were going to have a quiet service, but then I saw the cameras and I realized it was just a media event. I was doing pretty well until that charade. They had this little Christmas tree in the corner, and they had cards and glitter and stuff hanging around. I was in a state of shock. I was thinking, "My God, this is Christmas! I can't believe we're still here!"

JOHN LIMBERT (*political officer*): I saw Reverend Howard from the National Council of Churches of Christ. He was obviously exhausted, but he managed to conduct a short ceremony. There were four of us together, and we sang some Christmas carols. Then Reverend Howard asked each of us who we were, and we told him. While we were talking with him, the students hovered over us to make sure that no news was passed. In spite of that, Reverend Howard was able to get the idea through that people did care about us at home, and that the concern wasn't limited to our families, but that others were thinking of us as well. So that was positive. I know that there have been lots of criticisms about the presence of the clergy, but I definitely think that Dr. Howard's actions were entirely appropriate. He was very sincere.

Anyway, before we left, we took some cookies and fruit and stuffed as much as we could into our pockets. Later, I learned that the cookies were made by some American ladies in Tehran.

CPL. WILLIAM GALLEGOS (*marine security guard*): The Iranians had all this food and candy spread all over the place, but I didn't get any of it. I know some other people did, but I went in there with three other marines, and they didn't give us anything. One guy in our group grabbed a candy bar on the way out, but the guards searched us in the hallway before they took us upstairs and they found the candy bar and took it away. I remember when I first walked into that room I thought, "Oh, great. Here's a big shindig that the Iranians are putting on camera." I knew right away that it was a bunch of bullshit. I don't know how the films looked back here, but it was total bullshit.

JOE HALL (*warrant officer*): I wasn't doing too badly until they took me in there. I saw the Christmas tree and all the festive junk they had put up, and I got all choked up. I had a lump in my throat, and when I saw all that stuff, I couldn't stand it. It was very emotional. Everybody was crying. I missed my wife so desperately that it was ridiculous. I knew it had to be just as bad for her as it was for me, if not worse. I was really depressed because I was separated from my wife and family. That was the real strong emotional pull. I loved them and missed them. And I regretted what they were having to go through. I was just about as low as I could get. There were peaks and valleys. Christmas was a real valley.

COL. LELAND HOLLAND (*army attaché*): My interrogations went on until fifteen minutes before midnight on Christmas Eve of 1979. Then they said, "It's Christmas, and there's a priest here. He wants to see you."

I think the lowest my morale has ever been in my whole life was Christmas Eve of 1979. I'd had the threats with the guns, and they'd been picking at me pretty hard. I was a beat and exhausted guy. Then they said, "We're going to stop now."

I was wearing a T-shirt and had bare feet. So they took me back to get some clothes on. Then when I got in to meet with the priest, there were TV cameras in the room, and there was a Christmas tree and food, and that type of thing. It was obvious that they wanted the world to see that the hostages were living in Fat City. At this time, I hadn't had any mail or news. Nothing. One of them handed me a Christmas card and said, "You may write a note to your family, and the priest will take it back with him." So I wrote a quick note to Mary and finished up by saying, "The Irish never say die." That sort of thing. I had a pretty wet face when I handed that card over. I've never felt rock-bottom lower in all my life.

JOHN LIMBERT (*political officer, at the Mushroom Inn*): On Christmas Day one of the leading clergymen of Iran, Ayatollah Montazari, came around and visited the Mushroom. At the time, he was the Friday prayer leader of Tehran, and he is now sometimes referred to as Khomeini's successor. When he came into the Mushroom he was accompanied by a television crew. He doesn't speak any English, so he spoke to us through an interpreter. He said that he had been in prison at one time, and that we really shouldn't worry about anything, but that we should just do as he had done and spend our time in prison without worrying about things. I felt that his coming into the Mushroom was a good sign, in the sense that I didn't think we would be taken out and shot the next day when a leading ayatollah was coming around to meet with us in front of a television crew. In fact, I had the impression that he was genuinely interested in seeing that we were all right.

After he finished speaking he came around and shook hands with each of us. When he got to me, he was introduced, and I said, "Oh yes, we've met before." About a week before the embassy was taken, I had gone to meet him with one of our State Department visitors. I had served as an interpreter. Ayatollah Montazari said that yes, he remembered. Well, when the students heard that their mouths dropped open. They couldn't believe it.

JOE HALL (*warrant officer, at the Mushroom Inn*): I remember when Ayatollah Montazari came through the Mushroom. Rich Queen and I used to call him Raving Monty, because he was the Friday prayer leader and we could hear him driving the crowds into a fever pitch. The guy was a real orator. His voice had all kinds of octaves. It would rise and fall, thunder and soften.

He was a short little guy with about nine million blackheads on his nose, and he looked like he'd never plucked a hair from his ear in his life. He was a gross little cretin, but the students just absolutely revered him. When he came in they were all around him, bowing and scraping, and I guess they assumed we would hold him in the same state of awe. He came over and was introduced by an interpreter. "This is Ayatollah Montazari."

I remember thinking, "So what?"

I was kind of confused about how to behave. I thought, "Well, I should just stand here and act like an adult, and conduct myself with dignity." But then I'd get upset because I took so much bullshit off of them. Anyway, I just stood there and he said a couple of words, and the students translated for him. He said, "How are you?" Then he said something like, "I stayed in the shah's prison for two years. I came out alive, and so will you."

I thought, "Two years!" That was not what I needed to hear.

CORT BARNES (*communications officer, at the Mushroom Inn*): I saw Ayatollah Khalkhalli* when he came through. I heard that this bigwig was in the Mushroom Inn, and he was coming around. I was freezing. I was cold. I had a little foam-rubber mattress, when everybody else had a regular embassy mattress. The food was poor. We had no communications with our relatives. Everything was poor. We were all miserable.

Khalkhalli was a short, fat little guy. He was trying to be jovial. Instead of reviewing the troops, I guess he was reviewing the enemy. He came in and Colonel Holland stood up and greeted him. But I refused to acknowledge that he was in the room. I had a book, and I read the same line over and over about fifteen times. I couldn't concentrate with this fat ayatollah standing there.

Finally he reached down and tried to shake my hand. I wouldn't let him. He said something in Farsi to one of the guards who was with him, and the guard said to me, "He wants to know how you're doing."

I looked up and said, "Tell him I'm too fucking cold."

Apparently the guard told him, because Khalkhalli ordered them to bring me a blanket. And they did. A nice one, too.

He kept trying to shake my hand, but I kept my hand firmly on the book. I wasn't about to shake hands with that guy. Khalkhalli walked around and viewed the place, then he came back. One of his escorts said, "He says this place is very clean compared to the SAVAK prison he was in." Apparently he'd been thrown in prison by the shah, and he was trying to tell me that our treatment was humane, that things

---

* Ayatollah Khalkhalli presided over numerous revolutionary tribunals in Iran. He frequently boasted of having personally ordered the execution of more than 200 high-ranking officials in the shah's government, including the former prime minister, Amir Abbas Hoveyda.

had been a lot worse for him. But I didn't want to hear it. When you feel bad yourself, you don't care how somebody else felt at some other time—especially when that person is partly responsible for your misery. I knew I wasn't being treated well, and I didn't care what he had to say about it.

At the time, I didn't know who Ayatollah Khalkhalli was. Later I learned that he was Iranian's famous hanging judge. When I heard that, I was glad I'd used profanity and ignored him. It made me feel as if I'd raised the flag in front of the hanging judge.

BILL BELK (*communications officer*): On Christmas Day, I was tied to a straight chair because of my escape. I was still in solitary, and I was very tightly bound hand and foot with nylon rope. My ankles were tied to the legs of the chair and my wrists were tied to the back of the chair. I couldn't move an inch. There wasn't a bit of slack in that rope.

One of the guards brought in a little twig that he called a Christmas tree. Even in the situation I was in, they brought in this evergreen branch with two or three Christmas decorations on it, and set it in the corner for me. They also brought around some sweet potato pie with marshmallows all over the top of it, and some hot tea. They untied my hands long enough to let me eat, and then tied me right back up. I thought it was rather ironic that they would do this, since I was being punished for trying to escape. And Christmas isn't a Moslem holiday to begin with. It just isn't their thing at all. I was sitting there tied to my chair, thinking, "What a hell of a place to be for Christmas. I should be at home with my family. What the hell am I doing here?"

Another thing that was really a kick in the teeth during this time was that I remember hearing Joe Subic in the room next to me. He was busy talking to the guards about getting Christmas cards to all of his relatives and friends. I was wondering why the guards were being so nice to him, and how in the hell he could get Christmas cards written. I could hear him talking, and I could also hear that he had a typewriter in there. He was actually typing. That really shocked me. I figured there must have been some sort of capitulation or something. Then later on I learned that Subic had allowed himself to be used for propaganda purposes, and that in return he was given special treatment.*

They kept me tied up like that for several days. The only time they

* During their period of captivity many of the hostages witnessed Sgt. Subic voluntarily assisting their captors in a variety of ways. He identified American embassy personnel on the day of the takeover, and in the weeks that followed willingly assisted the militants in their propaganda efforts. Perhaps his most glaring indiscretion came in a thirty-four-minute film produced by the Iranians in which Sgt. Subic "confessed" to being a CIA spy, even though he was never affiliated with the CIA in any capacity. Further, Sgt.

untied me was to let me go to the bathroom or to let me eat—and with the exception of that Christmas pie it was strictly a bread and water diet. They'd give me a couple of minutes to eat, then it was back to the ropes. After a couple days of this I was going nuts. Day after day would go by with me tied to that chair. You can't imagine what it's like when you have absolutely nothing to do but sit there blindfolded and wait for somebody to come in and blow your head off. Some things get beyond words. I don't quite know how to explain what that misery was like. I was sore, I was tired, I was angry, and I was bored. I'd think about anything and everything just to keep my mind occupied. I planned a swimming pool for my back yard, and I'd think about my wife. I'd wonder what she was doing. I'd also think about my father, who had been dead for seven years.

There's also a bit of irony in this, because I'd think about an old friend by the name of Danny White. I knew Danny back when I was an airman in the air force. For a while they made me a turnkey and put me down in the stockade. Can you believe that? I used to be a prison guard. I was the bad guy down there in the jail, turning the key on all the other bad guys.

After a while, they brought in my friend Danny White. He had gone AWOL and had been given thirty days. He tried to escape and made it over the wall, but the MPs found Danny and brought him back. He was thrown into solitary confinement and put on a bread and water diet. This was 1955, and back then military justice could be pretty harsh. They did things then that they wouldn't do now. Danny was put in a very small cell, and his bed was nothing but a steel frame that slanted out from the wall. He was given one blanket and a pot to go to the bathroom in. That was it. The walls were bare and he didn't have anything to read. He couldn't go anywhere, and he couldn't do anything. All he had to eat was bread and water. He wasn't even allowed to sleep

---

Subic identified several other Americans by name who he claimed were either CIA or American espionage agents. The film was shown on Iranian television and was offered for release in the United States, but all three major American networks refused to air it.

When the hostages returned to the United States, Sgt. Subic denied that he had participated in the film. In an interview with the *Radford Observer,* he said: "The militants spliced used film footage of me taken on various occasions during my captivity, and one of them faked my voice in the film where I supposedly admitted to the militants as being a CIA agent."

Because of the behavior they witnessed in Iran, several of the hostages have stated that they feel Sgt. Subic should have been court-martialed upon his return to the United States. Although the army did not pursue a court-martial, Sgt. Subic was the only hostage who was not awarded the National Medal of Honor.

well, because every thirty minutes someone would go in and make sure that he was awake. I felt sorry for Danny, and thought it was a cruel punishment. I really did. But when I was on duty I had to go in there and wake Danny up. I was told to. I was just a flunky turnkey, and the sergeant made me go in and do it. Every thirty minutes I'd go into the cell and say, "Get up, Danny! Get up!" He was supposed to stand up on his feet whenever someone went in there. He had to go through thirty days of total and complete isolation with absolutely nothing to do, and frequent harassment. It's a wonder he didn't lose his mind.

Well, the irony is that twenty-five years later I was the prisoner who was suffering harassment on a bread and water diet with absolutely nothing to do. I was the prisoner who had tried to escape. I'd sit there blindfolded and tied to the chair, and I couldn't help but wonder, "Is it going to be thirty days before I'm released from this torture? Is it going to be thirty days before they untie me and take this godforsaken blindfold off?" I'd think about old Danny White and would regret that I hadn't let him sleep, regardless of what that sergeant had said. You know, I could've just gone in there and told him to get up without really bothering him. I can't imagine how Danny put up with that for thirty days. During the time I was tied to the chair, I realized what a terrible thing that was. At least I could sleep.

On the seventh day, those assholes came in and took my blindfold off and untied me from the chair. After that, nobody bothered me. I was still in solitary, but they gave me some books to read and pretty much just left me alone. After seven solid days of being bound and blindfolded, you can't imagine how nice it was to be able to walk around the room and have something to read. To be able to stretch or lie down. Even though I was still in solitary, it was wonderful just to have something to do.

Part Five

In Hiding
with the Canadians

November 8, 1979–
January 25, 1980

AT THE AMERICAN embassy, the student militants responsible for the takeover never discovered that six American diplomats had escaped capture and were hiding in Tehran. On November 8, 1979, as the homes of the American hostages were being broken into and searched by Iranian militants, Robert Anders had called John Sheardown, the chief immigrations officer at the Canadian embassy, and explained that he and four other Americans had run out of places to hide. John Sheardown immediately offered to take the Americans into his home, and did so without regard for his own personal safety. After receiving the phone call from Anders, Sheardown immediately informed Ken Taylor, the Canadian ambassador to Iran, of the situation. During the course of the next two days Ambassador Taylor transmitted a series of top secret communications to his superiors in Canada, and within forty-eight hours hiding the American diplomats became an official act of Canadian policy.

Two of the Americans, Joe and Kathy Stafford, moved in with Ambassador Taylor, while the four others remained at the Sheardown residence. Meanwhile, Bruce Laingen, Victor Tomseth, and Michael Howland remained at the Iranian Foreign Ministry. Ambassador Taylor was able to visit them, and informed them of the protection being provided to their colleagues.

In the United States, plans were initiated to extract the six Americans from Iran. In conjunction with these plans, the Canadian government decided to close down its embassy in order to protect its personnel from possible retaliation for the American escape. What follows is an account of the eleven weeks subsequent to the arrival of the American diplomats at the home of John Sheardown on November 8.

MARK LIJEK (*consular officer, in hiding at a private residence in Tehran*): The six of us in hiding were kept at two different residences. Ambassador Taylor felt that it was important for some of the Americans to stay at his house. In the event that we were caught, he wanted it to be clear that offering us protection was an act of Canadian policy and not something that John Sheardown had decided to do on his own. So Joe and Kathy Stafford stayed at Ambassador Taylor's residence, while Bob

Anders, Lee Schatz, and Cora and I stayed at John Sheardown's house with John and his wife Zena.

John Sheardown was the number two man at the Canadian embassy, and while we were in hiding he continued to go into work every morning. His house was a terrific house to hide in. In front, the garage was at the base of the house, and there was a long flight of stairs leading up to the living area. The back of the house was built into a hill, so that in the rear the roof was at ground level. This was important, because it meant it was difficult for anyone to see what was going on inside the house. I think there were seventeen rooms, so there was plenty of space. There was also a totally enclosed courtyard, so that we could go out and get a little bit of sun without anybody seeing us. We settled in and were able to live very comfortably in that house.

Our hosts were very interested in helping us. They knew we were in a difficult situation. The food was always very good and there was always plenty of liquor. In the evening, when he got home from work, John would always come in and sit with us. He'd give us the latest news, and all the newspapers and magazines he could get hold of. Given the fact that we had to be in hiding, I cannot imagine being in more comfortable circumstances, or being with nicer people.

CORA LIJEK (*consular officer, in hiding at a private residence in Tehran*): John made an effort to make us feel secure. He said if anyone ever came to the house and we had to leave in a hurry, there was a way to get out the back of the house. Then he showed us how to get up on the roof and over the back hill. This made me feel more secure. If someone came to the house looking for us, or if something happened, we knew we had an escape route planned.

MARK LIJEK (*consular officer, in hiding at a private residence in Tehran*): Strangely enough, there was another *komiteh* gardener who worked at the Sheardowns' residence. He had a key to the front gate and could walk into the yard whenever he wanted. So we had to be careful about him.

There was a big glass door in the kitchen, which we covered over with white shoe polish so that we could sit in the kitchen and have breakfast without having to worry about him seeing us. We spent most of our time in the den at the back of the house, which opened on to a closed courtyard. When we were back there we didn't have to worry about the gardener too much.

We had arrived at this house about six days after the attack, and I think most of the people involved were still anticipating—or at least hoping for—a general release in which all of the hostages would be freed. The only policy that we heard from the Canadians in regard to our own situation was that in the event that the other hostages were released, we would be taken down to the airport under the protection of a group of six ambassadors and delivered to the Iranian government. Hopefully, they would allow us to board the plane and leave with the rest of the hostages. This was the only thing we were told in terms of any strategy planned to get us out. So all we could do was wait. But I don't think any of us ever anticipated the amount of time that would be involved.

VICTOR TOMSETH (*chief political officer, at the Iranian Foreign Ministry*): At the Foreign Ministry Bruce Laingen, Mike Howland, and I did undergo a transition period during which time our status changed from diplomats to hostages. Once Ibrahim Yazdi, the foreign minister of the Provisional Government, conceded that the Foreign Ministry had an obligation to provide us with protection, our status in the eyes of the people in the Foreign Ministry was that we were their guests living under their protection. For a period of time, I think that if we had announced that we were leaving and walked out the door, we would not have been prevented from doing so. The shift on that didn't come until Sadegh Ghotbzadeh became foreign minister in December. At one of his first press conferences he was asked about the status of the three of us, and it became clear that if we tried to leave we would be prevented from doing so. The rationale given to us would not have been that we were hostages, but that the Foreign Ministry could not provide us with protection if we were out on the streets. But whatever the rationale, it was very clear that we were no longer free to leave.

In that early time period, we went through a breaking-in process of learning how to cope with the physical limitations of our environment. We had to figure out how to manage the sleeping arrangements and how to take care of our basic needs. On the second day we received a care package from the Danish ambassador, who brought us some shaving gear so that we could shave. A little later we were able to obtain some clean clothes. We did have access to a lavatory that had toilets and a sink, but no bathing facilities. So we had to clean ourselves at the sink until other arrangements were made. After about two weeks we finally managed to get a bath. There was a tub in the kitchen area that the Iranians used to throw stale bread in. They cleaned that out and heated up some bath water for us in the kitchen, and filled up the tub. So, in that fashion, we managed to get a bath. But we all three had to use the same water. Initially, we went on a rank basis. Bruce was first, I went second, and Mike was third. After that we rotated the order, and took turns at being the first to climb into the water. There was also a problem in that we had no towels. The best the Iranians could come up with were a couple of sheets. So we had to dry off with sheets rather than towels, and manage as best as we could. Learning to cope with the environment was a major preoccupation for the first two or three weeks. After that, we managed to more or less settle into an established routine.

LEE SCHATZ (*agricultural attaché, in hiding at a private residence in Tehran*): On the whole, I'd say it was easy to be living in hiding. For the most part, I felt safe. The house was a multileveled house built into a hillside, and you couldn't see from one yard into another. So there was no real problem from neighbors. We settled into a routine of sleeping late, standing out on the closed patio in the morning to catch some sun, and playing cards. Right in the center of this multileveled house, there was an open courtyard. We could go outside in the morning, lean back against the rail, and get some sunshine. Even when there was snow on the ground, it was warm enough so that we could go out there and read for a couple of hours in the morning.

During the day, we pretty much stayed out of the front part of the house, because when the gardener came in we had to make sure we were out of sight. So the four of us spent most of our time in the den, which had a table, some chairs, a sofa, and lots of books. I've often thought that it would be nice not to have to do anything, but to just have all of your time to yourself. But I never imagined that I'd find myself in a situation where I had to do it all in one spot. And when that happened it got to be boring pretty quickly. Very boring. The four of us spent a lot of time reading, and we drank a lot, too. I guess we had to dull the senses out of boredom, and we drank to help pass the time. We had to be careful about throwing away our garbage that had beer and whiskey bottles in it. Either the garbage man or the gardener could have posed a problem. We stored the beer and whiskey bottles in a back courtyard, which was where the trash sat. Then, when John went to work in the morning, he'd take the garbage with the beer bottles in it and throw it in some garbage dumpsters himself, so that the garbage man didn't have to deal with it. And when the gardener came around, we were careful to stay in the back of the house.

VICTOR TOMSETH (*chief political officer, at the Iranian Foreign Ministry*): After we were no longer active participants in the negotiating process, there were basically three groups of Iranians that we dealt with. Their reactions to us varied. The chief of protocol was put in charge of us, and we would see either him or people from his office fairly regularly.

These people were professional diplomats. They'd had assignments abroad, and they were acutely embarrassed by the whole incident.

The second group of people we dealt with regularly was the janitorial force. They were all literate, but not very well educated. Several of them had been long-term government employees. Their feelings were rather mixed. There were a couple who very quietly made it known to us that they didn't have much use for the Khomeini regime. On the other hand, some of the others thought Khomeini was the greatest thing since sliced bread, and with them we had some rather long and heated discussions on the merits of the hostage case. They would say things like: "The United States should give back the criminal shah so we can execute him." Or, "Of course we all know that the CIA worked hand in glove with SAVAK to torture and kill innocent Iranians."

None of these people were openly hostile to us. Quite to the contrary, most of them assured us that they liked us fine, and were sorry that we were being put through this ordeal. Yes, they understood that it was difficult on our families, but after all, the shah was a terrible person, and the United States government had supported him. Somebody had to pay.

The third group of people we regularly saw were the armed guards. They were comprised of the regular Foreign Ministry security force and army personnel. Again, they were not terribly well educated, and there seemed to be a division in feeling among them. There were a few who were not at all enthusiastic about either the Khomeini regime or the seizure of our embassy, and they would tell us so.

By and large, I would say that we weren't mistreated, and our relations with the people we saw were reasonably amicable. The people we had contact with at the Foreign Ministry were certainly more sophisticated than the students holding our people at the embassy. There weren't any ridiculous claims that an Islamic tidal wave was going to sweep the United States, or anything like that. The interesting thing to me was that over time some of the people who had been the most supportive of Khomeini began to have second thoughts about Khomeini-ism. Not all of them, but some of them did. I thought that was interesting.

CORA LIJEK (*consular officer, in hiding at a private residence in Tehran*): To help pass the time, I slept a great deal. Sleep was sort of my escape. And I remember Bob Anders exercised more than any of us. He'd go out in the courtyard and do push-ups and calisthenics even when there was snow on the ground.

MARK LIJEK (*consular officer, in hiding at a private residence in Tehran*): I spent the vast majority of my time reading. Fortunately, John Sheardown had a pretty good library. I kept a list of the books I was reading, just so I'd feel I was accomplishing something. By the time we left, I had fifty-five books on that list, ranging from Kissinger's treatise on Metternich to a lot of ghost stories, and almost every spy novel that John LeCarré had written.

LEE SCHATZ (*agricultural attaché, in hiding at a private residence in Tehran*): I read some of John LeCarré's novels. That's a strange type of book to read when you're living undercover. I kept getting all these great ideas on how we might be able to smuggle ourselves out of Iran. I'd read all of the derring-do in his books, and begin to think: "Turkey is a nice NATO country. Can't we get close to the Turkish border, and have an airplane fly out into the middle of the desert and pick us up in the blackness of night?" Or, "What would be the option of hiking into Pakistan? Could we do that?" Or, "Could we get a boat and cross the Caspian?" Reading his books would trigger fantasies about these sorts of things, and some of these scenarios didn't seem all that far-fetched. Some of them seemed like they might be realistic solutions to our problem.

Basically, we were told that it was a waiting game. That when everything was all worked out and the hostages were released, a group of foreign ambassadors would escort us to the airport at the same time the others were being released and try to put us on the same plane. I have to admit, that never did sound like a really great idea. It was one of those things that could have fouled the whole deal. But we were under the assumption that that was what was going to happen.

VICTOR TOMSETH (*chief political officer, at the Iranian Foreign Ministry*): Quite naturally, there were lots of meetings going on at the Foreign Ministry. Bani-Sadr would summon foreign diplomats, or Ghotbzadeh would have the press in. The three of us were being kept in a complex of rooms that were like the diplomatic reception rooms at the State Department. The room where the Iranians held their meetings was directly adjacent, and they would sequester the three of us off in a corner of the complex so we wouldn't be anywhere near the meeting room. We were sort of treated like lepers. But everyone knew we were in there, and after the meetings various ambassadors would come in and see us.

As this thing began to drag out, the three of us passed most of our time by reading. Initially, when the foreign ambassadors were allowed in to see us, they usually brought some pocket books in with them. Very quickly, I started zeroing in on how thick the book was. One of the best books I read was *The Far Pavilions* by M. M. Kaye. It's a novel set in late-nineteenth-century India, and I have a long-standing interest in India. So that was enjoyable. But basically, I didn't care what the subject was or who the author was, but was interested in how thick the book was. Books like *Shogun* and *Tai-Pan* by James Clavell were fun. They were also very long, and the thicker the better.

In addition, we had some other things to do. Somebody sent in a set of paints, and Bruce Laingen and Mike Howland painted a great deal. Bruce had done some painting prior to our time in Tehran, and he's a rather talented artist. So he took advantage of the time to develop his skills even further.

The room we were in was large enough so that you could actually jog around it. It must have been about seventy feet long and forty feet wide. Bruce and Mike would jog for exercise. That didn't appeal to me, so I used to lie on the sofa and wave at them as they ran by.

It may sound surprising, but most of the time I was not terribly unhappy. I didn't brood a great deal. Having access to newspapers, magazines, radio, and television, and being able to exchange views with at least a few Iranians was all rather interesting. It's heady stuff to be in the midst of a revolution.

CORA LIJEK (*consular officer, in hiding at a private residence in Tehran*): John and Zena tried to take care of our social life, to the extent that it was possible to have a social life. About once every two weeks, John would drive over to Ambassador Taylor's and get the Staffords, so that Joe and Kathy could come over and spend the day with us. There were also some people from some of the other friendly missions who came over from time to time. There weren't many, but a few people did know about us, and they'd come over and visit every now and then. So that helped.

LEE SCHATZ (*agricultural attaché, in hiding at a private residence in Tehran*): On the weekends, all six of us would get together and play cards and talk out our frustrations. Then we'd cook up a big Sunday dinner. One evening after dinner, I rode over to Ambassador Taylor's with John Sheardown when he took Joe and Kathy back. We dropped them off, had a drink with Ken, and talked for a little bit. As an ambassador, Ken had to have receptions and do some entertaining, which was all a normal part of diplomatic protocol. Whenever Ken had a reception downstairs, Joe and Kathy were kept hidden upstairs. I remember Ken telling us some of the things that had gone on when people were downstairs, while Joe and Kathy were hiding upstairs. One time a television correspondent from the United States was over at Ken Taylor's for a reception. Ken thought that was great. The whole time this newsman was being entertained in the living room, one of the biggest stories of the whole situation was sitting very quietly right above his head. I remember hearing Ken tell the story and cracking up over it. He thought it was hilarious.

VICTOR TOMSETH (*chief political officer, at the Iranian Foreign Ministry*): On one of his visits, Ken Taylor brought in a bottle of cologne that was actually whiskey. As I recall, that bottle was replenished several times throughout the course of our stay, not only by Ken, but by others as well. I don't drink whiskey, so I didn't really care. But Mike and Bruce did enjoy an occasional drink. I think the pleasure was not in the drink itself, but in the idea of doing—of putting one over on these Islamic zealots. That was the part of it that was fun.

CORA LIJEK (*consular officer, in hiding at a private residence in Tehran*): When Christmas rolled around, I decided that we should make cookies to be in the Christmas spirit. John and Zena had a huge kitchen. They had more counter space than I've ever seen in any kitchen. After we got going we had almost every counter in this huge kitchen covered with cookies. All of the men were decorating the cookies, when all of a sudden one of the Iranian secretaries from the Canadian embassy showed up at the door. None of the Iranian embassy staff knew about our being in hiding, so we had to run up to our bedrooms and shut the doors. The secretary had come over to bring John and Zena a Christmas gift. She came in, saw all of the cookies in the kitchen, and said to Zena that she'd always wondered what Zena did at home all day long. Now she knew that Zena stayed home and made cookies. We all laughed about that.

LEE SCHATZ (*agricultural attaché, in hiding at a private residence in Tehran*): At Christmas, I bought worry beads for everyone. I asked John to pick them up for me so I could give everyone a set of prayer beads for Christmas. Somehow it just seemed appropriate. I also bought some small Khomeini prayer rugs, about two feet by three feet, and gave everyone one of those. They were good for some black humor value. I said I was going to use mine to train a new puppy on, or use as a doormat.

The most amazing thing about that day was that John Sheardown had managed to buy a turkey. God knows where he got it. I think there was one farm in all of Iran that raised turkeys. It cost $130, and was the biggest turkey I've ever seen. John and I spent a good portion of the day in the kitchen working on the turkey. We made the dressing and gravy and some fixings. John was a great cook, and we fixed a turkey dinner with all the trimmings.

Joe and Kathy Stafford came over with Ambassador Taylor, and we also had some friends in from other embassies—friends who already knew where we were. John made hot wine, and we all sat down to a real feast. That was a good day.

MARK LIJEK (*consular officer, in hiding at a private residence in Tehran*): During those three months, time was not a very important factor to us, except in the sense that it was something that we had to try and get through. We were all just marking time. We were glad to be safe, and we were glad to have a comfortable place to stay. But we also knew that we couldn't stay there forever. Eventually something would have to be done.

LEE SCHATZ (*agricultural attaché, in hiding at a private residence in Tehran*): In the morning we'd get the BBC report, which was usually the only news we'd receive until the evening, when we'd listen to the BBC again. When John came home from work, he'd bring us everything he'd been able to lay his hands on, ranging from *Time* and *Newsweek* to some of the press clippings and cables the Canadians had received at their embassy. All of that was made available to us.

MARK LIJEK (*consular officer, in hiding at a private residence in Tehran*): I had a bad habit of oversleeping the early BBC news summary, and every morning I'd come down and ask Bob Anders what had been on the news. Of course, the news was always the same. Nothing had happened. Our government wasn't doing anything. Getting that morning news from Bob always depressed me. The announcements that we heard from the United States were always very weak, and we could tell that any steps being taken were going to be ineffectual. For me, that was always a cause of great frustration. Day in and day out nothing of consequence was coming out of Washington. After a while I think Bob was afraid to tell me what the news was.

LEE SCHATZ (*agricultural attaché, in hiding at a private residence in Tehran*): In the first few days immediately following the takeover, I was in contact with people from some of the other embassies, and they were scared to death because they figured there would be an incredible military reaction on the part of the United States. They were afraid that there would be some sort of chest-beating reaction. You know: "What if Carter just writes off all of the hostages and takes out the whole goddamn downtown section of Tehran? Or what if he lights up the entire mountain on the north side of Tehran, and says, 'Turn our people loose!' " But then we read in the news that he ruled out force almost immediately. Psychologically, I thought that was a poor negotiating tactic, because it eliminated that element of fear that was so visible in those first few days. There's a certain power that comes with bluster, but Carter eliminated that kind of leverage when he ruled out military force. I personally thought President Carter should have mined the harbors. You know, just shut the country down. A total embargo. But then, the Iranians were just crazy enough that that might have heightened their reaction and led to a total disaster. It is easy to criticize in hindsight, but I do remember while we were there in hiding his actions seemed to be way too soft. I kept waiting for him to do something dramatic that would make the Iranians realize that they had to resolve this issue a lot more quickly, but all of his actions seemed to signal weakness.

MARK LIJEK (consular officer, in hiding at a private residence in Tehran): From reading the Tehran Times it was obvious to us that President Carter's actions were considered weak by the Iranians. They viewed every step Carter took as a triumph for themselves. They gloried in the demonstration of American impotence, and they were not fooled by any rhetoric. They knew that President Carter was not going to do anything meaningful, anything that would cause them serious harm. I'm not sure that military force should have been used, but the threat should have been there. When President Carter publicly stated that the safety of the hostages was our primary concern, he pretty much told the Iranian people that they didn't have anything to worry about. They didn't have to worry about the United States coming in with any type of force, and I think force was the only thing the Iranians would have been afraid of.

VICTOR TOMSETH (chief political officer, at the Iranian Foreign Ministry): There certainly was a wave of fear in Iran following the takeover. The Iranians were quite concerned about what might happen to them as a consequence of the seizure of the embassy. I felt very strongly from the beginning that the most critical and dangerous period was the initial ten days, and this had to do with the fear on the part of the Iranians that something very bad was going to happen to them. In those circumstances Iranian behavior was extremely unpredictable, and a heightening of the rhetoric from the United States might have served to exacerbate that tension and uncertainty. But once the initial period passed, and the students realized what a tremendous political asset they had within the Iranian political context, I became fairly confident that they would never willingly harm the people they were holding, and that barring an accident, it would ultimately become possible to negotiate a settlement.

In assessing whether or not President Carter should have tried to exploit the fear within Iran, I think it is important to first determine what American priorities should have been. The Carter administration chose to make the release of the hostages its top priority. Speaking as one who had a vested interest in that decision, I am quite happy with the order of priorities President Carter chose. But I can also understand why others would have liked to have seen a different set of priorities. A number of people that I have talked to have suggested that America's primary objective should not have been the lives of the hostages, but rather should have been to punish the Iranians for taking our people captive. If that had been done, then I certainly think that most if not all of the hostages would have been killed. Further, I don't think that the United States would have gained any credit worldwide. Personally, I was glad that it was Jimmy Carter in the White House on November 4 and in the days immediately thereafter, and not someone like Richard Nixon. President Carter was not inclined to act rashly, whereas someone else might have. His caution in those initial stages may very well have saved all of our lives.

MARK LIJEK (*consular officer, in hiding at a private residence in Tehran*): It was pretty clear to me that Khomeini was using the hostages to consolidate his own political position within Iran. During this time, a constitution was completed, and ratified by the public, and a president was elected. So they went a long way toward building the Islamic republic that the ayatollah wanted. Having the hostages in Tehran provided a very convenient focus for public hostility and directed attention away from the poor state of the economy and any other domestic problems. In the hysterical atmosphere that prevailed, it was very difficult for anyone to oppose Khomeini.

LEE SCHATZ (*agricultural attaché, in hiding at a private residence in Tehran*): Of course, our biggest fear was that we would get caught while we were with the Canadians. At one point, the house we were staying in was put up for sale, and on one occasion we had to move over to another Canadian residence for the day. It was fun to get out, and yet the whole time we were driving along in this crazy Iranian traffic, all I could think was: "What in the hell are we going to do if we have an accident?" We didn't have any documents at all, and it was easy to imagine the worst. That kind of paranoia was always there. On one other night, we had come back from Ken Taylor's after a snowfall, and

Bob Anders, Mark Lijek, and I all got out of the car and started scooping up snow like a bunch of kids. You know, we couldn't just let it lie there, and we started pitching snowballs at a street lamp. Then all of a sudden we just froze and looked at each other. It was as if we were all three thinking, "Oh Christ! What if we break the light and someone reports us?" That was the kind of thing that could have brought the local *komiteh* around. I remember standing there and thinking, "Whew! This is really dumb!" Right away, all three of us went back into the house.

Another time a helicopter came right over the top of our house. I was outside in the courtyard when this helicopter started crisscrossing the neighborhood. We had no idea of what was going on, and of course we were concerned that they might be looking for us. But as it turned out, a mullah had been shot, and they were looking for someone who had escaped on a Honda.

That type of fear was always there. It never went away. If we had been caught we knew that the people who were hiding us would probably have been in just as bad a situation as the rest of us, maybe worse. Diplomatic immunity didn't mean a thing in Iran. It was rough knowing that the people who were doing what was right could have gotten into serious trouble because of us. Maybe that was the worst feeling throughout the whole thing.

As time continued to drag on, we became frustrated, and began to develop feelings of, "Look, there are two situations here. There's the problem downtown, and there's our problem. They require two different solutions."

MARK LIJEK (*consular officer, in hiding at a private residence in Tehran*): It became more and more difficult to just continue reading books and playing Scrabble. I think we all shared a feeling that we had been in hiding for too long, and even if the hostages were released it wouldn't necessarily help us. The students hadn't had a chance to interrogate us, and if we were taken down to the airport in the event of a general release, they might conclude that we were the real spies by virtue of the fact that we were the only ones who had escaped. So we began to feel that our problem should be considered separately from that of the hostages, and that even if there wasn't a general release, something should be done to get us out of the country. We had no indication that any sort of an escape route or contingency plan had been worked out, and this worried us a great deal. We were all getting antsy. We didn't feel that we could stay there forever. In Iran, the political situation was bound to get worse, and we felt that a prolonged passage of time would only make it more difficult for us to leave.

In early January we got together and drafted a telegram that outlined these thoughts. Then we asked the Canadians to send it to the State Department. We wanted Washington to know that we felt something should be done.

In retrospect, I don't think that telegram was ever sent, because there was no need for it. State Department planning had been in the works for quite a while. As a matter of fact, we were already drawing close to departure, even though we didn't know it.

CORA LIJEK (*consular officer, in hiding at a private residence in Tehran*): At about this same time, John Sheardown came in one day and asked us if anyone had called the Staffords. We all said no, we hadn't. John handled this in a very nonchalant manner, so we never thought anything about it. But apparently his question must have been in regard to the phone call that Mrs. Taylor received from someone who asked to speak to either Joe or Kathy Stafford. That call got the Canadians very upset, because no one had any idea who had made it, and it meant that there was definitely someone who now knew that the Staffords were staying with Ambassador Taylor. That made for a dangerous situation.

LEE SCHATZ (*agricultural attaché, in hiding at a private residence in Tehran*): The Canadians were gearing up for the final closing of their embassy and were getting all of their dependents out first. So John and Zena Sheardown left Tehran in early January. This was an initial step, and within a couple of weeks the embassy would be closed and all of the Canadians would leave. But we didn't know those plans were under way. All we knew was that people with dependents were being evacuated out, and we had no idea that we would be leaving soon. I don't think John was aware of it either, because he really felt bad. He felt like he was letting all of us down, that the job wasn't over. But I said, "Hey, don't be crazy. We're happy for you. You should be glad that you're getting out of here." And, of course, we thanked them both for all that they had done. We felt very good for them.

BRUCE LAINGEN (*chargé d'affaires, at the Iranian Foreign Ministry*): We saw Ambassador Taylor two or three times, but we did not work out any arrangements with him to get the six Americans out of Iran. Ambassador Taylor knew of our concern. He knew we wanted to see them get out of Iran as quickly as possible, and that we were concerned they might be stuck there longer than we were. But we were not involved in the plan. That was entirely out of our hands.

MARK LIJEK (*consular officer, in hiding at a private residence in Tehran*): Shortly after we drafted the telegram that we'd asked the Canadians to send, Ken Taylor came to see us. He asked how we would feel about leaving the country through the airport. Then he asked how we would feel about doing it under American passports. We all sort of howled at that, because we felt it would be pretty risky. The idea of our leaving on Canadian passports was never mentioned. The only other alternative discussed was that the security officer had some sort of a plan to drive us to the Turkish border. But that would have been tough to do in the winter. There was a lot of snow up that way, and it would have meant a long journey over land. Then we still would have to have been smuggled across the border on false documents. In the final analysis, we figured that the airport was a better bet since that was a much more natural way for a group of foreigners to leave the country, rather than to cross into Turkey by car. So the primary emphasis seemed to be on getting us out through the airport. Ken was very sketchy and didn't give us many details, but at least we had an inkling that something was happening.

LEE SCHATZ (*agricultural attaché, in hiding at a private residence in Tehran*): When things happened, they happened very quickly. Before we knew it we had another meeting over at the house. Ken Taylor pretty much said, "Here it is." And he laid out the options. We had various proposals to choose from. Various stories had been put together that would give us the necessary cover to leave Iran. The documentation was incredible. There was everything that you would expect to find in someone's wallet, and all of it looked legit. I remember one of the possible stories was that we were a bunch of unemployed American schoolteachers looking for work at the American school in Iran. To us, it just didn't seem like a real good idea to have a bunch of unemployed schoolteachers walking around with $2,000 worth of airplane tickets in their pockets. But the thing that really blew us off was that we would have been Americans. There was just no way we were going to the airport as Americans. So we picked another option. All I can say is that we did have a phony alibi, and that in our documentation we were Canadians, not Americans.

After that meeting we had new identities to learn. That part of it was fun. As a participant it was something you could really get involved in. We had backgrounds, where we were born, where we were raised, maps of the cities we were raised in, schools we'd attended, jobs, employers, union cards, health cards, plane tickets, and names. I even had a nickname.

MARK LIJEK (*consular officer, in hiding at a private residence in Tehran*): From looking at the documentation, it was pretty clear that somebody had done a lot of work. Our passports showed us to have traveled through a number of places, and had stamps on them from different countries. It was a very professional job, and we all felt that no one would question our documents.

CORA LIJEK (*consular officer, in hiding at a private residence in Tehran*): On the night before we departed, the Canadians put us through an interrogation to see whether we had learned the information that had been given to us. The atmosphere was sort of like going through a school stage play. We felt pretty good about the plan, and we were pretty sure that it was going to work. Which was important, because if we weren't convinced that it was going to work, it probably would have showed up in our behavior. The interrogation itself was sort of like a game, and I think that was good because it kept us fairly relaxed.

MARK LIJEK (*consular officer, in hiding at a private residence in Tehran*): To illustrate the way we turned this into a game, most of us tried to disguise ourselves in some way. I had grown a beard while I was in hiding and I looked a lot different, so I didn't need a disguise. It was more of a problem for the visa people. Their faces had been seen by hundreds of Iranians every day, some of whom had had nothing to do but stand in line for hours and look at them. Consequently, there was some concern that an Iranian might recognize one of our faces at the airport, so we used those disguises, which just added to the gamelike atmosphere.

LEE SCHATZ (*agricultural attaché, in hiding at a private residence in Tehran*): After dinner on the night before we left, Roger Lucy* held an interrogation. He was an Iranian Nazi. We went through all the hoops as if we were going through passport control—and I blew it. I didn't know where my visa had been issued. But I managed to talk my way out of it. I told the interrogator that I didn't deal with those things. Other people took care of that stuff for me. I didn't care where the visa came from, I just used it. That seemed like an approach that would work.

That night, after our interrogation, I sat in the living room with one of the other Americans. He had some legitimate concerns about whether or not this thing would work. He was having some second thoughts, and suggested that there were too many things that could go wrong.

* Roger Lucy was an official at the Canadian embassy.

So he and I spent most of that night in the living room with him sitting in a chair across from me. We walked through every bogeyman he could think of. He'd say, "Well, what if someone at the airport decides to call the ministry to see if we really were in the country?"

"We're leaving at 6:30 in the morning. The ministry doesn't open until 9:00 A.M. Do you really think that some minor official is going to take it upon himself to have a group of foreigners miss a plane?"

"Well, what if there's something wrong with the documentation?"

We'd go through the documents, and I'd say, "Look, here are the plane tickets. We were in Bangkok on the seventeenth. Here's the entry stamp on the seventeenth. We left on the eighteenth, and here's the exit stamp on the eighteenth."

We walked through all kinds of things, to the point of having hypothetical conversations with Iranian officials. Things like, "What do you mean, you don't believe this is who I work for? Call the goddamn number in California, friend. Do it. Call it collect." If an Iranian had done that, the phone would have been picked up at the other end and someone would have verified our alibi. Someone would have said, "Yeah, he's in Iran today. He should be leaving soon." I mean, we were backed up all the way. I was convinced it was going to work. It looked good. It felt good. And I thought it was the right time to try. So the two of us sat up late and marched through all sorts of bogeymen. I think that helped to calm any lingering doubts.

CORA LIJEK (*consular officer, in hiding at a private residence in Tehran*): There was one member of our group who had some reservations about leaving, not because he wanted to stay in Iran, but because he felt we were abandoning the others. He wasn't sure that we should leave until everyone was free.

Of course, all six of us were concerned about our friends at the embassy. But the other five of us felt that we couldn't be of any help to them by staying in Iran. In fact, our continued presence only compounded the difficulties. If the others were released and we were still in Iran, then the six of us would be an additional problem. We weren't helping the hostages by being there, and we were endangering those who were giving us shelter.

So that night when we went off to bed, I think we all pretty much felt that the plan was the best we were going to have, and that we should go through with it. It would be best for everyone involved if we were out of Iran.

LEE SCHATZ (*agricultural attaché*): We got up early the next morning and got ready to go. The Canadians had given us enough clothes and stuff to put in our luggage so that it would look like we were bona fide travelers. When we got to the airport we were careful to overtip the porters so that they would take good care of us. The Iranians inspected my bags, and I went on to the ticket counter. I requested a seat in the no-smoking section, and the other five all got seats in the smoking section.

Then I proceeded through the checkpoints. In Iran you have a temporary yellow slip in your passport, which is one of the last things they check. We had those slips, and they were authentic. In fact, somebody had actually stolen them from the airport. When we came to this checkpoint, the Iranian official was supposed to remove that yellow slip and hand me back my passport. That was the procedure. I handed this guy my passport. He opened it up, looked at it, and looked at me. Then he looked at the passport, and walked into a side room. That scared me. I was thinking, "Oh shit! Can they actually keep track of those yellow slips?" The other people were behind me, and I don't think they saw what was going on. They were progressing through their checkpoints. I was just standing there thinking, "Well, this could be where this whole thing goes sour."

Then the guy walked out, pointed at my passport picture, and said, "Is this you?"

It was me. It was the passport picture from my American passport. When the photograph was taken, I had a mustache that curled down around the corners of my mouth. So I kind of pulled on my mustache to demonstrate. He smiled, and handed me my passport. Then I walked slick on past the last checkpoint. The guy never stopped me. I left the country without an exit stamp.

MARK LIJEK (*consular officer*): We had no difficulty in getting through our checkpoints, except for a perverse sort of problem. We couldn't find the immigration inspector. He was supposed to stamp our passports "out," but he was having tea in a little room behind the counter. We had to go in there and get him because he wasn't at the counter doing his job. We probably could have walked past him without ever having our passports stamped, but we saw no reason to do that. We were confident our documents would stand up, and we didn't want it to appear that we were sneaking on past, on the off chance that someone would notice. So we went in and got him, and had him stamp our passports.

LEE SCHATZ (*agricultural attaché*): I walked into the departure lounge. Along one side there was a duty-free shop, and along the other there was a caviar stand and a walk-up, European-style coffee bar, where you could buy tea and sweet cakes and stuff like that. There was a guy over there from another embassy who I recognized. I knew he was supposed to be there observing, watching for anything that appeared to be unusual. I walked over and stepped up beside him as if he were a stranger. I introduced myself using my alias, and he nodded, "Yes."

I said, "Where are you flying today?"

"I'm not traveling. I'm here to meet someone."

I couldn't resist. I asked, "Then what are you doing in the *departure* lounge?" I was having a great time, because I felt the pressure was off. You know, we had passed through all the checkpoints and all we had to do was walk onto the plane and fly out of the country. But this guy didn't think I was being very funny. He just walked away.

I met the others in the middle of the departure lounge. We pooled our money, and Joe and Kathy Stafford went over and bought some caviar. We figured that was a good tourist-type thing to do. And Bob Anders and I got some coffee. At that point I was feeling pretty good.

MARK LIJEK (*consular officer*): While we were waiting to board the aircraft, it was announced that there would be a three-hour delay. Apparently there was a problem with a leaking fuel line on our flight, and we were told that we would have this delay.

CORA LIJEK (*consular officer*): I was concerned because I had worked in the visa section and I had been seen by a lot of people in Tehran. I was worried that someone might come into the airport and recognize me. So I didn't relish the thought of sitting there for three hours. I was also worried because sometimes an airline will tell you that a flight has been delayed for an hour, and then eight hours later you find you're still sitting there in the airport. So that was not a very pleasant thing to hear. After having passed through all our obstacles, we just didn't need that kind of news.

MARK LIJEK (*consular officer*): Once we were in the departure lounge there wasn't much we could do. We did have back-up reservations on another flight, but we thought that it might raise too many questions if we tried to leave the departure lounge and get on another flight. So we just had to wait it out. As luck would have it, the problem was fixed in twenty minutes. It would've been a nerve-racking three hours if we'd had to sit there that whole time. But as it was, we were able to board the plane and settle into our seats.

LEE SCHATZ (*agricultural attaché*): We ordered Bloody Marys as soon as we were in the air. When we crossed over into Turkish airspace, I looked back into the smoking section and raised my glass in a toast. I felt an incredible adrenaline high, and had a great big grin on my face. With an Iranian sitting on either side of me, I toasted our departure out of Iran. I remember thinking, "Even if the engines fall off this plane, we're going to go down in Turkey—not Iran!"

We flew into Switzerland, and when I stepped onto European soil I stomped my foot so hard it hurt. It was the most wonderful feeling to be out after having been cooped up in hiding for those three months. We passed through the Swiss customs and immigration using the same documentation that we had used in Tehran. Then, when we walked into the lobby, there were some people from the State Department there to meet us. You could have painted these guys blue, that's how clearly they stood out. I mean, it was just obvious who they were. Of course, we figured, "We're out! Things are over! We're free!" But within our first few minutes it became apparent that that was not the case. The American government did not want our escape to become public knowledge, and arrangements had been made to have us taken to a military base where we would be sealed from contact with anyone until the entire situation had been resolved.

From the airport we were taken over to the American embassy, and we spent the night at the ambassador's residence. Bob Anders and I shared a bedroom, and after the lights were turned out, we started talking about the idea of being quarantined. I said, "You know, my family has been worrying for too long. I have got to make a couple of phone calls and say, 'Look, I'm safe. I can't say anything more than that right now. But I am safe, and I'm no longer in Iran. It's over. So don't worry about me.' " Bob had a wife and children, so he felt the same way I did. We decided that we were going to request that we be allowed to make some phone calls the next morning, and then we went to sleep.

As it turned out, Sheldon Krys* walked in the next morning and the first thing he said was, "Well, it looks like you people are known. Your story has broken." We were all over the news. So we didn't have to worry about any phone calls.

Our original plan had been to stay in Europe for a couple of days, but within an hour we were put into a van. The State Department wanted to get us out of Switzerland. For security reasons they didn't want the Iranians to suspect that there had been a Swiss connection in any of this, because the Swiss still had an embassy functioning in Tehran. So we hit the road. I remember sitting in this van and hearing the first news reports about our escape—you know, there were some Americans who had never been captured and they had escaped from Iran. And

---

* Sheldon Krys was an American State Department employee.

right now these Americans were in Europe, but no one knew exactly where. Well, at the time that we were listening to that news, we were roaring down the autobahn in a Volkswagen van, carrying on and having a good time driving right through the night.

We spent a night in Germany and then flew back to the States. We were told that we were going to be put on a military flight, but it turned out that the flight they wanted to put us on was loaded with soldiers who were being shipped back to the United States after having been picked up AWOL. It was a big prison ship flying back to the States.

The State Department decided they could do better than that, and acquired the jet that the American NATO general had assigned to him. That plane was tremendous. It had sleeping compartments and a huge galley with a table and big comfortable chairs. On that flight we were treated like absolute royalty.

I went to get a drink and started talking to one of the flight attendants. He said, "You know, this plane was torn down this morning. We were told to put it back together as fast as we could because we had some very important people we had to get to Washington."

I said, "Oh?"

He said, "I read about some people in *Stars and Stripes* this morning. But there are too many of you here."

"Well," I said, "maybe those people you read about have picked up a few escorts." He smiled and nodded.

MARK LIJEK (*consular officer*): On the day we returned to Washington, there was a welcoming reception for us at the State Department. Bob Anders read a short statement that we had all written, and we didn't take any questions from the press. We were taken upstairs to meet with Secretary Vance. Our parents were there, and it was all very nice. We couldn't have asked for a better welcome.

While we were at the reception, we were informed that we were going to be taken over to the White House to meet with President Carter, which we did. The president spent about fifteen minutes with us, which is a long time for a president. He was glad to see us, and I think he had been genuinely concerned about our predicament. Yet I have very ambivalent feelings about our meeting with him. I sometimes suspect that the reason we weren't given any advance notice of the meeting was that there was concern at the White House that we might refuse to go. If our group had been given the opportunity to discuss it among ourselves, some of us—in particular Cora and I—might have decided that we didn't want to go. There was a feeling that President Carter wasn't handling the crisis in an adequate way, and some of us might have chosen not to be put on display for political purposes. There was also a bit of resentment about our having been put in that situation to begin with, and the decisions that were made in October of 1979. I happen to think that the shah should have been admitted to the United States, but once that decision was made some steps should have been taken to provide for the security of American personnel at the embassy. If nothing else, nonessential personnel should have been filtered out. But nothing was done. So there was some resentment about that, and I think some of us would have raised objections to meeting with President Carter had we been given any notice. But as it turned out, the meeting was a positive thing. We got to see that President Carter was genuinely concerned about our predicament, and hoped for the safe return of our colleagues.

BRUCE LAINGEN (*chargé d'affaires, at the Iranian Foreign Ministry*): When we heard the news that they were gone, there were no happier people than the three of us. Although I can honestly say that we were not involved in the planning, the Iranian authorities were suspicious that we had been involved. I can understand why, because Ambassador Taylor had been in to see us. They terminated our telex arrangements, and it ended our contacts with Washington through any visiting diplomat or telephone connection. For a period of about five or six weeks, the Iranians effectively terminated our contact with the outside world, due, I think, to their suspicion that we had somehow been involved.

Part Six

Waiting

1 Winter 1979–80

In early December, the Carter administration decided it would be virtually impossible to achieve a resolution to the hostage crisis as long as the shah remained in the United States. However, during his convalescence at New York Hospital the Mexican government revoked the shah's visa and announced that he would not be permitted to return to his residence in Cuernavaca. Because of the attack on the American embassy in Tehran, other governments feared that offering asylum to the shah would subject their diplomats to possible terrorist attack. In search of a way to relocate the shah, President Carter sent his chief of staff, Hamilton Jordan, to Panama to issue a direct appeal for assistance. Jordan had established a close personal friendship with the Panamanian leader, Omar Torrijos, during negotiations on the Panama Canal treaties, and Torrijos agreed to accept the shah in Panama as a favor to the United States government. In mid-December of 1979, six weeks after the attack on the embassy, the shah left the United States.

The Carter administration wanted to engage in direct negotiations with the Iranian government and tried to establish an open line of communication through a variety of diplomatic channels, but met with little success. As the New Year dawned, the United States and Iran remained caught in a seemingly immobile deadlock. At this time, most of the hostages were being held in empty offices in the main chancery building or in the Mushroom Inn.

WILLIAM ROYER (*director of academic courses, at the chancery*): It became clear to me that the guards were concerned about our welfare, and that we were valuable as their only negotiable instrument. This observation came from a near set-to I had with one of the guards. At one point, when I was being kept at the ambassador's residence, this fellow made an obscene gesture to me and I returned it. Then later, in the basement of the chancery, I saw this fellow again. At this time we all kept our own plates and spoons, and we had to wash them after every meal. This one guard came in to get my plate so he could bring me some dinner. He wasn't at all civil and he didn't say anything, but just demanded the plate by coming in and gesturing. So I ignored him. Finally, he grabbed the plate and gave me another obscene gesture. I didn't say anything, but sort of sneered at him. This seemed to get his goat, and as he headed toward the door he gave me a quick karate kick to the face. I ducked back, and his foot grazed my forehead. Then I lunged at him. He jumped into the hall, and I slammed my fist against the door, which made a terrific amount of noise.

After a while the guard who was in charge down there came in, and in a very quiet way said, "You seem to have some trouble with my friend."

I said, "Yes, and if he comes back in here I'm going to hit him."

"Oh, no, no, no. You cannot do that."

"If he comes back in here I'm going to hit him."

This sort of conversation went on for a while, but the end result of it was that the guard who had caused the disturbance did not come into my room after that. He never again served us. So from that I was able to deduce that our safety and welfare was important to the students. And this was not the only instance. There were several indications that we were valuable to them for the purposes of negotiation. So I didn't feel that I was going to be taken out and shot, or come to any immediate harm.

CDR. ROBERT ENGELMANN (*naval supply corps officer, at the Mushroom Inn*): After all the excitement of Christmas, I think a lot of people had their hopes up for a release, and when those expectations weren't realized they went into a depression. So I just took it one day at a time. I'd wake up in the morning and say, "Okay, one more day."

I had some aluminum foil from the back of a Gelusil tablet, and used the tooth of my comb to etch a mark onto the aluminum foil. That way I could keep track of the days. If the Iranians saw that I was writing something, I'd be able to wad the aluminum foil up real quick so they couldn't read it. It would just be a piece of trash. I got up every morning and put another mark on the calendar.

WILLIAM ROYER (*director of academic courses, at the chancery*): With its barred windows and bulletproof bastions in the lower sections, the chancery was now a full-fledged prison. Previously, these security devices had been intended to protect us from people on the outside, but now they were serving in reverse by keeping us locked up with the people they'd been designed to protect us from. There was some irony in that. We all settled into this quasi-prison atmosphere.

The feel of a long haul had also settled in. Things were becoming organized, and I sensed that the students anticipated a long period of incarceration. They put padlocks on all the doors and fixed up the rooms as if they were prepared for a long period of waiting—just waiting, that's all there was to do.

SGT. PAUL LEWIS (*marine security guard*): Just before New Year's Eve, J. D. McKeel and I were taken out of the ambassador's residence and put in a basement room in the chancery. It was a tiny room. With two mattresses on the floor there was just barely enough space for one guy to walk between them. When they threw us in there, the window was open and it was extremely cold. This was the middle of winter, and it can get very cold in Tehran. Of course, the window was barred so there was no way we could crawl out. Not only was this window open, but these guys had busted out a few panes, so that when we closed the window the cold air still came rushing in. There was still glass on the floor from where these guys had broken the window. They had taken our shoes away, and didn't care about cleaning the glass up. They just expected us to live in it.

I don't know if they stuck us in that room to punish us or not. They never did say. But I guess we didn't participate well enough in their Christmas ceremony—we wouldn't sing and hold hands and act like we were happy.

DON HOHMAN (*army medic, at the chancery*): They jerked me out of the ambassador's residence and took me over and threw me in the basement of the chancery. Way in the back of the basement. I didn't have a bed or a mattress in there. It was just a rug on the floor, and that rug was filthy.

I went on a hunger strike down there. I didn't eat for twenty-one days, and I dropped a lot of weight. I remember in the middle of that hunger strike, they took me over to the ambassador's residence for a shower. When I stepped out of the shower stall there was a mirror across from me, and I couldn't believe what I saw. I didn't even think it was me. By holding my breath I could see my spine through my abdomen. I thought, "Whooh!"

That hunger strike worried the rag heads. They wanted me to eat. But I was getting really radical about it. I was screaming and yelling and cussing at every rag head that came in with food. It got to the point where they were afraid to come into my cell, because they'd have to listen to me rant and rave. I don't know why they didn't punch my lights out.

BILL BELK (*communications officer, at the chancery*): After thirty-four days in solitary, I was moved into a basement room in the chancery with Don Hohman. It was the very room where the students had broken into the embassy on the fourth of November. When I was moved in there, the window was still broken and had a hole in it. This was the dead of winter, and it was cold. Terribly cold. And that broken window made it even colder. Don and I stuffed a piece of paper and a rag in there to try and patch it up and keep the room as warm as we could. But it didn't do much good. We were both freezing, and we didn't have any warm clothes. As a matter of fact, I was wearing a short-sleeve shirt that had been given to me in the Mushroom Inn. It had belonged to somebody else, and was too small for me. That was all I had.

The carpet in that basement room was filthy. Cleanliness was always a problem, and it got progressively worse as time dragged by. I couldn't believe the filth those guys expected us to live in. Here we were sleeping on the floor, and the militants would never wipe their feet before they came into the room. If it had been their own home, they would have taken their shoes off. But for us they just tracked in all kinds of mud and dirt and dust. Every time they came they kicked in a little more filth.

DON HOHMAN (*army medic, at the chancery*): I hate being cold. God, I hate it. I'd rather be whipped than be cold. And they'd leave us sitting in there with a hole in the window and snow on the ground. The only time I ever got out from under my blanket was to drink some hot tea. The rag heads had a guard sitting in there reading a book twenty-four hours a day to make sure that we didn't talk. He'd sit in there with all his warm clothes on and watch us freeze. Every now and then he'd get up and go out in the hall and sit next to the heater and one of his buddies would come into our room. It amazed me how those guys would do that. Some of them were less than human.

SGT. PAUL LEWIS (*marine security guard, at the chancery*): They left McKeel and me in that basement room with the busted-out window for two or three weeks. There wasn't much I could do to keep warm except huddle up in my blanket. I only had one thin little blanket, and it was probably thirty degrees in there.

None of the guards seemed to know how to speak English very well. Through pidgin English and gestures we asked them to fix the window. All they would ever say was, "I have to ask my friend." Which meant that it wasn't going to happen. Whenever they had to ask permission, we knew we could forget it. We just had to live with the busted window.

McKeel and I had picked out the guards who were more or less the shift supervisors, and when they'd come in we'd have our shirts off and would be exercising as if it were seventy degrees. We'd act like the cold didn't bother us a bit.

I remember McKeel found a picture of a Polaris missile in one of the books that was lying on the floor. He tore that picture out, licked the back of it, and stuck it up on the wall. Every time one of the guards came in, McKeel would remind them that those missiles were out in the Persian Gulf. We made sure they knew the Sixth Fleet was out there—and the military might of the United States was something that did concern them. They would ask about Phantom jets, and they wanted to know how many planes an aircraft carrier could carry. McKeel and I exaggerated. We told them that a single carrier could house 150 planes, when the actual capacity was only about 89. They'd ask about the ships in the Sixth Fleet and the planes on an aircraft carrier, and we'd tell them how easy it would be for the United States to blow up a few Iranian cities.

Sometimes it's hard to believe those guys were college students, because they never took that picture off the wall. They just let it stay up there, and let us go on telling them about what a Polaris missile could do to one of their cities, and how easy it would be for a few Phantoms to come in and take out Tabriz and Tehran.

Anyway, by the time they moved us out of there, I had a bad case of bronchitis. I was stopped up real bad.

CDR. ROBERT ENGELMANN (*naval supply corps officer, at the Mushroom Inn*): As the days went by, it was important to fight the boredom. I think there's a fine line between boredom and depression, and of course depression can become very acute. It can lead to suicide or all sorts of severe problems. One of the manifestations of depression is sleep, and there were people down in the Mushroom Inn who were sleeping eighteen or twenty hours a day. They were escaping by sleeping. But I made an attempt to get up every morning, stay up during the day, and sleep only at night. I maintained a routine to try and prevent myself from becoming too bored. I'd force whatever self-discipline I could. If I had a book that I didn't want to read, I'd read it anyway. I'd force myself to.

If you just sat there and thought about how bad it was—thought about being tied up in a basement in the middle of Tehran 10,000 miles from Mom and Dad, and it was thirty-five degrees and some guy had taken your shoes and you didn't have any warm clothes and all you had was a blue blanket—it would get depressing real fast. There was enough objective information there to throw you into a deep depression. But if you fought it, and forced yourself to think positive thoughts, then that made things a little easier. Instead of dwelling on how bad it was, I'd think, "Hey, here we are four months into this thing, and I'm still alive. I'm still healthy. That was a good book I just read, and I'm reading a decent book right now. I've got my blue blanket to help keep me warm."

No matter how bad it was, you had to look for whatever positive things there were. If you made the best with what you had—with what very little you had—then it was easier to get through the day.

COL. CHARLES SCOTT (*chief of the Defense Liaison Office, at the Mushroom Inn*): If you wanted to drive yourself nuts with worry, that was easy to do. There were a lot of different scenarios you could imagine that would have resulted in all of us getting killed. The Iranians were threatening us with spy trials, and you could sit there and dwell on that. Of course, we all knew what the result of one of their kangaroo courts would be. Or you could ask yourself: "What if the United States decides to up the ante and takes out an Iranian oil refinery? If that happens, will the Iranians take us out and shoot us? Or what if a radical opposition faction in Iran decides to come in and clean us out—just comes in with guns blazing?"

In order to deal with such fears, I tried to regiment the amount of time that I would allow myself to think about them. You couldn't get these worries out of your system by talking about them, because there wasn't anyone to talk to, so you had to do it all within your own mind. I'd set aside an hour in the evening when I'd try to get all of that out of my system. I would go ahead and imagine the worst. I'd visualize scenarios where they would put me in front of a firing squad, or put me on trial in front of a revolutionary court. In doing that, my fantasies became cathartic. Because once you've faced these fears you discover that you can handle them. I knew that even in front of a firing squad I could maintain my own personal integrity and my faith in God. I dealt with death by accepting it as a real possibility. Which it was.

I found that to go ahead and think about these things was much less debilitating than to try and keep them all bottled up by denying them. If you do that, your fears will keep creeping into your mind while you're trying to read a book, and then pretty soon you find that they never leave your thought pattern. But once you accept something and realize you can handle it, even something like death, then you can dismiss it and get on with maintaining a constructive routine.

GARY LEE (*general services officer, at the Mushroom Inn*): I hit a low point after Christmas. It was depressing as hell down in the Mushroom, and I just turned the whole thing over to God. I said, "Hey, this is too big for me. God, if You are out there—and I think You are—You deal with it. I'm putting this in Your hands." And that helped ease my anxieties. It gave me some peace of mind. I don't mean to suggest that I quit worrying about what was going to happen, or whether or not I was going to be taken out and shot. But I developed a more fatalistic attitude. I'd remind myself, "Hey, whatever happens, happens. There's nothing I can do about it. This one is in the hands of God."

Prayer and faith definitely helped me during those grim months down in the hole. I think it's the reason I was able to weather the storm.

WILLIAM ROYER (*director of academic courses, at the chancery*): My initial reaction was anger. I was very irate, and it was difficult to keep all of this anger and tension within myself, but I couldn't vent it to anyone other than myself. In my dreams, I killed the Iranians many times over, especially one or two of the guards that I didn't like. I would construct elaborate fantasies in which I bashed them over the head with the butt of a gun, or there would be a great military rescue with everyone grabbing guns and *rat-tat-tat*-ing their way out.

Due to all this anger and hatred, I became afflicted with internal tension pain and muscle spasms. I couldn't sit comfortably at all. A couple of times I woke up with a completely dead arm, and I had a tingling sensation in my hand that was connected with this pain. I was aware that this was tension induced and that I'd created much of it myself, but I couldn't control it. Finally, I realized that these violent dreams and fantasies were working to my detriment.

Consequently, I began to spend less time hating and creating all these violent fantasies. It was much better to distance myself from the immediate situation, and to think pleasant things. I would think about visiting places I'd enjoyed, and created trips and vacations, and spent time with people I loved. Or I would build a house or pave a road—anything that was pleasurable and a diversion. In short, I began to live in another world out of necessity.

RICHARD QUEEN (*consular officer, at the Mushroom Inn*): Down in the Mushroom, I would escape by reliving my past, particularly my college days. The best years of my life were at Hamilton College, and those were the years I relived. I would take an incident or an event and from my memory of that event, I would build a whole scenario around it: how things might have changed if I had done this or done that. Some of my most basic fantasies revolved around a couple of women whom I'd had passionate crushes on. Unfortunately, because I was so painfully shy, none of those crushes ever came to fruition. But I would develop fantasies on what might have happened, and what life would be like if something had developed from those crushes. I knew who the people were and what they looked like, and how they would probably react. So I used them to construct scenarios. I withdrew from reality that way, by building a world out of my past.

Another thing is that I set up a college schedule for myself. I would set a time aside for studying French from a high school text I managed to get hold of. It was actually the same text I had when I was in high school. I'd spend two hours a day studying French. I'd also spend time reading history, and then I'd study an English novel. I'd read several books simultaneously, just like when I was taking college courses, because in my mind I was back at Hamilton College. That was my way of fighting depression. I was so successful that my roommate, Joe Hall, once said, "When we're released, you won't mind if I leave, will you? You can stay here with your books, but I'd like to go home and see my wife again."

GARY LEE (*general services officer, at the Mushroom Inn*): I was just trying to get through each day one hour at a time. It was miserably cold, and I'd crawl under my blanket with a book. That's how I survived. Somewhere along the line, I discovered that I read at a rate of forty-five pages an hour. No matter what size the print or what the topic was, I'd pretty much stick to that average. I was not so much interested in reading a good book as I was in getting through those pages. Forty-five pages was the primary goal. Every time I finished a section of forty-five pages it meant that I'd gotten through another hour, and I was just trying to get through one hour at a time. I'd divide my day between reading hours and the four or five cigarettes we were given each day. After getting through an hour of reading, I'd either light up a cigarette or start in on a fresh forty-five pages. That was my routine in getting through.

CORT BARNES (*communications officer, at the Mushroom Inn*): For three or four days they took away my reading privileges while I was down in the Mushroom. Only certain people were allowed to have books, and I wasn't one of them. They took all of my books away from me, which meant there was nothing for me to occupy my time with. So I just started walking in a little rectangle in my cubicle that measured three yards by one yard, which meant that one loop totaled eight yards. I had read a book called *Alexander Dolgun's Story: An American in the Gulag*. He had been kept in a very small cell in a Soviet prison, and in his book he described how he had walked out of Russia in his mind. He was familiar with the surrounding terrain, and established a route map so that when he walked so many kilometers in his cell he knew where he would be on his road map. Each day he would keep track of his progress. I figured I'd do the same thing, and walk out of Iran. Unfortunately, I didn't know anything about Iranian geography. All I knew was to head north toward the Caspian and then start swimming. So I couldn't plot a route map the way Dolgun had done. But that didn't stop me from walking. By looping my little eight-yard rectangle, I walked twenty-seven miles in three days, which had me thinking, "Geez, I must be outside of Tehran by now."

After three days, I was allowed to have books again, and I pretty much gave up on my walking. I didn't see any need to go further. Instead, I settled down with a book by Leon Uris, and started reading *Armageddon*.

CAPT. PAUL NEEDHAM (*air force logistics officer, at the Mushroom Inn*): There were periods when they would give us books, then they'd take them away for a while. Then they'd give us books again. I guess reading was something to pass the time with. But it didn't make much difference to me. I'd start reading a book, and I'd get bored with it. Even if it was a real good book. It just didn't matter what I was reading. I'd have to set it down. I'd get up and walk. I was too impatient to read. I wanted to do something. I was not willing to resign myself to being a hostage for a long period of time. I wanted out. I did not say to myself, "Well, it looks like I'm going to be here for a long time, so I'm going to do this or that during my time here." Instead, I kept thinking, "How am I getting out of here?" And I would get up and walk. Back and forth. Back and forth.

While I walked I would rehearse different scenarios for an escape. I would think: "How do I get past that guard? What do I do once I get outside? Am I going to have to take a gun and kill somebody? Where am I going to go? How do I hot-wire a car? Do I remember how to survive in the desert? Do I remember the winter survival course I learned up in Minnesota?" I'd think about all these things and use them to put together different scenarios. I spent a lot of time designing new escape routes, and this helped to pass the time.

BILL BELK (*communications officer, at the chancery*): I can honestly say that I was never happy. Never. Not once during the entire time that I was held was I actually happy. I did anything and everything I could to pass the time. I read a lot and I exercised, but it never took me away from where I was. Hour after hour would go by with me and Don Hohman cooped up in that little hole. And there was always a guard in the room, twenty-four hours a day, watching my every move. Always a pair of eyes on me. The guard sat there in a chair so close I could feel his presence.

DON HOHMAN (*army medic, at the chancery*): I figured the best way to deal with the rag heads was to push them—you know, find out how much I could get away with. I figured they might come in and beat me, but so what? I'd been beat before, and I figured I'd get beat again. I wanted to find out if I could push them to the wall or not. I wanted to find out what the limits were. So I would talk and read out loud. The Iranians would tell me to shut up, but I wouldn't pay any attention to them. I'd keep on talking. I'd talk to Bill or I'd talk to myself. They would say, "Shh! Don'ta speak! No talk! No talk!" But I wouldn't stop. When I wasn't talking to Bill, I'd walk back and forth across the cell and literally hold a conversation with myself. I'd rattle on just to piss the guards off. Or I'd sit down and read out of a book. If I ran out of things to say, I'd read out loud.

The amazing thing was that after a while the guards gave up on me. The people in the rooms around us still couldn't speak, but pretty soon instead of telling me to shut up, the guards were saying, "Don'ta speak so loud." They'd gesture with their hands and say, "Not so loud." So that's how Bill and I got to talk. I just refused not to speak. He and I would carry on conversations whenever we wanted to, and the guards wouldn't bother us. Bill and I became pretty close that way. We talked about all kinds of things. We talked about our lives back in the States, our families, and what was going on around us. And we'd cuss the rag heads.

JOHN LIMBERT (*political officer*): On January 18, I was moved out of the Mushroom and put in solitary down in the basement of the chancery. I didn't care for that move. I found it to be unsettling. Solzhenitsyn talks about the notion of "first cell, first love." No matter where you are, you eventually get used to your surroundings. It may be bad, but you develop a routine and you adapt to a particular area. You more or less settle into a place, and you never want to be moved, because being moved means readapting to a new place. It also reminds you that you're still a prisoner. So none of us liked to be moved. As bad as life in the Mushroom Inn was, it was tolerable. It was the devil I knew. While I was down there the students had brought in some board games. Gary Lee and I found that we played chess at about the same level, so that made a good match. We usually had a game or two after dinner, and that was a good way of passing the time. With the move, all of that went and that was upsetting.

Physically, my new room was not a very good place. It was a small basement room maybe ten feet by ten feet. No windows. At one time it had been part of a larger room, and the walls were made of a very thin partition, as the one room had been partitioned into smaller rooms. In the room next to me were two embassy people, Don Hohman and Bill Belk. I could hear the two of them talking, and the guards made no attempt to stop them. This was the first time I'd heard any Americans talking, so that was good. They were giving the guards a hard time, and I enjoyed listening to that. Don Hohman, in particular, was giving them a hard time about his diet. He told them that he couldn't eat any red meat, and they would continually forget this or disregard it. When that happened, he would ridicule them. He would say, "Can't you people do anything right? I told you about this the last time! Don't you talk to each other?" He would take a domineering attitude with them, and since their command of English wasn't very good, they weren't at all sure of what he was saying to them. From what I heard, Don had them completely confused. They didn't know how to deal with what he was saying, and I enjoyed listening to that.

DON HOHMAN (*army medic, at the chancery*): I have something called hypoeurocemia, and I need to take regular medication for it. The Iranians let me have my medication for about the first thirty days, but after that they wouldn't give it to me, or they would only give it to me intermittently. I knew that could cause problems. I figured that instead of running the risk of a full-blown gout attack, I'd just quit eating meat. I told the Iranians that because of my hypoeurocemia I couldn't eat any red meat. Vegetables and rice weren't any problem, and beyond that I needed seafood. I knew we had lots and lots of cocktail shrimp and canned sardines over at the commissary. So I told the Iranians where they could go to get this stuff, but a lot of times they'd keep on bringing me red meat. No matter how many times I told them I couldn't eat it, they'd keep bringing it in. I'd get pissed off and rant and rave at them. To show them I wasn't about to eat any red meat, I'd dump my bowl on top of their desk or throw it out in the hall. That would get them pissed off, but I'd just tell them that it was their fault. I wasn't getting my medication as regularly as I needed it, and if they'd quit bringing me meat that would solve the problem. Finally they came in with some seafood. They brought in jars and jars of shrimp and let me keep it in the room. After a while, I had my own private supply of seafood.

JOHN LIMBERT (*political officer, at the chancery*): One of the things about prison life is you become a pack rat. Everything you get your hands on you squirrel away somewhere, because you never know when you can use it. So every time the students gave me a pen or pencil so I could write a letter or work a crossword puzzle, I'd squirrel it away. A lot of times they would forget to ask for it back. So eventually I had a collection of pens and pencils hidden in one place or another.

Shortly after I was moved into this basement room, I established written communication with Bill Belk and Don Hohman. There was a small space at the back of the wall, which was really a partition, and when I realized that there wasn't a guard in their room we started passing notes through this space in the wall. I gave them what little news I had and they gave me what news they had, which wasn't very much because the students were making an effort to keep us isolated from news. However, I did pick up a few bits of information that I was able to pass along. Because the air was bad down there, I asked the students to keep the door to my room a little bit ajar. Some of them were willing to do this, and there was always a guard sitting in a chair right outside my door. On one or two occasions the guard got up to do something in the hall, and when he did so he left a newspaper on the chair by the door. When that happened I would go over to sneak a look, and in this way I learned about the election of Bani-Sadr as president of Iran,* and I also got the news about the people the Canadians had smuggled out. I could just see the headline and that was all, but it did confirm that six Americans had gotten out of Iran through the Canadian embassy. I didn't know who the six were or how they had managed to get away, but it was the sort of news that made me feel very good. Very good indeed. This information was passed along to Bill and Don in the room next door. Then one day, much to my surprise, a note came back through the wall that asked if I wanted a radio.

DON HOHMAN (*army medic, at the chancery*): Those rag heads could never keep track of their property. They'd come in the room and sit at the little desk to read, then they'd change guards and leave their objects lying there. So Bill Belk would steal stuff from them. One time he stole a jacket off of them, a big, fluffy jacket. Of course, he couldn't wear it because they would've seen it, so he stuffed it up a pillow case and used it as a pillow. I didn't even know he had it until a couple of weeks later, when he pulled it out and showed it to me. He said, "Look at this. Some dumb rag head left it in here." I couldn't believe it. I thought it was great. Then another time he stole a radio from them.

BILL BELK (*communications officer, at the chancery*): This one guard used to sit in the room, and he'd hold a little transistor radio up to his ear. He was one of the worst of the lot, a really surly SOB. And he was so secretive about listening to his radio that it pissed Don Hohman and me off. He was acting like he didn't want us to hear any news, but we couldn't understand Farsi anyway, so it didn't matter. This character loved to sit in there with his transistor. I knew damn well that he had

---

* Abol-Hasan Bani-Sadr was elected president of Iran on January 25, 1980.

taken that radio out of the commissary store on the compound. All of the students took radios and cameras and watches out of the store. I swear, every militant who was guarding us was walking around with a brand-new watch on his wrist. Anyway, this one guy was sitting in the room with his radio one time, and he went to sleep. He just nodded off in his chair. The radio was on the desk, and while he was sleeping I crawled over and hid the radio inside a little cubbyhole of the desk. There was a space that could be used as a letter file, and I hid the radio in there. After a while, this fellow woke up and he didn't think anything of it. He didn't even miss his radio. When they changed guards, the radio was still sitting inside that desk area. I left it in there the next day, and no one came looking for it. On the day after, I took the radio out of the desk and hid it in another part of the room.

DON HOHMAN (*army medic, at the chancery*): A couple of days later, the kid came back and looked for his radio. He didn't say anything to us about it, he just came in and looked around the room. We knew what he was looking for. But he didn't find it. By this time, Bill had the radio stashed away. The only trouble was Bill couldn't figure out what to do with it. Neither one of us could speak Farsi, so it didn't do us any good.

BILL BELK (*communications officer, at the chancery*): I didn't want to steal a radio that I couldn't use. I knew that John Limbert was in the room next door to us. I didn't know John very well, but I knew that he could speak Persian because I could hear him talking to the militants. Sometimes they'd talk in English, and sometimes they'd talk in Farsi. They would talk about politics and literature, and all kinds of things. I figured if we were going to get any news at all, I had to get that radio to somebody who spoke Farsi.

JOHN LIMBERT (*political officer, at the chancery*): Bill Belk passed a note through the space at the end of the wall that said, "We know you can speak Persian. If I can get you a radio, would you like that?" Well, is the pope Catholic? Of course I wanted a radio. One of the things that was difficult to deal with was that from the time we were taken we had absolutely no news at all. We didn't know what was happening. So I immediately sent Bill a note back: "Yes, of course. I'd love a radio."

BILL BELK (*communications officer, at the chancery*): The next time I went down to the toilet, I stuffed the radio in my pants and took it down to the bathroom with me. I hid it in a very, very dark spot underneath the radiator. It was impossible to see it unless you got down there on your hands and knees, and the bathroom was filthy. Nobody was going to go crawling around in there, so I knew that radio would be safe until John could go in and get it. After going to all the trouble of stealing it, the last thing I wanted was for an Iranian to find it. So I was very careful about hiding it.

When I got back to the room, I passed John another note and told him where I'd hidden the radio. I even drew a little diagram. It was like passing a little treasure map through the wall.

JOHN LIMBERT (*political officer, at the chancery*): I took a trip to the bathroom and picked the radio up. In my room I had a mattress on the floor, and I had an upholstered foam rubber cushion that I was using as a pillow. That was where I hid the radio. There was a zipper along one side of the cushion, so I unzipped it, tore out some of the foam rubber, and stuck the radio in there. To listen to it, I'd put my head down on the cushion, and keep the radio volume turned way down so that none of the students could hear it out in the hall. I'd press my head right against the cushion. It was important to save batteries, so I'd only turn the radio on for news broadcasts. I developed a routine where I'd listen three times a day. I'd listen at two o'clock, eight o'clock, and twelve o'clock at night. I didn't have a watch, so Bill Belk or Don Hohman would give me a two-minute warning. One of them had a watch, and they would tap on the wall two minutes before the news hour. In that way, we were able to get a regular news service going. I'd put my head down on the pillow, listen to the news, and then write a summary of whatever was going on for Bill Belk and Don Hohman.

After having had no news at all for such a long period of time, that radio was a godsend. We were getting regular news reports while the students were making a big pretense of keeping us completely isolated from news. It was a wonderful way of putting one over on them.

BILL BELK (*communications officer, at the chancery*): I knew John didn't have any trouble finding the radio, because he sent me a note that said that stealing it was a "marvelous coup." He was very happy to get it, and very graciously kept us informed about all the news he was hearing. About ten minutes after every news broadcast, John would slip a little press release through the wall.

I remember one of the first bits of news we got was that Khomeini was in the hospital with a heart condition. The Iranians devoted a lot of attention to that, and there was a lot in the news about Khomeini's health. They played that for all it was worth. Every note Limbert would pass through the wall had something in it about Khomeini's heart.

VICTOR TOMSETH (*chief political officer, at the Iranian Foreign Ministry with Bruce Laingen and Michael Howland*): Khomeini became sick and there was some question as to whether or not he would survive. During this period the Iranian newspapers were all printing offers that had been made by the revolutionary faithful to donate their hearts to Khomeini, if that was what was needed to save him. At the Foreign Ministry we got the newspapers regularly, and on one occasion I decided to sit down and write a letter to the editor of one of Tehran's newspapers. In this letter, I said that I had read about the various people who had offered to donate organs to Khomeini with a great deal of interest. I thought it was a splendid idea, because it was obvious that Khomeini could do very nicely with a new brain, but as to a new heart, he had demonstrated by his behavior in the previous months that he could get along very well without one. The three of us got a laugh out of that, and then very promptly tore up the letter.

BILL BELK (*communications officer, at the chancery*): The window in our room had a little cement culvert that led down from the outside. The actual window was below ground. It was like being in a pit. But Don Hohman and I could look up and see the sky and the tops of trees. That was about it. We couldn't see anything else. But at least we could see what the weather was like. We could see when it snowed, and we could see when the sky was blue and clear, or dark and stormy.

It was tremendously cold, and one time I was looking out at the trees and I saw the snow coming down, which was very pretty. I was watching the snow when all of a sudden I heard this female voice holler in to me: "Hello, how are you doing? It's snowing." There was a girl right there in front of the window. An Iranian girl with a G-3. I could barely see her. She was the outside guard, and she was very friendly—although I'm sure that if I'd tried to go out that window she would have blasted my head off. She said, "It's beautiful. The snow is beautiful."

I hollered up, "Yes, it is beautiful. I wish I could be out there in it."

She scooped up some snow and made me a little snowball. Then she pushed it through the broken glass so I could have some snow. So I guess there was some kindness that went along with all the bitterness of it.

CAPT. PAUL NEEDHAM (*air force logistics officer, at the Mushroom Inn*): During the month of January things started to ease up. The Iranians took the ropes off our hands, and they brought in some games that we could play to help pass the time. Of course, we'd use the games to try to communicate with other hostages. We'd drop notes in gum wrappers and try to pass around what little information we had. Joe Hall and I were playing checkers at this time. We'd play on his bed in the back of his little cell, and we managed to talk a lot while we played. We didn't play in my cubicle because it wasn't as easy to whisper. Toward the end of January things really started getting loose.

BILL BELK (*communications officer, at the chancery*): There was a big high-walled courtyard at the ambassador's residence, and one day I was taken over there. I had no idea what was going on. Without a word of explanation these guys came in, blindfolded me, and threw a blanket over my head. Then I was taken over to the courtyard. It had a rocky gravel base, and as we walked in I could feel the rocks under my feet. The guards stood me against the wall and I thought, "Oh Christ, this is it! They've taken me out to shoot me!"

But I didn't have time to react. What could I do? I was blindfolded and tied up. We all knew that the students could take us out and shoot us at any time. That was always a possibility, and that's what I thought they were going to do. I just went kind of numb. There was no real sense of terror or fear. I stood there for a minute, but instead of shooting me, they took the blanket off my head and undid my blindfold. I could look around and see the sky and the trees beyond the wall. Then it was great! Fresh air! What a nice feeling it was to be outside for the first time in over three months. The guard told me that I was there so that I could exercise. They were doing this to be nice. So I walked around the courtyard a couple of times, did some stretching, and felt the wind on my face. After about seven or eight minutes they put my blindfold back on, threw the blanket over my head again, and took me back to the chancery. That was it. That was my trip outdoors.

JOE HALL (*warrant officer, at the Mushroom Inn*): In mid-January the Iranians took me outside for the first time, so I could get some air. It had been snowing, and it was cold and crisp. Just beautiful. They took me over to the walled-in courtyard behind the ambassador's residence. It had big tall walls, so I couldn't see anything except the blue sky. There were lots of birds on the compound, wild parrots and pigeons. I remember I was savoring the sun and saw birds flying free and clear. They were so pretty that I got all choked up. I couldn't help it. I started crying.

RICHARD QUEEN (*consular officer, at the Mushroom Inn*): I remember the first time we were taken outside. To see the sun and feel its warmth and hear the birds was really quite an experience. In the Mushroom Inn, not only couldn't we see anything, we couldn't hear anything. It was like living in a tomb. So when we went out, I remember listening to the green parrots and looking at the birds flying against a cloudy gray sky. It was a beautiful and moving experience.

2 The Mock Executions

JOE HALL (*warrant officer, at the Mushroom Inn*): One night I noticed something strange. We were just about ready for bed, and I came back from the bathroom and saw that the metal door between our room and the larger room across the hall was closed. I'd never seen that done before. I thought, "That's strange. I wonder what's going on in there?"

I sat down on my mattress, in the same position I'd been in for three or four months, when I heard the door open, and I saw a group of Iranians go across the hall and into the big room. That's where they went first.

CHARLES JONES (*communications officer, at the Mushroom Inn*): It was strange, because there were very few guards around. A lot of them had disappeared. Then all of a sudden these guys burst in with masks over their faces. They were wearing fatigues, and they had guns. That was the big thing—they all had guns! They started hollering and screaming, "Get up! Get up! Move! Move! Move! Don't take anything! Get up! Move! Move! Move!"

Two of them grabbed me—one guy on each arm—and they jerked me out. I could tell where they were taking us, because we had to go up the steps.

JOE HALL (*warrant officer, at the Mushroom Inn*): I could see these guys pushing people around, and then they came in and got me. I had my hands up, and they propelled me down the hall and through the room where all the other hostages had been. That room was completely cleared out. There was a lot of gruff talk and pushing. I got kicked in the ass and pushed in the back with a gun as I was propelled along.

They took us up into the area where we used to play Ping-Pong and had a TV set prior to the embassy being taken. There were a lot of guards in that room, and they all had guns. They wore masks and shouted, "Get your hands on the wall! Do not for to speak! Get your hands on the wall!"

CHARLES JONES (*communications officer, at the Mushroom Inn*): They lined us up along the wall and made us spread our feet and put our hands on the wall.

CDR. ROBERT ENGELMANN (*naval supply corps officer, at the Mushroom Inn*): Those guys were really excited. When they lined us up against the wall, the first thing I thought was, "Negotiations must have broken down. They've got us lined up and this is the end. Negotiations must have broken down real bad."

JOE HALL (*warrant officer, at the Mushroom Inn*): They kicked my legs apart and pushed my arms up higher. It was scaring the shit out of me. They brought Rich Queen in and put him in line two or three people down from me. He couldn't get his arm up on the wall. The guards who were doing this didn't realize that he had a medical problem and couldn't get his arm up on the wall.

RICHARD QUEEN (*consular officer, at the Mushroom Inn*): In the first month or two after the takeover I used to fantasize that I was going to be shot. I'd fantasize that we were all put in front of a firing squad, and I could see that I was dead. In the fantasy, I'd say to myself: "Well, if you're going to go, you might as well go with some dignity."

And now it was happening. They literally had us up against the wall in front of a firing squad.

CHARLES JONES (*communications officer, at the Mushroom Inn*): They made us all stand there, and I could look slightly to the right and slightly to the left. I could see Rich Queen standing beside me. They were telling him to keep his arms up, and Rich kept saying, "I can't. I can't." His arm kept falling because of his disease. And Commander Sharer was giving them a hard time. He was saying, "If you bastards are going to shoot me, you're not going to shoot me in the back!" They kept telling him, "Turn around! Turn around!" And he said, "No! If you're going to shoot me, you're not going to shoot me in the back! You're going to shoot me face to face! I'm going to face you like a man!"

I'll be quite honest with you, I was frightened. I was extremely frightened. But what I said to myself was, "Okay, if they're going to shoot me, they're going to shoot me. And there is nothing, absolutely nothing, that I can do about it. At least they're not going to torture me first. They're just going to shoot us."

RICHARD QUEEN (*consular officer, at the Mushroom Inn*): I was sure that I was going to be shot. I had the normal animal reactions. My knees knocked, and I couldn't stop them. I heard the bolts snap shut and the metallic click of the safeties being taken off. I said the Lord's Prayer, which helped. It greatly comforted me, and took my mind away from the scene. Although my knees were still shaking, my mind sort of left the scene. I'd imagined what it would be like to go before a firing squad, and now I was in front of one. I can't say that I had previous experience, but the fantasies helped calm me. It was like I'd had practice. I was resigned to being shot. Fatalistic. In my mind, I knew that I was dead. I stood there waiting for what I assumed would be a loud crash, and things would sort of fade out.

JOE HALL (*warrant officer, at the Mushroom Inn*): Boy, if I have ever talked to God, I was doing some talking right then. All I could think was, "Oh God, please take care of my wife! Please take care of Cheri!" I kept saying, "Please, dear God, take care of Cheri! God, take care of Cheri!" My knees were banging together. It got very, very quiet. Almost perfectly still. It seemed like the moment was approaching. I couldn't tell if the Iranians were taking aim or not. Then suddenly my knees stopped knocking. I was steeling myself for the blast. My whole body was clenching, waiting for it to happen.

It seemed like the moment is right now! It's going to happen! We came right up to the moment when I thought they were going to fire. And then nothing happened. The moment passed. I was standing there thinking, "Well?" And then another moment passed. I was still frightened, but it seemed like the opportune moment was slipping away. A couple more seconds ticked off, and I started getting hope back. I was still terrified—this entire ordeal was still terrifying, but it was gradually becoming obvious that we had passed the point where they were going to execute us. I heard some noise behind us. Then some more noise—feet were shuffling, and someone was talking. I heard the guards telling people to move. Eventually they came up and knocked my hands off of the wall. I was so limp they practically had to pull me off of the wall.

CHARLES JONES (*communications officer, at the Mushroom Inn*): The next thing I knew, they grabbed me and very roughly took me into a little room off the library. They made me take my clothes off. There were two militants in there doing a strip search. I stripped down to my shorts, and these guys went through all of my pockets. They examined every article of clothing. Then they made me pull my shorts down so they could make sure that I wasn't hiding anything on my person. After that, they blindfolded me and took me back to my mattress area.

JOE HALL (*warrant officer, at the Mushroom Inn*): Eventually the guards got me back to our room, and I saw that it had been completely ransacked. Everything had been tossed. It was an incredible mess. The Iranians had run their grubby hands through everything and kicked things around. Not only had the room been tossed, but the mattresses weren't even the same. They'd even dragged the mattresses around. It was obvious that everything had been very thoroughly searched.

CHARLES JONES (*communications officer, at the Mushroom Inn*): When I walked in the room there was complete silence. Everybody was sitting around stunned. Completely stunned. And the room was a mess. Everything we had accumulated up to that point was gone. All of our books, letters, cigarettes, and things like that had been taken from us. Our mattresses had been kicked around and the sheets torn off. I had a little green New Testament, and that was the only book of mine they left. I sat down on my mattress, and I was still shaking. I was still upset. You know, still frightened. That's not the kind of thing you get over in a minute or two.

BILL BELK (*communications officer, at the chancery*): After they went through the mock executions in the Mushroom, they came over to the chancery and got us. I'm not sure if it was that very same night or the next night, but they did come and get us very late at night.

JOHN LIMBERT (*political officer, at the chancery*): I had my radio hidden in the cushion and I'd listened to the late news, which was over at about 12:30. After the news, I'd usually stay up and read for a couple of hours. That was a good time to read *War and Peace,* which is what I was doing that night. It must've been about 2:30 in the morning when I turned off the lights and got into bed. Just a few minutes after that, these guys burst through the door. I was still awake and alert.

ROBERT ODE (*consular officer, at the chancery*): I was in a room with Bob Blucker and Barry Rosen. At about 2:30 in the morning we were routed off our mattresses and out of a deep sleep by these guys shouting, "Stand up! Stand up! Stand up!" The terrorists were wearing camouflage uniforms and masks over their faces. One of them had his gun leveled right at me.

I looked up. "Don't point that gun at me!"

He said, "Don'ta speak! Don'ta speak!"

BRUCE GERMAN (*budget officer, at the chancery*): These guys burst through the door with their weapons and their green jackets. They all had masks on. They said that they were from security, and that they were looking for weapons. They didn't give us any choices. They said, "Stand up! Stand up! Stand up! Take your clothes off! Hurry! Right now! Right now!" They shoved us out in the hall, and we had to stand up against the wall and assume the classic spread-eagle position.

BILL BELK (*communications officer, at the chancery*): Somewhere during this time they showed me a picture of some naked people who had been executed. The people in the photos were completely nude, and they'd had their heads blown off. Then in that hallway, they told us to strip off all of our clothes. There was a guard behind each one of us with a gun to our heads. I remembered the pictures, and I thought, "Oh my God, what is this?" Don Hohman was right next to me, and they said, "Put your head against the wall!" They wanted our heads touching the concrete, and Don hadn't moved his head close enough, so they smacked his head against the wall. Smacked him hard.

MALCOLM KALP (*economics officer, at the chancery*): I put my head against the wall. They were behind me with their rifles. My thought was: "Well, they've got a G-3 rifle and it has a large-caliber slug in it. When they shoot me I won't feel a thing. I'll go fast."

BRUCE GERMAN (*budget officer, at the chancery*): They kept cocking the guns and cocking the guns. Threatening us, and cocking the guns. I was standing in my drawers in this cold hallway, and my legs were trembling. I thought that was it. When I heard them cocking those weapons a few feet from my head, I assumed they were going to execute us. So I just started praying. I started praying for all I was worth, which helped take my mind off what was going on behind me. I felt worse for my family than I did for myself. At least I knew what was going on. But they were back home and would have to wake up to the news that I'd been shot. I thought about what a terrible disaster it was going to be for them.

DON HOHMAN (*army medic, at the chancery*): In the moment before you think you're going to be shot, everything stops. Your heart stops. Your breathing stops. Your pulse stops. It's like you're totally suspended in air—like jumping off a mountain, and all you feel is the flip-flop of your stomach.

JOHN LIMBERT (*political officer, at the chancery*): It was cold, very cold, standing there in the hall, I remember that. And I remember being scared. Even though I was frightened, I also remember thinking, "They probably won't shoot us here." If we were out in a courtyard somewhere it would have seemed much more plausible, but not in a basement where bullets could ricochet around. It just didn't seem logical. If you're going to execute people, you take them outside—at least that had been the pattern established in the revolution. People had usually been executed in courtyards or on the roofs of buildings, but not inside. They were chambering the rounds behind us, and I can't say I wasn't scared, because I was. And I remember thinking, "Maybe we are going to be shot. Maybe it is going to happen." It was certainly very possible. But I was also thinking, "Probably not. Not in here." There was such a flair for the dramatic in this sort of action. Remember that many of the people in charge of us had spent time in jail themselves, and this was the sort of thing that had happened in the shah's prisons. A common tactic in the SAVAK jails was to have things happen after midnight. They would try to get to people when they were asleep and psychologically least prepared—get to them when their resistances were down. So there was this sense of the dramatic in what the students were doing. And I knew that this sense of the dramatic was something the students wanted.

ROBERT ODE (*consular officer, at the chancery*): We stood there for what seemed an interminable period of time. Then I was pulled out of line, and the terrorists took me down to the end of the hall and into another room. I was told to strip completely, and they gave me a GI-style examination. They took my belt off of my trousers and went through everything. They didn't leave a stitch untouched. I had two letters in one of my pockets, and they confiscated both of those. Then they gave me my clothes and told me to get dressed again.

DON HOHMAN (*army medic, at the chancery*): We had one guy who literally went into shock. That mock execution scared him silly. And I don't blame him, because I was scared too. He was down on the floor doing push-ups like crazy. His adrenaline was driving him so hard that he couldn't settle down. He was practically driving himself through the floor, and I was trying to get this guy to settle down. I had some Atarax in my pack, and I gave him three of those. I think the stress of the entire situation had been building in him. The stress was getting to everybody. After a while, stress can have an effect that's sort of like building blocks, and this firing squad routine, on top of everything else we'd been through, sent this guy shocky.

ROBERT ODE (*consular officer, at the chancery*): Everything in our room was utter chaos. Our mattresses had been overturned and everything was scattered about. We got things sort of back in order, and I lay down on the mattress. I must've had a delayed reaction to fright, because my heart started pounding so hard that I thought it was going to burst out of my chest. My heart was just hammering away. I thought I was having a heart attack. I was sure that was what was happening. I laid there perfectly still, because there wasn't anything else I could do, and I thought, "This is the end. I'm finished now." My heart just kept pounding and pounding at an incredibly rapid rate. This went on for several minutes. Then, after what seemed like an eternity, my heartbeat gradually began to slow down. Finally it settled back into its normal beat, and I was all right.

After a while I had to go to the toilet, and one of the guards who was a little more lenient took me down to the bathroom and then brought me back. He didn't speak English very well, but on the way back to my room he did say, "These men were not ours. They were very angry." What precipitated that raid I don't know. But this one guy did offer a sort of semi-apology by saying it wasn't their group that was responsible, but that it was an outside group. What faction they were, or what they were angry about, I don't know.

JOE HALL (*warrant officer, at the Mushroom Inn*): The next day, the guards took me into the room where they'd had the Christmas ceremony. As a matter of fact, the Christmas tree was still in there. This was a month and a half later, and they hadn't gotten rid of the tree. I was with five other hostages. Hamid the Liar was standing in front of us, and of all things, he gave us some mail. I thought that was odd. This was only the second time I'd received any mail. The other time was at Christmas. He was trying to be very nonchalant and act like nothing had happened. I said, "Now what the shit was that about last night?"

Hamid said, "Oh, that was just a joke."

"Some goddamn joke. Why did you do that?"

Hamid told us that was a different group of guards. He said it was the exterior guards who came in and did it, it wasn't our regular group of interior guards. He told us that the interior guards had tried to talk them out of doing it, but the exterior guards came in and did it anyhow. Now I don't know whether that's true or not, or what their purpose was in doing it. But Hamid was sort of apologetic, without really coming out and apologizing. His disavowal of any responsibility was sort of like an apology.

DON HOHMAN (*army medic, at the chancery*): I don't know why the rag heads took us through that mock execution. Later some of the guards told me that it was the perimeter guards who had done it. They were saying, "We're sorry. We didn't know that was going to happen." And I could sense that they were actually sorry. They were embarrassed by it. I didn't realize there were different factions of guards right there on the compound until that moment. That was an eerie realization. It just added to all the uncertainty we were living with.

JOHN LIMBERT (*political officer, at the chancery*): They had searched my room and had taken a heavy water pitcher and a fork. The radio was still hidden in my cushion, but they didn't find it. So I still had the radio. I don't know if they thought the pitcher or the fork could be used as weapons of some kind or not. In the next room, I can remember hearing one of the students refer to this as a "shakedown." I thought that was interesting, because it was a piece of slang that most of them wouldn't have known. It suggested that they were looking for hidden weapons or something like that. But who knows what they were after? The whole thing had the feel of something out of a prison movie. They liked to create this flair for the dramatic.

Over the next couple of days I tried to get my eating utensils back from them, and was able to do so. When they brought me my meal, I'd say, "Hey, give me my fork. What am I supposed to eat with?"

The guard who had brought the meal would say, "Well, where is it?"

"Your friends took it away."

They were sort of apologetic at that point. I had the feeling that another group had been responsible for all of this. So the guard said, "Okay, I'll see what I can do." Then he went out and managed to dig up a fork for me. Within a couple of days my water pitcher was also returned. In a sense, their own disorganization was a godsend. It helped to make life tolerable. If one group of guards decided that they were going to take your fork away, the other group wouldn't know about it and would give you your fork back.

BILL BELK (*communications officer, at the chancery*): Later, I was told that one of the hostages had tried to commit suicide by slitting his wrists, and that was why they had their terror raid and ransacked all of the rooms. That happened the night before the raid. Apparently someone managed to get his hands on a very sharp object. The Iranians were extremely paranoid to begin with. When they realized that this one guy had a weapon, they were afraid there might be some more weapons lying around, and they went berserk!

MALCOLM KALP (*economics officer, at the chancery*): No matter where I went, I had a weapon. I lived by the two Ws: a weapon and a wedge. My thinking was that if the United States ever sent a rescue team in after us, I wanted to have a wedge to brace the door and a weapon to fight for my life with. I figured I'd wedge the door closed until I heard an American say, "Who's behind that door?" Then I'd step out and say, "Hey, here I am."

A weapon and a wedge, the two Ws, stayed with me the whole way through. The weapon could have been anything I could use to fight with, ranging from a heavy cast-iron tape dispenser that I found, to a piece of glass or a twenty-penny nail. As a matter of fact, I had a knife belt* that I kept for ninety-three days. I kept that knife until the night in February when the terrorists came bursting through the door and put us up against the wall. They ransacked my whole room, and they found my knife belt on my pants, which were under my pillow. They took it and never said a word to me about it. Later on, I found that one of the Americans had tried to commit suicide, and that was the reason for the shakedown. The Iranians were looking for weapons.

CDR. ROBERT ENGELMANN (*naval supply corps officer, at the Mushroom Inn*): If I had to pick a worst time, that was it, when they lined us all up against the wall. The experience itself wasn't so bad, but after it was over I started to question my ability to survive the entire ordeal. That convinced me that these guys were going to shoot us whether they wanted to or not. They were crazy. Literally crazy. Up to that time it had just been a joke—a bunch of amateur terrorists running all over the place. But after that, I knew that if they were told, "Go in there and shoot the hostages," these guys would have done it. The same guy that smiled at you in the morning while serving tea would have smiled at you as he put you up against the wall. There was no doubt in my mind of that. Had that mock execution not happened, the ongoing period of captivity would have been much less demanding on me mentally and psychologically. Even though their threats were never realized, it worked on you and took its toll.

CHARLES JONES (*communications officer, at the Mushroom Inn*): Every now and then the Iranians would give us chewing gum, and we would use the little tin foil wrappers to write messages in. That was one of the ways we passed information while we were down in the Mushroom Inn. We'd roll the tin foil into a little ball, and as soon as the guard turned his head, we'd throw it to the guy across from us. He'd read the note and throw it to the next guy. So we had our own little grapevine going. The messages would say things like: "Colonel Schaefer has been seen. He's all right." Which was important news, because he had dis-

---

* A knife belt has a blade attached to the buckle that fits into the belt to keep it hidden.

appeared from the Mushroom and no one knew what had happened to him. So it was comforting to know that he was still all right.

The Iranians didn't like us passing notes at all. They wanted absolutely no communication among any of the hostages. That was something they were very strict about. So we had to be careful when we passed messages back and forth, because the guards threatened us with isolation if we were caught. That was one of the punishments. And I didn't want to be isolated from the others. The one good thing about the Mushroom was that I felt safety in numbers. It was very comforting to look around and see other Americans.

COL. CHARLES SCOTT (*military attaché, at the Mushroom Inn*): Even though we weren't supposed to talk with one another, we developed a pretty good communications system down in the Mushroom. We were writing notes in gum wrappers and passing them from cell to cell, and writing messages on toilet paper rolls. Then one night Joe Subic was moved into the Mushroom. I knew that Joe had helped the Iranians on the day of the takeover by identifying American personnel for them and that sort of thing. But that had been a very frightening time. I figured, "Hey, people screw up. Don't hold it against him forever." So I let Subic in on some of our communications, and included him in on the information that was being passed among us.

CAPT. PAUL NEEDHAM (*air force logistics officer, at the Mushroom Inn*): They moved one hostage into the Mushroom, and this guy seemed to have a free rein. Too free of a rein. He was moving around and talking, and was just too loose in his actions. Right away I realized what was going on. It was a set-up. I don't think too many of the other hostages realized it, but I suspected that the Iranians had planted this guy so they could identify who was communicating with whom and put a stop to it. So I stayed away from this particular individual. Others included him in on things.

COL. CHARLES SCOTT (*military attaché, at the Mushroom Inn*): Joe Subic was down in the Mushroom for exactly three days and two nights. On the afternoon of the third day, Hamid the Liar came down and told Joe to gather up his things. They took him out. When I saw that I knew we'd had it. Trouble was on the way. We'd been set up.

CAPT. PAUL NEEDHAM (*air force logistics officer, at the Mushroom Inn*): This individual was moved out of the Mushroom at about eleven o'clock at night, and I had a feeling that something was going to happen. Then, sure enough, that night we had another shakedown and mock execution.

They lined us up, told us to put our hands against the wall, step back and lean into the wall. They had their guns behind us, and we were in the same position we had been in in February. Even though I was frightened, I knew they'd done this once before. I was thinking, "Come on, guys. Can't you think of something more original?"

CPL. STEVEN KIRTLEY (*marine security guard*): I was with Jim Lopez when we had one of the mock executions, and Jim was kind of radical. The Iranians came in, put their guns on us, and led us out into the hall. When those guys stuck a rifle in my face and told me to get up against the wall, I got up against the wall. But not Jim. He was screaming at them: "Hey, what the fuck's going on? What are you guys doing? Get your hands off me!" He was saying these things, and I was thinking, "Jim! Jim! Shut up! Shut up! They're going to shoot you in the head! Shut up! Man, shut up!"

SGT. JAMES LOPEZ (*marine security guard*): They lined us up against the wall, and there were people behind us with masks over their faces and rifles to the back of our heads. I turned on the guy behind me and knocked his hands away. I said, "Fuck this shit!" And I sat down.

The guy pointed his rifle at me and said, "You must stand! You must put your hands on the wall!"

"Fuck you!" I said. "What are you going to do, shoot me?" I just sat there.

They didn't know what to do. Pretty soon, they told everybody else to sit down.

JOE HALL (*warrant officer, at the Mushroom Inn*): There was all the pushing and shoving and running us up to the wall again, but that second mock execution never did take on the atmosphere of the first one. After it was over, the guards were very hostile to us for about three or four days. They took all our books away, and we had nothing to do but sit there on our mattresses in that underground tomb. I swear, I've never been so bored in all my life. There was absolutely nothing to do. Even though the guards were denying us reading privileges, they had books stacked up on shelves to keep people from seeing the person next to them. Jim Lopez took a book off the shelf and started reading it. One of the Iranians came up and yanked it out of his hands. Jim was angry to begin with. He was always very hostile toward the Iranians, and when that guard grabbed the book away from him he was practically frothing at the mouth. Jim jumped up and took a swing at the guy.

SGT. JAMES LOPEZ (*marine security guard, at the Mushroom Inn*): They handcuffed me and stuck me in one of the back rooms. This was still winter, and very cold. All I had on were my Levis. I wasn't wearing a shirt, so I was really cold. I bent my handcuffs all to shit. I was trying to get my hands free, but I couldn't quite pop the rivet. They gave me an old cushion to sit on, and I tore the cover off of it and used that ratty old cover as a blanket.

This one guard, who was a real asshole, would come in with my food like he was doing me a big favor. I told him to stuff it up his ass, and started to argue with him. I said, "You're either going to have to kill me or let me go. If you kill me you're going to get a bad public reaction. If you let me go, I'm going to tell the world what you're doing right now."

They kept me in that room for about two weeks. I can't even remember how I killed the time. I just kind of blanked out on it. I really did.

COL. CHARLES SCOTT (*military attaché*): After the second mock execution, I was moved out of the Mushroom and thrown into solitary confinement in the chancery. Of course, the obvious inference was that Joe Subic had been planted in the Mushroom by the Iranians so they could find out who was communicating and how they were doing it. As soon as he reported to them, I was identified as one of the ringleaders and taken out altogether.

They threw me into the money vault down in the basement of the chancery. It was a sealed vault, and there was no light in there at all. The Iranians tossed me in there and left me sitting in the dark. It was so black that I couldn't even see my hand in front of my face. I had a mattress on the floor. There were some rats in the vault with me. The rats were annoying at first, but after a while I got used to them.

The guards kept the lights off for about two weeks. That was part of my punishment for passing notes. Of course I couldn't read, but I could still exercise. I pretty much divided my day into two big exercise periods, and I would do all of the exercise that I could handle. I'd run in place, do sit-ups, push-ups, and run in place some more. I'd keep going until I was wringing wet. Vigorous physical exertion was a big asset in controlling nervous tension. It also helped me sleep at night. And I did sleep well during those two weeks. Of course, another reason for exercise was that if a situation ever presented itself where I could escape, I wanted to be in good enough shape. There were many, many times in that vault when I envisioned myself getting free and walking west—walking miles and miles away from Tehran.

3 Rumors of Release

IN LATE JANUARY of 1980 an avenue of communication finally opened between the United States and Iran. At the behest of Foreign Minister Sadegh Ghotbzadeh, a French attorney and an Argentine businessman served as intermediaries. In a series of clandestine meetings that took place in four different countries, with the intermediaries shuttling back and forth between representatives of the two governments, the United States and Iran developed a scenario to resolve the hostage crisis. The plan called for a United Nations Commission of Inquiry to be sent to Tehran on a fact-finding mission to investigate Iran's grievances against the shah, and to visit each of the American hostages. As soon as the commission completed its inquiry, the Iranian government would transfer the hostages from the custody of the militants to its own protection. The commission would then leave Iran and deliver its report to Secretary-General Kurt Waldheim for publication. Two days later, the hostages would be flown out of Iran and Secretary-General Waldheim would release an exchange of statements between the United States and Iran. The American statement would reaffirm Iran's right to self-determination, pledge noninterference in Iran's internal affairs, and recognize the grievances of the Iranian people. The Iranian statement would admit to "the moral wrong of holding hostages," and promise to "respect international law."

In order to initiate the process agreed upon in this scenario, the United Nations commission flew to Tehran on February 23, 1980. For the next two weeks, the Commission of Inquiry reviewed government documents, received affidavits, and listened to testimony from a variety of sources, including hundreds of witnesses who claimed to have been tortured by the shah's secret police, SAVAK. As the commission proceeded with its task, the hostages remained in the custody of the student militants at the embassy.

BILL BELK (*communications officer, at the chancery*): After the mock executions, everything settled back down and the guards tried to pretend it had never happened. For some reason, they were being much more congenial. They brought a little space heater into the room to help keep us warm, and they brought us plastic cups of hot tea in the morning. Don and I slept late because we didn't have anything else to do, and the guards set our tea in front of the space heater to keep it warm for us. Maybe they thought a release was in the wind. I figured that was why they were trying to be nice.

The most amazing thing about the mock executions and the way they searched our rooms was that John Limbert kept the radio. That really surprised me, because they did a very thorough search. There wasn't an article of clothing or piece of bedding left untouched. They'd even gone so far as to shine a flashlight up my asshole, to make sure I hadn't hidden anything in my rectum. But John still had his cushion with the radio stuffed in the foam rubber. That was great. Our press releases kept coming through the wall. I remember it was obvious that there was still a lot of factional infighting going on within Iran. There were political assassinations and bombings and things like that reported in the news. It was apparent that the revolutionary situation was still very chaotic.

JOHN LIMBERT (*political officer, at the chancery*): At one point, Bill Belk and Don Hohman got caught passing a note through the wall. It was actually very funny. I had been taken out for a shower, and while I was gone they sent a note over. Not realizing that I was gone, when I didn't pick the note up, they banged on the wall. I guess the students were searching the room, and there was a guard in there who saw the note and took it. The note had some things in it about the U.N. commission. It was the sort of thing that let them know that we were getting news from somewhere, when they were trying very hard to isolate us from news. This was precisely the type of thing that we weren't supposed to know about. But they never said a word to me about that note. Not a word. They did search the room, but they never found the radio. If that note caused them to be puzzled as to how we were getting news, then so much the better.

CAPT. PAUL NEEDHAM (*air force logistics officer, at the Mushroom Inn*): In February there was a lot of commotion. It seemed like something big was going on. Somebody had picked up some information that a big commission was in Iran and negotiations were going on. We should hear something in a couple of weeks. That's the kind of news that was being passed around.

VICTOR TOMSETH (*chief political officer, at the Iranian Foreign Ministry with Bruce Laingen and Michael Howland*): We did meet with the members of the United Nations commission at the Foreign Ministry. They had just arrived in Tehran, and they were reasonably optimistic. They had already had some meetings with Iranian government officials, and they emphasized that they had obtained an agreed-upon scenario—agreed upon not only by the United States, but by the Iranians as well. So they were hopeful that they were going to be able to bring about a resolution.

DON HOHMAN (*army medic, at the chancery*): We'd get the news from Limbert, and one day everything would be looking good, and then the next day we'd get a news report saying there was a snag in the negotiations.* Then we'd get a note saying that there was going to be a breakthrough any minute. It was up and down, up and down. Whenever the news was good, Bill would get excited. He'd say, "We're going home. I just know it. We're going to be out of here in two weeks."

I'd say, "Wait a minute, Bill. These are Iranians we're talking about. They don't know what they're doing. Nobody in the government has any power. It's all up to Khomeini. Those negotiations might not mean a thing." No matter whether the news was good or bad, I was a pessimist. I had a feeling that the time wasn't right. I didn't think that the Iranians were going to follow through.

As a matter of fact, I got to where I hated that radio, because it was such an up and down thing. It was like a roller coaster ride with your emotions. And that's hard to live with.

BILL BELK (*communications officer, at the chancery*): There had been rumors all along, but in early March, all of the news that we were getting from the radio was good. After two or three weeks of confusion and contradictions, the United Nations commission had arrived in Iran, and discussions with them did take place. So that was a time of great hope.

I think some of the students even thought we were going home. They normally didn't talk about any of that with us, but a couple of times they let things slip. They'd hint that negotiations were going on, and we'd ask them about it. We'd say, "Hey, when is something going to happen? When are we getting out of here?"

They'd say, "Maybe tomorrow." Or, "Soon, soon." That was their favorite word. "Soon."

* After the arrival of the United Nations commission on February 23, 1980, numerous contradictory statements were made by members of the Revolutionary Council, the Iranian government, and Ayatollah Khomeini, who suggested that the fate of the hostages would be determined by the yet-to-be-elected Iranian parliament. In spite of all the confusion and political infighting, the United Nations commission continued with its appointed task, hoping that President Bani-Sadr and Foreign Minister Sadegh Ghotbzadeh would eventually be able to engineer the scenario through to its agreed-upon conclusion.

WILLIAM ROYER (*director of academic courses, at the chancery*): In the chancery I was rooming with Bill Keough and Cort Barnes. Every morning we could hear chanting outside. I think the Iranian army had put soldiers or revolutionary guards on the compound, and every morning they would do their calisthenics—"Ump-two-three-four." And we could hear them. One morning shortly after sunrise, they were running at double time around the parade field in the center of the compound, and chanting: "Let the hostages go! Let the hostages go! The other half! The other half!" I heard this very distinctly.

I deduced that they represented the half of the population that was in favor of letting us go. I understand that there was a great deal of debate going on at the time, and even among the revolutionary guard types there was a cadre that would have been happy to see us on our way.

JOHN LIMBERT (*political officer, at the chancery*): At the time of the United Nations commission's visit to Iran, things looked very good for a while. I heard on the Thursday noon news that the students had made an announcement and said that they were going to turn us over to the Iranian government. Prior to this announcement there had been a dispute. The government wanted to allow the United Nations commission to come in and see all of the hostages, and this was something that the students objected to. It more or less reached a stalemate; then the students finally said, "All right, we are simply going to wash our hands of the whole matter." And the announcement was made that we were going to be turned over to the government, which I heard on the Thursday noon news.

VICTOR TOMSETH (*chief political officer, at the Iranian Foreign Ministry with Bruce Laingen and Michael Howland*): At this time, Sadegh Ghotbzadeh was working to have the hostages transferred from the students to the custody of the Iranian government. He was very interested in having the commission succeed. In many respects, it was his baby. He recognized that the continuation of United States diplomats being held hostage was doing far more damage to Iran than it was to anyone else. He wanted to put an end to it, and he worked very assiduously toward that goal. He did so not because he liked America or because he thought the holding of hostages was morally wrong, but because he thought that it was in Iran's best interest to end this thing. At one point Ghotbzadeh himself was quite confident that this was going to happen. That was the first time Bruce and Mike and I met him. He came into our room and very confidently told us that all of the hostages were going to be delivered to the Foreign Ministry within twenty-four hours. Immediately thereafter, some metal lockers were very, very hurriedly brought into the room where we were staying, and they were put up in preparation for the arrival of the others. Bruce and Mike and I discussed some of the logistical problems that would result from our having over fifty people in this one room, and we made some initial preparations, such as creating a schedule for the use of the washrooms.

BILL BELK (*communications officer, at the chancery*): The news we were getting from the radio was extremely optimistic. All of the signs were positive. After it was announced that the students were going to relinquish the custody of the hostages and turn us over to the Iranian government, I was absolutely certain that a release was at hand. I was sure of it. This was an extremely positive sign. I was pumped up and ready to go.

CAPT. PAUL NEEDHAM (*air force logistics officer, at the Mushroom Inn*): On the seventh of March, we had a visit from someone in the Iranian government. The students came around at about nine o'clock in the morning with a piece of paper for us to fill out. They had all these questions on it: How have the students been treating you? How was the food? Things like that. I answered truthfully, saying that I hadn't actually been physically tortured, but I'd suffered everything short of it. After a while the students came around and picked up the questionnaires. I guess they weren't very happy with our answers, because I think most of us answered truthfully.

Later, I came to find out that we were supposed to have been handed over to the Iranian government on that day. Who knows? Maybe we sank ourselves. But I doubt it. Anyway, we thought something was going to happen.

*

BY MARCH 8, 1980, the United Nations Commission of Inquiry had completed its investigation into the alleged crimes of the shah. The next step in the agreed-upon scenario was to have the hostages transferred from the embassy into the protective custody of the Iranian government. Iranian President Abol-Hasan Bani-Sadr and Foreign Minister Sadegh Ghotbzadeh were both in favor of proceeding with the transfer, and Ghotbzadeh indicated that he had the support of Ayatollah Khomeini. However, some of the radical members of the Revolutionary Council, such as Ayatollah Behesti and Ahmed Khomeini, wanted to thwart the transfer of the hostages and sabotage the agreement.

At 11:30 in the morning on March 8, 1980, a letter from Bani-Sadr was delivered to the student militants ordering them to release the hostages to the Iranian government. As preparations for the transportation of the hostages to the Foreign Ministry were being put into effect, Ahmed Khomeini, the ayatollah's son, intervened by saying that his father had never approved of the transfer as Ghotbzadeh claimed. Demonstrators soon arrived at the embassy to protest the transfer, and the student militants said Ghotbzadeh was "a liar" and refused to make the hostages available to the Iranian government.

The following day, an emergency session of the Revolutionary Council was convened in which the transfer of the hostages was bitterly debated. The end result of the meeting was that Ayatollah Khomeini demanded that the United Nations Commission of Inquiry issue a statement of its findings prior to its departure from Iran, so that Khomeini could be certain that the commission had done its work "honestly." If Khomeini was pleased by their statement, he would order the students to let the commission visit the hostages. The question of whether or not the hostages would actually be transferred or released was not addressed.

The members of the commission felt that Khomeini's demand for a preliminary statement was a serious deviation from the agreed-upon scenario, which amounted to political blackmail and compromised its integrity. On March 11, 1980, the Commission of Inquiry left Iran without ever visiting the American embassy. The scenario had fallen apart, and the hostages remained in the hands of the student militants.

BILL BELK (*communications officer, at the chancery*): Within forty-eight hours of the students' announcement that they were going to turn us over to the government, it came over the news that the deal had fallen through. I guess the Revolutionary Council met and decided that the positions of the Iranian government and the U.N. commission were not in harmony with the thinking of some of the more radical clergy. There was obviously a great deal of in-fighting going on in Iran between the government and certain members on the Revolutionary Council. Khomeini sided with the more radical faction, and that sealed our doom.

JOHN LIMBERT (*political officer, at the chancery*): To say that I was disappointed would be an understatement. Not only did I hear on the news that the whole thing had fallen apart, and that we were going to remain in the hands of the students, but I could hear the demonstrations outside the embassy. What I could hear was a demonstration of a very different quality from the normal ones. It was very hysterical, and it sounded small and less organized. It was clearly a very hard-core group of people who were determined to stay out in front of the embassy, as if to say that we were going to be delivered to the government over their dead bodies. It had that kind of hysterical atmosphere. It was not like the previous very well-orchestrated demonstrations that had been going on in the past.

VICTOR TOMSETH (*chief political officer, at the Iranian Foreign Ministry with Bruce Laingen and Michael Howland*): When the United Nations commission initiative collapsed in March of 1980, Ghotbzadeh was terribly disappointed. He went on Iranian national television and roundly castigated the students for having sabotaged an arrangement which he believed served Iran's interests. The very act of his doing so showed a considerable amount of political courage, at a time when exhibitions of political courage in Iran were extremely rare. But he didn't care a whole lot about the consequences or possible repercussions.

I think this incident demonstrated rather dramatically that Ghotbzadeh and Bani-Sadr were not able to deliver the goods. They just didn't have the necessary constituency to pull a resolution off. The process of their being pushed aside by the more radical Islamic types had already begun. More than any other people, the failure of this initiative served the interests of the radical Islamic types such as Ayatollah Behesti and Ayatollah Khameini*—and did so at the expense of Ghotbzadeh and Bani-Sadr.

4 Surviving

BILL BELK (*communications officer, at the chancery*): After the collapse of the United Nations commission, we fell into a pattern of continuous boredom. Absolute boredom. Everything was boring. The books, the food. Everything. I think we had brussels sprouts for forty straight days. I hated the damn things. I called them "little green awfuls," and tried to throw them through the crack in the window just to get rid of them. During that same stretch we had chicken noodle soup for fifty-seven consecutive days. We'd have bread and tea in the morning, and soup in the evening.

In order to help pass the time, I'd do a lot of drawing. I can't just sit down and draw from my mind's eye. I have to have a picture. I need

* Ayatollah Ali Khameini, a member of Iran's Revolutionary Council, should not be confused with Ayatollah Ruhollah Khomeini.

something in front of me. Well, one day I was incredibly bored and I drew a picture of Khomeini onto the wall, because it was the only picture in the room. And I had to draw on the wall because I didn't have any paper. Ahmed, one of the guards, came in, saw the picture of Khomeini, and said, "Oh, that is very good. I will bring you something."

The next thing I knew, I had pencils and paper so I could draw. I even had Scotch tape. They gave me some propaganda books that had pictures in them, and I drew from those pictures. I drew pictures of Ayatollah Behesti, Mohammed Mossadeq, and another picture of Khomeini. The students got real excited about that. I guess they thought that psychologically I was coming over to their side or something. In fact, they liked the pictures so much that they put them into one of their little revolutionary magazines. When this publication came out, they brought it in to me and showed me eight or ten pictures in there that I had drawn. They wouldn't tell me what the printed text said underneath the pictures, and I couldn't read Farsi. But later on, I learned that it said I was thinking along the lines of the great Khomeini and all this other bullshit. Which I wasn't. I was just drawing to pass the time, and those were the only pictures I had to draw from. To me a face was a face. It didn't matter who it was. It was just a way to pass the time.

The militants kept coming into the room to look at my pictures. I had them taped up on the wall, and pretty soon the students started requesting that I draw pictures of them. Which I did. I'd sketch a portrait, sign it, and date it.

I recall one guard in particular. We had to ask permission to go to the toilet, and for some reason this guy would never touch us. All of the other guards would take us by the arms and lead us out the door. But this guy would blindfold us, then take two paper towels and use them to guide us down the hall so that he would never have to touch us. I guess he thought we were dirty Americans who had lots of germs. He came in and wanted me to draw a picture of him.

I said, "Why would somebody who doesn't want to touch me want a picture I've drawn?"

He said, "I will pay you. I will pay you."

"What are you going to pay me?"

He went out, and came back with my own watch. It was the watch they had taken away from me in November. He held it up and said, "This—for you drawing picture."

I figured, "What the hell? It's worth it to get the watch, even though somebody else will probably come in and take it away again later." So I drew the guy's picture and got my watch back.

This went on for quite a while. The students kept coming in and wanting me to draw for them. Which is how I spent a lot of my time.

COL. THOMAS SCHAEFER (*defense attaché, at the chancery*): I spent approximately 100 days in solitary confinement. After my interrogations ended, I was taken over to the chancery and kept in a room there. While I was in solitary, I developed a schedule that kept me busy practically every minute of the day. On my first trip to the library, I found four German-language textbooks, and I thought, "Gee, this is beautiful." And I proceeded to learn German.

My basic routine was as follows. I'd get up in the morning, and after breakfast I would spend two or three hours studying German. Then I would do an hour of yoga, and would spend an hour walking around the room. I measured every room that I was kept in, and determined how many laps equaled a mile. In one room I was walking 146 laps per mile, and I was usually walking at a pace of about three miles per hour. I had a deck of cards there, and as I walked I would turn over a card every ten laps to help me maintain my lap count. I would also try to keep my mind active. I did a lot of what is called "constructive visualization." As I was walking around the room, I would visualize hikes I had taken in Yosemite National Park with my family, or I would visualize and redrive family trips. It was important to remember the warm things, things that were uplifting to me. I also did a lot of singing when I walked. I'd sing hymns, or popular songs, or patriotic songs. Any kind of song. I'd sing out loud until the militants told me not to. They honestly thought that I was sending out coded messages in my songs, and they would come into the room and tell me not to sing. When they did that I would just keep on walking, and mouth the words as I went and sing in my mind.

After my morning walk it was usually time for lunch. I would eat, and then begin the afternoon by reading. I enjoy challenging books, and I love history. So I set aside some time for serious reading. It was during this time that I would catch up on the "Great Books." That collection was in our hostage library. I read Herodotus and Thucydides, and a lot of the great classics, a lot of history and philosophy. After reading for two or three hours, I would give myself a couple hours of free time. That's when I would play cards or write letters. I found it was very therapeutic for me to sit down and write. Even though I knew most of my letters were not being mailed back to the States, I would write to my wife and tell her how my day was going. I'd try to focus on the positive things, and tell her about the books I was reading, or the amount of exercise I was getting. I would then do some more exercise, and some more reading. That was how I structured my day and spent the majority of my time.

In the evening, I kept a record of each day, which I recorded in my diary. Somewhere between Christmas and the first of January, I was able to get my hands on a Good News version of the Bible, and I got the idea that I could use this Bible as a diary by poking pinholes on certain pages. Each page represented a single day in captivity, and it was here that I would record the events of my day. My code was as follows: on the first line of the page, I would put a dot over the number of miles that I walked. If I had walked six miles, then I'd make a pinhole over the sixth letter of the first line. On the second line, I would record the total number of hours that I spent exercising. And on the third line I recorded a self-evaluation. This was one of the most important things I did. That self-evaluation helped me more than anything. It was based on a scale of one to five. Number one was a very good day, two was a good day, three was a satisfactory day, four was a bad day, and five was a very bad day. At the end of each day, I would ask myself: "How did Tom Schaefer do today?" Then I would put a pinhole over the letter corresponding to the number of my evaluation.

During the time in captivity, my evaluations ran the entire range. I had number one days to number five days. But when I decoded my diary, I found that about 90 percent of my days were number three or better. Satisfactory or better. That's because I didn't need much to have a satisfactory day. Basically, I only needed three things: a warm room, enough food to stay alive, and a book to read. If I had those three things, then that would normally be a number three day or better. A letter from home could give me several number one days in a row. That was something that would keep me going. I think my wife wrote me over 200 times, and I received four of those letters. So those four letters were very important.

It may sound surprising, but in going through my routine there were times in solitary when I was actually happy. There were days that didn't seem long enough. I would want to accomplish more, and wouldn't be ready to go to bed. I also found that because my days were productive, I slept well at night. I'd go to bed feeling very good about the fact that I'd had four hours of exercise, and that I'd read a good book. I was proud of the fact that I was learning German, history and philosophy. And most of all, I was proud of the fact I was doing well. That self-evaluation was important, because the momentum begins to build on itself. Each night you're saying to yourself: "Hey, you're doing all right. You can handle this. You're going to survive." One of the things I learned in the "Dynamics of International Terrorism" school was that the longer you're in captivity, the better your chances are of coming out alive. The most dangerous time is right after you've been captured. That is when most of the killings occur. The second most hazardous time of any captive period is the release, so I was aware of that too. But all the time I was staying in solitary, I knew I was slowly improving my chances of getting out alive.

JOE HALL (*warrant officer, at the Mushroom Inn*): The whole time that Rich Queen and I were together in the Mushroom Inn, we were never allowed to speak. We did a lot of whispering whenever the opportunity presented itself, and he kept me pretty well informed of what he'd been hearing. But we never had a chance to carry on a true conversation. In spite of this silence, our friendship started to develop. The initial stages of his disease also began to surface. He lost sensation in his right hand, and he wobbled when he walked. He also had problems with nausea.

I was very concerned about him, and I tried to help him as much as I could. When he lost complete control of his hand I'd help him with his pipe and button his shirt for him—little things like that. I just felt terrible for him. The guy had more reason to be in the dumps than any of us. Not only was he a hostage, but he had to cope with a strange disease. It would have scared me to death, but Richard had a remarkably optimistic outlook. He just kept looking for the bright side, and he did a great deal for my morale. I like to think that in some small way I helped him out too.

RICHARD QUEEN (*consular officer, at the Mushroom Inn*): I first noticed a faint numbness in my left hand in early December. I thought, "You slept on your arm. It'll go away in a day or two." Well, it didn't go away. As a matter of fact, it got worse. The numbness spread from my hand to my arm and up my shoulder, until eventually it affected my entire left torso. By this time, I realized that it wasn't caused by sleeping wrong. I called one of the guards and I said, "I'd like to see a doctor." One of the militants was a pharmacy student, and he came around and looked at me. He said, "Maybe it's caused by a draft." So we closed off a little vent that we had been keeping open to let cool air in. But the numbness didn't go away.

At its worst the numbness affected an area from my left knee up to my shoulder, and only on the left side of my body. The right side remained normal. Eventually, the numbness grew to be rather severe. I couldn't hold things in my left hand. For example, I couldn't tell when I had my pipe in my hand. It would slip, and the only way I'd know that I'd dropped it was I'd hear it hit the ground. And I'd itch something awful around my neck and chest. I'd scratch so much that I'd start to bleed. That happened several times. There wasn't anything I could do about it, so I tried not to think about it—just hoping that maybe it would go away.

DON HOHMAN (*army medic, at the chancery*): The Iranians brought medical problems to me. I treated people several times without having the slightest idea who they were. There were a lot of flu and cold symptoms and I'd prescribe whatever medication was available. It was the wrong way to practice medicine, but it was the only way the rag heads would let me do anything. They'd come to me with symptoms and I'd tell them what vital signs I needed. Then one of the medical students would go out and take someone's blood pressure, or get a temperature, and relay the information back to me. I treated quite a few people that way. But I knew that if somebody had a heart attack, or a serious illness or injury, all I had to work with was my hands. I didn't have the necessary medication or equipment to deal with a serious medical problem. The dispensary had been trashed. Those people had destroyed that place, and had stolen a lot of the drugs and equipment we had in there. It was just pure vandalism. There was enough medicine to handle colds and the flu, but when they'd bring the minor problems I'd wonder, "Hey, what if somebody gets seriously hurt or becomes seriously ill? What the hell am I going to do?" That thought was always in the back of my mind. I'll tell you, somebody must have been watching over us, because it's a miracle that nobody died.

RICHARD QUEEN (*consular officer, at the Mushroom Inn*): Eventually they brought in a doctor. He might have known what he was doing, but I thought he was a quack. He was working hand in glove with the militants. He used to come by with the pharmacy students once every two or three weeks to check me out. I was starting to have some double vision, and I mentioned that to him, and he looked in my eyes. Supposedly, the eyes are one of the first places you can tell if some sort of neurological problem is developing. He knew something was wrong, because when he first looked in my eyes he slightly pulled back. I could see that he was startled. He pulled his head back, and then leaned forward again to check my eyes more closely. But after he was finished, the quack doctor said, "Ah, it's nothing. I have the same problem. It's a twist in your spine. A slight twist in your spine. It will go away. I had the same problem once." He just sort of laughed it off. "Ah, a twist in your spine."

But I knew something was wrong. He told me it was nothing, but I knew it was something. At that point, I was very fatalistic. There was nothing I could do, so I just sort of shrugged my shoulders. There was no use fighting it.

JOHN LIMBERT (*political officer, at the chancery*): I could hear the students in the other room. Don Hohman was always giving them a hard time. At one point he went on a hunger strike. The students would threaten him and tell him that if he didn't eat they were going to punish him. When that happened, Don would simply say, "What are you going to do to me? Go ahead and do it right now." And that disarmed them completely.

DON HOHMAN (*army medic, at the chancery*): I went on three hunger strikes. The first one lasted twenty-one days. Then later I went on a second one. I'd do it because it pissed the Iranians off. I wanted to protest the way we were being treated, and I was hoping that other people would join me. I left some notes in the bathroom about it. I wanted to get a big hunger strike going.

I'd done fasting before I went to Tehran, just to diet and lose a little weight, and I knew that after the first forty-eight or seventy-two hours your hunger disappears. It just goes away. After about ten days into my second hunger strike I was lightheaded, and I didn't want to stand up real quick, but other than that I was doing okay. I was still doing my exercises. I'd do my sit-ups and my push-ups, but, of course, the further along I got into the hunger strike the more difficult it became because I was losing strength. I was also jumpy and irritable, which is a sign of someone who is on a hunger strike. I don't know how Bill ever put up with me.

JOHN LIMBERT (*political officer, at the chancery*): I joined Don Hohman on one of his hunger strikes. Given the conditions that we were living in, a hunger strike was one of the few gestures of protest we had. So one day I quit eating. The students responded by trying to ignore the fact that I was not eating. They would come into the room at mealtime and leave my food in the room. They would just set it there as though I had been eating all along. After three or four days of not eating, it got pretty tough, especially with the food sitting there in the room. I found that the hunger strike affected my nerves. I became very short-tempered, and yelled at the students for no particular reason. I didn't think too much of myself for doing that, either.

Seven or eight days without food was about all I could take. So I went ahead and broke my hunger strike. The students were still bringing my meals in, and one day I just started eating again. I remember they made a great pretense out of not acknowledging this fact. They just pretended that they had never noticed.

DON HOHMAN (*army medic, at the chancery*): I kept my hunger strike going. The rag heads would bring the food in, place it down, and say, "You must eat!"

I'd say, "No." And I'd just let the food pile up. I left a note in the bathroom about my hunger strike, hoping that somebody would find it. I was hoping it could get to the point where flat nobody was eating. I wanted to spread the word.

Apparently somebody did pick up my message, because Jim Lopez, one of the marines, erased a line out of a book and then wrote in the blank space, "The Marines started a hunger strike on—" and he gave the date. I couldn't believe it. I was sitting there reading *The Dunes*, and then all of a sudden I read Jim's message. It was beautiful. Jim is a great artist, and his printing was exactly like the text. It was incredible. The guards always used to search the books for notes. They would shake them and flip through the pages to make sure notes weren't being passed when we exchanged books, but no one would ever think to look directly at the text. But my message must have been picked up kind of late, because by that time I was already two weeks into my second hunger strike, and they had been on theirs for two days. By that point I knew I couldn't keep up with them for however much longer they were going to go.

My first hunger strike was in December, and it lasted twenty-one days. After about fifteen days on my second hunger strike I could feel that I was getting weaker. I figured I was probably starting to eat into my muscle tissue, and that worried me. It worried Bill, too. Over a two-month period I'd gone thirty-six days without food. Bill was getting pretty concerned. Then on the sixteenth night of the second hunger strike, I was sitting on my thin little mattress on the floor, and I got up and reached for a pitcher of water that was on the window—all of a sudden it was blackout time. I was holding onto the pitcher and everything went black. I was standing there shaking. I remained conscious and knew what was happening, but there was nothing I could do to stop shaking.

Bill was sleeping, but he woke up. He saw me shaking and got up to help me. Finally I was able to sit down, and Bill said, "Man, you've got to stop this. You're scaring the hell out of me. You've got to stop this, or you're going to die. I don't want you to die."

So I said, "Okay, I'll stop."

Bill called the guards in right then. He told them, "Hey, he wants to eat."

That really shocked the rag heads, because I hadn't eaten in over two weeks. There were plates on the desk that had been left sitting there with food on them. But I knew I was starting some body damage, so I went back to eating.

5 Closing Down the Mushroom Inn

JOE HALL (*warrant officer*): In March, one of the guards came into the Mushroom and told Rich Queen and I that we were going to be moved. He said, "This is a good thing. You are going to a much better place. You should be very happy." Well, any time something like that happened I dreaded it, because I never knew what was going to happen next. The constant uncertainty was one of the things that made the situation so unpleasant. In telling us about this move, the guard indicated that Rich Queen and I were going to be separated. I remember he told Rich, "You will be put with some important people. You will be able to play cards."

Rich said, "I don't want to move in with any important people. I want to stay with Joe. We get along well, and we both want to stay together."

RICHARD QUEEN (*consular officer*): They said, "Get ready! Get ready! You're moving right now!" Then we sat there for hours. We didn't know where we were going or what the move meant, so that was a little bit unsettling. Then once things got under way, it was obvious that there was a lot of movement going on. All of the hostages were being taken out of the Mushroom Inn.

JOE HALL (*warrant officer*): They took us out one at a time. We each had our little bundles packed up with our letters, pictures from home, and what little we'd managed to accumulate. I remember they took Rich out first. It must've been about midnight when they came back, blindfolded me, and put me in a car with some other Americans. We drove around in circles on the compound for about thirty minutes, and then the Iranians took me out of the car and sat me down in a hallway inside the chancery building. It was only about 150 yards from the Mushroom to the chancery, but the guards made a big charade out of driving around in circles. I guess they thought they were confusing us, which was ridiculous. We knew exactly where we were. In order to blindfold me, they had draped a big wool blanket over me, and as I sat there in the hallway I could look underneath the blanket and see feet walking past me. Some of them were hostage feet, and some of them were Iranian feet. They kept shuffling me around. I sat in the hallway for a while, then they took me somewhere else and sat me down, and I had nothing to do but wait and wait. Finally, they put me in a room, and when they pulled the blanket off my head, I was looking right at Rich Queen. They had decided to leave us together after all. We were both really happy about that.

CDR. ROBERT ENGELMANN (*naval supply corps officer*): They moved us all out of the Mushroom Inn and put us into the chancery. I was stuck in an office up on the second floor with Gary Lee. That was it. Just the two of us in this room, and they shut the door. This was the first time that we didn't have an Iranian guard in the room with us. I looked at Gary Lee, and he looked at me. Gary silently mouthed the words, "Can we talk?" I thought that was funny, because there wasn't anyone else in the room. But for the previous 135 days, every time we turned around it was, "No esspeak! No esspeak!" We weren't sure what we could do. So we went ahead and started to talk and whisper.

JOE HALL (*warrant officer, at the chancery*): When Rich Queen and I were put into that office in the chancery we were all alone. There wasn't a guard in there watching over us, and it was the first time we could talk openly. We couldn't talk fast enough. We talked each other's ears off. It was constant talk. I mean talk, talk, talk, talk. We tried to rehash everything that had happened, and were trying to guess what it could mean. We spent hour after hour talking. Rich and I must've sat up and talked for twenty-four consecutive hours. We told each other anything and everything that came to mind. We talked about our families and our lives back in the States, and we talked about what was going on in Iran. We'd been together down in the Mushroom for four months, but this was the first time we carried on an actual conversation.

WILLIAM ROYER (*director of academic courses, at the chancery*): I was in a room with Cort Barnes and Bill Keough when we were first allowed to talk, and the three of us talked up an uninterrupted stream of speech for a solid eight hours. We talked about personal tidbits, and what we'd been able to deduce from what had transpired over the previous three months. I remember a great sense of relief at being able to speak. A lot of what we were rattling on about wasn't of any importance to any of us. It came out in almost a stream of consciousness-type delivery.

But with it came a great sense of release—and the opportunity to utter a few choice words about the Iranians.

BARRY ROSEN (*press attaché, at the chancery*): They moved all three of my roommates out—Bruce German, Bob Ode, and Bob Blucker—and I was in the room alone for a while. Then they moved another hostage in. This fellow was having a lot of problems. I thought I was having a hard time coping with the situation, but he was really bad. We had a water pitcher in there, and his hands were shaking so badly that he couldn't pour himself a glass of water. Absolutely couldn't do it. He looked terrible, too. Really bad. Our guard was no longer sitting in the room twenty-four hours a day, like they had been doing for the previous four months, so it was a great moment to have somebody to talk to. This was my first real opportunity to talk, but this fellow didn't want to. He said very, very little, and would kind of clam up off in a corner by himself. I thought, "My God, this is sad. Really sad."

JOHN LIMBERT (*political officer, at the chancery*): I was moved out of the basement and into a room on the top floor of the chancery. The room I was put into was a little bit bigger than my basement room had been, but I lost my radio. The students would not let me take the cushion I had it hidden in with me. I kept asking for it the whole time I was there. I'd say, "Gee, can I have my old mattress and pillow back? I really got used to that cushion and would like to have it back." But they never did get it for me. I lost the radio with that move, and I lost contact with Bill Belk and Don Hohman. So that move was not an improvement. I was still in solitary, and I hated losing that radio.

JOE HALL (*warrant officer, at the chancery*): Rich Queen and I were in one of the upstairs offices. The two of us spent practically the entire night and all of the next morning cleaning that room up. We had two great big leather chairs in there, and a big desk. It was very nice compared to the Mushroom Inn. Even though they had whitewashed over the window, it was still bright. We'd get sunlight shining through the whitewash, and the guards let us fold the upper part of the window down so we could get some fresh air. They told us not to look out the window, but they did let us open it. After four months in the Mushroom, it was nice to have that light and air. That part of it was great. But our eyes were bothering the hell out of both of us, and the longer we stayed in there the worse it got.

RICHARD QUEEN (*consular officer, at the chancery*): I had my pipe, and was smoking the pipe. I thought that was what was causing the eye irritation. As it turned out, the rug in there was full of tear gas. The more Joe and I walked around and cleaned the place up, the more we stirred up the tear gas in the rug. When the militants came back in, they nearly choked.

JOE HALL (*warrant officer*): They moved Rich and me out of there, and bounced us from room to room until we finally ended up in the basement of the chancery. The room they put us in was a dump. I mean, a real mess. Absolutely filthy. Two marines had been in there, and there were drawings and doodlings all over the walls. So Rich Queen talked the guards into bringing us some paint. He kept telling them, "There's a lot of paint over in the embassy warehouse. Couldn't you bring us some paint?" And believe it or not, Hamid the Liar brought us two gallons of white paint and some brushes. So Rich and I went to work and put two coats of nice, fresh white paint on the walls, and cleaned up the floors and everything, until we had that room all fixed up. The Iranians brought in two big leather chairs, and we also had a big desk and some bookshelf space. We put our family pictures up on the walls, and Rich even talked one of the guards into going out and getting an Alaska travel poster that he'd had hanging up somewhere, and we put that up in the room too. We got that room all fixed up and arranged the furniture, so that we were just happy as hell in there.

CDR. ROBERT ENGELMANN (*naval supply corps officer, at the chancery*): It definitely helped to be able to talk, and Gary Lee was a good person to be with. He had an extremely laid-back attitude, and I think he was coping with the situation as well as anybody could.

Our circumstances had improved to the extent that now we were just locked up in a room. We weren't tied up, and we were free to move around the room as we pleased. The Iranians had painted over the windows, but they hadn't done a very good job. We could look between the brush marks and see grass and trees on the embassy compound, and when there was a crowd in the street we could see them. Our horizon extended beyond a concrete wall, and that helped a little bit, too.

During this time, there were demonstrations going on in front of the embassy every day. We'd look out, and we could see that for the Iranians coming down to a demonstration was like a day at the fair. They'd have vendors out there selling balloons and snow cones, and a father would be walking along holding hands with his two little sons. They'd come down to this festival-type atmosphere at the American embassy and shout "Death to America!" for an hour or two.

Even when there wasn't an actual demonstration going, the militants had taped some of the previous crowds, and they would play those tapes of demonstrations and crowd noise over loudspeakers that they had set up around the embassy. So the crowd noise was constant, and it all sounded pretty ugly. The first time Gary and I realized that they were taping these things and playing them back was one afternoon when they had a big demonstration. People were out there screaming and chanting for a couple of hours, and right at the end of the demonstration a jet flew straight down Takht-e Jamshid. That surprised us. It made a lot of noise—a great big *whooosh* as it flew right over the street. Then everyone cheered. Gary and I laughed about that, and commented: "Those turkeys have been out there shouting 'Death to America!' for two hours, but when an American-manufactured jet flown by an American-trained pilot flies over their heads, they all jump up and cheer."

Later on, the shouting and chanting started up again, and it was virtually impossible for us to tell one demonstration from another. They all sounded alike. But at the end of this demonstration, we heard that jet fly over again, and all of the cheering—only this time a jet never came down Takht-e Jamshid. It was obvious that this was a tape of the previous demonstration. We heard that same tape a few more times, and realized that a lot of the crowd noise we were hearing was nothing but smoke. It was just stuff that the guards were playing over loudspeakers.

CPL. STEVEN KIRTLEY (*marine security guard, at the chancery*): It seemed like we were still hearing a lot of crowds outside. Those demonstrations were going regular as clockwork. Then we got smart and listened to some of them, and realized that the Iranians were playing tapes over the loudspeakers. They'd play the same tapes over and over again, and we'd hear the same imperfections or static in the tape at the exact same time in the demonstration. So we knew what they were doing. One time one of the militants came into the room, and we said, "Hey, why don't you turn off that noise outside?"

"What do you mean? There's a demonstration going on outside."

"Bullshit! That's a tape. There isn't any demonstration outside."

"No, there's a demonstration."

Then about fifteen or thirty minutes later the noise stopped. After they realized that we knew what they were doing, they didn't play those tapes quite as much.

JOE HALL (*warrant officer, at the chancery*): Every now and then the Iranians would make a big show out of giving us mail, and any letters that I got from my family were very, very important to me. Unfortunately, the majority of my mail was from people I didn't know. Those "Dear Hostage" letters meant very little to me. There was never any news or information in them, and a lot of them were from school kids. I remember one letter from a little boy that started out: "Hi, my name is Jimmy. I am eight years old, and I am writing this letter to you because my teacher says I have to." And that was typical. I'd get a lot of letters where it was obvious that the classroom project for the day was to write to the hostages in Iran. The guards would give some of those to us. The kids would always ask: "What do you eat?" Some of them would say: "I hope you don't die."

CDR. ROBERT ENGELMANN (*naval supply corps officer, at the chancery*): Iranian family ties are very strong. That's a big part of their culture. And some of us received mail with family pictures in them. When that happened, we would take the pictures and hang them up on the wall. The guards would look at our families, and it seemed to change their attitude toward us a little bit. It would soften the way they treated us. I guess it gave a human aspect to who we were. We were no longer just the big American spy, or the "Great Satan," but we were people who had families. We had a mother, a wife, and some of us had little kids. At the time, I wasn't married. But some pictures were sent over to Iran that had been taken at one of the State Department family briefings in Washington, D.C. The guards had these pictures, and one of them came around and told me that he had a picture of my wife, and he gave me a picture from this briefing where my mother was sitting at a table with Joe Hall's wife Cheri. He obviously thought that Cheri Hall was my wife. So I said, "Oh yeah, there she is. That's my wife." And I taped the picture up on the wall. I adopted Joe Hall's wife as my wife, so the Iranians could see that I had a family, too.

JOHN LIMBERT (*political officer, at the chancery*): Mail was very irregular. It was very sparse. However, I did get a few letters from my family, and in reading those it was obvious that my mail was not getting out. I had written several letters, and none of them were acknowledged. Mail was very strange, because you might get something and you might not. I remember on one occasion the students brought in a box that had been sent to Tehran by an American Indian activist, and gave it to me. It was a care package sort of thing, and it had some books in it. The interesting thing about the books was that they were all at least 1,000 pages long. There was *War and Peace, The Brothers Karamazov, David Copperfield, Middlemarch,* and *Tom Jones.* I remember looking at those books and thinking, "Wow! Whoever sent this package must think that we are going to be in Iran for a very long time."

CPL. STEVEN KIRTLEY (*marine security guard, at the chancery*): For a while there I was really feeling depressed. I had kind of lost hope. I couldn't keep on saying, "Maybe tomorrow. Maybe something will happen tomorrow," because nothing was happening. I was really low. I went to the bathroom one time, and when I came back Jim Lopez was sitting on his mattress on the floor reading a piece of paper that the Iranians had given him. I said, "What's that?"

He said, "Just a minute and I'll let you read it. It's telling about all the great stuff Americans are doing back home."

Jim gave it to me, and it turned out it was a letter that one of the militant students in Iran had written to a newspaper. It was denouncing the American people for some of the atrocities that had occurred against Iranian students who were studying in the United States. It gave some examples, like someone had sicced their attack dogs on an Iranian, and a couple of Iranian students got the shit beat out of them in Texas bars. Things like that.

Boy, I was really feeling depressed until I read that letter. But it made a world of difference. I felt much better. If the American government was doing anything we didn't know about it, so it was good to see that the American people were upset about what was happening. After what the Iranians had done to me, it made me feel good to know that people back home were angry and doing these things.

SGT. JAMES LOPEZ (*marine security guard, at the chancery*): I'd just treat the Iranians like the assholes they were. When they came into the room, I would intimidate them by standing above them to make them feel small.

There were lots of little things that we'd do to piss them off. When we were living in the chancery, the rag heads used to take us over to the ambassador's residence every ten or fifteen days to let us take a shower. We knew that the students were living in the residence, and that they were using those bathrooms. So we'd plug up the sinks and plug up the toilets. One time I noticed that they had their dishes stacked in the sink, so I urinated on them.

Every now and then, Steve Kirtley and I would blow out a fuse in the chancery. We'd get a fork and stick it in the socket just to drive the rags crazy. They'd start running up and down all over the place, because they wouldn't know what was going on. We'd hear them playing with the circuit breakers, and lights would be flashing on and off all over the place. They were not all that bright, and it would take them a while to figure out which circuit was blown.

Kirtley and I were very rude to them. Steve was having a problem with flatulence because of the food, and he'd stand right next to them and cut loose. Really loud ones just to try and degrade them. They'd get pissed off, and a bunch of them would come running in with their rifles. They'd take Steve away and talk with him.

There were a bunch of little things like that that we did to piss them off. They were assholes, so we treated them like assholes.

CPL. WILLIAM GALLEGOS (*marine security guard, at the chancery*): We used to do things to piss the guards off. While we were being kept there in the chancery they let us open the windows a little bit so we could get some fresh air. Of course, there were big thick bars on the windows, so we couldn't get out. But we did get a little fresh air. For some reason, the guards used to bring Geritol pills in for us. We had bottles of Geritol all over the place. There was also a desk in the room. It was completely empty except for one drawer, which had some rubber bands and some pencils in it. One night Rocky and I were messing around. From the window we could see that there was an armed guard outside near the side of the building, and there was another guard out toward the back part of the compound. Rocky and I took the rubber bands from the desk and made little slingshots out of them, and we used the Geritol pills as ammunition. After lights out, we climbed up to the window and shot these pills out at the outside guards. The pills ricocheted off the walls, and the guards didn't know what was going on. There were some trucks parked back there, and the pills hit the trucks and *ping!* They pinged right off the end of them. It was fabulous. The guards didn't know what was going on. They fired their weapons and shouted "*Est! Est!* (Stop! Stop!)" Of course, they couldn't see anybody because there wasn't anybody out there. We let go with another Geritol pill, and *ping!* These guys just started blasting. They were shooting in the dark at where the noise was coming from. They had no idea what was going on. Pretty soon Iranians were running around all over the place. We could hear them talking into their radios, and shouting, and firing their weapons outside. They were all excited. Rocky and I jumped down from the window, and when the guards came around checking the room we were lying on our mattresses like nothing was going on. That was pretty funny.

SGT. PAUL LEWIS (*marine security guard, at the chancery*): One time J. D. McKeel and I got ourselves into trouble. The students had come in and put pictures of Khomeini all over the walls. These pictures were plastered all over the room. When the students went out into the hall, McKeel and I took them down and put them in a neat pile on top of the desk. Then one day we had macaroni and tomato sauce for lunch, and I spilled mine. There was tomato sauce all over the bed and floor, and on one of those pictures of Khomeini. So I took the picture and scooped up as much of the sauce as I could—cleaned things up and threw the picture in our trash bag. I guess these guys looked through our trash to see what we had in there, because they came in with that picture thinking that we had defaced it. All of a sudden that room filled up with Iranians. I mean *whomp*! There were a bunch of them in there, and they were rabid. I'd never seen them so angry.

They tried to handcuff us, and we wouldn't let them. But they grabbed us and put the handcuffs on us anyway. That was one of the few times when we resisted that they got physical. They cranked those handcuffs down tight, too. They were as tight as they could get them, and it hurt.

McKeel and I tried to act like nothing was going on. We were handcuffed in front, so we got out our chess board and played a game of chess. We talked to each other, and the guard told us not to speak. But we ignored him. We pretended like he wasn't even there, and we had a friendly game of chess.

After about four hours, one of the more reasonable guards came into the room. We talked about what had happened, and I explained to him that I hadn't purposely tried to deface the picture. I'd just spilled tomato sauce on the thing. He left, and I guess he went off to talk to some of the other guards, because within an hour they came in and took the handcuffs off.

SGT. KEVIN HERMENING (*marine security guard, at the chancery*): I was in solitary for over forty days, and then they put me in a room with Al Golacinski. I really liked Al. We became good friends. We shared our mail with each other, and talked very candidly about how we were feeling and what our lives were like before Tehran. Al was ten years older than me and as the security officer he was my superior, but that never seemed to matter. Age and rank didn't interfere with our friendship.

As Easter approached, Al and I knew that we were going to have a religious service on Easter Sunday with American clergymen like they had done on Christmas.* The guards told us they were coming. We

* A delegation of four clergymen was invited into the embassy by the Iranians for the purpose of conducting an Easter service. This group included three Americans and Archbishop Hilarion Capucci of Israel, who had previously been imprisoned for running guns across the Lebanese border to the PLO. The Americans were Rev. Jack Bremer of Lawrence, Kansas; Rev. Nelson Thompson of Kansas City, Missouri; and Father Darell Rupiper, a Catholic priest from Omaha, Nebraska.

decided to try and pass a note to one of the religious leaders. Each of us wrote out a note on the inside of a chewing gum wrapper that said we wanted the American people to know that some truly inhumane treatment was taking place: hostages were being kept in solitary confinement, sanitary conditions were terrible, and we were continually being blindfolded and handcuffed. Basically, we wanted them to know that the situation the students set up for the television cameras was not an accurate indication of the way we were being treated. We were living in a hellhole, and we wanted to have something done to get us out of there.

We folded the notes up real tight. I was wearing a pair of dark blue slacks that had a tear in the cuff, and we hid the notes inside the cuff of my pants until it was time for the Easter service.

CDR. ROBERT ENGELMANN (*naval supply corps officer, at the chancery*): When you are in a situation like the one we were in, and you are told that you're going to have a chance to meet with and talk to an American clergyman, it's inevitable that your expectations are raised a little. I remembered meeting Reverend Howard at Christmas, and given the circumstances, I thought he did an excellent job. Prior to coming over to Iran, he had tried to talk to as many of the parents and wives as he could so he could deliver some family greetings, and asked each of us if we had any messages that we wanted to give to our families. In spite of the difficult circumstances, with the Iranians watching over his every move, I think he was a good person who had our well-being at heart. But those guys that came in to see us at Easter were a completely different breed. That's particularly true of Darell Rupiper. He was not there to give us any comfort at all. He was there to make headlines for himself. I guess he had spent some time down in Brazil, because at this Easter service he started telling us about human rights violations in Brazil. He wasn't the least bit concerned about what was happening to us; he just went on and on about how bad it was in Brazil. As he talked, his whole attitude was very sympathetic to the Iranians. I remember sitting there thinking, "I don't need this. I don't need this at all." Rupiper really disappointed me.

CHARLES JONES (*communications officer, at the chancery*): I didn't care about seeing the ministers, but I did want to get some of the goodies. Greg Persinger and I were roommates that Easter, and when the guards came in and told us the ministers were there, we went in to see if we could get some food. We walked in, and of course the Iranians had the TV cameras going. Father Rupiper, the Jesuit priest, was there and he asked us, "How are you doing?"

I said, "I haven't been physically tortured, but I've suffered everything short of it. The conditions have not been good. The only thing any of us are interested in is getting the heck out of here."

Well, Rupiper commenced to tell us about the time he spent in Brazil. He said that he had seen some of the prisons there, and that our conditions weren't nearly as bad as the conditions in the Brazilian prisons. He told us about human rights violations in Brazil, and all sorts of crap. Of course, the Iranians just loved that. The implication was that by comparison we were being treated well. Rupiper obviously felt a great deal of sympathy for the Iranians, and it was very demoralizing to have to sit there and listen to that garbage.

SGT. KEVIN HERMENING (*marine security guard, at the chancery*): When we walked in for the Easter ceremony, there were lots and lots of television lights, and they had anti-American posters and slogans plastered all over the walls. It was "Death to Carter!" and "Death to the Shah!" And there were also a couple of big pictures of Khomeini.

Three ministers were in there, and they gave us a short service. At Christmas, I had been allowed to read from the scripture book, so I asked the ministers if I could give another reading at this service. They agreed, and Father Rupiper gave me the book. I had my note in my hand, and while I was reading I slipped the note between the pages of the scripture book. I did that and kept on reading. When I finished, I started to give the book back to Father Rupiper, but he reached for it in a very casual, limp-wristed way. I was afraid that the note might fall out. As he took the book back from me, I held onto it with two hands and looked straight into his eyes. I was trying to get him to take hold of the book and secure it. But my message wasn't getting through. He took the book and started flipping through it to get ready for another reading. So I leaned right up to his ear and whispered, "There's a note in there."

Rupiper jumped away from me like I was a poison snake or something. He got all flustered, and made it obvious that he didn't want to have anything to do with my note. I was surprised that the Iranians didn't come running right up to us to find out what was going on.

ROBERT ODE (*consular officer, at the chancery*): It's important to remember that the clergymen who came to see us were brought over to Iran by the Iranians. None of them were selected by the United States government. They were chosen by the Iranians for their political views, and they were all far more sympathetic to the terrorists than they were to the American hostages. That was apparent in their general attitude. They had a little Easter service for us, and while we were sitting in front of the television cameras, I told the ministers, "We need more than prayers. We need action. That's what we really need." I wanted them to know that while prayers were appreciated, we were all much more interested in hearing about some tangible measures that were being taken to get us out. That's all we cared about. And I didn't think that any of them were doing us any favors by being there.

SGT. KEVIN HERMENING (*marine security guard, at the chancery*): After we were taken back to our room the Iranians were given the note that I had hidden in the book. I have to assume that Father Rupiper gave it to them, because they told me they had it, and I don't think they searched him to get it. Someone had to give it to them. That really ticked me off. I was totally disgusted by Father Rupiper and his actions at that service. He certainly wasn't providing us with any solace or comfort. I thought he was disgusting and revolting. He did us a great disservice by being there.

RICHARD QUEEN (*consular officer, at the chancery*): Easter came and went, and nothing changed. The guards would just lock the door and pretty much leave us alone. So we had our own little world right there in our cells. The only events that my roommate and I knew about were the events that occurred within the walls of our own room. We lived pretty much by ourselves. That room was like a small world within the greater world.

JOE HALL (*warrant officer, at the chancery*): Even though we were in the basement, we had a window that we could open to let in fresh air. In the morning, sunlight would come streaming into the room. This was April, and the climate was getting warm. Spring is a very nice season in Tehran. We could hear birds singing, and traffic, and outside noises. After being locked up in the Mushroom, you can't imagine how nice that was.

Rich is a morning person. He liked the early morning sunlight, and he would get up and smoke his pipe and read Shakespeare while I usually stayed in bed until they brought breakfast in. Then I'd eat, do my exercises, and bathe at the sink in the bathroom across the hall. By this time, I'd had so much practice that I could take a complete bath standing right at the sink. It didn't bother me at all.

Rich and I spent a lot of afternoons playing games and reading. But the evening was a special time for us. The Iranians would usually bring us tea after dinner. They'd come in with big tall glasses of very strong, very hot tea. I really enjoyed that freshly brewed Iranian tea. We had a little lamp on the desk that gave off a soft, pleasant glow. We called it our smoking lamp. When the Iranians came in with the evening tea, we'd turn on our smoking lamp, sit back in our big leather chairs, drink tea, and smoke our pipes. That was very pleasant. During that time, Rich and I learned a great deal about each other. We'd talk about everything that had ever happened to us before the embassy was sacked. We'd talk about where we grew up, where we went to school, what our families were like, and who and what we were. In talking about times past, Rich came to say that he thought he knew my wife, Cheri, even though he'd never met her, and I felt the same way about his parents and brother. I knew exactly what he meant. In its own bizarre way, that was a very special time for both of us.

JOHN LIMBERT (*political officer, at the chancery*): After Easter I was moved into a much nicer room on the first floor of the chancery. I had a window with a nice view that looked out on the back side of the embassy. I could also get some fresh air. That was April, which is a nice time of year in Tehran. So my circumstances were much improved. By the standards we were living under, it was a reasonable setup. In fact, I even had a typewriter in my room, which was a nice thing to have. I had access to books, and the students had set up a Ping-Pong table in one of the rooms. Occasionally I'd play Ping-Pong with them. I was still being kept by myself, but the circumstances were improved. Having the light and the air in the room was good. But of course nothing lasts. All good things must come to an end.

Part Seven

Dispersal

1 Aftermath of the Rescue Mission

THROUGHOUT MARCH OF 1980, the Carter administration continued to engage in a series of secret negotiations aimed at resolving the hostage crisis. Iranian foreign minister Sadegh Ghotbzadeh was very active in these negotiations, which were once again conducted through two intermediaries. Shortly after failure of the United Nations commission, Ghotbzadeh approved a second plan to secure the release of the hostages. On April 1, 1980, Iranian president Bani-Sadr once again announced that the hostages would be transferred to the "care and custody" of the Iranian government. However, this plan was once again derailed by radical members of the Revolutionary Council. Within twenty-four hours Bani-Sadr reversed himself and said that an agreement between the United States and Iran was not possible.

Ten days later, President Carter approved a military rescue operation designed to free the hostages. On April 24, 1980, eight navy helicopters took off from the flight deck of the aircraft carrier USS *Nimitz*. They were to rendezvous with six American C-130 transport planes at a remote desert staging area code-named Desert One. The American C-130s arrived safely at Desert One, but the helicopters encountered severe dust storms en route. One of the helicopters was forced down approximately seventy miles inside Iran, while another returned to the USS *Nimitz* because of a navigational instrument failure. A third helicopter developed hydraulic problems in flight, and was scratched from the mission after arriving at Desert One. President Carter was informed that only five helicopters remained operational. From the White House he ordered that the mission be aborted.

As the rescue team was evacuating the staging area, a C-130 collided with an airborne helicopter, and eight American servicemen were killed. At 1:00 A.M. (Washington time) the White House issued a brief statement announcing that the rescue mission had been undertaken and then aborted due to "equipment failure," and that eight Americans had died in the attempt.

VICTOR TOMSETH (*chief political officer, at the Iranian Foreign Ministry with Bruce Laingen and Mike Howland*): We had a radio at the Foreign Ministry, and we regularly listened to the Voice of America in the morning. Because of that radio, I suspect that the three of us knew about the rescue mission as soon as anyone in Iran, with the exception of the forty-four people on the bus and whoever was in the pickup truck that sped away from the scene.* When the operation was canceled, there was an announcement out of the White House in the very early hours, Washington time, to the effect that there had been a rescue attempt, and that it had been aborted. That announcement was immediately picked up by the wire services, and the Voice of America carried it.

When we heard that news, we really thought the shit would hit the fan. We thought there was a very real possibility that we might be turned over to the students. There were any number of things that could have been done to punish us. But the only thing that happened was a Ping-Pong table that had just recently been brought up for our use was taken away. That was the sum total of our punishment.

JOE HALL (*warrant officer, at the chancery*): We knew something was strange that day. First of all, breakfast was very late. That broke a five-week-old routine, and the guards were kind of surly when they finally did bring stuff in. They were in a nasty mood. Lunch didn't come at all. We didn't get anything to eat that afternoon. And there were crowds out in front of the embassy. Big crowds. I mean, it was a massive demonstration. We couldn't figure out what the hell was going on.

CPL. STEVEN KIRTLEY (*marine security guard, at the chancery*): I didn't have any idea about the rescue mission, but there was a big, big demonstration, bigger than anything I'd heard before. We hadn't had a big demonstration in a long time, and I remember thinking, "Jesus Christ, Carter must've broken down and done something."

I was with Bert Moore, and we were trying to figure out what was happening. I said, "What's going on, Bert?"

He said, "I don't know. Maybe Carter did something. Or maybe Miss Lillian said something about the ayatollah."

JOE HALL (*warrant officer, at the chancery*): At about three o'clock in the afternoon, Hamid the Liar came in and told us to get our stuff together, that we were being moved. So we packed up our stuff, our books and what little we had. I remember Rich Queen and I were really concerned. We didn't know what the hell this move was all about, and we didn't

* At Desert One, the American rescue force observed an Iranian bus on a nearby road; its forty-four passengers were temporarily detained. A pickup truck was also observed. When it refused to stop warning shots were fired, but the truck managed to race away from the staging area.

want to be separated. We thought it was possible that maybe we were going to be released, but things didn't feel right for that. And we didn't know what those demonstrations out front were about. To tell you the truth, it was scary.

ROBERT ODE (*consular officer, at the chancery*): That afternoon the terrorists came in and told us to get ready, that we were going to be moved in ten minutes. Ahmed, the supervisory guard who I always referred to as Shovel Face, said, "You are going to be taken to a much, much better room."

I thought, "Great, an agreement has been reached!" I figured we were going to be taken to a hotel. At the time of the February 1979 evacuation the Americans were taken to the Tehran Hilton. I was thinking, "This is it! An agreement has been reached, and we are going to be released. They don't want the public to know how we've been treated here, so they're going to take us to a hotel from where we'll be released." That was the picture I had in mind.

CDR. ROBERT ENGELMANN (*naval supply corps officer*): We had been moved four or five times prior to this, and I thought it was just going to be another move. I probably should have said to myself, "This is unusual." Because in the afternoon they took me out and sat me in a van with some other Americans. Then they just left us sitting there. We were blindfolded and tied up, and left sitting in the van. Instead of using handcuffs, they had taken some nylon cable binders that you can pull to tighten the loop, and those things were worse than handcuffs. Not only were they tight, they also cut into your wrists. They used those things to tie us up, and left us sitting blindfolded in the van for an hour and a half or so until it was dark.

SGT. PAUL LEWIS (*marine security guard*): It seemed like we sat in the van forever. When we finally did take off, underneath my blindfold I could see blue lights flashing on top of police cars. So I knew we had a police escort when we left the embassy. That made me think we were going to the airport. I couldn't help but hope that was where we were going. But after we'd been on the road for a while I knew we'd gone too far. Every time you let yourself get your hopes up, it always ended in disappointment.

COL. THOMAS SCHAEFER (*defense attaché*): I did one thing right on that trip. I took my little Sanka coffee jar with me. I had it in my coat pocket when the militants threw me in the back of a van with about eight other Americans. I remember Dave Roeder was in there, and so was Bob Engelmann. When the Iranians came into the room and told us we were moving, I put on every article of clothing I had. I didn't want to leave any of it behind, so I was wearing two pairs of pants. Previously, one of the ways the militants had harassed me was to not let me go to the bathroom when I needed to. In some of the cold rooms they kept me in that was quite a problem. Eventually I got my hands on a Sanka jar, and whenever I had to relieve myself in my room, I'd just do it in the Sanka jar. Then when the Iranians did let me go to the bathroom, I'd hide the jar and carry it down with me and empty it. Anyway, I had that jar when I was thrown in the back of this van. We drove for about four hours, and there weren't any rest stops along the way. I had on my extra clothing and my hands were strapped with cable binders, but I managed to manipulate my Sanka jar, grapple with my clothes, and do what I needed to do in the back of the van while we were driving.

COL. LELAND HOLLAND (*army attaché*): All night long we were rocking and rolling and bouncing along. I was handcuffed to the seat right behind the driver in a Dodge van. Even though I was blindfolded, I could see the glare of headlights from oncoming vehicles, so I knew we were on a highway that had a double-stripe line divider. Our driver was going on and on like a son of a bitch. Hour after hour, he'd be droning on, and all of a sudden we'd hear the blare of a horn—*honk! honk! honk!* And this guy would make a vicious swing, like he'd been way over on the wrong side of the goddamn road. I'd think, "Jesus! If he gets hit there's no way we can get out. I'm handcuffed to the seat." That was a frightening trip.

JOHN LIMBERT (*political officer*): There are only so many directions you can travel out of Tehran, and I had a pretty good idea that we were going south because I knew that road very well. I had traveled it many times when I was a teacher in Iran. I could see enough lights and things from under my blindfold to know when we reached various towns, and we were also traveling over a fairly level piece of highway. From the timing of the towns and the nature of the highway, I had a pretty good idea of where we were. We must've left Tehran at about eleven o'clock that night, and we arrived at our destination the next morning. The students never told us where we were, or why we had moved. But the flatness of the road and the timing of the drive gave the location away. I knew we were in Isfahan.

JOE HALL (*warrant officer*): It was late at night, and I was asleep when they came in and got me. They had already taken Charles Jones and

Rich Queen out. I had my little bundle all packed up ready to go, but they left me sitting there. It must've been about two or three o'clock in the morning when they finally came in, blindfolded and handcuffed me, and took me downstairs. When they put me into a van, I could tell that I was sitting next to another American. I whispered, "Who are you?" The guy whispered back, "Persinger." So I was sitting next to Greg Persinger. The Iranians handcuffed the two of us together. One of my hands was handcuffed to the seat, and the other hand was handcuffed to Greg. By peeking out from under my blindfold I could tell that there were two other Americans in the seat in front of us. I don't know if anyone was sitting behind us or not.

Eventually, these guys took off and drove us through the streets of Tehran. We ended up at what had once been a very elaborate home in northern Tehran. It was a great big place. As we were being taken in, I could see from under my blindfold that we were being led up some wide marble steps—I mean, a big, sweeping circular stairway that must've been about ten feet wide. This had obviously been a fantastic house.

When they finally took my blindfold off, I was in a very large bedroom, the largest bedroom you can imagine. It was huge, and had plush carpeting, and the walls were upholstered with a very ornate fabric. There were a couple of beautiful big chandeliers hanging from the ceiling. All of the furniture had been moved out, and about thirty steel military bunks had been brought in. That's all there was in the room.

Greg Persinger and Jim Lopez were in there with me. The guards wouldn't allow us to talk. They spread us apart. They took some of the bunks and stood them up on their ends to create partitions so that we couldn't see each other. Then they told us to go to sleep.

ROBERT ODE (*consular officer, at the chancery*): I was still at the embassy. Instead of sitting there for about ten minutes like Shovel Face had said, Bruce German and I sat in our room for about seven hours, waiting to go. I was still thinking that an agreement had been reached and that a release was pending. Finally, in the middle of the night a couple of terrorists came into the room and took Bruce out, and left me alone. My thought at the time was, "Bruce is going home. Some of the hostages are getting their freedom, and I'm being left behind. They're not letting me go, because I've been cantankerous and uncooperative." As the terrorists were taking Bruce out, I started calling them every name I could think of. I used language I didn't even use when I was in the navy during World War II. I really let go. I screamed and railed at them, and called them all kinds of dirty names.

The only answer I received was, "Older men should be more polite."
I crawled back on my mattress and tried to sleep.

WILLIAM ROYER (*director of academic courses, at the chancery*): I sensed
that many of us were being moved, and I actually thought that at long
last we were on our way home. I was blindfolded and handcuffed, and
I sat down on the floor of a van. When we left the embassy compound,
I thought we were headed for the airport. I was very excited, and
thought, "This is finally it!" But then the van turned north, and we
were climbing. I could tell that we were on one of the main arteries,
a boulevard that sort of circumnavigated to the north. So I knew we
weren't headed toward the airport. I thought, "Well, maybe we are
being taken to the Hilton Inn for an overnight stop before they load
us onto a plane in the morning." That seemed logical, and I still hadn't
given up hope.

When we finally came to a stop, the Iranians put a canvas bag over
my head. I was still blindfolded, and they put this bag over my blindfold.
Then they marched me down a curious number of steps into a sort of
cold, resonant atmosphere. I knew right away that we weren't in a hotel.
There was no carpeting on the floor, and we were led down these very
long concrete corridors.

All of a sudden I was told to lower my head and step in to the right.
I did so, and heard the clank of a door behind me. I was still blindfolded,
and I stood there for a minute before I realized that I was alone. When
I took the bag and blindfold off, I was standing in a dimly lit prison
cell. There was about a fifteen-watt night light way up in the ceiling,
and there was a pallet on the floor. There was also a stainless steel
toilet, and a little stainless steel sink. That was it.

I stood there and thought, "Well, this is their little joke. The guards
led us to believe that a release was imminent just so that they could
transfer us from the embassy to the prison without encountering any
resistance from us. They wanted to make it as easy as possible on
themselves. And now they've got each of us in our own little prison
cell."

It was a very stark and frightening position to be in, but I didn't want
to let myself feel frightened. It was already late at night, and I told
myself, "Just lie down and go to sleep. Don't worry about it. Worry
and fear won't help. So just go to sleep."

BRUCE GERMAN (*budget officer*): I was taken to a maximum security
prison, and the scene I am going to describe to you was as frightening
as anything I've ever experienced. The cell was about six by eight, and
there was a thin mattress on the floor. In one corner there was a stainless

steel commode with no seat, and a stainless steel sink. At the top of the cell there was a little grille where some light could come in in the morning, and above my head was a lightbulb which burned twenty-four hours a day. It never went out. There was a slot at the base of the door which the Iranians could slide food through. That's how you got your food. You weren't allowed to see anybody, and you weren't allowed to talk to anybody. You did all that you had to do inside that cell. You had a toilet and a sink—what else do you need?

The guard shut the door, and I sat down on the mattress. I have never felt so alone in all my life. I was totally and completely alone. There was no one I could appeal to, and no one I could talk to. It's a terrible thing to feel an aloneness that total. I sat there on the mattress, and I'm not ashamed to admit that I cried. I cried and prayed and cried, and finally fell asleep from emotional exhaustion.

CAP. PAUL NEEDHAM (*air force logistics officer*): I was taken up to Evin Prison, where I was put in solitary confinement. I was pretty sure there were other Americans around, and I figured that something had happened. It was obvious. The Iranians were scared, and because of the way they were acting I thought there might have been a rescue attempt. But I didn't want to admit that to myself, because if there had been a rescue attempt it had obviously failed.

WILLIAM ROYER (*director of academic courses, at Evin Prison*): A couple of hours later one of the guards came in and woke me up. He told me that we were just going to stay in this prison temporarily. I laughed at him. I laughed right out loud. I didn't believe him for a minute.

He said, "Oh, no, no. It is temporary. We will be leaving soon."

Well, after he left I got my hopes up again. I was thinking, "Maybe this is just an intermediate stop, and we were brought here for our own safety." I had heard a lot of demonstrations going on outside the embassy and had been told that the demonstrators wanted to get hold of us. They wanted our guts. So I figured that if a release had been negotiated, it was likely that there was a radical revolutionary element that did not want to see us go. Suddenly it seemed possible that the students had put us in the prison for our own safety until they could get us on a plane. So once again I started hoping that a release was pending.

ROBERT ODE (*consular officer, at the chancery*): I wasn't moved at all that night, and in the morning when I woke up the chancery building was as quiet as a tomb. It was as if the whole place had been deserted. One of the terrorists came in and brought me some breakfast. He wanted to know if I wanted my typewriter in the other room.

I said, "What other room?"

He said, "You are being put in another room."

They took me down the hall and put me into an office that apparently had been vacant the whole time. It was extremely dusty. So I said to Hamid the Liar, "Ahmed said I was going to a 'much, much better room.' What do you mean, a better room? This place is a dump!"

Hamid said, "You have cursed the students, and I am not speaking to you."

BILL BELK (*communications officer, at the chancery*): I sat in the embassy for that entire night and all of the next day. In the middle of the night a couple of guards had busted into the room and told me to pack up my essentials—you know, pencils, papers, books, and clothes. They said everyone was being moved. But I just sat there waiting for them to come and get me. They never did. I sat there all that night and all of the next day.

On the second night Ahmed came in. He was one of the guards that was usually pretty easy to get along with. But his attitude had completely changed. He was very angry. I had taken what little I had accumulated, folded it into my blanket, and tied the blanket up into a little bundle. Ahmed ripped the blanket open and started throwing stuff around. He was throwing books and clothes all over the room. I thought he was doing it just to be real rotten. I didn't know anything about the rescue attempt. And I didn't know what this move was all about. He was just going crazy throwing my stuff around the room.

Some more guards came in, blindfolded me, tied my hands up, threw a blanket over my head, and led me out. All the stuff that I had packed up was left scattered all over the room. I didn't get to take it with me. I was led outside and put into a van with about five or six other people. I know that Joe Subic, Malcolm Kalp, and Gary Lee were in the same van. There were also a couple of others, but I don't know who they were.

The guards told us that we were being transferred a very long distance, and that we were not to speak. Fortunately I went to the toilet just before we left, because we drove for twelve solid hours without stopping. They never let us get out of the van to stretch our legs or go to the toilet. They taped newspaper over all of the windows so that no one could look in and see us. They obviously didn't want anyone to know who we were or where we were going.

CPL. STEVEN KIRTLEY (*marine security guard, at the chancery*): Bert Moore and I were sitting in the embassy for a full twenty-four hours before they finally came and got the two of us and another guy, and put us into a Chevy Blazer. That night we started out on a long-ass drive. I thought we were going to the far southern edge of Iran or something. We drove for sixteen consecutive hours. We must've started out at about 2:30 in the morning, and we drove all through the next day. During this time, I only got out of the car once. I got out, went out into the middle of the desert, and urinated. The rest of the time the three of us were sitting in the back of this Blazer. We were going through the middle of the desert, and it was hot! The Iranians had put blankets around all the windows, and a blanket in front of us to separate us from the front seat. There were three of us sitting back there shoulder to shoulder. We were handcuffed together, and we had our blindfolds on. There was no backseat. We were just sitting on the floor.

Damn, that was a miserable trip. The Chevy Blazer kept breaking down. The Iranians would stop, get out, look at the engine, and talk for half an hour or so. Then they'd get in, drive a little longer, and the thing would break down again. They never could figure out what was wrong. I remember sitting back there thinking, "Maybe they'll ask me if I know something, and we can fix it and get the hell out of here." Because we would just sit there in the middle of the damn desert. And it was miserably hot. One time, I heard all three of the Iranians get out of the front, so I adjusted my blindfold and pulled the blanket back a little bit. I looked outside, and all I could see was desert. I looked over to the right and there was nothing but sand everywhere. I looked over to the left, and it was sand and more sand. Dunes and sand.

BILL BELK (*communications officer*): After driving for twelve solid hours we spent the night at a school of some sort. There were lots and lots of trees around this place. I think there were six people in the van, and we were taken down to this secluded little area. It was very pretty with all the trees, and the guards let us walk around outside for a little bit. I thought there was something strange about that, because the guards were taking pictures of us. After being royal assholes on the drive, all of a sudden they were trying to be real friendly and they wanted us to smile. I figured, "Screw you!" I'd flip the bird at the camera, and I wouldn't smile. I don't think any of us did. But they were taking lots of pictures. You know, here we are in these nice surroundings, and it was the first time I'd been outside in months. I figured they wanted those pictures for propaganda purposes, so I just kept flipping the bird. They didn't like that, but they didn't try to do anything to me, either.

I imagine at one time the school we were at was pretty nice. But by the time we arrived it was run-down and deserted. It had probably closed down when the shah left the country. We stopped for the night, and I was put into a room with Joe Subic. There was a window in the room, but the students had covered it up with some boards and paper siding so that we couldn't see out. Well, a strong wind came along and blew the paper siding off the window. Joe Subic popped up and he was looking out for all he was worth. There was a guard out there, and he saw Subic looking out the window. So Ahmed came storming in and told Subic, "If you look out that window again, I'll blow your head off!" He actually told Joe that he would kill him.

I couldn't believe it. I thought, "Oh, man, what's with Ahmed?" He was really breaking hard on Subic. Of course, this was right after the rescue attempt, and the guards were all pissed off. But I didn't know anything about the rescue mission. I didn't know what made them so angry. But Ahmed made a believer out of Subic. Joe stayed away from the window after that.

The room we were in was real bad. There were no mattresses and no chairs. All we had there was a hard concrete floor. So we had to sleep on the floor that night. Then the next day we were blindfolded again and taken to a small police jail. It was a little precinct jail, a small place with bars on the windows. Subic and I were put into a cell there, and nobody else was around. We were isolated from all of the other Americans. We didn't know where we were.

CAPT. PAUL NEEDHAM (*air force logistics officer, at Evin Prison*): Being thrown into solitary at the prison was quite a transition. I didn't know what was happening. I just kind of resigned myself to the new situation. I figured, "Okay, they're going to make things rough for a while. That's just the way it's going to be." They could take everything away from me and make me lie on the floor. So what? That was no big deal.

I kept reflecting back on what the POWs had gone through in Vietnam. On October 9, 1979, the night before I left for Iran, the last movie I saw in the United States was *When Hell Was in Session*. It has Hal Holbrook portraying Jeremiah Denton, who was a prisoner of war in Vietnam. That movie was on television and I watched it. The whole time I was in Iran I'd think about that movie. Whenever something bad happened, I'd remember what those guys went through in Vietnam. I'd say to myself, "Those guys went through a lot worse and they survived. Seven years, nine years as a POW, whatever. They made it through. I can survive, too. I'm going to survive." I knew that what I was dealing with wasn't as bad as what they had had to endure. I kept on thinking, "Those guys made it, and they had it a hell of a lot worse."

And actually, there were advantages to being in solitary. I didn't have to ask the Iranians to go to the bathroom. I had a toilet right there, and a sink. I had water. I didn't have to ask for anything. They shoved food through a slot in the door, which was nice. I didn't have to look at any of those rag heads.

CHARLES JONES (*communications officer*): After two nights in Evin Prison, the Iranians came and got me. They blindfolded me and then put a prisoner's hood over my head. That prisoner's hood was one of the worst things I've ever experienced. It was made of heavy canvas on the outside and rubber on the inside. It was absolutely suffocating. I was handcuffed and put in a van with some other Americans. I knew Bruce German was there, because we whispered to each other, and I knew Cort Barnes was there because I heard him laugh. I also knew there were some other Americans, but I didn't know who they were. We took off in the van and must've drove for thirty minutes. They took us out to an airfield. I could hear airplanes, and I thought that was strange. I couldn't figure out why they were taking us to an airport. I thought, "What are they doing? Certainly they're not about to release us. If they were going to release us, they wouldn't handcuff us and put hoods over our heads. They would be treating us much, much better." But they took us out of the van and walked us across the tarmac, and actually put us on a plane, a commercial jetliner. Once we were settled in our seats, the guards took the hoods off our heads, but they kept the blindfolds over our eyes. I worked my blindfold up so that I could see underneath it. I had a guard sitting on either side of me, and about five rows up I could see the back of a very tall American sitting there in a white shirt. It was Bill Keough. By peeking around, I saw enough to know that we were on a 727, and there were about twenty-five guards on board with five hostages. But I had no idea where we were going, or why they had put me on this airplane. All I knew was that the plane started rumbling down the runway, and off we went.

BRUCE GERMAN (*budget officer*): Five hostages and twenty guards were flown out in a 727. I had a guard sitting on either side of me, and even though I was blindfolded I knew there were stewardesses on board because I could hear their voices. Every now and then I would scratch my ear and lift the blindfold a little, and I could see feet walking up and down the aisle. These were obviously female feet, and they were serving the goons, giving them things to eat and drink.

There weren't any other civilian passengers on board. This flight was strictly for us. They wanted to get us the hell out of Tehran as quickly as possible. So it was obvious to me that someone other than the goons was running this whole show. It was obvious that the government was involved. I mean, you don't get yourself a full flight crew and a 727 unless you've got some powerful support.

CHARLES JONES (*communications officer*): When we landed, I knew we were out in the country somewhere, because it was very quiet. Even though we were blindfolded, I could tell there weren't any city lights, and I couldn't hear any traffic. Everything was very still. Instead of a bunch of hustle and bustle, the only thing I could hear was the chirping of insects. The terrorists took us to an old abandoned house and kept us there overnight. That place was awful. The walls were crumbling, and the floors were part dirt and part linoleum.

Early the next morning, we were blindfolded again and driven into a city. When we stopped, the guards led us into a building and we started climbing stairs. We were still blindfolded, and we went up one flight after another. I was counting them as we went. We were all huffing and puffing, and finally, after going up the ten flights, the Iranians put Bruce German and me into a room on the tenth floor. Bruce and I figured we were in a hotel that had never opened, because this was obviously a brand-new building, and they had never finished painting the inside. From the tenth story, we had a nice view of the city. At that time, I still didn't know we were in Meshed. Bruce and I thought we were in Tabriz, and we figured the room we were in wasn't too bad. We could make do there for a while. It was certainly better than the old abandoned house they had put us in the night before, and it was a major, major improvement over Evin Prison. But as it turned out, we only stayed there for a couple of nights.

The thing I remember the most about being kept in that hotel is that the idiots who were taking care of us actually built a fire in the bathroom to cook over. They built a fire on the bathroom floor. They didn't use a propane stove or a hot plate, but built an honest-to-God fire! When I walked in the bathroom the next day, I could see soot had blackened the walls, and I could see the spot on the floor where the guards had built their fire. Iranians are famous tea drinkers, and these guys built a fire on the floor to heat water for their tea. I saw that and couldn't believe it.

Anyway, after two days they moved us again. We ended up at what was once the Chamber of Commerce building in Meshed, where we stayed for the next two and a half months.

CPL. STEVEN KIRTLEY (*marine security guard, in Isfahan*): The Iranians took us to a big compound of some sort. They took us inside a building, and I remember walking down some stairs. When the blindfold came off, the three of us were in this great big subterranean room. It was huge. The guards left the three of us in there, and we had three little cots with thin little mattresses. Those cots were real dinky. When you got on them they'd sag like crazy.

I checked the place out, and I could see that the rag heads had just put bars in the windows, because the cement was still a bit damp. There were five windows, and all of them had been painted over. But by looking through the cracks, I could see that there was an armed guard outside each of those five windows. I pulled on the bars, but even though the cement was still damp, I couldn't move them. I remember thinking, "Jesus Christ, they made this place up especially for us. Those bars are brand new. It looks like we're going to be here for a while." I felt very depressed about that.

SGT. PAUL LEWIS (*marine security guard, somewhere near Qöm*): I think we were kept at some sort of pasdaran station. It looked like a military encampment or police station. John McKeel and I were put in with Colonel Schaefer and Steve Lauterbach. We were in a ground floor room, and it was hot there. The Iranians put a blanket up over the window so that we couldn't see out, and it got real stuffy. The food was awful, and McKeel and I got dysentery pretty bad. But the thing I remember the most about Qöm was that there were floggings in the courtyard. They took place almost daily. When we first heard the screams and lashes, we were afraid that maybe they were flogging some of the hostages. In order to see out, we had to look around the blanket and angle ourselves so that we could see through a louver. Eventually, we were able to find a position where we could see that it was Iranians who were being flogged, and not Americans. They weren't but twenty yards from our window, and we could hear the lashes and the screams. That was enough to make your skin crawl. Hearing that always made me queasy. Then the Iranians would cleanse the person after flogging them. To do that they'd chant, "*Allah Akbar! Allah Akbar!*"—you know, "God is great! God is great!" right after flogging some guy.

There was a guard there by the name of Azim. He had spent quite a bit of time in the United States, and we could tell that these floggings embarrassed him. We asked him who was being flogged and why, and he pretended that he didn't know what we were talking about. He'd say, "What flogging? I didn't know there was one." He was really ashamed of it. We also asked some of the other guards, and they told us that these people were being flogged for having had premarital sexual relations. It was ten lashes for premarital sex, and twenty-one lashes for adultery.

JOE HALL (*warrant officer, at a house in northern Tehran*): They kept Greg Persinger, Jim Lopez, and myself in the big bedroom of a huge house in northern Tehran for about a week. The day after they put us in there, the guards came in and started moving the bunks out. They must've had thirty bunks in there at first, and they pulled all of them out except three.

The strange thing was, we ate like kings during the week that we were there. We were fed three good meals a day. We also had a bathroom to ourselves, and we had this big huge room. We couldn't figure out what the hell happened and why the guards were feeding us so well. Not only was the food good, there was a lot of it. We didn't know what was going to happen. We thought maybe all this good treatment was a prelude to being released.

SGT. PAUL LEWIS (*marine security guard, with three other hostages at a location near Qöm*): It was nice for me to spend a week with Colonel Schaefer. He was with us in the pit. While we were there, we all got into a pretty rigorous exercise routine. We'd walk around in circles for a couple of hours each day. I mean, we'd walk until we got dizzy. Then we'd turn around, walk the other way, and try to get undizzy. Colonel Schaefer was a new face for McKeel and I, and we talked with him a great deal. It was a chance to compare notes on what had been going on.

One thing that was sort of funny was that the Iranians couldn't stand to see us show any respect to Colonel Schaefer. We would always refer to him as either sir or colonel, and a couple of the guards took exception to that. They would say, "You don't have to do that. Everyone here is an equal." Of course, we'd jump all over them for that. We'd ask, "Are you an equal too? Is that why you're free to come and go when we have to stay in this stinking room?" We told them that addressing him that way was a sign of respect, and that we were going to give him all the respect he was due. They'd hear that, and would go off on a tangent and make a big deal about Colonel Schaefer being a war criminal because he had been attached to a bomber wing in Vietnam. When he was in Vietnam, Colonel Schaefer never even flew tactically. He wasn't a fighter pilot, but the Iranians didn't understand that. They accused him of murdering babies and all sorts of nonsense. They were always threatening to turn him over to the Vietnamese embassy for extradition to Hanoi as a war criminal. It was really ridiculous.

Of course, when we found out that it bothered them that we showed him respect, we played that to the hilt. Whenever we walked our circles for exercise Colonel Schaefer was always in front. He was the leader, and we were always very deferential. We continued to call him colonel or sir. When they'd bring him back from the bathroom, we'd all be standing at attention. We'd be in a line as if he had made us fall out, and we'd salute as he came back into the room.

As individual marines, McKeel and I had been on our own for a long time, and it was good for us to be able to sit and talk with a senior officer. He reassured us about the way we had handled some of the things that had gone on, and he gave us some guidelines for situations that might come up in the future. He'd been in the service for close to thirty years and had a lot of experience. Even though he was a senior officer, I found that he was easy to talk to. He's a very nice man. He downplayed a lot of the things that had happened to him, and acted like he'd had a fairly easy time of it. But we knew the militants had been going after him pretty bad. He was the defense attaché, and they thought he was some sort of master spy. We used to tease him all the time about being a three-time hostage.* We'd tell him, "You know, Colonel, I can understand it happening to you once, or even twice. But after that second time we'd think that you would have learned something." He always laughed about that, and he definitely helped my morale. I wish I could have had more time with Colonel Schaefer. But like I said, the Iranians didn't like us showing respect to him. So one night they pulled him out of there.

JOE HALL (*warrant officer*): We stayed at the house in northern Tehran for exactly one week. Then the guards came in and told Persinger and me to get our things together. They said, "You're leaving on a long trip."

I thought, "Aha! How long? Are we going by air?" You know, we thought that maybe we were going home. I was really excited. I was so excited that I didn't want to discuss it. I was thinking, "This is it!

---

* Colonel Schaefer had been held hostage on two previous occasions. He was present at the time of the February 14, 1979, attack, when the embassy was briefly surrendered and the staff was held hostage for approximately two hours. Three weeks later, in March of 1979, a group of Iranian militants stormed an American listening post near the Soviet border and took twenty hostages. Colonel Schaefer was dispatched to the scene as a negotiator, and when he arrived he was taken captive at gunpoint. Later that day, he was able to bribe the militants and negotiate the release of everyone being held.

They're releasing some of us!" That was one time when I really thought I was going home.

They put me in a van, and I could hardly wait for them to get started. They kept messing around and messing around, and we were just sitting inside the van. I wanted them to hurry up and get the show on the road. Then after an hour on the road, I became very, very disappointed, because I knew we weren't being taken to the airport. It was always a big letdown whenever you let yourself get your hopes up. I just sank into a depression.

We were on the road for about eighteen hours. After a few hours, I had to urinate so badly that my kidneys were killing me. We asked them to stop several times, but they wouldn't do it. They just said, "Don'ta speak! Don'ta speak!" Or, "No es speak!" I was really uncomfortable. We were driving over some incredibly bumpy roads, and my bladder was about to burst. I was hurting. Finally, after about twelve hours, I told them that we had to stop. I couldn't last any longer. So they stopped and got me out of the van. It must've been in the early morning, because underneath my blindfold I could tell that it was light outside. The sun was coming up behind my right shoulder. They got us all out so that we could relieve ourselves. The only trouble was that by this time my kidneys were too swollen for me to just pop out of the van and go. I was standing there beside the road with my damn blindfold on, and the guards were standing around watching me try to urinate. My kidneys were too swollen and sore for me to be able to relax enough to do anything. I was in too much pain. After straining and straining and only getting a little dribble, they said, "Okay, enough!" Then they grabbed me and put me back into the damn van. I sat down, and when they finally got us to where we were going the first thing I did was say, "Hey, can I use the restroom?" So they put me in there, and I swear it must've taken thirty minutes before I was able to urinate satisfactorily. My kidneys were just too swollen and sore from that damn drive.

BILL BELK (*communications officer, at a rural precinct jail*): While Joe Subic and I were being kept in the small police jail, the food went downhill—way downhill. The students would come in with a can of something and hand it to us. They'd show us two or three cans and say, "What you like?" Then they'd hand us one. God, you can't imagine what it's like when somebody gives you a can of cranberry sauce and says, "Supper." Or a can of cold pork and beans. "Here is supper." Man, that was lousy. I knew that this wasn't going to make it. We had to have more to eat than what they were giving us. I'd already lost about twenty-five pounds due to stress and inactivity. I could see the handwriting on the wall. I knew we were in serious trouble unless we got more to eat. I told the guards, "Hey, we've got to get more than this or we're going to starve to death." And to make matters worse, the room we were in was very, very small, and hot as blazes. I mean, it was stifling in there. I'd sweat all day long and never get enough to eat.

WILLIAM ROYER (*director of academic courses, in Meshed*): The food wasn't very good during the period that we were in Meshed, because we had to live off the local economy and we ate the local food. Basically, we were given a lot of rice. There was very little fruit on the local market, and consequently we began pushing for vitamins. Charles Jones was in the room next door. He had high blood pressure, and was in need of having a doctor check him periodically. Arrangements were made to have this doctor come in, and I remember that he wasn't very satisfactory as a doctor. He thought that we were getting enough vitamins in our regular food, and suggested that 75 milligrams of vitamin C per day was more than enough. Bill Keough scoffed at this, and told him that he normally consumed hundreds of milligrams a day.

Our diet was a little project that we could goad the students with and use to make them continually feel that they were not meeting our needs. It was a game of wits. We'd challenge them a little bit to see how they would respond, and then they would either accommodate us to a certain extent or deny us something we had asked for.

One of the guards, who left and I never saw again, left us a note after we had engaged him in some conversation. The import of his note was that he wasn't pleased with the status quo, and he did not support our continuing to be held hostage. But he also let it be known that he felt the United States had been responsible for undermining Iran, and he didn't like the way we had demanded things from him and his fellow students as though they were our servants. But in fact, this was the way things had come around. The students had placed themselves in the position of having to take care of us and we, in turn, had become demanding. There was always some little thing we could find to ask for to keep the pressure on them, and I think they grew frustrated with the task they had taken on. They wanted their job to be finished. Of course, we took great pleasure in seeing that, and didn't fail to remind them that the venture they had undertaken had been foolhardy from the very beginning.

CAPT. PAUL NEEDHAM (*air force logistics officer*): Around the seventh or eighth of May, I was moved out of Evin Prison and six of us were moved about 200 miles outside the city of Tehran. Then, three days later, Mike Moeller, Bill Daugherty, and I were moved again. I still don't know exactly where we were, but it was another three or four hours away. I guess we were about 250 to 300 miles to the northwest of Tehran. I could tell we were quite high, because my ears were popping from the pressure changes in elevation.

We stayed in this place for about five weeks. We were inside a hotel room, and while I was there I lost about twenty pounds. The food was not very good. It was definitely different. We had a lot of rice. Then for supper we had something they called *osh*, which was a type of soup. We had another name for it. We just added an "it" to it, and changed the emphasis a little bit. Called it "osh-it." I remember sometimes there would be worms in our food. These little white things crawling around in it. We'd just brush them off and go ahead and eat.

CPL. STEVEN KIRTLEY (*marine security guard, with two other hostages at a location near Khorramshahr*): When I was down in that subterranean room, I had a bad case of food poisoning. They started feeding us Iranian food when they moved us away from Tehran. For breakfast they'd bring us some kind of bread and butter. Then for lunch, which was the main meal, they'd usually bring in some kind of Iranian rice dish. And I mean they came in with some of the strangest shit. Then for supper it would be a can of soup. They'd come in with Campbell's cream of mushroom or cream of cheddar soup. I loathe cream of mushroom soup, and I feel the same way about cream of cheddar. What the Iranians would do is cut the top off the can, put the can on a burner to heat it up, and stick a spoon in it and give it to us. That was the way we had to eat it. God, I hated that stuff.

One of the Iranian dishes they gave me had something in it that made me real sick. I had a bad case of dysentery. I would repeatedly have to bang on the door and get the guard to come and get me. The guard would come in, blindfold me, and help me get up the stairs. Twenty-one stairs. I had to climb all those goddamn stairs every time I got sick. I'd get in the bathroom, and I'd have bouts of diarrhea and I'd throw up, and then have more diarrhea. I was hurting. I was really sick. When I was finished, I'd be so weak that I'd just pull my pants up and lean back against the wall and rest. I didn't have enough energy to go back downstairs. I'd feel so bad that I'd just sit there for a while. Then finally I'd knock on the door and the guard would come in, put my blindfold back on, and help me back down the stairs.

The worst part of being sick was at night. I'd wake up at 2:30 in the morning, and there would just be one guard on duty. I'd bang on the door, and he'd be walking around the building or would be asleep on the other side of the hall or something. I'd beat on the door and beat on the door, and would wake up the two Americans who were down there with me, and nobody would come. I had diarrhea, and I was hurting. I'd stand there and beat on the door for half an hour sometimes. That was painful. I'd just stand there beating and beating and beating on that door. When the guard finally came I'd cuss at him, but it would only be two or three words because I'd be doubled over in pain. I was hurting so goddamn much that would be all I could get out.

After three or four days of this, they brought in a doctor. He gave me some pills for my upset stomach and diarrhea, and made these guys move me upstairs to a room that was on the other side of the bathroom so I didn't have to walk up all those steps. He also changed my diet. They wouldn't give me anything but yogurt and rice. When they started feeding me that shit, I told myself, "Goddamn, man, you've got to get better, because you can't live off of this."

CDR. ROBERT ENGELMANN (*naval supply corps officer, at a location near Qöm*): I spent about a week in this place we called the White Hole. I was there with three other guys. As far as we could tell, the White Hole was a men's locker room in a police station. It had white tiles on all of the walls, and there was a drain in the floor. There were a few holes in the wall that had been plugged up with paper where it looked like showers had been. This place was a real pit. The Iranians put four bunks in there, and it was like four guys living in a closet.

They were serving a lot of rice with lamb and stuff in it, and it would come in an inch of coagulated fat. When we were finished, we didn't have any hot water to wash our dishes with. We had to wash everything in cold water in the bathroom. So it didn't take long before everybody was sick. We all got the Shah's Revenge down there in the White Hole.

I remember they brought a doctor in. He was a cardiologist. This guy came in and told us that he was Khomeini's cardiologist. Whether that was true or not I don't know, but that's what he told us. Then he listened to my ticker and said, "You are fine." I couldn't believe it. I've got dysentery and he listened to my heart.

I told him, "Doctor, I don't need a cardiologist. I need a cork."

He wouldn't do anything for us. He just left us alone, and wouldn't give us any medicine. But everybody was getting sick down there, even the guards. We finally talked one guard into going out and buying some Entero-Vioform. It's a medicine that's not sold in the United States, but is sold in Europe. In large quantities it's supposed to destroy your central nervous system, but it will also get rid of dysentery real quick. It's a strong antibacterial agent. I knew that for eighty cents we could solve the problem. Finally, the guard went out and bought some of this. We'd all take two tablets, and within a few days we were back together again. It was a case where the doctor wouldn't do anything for us, so we cured ourselves.

JOE HALL (*warrant officer, in Yaz*): We were sick all the time. The food was piss poor, and we had bad, bad dysentery. The food and the water were getting to us. I think the water down there was something that our systems just couldn't handle, because we were sick all the time. John Graves, Greg Persinger, and I were together in a place called Yaz. The windows in our room were painted over, and it was hot and stuffy in there because that place wasn't ventilated worth a damn. We'd just lie around in a sick daze all day long. Hour after hour would pass, and we'd lie there too sick to move. We were suffering through some lousy chow, and lost a lot of weight. I was as light as I'd been since I was a small kid. Greg Persinger was losing weight too, and the Iranians finally put Greg on an IV. But the idiots set the thing wrong, and he sucked all the fluid down in about ten minutes. It was ridiculous. They wanted to give me an IV too, but I said, "Bullshit! I'll take my chances without one. No Iranian is sticking a needle in me!"

COL. LELAND HOLLAND (*army attaché, in Jahrom*): These students were typical Persian males. From the time they were babies, they had been waited on hand and foot. They were typical products of that kind of environment. They couldn't boil water without screwing it up. And we were at the mercy of these guys and their capabilities for our food. That summer the sanitation was bad and the food preservation was bad.

I was in this jail cell when I got a horrible cramp in my belly. I knocked on the door and said, "Toilet." They took me down, and boy, I just made it. I was sick. I got back to my room, then all of a sudden I had to go again. I was thinking, "Holy mackerel! What kind of bug have I got? I've got to go again." I banged on the door and said, "Toilet!"

The guard slammed the door in my face and said, "No."

I beat on the door and said, "It's an emergency!"

"You make joke," he said, and he slammed the door again.

Well, what could I do? Here I am. I've got to go. I figure I've got two choices. I can go in my britches, or I can go in the corner. I had a big Hefty trash bag in there that they had given me to put junk in. So I went over, pulled down my pants just like I was out in the woods, opened up the trash bag, and crapped in the bag. No sooner was I finished than I thought, "Hey, this deserves a good turn."

So I knocked on the door, and the guard came over. I held the bag out to him—literally a bag full of shit—and I said, "Would you empty this?"

God, did he get mad! He was furious! He said, "You must let us know! You must let us know!"

"I tried to tell you," I said.

After that, when I knocked on the door they took me to the bathroom. I made twenty-four trips in twenty-two hours. To me it wasn't a case of being crude or coarse. You fight the sons of bitches with whatever you've got—even when all you've got is a bag of shit.

BARRY ROSEN (*press attaché*): From the White Hole, Dave Roeder and I were separated from the others, driven out in an embassy Ford to a location near the town of Mahalat, and put into a place that we called the Tan Hole. It was so dark in there that we could barely read. The Tan Hole was an L-shaped room that was wide and long. There was a narrow opening in the ceiling that was sort of like a skylight, and it provided a shaft of light. In the room, there were two mats on the floor, a table, and two chairs. That was it. There was a guard with an automatic rifle who stayed in this skylight hole above us twenty-four hours a day. We'd get up in the morning and wave to him, but all he would do was turn his back and look away.

Every few days, we'd hear a demonstration outside. So it was obvious that the local population knew we were there. From the balcony of the building that we were being kept in someone would lead these people in their chants. During one of the demonstrations, I heard something being said about the American Sixth Fleet and a threatened invasion. Of course, we didn't get any news about the rescue attempt, and didn't know anything about it. But apparently the Iranians were conjuring up possibilities of what the Americans might be doing in the wake of the failed rescue mission. I remember listening to the demonstration and saying to Dave, "They're telling everybody about a threatened invasion by the American Sixth Fleet."

We didn't know what to make of that. We were sitting there wondering, "What the hell is going on?" We thought that most everybody else was still at the embassy. We didn't know that everyone had been dispersed all across the entire country. Instead, we figured that we were being kept apart as the ace in the hole. If an attack came we were afraid we'd be the only two Americans left in Iran.

JOHN LIMBERT (*political officer*): I was taken to a little one-story villa near the Zayandeh Rud (river), which flows right through the middle of Isfahan. There were other Americans being held in the villa, but once again I was in a room by myself. I was still in solitary. Unfortunately, the accommodations were very modest. The room was small and there wasn't much light.

While I was there I could overhear small snatches of news when the students listened to their radio. At the embassy the students had always been careful to keep the radio volume down when I was around. But in Isfahan I occasionally overheard snatches of things. I remember I thought I overheard something about an unsuccessful rescue attempt, but I wasn't sure. The radio kept fading in and out, and I wasn't quite sure of what I was hearing.

I'd been in this place for about ten days when one day I went in to take a shower. One of the students had been in there before me. He had spread a Persian-language newspaper out on a shelf and left it there. At the time, the paper was about a week old. It was dated around the first of May, and it carried a story in Persian that was compiled from wire service reports about the rescue mission. It was just enough for me to know that there had been a mission, that it had been unsuccessful, and there were American casualties. That was it.

Eventually I established contact with Malcolm Kalp, who was being kept in the same building. I passed the news on to him. By exchanging notes we talked about what I had learned, and the logistics of rescue possibilities. Knowing that such an attempt had been made, we figured that it was possible the United States might try again. That was a thought that was always in the back of my mind, and we discussed possible logistics in our notes. Then one night at about eleven o'clock, I heard a couple of students talking outside my window. They were saying things like: "If something happens, make sure the explosives are in the right place," or words to that effect. What they were saying wasn't completely clear, but they seemed to indicate that if there was another rescue attempt they were going to try to put us all in a place where they could blow us up. As I look back on it now, I think they might have been deliberately talking right outside the window because they knew I would hear them, and they were saying these things for my benefit. Maybe such explosives and plans did exist, and maybe they didn't. But hearing that didn't make me feel very good.

SGT. ROCKY SICKMANN (*marine security guard, in Shiraz*): We didn't know that a rescue mission had failed. But I kept a diary and when we got to Shiraz I wrote down everything that had happened. Then a couple of weeks later one of the guards came in with a *Time* magazine and showed us some pictures of the crash site and the eight men who had died in the rescue attempt. They wouldn't let us read the article. They just flashed the pictures in front of our faces, and told us that Secretary of State Vance had resigned. They also said that if the United States tried any kind of military intervention they were going to kill us right away. They told us that several times.

After the guards left, Jerry Plotkin, Bill Gallegos, and I sat there and talked about it, and I looked back in my diary to see what I'd written down. We came to the conclusion that the rescue attempt had probably happened on the night they moved us. I guess they moved everyone into different locations, although we didn't know that everyone else had been moved too. We just knew that there were some other people in the van when we were taken out.

There was one guard there that we called Santa Claus. He was the guy who had come in with the *Time* magazine. He was a liar and a bastard. He was kind of a head honcho among the militants. He was the sort of guy who would lie to us about when we were going to be released just to be a bastard and give us false hope. And he lied about what was going on in the news. A couple of days after he had come in with the pictures from the rescue attempt, he came in and told us that two F-14s had crashed over the Persian Gulf and that the pilots had been killed. He did that to us a couple of times. He'd come into the room and say that two more Americans had been killed. He just lied and lied. He loved to play with our minds. We didn't know what was going on outside.

WILLIAM ROYER (*director of academic courses, in Meshed*): In Meshed we were kept in a small office building. From an envelope that we found, we determined that at one time the building we were in had housed a local Iranian version of the Chamber of Commerce, involved with import/export business, or something like that. Three of us were put into a large room where the windows had been whitewashed over so that we couldn't see out. We tried to find cracks near the panels where the students had missed whitewashing in order to get at least a partial view of what was outside. Then we discovered that some of the guards had scratched out a little bit of whitewash from the outside so that they could look in and see us at night. Of course, this gave us a peephole that we could look out in the daytime. Perched on the balcony outside our window, I could see a .30-caliber machine gun that was surrounded by a sandbag emplacement.

On one occasion, a helicopter flew over our building. Through our little peephole I could see that this caused a great deal of commotion outside, and the guards manned the machine gun. For a minute there, I thought there was really going to be some fireworks. But the helicopter passed on by. I chose to interpret this reaction on the part of the guards as further evidence of internal strife in Iran. The students obviously felt threatened by the appearance of this helicopter.

Our guards tried to tell us that no one knew where we were and that our whereabouts was being kept secret. But it became obvious to us that people knew where we were being held, because there were demonstrations outside our building. We'd hear the usual chanting: "Death to America!" and "Death to Carter!" These demonstrations seemed to make the guards very nervous. I sensed that they were worried for their own safety, and hence, there were always revolutionary guards there to help defend the students who were overseeing us. Of course, they didn't speak about these things within the range of our hearing, and they did a good job of keeping us uninformed. But it was obvious that there were different domestic Iranian factions at play, and the students felt threatened and in jeopardy from their own people.

JOHN LIMBERT (*political officer, in solitary confinement at a house in Isfahan*): Apparently no attempt was made to hide the existence of the place in Isfahan where some of us were kept. There was a banner outside which identified the place as the headquarters of the "Student Followers of the Imam's Line," and there were loudspeakers and sandbags around the building. Occasionally there would be demonstrations. In fact, I remember one demonstration that took place on a Friday. After their Friday prayers there was the usual chanting of slogans, and the usual fifteen- or twenty-point declaration was read. But the thing that interested me was that during this demonstration it was announced that type-A blood was needed for those people who were wounded in Kurdistan, and that anyone who was willing to donate blood should do so.

A couple of hours later one of the students came by, and I said to him, "I understand you need blood donors for the wounded. I have type-A blood, and I'd be perfectly happy to donate blood."

He got very upset. I wasn't supposed to know these things, and the fact that I did meant their system of keeping us isolated from news had broken down. I knew something about them that they didn't want me to know. I knew that there were disorders, that there was fighting going on, and that there were wounded. Which meant that all was not right in their revolutionary world. So I knew one of their vulnerabilities. This fellow was very concerned with how I found this out. He kept asking me, "How do you know? How do you know?"

All I said was, "I just know." I wouldn't tell him. If he wanted to think that one of his own people had told me, then that was just fine with me. I figured, let them be suspicious of each other, and let him chase after whoever he thought made the leak.

Because I knew this was a vulnerability, I kept after him about my offer. I'd repeatedly say to him, "I'd be more than happy to donate blood, and I'm sure some of the other hostages would be perfectly willing to do so too, if you would only ask them." It was worth doing this just to watch how upset this fellow got.

BILL BELK (*communications officer, at a rural precinct jail*): Subic and I were about an hour or so outside of Isfahan when we were being kept in the little precinct jail. But I don't know where. All I know is that we were near a school, because during daytime we could hear kids playing across the street. We could hear them hollering to each other and laughing and going out for recess. The guards boarded up the window in our cell so that we couldn't look out. But in the bathroom there was a window way high up on the wall. It had bars on it, and I would jump up, grab the bars, and pull myself up to see out. There was a big excavation pit that had been dug for construction right next to the little building that we were being kept in. The construction had stopped, and this big pit was just sitting there deserted. Beyond the excavation pit was a wall, and beyond the wall I could see the tops of a few huts in the village. That was about it.

At first, I don't think anybody in the village knew the students were holding the two of us there, because it was pretty quiet. The worst thing was the desert heat and the food. The food was real bad. The students did give us some cards and a game of checkers. So Subic and I would spend a lot of time playing checkers. It was too damn hot to do anything else.

Then somehow the local population found out that we were being kept there, and crowds started to gather in front of this little jail. Hundreds of people would stand out there and chant, "*Marg bar Amrika! Marg bar Amrika!*" Pretty soon the crowds got so big that it sounded like they were going to cave the walls in with all of their yelling. They'd chant, "*Allah Akbar! Allah Akbar!*" Then they'd start to shout for our blood. Death to this. Death to that. Those people were obsessed with hollering for death. I think the major form of recreation throughout the entire country was to go out and holler for somebody's death. Death to the shah. Death to Carter. Death to the hostages. It would go on and on.

Then all of a sudden rounds of ammunition started going off in addition to the chanting. We heard gunfire and explosions, and started taking incoming rounds. Bullets were bouncing around all over the place. That was an amazing situation to be in. There was a lot of dissension among the population, and we figured that there was a radical faction out there that wanted to come in and kill us. The students were very frightened. They were receiving incoming sniper fire, and they were obviously afraid that they might get killed or that we might get killed. They didn't like us, but they were concerned about the consequences of our getting shot. If hostages started turning up dead, they were afraid that President Carter would level the whole damn country. Just remove Iran from the map.

Subic and I would sit there and talk about it while all this shooting was going on. We figured, "Hell, there's no way we're getting out of this. These people are fighting among themselves, and we're sitting here caught in the middle. The idiots who are holding us are trying to protect their own asses plus ours." I figured there was no damn way we'd ever get out of there alive.

JOE HALL (*warrant officer, in the village of Yaz with Greg Persinger and John Graves*): Periodically we'd hear bursts of machine-gun fire, and we'd hit the floor. We were afraid that bullets would come winging in the window. It was very obvious that our guards were afraid for our safety. There were rifle attacks at night, and we could actually hear the bullets plugging off the walls. We thought that somebody else was trying to get hold of us, and it was difficult to know who in the hell to root for. There was a power struggle going on among dissident groups, but we didn't know who the students were fighting or what other groups wanted to do—or would do if they ever got us.

JOHN GRAVES (*public affairs officer*): While we were being kept in Yaz, the students were very, very jumpy. They were under attack and didn't feel secure. I used to sit there and wonder, "Will we be better off if the guys outside win? Or worse off?"

BILL BELK (*communications officer, at a rural precinct jail*): That was a confusing time. We didn't know what was going to happen. The bullets were flying hot and heavy, and I was afraid that the guys who were guarding us would just cut and run, and leave us sitting there in the jail. Every night there was gunfire, and we didn't know if the students could hold out, or for how long. They were very frightened—hiding behind concrete walls with their rifles. Then one night there was a great explosion. I think somebody fired a rocket-propelled grenade at us. Within an hour, the guards snuck us out of there in the middle of the night. They put us into a van and drove us to Isfahan.

JOE HALL (*warrant officer, in the village of Yaz with Greg Persinger and John Graves*): On May 30, the Iranians came in and told us to get our stuff together, that we were being moved again. They took the three of us and put us in the back of a Ford Bronco, and we went on another all-night ride. We were cramped into the back of that thing and could feel practically every bump on the road. That was another miserable ride. They took us from Yaz to Khorramshahr, and put us in what looked like an old gendarme headquarters. It was an old adobe building with real thick walls and bars on the windows.

Fortunately, we never did hear any gunfire at this place. I assume that's why the guards moved us. They were obviously concerned about our safety in Yaz.

BILL BELK (*communications officer*): It was still dark when we arrived in Isfahan. The Iranians took Subic and I into a huge mansion. I remember being led up a very long spiral staircase and put into a bedroom on the second floor. There was only one bed in the room—one great big huge bed—and the Iranians told us that Subic and I were going to have to sleep on the bed together. Well, I wasn't too wild about crawling into bed with an army sergeant, and he wasn't too crazy about getting into bed with me. So we talked the guards into dragging another mattress into the room, and Subic slept on the mattress and I slept on the bed. The most amazing thing about that place was that the guards brought us sheets—clean sheets! I couldn't believe it. That was the first time I'd seen sheets in over six months.

2 At the Embassy: May–July 1980

IN THE WEEK that followed the rescue attempt, forty-four of the hostages were dispersed throughout various locations in Iran in order to prevent the United States from attempting a similar mission. Only five hostages remained in the embassy compound. They included the two female hostages, Katherine Koob and Elizabeth Ann Swift, and three men: Robert Ode, age sixty-six; Richard Queen, who was seriously ill with an undiagnosed disease; and Don Hohman, the army medic. All five hostages were housed on the second floor of the chancery building, along with a detail of Iranian guards.

RICHARD QUEEN (*consular officer*): It was very quiet in the chancery. We didn't hear any of the normal hostage sounds, the knocking on doors and the footsteps in the hallway. At first, I just figured that the Iranians had moved everyone out of our wing of the building. But we were eventually able to figure out that everyone had been moved off the compound, and that there were only five of us left at the embassy. It was myself, Bob Ode, and Don Hohman, along with the two women. Kate Koob and Ann Swift were being kept across the hall. We weren't allowed to see them, but we knew they were there. That was it. Just the five of us remained. So it was very quiet.

ROBERT ODE (*consular officer*): For a while, one of the militants had been doing our cooking. Then one day he disappeared and one of the terrorists brought in a note from Kate and Ann saying that they were going to cook for us. They wanted to know what type of things we would like to eat. So we sent them a note back letting them know what our likes and dislikes were. Kate Koob was an excellent cook, and Ann Swift was willing to help her. Due to Kate's culinary skills and her ability to work miracles with the facilities and supplies available, the three of us men lived pretty high off the hog.

It was sort of funny, because the terrorists wouldn't ever let us see the girls or talk to them. But they did let us write notes requesting certain meals, as long as we didn't sign these notes. The arrangement that developed was that I would address the notes "Les Girls," and then sign them "The Boys in the Back Room." The Iranians passed these notes right along. In this way I let Kate know one time that one of my favorite foods was stuffed peppers, and shortly after that we had some wonderful stuffed peppers. Kate and Ann made us a lot of great meals. Kate would even make doughnuts for us. During this period of time, I'm sure that we three men fared much better than any of the other hostages.

DON HOHMAN (*army medic*): At the embassy, we had one guard who was particularly obnoxious. He was in charge there, and Bob, Rich, and I all hated him. We called him Hamid the Liar. He used to love to come into the room with his hands full of mail and very deliberately make a big show out of giving mail to Rich Queen and Bob Ode. Then he'd say, "You don't have anything, Mr. Hohman. No one has written you."

I'd say, "You asshole! I know better than that!" I knew that my wife, my daughters, and my mother were writing.

But Hamid loved to pull that kind of stuff. Bob Ode and Rich Queen would try to talk to him about it. Rich in particular would appeal to Hamid in his bad Farsi. Poor Rich. His Farsi was terrible. The Iranians would laugh at him because it was so bad. I think my Farsi was better. I had this little phrase book that I used. It was the only way I could get the Iranians to get me the kinds of food I wanted because I wasn't eating any meat. But Rich and Bob tried to reason with Hamid about my not getting any mail. It didn't do any good, but they gave it their best shot. The three of us were tight. We were real close.

Rich Queen was the only guy I ever saw who never got pissed at the rag heads. Different people react to captivity in different ways. I was raised on the streets, and I reacted to them the way I would've reacted to any punk on the streets. If they came in to feed me a line of shit, I'd cuss them out. Especially Hamid. I'd say, "You're just a bunch of lying punks! Now get the hell out of here!" But Rich Queen was totally the opposite. He was always calm. He'd just sit back and relax, and read a book or play one of his games. He got by day to day, and hardly ever raised his voice. Of course, he was having trouble with his illness, and in a way I guess he had more reason to be miserable than anyone. But he never complained. You know, being there was driving me nuts, but Rich never got shook. Even when he was seriously ill, he took what came.

RICHARD QUEEN (*consular officer*): When I was living with Bob Ode and Don Hohman, we had a room with a view of the mountains to the north of Tehran. It was a very beautiful view. One evening we could see some very dark clouds slowly moving toward us. A thunderstorm was rolling in over the mountains. We turned the lights off, and sat there and watched the storm come down toward us. Lightning was cracking over the mountains, and that was a beautiful sight. The three of us sat there in front of the window and watched the storm. We didn't say much. We were very quiet. We wanted to see as much of the world outside as we could. Watching the storm made me feel calm and serene. It was comforting to see an everyday occurrence like that, because it was the part of the world that we were being denied. It felt familiar, and was the sort of thing we could have seen in the States.

DON HOHMAN (*army medic*): The days would pass ever so slowly. One day after another would slip from our lives. We were already in the middle of summer, and not much was going on. Rich Queen, Bod Ode, and I got into daily games of Scrabble. I never played so much Scrabble in my life. We literally got to the point where we would play four, five, or six hours of straight Scrabble. Rich Queen was really good at it. He could read the board upside down, and he was always figuring out his next play, and he knew exactly what he was going to do before his turn came. The guy amazed me. He's incredibly bright, and he had a huge vocabulary. The only way we could catch him was because he couldn't spell worth a shit. He's got a master's degree in history, and he can't spell.

We played Scrabble to pass the time, but we were also concerned about Rich. He was a very sick man.

RICHARD QUEEN (*consular officer*): For a while, my symptoms did recede. Slowly but surely I was getting better. Of course, Don Hohman didn't have any of his equipment and he couldn't give me a complete examination, but he said, "I think you've had a stroke." That was because of the way the numbness had only affected the left half of my body. So I thought I'd had a mild stroke.

Once the quack doctor I'd seen before came in with an Iranian medical student who was missing one of his fingers. The medical student agreed with Don Hohman; he thought I'd had a stroke. He said, "We're sorry. We should have done something. We should have taken you to the hospital." But by that time I was getting better.

Then the same slight numbness that I'd felt on the left side of my body started to affect my right hand. I said, "Don, what's going on?" He didn't know. All he could say was, "I don't know. I don't know what you have."

DON HOHMAN (*army medic*): I had my Merck manual, and I kept reading it and reading it, and a lot of what was going on with Rich didn't seem right for a stroke. If it was a stroke, he should have had a sudden onset, whereas his symptoms had increased very gradually.

I knew Rich was seriously ill, but I didn't know what he had. I started thinking brain tumor. I thought maybe a tumor was pinching somewhere. His symptoms could have been consistent with a brain tumor, but I didn't have any equipment to diagnose him with, or the knowledge to put it all together. All I had was this little Merck manual. I was thinking, "Jesus Christ, I don't know what he's got." All I knew was that he was seriously ill. His balance was totally off, and he had numbness in both of his hands. His vision had doubled.

RICHARD QUEEN (*consular officer*): We used to walk around the room for exercise, and when I was walking I started to get dizzy and my balance wasn't too good. The dizziness increased in severity very quickly. It got to the point where I could only sit down. I couldn't walk any more. About once a week the guards took us out to the courtyard to walk around and give us some fresh air. I had to stop going outside. I couldn't walk without getting sick. I had to either sit still or lie down. If I turned my head too quickly I became nauseous. Then my symptoms quickly got much worse.

DON HOHMAN (*army medic*): At one point they brought their stupid rag head doctor in, and he looked at Rich and said, "Maybe he has an inner ear infection."

I said, "Bullshit!" That doctor spoke English, so he knew exactly what I was saying. I said, "That's bullshit! And you know it!"

I'd looked in Rich's ears, and I knew he had something much more serious than an ear infection. There wasn't anything wrong with his ears. But this doctor gave Rich some Dramamine. I told him, "No, this isn't going to work." I knew it had to be something neurological. And of course the Dramamine didn't slow his dizziness down at all. Rich just got sicker and sicker.

RICHARD QUEEN (*consular officer*): It got to the point where I couldn't move at all. I had to lie flat on my back and remain motionless. If I turned my head a little, I'd get nauseous and vomit, which I did a few times in my sleep at night, and then I'd suddenly wake up very nauseous. I couldn't touch any food. I couldn't keep anything down, so I didn't want any food. The absolute worst was having to go to the bathroom—that was incredible agony. My balance was so bad that I had to use my hand as a brace to keep myself steady against the wall. I remember I'd sing army marching songs to keep my morale up as I was moving down the hall to the bathroom. Inevitably, when I got there I'd be dizzy and nauseous, and I'd have to vomit. Then I'd crawl back to my bed and lie flat on my back.

DON HOHMAN (*army medic*): Finally, it got to the point where Rich couldn't get out of bed. Bob was yelling and screaming at those stupid rag heads to do something for him. We repeatedly told those rag heads that Rich was seriously ill, that he needed a hospital, that nobody could do what needed to be done in that room. Rich needed tests. But they wouldn't do a goddamn thing. Finally, I took Akbar aside and I said, "Akbar, if you don't do something for Richard, he's going to die. You've got to get him to a hospital. I mean that. He's going to die." Akbar knew I wasn't trying to bullshit him, and I think that scared the rag heads.

RICHARD QUEEN (*consular officer*): Don Hohman told the Iranian medical student that he thought I was dying. The medical student must have conferred with his superiors, because they brought in a regular doctor. I remember the doctor came in the door, and the first thing I did was turn my head to look at him, which made me nauseous, and so I vomited. Made a mess next to my mattress.

The doctor looked at me, and he asked me to do some basic tests:

"Can you walk? Can you put your toe to your heel?" I couldn't do that at all. I was very unstable. The next morning a couple of militants came in and told me I was going to the hospital. I didn't take anything with me, because I thought I would just be there for the day.

DON HOHMAN (*army medic*): It must have been about nine o'clock in the morning when the doctor came back in with a couple of other guys. Rich was still vomiting, and he really looked bad. They wanted to get him up and walk him out to the ambulance. I said, "No. There's no way you are going to do that to him. He's got to have a stretcher."

As soon as I said that, Bob Ode started ranting and raving at them. He was saying, "You'd better get a stretcher for this man. We're not letting you move him unless he's on a stretcher." Bob was just like a high school principal chewing these kids out. He was shaking his finger under their noses, and telling them to get a stretcher.

They finally went out and got a stretcher, and I helped them move Rich onto it. I remember saying good-bye to him as he left, but I don't know if he understood me. I don't think he knew where he was. He was a very sick man. I don't know how he managed to survive in captivity for as long as he did. He'd had most of his symptoms for a good six months. As I watched them take him out on the stretcher, I thought he was dying. I was still thinking brain tumor.

RICHARD QUEEN (*consular officer*): I was taken to a hospital in northern Tehran. I was still very nauseous, and while they were conducting tests, I continued to vomit. I couldn't eat any food at all, so they fed me intravenously.

Every morning I'd get a whole bucket of pills. The nurse would come in with a bunch of pills, and I'd eat them all. One of those drugs, which was used to try and control my nausea, had a horrendous side effect. I lost control of my neck muscles and couldn't stop turning my head. My head would continually drift slowly to the right, and I couldn't stop it. I'd take my hand and physically force my head straight, but the minute I moved my hand, my head would slowly drift to the right. That was the one time when I really thought I might be dying. I was just lying there in my hospital bed, going back through my memory and singing old army marching songs to myself to keep my mind occupied. That was the one time I thought I was going under.

At the hospital I wasn't getting any better. As a matter of fact, I was getting worse. The neurologist said that my disease had been narrowed down to either multiple sclerosis or encephalitis getting near the acute phase. None of that meant anything to me. I didn't know what those things were.

Then shortly after that, someone came in and said that I was going back. I said, "What? Back to the compound?" I was sure that's where I would go after I was cured. I thought they were going to send me back to the embassy. I said, "I can't go back yet." I was still being fed intravenously, and I thought it was too soon for me to leave the hospital.

I was told, "No, you're going back home. Ayatollah Khomeini has released you to your parents." Just then, the news was on the radio, and I listened. I could make out enough of the Farsi to understand the broadcast. I recognized my name and the name of Ayatollah Khomeini. I understood that I had been released to my parents for medical reasons.

Pretty soon, a representative from Bani-Sadr's government arrived, and I was signed over to him. I was helped down to the car, and then this guy drove like a bat out of hell to the airport. I remember him saying, "We've got to hurry. Swissair is holding a plane up for you. It's costing the Swiss a thousand dollars a minute to hold that plane up, and you know how the Swiss are about their money." When we got to the airport, we didn't go into the lobby or anything. There was no waiting in lines. We rode right out onto the runway in the car.

The press was there waiting. There was a Japanese reporter, an Iranian reporter, and a Danish reporter. The Danish reporter turned out to be a stringer for CBS. The film that was shot of me being transferred onto the plane was shown almost immediately in the United States, and the Iranians were furious about that. They wondered how CBS got that film. American reporters were not allowed in Iran,* so they traced the film to the Danish reporter, and they threw the reporter in jail. They threatened to execute him as a CIA agent. Then, a few days later, they threw him out of Iran.

Anyway, I was met at the ramp by the head of the American Interest Section at the Swiss embassy, and he helped me up the ramp. I went into a remission the minute I got on the plane. It was just miraculous. I was seated in first class, and the stewardesses started wheeling out food for all the passengers. I was famished—and yet, an hour and a half earlier it would have been impossible for me to have even thought about food. I was too busy vomiting. But on the flight, I was feeling so much better that I went ahead and ate breakfast. Being in first class, they served crepes and fruit and little filet mignon steaks. Then they kept wheeling out pastries, champagne, and caviar. Finally, they offered me a tray full of cordials and Schnapps. I thought, "No, I'm not going to push myself by going that far."

It was just a miracle. I was getting so much better on the flight out.

---

* American correspondents were expelled from Iran on January 14, 1980, and Richard Queen was released on July 11, 1980.

I had a little vertigo, but it wasn't too bad. Everything was happening so fast that it still hadn't sunk in that I was no longer a hostage. That I was free, and flying out of Iran to meet my parents.

In the hospital in Zurich, I got a call from President Carter and Rosalynn Carter. We had a very informal conversation. He wanted to know, "How are you doing? How are you feeling?" That sort of thing. Then a little later I got a call from Secretary of State Muskie. It shocked me when he introduced himself as the secretary of state. I had no idea that Cyrus Vance had resigned. For nine months I'd been like Rip Van Winkle. No news at all. I didn't have any idea of what was going on.

When I got back to the United States, I met with President Carter in the White House. He wanted to know what it was like in Tehran. So I told him as much as I could. I just went on and on. I did almost all of the talking, and he listened. I told him how we were put in front of the mock firing squad in February, which is something I didn't mention to the press or any of the hostage family members. I didn't see any point in making that public, and scaring the families when there was nothing they could do about it except worry. But I did tell President Carter, and when I described that to him I could see that he was very moved. My God, he was moved. He's a very humane man, and he was very genuinely caught up in the hostage crisis.

ROBERT ODE (*consular officer*): Don Hohman and I were never told that Richard Queen was evacuated to the United States. Every time we'd ask one of the terrorists how Richard was getting along, we'd always get the same stock answer: "Oh, he's getting along just fine. Just fine. He's doing very well."

We'd ask, "Well, when is he coming back?"

"Perhaps in a week or so," they'd tell us.

We thought Richard was going to return to the embassy. Of course, by this time he was already back in the United States, but we didn't know that. After they took him to the hospital, I took all of the bedsheets off his mattress, his pillowcases, and his underwear, and gathered up all of the clothing he had there, and took it down to the toilet and washed everything. I dusted his room and took care to get everything in order for him to come back. I wanted the room ready in anticipation of his return. But of course he never came back.

RICHARD QUEEN (*consular officer*): When the doctors told me that I had multiple sclerosis, I didn't really care. After I was released from Tehran, my health improved so rapidly that I just assumed it wasn't important. All of my symptoms receded, and I left the hospital much sooner than the doctors had originally thought I'd be able to.

Of course, the hostages were always on my mind. I was constantly thinking about them. I met with as many of the family members as I could and tried to answer their questions and give them any news I could. I also went up to Alaska to visit two of my very close friends. We went fishing and relaxed in the wilderness and talked. It was really good to get away from everything. To escape. I think what I really wanted was to turn the clock back to before November 4, 1979. I wanted to continue my life as though Tehran had never happened. There were times when I would feel horribly guilty. I'd ask myself, "What am I doing out?" And I'd think, "I'd much rather be with them in Tehran." Meeting with the families of those who were still back there was especially difficult. Of course, they'd tell me, "You have nothing to feel guilty about." A couple of the mothers held me with tears in their eyes and said, "My son is locked up. Until he returns, you are my son." But all the same, I felt horribly guilty. There were times when I'd think, "Those still in Tehran are the lucky ones—I'm not. I'd much rather be with them."

DON HOHMAN (*army medic*): We thought the Iranians would treat Rich at the hospital in Tehran and then bring him back to us. That's what they always told us they were going to do. They said that he was coming back. We didn't learn until four months later that he had gone home. Bob Ode got a letter from a little girl in the States—you know, one of those "Dear Hostage" letters—and in it she mentioned something about Richard Queen being in the United States. We read that with the greatest of joy. We thought, "All right! Somebody made it home!" I was very glad to see that he had gotten out. But at the same time I was wondering how his health was. I knew he must have been in a pretty serious condition for them to let him go.

3 Life after the Dispersal: May–July 1980

BILL BELK (*communications officer, with Sgt. Joe Subic at a mansion in Isfahan*): I still didn't know anything about the rescue mission, and I didn't know that all of the other hostages had been scattered all over Iran. We were like so much dust blown by the wind. Nobody knew where we'd landed. I didn't know a thing about the others. I was only aware of what was going on in my immediate surroundings.

At this house in Isfahan Subic and I more or less settled back into a routine. Outside it was very quiet. We didn't have to put up with any more crowds or gunfire. I'm sure the students were trying to hide the fact that we were there. They didn't want anyone to know about us. In the bedroom they put contact paper on the inside of the windows so we couldn't see out—on the inside, not the outside. That's how stupid they could be. We just cut little slits into the contact paper so that we could look out. We were on the second floor of a gigantic house. We could stand at the window and watch the comings and goings of people in the street. We'd see them walking around or driving around, and going about their daily business. After taking all that gunfire and putting up with all the chanting, I thought it was a little peculiar how these people would come and go by this house and never pay us any mind. They obviously didn't know what was going on inside.

One time, Subic peeled back a little corner of the contact paper so that he could look out. He peeled it back too far and one of the outside guards saw that he was looking out the window. All of a sudden, this absolutely filthy, grotesque character flew into the room. He couldn't speak English at all, but he tried to put a few words together. He was saying something like: "We student security. We shoot. You look out window. We shoot you." In a way it was kind of funny, because this guy was having so much trouble with his English. He was a big goon, and he was standing there pointing at his head saying, "We smart. We security. We smart." It was like something out of a very bad movie— *The Ape Man Cometh to Isfahan* or something. But broken English and all, he let us know that we weren't supposed to look out the window.

While we were in that room, another funny thing happened. We found a little tiny mouse on the rug next to Subic's mattress. A little brown mouse. Now I never realized that a grown man could be afraid of a mouse. But when Subic saw this mouse he started jumping around on his mattress and pointing at it. "Ooh! Ooh! A mouse! A mouse!" He was scared to death. I thought that was one of the funniest things I ever saw. I'll never forget seeing this big bad army sergeant jumping around in front of that little mouse. I cracked up. I wasn't about to get up and chase the mouse away. It was too damn funny watching Subic jump around. That was definitely the highlight of our time in Isfahan.

The routine we settled into more or less resembled the routine that had been established back at the embassy. The students would come in with the normal breakfast, which was some hard bread and jelly. Then for lunch we started to receive a lot more rice. They were trying to prepare better meals than we'd had at the precinct jail. Instead of coming in with a can of cranberry sauce, they were bringing us some Iranian rice dishes. I think we were eating the same things that the students were eating. We needed that better diet, too, because I'd lost quite a bit of weight. I tried to convince Subic that we should get an exercise program going, but there was no way he was going to exercise. So I started my own program of exercises that I would do every day.

At one point, the students brought a cassette player into our room, and they let us listen to some music. That was the first time they'd ever done anything like that. They brought in a Charlie Pride country music tape, and we listened to that. We also had a table with two chairs, in addition to a comfortable easy chair. It was unbelievable that we had so much luxury. These were the best accommodations I'd had the whole time I was there. Subic and I would sit at the table, play rummy, and listen to country music.

JOHN LIMBERT (*political officer, in solitary confinement at a house in Isfahan*): I had lots of conversations with the students, and those conversations varied as much as the person I was talking with. I do remember one fellow by the name of Mohammed that I got to know fairly well. He decided that he was interested in improving his English, and I told him that I was willing to teach him. Several of them mentioned this, and I was willing to teach whoever wanted to learn. Mohammed, in particular, was serious about learning the language, and he worked very hard at it. He and I would pick a subject and work on the vocabulary of the subject. For example, one time we might talk about food, and different names for various kinds of food. Another time we might talk about travel. He was very interested in traveling, so we would work on his English while talking about various trips, and where he should go and what it would be interesting for him to see.

My tuition for teaching him English was to have him play chess with me. I'd been in solitary for quite a while, and getting someone to come in and play chess with me was a way to help pass the time.

We would also talk about religion. In the context of teaching Mohammed English, I would ask him to prepare a talk about one of their religious figures, or about the history of their religion. Interestingly enough, for all their religiosity, I found that the students didn't know much about the history of their religion. To them history was not interesting. What interested them was "religion." The facts and the lives of their various heroes—where they had lived and what they had done— was not of great interest to them. What was more interesting for them was to list a series of virtues about one of their religious heroes. For example, they might want to list things that illustrated the virtue of Ali, their first imam. At the time of the twentieth of Ramadan, which is the day of Ali's death, I asked Mohammed to prepare a talk about Ali. As it turned out, he got so emotional that he couldn't do it, but he did bring me some literature on Ali. Perhaps he thought he was going to convert me, I don't know.

I can honestly say that I didn't dislike Mohammed. In fact, I didn't dislike most of the students who were holding us. I felt sorry for them, and I was frustrated by them. I thought that they were misled. While they were not necessarily stupid people, they were led by their stupidity. There's a proverb that says, "Against stupidity the gods themselves labor in vain." And these people had been led into stupidity. For me it was not really a question of liking or disliking them, although there were some of them that I actively disliked. It was more a situation where I was frustrated by their insistence that what they were doing was right. They were not experienced hard-line terrorists. That was a role that was unfamiliar to them, and I was frustrated by their naïveté. Instead of disliking them, I felt sorry for them.

CDR. ROBERT ENGELMANN (*naval supply corps officer, in a rural location with three other hostages*): One day a couple of guards came in and told us to pack up, we were moving. At the time, we were still suffering from dysentery, and we said to the guards, "Listen, guys, we've got a real problem here. How far are we going to go? This better not be a very long move, because we can't hold it for very long."

They said, "Not far at all. Not far at all."

Well, it turned out it was only about a ten-minute drive. The way things worked, every time you were moved it was sort of like playing "Let's Make a Deal." "Behind this door is—" and then they'd take your blindfold off and you'd look to see who your new roommates were. At the new place, I thought I had real problems when they took off my blindfold and I saw I was with Colonel Schaefer and Barry Rosen. Here I am surrounded by bloodthirsty Moslems, and I'm being kept with Barry, who is Jewish, and with the defense attaché, who was a marked man if ever there was one. The Iranians had him pegged as some sort of master spy. I thought, "I'm in with a bad crowd now. These two guys are marked men. We might be in for some trouble."

BARRY ROSEN (*press attaché, in a rural location with three other hostages*): Interestingly enough, I don't think my being Jewish affected the way I was treated in any way, which is surprising. Very surprising. The Iranians would make remarks about my being Jewish. They would say that I was a Zionist this or a Zionist that, and one guy came in and asked me if my wife was living in Jerusalem. But I don't think they were any more severe in their treatment of me than they were on most of the others. And I honestly don't know why. I would've expected different from them. But that was not the axe they chose to grind. They were much more concerned about "spying" and identifying American spies. That put a lot of us in the same boat, because by their definition we were practically all spies of one sort or another.

CDR. ROBERT ENGELMANN (*naval supply corps officer, in a rural location with three other hostages*): We called our new place the Pink Palace. It was a house where all of the walls were pink. The Iranians had welded steel up against the windows to make sandboxes, which they filled full of gravel and steel. Consequently, our room was full of grit, gravel, and little pieces of metal, because the guards never cleaned up. But in spite of that, the Pink Palace was luxury living. We had free access to our own bathroom, and that was a real benefit. We didn't have to pound on the door and be blindfolded every time we had to use the toilet. Previously, there had been times when you could pound and pound on the door and the guard would never come, or would tell you that the bathroom was being used. So you'd have to wait 30 or 40 minutes. That can pose quite a problem when you've got dysentery.

COL. THOMAS SCHAEFER (*defense attaché, in a rural location with three other hostages*): While we were at the Pink Palace, we could hear the demonstrations outside. There was always a lot of chanting and screaming and hollering going on. One day we'd have a large crowd out there, and then other days it would be a small group. We even had a marching band go by one time. That marching band consisted of one drum and one bugle. It was a large crowd that day, and I guess the Iranians thought that this drum and bugle were playing music. The crowd was chanting, and there was one guy pounding on the bass drum and another guy playing the bugle. They were horrible. They were so bad it was funny. We used to laugh about that.

GARY LEE (*general services officer, in Jahrom*): Down in Jahrom, Lee Holland and I were together for about a week. Then they moved him out, and we were both in solitary. It was during this time that a couple of guards burst in and accused Lee of passing messages to me by using "eu-rine." They wanted me to tell them about these messages.

I said, "Eu-rine? What is eu-rine?"

"You know! Eu-rine! Eu-rine!"

I couldn't figure out what the hell they were talking about. Finally, I realized that they were accusing Lee of writing messages in urine. I thought that was hilarious. I laughed out loud and told them they were crazy.

COL. THOMAS SCHAEFER (*defense attaché, in a rural location with three other hostages*): To the best of my knowledge, when we were at the Pink Palace we were somewhere near Qöm, although I'm not certain. There was just no way to know for sure. Those were the few months of my life when I didn't know exactly where I was.

An interesting thing happened while we were there. I received a letter from my son that was addressed "To the Greatest Dad in the World, Somewhere in Iran." That's all it said on the envelope. And I got that letter. It was surprising some of the things that they would allow through. That letter in particular, not only because of the way it was addressed, but because it talked about some of the things that were going on back in the United States. It was unusual for them to give me mail that contained any kind of world news. In that letter my son was trying to tell me how much our being held hostage meant to the American people. He said, "Dad, you won't believe the changes we are seeing in the United States. There is renewed unity and patriotism. We are all praying for you." I have to admit that I don't think I believed it at the time. I didn't think that our being held was all that important to the American people. I thought it was important to the immediate families, but beyond that, I didn't think that there would be much concern. I didn't realize that the entire country was agonizing over the fact that we were being held in Iran. It was amazing that letter got through, because it was the type of thing the Iranians didn't want me to know. I guess one of the militants had a little bit of heart that day. From the envelope they could see that it was a letter from my son, and in one of their softer moments figured, "We'll let him have this one letter."

JOHN LIMBERT (*political officer, in solitary confinement at a house in Isfahan*): That period in Isfahan was a long stretch. I was there from late April through late August. I was in solitary all this time, and that part of it was not easy. Being alone and being without news were probably the two hardest things I had to deal with. In terms of depression, those four months in Isfahan were the most difficult. The days just dragged on. Being outside of Tehran didn't give me much cause for hope, because it meant that there was no immediate prospect of a release. If there had been any reason to hope, then why would they have brought us down here and kept us that far away? I figured that we would be released from Tehran, and being away was not a promising sign.

One night during the middle of Ramadan I was sitting in my room when all of a sudden a lot of car horns started honking. People were driving around in the streets honking their horns. In Iran, this means that something good has happened. It's the sort of thing that you would normally hear after a wedding, but they don't have weddings during Ramadan, so I knew that something had happened.

During that summer the students had set a tent up in the yard, and they would sit out there and watch the news on television. Occasionally they would get a little careless about keeping the volume down, and the sound would carry pretty well in the night air. I knew the news came on at nine o'clock, so every night I would stand by the window and try to pick up what little bits of news I could. So the night after I heard all the honking of horns, I listened very carefully and heard the news broadcaster talking about the death of "the vampire of the age," and "the bloodsucker of the age." And I knew that the shah had died.

Later that night Mohammed came in. We were sitting there talking when the car horns started blasting again. I said, "What's going on?"

"Oh, it's a wedding."

"Really?" I said. "A wedding in Ramadan? Those people must have been in an awful hurry to get married."

Even though I knew that the shah was dead, I didn't want the students to know that I knew he was dead. They were trying to isolate us from news, and I was curious to see what Mohammed would say. But I didn't push him too hard, and I didn't delude myself into thinking that this would solve our problem and that we would be going home soon. I knew that the shah's death might open some possibilities, and that while he was alive it would probably be a bit more difficult to get us out of Iran, but I didn't let myself start thinking that a release was imminent.

Then Mohammed said something that I thought was very interesting. He wanted to know, "When you leave here and go home, what are you going to say about us?" He was extremely concerned that I would not speak ill of him and his people, and was genuinely concerned about what my opinion of him was, and what American opinion of Iran was. They were all concerned about this. It was something that was very important to them. In a polite way, I told Mohammed that when I got home I would tell the American people that some of the students were human beings, and some of them were filth. Their action in seizing the embassy fell into the latter category, but there were individuals there who could be taken either way. That wasn't the answer he wanted to hear. It didn't satisfy him.

If I had just said, "Mohammed, everybody hates you for what you have done," then all doubt would have vanished, and this might have been less of a concern to them. I thought it was better to leave a little ambiguity in my answer, because I wanted them to worry about it, and I wanted them to think about it. Not only could it improve our treatment, but it might also impart some sense of guilt, and put some doubt in their minds.

CORT BARNES (*communications officer, with two other hostages in Meshed*): There was a guard that used to carry a .45 with him. We called him Bug Eyes or Crazy Eyes, because he had bulging eyeballs, and he looked like he could go off the deep end any minute. I didn't know it, but he was one of the revolutionary executioners. I found that out later from one of the other hostages, who had seen Bug Eyes in a newspaper. His picture had been taken at a trial of one of Iran's big four-star generals, who was put before a revolutionary court, and then immediately taken up to the roof and shot. In the picture, Bug Eyes was guarding this four-star general, and he was one of the people who went up and performed the execution.

I got to know Bug Eyes while we were in Meshed. He was a pretty fanatical guy, and he was the commander of the guard detail there in Meshed. He didn't speak very good English, but he could understand it. One time I had a run-in with him. Bill Keough, Bill Royer, and I were taken down to our "exercise room," which was a room that didn't have any paint over the windows, so that the sun could shine in. The guards took the three of us down there when they wanted to search our stuff upstairs. They told us it was so we could get "sunshine," but what they were doing was searching our stuff. Anyway, the three of us were down there playing cards when Bug Eyes came by and recognized the game. He knew how to play, and he wanted to be dealt in. So he sat down, and while he was playing he started spouting his radical lines about how America was responsible for all of the evil in the world. I'd heard about all I could take from him, and I threw my cards down on the table and told him that he was a "fucking jerk."

Bill Keough said, "Hey, cool it, Cort." He wanted me to calm down.

Bug Eyes said, "What do you mean, Turk?" Because calling an Iranian a Turk is about the worst insult you can give them.

I said, "I didn't call you a Turk. I called you a jerk."

Bug Eyes looked me square in the face and said, "You ought to speak better English, so we can understand what you are trying to say."

That was the kind of bullshit we had to put up with. If I'd known he was an executioner I might have been a bit more deferential, but as it was, I used a lot of profanity in front of him and didn't try to hide my contempt.

COL. LELAND HOLLAND (*army attaché, in solitary confinement in Jahrom*): Here it is, the summer of 1980, and I'm down in this goddamn rat hole. I mean, it was a dungeon. The ceiling was about six and a half feet tall, and the floor was made up of imitation concrete tiles. Each tile was about five inches square, and the room was about thirteen tiles long and eight tiles wide. There was a jail cell door. That was my room.

I'd pretty much had a break from the interrogations ever since Christmas, but down in that dungeon they started in on me again. They put me down there to try and get me to sign a confession. The guard who ran that interrogation was one of the rattle heads. His approach was shock action. He threatened me with all sorts of nasty consequences if I didn't sign. You know, it was if you don't do what I say, then *bang*! He told me that there was an American woman named Cynthia who had been captured by the police, and that she had confessed to being a spy.* He said that she was going to be executed, and that she had implicated me as being her contact inside the embassy for passing things back and forth. He wanted to know, what did we pass? How did we do it? That sort of thing. I literally did not know a woman named Cynthia. I had no idea what he was talking about. But I wasn't going to sign any confession. If I had, who knows where this girl would be today? Who knows what they would have done with her? A signed confession from me could have been the administrative thing they needed to go ahead and do her in. He would shout at me, and I'd shout right back. We got into a shouting contest, and it ended with him finally telling me that I was going to stay in that room until I signed the confession.

That place was a real rat trap, too. It was littered with all kinds of junk and broken glass, and it was full of bugs. I hauled back the crap and swept off a little section of floor that was just long enough and wide enough for me to lay my body on the floor, and I slept on the concrete floor for four weeks. They kept coming in and telling me, "If you sign this confession, you can go to the good room." I'd just say, "Stuff it up your ass, you son of a bitch!"

Then they started to come in and play their nice guy/hard guy routine. One guy looked around and said, "Bad place. You must clean this room." Then he gave me a broom and said, "You must clean it!"

I said, "Bullshit!" And I refused to clean the room.

A little later, they brought in a chair and a small table. I refused to

---

* Cynthia Dwyer, an American free-lance writer, was picked up in Tehran on the morning after the aborted rescue attempt. At this time, all American reporters had been expelled from Iran, and Iranian authorities accused Ms. Dwyer of being an American spy sent to Iran to assist in the rescue operation. She was jailed for ten months, repeatedly interrogated, and was not released until February of 1981, one full month after the hostages had returned to the United States.

use them. I took them over to the corner and turned them upside down. The guards were really upset by that. They said, "You must use! You must use!"

I said, "You get those fucking things out of here! If you bring them in here again, I'll break them over your goddamn head!" I railed them up one side and down the other. They didn't understand all of the profanity, but they got the emphasis. I wasn't about to accept any favors from them. They were trying to get me to sign this confession, and they wanted to butter me up. I refused to have any part of it. I wouldn't clean the room, and I wouldn't use the furniture.

Then, one time I was in the bathroom, they went into my room and swept it out for me. They cleaned the place up. I came back and gave them hell. I was shouting and ranting and raving. "You did this! You assholes!" God, I gave them hell and called them all sorts of names. They tried to calm me down, but I wasn't about to let them off the hook. That was a very important thing for me. They had put me in this position and I was going to fight back. I didn't have a gun and I didn't have a club, but I was going to fight them in any way I could. I absolutely refused to accept any favors from them. They were trying to do something that I would be grateful for, but I refused to play that game. I snubbed every bit of their hospitality. In the beginning they had come on strong and I met them head on. Then they backed off and tried to start negotiating by bringing me these physical comforts. I wouldn't have any part of it. Those sons of bitches started a tough war, and by God it was going to *be* a tough war. They were going to do it my way. I wasn't going to do it their way. And this bothered them. I wouldn't sweep the damn floor, and I wouldn't use the damn chair. And I wouldn't sign any confession. This really upset them. I'd stood up to all their threats and refused all their favors, so there wasn't much else they could do.

JOHN LIMBERT (*political officer, in solitary confinement at a house in Isfahan*): The difficult thing about being in Isfahan was the long period of time that I was there. It just seemed endless. For a while there the students would turn their radios up every afternoon and broadcast a cleric giving a speech. He would rant and rave, and go on and on for about two hours. His voice would rise and fall, and there would always be a crowd that he was whipping up. That was the kind of thing that would get on your nerves.

By this time, we had all become pretty good at establishing contact with each other through one form of communication or another, but in Isfahan there were long periods when I didn't have any communication with other Americans at all. I wouldn't even hear anyone else.

I didn't know if I was in this house alone, or was just unable to establish contact. I'd sit there and wonder: "Am I the last person here? Is everybody else gone? Is everybody else dead?" You couldn't help but think about these things.

Of course, this was part of the students' idea of isolating you from news and from contact with each other. After a while it works on your mind. You begin to worry about these things, and presumably you become more vulnerable.

What little news there was, was very hard to come by. I'd hear little bits and scraps when the students would get careless with the volume of the radio or the television, and what I did hear didn't seem to have anything to do with us. It was as if we had faded from the front of everyone's consciousness. It was like I'd just been left there and forgotten.

There was a young fellow there by the name of Hamid, and during this long stretch he came in and asked me the meaning of three or four words. He said, "What does X mean?" I wasn't sure what he was asking, and I knew from my years of teaching English that sometimes students could read a label and see a trademark like FTD Florists or 3M Company, and they'd want to know, what does FTD mean? What does 3M mean? Teaching had prepared me for that sort of thing. So when Hamid came in and asked me for the meaning of some words, I said, "I can't tell you out of context. Bring me the words either written down, or say them in a sentence so I'll know the context." Hamid went off and came back with several words written on a piece of paper. They were words like "rag head" and "bozo," and a few other derogatory expressions. I thought that was great. It meant that there were some marines around, and I wasn't alone in this place. It could only be marines who would come up with a vocabulary list like the one that was given to Hamid. They were obviously trying to buffalo him. I looked at him and I said, "Hamid, I'm not familiar with these words. Are you sure these are English?"

That was amusing. It was good to know that I wasn't alone. It eased my anxieties a bit, and I was in a situation where I had to take my amusement when I could get it.

BILL BELK (*communications officer, at a mansion in Isfahan with Sgt. Joe Subic*): In Isfahan, Malcolm Kalp was being kept in a room across the hall and down to the left of the room Subic and I were in. We developed a system for passing notes with him. One of the tiles in the bathroom was loose, and we hid our notes under that loose tile. It amazes me that the Iranians never figured out what we were doing. We used that drop for several weeks, and they never caught on. In one of his notes, Malcolm told us that he wanted to try to escape.

MALCOLM KALP (*economics officer, at a mansion in Isfahan*): Ever since I was a six-year-old kid, I fooled around with locks, trying to pick them, and never in my life was I able to pick a lock. In Isfahan we were put into a big house, and I started fooling around with the lock on the window. Never in my life had I picked a lock. But suddenly I picked that lock, and the window opened. The terrorists had painted over the window from both the inside and outside, and all of a sudden I could look out. We were in a lower-middle-class housing area, and I could see that there was no guard in sight. There weren't any demonstrations at this place, and the guard force was reduced. I didn't see any guards outside at all. They had a watchdog chained below me and a big wall around the place, and that was it.

I started passing notes with Bill Belk and Joe Subic, and we decided that we were going to try to escape. I made a detailed reconnaissance of everything I could see from my window, and passed that information to Subic and Belk in my notes.

BILL BELK (*communications officer, at a mansion in Isfahan with Sgt. Joe Subic*): On one occasion Malcolm dropped us a note that told us how to pick the window locks. He drew a little diagram that showed us how to do it, and described how to insert a paper clip and run it down inside the lock to close off the toners, and then how to stick a very small, flat piece of metal on top of the paper clip to hold the lower tumblers so that you could turn it and pop open the lock. After getting the note, I practiced for a little while, and by following Malcolm's instructions I learned how to pick the lock. I was surprised at how simple it was. It was as easy as following a recipe.

From the window in our room, Subic and I had a thirty-five- to forty-foot drop to the ground, and if we made it to the ground we would have had to scale a twenty-foot-high wall. Yet the wall was only about ten feet from our window. So I started trying to figure out a way for us to get directly from the window to the top of the wall. I decided that I could make a rope, tie it to the radiator under our window, and that we could swing across to the top of the wall. I didn't think any of the guards would see us if we went out in the middle of the night. They dozed off all the time when they were on guard duty, and I figured we could make it directly to the top of the wall and be gone in less than a minute. Just sail on out.

The students had given us some bed sheets, and for some strange reason we had a large supply of them. They were just folded and left in the room. Well, I know how to braid a rope. Which is exactly what I did. I tore the sheets into long strips that were about an inch and a half wide, and I'd wet them down so that they would bind real tight. Then I'd braid three of them together. I made a twenty-five-foot rope that way. If we were going out the window, I wanted to be damn sure that the rope would be strong enough to hold our weight. So I braided an additional three strips into the three I'd already braided. That was a very strong rope. I was confident that it would hold our weight without any problem.

As we were formulating our escape plans, Subic and I tried to accumulate whatever food we could. The students used to give us little boxes of raisins and cigarettes and stuff, and we would hide whatever nonperishable food we could get our hands on behind the cushion of an easy chair we had in the room. There was a little area in the back of the chair that was a very safe hiding place. That's also where I hid the rope.

Of course, one hitch was that Malcolm couldn't go out of our bedroom window with us, because he was being kept on the other side of the house. But he knew how to pick the window lock in his room, and he figured that he could jump out of the window without injuring himself and make his way to the wall. The plan was for Malcolm to go first, and when he made it to the wall he would signal us and then we would go out our window.

MALCOLM KALP (*economics officer, at a mansion in Isfahan*): The first thing I had to do was take care of the dog chained up under my window. The Iranians were giving me tranquilizers because I couldn't sleep. So I started hoarding tranquilizers, and figured I could pack them into a piece of meat and throw them down to the dog, knock him out, and climb out the window. Subic or Belk had stolen a flashlight with a red lens. The plan was for me to go out my window first, and when I got to the wall I was going to signal Subic and Belk with the flashlight. They'd come down a rope from their window, and off we'd go. The idea was to get into the immediate residential area, hit some guy over the head with a brick, steal his car and his money, and head for the Persian Gulf. If we made it to the Gulf, we'd steal a boat and head for international waters with the hope of hooking up with an American warship.

I thought our chances of getting over the wall were about 50 percent, and our chances of ever getting to the Persian Gulf about 5 percent. So it was a long shot. We all knew that. But I was ready to give it a try.

BILL BELK (*communications officer, at a mansion in Isfahan with Sgt. Joe Subic*): By mid-June we had our rope, tranquilizers, and everything ready, and we decided that we were going to go at three o'clock in the morning on the twenty-third of June. I remember the date, because it was the six-month anniversary of my first escape attempt back in December. So the twenty-third came, and we were all set, all psyched up and ready to go. I was prepared to do whatever was necessary. If it came down to having to disarm a guard and shoot him, or hitting somebody over the head to steal a car and some money, then that's what I was ready to do. We knew that the odds were against us—the chances for success were extremely slim—but we were ready to give it a try anyway.

Well, I've got to admit that that escape attempt got off on the wrong foot before we even popped the window open. Joe Subic had a compulsion about being prepared. He wanted to be ready, and at midnight—a full three hours before we were going to go—he put on his military utilities. I told him he was crazy. This was the dead of summer in Iranian desert country, and it was hot as blazes. It was so hot that we were always walking around in our drawers. There was no way we were going to wear long pants when we were cooped up in that house with all the windows shut. It would get up to 100 degrees in there every single day. And if we weren't wearing pants when we were awake, we sure as hell weren't sleeping in them. But Subic had those goddamn utilities on, and he put his stupid socks on, too. I couldn't believe it, and told him so. But he wouldn't listen to me. Well, as luck would have it, a guard came into our room to check on us, and he saw Subic sitting there all dressed up. That was like a telegraph key sending out a signal. I think Joe wanted to get caught. It was like he was afraid to really go through with it. The guard didn't say a word; he just looked around and then backed out the door. But I'll bet he could sense that something was in the wind. I said, "Goddammit, Joe, you're going to give us away unless you get into bed immediately. You just get in bed and lie there until it's time to go." So Subic took his pants back off and got down on his mattress.

Even though I was afraid that Subic had tipped off the guards, I was also hoping they were too stupid to figure out what was happening. Plus I knew that Malcolm was set to go, and I didn't want to back out on him at the zero hour. I couldn't talk with him and revise the plan. It was too late for that. Malcolm was going to go out his window whether we went out ours or not.

MALCOLM KALP (*economics officer, at a mansion in Isfahan*): On the night of June 23, I got everything all set. Stuffed the tranquilizers in a piece of hot dog that Belk and Subic had smuggled to me, and threw them out to the dog. The dog jumped up, ate them, and went out like a light.

At a quarter to three in the morning, I got dressed and everything, and picked the lock on the window. Opened the window, looked out, and everything was beautiful. I couldn't see any guards, and the dog was asleep. I had a pillowcase that I used as a bag, and I put some stuff in there, including a forty-eight-ounce bottle of water. I lowered it gently out the window by a long piece of string. When the bag hit the ground, that was my moment of decision. If I let the string go there was no turning back, because there was no way I could explain to the terrorists what all of my belongings were doing on the ground. So I asked myself, "Do you want to go through with this or not?" I took a deep breath and let the string go. Then I crawled out the window.

BILL BELK (*communications officer, at a mansion in Isfahan with Sgt. Joe Subic*): When the time to go came, I got the rope out and tied it to the radiator. Malcolm was on the other side of the house, and right on schedule he jumped out of his window.

MALCOLM KALP (*economics officer, at a mansion in Isfahan*): By hanging onto the window frame, I lowered myself down. There was a ventilation ledge that I swung onto, and as soon as I hit that ledge the dog went crazy. I mean absolutely crazy. That dog was charging at me from the end of a steel chain. He didn't get to me, but he was making one hell of a racket, barking and yapping and going crazy. I hit the ground and ran around the east side of the building. For a moment it looked clear, but the dog woke up all the guards. I was running toward Belk and Subic's window, when I saw someone kneeling in the shadows with a rifle pointed right at my stomach. He yelled something in Persian, and I put my hands up.

He was screaming, and a bunch of other terrorists came running. I stood there saying, "Good morning. Good morning," and nodding to each of them.

BILL BELK (*communications officer, at a mansion in Isfahan with Sgt. Joe Subic*): There was a horrible racket. We could hear the dog barking, and we could hear the guards racing around the building shouting and clicking their weapons. There were a whole bunch of them outside, just like they'd been sitting there waiting for something to happen. Then we heard a bunch of bloodcurdling screams and an agonized series of groans. All of the guards were hollering, and we knew they were beating the hell out of Malcolm. From the sounds it was obvious that they were hurting him.

Very quickly, I untied the rope from the radiator and hid it behind the chair cushion, along with our little bag of food. Then I locked the window back up. Subic was just standing there looking out the window like a dummy. I told him to get his clothes off and get back on his mattress like nothing had happened. So he ripped off his clothes and jumped in the rack.

MALCOLM KALP (*economics officer, at a mansion in Isfahan*): The terrorists were so nervous that it took them five minutes to tie me up and blindfold me. They took me down into the basement, and a couple of revolutionary guards started working me over. They hit me and kicked me. I screamed and hollered. The terrorists yelled, "Shut up! Shut up!" and kept beating me.

BILL BELK (*communications officer, at a mansion in Isfahan with Sgt. Joe Subic*): Pretty soon a couple of guards came into the room with their Uzi submachine guns. We were just lying there in bed. One of them checked the window and saw that it was locked. They didn't say anything to us. Not a word. But these two guys stayed in the room with their machine guns for the entire night. They stood right beside the door. When they didn't say anything to us, I started thinking that maybe they were just taking extra precautions to guard us, and didn't know that we were involved. I thought it was odd that they weren't trying to rough us up like they were doing to Malcolm. I could remember my first escape attempt, when I'd been beaten and forced to spend seven days blindfolded and handcuffed. As soon as Malcolm was caught, I expected trouble, but nobody did anything.

MALCOLM KALP (*economics officer, at a mansion in Isfahan*): After thirty-six hours of being handcuffed, tied, and blindfolded, they started asking me about the note-passing system. Underneath my blindfold I could see six pairs of feet, so I knew there were six terrorists in there. I denied everything they said. They were beating me, kicking me, banging my head against the wall, and kicking me in the groin. But I just kept on denying their accusations. They had a note that I had passed to Belk and Subic, but at that time they didn't show it to me. So they kept beating and kicking me. Finally, after a couple of hours they saw that I wasn't about to confess to anything, and they gave up. They stopped, and left me tied up and blindfolded.

BILL BELK (*communications officer, at a mansion in Isfahan*): One of the guards came into the room, pointed his finger at me and said, "You come!" I was blindfolded and taken way down into the basement of this house. I mean, I was in the bowels of this mansion. Two Iranians were down there, and they questioned me about the escape attempt. Of course, they couldn't do this without playing their stupid little games. They had one guy sitting there trying to play the heavy. He would only speak in Persian. He'd say something, and the other kid would talk to me in English. "*He* wants to know why you were trying to escape! *He* wants to know where you were going!"

I denied being involved. I said, "You're out of your goddamn mind. I wasn't trying to go anywhere."

They said, "No! You lie! Why did you do this? Where were you trying to go?"

"No way, man. Not me. I wasn't going anywhere."

"You lie! It is possible we might shoot you!"

Even though I was blindfolded, I knew exactly who I was talking to. I recognized their voices. Ahmed was one of them, and I knew they weren't going to shoot me. I wasn't scared a bit. I knew they could make things tough on me if they wanted to, and they could have their sadistic Moslem brothers come in and beat me around, but I hadn't the slightest fear in the world that they were going to kill me.

As it turned out, they found the rope that was hidden in the chair, and they also found some notes that Malcolm Kalp had written to us about the escape plans. Instead of destroying these notes or flushing them down the toilet, Subic hid them under his mattress and the Iranians found several of them. So they knew the entire plan. When they showed me those notes, there wasn't much I could say to that, except tell them to go fuck off.

After questioning and threatening me for about two hours, they took me and put me into a basement room. They left me there without any books and with nothing to do. That was my punishment. They didn't like me at all. They left me sitting in this room alone, with nothing to do.

JOE HALL (*warrant officer, in Khorramshahr with Greg Persinger and John Graves*): When we first moved into the place in Khorramshahr, the Iranians told us that there weren't any other hostages in the building. But we knew that was bullshit, because we could hear them in the bathroom. Then one time the guards made the mistake of putting me in the bathroom when Steve Kirtley was trying to brush his teeth. All of a sudden, I was standing right beside him and I said, "Hi, Steve.

How you doing?" The guard realized the mistake and pulled me right back out the door.

After that, they went ahead and told us that there were three other Americans in the building, and they let the three of us play cards with them. The other three were in a big room downstairs that was a real dungeon-type place, but it was cool compared to the upstairs rooms we were in. Upstairs it was stifling hot all the time. For a couple of weeks we'd get to visit the others, shoot the bull, and play cards. One of them would come up to our room, while one of us went down there. They never let all six of us get together at one time, and always kept us in two groups of three, but they would shift us around so we could visit. Then one day the students wouldn't let us go see the other hostages.

We asked, "Why not?"

The guard said, "Because they're not there anymore. They've been moved."

CPL. STEVEN KIRTLEY (*marine security guard, in Khorramshahr*): I had my bout with food poisoning when we first moved into the subterranean room; then later on Bert Moore got real sick. He had the same damn thing I did. Only the militants brought in a doctor for him right away. But Bert didn't get any better. He just kept getting weaker and weaker. Finally, the Iranians took him out. I guess they took him back to Tehran or to a hospital.

So that left two of us down in that big subterranean room, me and another guy. A few days after Bert left, something bad happened to the other guy, too. The militants were giving him a real hard time. They were constantly threatening him and trying to get him to sign a confession. They were making all kinds of accusations. It was just too much for him to take. One morning I noticed he was acting kind of funny. Ali came into the room with some lunch, and this guy told Ali that once our ordeal was all over he hoped the real truth would come out. He was walking around, and all of a sudden he ran straight toward a protruding corner of the wall, and dove at it head first. He was trying to kill himself, and he tore a giant eight-inch split in his scalp. I jumped up and ran over to him, and I listened to his heart to make sure it was still beating. Ali was standing there looking down at us. I said, "Go call an ambulance, Ali! Hurry! Call an ambulance!"

This guy was lying on his back. His scalp was torn open and laid to the side. I looked to make sure there was nothing underneath his skin, and folded the scalp back on top of his head. Fortunately, I'd just washed a towel the day before, and I got my clean towel, put it on top of his head, and applied a little pressure to try and stem the bleeding. Within a couple of minutes he woke up. He opened his eyes and looked around. I kept talking to him. I was trying to get him to say something to me, and trying to reassure him.

Within about ten minutes, the ambulance got there. I was surprised by how quick they got there. But the two idiots that drove the ambulance must have been dirt farmers. I think ambulance duty in Iran must be like jury duty in the United States. They just pick two people off the street and stick them in an ambulance, because these two guys didn't know their ass from a hole in the wall. I knew more about what to do than they did. It took all fucking day for them to put a little wrap around his head and get him into the ambulance.

The guy who tried to kill himself was fortunate. If he had hit the wall at a different angle it could have easily been fatal. But luckily he turned out to be all right. He was a real nice guy. When he was down there he'd been reading a Bible that somebody had sent to me. When they put him in the ambulance, I gave the Bible to one of the guards and told him to make sure this guy got it.

After they took him to the hospital, I was all alone in that big subterranean room. I spent a couple of days just walking around in circles by myself.

Part Eight

Prison

1 Return to Tehran

THE DISPERSAL OF the hostages throughout Iran created more problems for the militants than it solved. Resources were severely strained, sanitation was bad, and security was a problem at several locations. Throughout the summer of 1980 the hostages were gradually returned to Tehran and put in the downtown Komiteh Prison.* The prison was a massive concrete structure built in a series of concentric rings, with circular two-story cell blocks located one inside the other. It was infamous as one of the shah's political prisons, and after the revolution it was closed down because of its reputation for torture and repression. However, it wasn't long before the prison was opened again and put to use jailing opponents of the revolution.

The militants were concerned about another rescue attempt, so they returned the hostages to Tehran with as much secrecy as possible. They did not want the United States government to know where the hostages were being kept, or how many of them were actually in Tehran.

CORT BARNES (*communications officer, with two other hostages in Meshed*): Meshed was the low point of the entire ordeal. We figured that there wasn't much hope of going from Meshed to freedom. If freedom came, we thought it would probably come from Tehran. So Meshed was like a transfer to oblivion. To make matters worse, the selection of books was very poor. So there wasn't much to do except walk around the room. That was a time of very little hope. We all knew that going back to Tehran would be a good sign.

CHARLES JONES (*communications officer, with one other hostage in Meshed*): One day the guards came in and told Bruce German and me to get our stuff together. Then Bruce and I were put into a van with Cort Barnes, Bill Keough, and Bill Royer. The guards took the five of us out to a villa, where we waited until dark, when we took off on a long trip.

Along the way, we stopped in some small town and picked up Kevin Hermening and Don Cooke. Then a little later, the guards stopped at

* The only female hostages, Katherine Koob and Elizabeth Ann Swift, remained at the embassy compound until December of 1980. Three male hostages were also being housed in the chancery building, and in October of 1980 they were transferred to Komiteh Prison. Throughout the entire year of 1980, Bruce Laingen, Victor Tomseth, and Michael Howland remained at the Iranian Foreign Ministry.

a filling station, and we heard the driver ask directions for the road to Tehran. As soon as he said "Tehran," we all started coughing. It was cough, cough, cough, clear your throat and cough. We were signaling to each other: "Did you hear hear that? We're going to Tehran!"

My spirits soared! I thought that going back to Tehran was a good sign. We picked up Don and Kevin along the way, so it looked like they were reuniting the hostages. I thought, "Boy-oh-boy, this has got to be the beginning of the end!"

JOE HALL (*warrant officer, being held with Greg Persinger and John Graves at Khorramshahr*): One day the guards came in and told the three of us that we were going back to Tehran. They didn't tell us why, they just told us that we were going to Tehran. Immediately, that raised our expectations. After two months of living under adverse conditions, going back to Tehran was a hopeful sign, although we weren't entirely certain what it meant. They'd threatened us with spy trials, so it was possible that we were going back for these trials. In late April, after we'd been moved out of Tehran, they had talked about putting us on trial, and had said that some of the hostages might be killed—executed for crimes against Iran—but that those of us who had no real spy involvement would be released. Well, I worked for the Defense Intelligence Agency, and I was concerned as to where they would place me in the embassy hierarchy. I thought I'd pretty much convinced them that I was only an administrator and not an intelligence collector, but if there were trials I didn't know what sort of association they would try to pin on me. Regardless of that possibility, I figured that even if they did take us back to Tehran for some kind of show trial, at least it would bring an end to what was going on. One way or another something would happen. So basically I felt it was a good sign that we were being moved back to Tehran.

After nightfall they moved us down out of this building and put four of us into a Dodge van. It was one of the vans that had belonged to the marine guards back at the embassy.

CPL. STEVEN KIRTLEY (*marine security guard, in Khorramshahr*): They came in at nine o'clock one night and took me out of that subterranean room. Joe Hall, Greg Persinger, and John Graves were upstairs, and they put me into a van with the three of them. I didn't know where we were going.

JOE HALL (*warrant officer*): Of course, we were blindfolded. They handcuffed Persinger and myself together, and they handcuffed John Graves to Steve Kirtley. I remember Kirtley said something and the guards told him to shut up. But that's how we knew Steve was with us. When I heard him, I remember thinking, "Where have you been?" I thought he had been moved away, and didn't know that he was still being kept downstairs. I was glad he was there with us, but I didn't know where the other two guys were that had been kept down there with him. Anyway, they got us all into the van, and we took off on this long, torturous trip back to Tehran.

CPL. STEVEN KIRTLEY (*marine security guard*): The road was bumpy and the driver was crazy. We'd stop at various places for gas and eats for the chauffeurs. At about five o'clock in the morning, right when it was just first getting light, we were driving along, and all four of us were laid back—you know, just rolling and jostling along. I think the rag heads were all asleep. Greg and Joe were handcuffed together, and I was handcuffed to John Graves. I was sitting there on the verge of going back to sleep, when I noticed the driver was making a sharp, bumpy turn. We were going over something real bumpy. And I don't mean your average bumpy. I mean, *blam-blam-blam-blam!* I thought, "Holy shit! This guy is trying to go four-wheeling!"

JOE HALL (*warrant officer*): I had finally managed to doze off. Suddenly I woke to a nightmare. The driver had gone to sleep at the wheel and had driven off the road. When I woke the van was rolling, and we were being tossed around inside it. To wake to something like that is incredibly bizarre. I didn't know what was going on. Although it was over in a matter of two or three seconds, it seemed like it lasted forever.

CPL. STEVEN KIRTLEY (*marine security guard*): The van twisted around and flipped twice. We were lucky that we were so relaxed, because we were banging around in there like bingo chips. It flipped over twice and finally came to rest. The windows were all busted out, and we were just kind of lying there.

JOE HALL (*warrant officer*): I don't know if I was knocked out or not, but I finally came to. I was in the bottom of the van, lying in this thick dust. My blindfold had been knocked off, and I was looking around trying to orient myself. Persinger and I were staring at each other. Both of our blindfolds had been knocked off. We each had a few cuts and blood was streaming from here and there and soaking through our clothes.

I don't know how we got out of that damn van. But the next thing I remember is standing on the outside looking down at the wreck. I looked through the door, and I could see a leg in a very strange position.

My first thought was, "My God, it's been torn off! Somebody has lost a leg!" But as I was looking at it I saw it move, and Steve Kirtley crawled out of that tangled mess. It was his leg, and he was dragging John Graves out with him.

CPL. STEVEN KIRTLEY (*marine security guard*): All four of us got out. Two of the guards were obviously hurt. One was lying down in the dirt, and the other one was hobbling about. The first thing that came to my mind was, "Let's get out of here. Let's escape." But the landscape was just like a repeat of the trip out of Tehran—nothing but desert everywhere you turn. You look to the right and it's desert, nothing but sand. You look to your left, more desert and more sand. You look behind you and it's a long stretch of desert with some mountains way, way in the background. There was no place to go. So we just stood there and looked at each other.

JOE HALL (*warrant officer*): I was still handcuffed to Greg Persinger, and Steve Kirtley was handcuffed to John Graves. I don't remember seeing any of the guards. There was no one around. Both Greg and I had to urinate desperately, so we started walking. We took a leak, and then we walked back and stood there looking at the van. The thing was a mess. It was totaled. I think the only thing that kept us from being killed was that it had been bulletproofed. It must have beefed the thing up just enough so that it kept us from getting crushed inside. It still amazes me that we walked away from that van, the way it was totaled.

I don't know where the guards were. We never did see the driver again. Later I was told that he was killed, but I never had that confirmed. So I don't know if he was killed or not.

Big Ali was one of the guards who had been friendly to us, and he had been riding in the front next to the driver when the van flipped. He suddenly materialized from nowhere and told us not to wander off. I remember he had a gun. That surprised me. It was the first time I'd ever seen Big Ali with a gun in his hands. Just about the same time, an ambulance pulled up. I thought, "Boy, that's quick work, getting an ambulance out here that fast."

CPL. STEVEN KIRTLEY (*marine security guard*): What happened was an ambulance was following our van carrying the hostage who had tried to kill himself a few days earlier. They were driving behind us. So the ambulance stopped, and the guards stuffed the four of us into the back of the ambulance.

JOE HALL (*warrant officer*): They put us in the ambulance, and there was another American lying on the stretcher in the back. They packed Steve Kirtley, John Graves, Greg Persinger, and myself in around him. Then they said, "Put your blindfolds on!"

I said, "Screw you. I'm not putting my damn blindfold on. To hell with you." And no one else did, either. We all refused.

The guards didn't force the issue. They were very nervous. We could see that they were shaken up. Maybe the driver of the van was killed, because those people were basket cases.

CPL. STEVEN KIRTLEY (*marine security guard*): We took off in the ambulance, and the driver started going as fast as he could. He was a reckless son of a bitch. He headed into a big curve doing ninety miles an hour, and swerved off into the other lane where another car was coming around the curve right at him. He tried to shift, and cut it back real sharp to the right lane, and the ambulance went up on two wheels. He almost rolled the damn thing. All four of us started screaming at the driver, "Shit, man! Slow the fuck down! You're going to kill us all!"

JOE HALL (*warrant officer*): We were only fourteen kilometers from Qöm. No sooner did we take off in this ambulance than I saw a road sign. It had something in Farsi, and then underneath it in English it said "Qöm 14." We arrived there very soon, and drove through the streets of Qöm in the early morning light. The guards were holding pieces of cloth up in the windows so that no one could look into the ambulance and see all of us sitting there. They were still nervous as hell, and then they got lost in the city. They were having a hard time finding the place that they were looking for, and we drove around the city for a while.

Finally, we pulled down a little narrow street, and there were a bunch of Iranians waiting there. I'd seen some of them before and knew they were guards. They put us into a room that had recently been occupied by some Americans. We could tell from the dishes and things that were left behind. There was a dish drainer where some other hostages had washed and stacked their dishes, and there were foam rubber mattresses on the floor. It was obvious that they had just removed some Americans, and put us in there after vacating them.

It must've been about seven o'clock in the morning when we got settled in there. They brought us some breakfast, and we cleaned ourselves up. We were filthy from all the dirt and dust that had been kicked up in the wreck. That stuff was just caked on us. Plus, each of us had some cuts and gashes. Both Greg Persinger and Steve Kirtley had some nasty cuts. We didn't have any medication, and had to do the best we could. The Iranians didn't bring us a thing. I tried to doctor a cut on Greg Persinger's back. I washed it out with soap and water, and then smeared toothpaste on it. He said that the toothpaste stung, and I figured if it was stinging it was doing some good. I thought maybe the fluoride would act as a cleansing agent. There was nothing else there to use.

We were all tired. We had driven all night long, so we'd missed a night's sleep. When something really emotional and physical like that happens, it exhausts you, and we all fell into an exhausted sleep. We slept most of that day. I remember the guards brought in some dinner at night, and we got up and ate. We had calmed down, and the fellow who had been riding on the stretcher told us what he had tried to do to himself. He had tried to commit suicide, and had come very close to succeeding. He was very, very despondent. The Iranians had interrogated him very intensely for a period of months. He'd been pushed to the limit, and he thought he'd heard his name being chanted by the crowds in their calls for death. As far as the Iranians were concerned, he was in a nasty position. They accused him of being CIA and really went after him. Having been through one of those interrogations myself, I don't blame him for anything he might have said or done. But he was obviously feeling a lot of self-doubt and guilt.

When we woke up the next morning, we were all banged up. We were just barely able to crawl around. We had cuts and bruises from the wreck, and I was urinating blood, so I knew my kidneys were bruised. John Graves hurt his back, and it bothered him for quite a long while after that. I think he was probably hurt the worst. It beat the hell out of all four of us. We could hardly get around that morning. Luckily, none of us had been crippled or killed.

Two and a half days after our car accident, the Iranians decided that they were going to take us the rest of the way to Tehran. Well, we didn't want to go. The thought of being blindfolded, tied up, and getting back into a van with those guys terrified us. No sooner did we take off than all three of us started yelling at them, "Slow down! Slow down! Don't go so fast!" We drove for several hours, jostling around on those Iranian roads, and we were constantly reminding them to stay awake and to drive slower. Even with our blindfolds on we'd tell them, "Hey, you guys, stay awake. Take it easy and stay awake."

We still didn't know what going back to Tehran would mean for us. We didn't know if there would be any of the spy trials the militants had talked about or not. But in spite of the uncertainty, we all thought that going back to Tehran was a good sign.

CPL. STEVEN KIRTLEY (*marine security guard*): My shoulder was sore and I had some bruises and scrapes on my leg, but outside of that I was all right. I remember when they came to get us and take us to Tehran, my shoulder was so sore that I could barely move it. Anyway, we had another long-ass drive into Tehran. When we got there, they pulled into some kind of big complex. With my blindfold on, I didn't know where we were. But the guards took us out of the van and started leading us through all these doors and gates. We could hear all kinds of noise. *Clang-clang! Boom! Clink, clang, bang!* And the guards were telling us, "Watch your step. Step over this. Step over that. Go up these steps. Turn to your left." And all the while doors and locks were closing behind us. *Clink, clang, clang!*

JOE HALL (*warrant officer*): When they took our blindfolds off, we were in a goddamn prison cell. An honest-to-God prison cell. I'll tell you, my spirits plummeted. I thought, "Boy, have we bottomed out now. After all this shit we've gone through we are finally in a prison—in a real prison." We'd been prisoners all along, but then we became prisoners totally. Somehow actually being in a real prison made a big difference. It kind of doubled the emphasis of the whole experience.

CPL. STEVEN KIRTLEY (*marine security guard*): They took Joe Hall, Greg Persinger, and John Graves and put them in a cell together, and they took me and put me in a separate cell by myself. We were in this big mass prison. The walls were a foot and a half thick, and my cell had a steel door. I started getting more depressed than I'd ever been before. I was even more depressed than when they first took me to Khorramshahr and stuck me in that subterranean room. I was looking around at the prison cell, thinking, "Oh, shit."

Then I heard someone at the other end of the hall beating on the cell door. *Bam-bam-bam!* And I heard Joe Hall yelling at the guards, "Hey, goddammit! Where the hell are you? There's a guy sitting in here who's about ready to shit on himself!"

Fortunately, they only kept me in that cell by myself for five or six hours. I didn't even spend an entire day in there. Before nightfall they came and got me, and put me in the cell with Joe Hall and Greg Persinger. We spent most of that evening talking together.

COL. THOMAS SCHAEFER (*defense attaché*): Once I was taken captive, I thought my chances for survival were about fifty-fifty. The reason I say that is not because I thought the militants were going to shoot me. I was quite confident that they would not purposely kill me, because we were valuable to them only as long as we were alive. But there were two things that concerned me. The first was that there was always a chance that the militants could not provide the security that was needed to keep us alive. Especially in some of those places like the White Hole or the Pink Palace, where we could hear crowds of people going by chanting, *"Marg bar Amrika! Marg bar Amrika!"* That told me that a lot of people knew that we were being kept there. If some group or faction wanted to come in and get us, the militants who were holding us might not have been able to prevent them from doing so. That was always a possibility. My second concern was that the Iranians were not trained in how to handle their weapons. I thought the inadvertent killing of a hostage was a high probability. The guards would just fan an entire area with a weapon when they had rounds in the chamber and their fingers resting on the trigger. They didn't think anything of pointing a loaded weapon at someone. They would even do that to their fellow militants when they were talking to them. So in addition to the inadequate security, there was always the possibility of an accidental shooting.

Then one night we were marched into the Komiteh Prison. I was blindfolded, with my hand on the shoulder of the fellow in front of me. I can honestly say that hearing those prison doors slam was an excellent sound. I said to myself, "By gosh, it sounds like we have proper security." And we did. We were in prison. I actually felt pretty good about that.

BILL BELK (*communications officer*): Six days after my escape attempt, the students moved me back to Tehran and put me in prison. I was put into solitary confinement on a cell block where the Iranians kept some of their political prisoners. There weren't any other hostages around. I remember it was hot as Hades in that cell, and I didn't have a thing. I mean nothing. No books. No cards. Nothing. Nothing but me in this gray prison cell.

After my escape attempt, the militants found several packs of cigarettes hidden in the back of the easy chair under the cushion. They'd questioned me about that, and wanted to know why I had so many cigarettes. Of course, I'd been ratholing them for the escape attempt. While we were in Isfahan, I kept asking and asking for cigarettes. The guards kept telling me, "You smoke too much. You smoke too much." But they'd always give me cigarettes when I wanted them. When a new guard came on duty, I'd ask for another pack of cigarettes, and hide them behind the cushion. Because I had done that, I thought that the guards were probably going to start denying me cigarettes in the prison. So I decided right then and there that I was going to quit smoking. I wasn't about to beg them for cigarettes and give them the opportunity to tell me that I couldn't have any. So the day I was thrown into Komiteh Prison was the day I quit smoking. In fact, I've never had a cigarette since that day.

In the prison cell, I didn't even have a mattress. It was just a plain gray concrete cell with nothing in it. I had to sleep on the bare floor. There was a light bulb in the ceiling, and there was a barred window way up high on the wall. From the outside, the window was covered with wire mesh, and it was so dirty that it was impossible to see out. It was just looking up at a square screen full of black soot. Over in the corner of the cell, I found a very, very small nail. It must've fallen out of the window frame. To keep from going nuts, I took that nail and started scratching my wife's name onto the walls of the cell. I wrote: "Angela. My love. My life. My wife." Then I just kept carving her name on the walls. I must've written her name a thousand different times. I was in pretty bad shape. That prison cell was grim. But for some reason all I had on my mind was Angela. My mind was channeled to the one thing in life that I held dear, and I just wanted to carve her name. Angela. Angela. Angela. I just wanted to make that prison cell remind me of her. The whole cell was nothing but gray, and I went as high as I could and as often as I could scratching her name on the wall. For fourteen days I did nothing except that. Nothing at all.

One time Ahmed came in there. The guy was such a bastard. He saw what I was doing, and he came up to me and said, "I don't think you should write on the walls." He was shaking his finger at me like a schoolmaster.

I said, "Go get fucked!" Just like that. By this time my nail was nothing but a little nub. I could barely hold it between my fingers. Ahmed was a sleazy bastard. He wasn't about to fight me to get that nail. But he did get back at me. When I had to go to the bathroom, I pounded on the door, but no one came. Nothing but silence in the hall. They just let me sit there. Every fifteen or twenty minutes I'd get up and pound on the door, but no one would come. This went on for three or four hours. Ahmed wasn't about to let me use the bathroom after I told him to go get fucked. Finally, after I beat on the door again, Ahmed showed up with a silly smirk on his face. He blindfolded me, and as he led me to the toilet he pushed to make me run, and he rammed me right into the wall. On two or three occasions he'd push and guide me so that I'd bang my head on the concrete wall. I knew better than to take a poke at him, but God, you can't imagine how much I wanted to. This was the same guy who brought me pencils and paper so that I could draw while we were in the chancery. Back then, he would come into our room and try to explain how he believed in

God, and how he felt that the takeover was a just and right cause. It was very important to him that we understood what the revolution meant to Iran, and how they were trying to right what they thought was a wrong. He was very patient and sincere in trying to explain his beliefs. Then his entire attitude changed after the rescue attempt. He became a real son of a bitch. Anyway, after he brought me back from the toilet, I took my little nail out of my pocket and went back to work carving Angela's name all over the walls.

While I was being kept in solitary confinement, I heard all kinds of agonizing noises. It was obvious that prisoners were being beaten. I could hear them screaming. With my very limited Persian language abilities, I could make out that one guy was being forced to say things like, "Khomeini is great!" "Death to the shah!" "God is merciful!" "Khomeini is great!" He was screaming these things, and I could tell that he was being tortured. I'd hear the cries of anguish, and then these slogans would be screamed under duress. It was like somebody was standing over him and forcing him to say these things over and over and over again. They were beating the hell out of him, and he would scream in pain. The guy was pleading with them to stop. I could hear him begging, "No more. Please. No more." Then they would make him holler more of the slogans: "Khomeini is great!" "God is merciful!" "Khomeini is great!" That was a frightening thing to hear. I was thinking, "Why? Why do they do these things? For what reason? Why would a human being do this to his fellow man?" It was just an awful thing to hear.

Then on other occasions I could hear women crying. It sounded like women were interrogating and torturing other women. All this time I was by myself. I didn't hear any of the other hostages on that corridor. What I heard were Iranian prisoners, and all of the torturing and crying that was going on. I also heard little children. Babies. I could actually hear babies crying in the prison. The only thing I could deduce was that some of the women were brought into the prison with their children, and they had a section or an area in the prison where the children were cared for while the mothers were questioned or did their prison time. Now I can't substantiate what was actually happening, because I never saw what was going on, and the guards wouldn't tell me anything. All I know is that I heard these things when they put me in the prison. I heard all of the torturing going on, and I heard the voices of women and children.

After fourteen days, I was moved onto another corridor in the prison where I couldn't hear these things anymore. I think that's why I was moved. They took me from one drab gray cell to another one that looked exactly like it, and I was still kept in solitary. The only difference was that I didn't have to listen to all that pain and suffering. That was a welcome relief. I could also hear the voices of other hostages in the corridors, and that too was nice.

2 Settling in at Komiteh Prison: Summer 1980

JOHN LIMBERT (*political officer*): The prison had been built by the Germans in the 1930s, and it was a place with very thick walls and great echoes. The cell doors were the sort you'd expect to see on submarines—big heavy doors set above the floor, with big thick latches on them. There was a long hallway with a bathroom at the far end, and we could hear the other hostages walk up and down the hallway as they were being led to the bathroom. It got to where we could identify an individual by his walk, and it was nice to know who was around. After that long stretch in Isfahan, it was good to be back in some sort of proximity with the others.

JOE HALL (*warrant officer*): In a way, prison was kind of a relief. We had a continuous and uninterrupted routine, and we didn't get sick from drinking the water. We ate fairly well, too. The food wasn't very good, but there was usually enough of it.

By the time we got back to Tehran, I was feeling a lot better about myself. I'd been through the initial shock of being taken hostage and held against my will, which is one hell of a jolt to the system. Then I went through the interrogation, a couple of mock executions, the firefights outside the place in Yaz where I'd been handcuffed and blindfolded, and the car accident on our way back to Tehran. After all of that, I started feeling like a survivor. I realized a lot of things about myself that I'd never known before. I was more aware of my fiber. I'd never really been tested before, but in Iran I felt like we'd all been tested about as much as an individual can be tested. You know, when you face the moment where you think you are going to be killed, I mean come right up to that moment where you have to face death, that's an extreme test. It's about all anyone can ask of you. The fact that we didn't die was just due to the grace of God. But I still had to come right to the point where I thought I was going to die, where I was absolutely certain that it was all over. Facing something like that changes you. It really does.

I felt pretty good about myself. I kept thinking, "I've survived all of this, and I'm in better physical shape than I was a year ago." I'd stopped caring about whether or not they were going to kill us, and I think I was slowly preparing myself for the eventuality that we would never leave. I felt like I could go on for a long time and continue to survive. I'd get up in the morning and mark another day on the calendar, and face the same old routine. I'd walk around in circles, exercise for three or four hours a day, bathe and eat. Pretty soon another month had come and gone. I knew it was possible that we would never get out.

GARY LEE (*general services officer*): I was put into a prison cell with Jim Lopez, Morehead Kennedy, and Rick Kupke. The four of us were trying to figure out where we were. We knew we were in Tehran, but we didn't know which part of the city. Then one night, by pure fluke, I climbed up on a chair to look out the window like I'd done many times before, only this time I recognized the microwave relay tower of the PTT* building across from me. Then I knew we were in the downtown prison, the Komiteh Prison in south Tehran. I told the other guys, and we all felt a little bit better. At least we knew where we were.

CDR. ROBERT ENGELMANN (*naval supply corps officer*): By the time we got to the prison, most of the guards were Iranian peasants. Most of the bloodthirsty guys—the real revolutionaries with the machine guns—were out of sight. They were still involved, but they considered it beneath their rank and station in life to serve Americans their meals and take them down to the toilet. Which is what these peasants had to do. It was their job to feed us and lead us down to the bathroom. In the revolutionary hierarchy the guards we were in contact with were probably lower on the totem pole than the American hostages. They were kind of like zookeepers, and not much more. Most of them were pretty passive people. There were a couple who were excitable, but for the most part it wasn't an antagonistic situation.

CPL. WILLIAM GALLEGOS (*marine security guard*): In the prison, the Iranians had a little TV room where they used to show TV videos. We had a bunch of tapes at the embassy before we were taken. They were just series-type TV shows, "Barnaby Jones" or "M*A*S*H." Stuff like that.

The Iranians would come in once or twice a week and take us down to another cell to watch TV videos. I went the first time or two, but after that I didn't go anymore. The guards would come in to take us

* Post Telegraph and Telecommunications.

down there, and I'd say, "I don't want to go. I want to stay here. I don't want to see those things." So everybody else would go, and I'd stay in the cell. I really didn't want to see that stuff. I'd been a prisoner for a long time, and I'd adapted to it. When they started showing us TV shows that had been filmed in the United States it didn't seem real to me. Didn't seem real at all. It didn't depress me, but at the same time I didn't want to be reminded of home. I didn't want to see all the cars and the women and the people having a good time. So I didn't go see those things. I liked it better in the cell.

SGT. PAUL LEWIS (*marine security guard*): They brought the VCR from the embassy over to the prison, and they would show us American TV shows. I really don't know why they bothered with that. I guess it was something to keep us distracted. When they first asked me if I wanted to go see movies, I said, "No, I don't want to see those movies again. I've seen all of your revolutionary movies." You know, I thought they were going to show us more of their revolutionary propaganda films. Then, when I found out they were talking about American videos, I went down to watch.

They had put the VCR in an empty cell, along with a stack of tapes. The guards would take us down there and put a tape in. Sometimes they would stay and watch, and sometimes they'd just lock the door and leave. Then other times they'd put snacks out for us—potato chips, popcorn, or dates we could munch on.

I'd go whenever they'd take us down there. It was nice to get out of my cell and do something different. One time, I remember they put on a "Charlie's Angels" episode. That surprised me. Those guys were always talking about how religious they were and how decadent America is. I didn't think they would let us see something like "Charlie's Angels." But when they put that on, the guards stayed and watched too. The Iranians liked "Charlie's Angels" a lot.

JOE HALL (*warrant officer*): The Iranians would take us over to another cell block and give us an hour of TV once a week. I remember they showed us "Three's Company" three or four weeks in a row, and they also showed us some NFL Super Bowl highlight films that were about thirty minutes each.

One time, Big Ali came in and said he had a film of Father Rupiper that he wanted to show us. So Kirtley, Persinger, and I went down there and watched it. We watched very, very solemnly. I remember later one of the other hostages said that he wanted to knock Father Rupiper on his ass. Now I don't know that I would ever want to knock a pastor on his rear end, but I would have liked to have had a serious talk with that man. I thought he did us a lot of harm. I remember when the three of us got back to our cell, we were thoroughly pissed off.

BRUCE GERMAN (*budget officer*): In Komiteh Prison the goons used to show us videotapes, and one of their favorites was an interview with Father Rupiper when he returned to the States after visiting us at Easter. It was a press conference sort of thing, and I remember that he went on and on pleading the Iranian cause. He gave some ridiculous number of people who had been killed, maimed, tortured, and imprisoned under the shah. Of course, he didn't mention what was happening under Khomeini, and he failed to address the issue of why we were being held hostage, or whether or not anything could be done to get us out. Instead he preferred to plead the Iranian cause. The goons just loved it. They thought it was good for our moral edification to sit there in Komiteh Prison and watch this trash.

SGT. PAUL LEWIS (*marine security guard*): Father Rupiper really disappointed me. I saw him when he came to visit us in Tehran. I remember I was really glad to see him. He came in with a church group, and they didn't seem to be controversial at all. I knew who Father Rupiper was, because when I was in the seventh or eighth grade, he had spent some time with the Newman Foundation at the University of Illinois. The Newman Foundation sent some priests down to our mission church. So I knew him from that, and I was really glad to see him. He was someone I recognized, someone I knew. I was thinking, "Hey, it's a small world."

At the time, we were led to believe that this church group was acting in a semiofficial capacity as intermediaries of some sort. Later on, I found out that was not the case. But I did have a chance to talk with Father Rupiper for a couple of minutes. We shook hands, and he promised to call my folks. I thought he was sincerely interested in our welfare.

Then, in Komiteh Prison, they showed us a tape of him being interviewed when he returned to the United States after visiting us at the embassy in Tehran. I couldn't believe the things he was saying. He claimed to have seen torture machines that SAVAK and the CIA used, and he claimed to have seen documents that supported the militants' allegations, and he went on and on, saying that they were just students who were busy studying all the time, and that they were really nice people. He didn't know anything about the conditions we were actually living under, and it was obvious that he was talking about things he had no knowledge and no understanding of. I couldn't believe what I was hearing. It made me angry, because I'd been so glad to see him when he came to visit us. I felt like I'd been betrayed. Basically, I think deep down he's probably a good man, but in this instance he proved to be very naive and overly idealistic. He certainly didn't know what he was talking about.

CHARLES JONES (*communications officer*): I woke up in the middle of the night one night to the sound of bloodcurdling screams. I heard screams and screams and more screams coming from the section of the prison that was directly behind us. I thought, "My God, what is going on over there?" It went on all night long, and I sat there and listened to it with my head between my legs. I tried to lie back down, but there was no way I could sleep. So I sat back up and put my head between my legs. That was a long night. "My God," I thought, "they've started torturing the hostages. Pretty soon they're going to come and get me."

WILLIAM ROYER (*director of academic courses*): We definitely heard torture taking place in another section of the prison, and we could tell that it was being used for interrogation purposes. Although we couldn't make out much of what was being said, we could hear them bring people in, and there was no mistake about the beatings. There would be a slapping sound, as though a rubber hose was being used, and we'd hear the screams. It was a horrible feeling to listen to these cries.

CHARLES JONES (*communications officer*): The militants told us that none of the hostages were being tortured, that what was happening did not concern us. We could hear that most of the screaming and interrogations were in Farsi, so we knew that it was Iranians who were being tortured. But one night, I heard somebody speaking in English. This was in the middle of the night, and everybody else in the cell was asleep. They were working some guy over, and I heard him say, "Oh God, somebody help me! Oh, God. Oh, God. Somebody please help me!" That scared me. When I heard him speaking English I sat bolt upright and thought, "Who is that speaking English? Is that an American? Is that Ahearn? Metrinko?" The guy babbled off, and he was mostly speaking in Farsi, but hearing that English was very frightening. I didn't know if he was a hostage or not, and I didn't say anything to the other people in the cell with me because I didn't want to frighten them.

JOE HALL (*warrant officer*): I'll tell you, the sound of someone being tortured is terrifying. When I first heard it, it scared the shit out of me. I've never heard anything like the cries of anguish and pain we could hear when we went down to the bathroom at the end of the hall. That was gruesome. Fortunately, we couldn't hear it in our cell. We could only hear it from the bathroom. At first, I thought it was an American being tortured. But by communicating with some of the other hostages I learned that this was something that had been going on for some time, and that it was Iranians torturing Iranians. Other Americans whose cells were situated differently had heard these sorts of screams and lashes at various times. When I learned that no Americans were involved it made me feel a little bit better. Hell, I figured that Persians had been committing these sorts of crimes against each other for over two centuries. There was nothing I could do about that.

CHARLES JONES (*communications officer*): The prison was arranged in rings or circles, and the cell I was in was on one of the inside circles on the second floor. It just so happened that this cell was directly across from one of the torture cells. I know some of the hostages couldn't hear any torture going on, but we could hear it very distinctly. Whenever the Iranians opened the door to that cell we could hear it, and when they turned on the light we could see it from our window. We couldn't see inside the torture cell, but we could see exactly where it was taking place. We'd hear the door open and hear them bring people in; then the interrogations and beating would take place. This went on constantly from July through September. I mean twenty-four hours a day. That was not a pretty thing to hear. Not a pretty thing at all.

They dragged one woman over there who was tougher than any of the others. She screamed and hollered at the top of her lungs. The guards would try to get her to say certain things. She would holler, "*Allah Akbar! Allah Akbar!*" And right after her the Iranians would holler out, "*Khomeini rah bar! Khomeini rah bar!*" They were trying to get her to say, "Khomeini is the leader! Khomeini is the leader!" But she refused to do that. They threatened and cajoled, and the guards would chant, "*Allah Akbar! Khomeini rah bar! Allah Akbar! Khomeini rah bar!*" That was a repetition they continually used. But this woman refused to acknowledge that Khomeini was the leader. She would holler, "God is great!" But she wouldn't go beyond that. She stood right up to those assholes and refused to do what they wanted her to do.

BARRY ROSEN (*press attaché*): From what I could hear, it seemed to me that there were specific rooms in the prison for torture. We could hear a tremendous amount of screaming both in our cell and in the bathroom, and it was obvious that these people were in a great deal of pain. Their screams would pierce right through me. While this was going on, we had a guard named Ahmed who was a very peculiar character. He liked to play classical music while these people were being tortured. He was trying to cover up the screams with music, but the music only made the torture that much more eerie. It was absolutely insane. One tends to think of classical music as being the best that culture has to offer, and then to have it used for that purpose would absolutely make your skin crawl.

CHARLES JONES (*communications officer*): Whenever we asked the militants what was going on, they would say, "Never mind. It is of no consequence. It doesn't concern you."

But we would taunt them and ask about all of this torture. We'd say, "Is this the Moslem way? Is this God's will? Is this how you demonstrate your concern for human rights?" A lot of the guards felt that the prisoners who were being tortured were enemies of the people, and they deserved to be tortured. But there was one guard we called Hamid the Cook, and he was a more compassionate person. He was embarrassed by the torture and didn't like the fact that it was taking place—didn't like it at all. But most of them would just deny that it was even happening, or would tell us that it was no concern of ours.

BRUCE GERMAN (*budget officer*): Every day in that prison was very much like the others. I mean, it was grim. Even though our cell was large, it was grim. There was nothing to see except those gray concrete walls. Solid concrete all the way around, the floors, the ceiling, everything. Thick, thick walls. And the only windows we had were way up at the top of one of the walls. They were covered with iron bars and wire-mesh screening. Along the ceiling there was a row of maybe six or eight light bulbs. We found out that this was one of the holding cells that had been used for political prisoners. The Iranians used to put thirty or forty people in one of those cells. It seemed like we were going to be there forever. It went on week after week.

The worst of it was the confinement—the knowledge that there was absolutely nowhere to go. Here we are spending our lives in prison when we've never been accused of a crime, never had a trial, and never been sentenced. That was tough to deal with.

There were times when I thought it would go beyond weeks and months and run into years and years. We'd talk among ourselves and say, "When is it going to end? Is there any end in sight?" It just didn't look like anything was being done. I couldn't understand why we were still there. But the days kept going by and going by, with all of us in this incredibly grim prison.

CPL. STEVEN KIRTLEY (*marine security guard*): In the prison our routine never changed. You'd wake up in the morning when they brought breakfast in, and you'd eat your bread and butter. Then you'd walk around in circles, go to the bathroom, read for a while, and talk for a little bit. Then you'd eat lunch, get up and go to the bathroom, read for a while, talk a little bit, and walk some more circles. By then it would be time for supper, and you'd have dinner, go to the bathroom, read for a while, play cards, and go to bed. That was it. The same old thing every day for six months.

It even got to where we'd talk about the same things over and over again. We'd talk about all of our old girlfriends, what we did in high school, and how we were always getting into trouble. We'd talk about all of the bad things we did. Stuff like that. I was with Joe Hall and Greg Persinger, and they were really good people. We got along well together. It was inevitable that there would be times when you'd get on each other's nerves, just because you were locked up in a prison cell. But we were in a situation where we had to get along, and we all knew that. So we did.

JOE HALL (*warrant officer*): It was myself, Steve Kirtley, and Greg Persinger in that prison cell, which was nothing other than a perfectly empty concrete box. We walked it off one time; the cell was thirteen feet by eighteen feet. Before the militants ever brought us to the prison, the Red Cross had been through on an inspection tour, and at that time the prison authorities had put some very cheap carpeting on the floor. So we had this tattered old carpet, and our three foam rubber mattresses on the floor.

Being with those two marines was good for me. They kept me exercising all the time. Even though I was ten years older than those two guys, I still think of them as brothers. When you're locked up in a cell like that, there's nothing that goes unsaid. We told each other about everything that we had ever done in our lives. Every fantasy, every hope, every desire we had was expressed. We knew all about each other's family, each other's love life, and each other's aspirations. Every day we'd lean our foam rubber mattresses up against the wall to have as much space in the cell as possible, and we'd walk around and around the cell in circles, just like Geronimo did when he was a prisoner. We walked so much that we could actually see a path we had worn into that cheap carpet. The three of us would always get up and walk together, and shoot the shit while we were doing it. We kept moving at a fairly good pace, and there was constant conversation as we turned our circles around and around that cell. Being with those two guys was a great benefit for me.

JOHN LIMBERT (*political officer*): I'd been in solitary for seven consecutive months. One of the interesting things that happened in the prison was that for a while they put me in a cell with Lee Holland. The conditions were lousy, but that didn't matter much. By this time I'd grown accustomed to living in lousy conditions, and being with Lee Holland was a great improvement. After seven months, solitary was getting to me. I don't know how I would have come out of the ordeal if I'd been in solitary much longer. Lee probably saved my sanity. He is a very strong person, and a very supportive person. The first night we were together we sat up and talked for several hours. After the rescue attempt, he had been down in Jahrom, a tiny litlte town in the southern part of Iran, and he had received some bad treatment down there. He told me about that, and talked about his time in Iran during the revolution, and about the time he had spent in Vietnam. He'd been in plenty of tight spots before, and nothing seemed to upset him. He just took everything in stride. His presence and easygoing attitude helped me. After seven months in solitary I felt very lucky to be with him.

BILL BELK (*communications officer*): I can tell you some terrible things about roommates. After several weeks in solitary the Iranians brought another American into my cell who I did not know very well. As a matter of fact, I'd never met him prior to the takeover. I'd only seen him one time, and that was in the first couple of weeks after we were taken hostage, when we were both being kept in one of those little yellow houses on the compound. I wasn't too impressed with this fellow because of the way he handled himself. If you want to know the truth about it, I took an immediate dislike to him. There was something in his manner that I didn't care for. He was very prissy in the way he smoked his pipe, and he had kind of a contrived erudite, manner when he talked to the students. I thought he was a real strange bird.

Anyway, they moved him into my prison cell, and my first thought was, "Oh Lord, I'm in trouble now. I hope they get this guy out of here soon." I didn't want to put the guy off or make him feel bad, because we were both in a shitty situation. I mean, it's no fun being locked up in an Iranian prison, and we all needed to support each other so we could get through the ordeal with our sanity intact. So I tried to get along with this guy and be friendly. But almost immediately he started to inflict his weird thinking on me. First off, he let me know that he expected me to exercise with him. He said that he was an "exercise buff," and that he had a routine of exercises the two of us could do together. Well, I have never seen anything more ridiculous in all my life than what he called exercise. He got up and demonstrated his little routine. He did this skip-to-my-lou kind of thing that is impossible to describe. What he was doing was skipping up and down on the balls of his feet and waving his hands above his head. It wasn't jumping jacks, because jumping jacks are fairly strenuous, but this wasn't. It was just his own fairy-tale kind of jump-around exercise. Here I was sitting in this stinking hot prison cell watching this guy jump around and wave his arms. I thought he was completely out of his mind. He looked like a goddamn sissy. And to make matters worse, he'd strip naked to exercise. He'd get buck-ass naked and hop around the cell. I thought, "My goodness, they have got to get him out of here in a hurry!" I couldn't believe I was locked up with this guy.

The way he ended his little series of exercises was even worse. He would stand there bare-ass naked, put his hands on his hips, and un-dulate his pelvic area. I thought, "Oh shit, this is unreal!" He would do these big circular undulations of his pelvis. It was absolutely gross—and he wanted me to do it with him. Well, I could just see two grown men standing there naked and undulating our pelvic areas. There was no way I was going to get up and exercise my pelvic area with that guy. In the first place, I was trying to forget how to use my pelvic area. I hadn't seen a woman in over ten months. But this guy was standing there doing that, not the least bit embarrassed.

I tried to be nice to him, just because of the situation we were in. But within two or three days I knew that we weren't going to make it as roommates. Exercise wasn't his only problem. He had this thing where he believed he was a little bit better than anybody else in the entire world. He didn't hesitate to tell me how great he was, and to put me in my position relative to him. He let me know I was just a middle-class American, whereas he was an upper-class American.

I said, "How do you define what somebody's class is?"

He said, "Well, for one thing, you wear short-sleeve shirts to work, and upper-class people don't do that. Upper-class people wear long-sleeve shirts." Now what the length of somebody's shirt sleeves has to do with the price of beef I don't know. But he went on and on about the difference between upper-class people and middle-class people. He talked about the size of his house back in the States, and the size of my house. He talked about who he had eaten dinner with, and where he'd been to school. Everything he said had a little twist to it, to illustrate how much better he was than me. And there wasn't anything I could do. We were stuck in this concrete box, and there wasn't any way I could get away from the guy. We were together twenty-four hours a day, every day. Think about it, every single minute of every single day with no place to turn.

I absolutely couldn't stand him, and after forty-eight hours I was in a frame of mind where I would find fault with everything he did. I would pass my time by sitting in the corner of the cell and making up

300 reasons to hate him. I'd say to myself, "I hate him because he's cross-eyed. I hate him because of the sucking noises he makes when he smokes his pipe. I hate him for the shape of his nose and the color of his eyes. I hate him for the way his little pinkie sticks out when he turns the pages of a book." On and on. I just kept making up reasons to hate him. "I hate him for the way he does his exercises. I hate him for his pelvic undulations. I hate him for the way he eats his food." On and on.

Well, he didn't like me either. It got to the point where we both hated each other so much that we wouldn't even talk to each other. The only thing we had in common was that we both played chess. We must've played hundreds of games of chess in that cell. Our dislike of each other carried over into our chess matches and made for some intensely competitive games. The most important part of my day was beating him at chess. Within the confines of the prison cell, that was the only thing that mattered. I hated it when he beat me, and I'm sure he hated it when I beat him. It was the type of situation where he'd reel off twelve straight wins in a row, and then I'd turn around and beat him twelve times in a row. So we were very, very evenly matched. We'd sit there and play in this cold, cold silence, each of us desperate to beat the other.

After our chess games, he'd always get up and do his stupid exercises, and start dancing buck-ass naked around the cell again, or he'd lean back and criticize the book I was reading and start telling me how I was only middle class. Well, in that type of confinement you can only take so much. After about ten days I decided that I had to do something about the roommate situation. When one of the guards took me down to the bathroom I told this little fellow Ali that they had better get that guy out of my cell or I was going to kill him. I told the guard I'd strangle the guy.

Ali said, "Oh, no, no, no. You cannot do that."

I said, "Get him out of there or I'm going to kill him. I mean it, Ali. I'm going to kill him." And I showed him my hands to demonstrate how I'd strangle the guy.

Of course, I never would have brought any harm to another American, but I had to get them to move this guy out. So I told this little Iranian that they had better do something. That very afternoon they moved the guy out and brought someone else in.

COL. LELAND HOLLAND (*army attaché*): When I was in solitary, there were times when I felt fortunate to be alone, because at least I had some privacy. There were hostages over there who had no privacy at all. Absolutely none. The Iranians would have four or five people in a single cell, and they would take them down to the bathroom together in a group. Speaking very bluntly, they couldn't even beat their meat in private, because there wasn't any privacy to be found. That was the kind of thing that could run you up a wall.

When you're living in captivity like that, there's a limit to how much you can take. In those close quarters you just get plain tired of other people. After a while, you're ready to jump up and punch somebody out. So it was inevitable that there were some roommate problems. There was one guy over there that caused everyone who was ever in a cell with him to go bananas. He had terrible eating habits and made a mess out of his food. He did all sorts of obnoxious things. Two different hostages who were put with him told me that they went to the guards and said, "You either move him out, or move me out. Get us away from each other, or I'm going to kill him." That was how they got away from the guy.

Now, with all the uncertainty inherent in our being held hostage, the last thing anybody needed was roommate problems. That was where I felt I had an advantage by spending so much time alone. When you're first thrown into solitary it's a frightening damn thing, but you can always live with yourself. Roommates can be a welcome relief, as John Limbert was for me, but they can also cause problems and get on your nerves. During those many months that I was alone, I really didn't mind it, because I knew I could always stand myself.

SGT. PAUL LEWIS (*marine security guard*): The big thing for all of us in the prison was information. To me, passing notes was a big help, a definite boost to morale. Way back when we were held in the basement of the embassy, Jim Lopez and I had exchanged notes. One day I noticed that someone had scratched FTR on the bathroom door, so I dropped Jim Lopez a note and asked him, "What does FTR mean?" He sent a note back that said, "Fuck the rags." Well, that got to be our signal. No matter where I was taken after that, if I saw FTR scratched on the wall, then I knew that Jim Lopez was there, too. It was also a clue to look for notes. In the prison, we'd scratch FTR on the wall in the bathroom to indicate where a note was hidden. That way we could exchange information between cells. Any news that Lopez had was news that I had, and vice versa.

Of course, we didn't know much. There just wasn't much news coming in. But there were times when I couldn't wait to get a note. I'd look forward to going down to the bathroom to see if there was a note there. Even though our notes were nothing more than a little scrunched-up piece of paper with a couple of scrunched-up paragraphs, and often-times very trivial, I enjoyed getting them. We'd tell each other little things, like when we got mail, or what one of the guards said, or what McKeel had said to one of the guards. You know, little bits of gossip. The important thing was that it was news from outside our cell, and somehow that made a big difference.

JOE HALL (*warrant officer*): While we were in prison, Kirtley, Persinger, and I fully developed the use of the tap code. It was the same code the POWs used in Vietnam. We'd tap out letters according to their position in a five by five box like this:

	1	2	3	4	5
1	A	B	C	D	E
2	F	G	H	I	J(K)
3	L	M	N	O	P
4	Q	R	S	T	U
5	V	W	X	Y	Z

The letter A would be one-one, the letter B would be one-two, and so on. We started using it to communicate with John Limbert, who was in the cell next door. At first, I found it was a very laborious process. You had to listen to the taps, jot the numbers down, and then decipher the code. But after a couple weeks of steady use all three of us grew to be very proficient. We could decipher it as we heard it. The militants kept John Limbert next door to us in solitary confinement for about three or four months. He had been in a cell with Lee Holland for a while, but the two of them got caught passing notes, so the militants split them up and put John back into solitary. We used to communicate with him several times a day. We even played chess with him by tapping through the wall. He asked the Iranians for a chess board, which was a little bit strange because he was by himself. But he told them he wanted to study the board and practice chess plays, so they gave him one. Then we asked for a chess board in our cell, too, and started to play chess with him through the wall. The students didn't want us communicating at all, and if they had been smart enough to put two and two together they could have looked at John's board and at our board, and seen that the pieces were in identical positions on both boards. But they weren't sharp enough to do that. So we continued to play together for the three or four months that John was in the cell next to us. Those chess games were always a source of amusement for us, but it was also an exercise in futility. John is a very good chess player. We must've played over 500 games of chess with him, and I doubt if the three of us won more than four or five of those games. Beating John at chess was a virtual impossibility.

We also used the tap code to pass what little information we had back and forth. But we ran out of new information pretty quickly, and when we didn't have anything else to say, we used the tap code to tease John. We'd tap out messages like: "Did you get ice cream with your cake today?" He'd tap back, "What cake?" Or we'd say, "Great mail call today." Even though we hadn't gotten any mail in over two weeks. Then later we'd have to tell him we were only joking, because we didn't want him to feel bad.

John was a pretty tough guy. We could hear him talking to the militants in his cell, and he never took any bullshit off of them. He was fluent in Farsi and he had been a teacher in Iran, so he was totally inside their heads. They couldn't fool him for a minute. I think John found it to be very difficult to have to take so much crap off a bunch of young punks, who were the same type of people he had been teaching a few years before.

CDR. ROBERT ENGELMANN (*naval supply corps officer*): Even though the Iranians were trying to seal us off from any news coming in from the outside, we did manage to get a few bits of information by communicating with other hostages or by reading everything that came into our cell. In the prison, the Iranians used to give us copies of the *Sporting News*, and that was how we first learned about the death of the shah. There was an article in there about a golf match, and in the article there was a sentence that said television coverage of the golf match had been interrupted because of the death of the shah. That was it. Just one little sentence buried in the text of an article, but it was a sentence that told us a lot.

Whenever we'd get a copy, we'd read the *Sporting News* from cover to cover. By picking out little things we were able to glean little bits of information. We learned about the inflation in oil and gold prices just from reading the *Sporting News*. There was something in there about the Hickcock Belt—which is an athletic award—and this article said that the value of the belt had been increased tenfold due to the rise in the price of gold. We read these sorts of things and then pieced some of this information together. So we knew that inflation was high back in the States, and that there were problems with the economy.

We learned about the rescue mission in a similar way. I had received a letter from a friend in New York, and in the letter she had enclosed some *New York Times* crossword puzzles. On the back of one of those puzzles was a portion of a TV listing. We were so starved for news that we'd read anything, even old TV listings. We passed our letters around the cell and shared them with each other. It was Steve Lauterbach who read the back of my crossword puzzle. The four of us were sitting there when Steve gasped and said, "You're not going to believe this." Then he was speechless. He literally could not talk. I was thinking, "That must be one hell of a crossword puzzle, Steve."

Then he showed us what he had found in the TV listing. It said there was going to be a network special which dealt with the CIA from 1952 through the aborted hostage rescue mission in Iran. That was big news. It was the first time we knew that an attempt had been made to get us out.

GARY LEE (*general services officer*): I first learned about the rescue attempt in a letter. It was from an army spec four, who was a total stranger to me. He was a member of my dad's church, which is why he had my name and was writing to me. The first page of the letter was the standard "I hope you are doing well" type of thing. But at the top of the second page was this sentence: "Any one of us would have gladly taken the place of the eight who died trying to rescue you." That sentence was actually in the letter. The Iranian censors had totally missed it. That was my first confirmation that a rescue attempt had been made. In the cell, we were extremely upset by that news. We had no feel for what had happened. We couldn't understand how eight Americans had died, and that was the end of it. No follow-up action of any kind. Nothing from the American government.

JOE HALL (*warrant officer*): John Limbert used the tap code to tell about the rescue attempt. That was the first the three of us had heard about it. I remember that hearing about the rescue attempt gave us some pretty bad moments. We didn't know what had happened back then, and when John told us that eight people had died that was hard to take. It had never dawned on me that people might have died trying to get us out.

MALCOLM KALP (*economics officer*): In captivity, the smallest things become extremely important. My greatest possession at the prison was a Fisher's cashew nut can that I managed to get my hands on. It had a lid on it, and why it was so important to me was that I could urinate in it. On a normal day, I'd go to the bathroom six times. I'd go after the three meals to wash my plate, and I'd go three times to use the toilet. But when I got my hands on that nut can, I'd urinate in it, put the lid on it, and carry it down to the bathroom and empty it when I went to wash my plate. That meant three fewer trips to the bathroom each day. Which meant three fewer times that I had to be humiliated by being blindfolded and led down there by one of the terrorists. That was important.

COL. LELAND HOLLAND (*army attaché*): Iranians are very big on modesty. Nudity just isn't a part of their culture. They find it to be very offensive. When we were being kept in the Mushroom, some of the guards would use the showers down there, and even when they were in the shower they would wear a pair of shorts. They'd never take everything off, because they were super modest.

While we were in the prison, they suspected that we were passing notes in the bathroom, and they were right. We were. But they would never come into the bathroom with us, because they were too modest. If they had come in there, we would not have been able to pass notes. So what they did was they brought a television monitor over to the prison that they had taken from the marine security desk at the embassy, and they mounted it up in the corner of the bathroom. They wouldn't come in there with us, but apparently they were willing to watch us on TV. I guess they felt that looking through glass made some kind of difference. That's how hypocritical they were.

BRUCE GERMAN (*budget officer*): They installed a TV camera in the john, and I resented the hell out of that. The bathroom is the one place where you want some privacy. I immediately told one of the guards that I wanted to have a meeting with Ahmed. He came to the cell and wanted to know, "What is it this time, Mr. German?"

I said, "You've got a TV camera down there, and I refuse to take a shower as long as that camera is in there."

"No, no," he said. "That's only for certain people. We have to watch them."

"That means you won't watch me?"

"No, no, no. We won't watch you."

"Well," I said, "I'll tell you what I'm going to do. I'm going to take a shower tomorrow and I'm going to cover that camera with my towel."

He said, "Oh, you shouldn't do that."

Then the next time I went down to the john, I put my towel over the camera and took a shower. They didn't like me doing that, but nothing was ever said to me about it.

COL. THOMAS SCHAEFER (*defense attaché*): When I saw that the Iranians had put a television camera in the bathroom, the first thing I did was harass them about it. It was great sport. I said to them, "You put that camera in there just because you want to see us naked. You want to see me naked, don't you?"

I'd say these sorts of things just to taunt and harass them. I said this to one of the guards, and I could see the hurt on his face. He said, "Oh, no. No. That is not why." His feelings were genuinely hurt by my saying this. I could have stabbed him in the stomach with a double-edged knife, and it would have hurt him less.

Then when I went into the bathroom, I'd pretend that I was talking into my watch. Initially, this was something that they were very paranoid about. They thought we had concealed microphones in our shoes and watches, so I'd stand in front of the camera and act like I was talking to Washington, D.C.

COL. LELAND HOLLAND (*army attaché*): When I saw that camera I figured, "I know what will bug them." Whether I had to use the toilet or not, I'd park myself on the throne and put on a little show. If that was what they wanted to see, I was going to let them see it. I'd sit there and wave at the camera while I was perched on the john. Then after taking a shower, I'd come out and stand right in front of the camera to dry myself off. They had a wide-angle lens on that thing, so I figured I'd give them a very good shot. I wanted them to see a good one. I'd turn my back to the camera and bend over and dry the hell out of my toes. I'd get my towel down in there between each toe, and took my time about doing it.

I'd use their own culture against them every chance I had. They had put me in one hell of an unpleasant bind, so I would fight back with whatever I had at my disposal. Pretty soon, some of the other hostages started picking up on it, too. We were all making moons at the camera. And it worked. It got to them. It was so bad that they came in and removed the camera.

JOHN LIMBERT (*political officer*): In many of the students, I recognized characteristics that I had seen in some of my own Iranian students ten years earlier. Basically, they were confused kids who were living in a very screwed-up society, and were looking for some way out of it. The students I'd had ten years earlier didn't take me hostage or threaten my life, but they were confused, and I could see the potential in them for following some kind of demagogue like Khomeini—for following someone who could offer them a way out of the confusion they were living in.

In his speeches Khomeini used to talk about something he called the "Mohammadan System." He kept saying, "We are trying to build a Mohammadan System." His reference was to the seventh-century city-state of Medina, where Mohammed sat in the mosque and gave judgments, made the law, received ambassadors, and led prayers. This was the sort of system that Khomeini wanted to reconstruct. That was his vision.

So while I was in prison I constructed a poster which listed Mohammed's system on one side and on the other side the students' system. I simply wrote down several of the very fine and generous things that Mohammed had done. For example, I listed how he had freed prisoners after his battles, how he had not bothered the people of Mecca, and how he had made sure that foreigners in his territory were protected. Then on the other side of the poster I juxtaposed examples of things the students had done. It was my way of using their religiosity against them and contrasting their way of treating people with Mohammed's way of treating people. Instead of protecting foreigners, I said that they had attacked defenseless people who were under their protection, and instead of being generous they had stolen property that did not belong to them. I listed all sorts of these things, and then I took this poster and put it up on the wall.

I also wrote some poems which were quite insulting to the students and put them up on the wall, too. There's a very famous and beautiful poem in Persian where the rhyme is *arezust* and I wrote my own poem with the same rhyme. *Arezust* means to desire something. In the Persian poem, that is the word that forms the rhyme. It's difficult for me to translate the poem I wrote into English, because the rhyme pattern and grammatical structure are different, but the gist of the poem I wrote would be something like this: "I am foaming at the mouth with violence and curses. I am a rabid dog, and I desire curses and a bone. / I am terribly fearful. I am scared to death of a fair fight. My desire is a cowardly attack in the direction of women. / I am tired of listening to the voice of human beings. My desire is the speech, the behavior, and the braying of donkeys. / I have disregarded the law of God and man. I desire the jungle and the character of the wild animal." And so on. This was a poem that I put up on the wall along with my posters. Even though nothing was ever said, I'm sure the message got through to the students that I had complete distaste for what they were doing.

In fact, this led to a rather interesting series of confrontations. There was one fellow there by the name of Gholam Reza, and he was one of the most obnoxious guards in the group. When Colonel Holland and I were together we used to call him Bedside Manners because he was gratuitously nasty. After I put my "Mohammadan System" poster on the wall he wouldn't come in and argue with me directly, but when I was taken down to the bathroom I'd occasionally come back and find that he had written something on the poster. He would leave a message, and then I would write an answer. For example, he might write, "Islam gives protection to diplomats, not to spies." Then under his comment I would write, "For example, a businessman, a secretary, and a medic are spies." Then the next time I was taken down to the bathroom, Gholam Reza would come in, read what I had written, and write another message for me. Then I would write another reply. This sort of communication between us went on for a long time.

The two of us must have filled up several pages with messages of this sort going back and forth to one another. But a word never passed between us. It was something that was done without ever being spoken of. I think it kept us from getting angry at one another, and was the sort of communication that worked out better for both of us. Finally, he had defaced so many of my posters that I took them down and recopied all of them clean, and stuck them back up on the wall. I also put up a sign that designated a free speech area, and indicated that if anyone had an argument or an opinion, this was the place for it. It was sort of like "Democracy Wall" in China. And we did continue to write messages and arguments back and forth, but still, a word never passed between us.

3 Autumn 1980

CAPT. PAUL NEEDHAM (*air force logistics officer*): July came and went; then August came around. I was thinking, "Maybe we'll get released before the election. Maybe Carter will pull something off." But still nothing happened. August passed, and we were into September, and still in prison.

In every letter I wrote home, I would ask for a Linebacker-Three game and D-models for Christmas. This referred to the bombings of Hanoi and Haiphong in December of 1972. That was called Linebacker-Two. Linebacker-One had been the earlier bombings in May of 1972. And D-models, of course, refer to B-52 D-models, which carry about 110 five-hundred-pound bombs. I thought that was the way to end the problem. Not nuke 'em, but just send over a few D-models and let them take care of the situation. Just keep a new load coming over about every thirty minutes and dropping. That would have gotten the Iranians' attention. By referring to Linebacker-Three games and D-models in my letters, I was saying, "Hey, military action is what's needed to end this problem." That's what I was asking for in every letter home.

In most of the letters that I received from my mother she would include some type of quote. In most of mine to her I would simply quote: "Is life so sweet or peace so dear?" I'd let it go at that. She knew the rest of it. It was from Patrick Henry's speech at the House of Burgesses in 1775, where he said, "Give me liberty, or give me death."

BRUCE GERMAN (*budget officer*): In September the goons started turning the lights out at night, and we couldn't understand why because we'd always been able to stay up late and read at night. But then they started having blackouts and giving us candles at night. That made reading very difficult. We had to read by candlelight, and that was bad for our eyes. We'd ask the goons about this. We'd ask them what was going on, and they'd say, "Oh, we're just checking the electricity in the city. That's all. Just checking the electricity."

Then there were times when the jets would fly in low overhead. I mean very low. I didn't know whose planes they were, but the prison windows would rattle and shake, and the whole building would vibrate. In the distance, we'd hear the guns going off. I mean big guns. They'd be booming away, and we'd ask, "What's that? What's going on now?"

The goons would say, "Oh, that's a celebration."

"Really? No lights? Loud guns? A celebration?"

VICTOR TOMSETH (*chief political officer, at the Iranian Foreign Ministry with Bruce Laingen and Michael Howland*): At about twenty minutes after two on September 22, the Iraqis dropped a couple of bombs on Mehrabad Airport. We were only a couple of miles away, and we heard the explosions and saw the smoke from the airport. We also saw two planes circle around and head back west toward Iraq.

We had a radio in the Foreign Ministry, and the BBC picked up the news faster than Tehran radio did. Within twenty minutes the BBC had a news report. We told the Iranian guards that Mehrabad Airport had been bombed. They said, "No, that's impossible!" Then about twenty or thirty minutes later the news reports were broadcast on Iranian radio as well.

JOHN LIMBERT (*political officer*): One night in September, the students turned on the television news, and it was loud enough so that I could hear the broadcast coming through the window. They normally didn't do that. I scrambled over to the window and listened to the news, and then in the middle of the broadcast everything stopped. We could hear an airplane flying above us. Lee Holland was in the cell with me. He was very good at identifying aircraft. He could distinguish between an F-4 or an F-5 or an F-27 transport. In the prison, we were on the flight path for Mehrabad Airport, and we heard lots of planes flying over.

Anyway, the news broadcast stopped and we heard the sound of this plane coming in. Then all hell broke loose.

COL. LELAND HOLLAND (*army attaché*): John Limbert and I were in the cell together when we heard this loud roaring *wa-wooosh!* I'd been on the ground before when attacking jets came in and dumped stuff in front of the lines, and that was a sound I'll never forget. That's just what this sounded like. We heard the *wa-woosh*, and then we heard the electric cannon on the plane burping away. Immediately I knew a bombing raid was going on. I didn't know who was doing it, but I knew exactly what was happening. Then we could hear the bombs. We heard a loud *boom!* Then right after that we'd hear the secondary explosions ignite—it was *boom!-kaboomb!* One right after the other.

I looked at Limbert and said, "Goddamn, John, they're playing our song!"

John is not a military guy, but he could hear all the noise. He said, "What is it? What's happening?"

CAPT. PAUL NEEDHAM (*air force logistics officer*): On the night of September 22 the bombing attacks started. That was a very pleasant night. I loved it. I thought they were F-4s flying overhead. I was just hoping they were F-4s. I figured that President Carter had finally called it quits, and that he was doing something that would help him in the election.

I heard jet passes overhead and I heard bombs dropping. I'll tell you, it's quite different being on the receiving end of a bombing attack. It was somewhat scary, but I really thought they were Americans, and that they would not bomb us because they knew where we were. It reminded me of Vietnam and the Linebacker-Two missions. The prisoners up in North Vietnam weren't afraid of bombs dropping near them, because the American pilots knew exactly where the POW camp was. The prisoners knew they weren't going to be hit. That POW camp was the safest place to be. I figured it was the same for us. We didn't have any problem.

CPL. WILLIAM GALLEGOS (*marine security guard*): I was pretty hyper. My adrenaline pumps real fast, and if anything happened I'd jump up right away. When those bombing raids started, some of the bombs landed pretty close, and the entire prison was shaking. We could see the Iranians shooting their antiaircraft guns into the air. It was lighting up the sky, and I was getting excited. At first I thought it was Americans, and I was ready to go. I jumped up and was just waiting for them to come bursting through the door.

GARY LEE (*general services officer*): All holy hell was breaking loose, and I figured, "This is it! America is finally attacking Iran, and I'm going to the wall." I knew there wasn't any way that we could survive an American attack, and I figured we would all be dying soon. But there wasn't any terror in that realization. I was way beyond that. It was more a feeling of, "Well, it's finally happening."

CDR. ROBERT ENGELMANN (*naval supply corps officer*): We were behind thick concrete walls, and when he had the blackouts it was really dark inside the prison. Pitch black. We heard the jets flying over at tree level, doing about 700 knots, and dropping their bombs. We were sitting in the dark wondering, "Hey, what's going on? What's happening?"

I didn't realize the degree of defenses the Iranians had around that prison. I figured we were surrounded by some goons with machine guns, but when those attack planes started flying over, the Iranians were firing some big guns from right outside our window. I mean heavy artillery. Hawk antiaircraft missiles were being launched, and all kinds of antiaircraft guns were going off. That really surprised me. I didn't know they had that kind of heavy artillery out there. But this stuff was going up right outside the window.

The funny thing about it was we heard one or two jets fly over, and then the Iranians kept on firing their weapons for the next thirty minutes. There was nothing up there. But they kept firing their antiaircraft guns into the dark long after the planes had disappeared.

At first, we weren't sure who had staged the attack. I didn't think it was an American attack, because too few bombs fell. These guys only dropped eight or nine bombs. If it was an American attack, I figured it would be a B-52 coming in with 104 bombs, or something big like that. At first, we thought maybe the Iranian military had turned against the revolutionaries, and that maybe they were fighting each other.

BILL BELK (*communications officer*): The students were scared shitless. They were running around and didn't know which way to turn. There must have been hundreds of guns going off that night. I was in a cell with John Graves, and we were very curious about what was going on. So when one of the students came into the cell, we asked him, "Who are you at war with?"

He said "There is no war. It is our troops. They are just practicing."

"Oh? They're practicing in the middle of the night? They're practicing right smack dab over the downtown area of Tehran?"

"Yes. Do not worry. It is only practice."

I just laughed. It was uncanny how those guys would lie. They'd come in and say these totally ridiculous things, and then expect us to believe them. What made it even more absurd was those guys were scared to death. You could see it in their faces. Their eyes were open wide. They were wired like they'd just been plugged in. This one guy who came into the cell was so frightened he was actually shaking—his hands, his lips, everything was trembling. And he kept saying, "Do not worry. It is only practicing."

COL. LELAND HOLLAND (*army attaché*): For the next twenty-four hours, the Iranians had a loudspeaker going outside the prison. They were broadcasting news, propaganda, and all kinds of religious junk. John Limbert could understand it perfectly, so we knew there had been an air raid, but it was a little while before we were sure who had done it. I knew it couldn't have been an American attack, because there would have been more than two airplanes. So I was sure that it wasn't American. Over the next twenty-four hours we heard all kinds of emergency broadcasts over the loudspeaker. Apparently, the Iran National Works had been hit and thirty-five people had been killed. The word was going out in these emergency broadcasts that people should not go to the hospital unless it was an absolute emergency. The hospitals were for real emergencies only. So it was obvious that this air raid hit them pretty hard. It wasn't long before Limbert and I were able to deduce that it had been Iraq who had attacked.

BARRY ROSEN (*press attaché*): From that time on we had blackouts every night. We heard a lot of artillery fire and commotion, and it was hard for us to know who was doing what to whom. Over the course of the next few days, we heard chanting in the prison courtyard where the Iranians gathered for their evening prayers. This was nothing new. They'd been chanting for some time, and the usual fare had been, *"Marg bar Carter! Marg bar Amrika!"* But after the bombing raids there was an added attraction. They were chanting something new. It was muffled and very hard for us to understand. It was a dense sound coming through the walls. We kept listening, and it sounded sort of like, *"Marg bar tum-tah, tum-tah."* I said to myself, "Now what the hell is that?" None of us could figure it out. I kept asking myself, "Now what can it be? *Marg bar tum-tah, tum-tah.*" By listening to the number of beats and syllables I was able to figure it out. I said, "Hey, guys, they're chanting *'Marg bar Sadam Hussein!'*" That was it. *"Marg bar Sadam Hussein!"* So immediately we knew that something was going on between Iran and Iraq, and that Iraq was doing the bombing.

JOE HALL (*warrant officer*): The students were shaken by these air raids. They were praying day and night. We could hear them out in the courtyard. They would get together in groups and pray and chant and carry on. All of a sudden they had a great burst of energy. They were at war, and they wanted to get in shape. They would be out in the courtyard at 5:30 in the morning doing calisthenics. All at once, everybody was in training. We'd hear them running on the roof, and then we'd hear them chanting and doing their prayers. All the while, you could see the tension in their faces. Those guys were obviously frightened.

CDR. ROBERT ENGELMANN (*naval supply corps officer*): When the war broke out the guards were up for two or three days straight. The jets flew over and they ran outside and shot at them with their rifles. The antiaircraft guns went off, and everybody went out shooting. They were really scared by all of this. They were pumped up and frightened.

You can only last so long, and after about three days without sleep the guards became exhausted. They started falling asleep in the hall while they were on guard duty. On the third night of the war, at about two o'clock in the morning, Bill Keough had to go to the bathroom, so he started beating on his metal door. Bill is a big guy. He's about six-nine, 300 pounds, and he was making plenty of noise, but there was no answer. We were in concrete cells, and when you beat on those metal doors it would echo and make all kinds of noise. I was asleep, but I woke up. I heard this *bang-bang-bang!* I realized that it was just somebody going to the bathroom. So I put my head down to go back to sleep. But the pounding kept on going. *Bang-bang-bang!* Bill was hammering that door. One of the things the Iranians used to say to us when we were making too much noise was, "Es-speak-a more slowly." They meant "softly," but they'd say "slowly." When Keough kept pounding on the door, one of the marines popped up and hollered into the hallway, "Speak-a more slowly."

Keough said, "Who's that?"

"Where the hell is the guard?" asked the marine.

"He's right outside the door, but I think he's dead."

The guy had gone to sleep in the hall. I guess he'd said his prayers and passed out from exhaustion. He'd been up for three days, and he fell into a deep, deep sleep.

So all of the Americans started shouting up and down the hallway. Everybody ran to their cell doors and hollered through the little barred windows. It had been almost eleven months since the takeover, and this was the first time any of us were able to talk with anyone other than those few in our own cells. I think there were twenty-seven Americans on that corridor. So this was the big chance—twenty-seven guys together! We were shouting and hollering and giving each other any information we had. There wasn't much news to give, because we hadn't heard much. I think a few people learned about the rescue mission for the first time that night, or about the death of the shah. Whatever information we had we passed, and we were sending greetings to our friends up and down the hall—just shouting and having a great time.

This went on for about ten or twelve minutes, which is a long time for that sort of commotion. Then in the middle of all this shouting the guard woke up. He was totally out of it. He didn't know what was going on. He started screaming, "No esspeak! No esspeak!" So the whole prison went deathly quiet. Total silence. Everyone settled back down and pretended nothing had happened.

Then a few minutes later, we heard this *bang-bang-bang!* It was Bill Keough knocking on his door, wanting to go to the bathroom. We thought that was hilarious.

JOE HALL (*warrant officer*): The bombing raids went on for two or three weeks, as regular as clockwork. At six o'clock there would be a blackout. The students would come in and make us snuff out our candles. They pointed at the candle and said, "Off that!" As if someone in a fighter plane could see a frigging candle through three feet of concrete. But the students were so paranoid they made us snuff out those candles. Twenty minutes later we could hear the jets come flying in. The Iraqis were flying F-4 Phantoms, and they had a very distinctive howl. They'd come howling in, and the air raid sirens would go off, and we'd hear the bombs falling. All kinds of antiaircraft fire would break loose all at once. We had three little windows that sat way up high in our cell, and we could see the antiaircraft fire. That was a spectacular sight.

Initially, the students were coming in and telling us, "It is only exercises. It is not war. It is only exercises."

After a couple nights of this, we jumped up in the morning and said, "Hey, they exercised the hell out of you last night, didn't they?" Or we'd try to play one off against the other. We'd say, "Ahmed told us that you shot down two Iraqi fighter planes last night." Of course, Ahmed hadn't said anything of the sort, but they would acknowledge these kinds of comments and say, "Yes, yes." We kept asking these kinds of loaded questions, and after a while they became more candid about the fact that they were at war with Iraq.

BILL BELK (*communications officer*): The crazy thing about the air raids was that the attack planes would always sneak up on the Iranians. Every time it was the same. We'd hear the bombs fall first and then the ack-

ack guns would go off. They'd really cut loose, and the sky would be full of return fire, but the Iraqi planes would already be gone. There was always a ten- or fifteen-second delay between the time when the bombs would fall and the return fire would begin. It was obvious that the Iranians didn't have any radar functioning at all. Because if they did, they would've locked in on the attack planes and started firing at them when they made their approach, not after they'd already finished their bombing runs. Those planes would hit their targets at will and be gone.

SGT. PAUL LEWIS (*marine security guard*): It was amazing how quickly the blackouts and air raids just became part of our routine. We'd hear the bombs fall, the sirens going off, and all of the shooting and shouting going on outside. In our cell, the four of us would just sit around our candle and play cards. We were used to it. At night, it was almost impossible for us to read, because there wasn't enough room for everybody to get around the candle in a position where the light was adequate. So instead of reading, we'd sit up and play Spades.

CPL. STEVEN KIRTLEY (*marine security guard*): Most of the air raids would take place at night. We'd have them four or five nights in a row, and then there wouldn't be anything for a while. I remember one time Joe Hall, Greg Persinger, and I were sitting there in our cell at 4:30 in the afternoon during one of those lulls in the air raids. We were playing cards, when all of sudden we heard a jet coming in even though it was broad daylight outside. That jet was flying low, too, and it sounded great! Absolutely outstanding. We had cards in our hands when we heard this *wawhoosh*! And then the bombing run. *Ba-boom! Ba-ba-boom!* We jumped up and rushed to the window and tried to see a little something through the triangle when the jet came screaming back. It sounded like it was right on top of us. *Whooosh!* It was so low that we thought, "Holy shit, this guy is getting ready to bomb us!" All three of us hit the deck. That jet was screaming, and some of those bombs landed so close to the prison that the walls shook. We used to love it when stuff like that took place, because it got the guards all excited. They'd be running around, jabbering real fast at each other in Farsi. I always thought it was kind of funny. Anything that frightened them was just fine with me.

JOHN LIMBERT (*political officer*): There was one daytime raid where a bomb went off very close to the prison. It was quite loud, and we could feel the tremors from the explosion. Later I learned that a bomb had hit a shopping passage about four or five blocks away. It killed about sixty people, and after the air raid we heard all the sirens.

JOE HALL (*warrant officer*): It got to the point where we would actually look forward to the bombing raids. If Tehran didn't get hit for several nights in a row, it would just depress the hell out of us. We liked the idea of them getting bombed. When the fighter planes came screaming in and dropped their bombs, we'd jump up and start clapping and cheering and hollering and carrying on. Everybody would do that. We could hear the other Americans up and down the cell block. Hostages would be shouting, "Give 'em hell!" "Flatten Tehran!" Or, "Buy Iraqi war bonds!" Things like that. We'd practically shake the prison with all of our cheering and clapping. It was always an event to look forward to, and when it didn't happen for a few nights in a row we really missed it.

CPL. WILLIAM GALLEGOS (*marine security guard*): When the militants would come walking into the cell after an air raid, I used to tell them, "That was good! I hope they blow us up. I hope they hit the prison and we all get killed. Because if that happens America will drop a nuclear bomb on this place."

They'd say, "No, no."

"Yeah, they're going to send a nuclear bomb in here. Do you know what happens when a nuclear bomb hits sand? It makes glass. It just turns everything to glass. All of you guys are going to be buried under glass. They'll turn this place into a museum, and people are going to walk over the glass and look at you."

That would always get them worried and pissed off.

4 Evin Prison

CAPT. PAUL NEEDHAM (*air force logistics officer*): At about 8:30 on the evening of October 22, I was moved over to Evin Prison and thrown into solitary confinement for three weeks. About fourteen of us were taken over to Evin Prison. I could count them by listening to the voices in the halls. I had mixed emotions about the company I was with. These guys were all high-level State Department, high-ranking military, or intelligence people—the hostages the Iranians would keep behind for a trial if they decided to do something like that. I was proud to be associated with those guys, but I was concerned about the possible consequences. I'd sit in my cell and think, "You guys have got me all wrong. I'm not important. You don't understand, I'm just not important." Then I'd think, "What the hell? It's good company."

COL. CHARLES SCOTT (*chief of the Defense Liaison Office, at Evin Prison*): Evin Prison is notorious for being one of the worst prisons in the world. It had been used by the shah to imprison and torture his political opposition, and Khomeini put it to use for the same purpose. In my cell there were places on the wall where I could read the last testaments of dying men, who had been tortured and were going on to meet their reward. There was an inscription right near my bed that was particularly depressing. It was written at an odd angle by a guy who obviously couldn't stand up anymore. It said, "Merciful God, please—" and then he never finished it. I could see how the guy had reached over and started to write on the wall while lying down, and then the angle tapered off. He didn't have the strength to finish. Seeing that sort of thing can work on your head. It can get you to thinking about all the other souls who have spent time in the very same cell you are in, and who are now dead. That's the sort of thing you don't want to dwell on. But when I first went into the cell, I couldn't avoid reading that stuff. It was sort of like seeing a street sign, in that you read it whether you want to or not. So that was very depressing. But after a couple of days, I got to where I didn't even see those slogans anymore. They were like so much wallpaper, and I was able to divorce myself not only from what they said, but what they meant.

JOHN LIMBERT (*political officer, at Evin Prison*): When I was put into my cell in Evin Prison, I remember there was graffiti all over the wall that had been written by other prisoners who had been held there. It was mostly from Mujihadin and Feda'iyen groups, along with a few things from Baluchi students. It was all recent, and I knew these were not the shah's prisoners, but postrevolution prisoners. From the graffiti it was very clear that there was a great deal of civil strife going on in Iran. The slogans said things like: "Forward for an armed mobilization of the masses!" That was obviously Feda'i-ye-Khlaq. Or, "Long live Masoud Rejavie." He is the Mujihadin leader who is now living in exile in Paris. There was another one about a student who had been taken from the University of Baluchistan and brought to the prison. The wall was just full of slogans and comments. So I added my name to the list. I wrote on the wall in both English and Persian: "A prisoner of Fascism, brought here in December of 1980—John Limbert."

COL. LELAND HOLLAND (*army attaché, at Evin Prison*): Being kept in Evin Prison was difficult because it was so cold in there. We were into another winter, and the prison was located way up north at one of the highest points in the city. It got very cold. One of the things I noticed was that because of the war, the students weren't getting some of the supplies they'd had previously. We were short on soap and a lot of other staples, and the food was lousy.

From my cell, I could look out onto a motor pool area. At night, I could see cars driving around with blue covers over their headlights because of the blackout conditions. It was obvious that the war was hurting the Iranians. There was no doubt about that. I remember there was a big truck out in this motor pool area that they took out to get refueled every day, and at night I could see a couple of guys run over to this truck with a hose to siphon fuel out of the tank and put in their cars. They were obviously short on gasoline, and were getting it in any way they could. The war had disrupted the economy, and was having its impact. Even from my little vantage point inside a prison I could see that.

COL. CHARLES SCOTT (*chief of the Defense Liaison Office, at Evin Prison*): Don Sharer and I were put in a cell together in Evin Prison. I knew that prime rib was Don's favorite food. So for a while there I got onto a kick where I would describe an absolutely glorious meal. I'd tell Don to imagine an inch-and-a-half-thick cut of medium-rare prime rib with horseradish sauce, a steaming hot baked potato with melted butter and chives, fresh green beans, and a chilled mug of beer with frost dripping down the glass. I'd go on and on, and describe the meal in minute detail. Don would pretend he was enraged. He'd say, "Hey, you really know how to hurt a guy."

"Yeah, but just think, Don, when we finally get out of here, that's exactly what we're going to be eating."

5 Winter 1980–81

JOE HALL (*warrant officer, at Komiteh Prison with Gerg Persinger and Steven Kirtley*): As miserable as life was in that prison, there were a few things we did to improve our surroundings. We never threw away anything the Iranians gave us, and one time Kirtley, Persinger, and I made a reflector to give us more light in our cell during the blackouts. The guards had come by and given each of us a can of Sunkist orange soda, and we kept the cans. Then we managed to talk one of the guards into bringing us a pair of scissors, which we used to cut open each of the aluminum soda cans. We also had an empty ketchup bottle that we'd pulled out of the garbage, which we used as a candle holder. Well, by carving a hole in the bottom of the soda can, we were able to fit it at the base of the candle, and we could spread out the aluminum sides of the can. That was our reflector. It was amazing how much extra light that simple little thing gave us. It practically lit up the whole cell. That made our nights a little easier to deal with. It was easier to play cards, and it was easier to get around.

SGT. JAMES LOPEZ (*marine security guard, at Komiteh Prison*): Occasionally the rags would bring us Sanka and hot water in place of tea. One day we asked for some Sanka, and the guard brought us a can of ground coffee. It took us a while to explain the difference, but when he finally realized what we were asking for, he went and got us the Sanka and we kept the ground coffee. Somehow, we managed to get our hands on a little four- or five-cup coffeepot.

At the time we were living by candlelight because of the power outages and blackouts due to the Iraqi war. We'd steal candles from the bathroom, and we'd scrape the wax when it melted to make our own little candles. We'd put the wax we scraped in little tin dishes. We propped the coffeepot on three books slanting edgewise. Then we'd stick a candle into the little space, and use that to heat up water. When it would get to boiling, we'd pour the coffee grounds in and let it simmer, let the grounds settle, and drink it that way. Cowboy coffee. It came out pretty good, and it helped keep us going.

After we finished with the first can of coffee, we talked the guard into bringing us another one. We used the empty can to make a stove. We cut a little door in the side of it, and had a little platform inside of it that we could raise or lower to adjust the flame. So that empty can became our stove.

COL. CHARLES SCOTT (*chief of the Defense Liaison Office, at Evin Prison*): As far as I was concerned, the war with Iraq was a positive thing. There was still a big internal power struggle going on in Iran, and from the very beginning the Khomeini regime and many of the radicals in power had very skillfully used the hostage crisis to their advantage. We were used to unify the people and rally them behind a cause, which meant directing attention away from some of the serious internal problems that plagued Iran. The war with Iraq performed a similar function. It required a mobilization of the masses for the war effort and gave Khomeini an excuse for the state of the economy. He could say that sacrifices had to be made for the war. It also meant that we weren't as valuable to the Iranian leadership anymore. They didn't need us. So it seemed logical to me that the war might signal the beginning of the end, and help us get out of Iran.

SGT. PAUL LEWIS (*marine security guard, at Komiteh Prison*): The closer the presidential election in the United States got, the more I wanted to know what was going on. We knew who was running, and I was really cheering for Ronald Reagan, not so much because I disliked President Carter, but because there was so little understanding between President Carter and the Iranians. I was afraid that if Carter was re-elected it would extend our stay. By this time, the militants were as exhausted as we were, and I had a feeling that the Iranians were looking for a way out. They wanted it to end, too. The shah was dead, and they were now at war with Iraq. The revolution had come full circle. There wasn't any purpose in continuing to hold us hostage. But I wasn't sure that the Iranians would reach an accommodation with President Carter. They just had too much dislike for the man. Which is sort of ironic, because Jimmy Carter was probably more fair in his dealings with the Iranian people than any of his predecessors. But I had a feeling that their dislike of him was one of the things that complicated any negotiations and prolonged our stay.

The Iranians listened to Voice of America all the time, and when the election returns were announced one of the militants came in and told us what had happened. I think the guards were glad that Carter was beaten, but at the same time they weren't sure that they were glad Ronald Reagan had been elected. They didn't know very much about him. They came into the cell and asked us, "What is Ronald Reagan like? What is Alexander Haig like?" McKeel and I would try to make them sound like warmongers. We'd tell the militants that Reagan and Haig would blow the hell out of Iran. When they heard those kinds of things, the guards would get kind of subdued. That made them look very thoughtful. It was not the answer they wanted to hear.

BILL BELK (*communications officer, at Komiteh Prison*): Once the elections were over, I was hoping maybe that would break up the logjam and help to get us out of there. I was confident that President Carter was doing everything he could to get us out of there, but the Iranians had an intense dislike for Jimmy Carter, and I didn't know if Khomeini would be willing to come to any kind of terms with him. But shortly after he was defeated one of the guards let it slip that negotiations were taking place,* and that there was reason to hope. He didn't tell me what was going on; all he said was, "They are talking. Things are looking good. Maybe you will go home soon."

BRUCE GERMAN (*budget officer, at Komiteh Prison*): At the prison in Tehran I once again encountered Mehdi, a skinny little guard who used to bring us extra food when we were in Meshed. Mehdi was the most humane of all the guards. He smoked incessantly, and his English was extremely limited, but I discovered that he was easy to talk to. He used to come on duty late at night. Whenever he did, I'd ask for permission to go to the toilet. He'd take me down the corridor away from the others and I'd take off my blindfold, and we'd talk for a few minutes before I used the bathroom. I'd say, "Mehdi, how are things? What's the status of negotiations?" And he'd give me dribs and drabs of information. Even though he was the most humane of the guards, he was still following Khomeini's line, and he was still a goon. He still hated the United States. He wasn't as fanatical about it as some of the others, but his contempt was still there. Because he was following Khomeini's line, he was very careful about what he'd say. But he would answer my questions and give me small bits of information, so at least I felt I was building some rapport with the guy. When I'd ask about the status of the negotiations, he'd say, "Oh, the Majlis is going to meet. They're going to talk about your situation." And he'd leave it at that. Of course that was more information than I could get anyplace else. I hadn't seen a newspaper or heard a radio in over ten months. Whatever little information I could get from this guy I'd share with my cellmates.

A week or two would pass, and I'd throw another question at him. I'd say, "Has the Majlis met yet?"

"Oh, they're still talking."

"What are they going to decide?"

Mehdi would say, "The situation is improving." Then sometimes, before leading me back, he would give me some extra bread or cheese, which I'd take back to the cell and share with my cellmates.

BILL BELK (*communications officer, at Komiteh Prison*): There were a couple of guards who had our well-being at heart. There was one guy

---

* In a radio broadcast Ayatollah Khomeini announced that the Iranian Majlis was responsible for determining the fate of the hostages, and the Majlis first considered the hostage issue in September 1980. However, the onset of the Iran–Iraq War resulted in a postponement of the hostage debate for approximately six weeks. In early November the Majlis established conditions for the release of the hostages that set the framework for the first serious negotiations between the United States and Iran since the aborted rescue mission.

named Ali who used to come into my cell late at night. I'd be sitting there with my little candle trying to play cards, and he would bring me a package of cookies or a Hershey's candy bar. He was a bedraggled sort of fellow, and I think he was from rural Iran. He was probably as tired of being a prison guard as we were of being his prisoners. He was very naive and idealistic. In the beginning, he had wanted very much for us to know Islam. He wanted me to know all about the Moslem prophets, and he had said that within five years Khomeini would lead America in revolution just as he had done Iran. First all the slave blacks would rise in revolt, then the rest of the people would follow. He had said, "We will teach you about Khomeini! We will teach you about Mohammed!" Then he would say, "We like the American people. It is your government we do not like. We will teach you about your CIA. We will teach you about what the shah and SAVAK did to Iran." Then he would come around with pictures of people who had been tortured and executed. But in the prison he stopped doing that. I think he became very disillusioned.

Once I asked him, "Why do you do this? Why do you bring me cookies?"

He said, "Sometimes the guys exercise too much." He spoke colloquial English just like that. It sounded funny in combination with his poor grammar. He said, "The guys—they exercise very hard. They get hungry. I bring cookies so maybe you guys not get hungry."

I hated some of the guards, but I could never hate a guy like Ali. He still believed in Khomeini, and he still believed that what America had done in Iran was very, very wrong, but at the same time he had a conscience. When he had joined in the overthrow of the American embassy, he hadn't thought that we would be held hostage for over a year. Khomeini and the takeover of the embassy had inspired him, because he thought he was fighting evil. But now he had become a part of the kind of evil that he had originally been trying to combat—and deep down in his heart he knew this, even if he wouldn't admit it to himself. In spite of all the revolutionary slogans that were rattling around in his head, his heart told him that holding us hostage was wrong. In some small way, he thought he had to do something a little extra for us to make up for the incarceration. The food was like an unspoken apology. He would come around late at night with cookies or dates or goat cheese. I'd hear the latch rattle on the door, then see his face in the glow of the candle. He'd say, "Hello, friend, I bring you present of goat cheese."

COL. LELAND HOLLAND (*army attaché, at Evin Prison*): Holding us hostage was drudgery for the students, too. One guy came into my cell, talking about the war and how things were not good. Then all of a sudden he said, "You're going home in a week or two."

Mike Metrinko was allowed to come over and visit me in my cell, and Mike was in there too. We both said, "Naw, it won't happen."

He said, "It must happen. I am leaving. In one week I'm going to be married."

A couple of weeks passed, and the fellow was still there. I chatted with him again. "Did you get married?"

"Yes."

"Where is your wife?"

"She has gone to the war."

I guess that's the way it was for them. All of the glory was gone. The luster and fun, the headlines and celebrity status of the whole thing had faded. This guy had just got married, and his wife immediately went off to the war.

COL. CHARLES SCOTT (*chief of the Defense Liaison Office, at Evin Prison*): While I was in Evin Prison, Akbar came in and told me that Hossein and Fazollah had been killed in the war with Iraq. They were two guards who had been with me in Tabriz after the rescue mission failed, and of course I had very vivid memories of them. Hossein was a kid who had wanted to be a soldier. He had a great romance with everything military, and even though he hated America, there were times when he and I would sit and talk for hours, because he wanted to learn as much about the military profession as he could. I also talked with Fazollah quite a bit, and had a good rapport with him. He was a simple peasant boy. Nineteen years old, and not much between his ears. But he had a good disposition, and tried to be helpful and make things a little easier on us. Both of those guys were killed very early in the war, and when Akbar came in and told me about them, I knew that a great many more would follow in their footsteps.

SGT. PAUL LEWIS (*marine security guard, at Komiteh Prison*): After the war with Iraq started several of the militants guarding us ran off to the front. One day Ahmed came into our cell and told us that Hamid the Liar had been killed.* We were very curious and asked what had happened. He said that some of the students who had been guarding us had formed a revolutionary guard unit, and went to the front to fight the Iraqis. Hamid had been one of them. Later on, I learned that Hamid

---

* Hamid the Liar was one of the student leaders responsible for taking care of the hostages at both the Mushroom Inn and the chancery.

wasn't alone. Several of those guys who were involved in the takeover were killed at the front in the first few months of the war.

RICHARD QUEEN (*consular officer, on assignment to the Pentagon after his release from Tehran*): After my release, I was working with the Defense Intelligence Agency for a while, and at the time of the first Iranian counteroffensive—the one that Bani-Sadr organized—we got some information concerning some of the students who had been guarding the hostages. Apparently, a bunch of these students volunteered for the war and were put in a revolutionary guard unit. They were fighting on the front lines, when all of a sudden the Iranian army withdrew from this area and left these guys sitting out there all by themselves. The Iraqis swept down, surrounded the student unit and killed them all.

This was the cause of some controversy in Tehran, because the army still had a lingering dislike of the revolutionary guards, and the revolutionary guards didn't trust the army. They were on opposite sides during the revolution, and some of the prerevolutionary antagonisms continued to exist from when the Iranian army was the shah's army. So there was some suspicion that the army had done this on purpose. Accusations were made in the Iranian media that the leading lights of the revolution had purposely been eliminated. The army claimed that they had tried to notify this student revolutionary guard unit that they were withdrawing, but the unit didn't get the word. At any rate, several of the students were killed during the first counteroffensive.

MALCOLM KALP (*economics officer, at Evin Prison*): I heard that Hamid was one of the first people killed in the Iran–Iraq War. When I heard that I was so happy that I literally did handstands. The terrorists would come into my cell and I'd ask them, "How is the war going?"

They'd say, "It is not good. I have lost many friends."

I'd clap and say, "Hey, all right! All right! I am very happy! I'll be happy when you go off to the war and get killed, too. That will make me very happy."

CORT BARNES (*communications officer, at Komiteh Prison*): Some of the guards would admit that Iran under Khomeini wasn't as good as they had expected. I remember one time after the election, Abbas was talking about President-elect Reagan. He had heard some rumor that Reagan was going to send a bunch of B-52s over to Iran as soon as he became president.

I said, "Good. Let them come. All I want is to see the flash."

Abbas was very despondent, and he said, "Well, who wants to live, anyway?"

He meant it, too. That kind of statement was indicative of the despair some of those guys had fallen into. They were caught up in something that they no longer had any control over. What they had wanted to have happen within the revolution wasn't happening, and there was absolutely nothing they could do about it. Nothing at all. They were stuck in the mess they had created.

BILL BELK (*communications officer*): It was amazing what the war did to the guards. They were absolutely worn out. Beat. Exhausted. I'd see the same faces day after day, and they knew that the only thing keeping them from marching off to the Iraqi front was that they were taking care of us. The war was very close to them, not just physically close, but in a personal sense as well. Not only were bombs falling on Tehran, but they had brothers and friends fighting on the front. Their friends and relatives were dying every day. They were careful to never talk about these things anywhere near us, but we could see it was taking its toll on them. All of their arrogance was gone, and they were very subdued in their treatment of us. We weren't getting any more of the revolutionary sermons. Then when Ronald Reagan was elected they became even more concerned. Ali would come in with our food and ask us about this "Cowboy Ree-gun." He wanted to know what we thought Reagan was going to do. I'm sure they felt that having the Iraqis drop bombs on their heads was enough. They didn't want more of that, so they were very fearful. Very grim. They had a lot to think about.

There were times when I actually felt sorry for them. And I always felt sorry for the Iranian people. They've been poorly led for so many years, and Khomeini is a total disaster. He offered them absolutely no hope for the future. Under Khomeini the Iranian people were like sheep being led to slaughter. Some of their battles with Iraq were nothing but mass suicide waves. Those kids were being cut to ribbons— yet they were so fanatical in their religion, they believed that if they were martyred on the battlefield they'd immediately go to paradise. That was a sad thing to see.

WILLIAM ROYER (*director of academic courses, at Komiteh Prison*): I have to admit that by the end of our incarceration I felt sorry for a number of the guards. In particular, I remember a fellow by the name of Ahmed. He had spent a great deal of time in the United States, was familiar with classical music, and had received a good education. Like many of the militants, he was a very complex character—someone who wanted to enjoy the benefits of the Western world, such as education and music, yet someone whose opposition to the shah's regime had been total. At the time of the revolution, I think he really felt that Khomeini's regime and the creation of the Islamic Republic was a just cause. It was something he sincerely believed in, and I felt sorry for him because I thought he had been duped. With the revolution evolving as it was in Iran, I think he was coming to see that the world wasn't as simple as he'd once believed. Of course, he wasn't going to admit that to any of us, and he was bitter and angry to the very end. But I think he was frustrated by the way things were turning out. The revolution wasn't necessarily the just cause he had believed in. So I felt a certain pity for him, and for many of the others as well.

CORT BARNES (*communications officer, at Komiteh Prison*): I never felt sorry for the Iranians. They could go outside when they wanted to, and they could always find a way to keep warm. I had an intense dislike for all of them—and I still feel the resentment. Before I went to Tehran, I always felt a little bit of Christian guilt if I actively disliked another person. It just wasn't the right thing to do. But I didn't feel that way in the prison. I hated the Iranians without feeling any remorse at all. As far as I was concerned, those guys could all go out and get ground up by the war. If they wanted to be martyrs, let them be martyrs. That was just fine with me.

CDR. ROBERT ENGELMANN (*naval supply corps officer, at Komiteh Prison*): One time we were sitting around in our cell talking about our guards. We were asking each other, "Do you really hate these guys? How do you feel about them? Is there anything you would want to do to them if you could?" In the cell there was pretty much a consensus that if they ever let us go, the worst thing that could happen to these people was that they would have to stay behind in Iran. We'd ask, "If somebody gave you a rubber hose, would you want to beat up on them?" The answer was, "No, let's just leave them in Iran. Because if we do they're going to kill each other, or get killed on the Iraqi front." That's how bad the situation was there. The worst punishment we could conceive of was the fact that they had to stay behind.

Part Nine

Liberation

1 The Guesthouse

BY NOVEMBER 1980 the stiff economic sanctions imposed on Iran by President Carter and the war with Iraq were placing a severe strain on the country. Ayatollah Khomeini and many of the hardline revolutionaries who had opposed the release of the hostages were finally ready to resolve the crisis. Following Khomeini's lead, the Iranian Majlis passed a bill on November 2 that listed four conditions necessary for the release of the hostages: the return of the shah's wealth to Iran, the cancellation of American claims against Iran, the unfreezing of all Iranian assets, and a promise by the United States to refrain from interference in Iran's internal affairs. The United States responded to the bill by accepting the Iranian conditions "in principle," and entered into a period of intensive negotiation. For the next ten weeks three Algerian intermediaries shuttled back and forth between representatives of the two countries in an attempt to hammer out an agreement that would address the four Iranian conditions in a manner that was consistent with American law. The negotiations were extremely complex, and were further complicated by differences in language and legal systems and the lack of face-to-face encounters between representatives from Iran and the United States. Yet steady progress was made. Sensing that a resolution to the crisis was near, the student militants moved the hostages out of the two prisons and relocated them one final time.

CAPT. PAUL NEEDHAM (*air force logistics officer, at Evin Prison*): The conditions in Evin Prison were bad. Very bad.

As time passed, I grew more and more disgusted. We were already into December. Christmas was coming, our second Christmas. I'd already turned thirty (I was twenty-eight when I'd arrived). So I'd sing my favorite, a Merle Haggard tune called, "Mama Tried." Only I'd switch the lyrics around a little bit, and sang, "I turned twenty-nine in prison doing life without parole." Then, after my birthday, I was singing, "I turned thirty in prison doing life without parole."

BRUCE GERMAN (*budget officer, at Komiteh Prison*): For some time Mehdi had been telling me that the situation was improving. When I'd ask about the negotiations, he'd say, "Things are looking good." Then one day in December he said, "You will go home soon."

Well, "soon" was a word we used to joke about. To the Iranians it was the equivalent of the Spanish *mañana*—you know, something that never happens. But this time when Mehdi said, "You will be going home soon," there seemed to be a new inflection in his voice, as if he really meant it.

Then a week or two later, Mehdi said, "You will be moving soon."

I said, "Soon? What does that mean? Tomorrow? Six months from now?"

"No, in a few days."

Then, sure enough, it happened.

GARY LEE (*general services officer, at Komiteh Prison*): On December 17, we heard a big commotion out in the halls, and it was obvious that another big move was under way. They moved all of us out of Komiteh Prison that evening. Morehead Kennedy, Jim Lopez, Rick Kupke, and myself were put in one of the embassy vans, and off we went. As we drove along, I was able to adjust my blindfold so I could look out and try to get some idea of where we were. But the entire city was pitch black. No street lights, no business lights, nothing. Just total blackness. I didn't have any idea where we were. All I knew was that we were climbing in elevation, so I figured that meant northern Tehran.

DON HOHMAN (*army medic*): We rode for a long time in one of the vans. It must've been about an hour's drive, and I didn't know where I was heading. I'd never been in northern Tehran before, but I could tell that we were heading up the mountain.

When we finally stopped, they led us into this great big mansion, and put me into an empty room with Bob Ode. There was a nice thick carpet on the floor, and we had our own private bathroom. This had obviously been a very fancy place before the revolution. Bob and I were busy settling in and getting our beds set up, when the door opened and in walked Bill Belk. God, it was nice to see him. It was the first time I'd seen him since the two of us had been together down in the basement of the chancery. It was great.

BILL BELK (*communications officer*): Don Hohman is a man for whom I have the deepest respect, and when they pushed me into that room and pulled the blanket off my head it was a beautiful sight to see Don standing there. I remember he looked a little worse for wear. His weight was way down, and his beard was practically as long as Khomeini's. But he hadn't changed a bit. He is the meanest, orneriest thing ever to walk on two legs, and he was still giving the Iranians a hard time. He was cussing at them about something when they brought me in. I heard that and just laughed and laughed. It was beautiful.

JOE HALL (*warrant officer*): That move was a major improvement, but it didn't really surprise me. Christmas was only a week away, and I thought it would be just like those sons of bitches to put us in much better circumstances and have some kind of big dog and pony show. They never missed a chance for a photo opportunity, so I figured that was what they were gearing up for.

We were all put into this big mansion that had previously been one of the shah's guesthouses.* It was near his palace, and it was kind of like being put into a fancy hotel room. We had a nice carpet on the floor and some chairs we could sit in, which was something new after the prison. We also had a great big wall-to-wall window. The students had mounted sturdy iron bars in front of the window, and there was a thin curtain between the bars and the glass, but we were able to pull the curtain back so that we could look outside.

We'd been moved in the middle of the night, and the next morning, I remember, sunlight came streaming through our window. I got up and looked out onto a big garden, and saw the most beautiful snowfall I have ever seen in my life. Of course, that was the first time I'd seen any sort of nature in a long, long time. The ground was completely covered with this pristine blanket of snow, and it was almost like a small forest outside the window. There were birds in the trees, and we could see the sky and the foliage.

CHARLES JONES (*communications officer*): The best thing about that move was that we had our own private bathroom right there in the room. That was great. It meant we didn't have to knock on the door, ask permission, be blindfolded, and all that other garbage just to go to the toilet. For the first time in over a year, I could get up and go when I needed to. You can't imagine what a luxury that was. On top of that, we actually had hot water in there. Oh my God, did that ever feel good! Hot water! After we all got settled in, the first thing I did was take a nice, long, leisurely bath.

---

* On December 17, 1980, thirty-three hostages were moved out of Komiteh Prison. One week later, on Christmas Eve, the fourteen hostages being held at Evin Prison were also transferred to the guesthouse, which was located on the grounds of the shah's Niyavaran Palace. The two women hostages, Katherine Koob and Ann Swift, were removed from the embassy compound and taken to the same location. At the guesthouse the hostages were kept in groups of two to six hostages per room.

Throughout this time Bruce Laingen, Victor Tomseth, and Michael Howland had remained at the Foreign Ministry. Shortly after Christmas they were turned over to the student militants and placed in Komiteh Prison for approximately three weeks before they joined their colleagues at the guesthouse on January 18, 1981.

GARY LEE (*general services officer*): Shortly after we arrived at this place, one of the Iranians came in and told us that we were going to have a visitor. This was no big surprise, seeing as how our living conditions had just undergone a dramatic improvement. So we told the Iranians that we didn't want any pictures taken. No cameras in the room when the visitor came.

Well, pretty soon the Algerian ambassador to Iran was brought around to our room. I guess he wanted to see all of the hostages and confirm that we were all still alive. When he came in, one of the Iranians had a camera, even though we had told them that we weren't going to stand for any pictures. Jim Lopez stepped up and practically shoved the camera down that guy's throat. He hit the guy and told him to get the hell out. The Iranians didn't do a thing to Jim because the Algerian ambassador was standing right there.

I remember the Algerians were very polite chaps. We shook hands with them and totally ignored the Iranian diplomats who were there as part of the entourage. We refused to shake hands with them or even acknowledge that they were there. Morehead Kennedy took the Iranians totally by surprise and spoke to the Algerian ambassador in very rapid-fire French. He was able to pass along the message to the ambassador that the living conditions he was seeing were brand-new and definitely not normal, that our treatment had not been good. I thought that was beautiful. I don't speak French, but I could tell that there was a little repartee going on between the two of them in which Kennedy was able to get this message across. None of the Iranians spoke French either, so they didn't know what was being said.

BILL BELK (*communications officer*): The Algerian ambassador spoke to us in very guarded terms. He was obviously under instructions from the Iranians not to say too much. But he did assure us that the Algerians were working as intermediaries, and that negotiations were in fact taking place. He refused to give us any details. All he would say was there was reason for hope, and he thought we would probably be released in the near future. So there was no firm commitment. Nevertheless, we were all delighted by his visit. At least we knew that serious negotiations were taking place. In the back of my mind I was thinking, "Hey, this just might be a Christmas release. It would be just like the Iranians to let us go on a big religious holiday."

GARY LEE (*general services officer*): In our room, we expected another Christmas propaganda show. Then, sure enough, one of the guards came into the room and said to the group, "Would you like to see a

Christian minister? You can make a Christmas film for your families. We will let you send a message back to America."

There were five of us in the room, and every single one of us said, "No. No way." After Easter and the shit Rupiper pulled, our attitude was: "Screw the Iranian TV cameras. We're not going to participate in another one of their dog and pony shows unless they have guns at our backs." After our previous experiences, we assumed that all of the other hostages felt the same way and would refuse to go, too. We said, "Look, no one else is going to go to this thing, so we're not going to go either."

BILL BELK (*communications officer*): I was in no mood to sing any goddamn songs, and I didn't want to pretend that I was buddy-buddy with any of the clergymen the Iranians brought into Iran. So I didn't really want to go to the Christmas service. But I hadn't gone a year earlier because of my escape attempt, and I wasn't part of the Easter thing. I'd never been in front of their TV cameras, and I knew that my mail wasn't getting out because I wasn't receiving any. So I knew that I had never been heard from or seen by anyone in the United States. I assumed that my wife and my two boys were probably thinking that I might be dead. Even though I didn't want to go to the Christmas service, it was something that I felt I had to do for my family. If there was any chance that they would see the film clips, then I had to be there.

ROBERT ODE (*consular officer*): I had made up my mind that I wasn't going to attend any more Christmas or religious services, because I considered them to be nothing but propaganda on the part of the Iranians. All of the American clergymen who had been brought over to Iran were selected by the Iranians because they were more sympathetic to the Iranians than they were to the American hostages. I thought their views were disgusting, and that the clergymen who came to Iran at the behest of the Khomeini regime did us a great disservice. So I made up my mind that I was not going to go, and I told the Iranians so. After they left the room, Bill Belk came over to me and said, "What's the matter, Bob? Are you trying to be unkind to your wife?"

I said, "No, of course not. Why would I want to do that?"

Bill said, "We all know that this is propaganda, but it's also the only way that anyone back in the United States is going to be able to see that you are still alive and well. If you don't appear on the TV screen it will probably cause your wife to worry, and wonder why you weren't seen."

So I thought about Rita and the effect it might have on her, and at the last hour I agreed to go.

JOE HALL (*warrant officer*): We were being kept up on a hill, and we had a big picture window. The city was in the valley below us, and we could see any lights that were twinkling in Tehran. It was a spectacular view. Shortly after dark on Christmas Eve, we were sitting around waiting for the Christmas ceremony, when all of a sudden we heard air raid sirens and the droning of jet engines. Then we saw some explosions down in the valley. Immediately, the sky lit up with antiaircraft fire. There were lots and lots of rockets and tracers going up into the air, and more explosions from falling bombs. We could see great big flare-ups on the ground when things were blown up, and we could hear the distant noises of the explosions. This went on for quite some time. The Iraqis didn't just drop a couple of bombs and fly off. They kept at it. They'd circle back and drop a few more bombs, and the antiaircraft fire and the tracers would keep going up. I think that attack was the longest and most sustained bombing that took place while we were in Iran. It was an incredible thing to witness. All of us just sat in front of the window and watched. The Iraqis really nailed Tehran that Christmas Eve.

About twenty minutes after the attack was over, the guards came into the room and took us to our Christmas festival.

BILL BELK (*communications officer*): There were six of us in the room, and five of us decided to attend the Christmas service; everyone except Don Hohman. The Iranians came around to get us, and Don refused to leave the room. He has the strongest convictions of anyone I've ever met in my life. Don does exactly what he wants to do, and that's the end of it. The Iranians got very upset when he refused to come with the rest of us. They said, "You must come! You must!"

Don said, "Fuck you. I'm not going."

"We'll put you in solitary," they said.

Don said, "I don't give a shit what you do to me. You can put me in solitary, or you can take me out and shoot me. I'm still not going."

And that was the end of that.

After we were blindfolded, they led the five of us down the hall to another room, which was all decked out for the Christmas celebration. Just before we went in the door, they took our blindfolds off. I remember the papal nuncio was there with two Iranian ministers. As soon as we walked into the room the clergymen wanted to embrace us and kiss us on the cheek, and carry on like we were long-lost friends. You know, they were very exuberant. But that kind of greeting wasn't for me. Those guys were total strangers. We didn't even speak the same language, and their reason for being there was very different from mine. So I stood back during all of the hugging and kissing.

We were seated at a table which had cakes and fruit on it, and the papal nuncio said a few words that I couldn't understand. Then he wanted us to sing some Christmas carols, which I thought was totally ridiculous. Here we were at this table looking across the room into a television camera, and behind the camera along the back wall were about forty or fifty militants standing there with their weapons. They were all staring at us like we were monkeys in a cage. Now how can five Americans feel at ease singing Christmas carols when they're face to face with all those automatic weapons? That really blew my mind. I refused to sing. I just glowered at the militants. I wanted anyone who saw me on TV to know that I was angry. I wasn't about to pretend that I was having a good time, and that I thought this was a nice little ceremony.

JOE HALL (*warrant officer*): The service was conducted by Iranian Christians. There weren't any Americans coming in from the outside, and I can't even remember if the Iranian ministers spoke English. I don't think they did. After they said a couple of prayers or whatever, I was allowed to say something in front of the television cameras. So I said to my wife, "Cheri, I'm still alive, honey. I can make it if you can. So hang in there." As it turned out, Cheri did see that film back in the United States. After saying my few words, I walked over to the table and took as much food as I could carry. There was some cake and pastry and stuff there that they had put out in front of the cameras, and I knew the guards wouldn't stop me from taking food in front of the ministers. So I was shoving stuff in my pockets and piling up all I could carry.

BILL BELK (*communications officer*): They let each of us deliver a short message to our families in front of the TV cameras. I said hello to my wife and told her that I was still alive. I also let her know that I had not received any mail. The whole time I was speaking, I kept glowering at the militants lined up along the back wall.

When the service was over, we were each given a present that was gift-wrapped and had our name on it. The Iranians filmed us receiving and opening these gifts. I remember there was a sweat suit and a couple of oranges in my box. Then when the television cameras were turned off, we were taken back out to the hall, blindfolded, and our gifts were taken away from us. We weren't allowed to keep them. They took that stuff and put it back on the pile with someone else's name so that there would be gifts for the next group when they came in.

GARY LEE (*general services officer*): After Christmas, we spent the next couple of weeks wondering when we were going to be moved back to the prison. I figured we had been brought up to this place so the Iranians could put on their propaganda show and bring the Algerian inspection team around so they could see that we were all alive. Now that all the activity was over, I figured it was time for us to go back to the local slammer. There was a lot of black humor in our cell. We had no idea what was going on in the negotiations. As far as we could tell, there didn't seem to be any progress. All we knew was that we had in excess of 400 days under our belts, and we were still sitting. We'd joke and say, "Hey guys, it looks like we're going to outlast the Siege of Leningrad." Which was 999 days.

BILL BELK (*communications officer*): After the visit of the Algerian ambassador, we were all hoping that a release was imminent. I was sure that something was in the works, and even thought that a Christmas release was possible. But I definitely expected to be out of there by the end of the year. I was dead certain of that. But the days came and went with all of us sitting in Tehran. We were in 1981 and still in Iran. That just boggled my mind. We kept asking the guards, "Hey, what's going on in the negotiations? What's happening?"

We'd always get the same stock answer. "They're working on it." That's all the guards would ever say. "They're working on it."

We'd ask, "Well, when is something going to happen? When are we going home?"

They'd say, "Maybe tomorrow. Do not worry. Maybe tomorrow." Or, "Soon, soon." Those were their favorite expressions. Of course, they'd been saying the exact same things back when we were being kept at the embassy. So I started getting very depressed. I was afraid that maybe the negotiations had fallen through, because the days just kept rolling by.

SGT. PAUL LEWIS (*marine security guard*): At the place up in northern Tehran the guards kept us better supplied with things like toothpaste and soap. I thought that was a positive sign. They were going out of their way to be nice to us. One time they even brought in some care packages from the Swiss embassy. I remember I was given a box of candy, which the four of us divided among ourselves. They were really playing the nice guy routine. If we asked for something like a deck of cards we'd always get it. Then they had some Super Bowl highlight films that they'd found at the embassy, and they would play those for us on the VCR in the evening.

The food was better, and there was more of it. They were definitely trying to fatten us up. They'd come in with a big pot and say, "You want more? You want more?" I thought maybe we were getting close to a major breakthrough, but I also knew that it was possible they might just be trying to fatten us up for somebody like the Red Cross to come in and look at us. You just couldn't be sure what was happening. It was one of those things where you didn't want to let yourself get your hopes too high.

BILL BELK (*communications officer*): Those first few weeks in January were particularly difficult, because we were living in such close quarters. There were six people in this one room, and a little friction among us was inevitable. We had all been in Iran for over a year now, and our nerves were frayed. We were sick and tired of being hostages. We kept hoping and hoping that we'd be released, but we were still sitting there. Because of that the degree of frustration was intense. Previously, I'd been locked up with one other person, and I'd been kept in solitary, and those kinds of arrangements were usually pretty easy to adjust to. But now we had six different personalities in the same room. Every morning we'd get up and there would be those fifteen or sixteen hours staring us in the face that had to be filled, and having that many people in such a small space made it difficult to establish and maintain a consistent routine. With those big steel bars in front of our picture window I felt just like I was in an animal cage at the zoo. We were all going nuts for being locked up like that.

I remember there was a girls' preschool right next door to us, and each day would begin with these five- and six-year-old girls gathering on the playground to sing, *"Marg bar Amrika! Marg bar Amrika! Marg bar Carter! Marg bar Carter!"* Every morning we'd hear the teacher leading these little girls in song. It was sad to know that an adult was standing out there on the playground and teaching those children to hate. I thought that was pathetic. But that was the way it was. Instead of saying the pledge of allegiance or singing the national anthem, those kids would sing "Death to America."

During this time, we had one hostage in our room who was in very bad shape. When they brought him in to the room, it was the first time I'd seen him throughout our entire ordeal. He had a great big scar on the top of his head. I thought maybe the Iranians had done something to him, or that he'd been in an accident. I asked him what had happened, and he just brushed me off. Then one of the other hostages told me that he had tried to commit suicide. Apparently, he went berserk and split his head open against the corner of a concrete wall.

He was extremely paranoid and had become delusional. He thought we were ganging up on him. I was very concerned, because I liked this fellow. I'd worked with him previously and thought he was a very competent and capable person, a very friendly man. But in the situation we were in, there wasn't anything that any of us could do for him. He'd go off into his own little world and no one could reach him. He'd lay down on his pallet and just turn his back to everyone else. He'd be off in a world of his own. Then all of a sudden he'd jump up and confront us with his very strange thinking. If anyone was talking, this guy would think that we were talking about him. He'd say, "Hey, you guys are talking about me!"

"No, we're not."

"Yes, you are! You guys are talking about me! I just read it in a book! I know what you're saying, because I just read it in a book!" He was totally divorced from reality, and all we could do was try to calm him down and let the outburst run its course. After a while, he'd go back to his mattress and lie down and start to cry. He'd totally withdraw from us again, and lie there on his mattress and weep for hours. It was a very sad thing.

Then there were other times when he would get an incredible burst of energy. There was an area in the middle of the room that we kept clear for exercising, and out of the blue this guy would jump up and start pacing. He would pace back and forth across the room in very short rapid steps—back and forth, back and forth, touch the window, touch the wall. He'd pace like that for one or two hours at a time, just burning energy. He didn't know where he was or what he was doing. It always frightened me when he got into one of his pacing moods because he was so paranoid. He was absolutely convinced that everybody in the room was out to get him, and I was afraid that he might try to commit suicide again. We had a short divider wall leading around to the bathroom, and it had a sharp protruding edge. When he started pacing, I'd sit there on my mattress and think, "Oh Christ, I hope this guy doesn't take off and try to flatten his head again."

COL. CHARLES SCOTT (*chief of the Defense Liaison Office*): Those days in January passed very, very slowly. There were four of us in the room, and we all knew that the twentieth of January was a key date. If the twentieth passed and we were still in Iran, then I could see Komiteh Prison and Evin Prison coming up in spades. By this time we'd been held hostage for over fourteen months. I remember it was difficult for me to read during that time. It was hard to concentrate. So Dick Morefield, Regis Ragan, Don Sharer and myself spent a lot of time playing bridge and poker. We did things as a group to keep ourselves occupied, and that helped, because we all knew how precarious our situation was.

CPL. STEVEN KIRTLEY (*marine security guard*): Our routine didn't change a whole lot from what it had been in the prison. We were just trying to get through the days one at a time. There were five of us in the room now, and we all got along pretty well. We'd talk, exercise, play cards, and read. Then every now and then the Iraqis would bomb Tehran.

We knew that Reagan's inauguration was coming up, and we figured that if Reagan didn't do something as soon as he became president we were lost. There were times when I thought it could run into years and years as opposed to months and months. So we started talking about escape. I knew we might get killed trying, but I figured getting killed was better than being locked up in Iran for the rest of our lives.

JOE HALL (*warrant officer*): In our room we hoped that a change in administrations would mark a turning point, but we were also getting ready to make a break for it in case nothing happened. Personally, I didn't anticipate being released before the inauguration. My big hope was that after Reagan became president, he would deliver an ultimatum to the Iranians. I knew they were afraid of him, so that worked in our favor. I was hoping that as soon as he became president he would say, "Release the hostages or suffer the consequences." But if he tried to negotiate or renegotiate then he was just putting the ball back in the Iranians' court and leaving it up to them. That could mean years. There were five of us in the room, and we were getting very desperate. We figured, "We'll wait through the change in administrations, but if Reagan doesn't do something to get us out of here soon, then this could drag on for two, three, or four more years." So we'd pretty much made up our minds that we were going to give Reagan one month. If something didn't happen by February 20, the four of us were going to try to escape.

Steve Kirtley, Greg Persinger, Don Cooke, and myself were formulating escape plans, but Bill Royer, who was also in the room, let us know he didn't want any part of it. Bill thought the best thing was for all of us to just wait the thing out. We discussed this with Bill and said, "Well, if we're still here on February 20 what we'll do is tie you up, and make it appear that there was nothing you could do. We tied you up to keep you from telling on us." Bill wasn't too happy with that idea, but it was about the only solution that any of us could come up with.

The four of us were very sincere in talking about making a break. Kirtley and Persinger were working on the bars in front of the window, and they had snapped a weld at the base of one of the bars. We knew we could pry the bar up so that we could slide under it and then walk out onto the balcony. From there we could drop to the ground and make a run for it. So getting out of the room wasn't a major problem. Our plan was to break up into two groups. Kirtley and Persinger were going to go together, and Don Cooke and I were going to head off in another direction. If we got out undetected in the middle of the night, who knows? We thought we might have six or eight hours before anyone realized we were gone. We figured we'd have to hold some guy up, steal his car and whatever money he had, and then head for the Turkish border. That was what we envisioned. I thought our chances for success were very slim. Close to nonexistent. But after fourteen months we were getting down to our last hope, and it would have been an act of desperation. The closer we got to the inauguration, the more difficult it became for me to even think about the escape. Just talking about it and proceeding with the planning made me very nervous, because I was afraid that we were actually going to have to carry it out. I knew that we might get killed trying, but by that time I was ready to go.

CAPT. PAUL NEEDHAM (*air force logistics officer*): It's hard to pick a worst time, because it was all bad. It was all just awful. But if there was a worst time, it was there at the very end, after Reagan had been elected and Carter was on his way out. Here it is the sixteenth of January and we're not out yet. The seventeenth, and we're still stuck in Tehran. I was thinking, "You stupid Iranians don't understand. Come the twentieth of January negotiations start all over again. You've got a new game in town." I figured either we were getting out right then, or we weren't—in which case we'd be stuck for quite a while. So as we got closer and closer to the twentieth, I was getting more and more anxious. Those last few days were just awful.

3 Release

By JANUARY 17, 1981, the United States and Iran had reached agreement on the basic terms necessary for a resolution of the crisis. The only outstanding issues were procedural. Over the weekend a step-by-step scenario was devised for the transfer of Iranian assets frozen in American banks and the simultaneous release of the hostages. On Monday morning the final details were in place, and at 7:00 A.M. on January 19, 1981, Deputy Secretary of State Warren Christopher signed the Declaration of Algiers on behalf of the United States. The question was no longer whether an agreement to free the hostages would be reached, but whether the complex terms of the agreement would be successfully implemented during the course of the next thirty-six hours.

JOE HALL (*warrant officer*): None of us knew a release was pending. On January 19, a couple of the militants came into our room and said, "One of you come with me." There were five of us in the room, and we all kind of looked at each other. Greg Persinger popped up and walked off with those guys. I was wondering, "Now what is this all about?" That left four of us just sitting there without a word of explanation. We were asking each other, "What was that all about?"

Then twenty or thirty minutes later they came back and said, "Next." Greg hadn't returned, and the militants didn't beckon a specific individual. They just said, "Next." I think Bill Royer went out with them this time. Then in a little while they came back for Steve Kirtley. I was the fourth one to go. It was Ali Akbar who led me away. I was blindfolded, and he was being very gentle with me. He took me in a room and closed the door. When I took my blindfold off, it was just the two of us sitting there. He was being as nice as he could be, and he said, "Well, Mr. Hall, how are you today?"

I thought, "Goddamn, this is strange. Something is going on." I said, "I'm fine. How are you?"

"I'm good. I'm good." Then he explained, "There have been some changes. I think we are going to release some people."

I was a little bit hesitant to believe him. I'd been through too many disappointments, and I didn't want to let myself get excited or hopeful. I asked, "How soon?"

"Very soon. Very soon. Maybe within eight hours. And I want you to know that right now you are a candidate for release." That's exactly the way he put it, "a candidate for release." Then he said something to indicate that they were not going to release all of us. I can't remember his exact words, but he gave me the impression that they were going to keep fifteen people in Iran, and that the rest of us would go. He showed me two issues of Tehran's English-language newspaper, the *Tehran Times,* and there was something about a hostage release right there in the headlines. You can't imagine how seeing that made me feel. *Boom! Boom! Boom!* My heart started pounding at about 180 beats a minute. I was thinking, "Holy shit, this is true! Maybe I'm getting out of here!" But I still didn't know what this bit about being a "candidate for release" meant. Ali Akbar said that he wanted me to do an interview, and then he took me down into another room.

MALCOLM KALP (*economics officer*): Late, late at night, one of the terrorist leaders came into our room. Blucker was sleeping, and this guard says, "Mr. Blucker, get up!"

Blucker doesn't move.

"Mr. Blucker, get up!"

"No."

"Get up!"

"No."

"You must get up!"

"No."

"You must!"

"Go away. I don't want to."

"Mr. Blucker, you must get up! You must take a test."

"I don't want to take a test."

This sort of conversation went back and forth for several minutes. The terrorist kept telling Blucker to get up, and Blucker kept telling him to get lost. Finally, Blucker says, "I can't go anywhere. You stole my shoes. I don't have any shoes."

Well, this terrorist kicks off his sandals and gives them to Blucker. Blucker refused to wear that guy's sandals, but he did get up. The two of us were blindfolded and led over to a building that was maybe 200 meters away. We had to walk through the snow and ice, and Blucker was walking along barefoot. He's a tough guy. I really liked Blucker. Once they got us over to this building, they put us into separate rooms.

I was sitting there, and this terrorist hands me an English-language newspaper that is published in Tehran. The headline is: "Hostages To Be Released."

He asked, "What do you think of that?"

"That's beautiful."

"Mr. Kalp, before you are released we want you to make a statement."

"No. No way. I have not made a statement yet, and I'm not going to make one now."

"Why not?"

"Because I haven't got anything good to say about you people."

Then he wanted to know, "Are you going to make any statements after you are released?"

"Absolutely."

"What will you say?"

I laughed and told him, "You just watch and seè."

BILL BELK (*communications officer*): Ahmed took me into a room and spoke with me individually, as they did with everyone else. He said, "I have some news for you. You are being considered for release. There is a strong possibility that some people will be released, but we haven't decided who we are going to let go. I want you to think about what you will say to your people when you go home. What is it that you are going to say?"

For some reason, this was something that was very important to the militants. They were extremely concerned about what we were going to say. They wanted us to speak well of them, which I thought was totally ridiculous. I said, "I'll tell the truth, Ahmed."

He nodded and said, "We have treated you good."

I said, "Ahmed, holding a man prisoner is not treating him good." Then I started to say something about the time I spent in the basement of the chancery with the busted-out window.

He very quickly interrupted, "But you have a nice room now."

I said, "Ahmed, six people in a room with steel bars all over it and a locked door is not a very nice room."

He obviously wanted me to strike a different tone, and he reiterated that I was being considered for a possible release. Then he said that I was going to be interviewed for television, and he made it clear that my release was contingent on my answers in the interview. In so many words he was saying, "If you want to go home, you'd better be good on TV." Then he let me sit there for fifteen or twenty minutes. He wanted me to think about it. I didn't trust that bastard for a minute, but in this instance I halfway believed him. I knew that the Algerians had been there and that negotiations had been going on. I didn't want to blow my chances with my mouth. That was very much on my mind when he came back into the room and said, "You will come now."

JOE HALL (*warrant officer*): They took me down into the interview room. Screaming Mary was standing there in front of a cameraman. The last time I'd seen her was thirteen months earlier, on December 5, 1979, during my interrogation. I hadn't seen a woman at all since then. She was the last woman I'd seen. I was still under the impression that they were only going to release some of us. I had it in my mind that thirty-seven of us would go and fifteen would stay. In the interview, I wasn't about to say a bad word against the Iranians. Not then. Not under those circumstances.

She asked, "How have you been treated?"

I said, "Fine."

"How was the food?"

"Fine. We were fed regularly."

"Were you mistreated?"

"Nope. Not me."

All Mary wanted to do was establish that I hadn't been mistreated by the Iranians, and all I wanted was to get the hell out of Iran. So I played through their little game, and tried to keep my answers as short as I could.

BILL BELK (*communications officer*): It was an amazing feeling to be sitting there for that interview. Aside from this one girl in the room, there were maybe fifteen or twenty armed guards standing along the wall behind the TV cameras. So I was sitting there looking at this one cameraman and all these other guys with their Uzi submachine guns. I still wasn't sure what was going on. I didn't know if I was going to be released, or taken out and shot. In the back of my mind, I had the vague notion that all of this might just be a pretext for a possible trial. They had threatened all of us with spy trials. There had been a couple of times when Ahmed had told me, "Some of the others might be released, but you are a spy. You are going to stay here and be put on trial." I'd been told so many things that I never knew what to believe. I thought maybe they wanted to get some answers on film to use against me in a trial. But I was also thinking about a possible release. At that point, nothing would've surprised me. One possibility seemed as likely as any other.

Then Sister Philadelphia started in with the interview. She was asking some leading questions, and trying to get me to say that our government had been in the wrong, and that the students had done the right thing in taking us captive. I can't remember exactly what I said, but I tried to make it clear that I didn't hold any animosities toward the Iranian people. I'm sure I buttered my answers up a little, because I didn't want to blow my chances of getting out. She wanted to know what I thought of the treatment I'd received, and I told her that I thought it was wrong to hold hostages, but I wasn't the sort of person to hold grudges or carry on a lingering hatred. It was that sort of thing. I felt like I was walking a fine line. I didn't want to say anything nice about them and play up to their propaganda, but at the same time what Ahmed had said about my being "a candidate for release" was on my mind. I was feeling very vulnerable.

SGT. PAUL LEWIS (*marine security guard*): My interview with Screaming Mary lasted about two minutes. I was sitting in a chair, and they had the cameras running. She asked, "Have you ever been tortured?"

I said, "No, I haven't been tortured. I've just been abused."

"Have you ever been beaten?"

"Yes. In the first couple of months I was beaten."

"Well, how about lately?"

I said, "You know as well as I do that we've been treated extremely well lately."

That was the end of my interview. They probably didn't put me on the air, or maybe they spliced the film and only used my answer to the last question on Iranian TV. But who gives a damn what they did with that stuff? It was all bullshit, anyway. And I knew it when I went in there.

BILL BELK (*communications officer*): After my interview I was taken into another room, and the guards were all being very friendly. They gave me some tea, and they were all smiles. But they also had me in isolation, and were making sure that I didn't have any contact with any of the other hostages who had not been interviewed yet. Even at that stage of the game they were doing everything they could to deprive us of contact with each other, and any sort of news or information. They weren't about to let us have any news if they felt that keeping us confused and uncertain was to their advantage. I sat there and quietly drank my tea. Then they came and took me in for my physical. Although I didn't know it at the time, every single one of us was given a physical by the Algerian doctors in preparation for our release. That was in the agreement that had been negotiated between the United States and Iran as part of the scenario for our release. A doctor listened to my heart, and a couple of nurses gave me a cardiogram. The whole time they were doing this the cameras were clicking away, and the students were hovering very close to make sure that I didn't have a chance to converse with the Algerian doctors. They didn't want the doctors to give me any information, either.

JOHN LIMBERT (*political officer*): While I was getting my physical, I spoke to one of the Algerian doctors in Arabic. I leaned toward him and whispered, "What's going on?"

"You're leaving."

"For sure?"

"Yes, it's certain."

"All of us?"

"Yes, all of you."

Then as I was being led back upstairs, I remember walking by a television set and hearing some news. I was blindfolded and couldn't see anything, but I could hear that an Iranian official was talking about conditions that had been set—he was explaining how money was going to be transferred to a certain bank at a certain time. So it was obvious that something was really going on. This wasn't just a charade.

MALCOLM KALP (*economics officer*): When I was being examined by the Algerian doctors, I spoke to one of them in French and asked, "When are we getting out of here?"

In French, the doctor said, "Haven't they told you?"

"They haven't told me a thing."

He said, "Tomorrow. Tomorrow."

SGT. ROCKY SICKMANN (*marine security guard*): That evening, after we'd gone through our physicals and everything, this one rag head came in who I despised very much. He acted like we were going to be in Tehran for another year, and that no one was going home. He didn't say that, it was just in his manner. He acted like a release wasn't even being considered. He said, "Okay, I've got the list of people who are going to be using the barbells for exercise. We want to make this list out and pass the weights around so that everyone gets a turn. We're going to use this schedule for the next few months." And he was asking us when we wanted to use the weights. He was doing that as a form of psychological torture. He was trying to mess with our minds. After he left, we just kind of looked at each other, thinking, "Hey, what's going on here?" In the morning Mehdi had come in and told us that things were looking very good, and then this guy came around with the weight list and implied that no one was going home. Some of those guys were messing with our minds and being purposely cruel right up to the very end.

CPL. WILLIAM GALLEGOS (*marine security guard*): I wasn't about to let myself get my hopes up. I didn't know what the Iranians were doing. I thought they were just playing games again. They didn't tell me anything, anyway. They just took me down there for those little medical examinations and didn't say anything. I thought, "Big deal. They just want these people to see that we're all right. It's just another show the Iranians are putting on." I didn't even want to think about going home. I said to myself, "Don't even think about it." Those guys were all a bunch of liars, anyway. We never knew what they were going to do.

Then that night, after our examinations, we were sitting in our room when this guy named Hamid came in. He said, "I have good news. You are going to go home."

I said, "Bullshit."

"No, believe me. Believe me. You are going home."

"Aw, bullshit. You're a liar."

JOE HALL (*warrant officer*): After my interview and physical and stuff, one of the guards told me that we would be leaving within eight hours. So I never did go to sleep that night. In our room all five of us were keyed up. We were talking about all the activity that was going on, and what we said in our interviews with Screaming Mary. We were just sitting up kicking these things around and speculating on what it meant. We stayed up that entire night.

MALCOLM KALP (*economics officer*): In the morning I woke up, and I said, "Blucker, today is the day!"

Blucker said, "No, I don't think so. We're going to be here another year. We've got another year to go."

"Oh, Blucker!" I said. "Don't say that!"

Then we ended up sitting there hour after hour, all day long. That was a nerve-racking damn day.

CAPT. PAUL NEEDHAM (*air force logistics officer*): On the twentieth, I woke up expecting to be released. Noon came, and no release. One o'clock came, nothing at all. Two o'clock, still nothing. At about five o'clock, we said, "Oh well, what the hell?" And Mike Moeller and I started exercising. We were getting back into our old routine.

JOE HALL (*warrant officer*): On January twentieth, we sat there all day. I'd been up for thirty-six consecutive hours and was on the brink of exhaustion. I'd stayed up all night and sat there all day. I think all of us in the room were starting to believe that the deal had fallen through, that we weren't going home. That made me feel despondent, but basically it wasn't anything unexpected. I'd been disappointed too many times before, and had been with the Iranians for too long to have any confidence in anything they said. So when it looked like a release wasn't going to happen, I wasn't totally crushed or anything like that. From the newspapers we had seen, I figured that at least the two governments had reached a stage where serious talks were going on. It was just a matter of continuing to wait it out.

JOHN LIMBERT (*political officer*): Right after sundown on the twentieth of January, we heard the call to evening prayer. We'd been waiting all day, and nothing had happened. We were afraid that maybe there had been some last-minute glitch, and that things had fallen through. Then at about 5:30 in the evening we heard some guns going off. It sounded like heavy artillery going off at regular intervals. What they were doing was saluting the great victory they had won over the United States. They had brought the Great Satan to its knees. The guns were still going off when one of the students came in and said, "Pack up. You're leaving."

BARRY ROSEN (*press attaché*): Ahmed came into our room and said, "Pack up!" So we took our letters and pictures and books and the few things we had managed to accumulate, and packed them into little bundles. Then Ahmed came back in, looked at our bundles and started to go crazy. He said, "This is too much! Too much!" He was stomping on our bags, tearing them open, and going crazy. He was screaming at us and losing control of himself. Just going insane. This was the same fellow who liked to play classical music while people were being tortured in the prison. A very peculiar character. He threw a big temper tantrum and ran out of the room.

Then when we were finally moved out, we were blindfolded and our bundles were just tossed aside. We were not allowed to take our belongings with us.

JOE HALL (*warrant officer*): Suddenly a guard came into the room and said, "Okay, right now! Get ready! We are going!" And just like that they started taking us out of the room one at a time. It was sort of funny, because none of us had any shoes. They had taken all of our shoes away from us. So when they led us downstairs, they took us into a room that literally had hundreds of pairs of shoes. They had gathered up all of the shoes they had taken out of our houses and apartments and threw them in a big pile. They took me in there and said, "Pick out a pair of shoes that fit." Well, shit, I could see five pairs of my own shoes in the pile. They'd stolen them from my apartment. I knew that everything I owned was gone, except for this one pair of shoes that they were going to let me put on. Anyway, I picked out my favorite pair, and I was still wearing the pants I'd been captured in, and I had on a clean T-shirt and the green sweatshirt that I'd been given at Christmas. Those were my going-home clothes.

BILL BELK (*communications officer*): I was blindfolded, and the Iranians led me out into a courtyard, where we stood around for a little while. I didn't have a coat, and it was very cold standing outside in my shirtsleeves. I could hear a bunch of people being moved around and the Iranians shouting to each other in Farsi. After a couple of minutes, one of the guards guided me over to a bus and helped me up. I couldn't tell how many Americans were getting on board. I'd been told so many things that I didn't know if we were all going to be released or not. But I could feel people being crowded in around me, so I knew that a substantial number of hostages were getting on the bus. That made me feel better.

The whole time the guards were putting us on the bus, they were telling us, "Don'ta speak! Don'ta speak!" I heard Ahmed say something very vicious to someone, and Mike Metrinko answered right back. In Farsi, Mike told Ahmed that his sister was a whore.

That caused quite a scuffle. Ahmed smacked Metrinko in the head, and a couple of guards helped him drag Mike off the bus. Outside they started punching Mike. We could hear them beating away, and Mike was screaming and cussing at the top of his lungs. He wanted everybody to know what was happening to him.

JOHN LIMBERT (*political officer*): They jammed us into some very fancy buses. I was blindfolded and couldn't see anything, so I don't know how many buses there were. But I remember I ended up sitting in the rear bathroom compartment. I guess that was the only seat they had available, so I rode out to the airport in the bathroom.

SGT. ROCKY SICKMANN (*marine security guard*): I was one of the last people to be put on the bus. The Iranians backed me onto a little ledge because there wasn't anyplace else for me to sit. I was blindfolded, so I couldn't see what was going on, but there were a lot of people already on the bus ready to go. Even though the Iranians had told me that we were going home, I still had a phobia that the whole thing would fall through. Those guys were a bunch of liars, and in a country as chaotic as Iran you never knew what to expect. The militants were always playing games with us, and I was reluctant to believe we were really going home. Even when I was on the bus, I was afraid that maybe it wasn't true.

BILL BELK (*communications officer*): The Iranians never did put Mike Metrinko back on the bus. When we started rolling he was still outside. I guess they were trying to scare him, and wanted to let him think that he was being left behind. They finally ended up taking him out to the airport in a car after all of us had been driven away.

SGT. KEVIN HERMENING (*marine security guard*): Whenever I could, I'd glance out from underneath my blindfold to see where we were. One of the guards had told us that we were going out to the airport, but just because he said it didn't mean it was true. We never could believe any of those guys. So I kept trying to glance out from under my blindfold to see if that was where we were really going. It was very dark outside, because of the blackouts due to the Iraqi war. Tehran was a totally dark city. So I couldn't tell very much.

SGT. ROCKY SICKMANN (*marine security guard*): The drive to the airport was sort of funny, because I had a huge hole in my pants. The militants had sat me down on that little ledge, and all of a sudden my rear end got very, very hot. I realized, "Hey, I'm sitting on a heat duct." It was burning my tail end off, because with that hole in my pants all I had for protection was my underwear. So on the ride out to the airport, I sat there shifting my buns from side to side.

JOHN LIMBERT (*political officer*): It was about eight o'clock when we drove out to the airport, and it was a very unusual trip because we never stopped. In Tehran traffic this is something that is unheard of. I guess they were either rationing gasoline, or an evening curfew had been imposed, because there was very little traffic on the road to the airport.

At the airport, we drove out onto the tarmac, and I could hear the airplane. I think that's the sweetest sound I have ever heard. Then they opened the doors on the bus, and the noise from the airplane was even louder. That was just beautiful.

BRUCE GERMAN (*budget officer*): We sat there at the airport, motionless, for what must've been thirty minutes. Maybe more. I don't know how long for sure, but it seemed like a long time. The goons were waiting until it was twelve noon in Washington, so that Carter would no longer be president. That meant it would have to have been 8:30 at night in Iran. So they were waiting for the official word that Reagan had in fact been sworn in before they said, "Let's move 'em."

JOHN LIMBERT (*political officer*): Back at the guesthouse the students had given me a copy of the *Tehran Times*, which was the local English-language newspaper, and I had carried it onto the bus with me. I wanted to keep it as a souvenir. But before they led me off the bus to board the airplane, the students took the newspaper away from me, and then they took everything I had in my pockets.

BILL BELK (*communications officer*): I was seated up near the front of the bus, so I was one of the first people to go. A couple of militants grabbed me and jerked me toward the door. They ripped my blindfold off, and there were bright lights shining right in my face. I could see the television cameras and a howling mob of idiots down there. About fifty or sixty of these guys had formed a gauntlet from the door of the bus to the base of the airplane ramp. It was sort of like being forced to run through an Indian paddle wheel. These were the dedicated sons of Allah, and they were all yelling and chanting, *"Marg bar Amrika! Marg bar Ree-gan! Marg bar Amrika! Marg bar Ree-gan!"* Before I stepped off the bus, I looked at those guys and raised my middle finger at them as a salute. They didn't appreciate that at all. It just made them chant that much louder. So I started chanting right along with them, *"Marg bar Khomeini! Marg bar Khomeini!"* The two students behind me pushed me forward and ran me through the crowd. I was chanting, *"Marg bar Khomeini! Marg bar Khomeini!"* and giving them the bird all the way to the plane. They were shouting right back and spitting and swinging at me.

BRUCE GERMAN (*budget officer*): I was moved off the bus and into the crowd. It was a relatively small crowd, but very antagonistic. They were shouting their slogans and threats. I understand that a few of the hostages got shoved around, but I didn't. I saw that plane with the Algerians standing in the doorway, and I just made a beeline for the ramp. I didn't look to one side or the other, but kept my eyes straight ahead.

JOHN LIMBERT (*political officer*): As I walked across the tarmac, there was a group lined up there chanting anti-American slogans. I thought that was really a sad way for them to end the ordeal. I remember thinking, "They can't even show a little class when they let us go." If they'd had any class at all, they would have given us flowers and shaken our hands. But they couldn't even do that. Walking across the tarmac, I remember thinking, "What a half-ass group this is."

SGT. KEVIN HERMENING (*marine security guard*): I remember seeing the plane and being entranced by it. I had a guard on each arm, and they pushed me through the crowd. Once I got to the stairs, the guards let me go and I went flying up those stairs. I took off running. The last thing I wanted was to get shot in the back at the last second. It would have been easy for someone to get a shot off from that crowd. So I raced up the stairs.

CPL. WILLIAM GALLEGOS (*marine security guard*): At the bottom of the ramp, two guys grabbed me and literally lifted me up the stairs. They kept saying, "You are safe now. You are safe now." I was looking at these two guys, and I didn't know who they were. They had foreign accents, and I looked under their parkas and saw that they had machine guns. I was thinking, "You guys are telling me I'm safe? I don't even know who you are."

On the plane everybody was sitting around. Nobody was exactly sure of what was happening. We were still kind of wondering, because nobody had told us anything. People were saying, "They're letting us go. This is it." And I was thinking, "I guarantee they're going to shoot a heat-seeking missile at us. They're just going to blast us out of the sky. This has got to be the all-time con." You just never knew what to expect from a country like Iran. They could blow us up and say that it was an accident.

SGT. PAUL LEWIS (*marine security guard*): When I got on the plane, I saw the guys with machine guns, and I wasn't sure if they were Algerians or Iranians. Then an older gentleman patted me on the arm and said, "You don't have anything to worry about. They won't get on this plane."

So I walked up into the passenger cabin, and I remember it was still pretty quiet. A lot of the hostages were sitting there, and I guess you'd expect a lot of noise and emotions, but there wasn't any celebration going on yet. We were all shaking hands and having some polite conversation, but I think everybody was still a little tense. We'd all been through so many periods of hope that ended with big letdowns, so no one was ready to actually believe that we were really going home. The plane was still on the ground, and we were waiting for the wheels to roll—we wanted to be on the way before we let any emotion out.

CHARLES JONES (*communications officer*): Once I was on the plane, I sat down and looked around. I wondered, "Is this a dream?" During the time we were being kept in Komiteh Prison, I had some very, very vivid dreams. There were several times when I'd dream of being free and back in the United States. So I wasn't quite ready to believe this was actually happening. The whole thing had a dreamlike feel to it. I had this nagging sense that I could wake up at any moment. So I sat there quietly, and watched the other hostages come on board, all the while wondering if they were just part of my dream.

MALCOLM KALP (*economics officer*): When I got on that plane it was a feeling of total euphoria and shock. I knew exactly where I was, and exactly what was happening, but it was sort of like I was suspended in a world of disbelief. Here were all these people who I hadn't seen in fourteen and a half months. They're all sitting right there. It was beautiful. There was a feeling of overwhelming joy and shock, and it didn't take long for that feeling of joy to turn into a crying binge.

BRUCE GERMAN (*budget officer*): We went around hugging and shaking hands. Then before the plane took off we made the Algerians count heads. They did it, and we did it, and then we took another count. We wanted to make sure everybody was on that plane. We weren't about to leave anyone behind.

SGT. ROCKY SICKMANN (*marine security guard*): When we were all on board and ready to go, there was a problem with the lights on the runway. The Iranians didn't want to turn them on because they were having blackouts on account of the war with Iraq, and the Algerian pilot couldn't take off without runway lights. So that caused some confusion and delayed us for a few minutes. Finally, the Iranians agreed to turn on the runway lights long enough for us to take off.

VICTOR TOMSETH (*chief political officer*): We sat on the ground for quite a while before actually getting underway. When the engines started up, there was a great cheer. Then when the plane began to move as we slowly taxied toward the head of the runway, there was another cheer. And when we began to really roll and lifted into the air, another great cheer went up.

BILL BELK (*communications officer*): When the wheels lifted off the runway there was a great shout of rejoicing. "We are off! We are free!" I think lifting off of that runway was the greatest thrill of my entire life. It was a moment of pure joy, and I joined in on all the cheering. I was hollering with the rest of 'em.

VICTOR TOMSETH (*chief political officer*): The Algerians had been unwilling to take on any food in Iran. I suppose they were afraid it would be poisoned or something, and would create an incident at the very moment that they were about to achieve their greatest diplomatic triumph. But they did have some cheese and a few things that they had brought with them. As soon as we were in the air, they started passing it around. United States-Algerian relations have never been better than they were on that day. It was absolutely beautiful. I felt great.

WILLIAM ROYER (*director of academic courses*): While we were in the air, we were told by the captain of the plane that the flight crew and the aircraft had been sitting in Tehran for several days. Initially, they had planned on giving us a big turkey dinner, but the food had been on the plane for too long, and they couldn't serve it. So they had to give us something else, which didn't bother me at all. I wasn't hungry, and I didn't care about food. I remember I was filled with a marvelous sense of happiness and relief, and for a while there were tears welling in my eyes.

BILL BELK (*communications officer*): People were just happy as hell to see and talk with each other. For the most part, these were people who we had been unable to speak with for the previous fourteen and a half months. Now we were free, and we were all getting caught up. I remember I was sitting with Cort Barnes and Bob Ode, and Joe Hall was there too. Everyone was talking at once. We were all sharing our joy with each other.

After about forty minutes, the captain came over the intercom and announced, "We have just cleared Iranian airspace. We are now in Turkey." A real roar went up when we heard that news. We were out of Iran!

CDR. ROBERT ENGELMANN (*naval supply corps officer*): Everybody breathed a sigh of relief when we crossed out of Iranian airspace, even the Algerians. We could see that they were happy to be out of Iran too. It was an incredibly chaotic situation for them, because there wasn't a government in Iran that was capable of functioning. You never knew if the people you were negotiating with had any power. So it was an extremely volatile situation, and even the Algerian emissaries were uncomfortable in that atmosphere. It was the kind of thing where they didn't know if someone would try to hose our plane with machine gun fire when we took off, or shoot us out of the sky. Anything could have happened. The Algerians had only been in Iran for a few days, but we could see that they were very happy to get out of there too.

BILL BELK (*communications officer*): As soon as we crossed out of Iranian air space, two Turkish fighter jets closed in alongside of us as escorts, and the word was passed that we were flying to Athens, Greece, to refuel. Then the captain brought out two big bottles of champagne. I remember Bruce Laingen stood up and offered a toast to the Algerians for their role in negotiating our release. So we all raised our glasses and drank to the Algerians. Then we had a couple more toasts.

CPL. WILLIAM GALLEGOS (*marine security guard*): When the stewardesses came back with some champagne I didn't drink anything. I thought it might be poisoned. I didn't want to swallow anything until everybody else had tried some. I watched them all eat and drink, and when nobody croaked or got sick I figured the food was okay. So I went ahead and ate my little sandwich and drank my glass of champagne.

BILL BELK (*communications officer*): After refueling in Athens, we flew to Algeria, which was an intermediate stop for us. That's where we were going to be officially transferred to the custody of American diplomatic personnel and put on American aircraft. It was about a two-hour flight from Athens to Algeria, and there were people on board who told us that there would be a big reception for us when we got off the plane in Algeria. At the time, I didn't think anything of it. I had no idea that we were a big news item back home. When I was told that there would be a welcoming reception, I figured that meant we'd get cookies and champagne at the airport. But when we landed and started coming off the airplane absolute madness beset us. There were hundreds and hundreds of people at the airport. They were all waving to us and cheering and jumping up and down. And my God, I'd never seen so many reporters in all my life. They were lined up behind yellow ropes, and it was like looking out into a sea of telephoto lenses. There were bright television lights flashing and moving around as cameramen tried to angle into position and film us coming off the plane. As we walked toward the terminal, all of the reporters were calling out to us from behind the ropes, "How do you feel? Are you okay?"

JOE HALL (*warrant officer*): We got off the plane, and they herded all of us toward the VIP Lounge in the terminal. I remember walking across the tarmac in a cool misty rain. I was absolutely beat. Just exhausted. I'd gone two nights in a row without any sleep, and I was feeling completely numb. The fact that I was no longer in Tehran hadn't sunk in yet.

There were a lot of people and reporters at the airport, and I was bewildered by all of the excitement. I think the entire American embassy staff was there to greet us, and there were lots and lots of lights and cameras and microphones. People were pointing at us and waving to us, and reporters were asking questions and filming us.

BILL BELK (*communications officer*): Deputy Secretary of State Warren Christopher was intimately involved in the negotiations to get us released, and he was at the airport in Algeria to greet us. The television cameras filmed all of us walking past him and shaking his hand, and shaking hands with other dignitaries. Some State Department doctors and psychiatrists were also there. They were part of our receiving line. I'm sure they were very concerned about us. Nobody knew what our health or mental condition was, and this was their first chance to get a look at us. We must've looked like a pretty bedraggled crew, because we were wearing the same tattered old clothes we'd been wearing for months and months. A lot of us had grown beards, and we'd all lost tremendous amounts of weight. It was a pretty rag-tag band of diplomats and military personnel that walked off that plane.

SGT. ROCKY SICKMANN (*marine security guard*): We shook hands with some of the diplomats who had worked so hard for our release. Sheldon Krys and Warren Christopher were there, and so was the Algerian ambassador. It was sort of funny because those guys were all dressed in nice business suits, and we were all real dirty and wearing messy clothes. The Algerian ambassador's wife was standing there crying, and I gave her a great big hug. She was a beautiful lady.

There in the terminal, everybody was staring at us in amazement. We were amazed too, and were staring right back at them. I had a huge hole in the rear of my pants, and the other hostages were joking around with me because my white underwear was showing. Here we were on national TV, and I was walking around with a hole in my pants.

JOE HALL (*warrant officer*): Inside the terminal there was a little ceremony for all of the people who had been involved in the negotiations to get us out. I guess the Algerians wanted to soak up all of the good publicity, and our State Department types didn't want to miss a chance to get in front of the cameras. We didn't know who any of these people were, so we were just kind of watching and looking around, trying to figure out what was going on. All of these senior government officials and ambassadors were getting up in front of the microphones and making little speeches and congratulating and thanking one another. I remember Don Hohman and I were leaning against the wall watching all of this take place. We thought it was really kind of ridiculous.

BILL BELK (*communications officer*): Television and radio reporters were sticking microphones in front of Bruce Laingen and Victor Tomseth, and trying to interview the two of them because they were up front. The rest of us were just sitting there watching the ceremony, and a few reporters were trying to get to some of us, too. I couldn't believe that there was so much media attention. I didn't really pay any attention to what was being said by the dignitaries up front. I was watching all of the reporters scramble around, thinking, "This is amazing. I can't believe these people are this interested in us." During this time, I looked over and saw that Don Cooke was so bored by all the speeches that he crawled behind the last row of chairs, lay down on the floor and went to sleep. The TV crews loved that. They zoomed right in on him for a closeup.

SGT. PAUL LEWIS (*marine security guard*): We were all sitting there in chairs, and camera crews were coming up to us, sticking microphones in our faces, saying "This is NBC live," and asking questions. That amazed me. Algeria was only an intermediate stop. I couldn't believe that network television was catching us there and bouncing it off a satellite live back to the United States. I really didn't have anything to say. I wasn't ready to talk to the press yet. It was too soon. We'd only been out of Iran for three hours, and I didn't have any idea of what was going on. No one had had a chance to brief us yet, but those reporters wouldn't leave us alone. I tried to stay back away from them as best I could and let others do the talking. But finally, we had to push some of them away from us. They were all zeroing in on us at once, and it was just too much too soon.

CHARLES JONES (*communications officer*): Once again, I have to refer to the dreamlike quality of what was happening. I was sitting in the reception area looking up at these big-wigs and their ceremony, and I said to myself, "This can't be real. It's not real at all."

While we were there, I made a comment to somebody about not being able to believe the reception we were getting, and he sort of scoffed at that, and said, "Oh, this is nothing. Wait until you get to Germany. And if you think that's a big welcome, wait until you get to the United States. You're in for a huge welcome. You people are heroes."

I said, "Heroes? We're not heroes. We're survivors. That's all. Just survivors."

SGT. ROCKY SICKMANN (*marine security guard*): There were three United States Air Force planes in Algeria to take us to Germany. We were divided up alphabetically by our last names, and assigned to our planes. After the ceremony, we were led back outside, and I remember we all started running to those American planes. We were so happy, we were screaming and splashing through the puddles like little kids. It was great.

CPL. WILLIAM GALLEGOS (*marine security guard*): I looked up and saw the planes had American flags on them and said United States Air Force. That was when I first started believing I was really going home. Seeing those American planes was great. We climbed on board, and the staff was real nice. They were shaking our hands and hugging us, being real warm and friendly. I remember sitting back and saying to myself, "Well, it looks like we're really going home." I was so used to feeling blah all that time, that it took a while for me to get excited.

JOE HALL (*warrant officer*): They loaded us on board those air force planes, and I think that was when I first started to feel free. We were on an American plane, and we were surrounded by Americans. That was the big thing. Up until this time, we'd been with the Algerians, and they were friendly, but they were still carrying guns, and it just wasn't the same. Seeing all those American faces and listening to people speak English made a big, big difference. When I got on board that plane, it was the first time in a long, long time that I wasn't surrounded by foreigners.

BILL BELK (*communications officer*): We were in big medevac aircraft, and the State Department must've thought we were all going to be a little loo-loo or something, because they had a couple of psychiatrists and four or five doctors on each plane. But they were all very friendly. They didn't try to question us right then or anything like that. They were more like a reception team, and they were being very kind. Of course, I hadn't seen any women at all in over a year, and I'll tell you, the nurses on those hospital planes were a sight for sore eyes. I remember sitting there absolutely entranced just to see a woman again. Everyone there was trying to make sure we were all comfortable, and help us get settled in. Some of them even had messages for us from our families and things like that. My God, you can't imagine what a good feeling it was to be with Americans!

COL. CHARLES SCOTT (*chief of the Defense Liaison Office*): On the flight into Germany, I felt like a nightmare was over. I settled into my seat with a tremendous sense of relief, appreciation, happiness, and fatigue all at the same time. Even though I was tired, I didn't want to go to sleep. There was too much euphoria for that.

BILL BELK (*communications officer*): The flight from Algeria to Germany was perfectly smooth. I sacked out for an hour or two and got a little sleep. As we were coming into Germany, I was talking to one of the doctors and I mentioned that the reception in Algeria was really unexpected. He said, "That was nothing. Wait until you get to Germany." He tried to explain that we were a major news item, and that the entire nation had been agonizing over our being held hostage. But it didn't sink in. He was trying to describe a situation that words could not possibly convey, and in spite of his very sincere efforts to tell me what a big deal this was to people all over the world, I had no idea of what was waiting for us.

JOHN LIMBERT (*political officer*): Our plane taxied up to the terminal at the Frankfurt airport at about six o'clock in the morning. Outside it was cold, dark, and snowy, but there was a big mob of people there. I looked out the window and wondered, "What's going on?" I didn't think that crowd had any relation to us. I had no idea we were a big news item. I was curious, and wanted to know what was happening.

SGT. KEVIN HERMENING (*marine security guard*): When we landed we could see thousands and thousands of people at the airport to greet us. It was still dark out, but there was this big huge crowd there, and banners were tacked up all over the place, and spotlights and flags and yellow ribbons. We'd only been free for six or seven hours, and it was kind of hard to comprehend and absorb all of this excitement at once. None of us were expecting to be welcomed as heroes. But there were mobs of people and reporters waiting for us at the airport.

BILL BELK (*communications officer*): We arrived in Frankfurt at some ungodly hour in the morning and were loaded onto some little buses to be driven in convoy from Frankfurt to Weisbaden. It was probably about twenty-five miles or so to the hospital, and all along that route the streets were lined with cheering people. That just amazed me. I think every American in Germany got out of bed that morning to come out and greet us. But it wasn't just Americans. There were a lot of Germans out there, too. I was amazed that our return from Iran was such a big deal to people who didn't even know us. I think that was when I had my first inkling that the press was really going to be after us, because our convoy of buses had a police escort, and we were being trailed by television crews and photographers. There was one television van that tried to swing around the police cars so that they could pull up parallel to us and get some television footage. The networks were so desperate for coverage that they were trying to break through police lines to get some film clips and pictures. The police ran that van right off the road.

When we arrived in Weisbaden, we received very warm greetings from the soldiers and patients at the hospital. A military band was playing as we walked in, and it was a very nice reception. Once again, there was a lot of hugging and kissing and shaking of hands. The band kept playing and a children's choir was singing in the lobby. It was all very festive. Very joyous. But the thing I remember the most was the huge number of letters that were waiting for us at the hospital. They had these letters stacked in boxes there in the hallway, and there were literally thousands and thousands of them. Big huge boxes full of mail. The whole time I was in Iran I received four letters. That was it. Ahmed kept telling me, "No one is writing to you. Your wife is not writing to you." I knew that was bullshit, but in the prison I think there were times when all of us felt like we'd been left there and forgotten. But seeing all of that mail stacked up at the hospital was amazing. It gave me an idea of how much people cared. That was beautiful.

SGT. PAUL LEWIS (*marine security guard*): At the hospital, a little kid came up to me and asked me for my autograph. I wasn't sure whether he was serious or not. Why would anybody want my autograph? I was just a marine from Homer, Illinois. But this little boy was too young to be a wise guy. So I gave him an autograph, and I remember I felt very self-conscious about signing my name and giving it back to him. It was almost embarrassing. That was something that took a while to get used to.

BILL BELK (*communications officer*): Of course, the first thing I wanted to do was get a bath and a haircut. They got us all checked into our rooms, and I took a long, long shower. I was getting all of the dirt and dust off, and I shaved my beard off just to get rid of that prison feeling. Then the most amazing thing was that after drying myself off I didn't have to step back into those same dirty clothes that I'd been wearing for the past year. We were all given clean clothing, and that was very nice.

Fortunately, we were sequestered from the press. They were kept down at the front gate of the hospital where they couldn't get to us. We were free to wander down there and talk to them if we wanted to, but we didn't have to. I remember Bruce German walked by the gate, and one of the reporters asked him if he'd ever go back to Iran. Bruce said, "Yeah, in a B-52."

SGT. PAUL LEWIS (*marine security guard*): I was in a hospital room with Jimmy Lopez, when one of the chaplains walked in and said, "Phone lines are available for you guys to call the States if you want to make some calls."

I looked at my watch, figured in the time difference, and said, "Not right now. It's already past midnight in Illinois."

Chaplain Evans said, "Paul, I don't think your folks will mind if you call them now."

I said, "No, I think I'll wait, and call them in the morning at a decent hour."

I think that was an attitude that a lot of us had. We'd been out of Iran for less than twenty-four hours, and the enormity of what was happening to us still hadn't sunk in. None of us knew what a big deal this was back in the States, and Chaplain Evans had to explain to me that my folks were expecting a call, in spite of the lateness of the hour.

BILL BELK (*communications officer*): They had forty telephones set up for us in one room, and we were told that we had unlimited access to the long-distance lines. We could call home as often as we wanted, and talk for as long as we wanted. So you'd better believe that one of the first things I did was call Angela. I could hardly wait to talk to her. I dialed the number from the hospital, and heard it ring at home in South Carolina. Angela picked it up, and I said, "Hi, honey, it's me."

Well, that was a very emotional moment for both of us. She broke down. She absolutely couldn't speak. I could hear her crying, and then I broke down too. Neither one of us could say a word. We just stood there and felt the love throbbing through the line.

ANITA SCHAEFER (*wife of Col. Thomas Schaefer*): Tom called from Weisbaden, and I remember our first conversation was very basic. The first thing I said to him was "How are you?" Now those are three words that we all frequently ask each other during the course of our daily lives. We literally ask that question thousands of times. But for the first time in my life I really meant it when I asked, "How are you?" That was something I needed to know.

PARVANEH LIMBERT (*wife of John Limbert*): I knew that John was going to call from Weisbaden, so I was waiting for his call. When the phone rang, I said, "That's John!" I picked it up, and said, "Hi John!"

"Hi!"

"How are you? Are you okay?"

"Yes, I'm fine."

I couldn't believe it. I was so happy. Hearing his voice was the happiest moment in my life.

I kept asking him, "Are you sure you're okay?"

JOHN LIMBERT (*political officer*): I think my wife was worried that something might be wrong with me. The first thing she asked was, "Are you all right?" I told her I was fine, and she said, "Are you sure you're all right?" I reassured her, and she asked, "Are you *really* all right?" I think by the tone of my voice and my manner, as well as by words, I was able to convince her that yes, I was still the same person.

Talking with the kids was great. They were so excited they were practically jumping out of their skins. The first news I got from my daughter was, "Daddy, we have a new puppy!"

Less than ecstatic, I said, "Oh? We do?"

SGT. PAUL LEWIS (*marine security guard*): I went in and called my folks back home in Illinois. I talked to my father for a little bit and told him that I was all right. I was just pretty much reassuring him that I was okay, and that I was grateful to be out. That was the big thing. At long last it was over. We were out. After a few minutes he asked me if I wanted to talk to anyone else. I thought that maybe a couple of our relatives had come over to the house, so I said, "Sure, let me talk to everybody who's there."

He laughed and said, "Paul, there are well over 200 people in the house." A lot of the neighbors had come over to watch our release on TV. It wasn't a planned celebration or anything like that; people just started showing up with food and champagne. They had TVs going in each room on the ground floor. There were so many people in the living room that my father was worried that the floor might collapse. I just couldn't conceive of that—I had no conception at all of what was going on in the States.

JOE HALL (*warrant officer*): I was walking around the hospital in a daze. I was totally wasted from fatigue. Of course, no sooner did we get checked in than all of the doctors and nurses wanted to start running medical and psychological tests on us. I was on the verge of collapse. I'd gone over sixty hours without sleep, and they had a battery of psychological questionnaires they wanted us to fill out. I worked my way through one of those things only to be handed another one. I was so tired that my hands were shaking. I answered three questions, and couldn't go any further. I turned it back in and said, "You can ask me this stuff later. I've got to get some sleep."

BILL BELK (*communications officer*): We met with some State Department psychiatrists as soon as we got to Weisbaden. All of those people were trying to pick my brain. They wanted to know what my emotional reaction was to this and to that, and they were asking all kinds of questions and having us take written tests. I really got tired of that. During my evaluation, the psychiatrist I was talking to said, "You were one of the hostages we were the most concerned about. We were really worried about you."

"Why were you so worried about me?"

"In the film clips from the Christmas ceremony, you looked very, very angry. We could tell you were glaring at the Iranians."

"Of course I was glaring at them. This was my second Christmas in captivity, and they were my enemy. They were the people who were holding me."

"But weren't you afraid of what they might do to you?"

That was the kind of question that really cracked me up. At that time, I couldn't imagine being in a worse situation than the one I was already in. I'd been held hostage for the previous thirteen months, and was way beyond fear. I didn't care what the Iranians thought of me or what they did to me. Fear didn't even enter into it. They could take me out and beat me, but so what? Physical pain certainly wasn't any worse than the extreme tension that comes from living under the conditions that we were being forced to live under. The only emotion I was capable of feeling was anger. I tried to explain this to the psychiatrist, and he seemed to understand what I was getting at. After we talked for a while he said that it looked like I was in good shape mentally, and gave me a clean bill of health. I think everyone was surprised by how well we were doing when we first came out. They expected more psychological problems than there were.

CPL. WILLIAM GALLEGOS (*marine security guard*): We had a lot of fun. We were told we weren't supposed to have any alcohol, but there was a little store in the basement of the hospital, and Paul Lewis, Rocky Sickmann, and I went down there and bought a bunch of beer. We didn't have a refrigerator, but it was really cold outside, so we put our beer on the balcony outside our room and let it get cold out there. Then we'd drink it in the hospital room. For us, that was a party, and we were having a lot of fun.

SGT. PAUL LEWIS (*marine security guard*): At the hospital the medical staff wanted us to take all kinds of tests. They measured everything. Every time we urinated, it was into a little jug so the fluid could be analyzed. That first day it seemed like they'd already drawn over a gallon of blood. At night, we were supposed to salivate into a jar before we went to bed. But none of us wanted to worry about that kind of stuff. We weren't supposed to have any alcohol, but we went ahead and partied in our hospital rooms anyway. We were really, really, really happy, and we had to let our joy go. So people were taking their little urinalysis jars and filling them up with grapefruit juice and water, and turning them in.

CPL. WILLIAM GALLEGOS (*marine security guard*): I remember waking up at the hospital on the first morning after our release, and I didn't know where I was. It was like being in a dream. I looked over at Rocky Sickmann, and then at Steve Kirtley, and they were both lying in their beds looking around the room like, "Wow! This is too good to be true!" I honestly didn't know where I was.

Then the door popped open, and in walked a bunch of nurses and medical technicians with test tubes and thermometers. They wanted blood samples and temperatures, and all kinds of things.

BILL BELK (*communications officer*): On the second day we had more tests. That morning the doctors were busy poking us and thumping on us, while the nurses were sticking needles in us, and the dentist was waiting with a drill for our teeth. But I was so happy, I didn't care what they did to me. I was just glad to be there. We were all walking around in our hospital gowns, and you can't imagine how nice it was to be able to walk down a hall without having a submachine gun pointed at your back.

I remember I filled out some psychological questionnaires, and got tired of that, so I left and went over to the PX, where I bought some Levis and some clean underwear. When we left Iran, everything we owned was left behind in the hands of some Iranian, so we had to start building our wardrobes back up from scratch. I didn't even have a pair of socks to my name. So I bought some clothes, and wandered around for a while with Rick Kupke. Then that afternoon they gathered all of us into a big room on the second floor of the hospital. We'd already met with several dignitaries, and it seemed like every time I turned around I was shaking somebody's hand. As we were walking into this room, somebody told me that President Carter was flying in to see us.

CPL. WILLIAM GALLEGOS (*marine security guard*): I remember when President Carter came to the hospital. I was standing outside on the balcony with some other marines. We wore our marine guard T-shirts and our hospital pajamas. We saw him when he got out of his limousine. We waved to him from the balcony. I thought that was great. Everyone was excited.

Inside the hospital, people were just kind of mingling around in this room where President Carter was supposed to come in and talk to us. The marines got into formation. We formed two lines and were standing at attention when he came into the room. He greeted everyone, and came over to the marines and gave each of us a big hug. He told us that he was proud of us, and I thought he was great. I never had any doubts about the man or what he did. I know some people have been critical of him for letting the shah into the country, or for this or that. Some people think that he didn't do anything that whole time, but those people weren't in Jimmy Carter's shoes. It's always easy to criticize in hindsight. Everyone knows that. If those people had been in President Carter's shoes, what would they have done? What could they have done? No matter what they tried, I'm sure people would have been critical of them, too. This was just one of those situations that was traumatic for the entire nation, and I'm convinced that President Carter did everything he possibly could for us. He did a lot. He really tried. So I admire the man, and I'm glad he came to Weisbaden. Meeting him was great.

SGT. JAMES LOPEZ (*marine security guard*): I didn't want to see the guy. I was ordered to be there. I thought he just piddled around and got people killed for no good reason, because he went at it half-ass. Personally, I think the whole thing could have been over a lot sooner if he'd taken a firm stand.

I just shook hands with him and was very polite. Then I left. Everyone else hung around for his speech, but I snuck out. I said to myself, "I don't want to hear this trash." I went down the hall and watched *Star Wars* on the video.

SGT. PAUL LEWIS (*marine security guard*): I didn't have any particular reason to be happy with President Carter, but at Weisbaden I felt sorry for him. I noticed how much he had aged in the fourteen months that we'd been in Tehran. I could see that the presidency and the hostage crisis had taken a toll on him. Then, after his just losing the election, the Iranians threw more dirt in his face by not letting us out of Tehran until after the inauguration. He didn't deserve that. He might not be the greatest president we'd ever had, but he is a sincere man, and I felt a little bit of pity for him. Looking into President Carter's face made me realize the enormity of the job he had faced for four years. Even though President Carter and I have very different political views, I'm absolutely certain that his actions during the Iranian crisis were guided by a genuine concern for our welfare. I won't criticize the man, because my friends and I are alive today.

VICTOR TOMSETH (*chief political officer*): The meeting with President Carter was a dialogue. It wasn't a situation where people jumped up and made wild accusations. Generally speaking, I do not think that President Carter is an eloquent man. But when he came in to meet with that group, and spoke for about twenty minutes, he was extremely eloquent. I think the reason he was, is that this issue was one he felt very deeply and genuinely about. That gave him the eloquence that he does not normally possess.

BILL BELK (*communications officer*): When President Carter came in, it was strictly us hostages in the room, and no one else. There were no State Department officials or doctors in there with us, and absolutely no press. After hugging each of us, President Carter made a brief speech, and discussed the financial terms of the deal that he had made to get us out. He also talked about the rescue mission. He assured us that it was a well-planned and well-executed attempt, but that everything that could have gone wrong did go wrong. He never said that it was a mistake to have tried, but said that logistical problems turned the mission into a dismal failure. He indicated that the weather, in particular, was a problem. President Carter is a very emotional man, and in talking about the rescue attempt he broke down and cried a couple of times. At the time, I didn't realize that eight people had died in the rescue attempt. I still hadn't been briefed, and didn't know much about it. Some of the other hostages had learned some of the details while we were still in prison, but not me. I was still in the dark, and I wasn't exactly sure what all the tears were about.

BARRY ROSEN (*press attaché*): In his talk, President Carter told us that the hostage crisis was the worst thing that had ever happened to him in his life—even worse than losing the election—and he expressed his feelings of terrible regret. It was easy to see that he had been genuinely concerned and genuinely affected by the situation. I think that because of his strict moral stance and religious convictions, he was very fixed on saving our lives. Khomeini was terribly inflexible, and was fixed on punishing America. That was what Carter had to deal with, and in his way he was equally inflexible. He wanted to save our lives no matter what. That might have cost him the election. If he had decided to save the presidency for himself and had bombed Iran in an act of retaliation, then I don't think it really would have mattered whether or not we lived or died. Everybody would have said it was a horrible thing, but I think that people would have also felt good about having inflicted some pain on Iran. If it had come down to a show of military force, President Carter's popularity would have probably risen. But he chose not to do that. I think his coming to Weisbaden and seeing all of us was something that he had to do for himself. He had to touch us and see that everyone was alive.

SGT. PAUL LEWIS (*marine security guard*): Nothing was sinking in fast enough. I lost all sense of time. On the first day we were out, it seemed like an entire week had passed, because our sense of time in relation to events was distorted. In prison nothing happened. We just sat there in our cells. But as soon as we were released, things were happening at an incredibly rapid pace. At the hospital, I didn't go to bed because sleep seemed like a waste of time. I wanted to be on the phone talking to family and friends, or watching videotapes of old news broadcasts so I could learn what had happened. It was just go, go, go. Constant movement and constant activity. Finally, on the second day at the hospital I had to go to bed. I was dizzy and exhausted, and went up to get my first sleep.

CPL. WILLIAM GALLEGOS (*marine security guard*): On our last night in Weisbaden some of the nurses came up to our hospital rooms and snuck a few of us out. They took us down to the basement and led us through a whole bunch of underground tunnels to get us out and over to their barracks. A bunch of nurses and medical technicians and hospital personnel were in a great big room, and they had a couple kegs of beer, and there was music and dancing. I remember it was sort of funny, because when we first got there some guy from ABC News climbed up on a ladder with a camera and peeked in at us. When we saw him, a bunch of guys from the army base went running out, grabbed him, and threw him out. After that, all of the curtains were closed, and we sat in there with the hospital staff and danced and talked and drank beer. That was great, because it was just like a party back in the States. Those people were all real nice. They were sensitive to what our situation had been, and they didn't ask us anything about Iran or what had happened. Nobody was coming up to us and saying, "What was it like? What did the militants do to you?" There was none of that. Instead they treated us like friends, and we talked about the things that friends talk about. We drank beer and danced and had a lot of fun. The only problem was our plane was leaving at 7:00 the next morning, so we had to get up at 5:30.

SGT. KEVIN HERMENING (*marine security guard*): We had a really good time, and I didn't sleep at all while we were in Weisbaden. For that entire three days I was busy doing things. Then right before we left for the United States, I went to bed and got about ninety minutes of sleep. That was it. Outside of that, I hadn't slept for a single minute while we were there.

COL. THOMAS SCHAEFER (*defense attaché*): On the flight back to the United States, I walked up to the cockpit and saw two majors sitting in the pilots' seats. I said, "Hey, guys, one of you is going to have to give up your seat, because I'm pulling rank on you."

They both laughed and said, "Come on in, Colonel." I settled in behind the controls and helped fly *Freedom One* back into American air space. I think that was the biggest thrill in my flying career. I was on the radio reporting our positions, and we got a call from someone who asked, "Are you the same Colonel Schaefer who was stationed at Westover Air Force Base?"

I said, "Yes, I am."

He said, "Well then, we have something here we want to play for you." Then they played "God Bless America" over the radio, which we piped back into the cabin. When that happened, there wasn't a dry eye anywhere on that airplane.

JOE HALL (*warrant officer*): When we entered American airspace we all knew that Colonel Schaefer was flying the plane, and that was a big boost for all of us. We thought it was great. As we approached New York messages were being piped back into the cabin from all over the United States welcoming us home. Boy, was that ever emotional! My whole body was zinging with chills and goose bumps.

When we landed at Stewart Air Force Base, we could see the crowds over by the hangar. Of course, I knew Cheri was there and I was trying to compose myself. Some of the hostages were grabbing their bags and jumping up to get off the plane. But I didn't feel a need to hurry. I knew I had the rest of my life stretching out in front of me, and I just wanted to compose myself before I walked off the plane.

BILL BELK (*communications officer*): I came down the ramp and saw my wife and two sons there waiting for me. My oldest son came charging up yelling and screaming, and as soon as my feet hit the tarmac he lifted me clean off the ground. Angela was right behind him. I was so pleased to see them. That was an incredibly good feeling. To be with them, look at them, touch them—that was a moment of great joy. It was a moment all of us had dreamed about many, many times, and everyone coming off the plane was being absolutely mobbed by their families— hugging and kissing and crying, and hugging and kissing some more. A few tears were only natural.

JOE HALL (*warrant officer*): I saw my wife, Cheri, when we touched down in the States. She was standing at the bottom of the ramp as we were coming off the plane. She was as strong as could be, and I was doing real well too—until I touched the bottom of the ramp. When we embraced I started sobbing uncontrollably. I was so choked up that I couldn't even carry on a conversation. The mental and emotional exhaustion of the previous fourteen and a half months hit me all at once, and turned me into a basket case. I was an emotional wreck, and Cheri was the Rock of Gibraltar. Secretly, I resented the fact that I was the one who was so emotional. I wanted to be the strong one, who had endured all those months of hell, and would come home and take care of her. But as it turned out, she was the one who was taking care of me.

PARVANEH LIMBERT (*wife of John Limbert*): When I first saw John, I was very, very happy, but it was also hard for me. Talking to him on the phone was much easier than seeing him face to face. For me it was a bit hard at the beginning because I am an Iranian. Thinking that my own people had done this to him—had taken him hostage—that made it very hard. Throughout the entire ordeal, I always had feelings of guilt, and I was frightened, because I wasn't sure how John would feel. There were times when I would wonder, "How can I face him?" But at the same time, I love him very much, and I was excited and happy. Fortunately, he understands me and what happened very well. Right away, when I first saw him, I knew that he was the same John who had left fourteen and a half months earlier. He looked exactly the same— his manner, his appearance, everything was the same. Nothing changed. I saw him, and I thought, "That's him! That's John!"

BILL BELK (*communications officer*): After we got off the airplane and were reunited with our families, we were loaded onto a couple of buses to be taken to West Point, and that trip from Stewart Air Force Base to West Point was the most amazing thing I've ever experienced in my life. There were thousands and thousands and thousands of people out to greet us. Every single mile the street was lined with people packed hundreds and thousands deep. They were screaming and cheering and waving flags and banners and yellow ribbons.

ROBERT ODE (*consular officer*): The streets were incredibly crowded. Absolutely packed with people. From our buses we were looking out onto a sea of people, and they were going wild. It was overwhelming and unbelievable. My wife Rita was with me, and I said to her, "Look, honey, some of those people are jumping up and down on top of their cars, just so they can see us. They're going to ruin their cars."

Then Rita, who is very practical, said, "Maybe they're jumping up and down on top of someone else's car."

JOHN LIMBERT (*political officer*): My wife kept telling me, "Wave to the people! They're expecting you to! They want to see you! Wave to them!" All of the way to West Point the street was just lined with people. It was the sort of reception you'd expect if you'd won the World Series, or had gone to the moon and back—but not the sort of reception you'd expect for having gotten out of jail. I found it to be absolutely amazing.

DON HOHMAN (*army medic*): That ride down Freedom Road was wonderful. I'd never seen so many people in all my life. It was miles and miles of people. As we passed along one stretch, they had our names lined up on placards right in a row, one name right after another. And there were fire engines with their ladders up and crossed out over the road. I don't think any of us expected that kind of reception. I looked around the bus, and everybody was overjoyed. Everybody was trying to hang out the window and wave. My arm was sore and tired, but I kept on leaning out the window and waving. It was unbelievable that so many people turned out. It was kind of like the whole United States was represented right there on Freedom Road.

PARVANEH LIMBERT (*wife of John Limbert*): Everybody was happy. The whole country was happy. There was so much celebration going on, but I was so glad to have John next to me that I didn't want to see anything else. I was sitting there thinking, "I am holding his hand. He is here beside me. I am the happiest person of all." It was a wonderful moment.

DON HOHMAN (*army medic*): By the time we got to West Point I was exhausted. We'd had a transatlantic flight, and that reception was an incredibly emotional experience. It must've taken us two hours or more to travel those seventeen miles. So I was pretty tired, and was glad to see the inside of a motel room.

BILL BELK (*communications officer*): West Point was a time to get reacquainted with our families. We were all put in the Thayer Hotel, and it was a good feeling to be with my wife and my boys again. We would sit together, or go for long walks on the West Point grounds, and it was just talk, talk, talk—it seemed none of us could talk fast enough. We hadn't seen each other in over a year and a half, and there was a lot of catching up to do. Of course, the greeting you give to a child is totally different from the greeting you give to a wife. Both of my boys were there, and I was struck by how much they'd grown. They were both bigger, stronger, and more intelligent. My only regret is that I didn't have a chance to greet each one of them separately. The excitement level was extremely high, and the demands for my attention were constant. It seemed I was never alone in a room with just one other person. We returned as celebrities and were constantly on the go—meeting people, giving interviews, going to press conferences, and going to receptions and dinners. It was go, go, go. Constant motion. I think that took away from the attention I should have been devoting to my wife and boys. If I'd had some time alone with each of them, I think it would have been easier for me to let them know how much I love them, and how much I missed them.

DON HOHMAN (*army medic*): I remember the day we got back to the States was the day of the Super Bowl. After we got checked into our hotel room, the first thing I did was get a couple of bottles of wine, and my wife and I settled in to watch the Super Bowl. That was nice. We'd talk, and drink our wine, and watch the football game. That was the year the Oakland Raiders beat the Philadelphia Eagles. After the game was over, I called the Oakland locker room. I told the operator who I was, and she put the call through. I wanted to talk to the Oakland quarterback, Jim Plunkett, and somebody in the locker room called him over to the phone. I told him that I was a hostage who had just returned to America, and I said, "Watching you play really made me feel good. I'm a Californian, and I was cheering for you all the way. You were great."

He said, "Well, we won that one for you. That Super Bowl is for the hostages."

CHERI HALL (*wife of Joe Hall*): Before the hostages came home, the wives and families had a meeting with some State Department psychiatrists, and they told about some things to watch out for. One of the things they said was: "Some of the hostages will have a tendency to want to remain hostages. They'll lock themselves in the bathroom, or they'll refuse to go outside. They'll want to stay cooped up in a room." Well, I was very intent on listening to everything the psychiatrists said, and when Joe came back I was constantly watching out for some of the symptoms they had warned us about.

At the hotel Joe started saying things like: "Let's stay in the room tonight. Let's call up room service, and have dinner in here."

I'd say, "No! We're going downstairs to eat in the restaurant." I wasn't about to let him stay in the room after what the psychiatrists had said.

Well, Joe suggested that we stay in the room and call room service a couple of nights in a row, and each time I refused to let him stay in the room. I made him get out. Of course, as soon as we went out the door we were immediately surrounded. There were people all over the place and that part of it was very exhausting.

Finally, when we had the same conversation one more time, Joe said, "Cheri, I'm tired. Aren't you tired? I'm very, very tired."

I thought about it for a minute, and realized that Joe wasn't trying to remain a hostage or anything like that. The poor guy was just exhausted. So I said, "Yeah, I *am* tired. Let's call room service and eat in the room tonight."

CPL. WILLIAM GALLEGOS (*marine security guard*): From our hotel rooms at West Point we could look out and see the police barricades that had been erected to keep people out. It was amazing how many people turned out to welcome us home. And it just kept on going. There were crowds out in the street waving American flags, and reporters and television crews were all over the place. Some of them would try to get into the hotel, and we could see the MPs push them back. It was incredible. None of us could get over what a big deal this was to the rest of the country. It was an incredible celebration, and I was surprised at how it didn't end, but kept on going.

COL. CHARLES SCOTT (*chief of the Defense Liaison Office*): I couldn't help but contrast my return from Iran with my return from Vietnam. When I came home from the Vietnam War, there weren't any brass bands and flags. Instead, we were greeted by demonstrators saying, "Get our troops out of Vietnam!" In the San Francisco airport, an old lady hit me in the chest and called me a baby killer and a murderer. That was the kind of return that was experienced by thousands and thousands of us for the thirteen years that we were coming home from that war. I'll bet that little old lady was out at the airport day after day.

So I really didn't expect the welcome home that we received. Even though we had been told what to expect, I took it all with a grain of salt. My memories were of a different era. I saw mobs and mobs of Americans cheering, and that did me a whole world of good. I could see that it was a reception that cut across all races and age groups. Black and white, young and old, were all involved. The same people who had been rioting in 1968 were now standing shoulder to shoulder celebrating the return of fifty-two of their brethren from an overseas imprisonment. To see and feel the rejuvenation of the American spirit was an amazing thing.

After all of the downers we've had in American politics since World War II, particularly in the Vietnam and Watergate era, the hostages became an international political issue where the United States was clearly in the right. That was important for our people. We needed it. Instead of being a divisive issue, it brought people together. Everyone felt the same way. So when we were finally released, it gave people a chance to celebrate America, and to celebrate the fact that we were in the right. I looked out at those crowds and crowds of people that welcomed us home and said to myself, "Chuck, they're not celebrating you. They're celebrating themselves. You're only a symbol of something that goes much, much deeper than the release of fifty-two people from a foreign prison."

CHARLES JONES (*communications officer*): The celebrations and receptions were continuous. It was like living through a dream. After a few days at West Point we all went to Washington, D.C., where we had a big ceremony at the White House and met President Reagan. That was nice. That was fun.

I think it was only after four or five days back in the States that I started to believe that I was actually and truly free—that it wasn't just a dream—because my daughters and relatives were there with me. Then in Washington a couple friends flew in from Detroit, and I remember sitting and talking with them, thinking, "Well, darn, maybe I really am free! Maybe I can go ahead and believe it at last!"

Then I went up to New York—and pop! It was right back into the dream world.

A large group of us spent three days in New York, and the pace never slacked off for a minute. We had the ticker-tape parade where over a million people showed up, we met the mayor, and we went to fabulous restaurants and Broadway shows. A commission was established to take care of us and show us around. Those people would get us up early in the morning, and we'd have breakfast, lunch, dinner, go to a Broadway show, then to a disco late at night—and during the day we'd have all kinds of official functions squeezed in where we received tributes and awards. The next morning we'd get up early again and keep on going. More restaurants, banquets, Broadway shows, and discos. I don't know when anyone thought we would sleep. But it was fun. They really rolled out the red carpet for us. The pace was so hectic that I fell asleep during *A Chorus Line*. I remember waking up and being surprised that the show was already over. They took us backstage to meet the cast, and one of the dancers—a real pretty little girl—came up to me and said that she was from Michigan and that she would like to have my autograph.

I said, "No, no. I should be asking for your autograph."

So we exchanged autographs, and went on to another exclusive disco. Then the next day it was still go, go, go. As a matter of fact, I fell asleep again the next night at a famous soul food restaurant in New York. Someone came up and took a picture of me sleeping in this restaurant. We were all having a great time, but we were also tired. Very, very tired. A lot of emotion and energy was spent in that first week home, and it wore me out.

RITA ODE (*wife of Robert Ode*): I don't think I realized how many crack-pots there are in the world until after Bob came home. Of course, the return of the hostages was a very, very public affair, so Bob received a great deal of media attention. He was willing to grant interviews and talk with people. The fact that he was so visible brought all sorts of crackpots out of the woodwork. We received quite a bit of hate mail and threatening phone calls, as well as an obscene phone call or two. It got to the point where we hated to answer the phone, because it seemed it was always a reporter or a crackpot. When we first started getting hate mail, my initial inclination was to throw it away. But then I decided that it would be best to save those letters. We have a huge cupboard that is full of hostage memorabilia—news reports, mail, awards, and the like. Someday we will probably give all of that to the Carter Presidential Library so that historians interested in the hostage crisis can have access to it. Instead of throwing our hate mail away, I decided to go ahead and put it in there along with everything else.

JOE HALL (*warrant officer*): I think the kind of attention that we were subjected to when we came home was more damaging to me than anything the Iranians did. There were just too many tugs and pulls for attention from too many people, and I found it to be a tremendous invasion of privacy. I didn't know how to deal with it. The whole time we were gone, the families were literally preyed upon by the media for months and months. Then as soon as we were back, they were just shuffled aside like so much garbage. The only people who seemed to matter were the hostages themselves. My wife never tried to compete with me for media attention or anything like that—in fact, she didn't want it. But all of the attention I was receiving interfered with our ability to relate to each other. I was carrying around a lot of pent-up emotion. My wife and I needed time to get reacquainted and to readjust, but living in that kind of environment made it virtually impossible to do. I think I expected to come back and have everything be exactly as it was before, and of course, it wasn't. While I was in prison, I had a romantic notion of what our release would be like, and that vision didn't include not being able to walk out the door without having a microphone shoved up my nose.

It was difficult for me to comprehend the feeling that America had for us. I guess the hostage situation united the nation, but that was something that I never experienced. My experiences inside the prison were completely different. It was hard for me to accept all of the attention I was receiving. I felt guilty about it. People were trying to turn me into a hero, and I didn't feel like a hero. I felt more like a victim, and a survivor. But not a hero.

You'd think that as soon as I was free, I'd be outside every minute, enjoying things and enjoying my newfound freedom. Instead, I practically went into hibernation, and the media had a lot to do with that. I was almost paranoid. Every time I walked out the front door I was on film, and reporters were constantly calling. Requests for speaking appearances were endless. I soon found that reporters would do anything to get an interview. An unlisted phone number didn't mean a thing. That was the easiest thing in the world for a journalist to get around. I couldn't go visit friends or relatives without having some journalist just happen to drop by, after he had already been told that it would be okay. That made interviews very hard to deny, and as soon as I granted one, somebody else's feelings were hurt because I had told them or one of their friends no. I was literally sick of talking about Iran. I didn't feel that I could go anywhere without being asked about it. Pretty soon, I was just plain sick of people.

The situation wasn't a whole lot better at work, either. I felt like I was being used as some sort of mannequin. A special billet was created for me, just because I was a former hostage. I became a sort of public relations plum, and I didn't care for that one bit. What I wanted was to get back into a normal routine with a job that had some substance and merit to it.

It took a long, long time for me to get over the shock—both of being held hostage, and then returning to America as an instant celebrity. It was several months before all of the attention began to fade and I was able to start enjoying life again. As a matter of fact, I can tell you exactly when I started to come out of my funk. It was the fall of 1981. I remember that was an absolutely beautiful autumn. My wife and I went up to the mountains and watched the leaves turn. All of that color was gorgeous. Breathtaking. Being up there alone in the mountains was when I first started to live again. That autumn was when I started to enjoy being free. Being in the mountains with all of that wonderful color made me feel lucky to be alive.

COL. THOMAS SCHAEFER (*defense attaché*): Being a hostage very definitely changed me. I now have a much greater appreciation of life. I understand that it's a great gift to be able to walk outside in the fresh air. That's a gift I took for granted for many, many years. I also have a deeper appreciation of prayer. I did turn to prayer in Iran, and it got me through some very tough days. But I think the biggest change in me is that I can enjoy each and every day with very little. Prior to being taken captive, I was always concerned about achieving my next promotion, and what my salary was. Things like that. But I've reevaluated that part of my life, and have discovered that those things aren't quite as important as I once thought they were. Being with my family has become a top priority. Just spending time with my wife and family—that's something that's very, very important to me.

CHARLES JONES (*communications officer*): In July of 1981 I was assigned to be vice consul in Vancouver, Canada. Before I left for the post, a couple of people told me, "It rains an awful lot in Vancouver. The weather up there is depressing. Don't be surprised if you go through periods of depression. It's not uncommon, because of the weather."

Well, it does rain a lot in Vancouver. There are probably only twenty or thirty days of solid sunshine a year. But that doesn't bother me a bit, not after Iran. During the 444 days in captivity, I only saw the sun in orbit on three or four occasions, and the moon only once. Now I can walk out and see the sun or the moon any time I choose. And that's special. I've found that since my release I'm much more appreciative of nature. I see the trees and grass and hills and beautiful landscapes, and I love it. The rain doesn't bother me. When it rains the important thing is to be able to feel it, and feel the breeze and the fresh air. I can honestly say that the two years following my release have been the best two years of my life. I think I've grown because of the hostage experience, and I've become a better and more tolerant person. Certainly, I'm much more appreciative of what life has to offer. Right now, my major goal is to finish my last tour in the foreign service, then retire, and do as they do in the fairy tales—live happily ever after.

COL. LELAND HOLLAND (*army attaché*): One of the questions I'm frequently asked is: "Would you ever like to go back to Iran?" And the answer is yes. Now that I've been manhandled in a very unusual way, I'd genuinely like to return to Iran someday. Prior to the takeover there were places that I grew to like, and would enjoy seeing again. Second, I was moved a total of twenty-seven times, and a large number of those trips were outside the embassy. Someday I'd like to go back and see some of the places where they had me holed up. I'd like to see them in broad daylight without a blindfold. It would be sort of like returning to the beach at Anzio thirty or forty years after D-Day.

CHERI HALL (*wife of Joe Hall*): There's an interesting story about the number 444. It's an uncommon number, and not one you'd expect to see very often. But Joe sees it all the time. He'll look up at the digital clock and it will be reading 4:44, or he'll be driving along and glance down at the odometer just as it flips up 444, or he'll be standing by a trophy case and see an award for Troop 444 of the Boy Scouts. He can check a price tag, or be reading an article in a magazine, and that combination of digits will jump out at him. I mean, he sees 444 all the time. And I tell him, "Hey, Joe, you know what that is, don't you? That's God tapping you on the shoulder. He's saying, 'This is your own personal miracle.' It's a miracle that you all got out alive."

Index

Afghanistan, 198
Ahearn, Tom, 79, 80, 81, 166
Ahmed (student guard), 279, 308, 310,
    351, 365–66, 372–73, 382
Akbar (student guard), 123 n, 331
*Alexander Dolgun's Story: An American in
    the Gulag* (Dolgun), 250
Algeria, stopover of released hostages
    in, 433–35
Algerian ambassador to Iran, 410, 434
Algerian intermediaries, 407, 410, 423–
    24, 430–33, 434, 436
Ali (the first Imam), 109, 337–38
Ali (Iranian medical student), 39, 136,
    137
Ambassador's residence (at the U.S. em-
    bassy), 33
    hostages held at, 84–90, 91–93, 94–
        95, 99–101, 102–4, 106–7, 108–
        9, 110, 119–21, 122–25, 126,
        127, 130, 138–39, 146, 149,
        166–68, 175–76, 179, 204, 206–
        11
America Held Hostage (Salinger), 3 n
American School in Tehran, 22
Anders, Bob
    in hiding, 114, 118, 139, 144–45
    on November 4, 1979, 73–75, 79
    return to the U.S., 234–39
Armageddon (Uris), 251
Athens, Greece, 432–33
Australian embassy, Tehran, 201
Azim (student guard), 313

Bakhtiar, Shapour, 8
Bangladesh, hostage from, 125 n
Bani-Sadr, Abol-Hasan, 174, 224, 254,
    273 n, 275–77, 301, 333, 401
"Barnaby Jones," 368
Barnes, Cort
    in the aftermath of the rescue mission,
        311
    in December 1979, 212–13
    in the first month of captivity, 121
    Komiteh Prison period, 357, 403
    liberation, 432

in May to July 1980, 342
on November 4, 1979, 39, 48, 60,
    72, 80, 82–83
in the winter of 1980, 274, 286
Bazargan, Mehdi, 8, 16, 26, 50, 119,
    121, 136
    resignation of, 123, 124, 133, 142,
        152
BBC, 190, 227
Behesti, Ayatollah, 134, 275, 277, 278
Belk, Angela, 365, 366, 439, 446, 448
Belk, Bill
    in the aftermath of the rescue mission,
        308, 309, 325–26, 327
    in December 1979, 184–86, 188,
        189, 200–206, 213–15
    escape attempt, 200–206, 213, 215
    in the first month of captivity, 103,
        104, 109, 121–22, 129, 131,
        132–33, 135–38, 148, 166, 167–
        68, 175
    Komiteh Prison period, 364–67, 375–
        77, 388–89, 391–92, 398–99
    in the last month of captivity, 408,
        410, 411, 412–13, 414, 415, 416,
        421, 422, 423, 426–27
    liberation, 428–29, 431, 432–33, 436,
        437–38, 439, 440–41, 443, 446,
        447, 448–49
    in May to July 1980, 335–37, 345–51
    as new arrival in Tehran, 19, 20–21,
        22–23, 24
    on November 4, 1979, 34–36, 40–41,
        43, 49, 53, 54, 55, 60–62, 63,
        65, 66, 67–69, 90–91, 94
    in the winter of 1980, 245–46, 251,
        252–56, 257, 258, 262, 266, 272,
        273, 275, 276, 277–79, 284, 287
Biafra, 191
Bijon Apartment Building, 33, 114
    on November 4, 1979, 41–42, 44–45,
        46–47, 52, 56–59
Black Americans
    Iranian students' beliefs about, 135–
        36
    release of most held hostage, 159–65

Black Friday, 3–4, 33–34, 138
Blucker, Bob, 166, 208, 262, 287, 420, 425
Brainwashing (Richardson), 111
Brazil, 294, 295
Bremer, Rev. Jack, 293 n, 295, 296
British embassy, Tehran, 6, 73, 74, 201
    protection of Americans who escaped captivity, 118, 139–41
    under attack, 118, 139, 140
Brothers Karamazov, The (Dostoyevsky), 290
Butler, Malcolm, 6

Canadian embassy in Tehran, 144–45
    American diplomats hidden and returned to the U.S. by, 144–45, 219–39, 254
    closing of, 219, 231
Capucci, Archbishop Hilarion, 293 n, 295, 296
Car accidents, 359–62
Carter, Hodding, 119
Carter, Jimmy, 127, 134, 168, 207, 227–28, 326, 428. *See also* Carter administration
    economic sanctions against Iran, 179, 407
    evaluations of policy followed by, 227–29
    meeting with Canadian-assisted Americans, 238–39
    meeting with released hostages, 334, 442–44
    1980 election, 385, 387, 397, 402, 443, 444
    Richard Queen and, 334
    the rescue mission, 301, 443–44
    shah of Iran and, 3, 25, 107, 138
Carter, Rosalyn, 334
Carter administration, 17, 25. *See also* Carter, Jimmy
    in December 1979, 179, 243
    in the first month of the hostage crisis, 99, 139, 154, 174, 227–29
    negotiations leading to hostages' release, 397–98, 407, 410, 418–19, 433, 434
    the rescue mission, 301–2
    in the winter of 1980, 271, 301

Central Intelligence Agency (CIA), 60, 87, 181, 191, 196, 223, 370
    hostages accused of being agents of, 92–93, 108, 111, 112, 126, 127, 138, 157, 165, 181, 205, 362
    Sgt. Subic's "confessions," 213 n–14 n
Chancery building (at U.S. embassy), 23, 33, 108
    hostages held in, 243–47, 249, 251–57, 258, 262–67, 271–72, 277–81, 282, 285–97, 307–8, 327–35, 357 n
    on November 4, 1979, 38, 39, 45, 48–49, 52–56, 59–72
"Charlie's Angels," 369
China, 111, 136
Christmas 1979
    for Americans in hiding, 226–27
    for hostages in captivity, 206–15, 245, 294
Christmas 1980, 409, 410–13
Christopher, Warren, 419, 433, 434
Clark, Ramsey, 134–35, 179
Coffin, Rev. William Sloan, 206 n, 208, 209
Communication among the hostages, 252, 253–54, 255, 256–58, 267–68, 270, 272, 281, 284, 286–87, 288, 293, 297, 322, 344, 345, 346, 350, 351, 363, 374, 375, 378–80, 381, 382, 390–91
Constantine (security official), 38
Consulate (at U.S. embassy), 33
    abandoning the, 72–78
    hostages held at the, 146, 149–57
    on November 4, 1979, 37, 43, 45, 50–52
Cooke, Don, 73, 75
    Komiteh Prison period, 357, 358
    in the last month of captivity, 417–18
    liberation, 434
Cooperation by hostage with the student guards, 92, 213 n–14 n, 268, 270
Coping, ways of, 247–51, 270, 277–80, 329, 337, 365, 368, 374, 416–17
Cottam, Richard, 153

Danish ambassador to Iran, 221
Daugherty, Bill, 318
David Copperfield (Dickens), 290
December 1979, 179–215, 243

Christmas in captivity, 206–15, 245, 294
escape plan, 200–206
the first ten days, 179–84
more interrogations, 194–200
the Mushroom Inn, 184–94
Defense Intelligence Agency, 358, 401
Defiance of the student guards, hostages', 243–44, 251–52, 253, 260, 269, 270, 283, 291–93, 314–15, 320–21, 324–25, 342, 343–44, 365, 382–83, 408, 410, 412, 427. *See also* Escape attempts
hunger strikes, 245, 283–85
Depression, 247, 291, 340
Desert One, 301, 302 n
Diary, keeping a, 280, 322
Diplomacy, 444. *See also* Carter administration; Foreign Ministry, Iranian; Provisional Government of Iran
Clark-Miller mission, 133–35
in the first month of the hostage crisis, 99, 133–35, 174, 179
leading to the release of the hostages, 397–98, 407, 410, 418–19, 433, 434
United Nations Commission of Inquiry, 271, 272–77, 301
in the winter of 1980, 243, 271, 272–77
Dispersal of the hostages, 302–27
Doctors for returning hostages, 423–24, 436, 437, 440, 441–42, 449. *See also* Illness
Doshen Tappeh Air Force Base, 8, 10
Dwyer, Cynthia, 343

Easter 1980, 293–96, 411
attempt to pass notes to religious leaders, 293–94, 295, 296
Economic sanctions against Iran, 179, 407
Egypt, 27, 48
Election of 1980, Presidential, 385, 387, 397, 402, 443, 444
Engelmann, Cdr. Robert
in the aftermath of the rescue mission, 303, 304
in the first month of captivity, 110–11, 170

Komiteh Prison period, 368, 380–81, 388, 390–91, 403
liberation, 432
in May to July 1980, 338, 339
in the winter of 1980, 244, 247–48, 260, 267, 286, 288–89, 290, 294
Escape attempts, 200–206, 213, 215, 345–51, 364. *See also* Canadian embassy in Tehran
thoughts about, 251, 360, 417–18
Ettelàat, 4
Evans, Chaplain, 438
Evin Prison, hostages held at, 306–7, 310–11, 312, 393–95, 396–97, 399–400, 407

Far Pavilions, The (Kaye), 224–25
Fighting among Iranian factions, 325–26, 327, 364, 394
Films aimed at indoctrinating the hostages, 190–91, 207
Firing squad. *See* Mock executions
First month of the hostage crisis, 99–176
Americans who avoided being captured, 114–18
the Clark-Miller mission, 133–35
George Hansen visit, 174–76
at the Iranian Foreign Ministry, 105–6
November 5, 1979, 99–104
November 6–8, 1979, on the inside, 119–33
November 6–10, 1979, on the outside, 139–45
November 7–9, 1979, on the inside, 135–39
November 7–16, 1979, on the inside, 145–59
November 17–19, 1979, 159–65
November 20–30, 1979, on the inside, 165–68
November 20–30, 1979, in Northern Tehran, 168–74
at the U.S. embassy, 106–13
Flogging of Iranians, 313–14, 366
Food, 188–89, 207–9, 210, 211, 213, 214, 215, 253, 277, 294, 296–97, 314, 316–17, 318, 319, 320, 328, 336–37, 367, 395, 399, 413, 415
hunger strikes, 245, 283–85
Foreign Ministry, Iranian, 219, 409 n

Foreign Ministry, Iranian (*cont.*)
the American diplomats as hostages at, 221–23, 224–25, 226, 228–29, 239, 257, 277, 301–2, 357 n, 386
change in the status of American diplomats at, 221
in the first month of the hostage crisis, 99, 105–6, 114, 115, 116, 118, 119, 134–35, 139, 140–41, 144
Ghotbzadeh at, 274–75
meeting of United Nations Commission and American diplomats at, 272–73
on November 4, 1979, 36, 37, 43, 44, 49, 50, 57, 58, 61, 78, 90

Gallegos, Cpl. William, 29
in the aftermath of the rescue mission, 323
in December 1979, 185, 187, 191, 210
in the first month of captivity, 108–9
Komiteh Prison period, 368–69, 387, 393
in the last month of captivity, 424
liberation, 429–30, 432, 435, 441, 442–43, 445, 450
on November 4, 1979, 53–54, 55, 61
in the winter of 1980, 292
Gast, Phil, 26
Geneva Convention, 173
German, Bruce, 23
in the aftermath of the rescue mission, 305, 306–7, 311–12
in December 1979, 189–90, 208, 209
in the first month of captivity, 110, 111, 149, 170–71
Komiteh Prison period, 357, 370, 373, 382, 386, 407–8
liberation, 428, 429, 430–31, 438
on November 4, 1979, 65, 69, 84, 92
in the winter of 1980, 262–63
Germany, stopover of released hostages in, 435, 436, 437–45
Ghotbzadeh, Sadegh, 179, 221, 224, 271, 273 n, 274, 275–77, 301
Gillette, Sam, 184
Goethe Institute, 115–16

Golacinski, Al
in the first month of captivity, 146
on November 4, 1979, 38, 43, 46, 49, 54–55, 58, 64–65, 66, 67, 79, 80
in the winter of 1980, 293–94
Graves, John, 47
in the aftermath of the rescue mission, 320, 326
in the first month of captivity, 136–37, 138–39, 154–55
Komiteh Prison period, 358, 359, 360, 361, 362, 363
in May to July 1980, 320, 326, 351–52
on November 4, 1979, 39, 47
Gross, Kathy, 56, 161, 162–63, 164
Gumbleton, Msgr. Thomas, 206 n

Haig, Alexander, 397
Hall, Cheri, 290, 297, 413, 446, 449–50, 452, 453, 454–55
Hall, Joe
in the aftermath of the rescue mission, 302–3, 304–5, 314, 315–16, 320, 326–27
in December 1979, 180–82, 189, 190, 193, 194–95, 206, 209, 210, 211–12
in the first month of captivity, 100, 102, 110, 119–20, 149–51, 166, 168, 169, 171–72
Komiteh Prison period, 358–60, 361–62, 363, 367–68, 369–70, 371–72, 374, 379–80, 381, 390, 391, 392, 393, 395–96
in the last month of captivity, 409, 412, 413, 419–20, 421–22, 425, 426
liberation, 432, 434, 435–36, 440, 446, 449–50, 452–53, 454–55
in May to July 1980, 351–52
as new arrival in Tehran, 18–20, 21, 23–24
on November 4, 1979, 37, 38, 44, 54, 56, 59, 60, 68, 69, 70–71, 86, 88, 94–95
in the winter of 1980, 250, 257–58, 259, 260, 261, 262, 265, 269,

281, 285–86, 287, 288, 289–90, 296–97
Hamid the Cook (Iranian guard), 373
Hamid the Liar (student guard), 265, 268, 288, 302, 308, 328–29, 345
   death of, 400–401
Hansen, George, 174–76, 185
Henry, Patrick, 386
Hermening, Sgt. Kevin, 21
   in the first month of captivity, 166
   Komiteh Prison period, 357, 358
   liberation, 427–28, 429, 437, 445
   on November 4, 1979, 38, 52–53, 56, 62, 64–65, 72, 79, 81, 82
   in the winter of 1980, 293–94, 295, 296
Hohman, Don, 20
   in the first month of captivity, 125– 26, 128–31, 132–33, 135, 166, 175
   in the last month of captivity, 408, 412
   liberation, 434, 447–48, 449
   in May to July 1980, 327–32, 334, 335
   on November 4, 1979, 38, 46–47
   in the winter of 1980, 245, 246, 251– 53, 254, 255, 256, 257, 263, 264, 265–66, 272, 273, 282, 283, 284–85, 287
Holbrook, Hal, 310
Holland, Col. Leland, 4–5, 6, 181, 182
   in the aftermath of the rescue mission, 304
   in December 1979, 180, 184, 194– 97, 198, 199–200, 210–11, 212
   in Evin Prison, 395, 399–400
   on February 14, 1979, 8–12, 13, 14, 15
   in the first month of captivity, 104, 127–28, 151–52, 169, 171–72
   Komiteh Prison period, 375, 377–78, 379, 382, 383, 384, 386–87, 389
   liberation, 454
   in May to July 1980, 339, 342–44
   on November 4, 1979, 52, 66, 71, 86
Hoseini, Ezz al-Din, 154
Hospitalization of Richard Queen, 332
Hossein (interrogator), 197
Hoveyda, Amir Abbas, 212n

Howard, Rev. William, 206n, 209–10, 294
Howland, Mike, 115
   in April to December 1980, 301–2, 357n, 386
   change in status from diplomat to hostage, 221
   in the first month of the hostage crisis, 105, 119, 134–35, 139
   knowledge of the Americans protected by Canadians, 219, 231, 239
   in the last month of captivity, 409n
   on November 4, 1979, 43, 49, 79, 90
   in the winter of 1979–80, 221–23, 224–25, 226, 239, 257, 273, 274–75, 277
Hunger strikes, 245, 283–85

ICA News Bulletin, 77
Illness, 125–26, 131–33, 167, 188, 247, 249, 260, 281–83, 287–88, 317, 352. *See also* Doctors for returning hostages
   dysentery, 313, 316, 318–21, 338
   mental. *See* Depression; Paranoia; Psychiatrists; Suicide
   release of Richard Queen, 327–35
India, 198
Indoctrination, attempts at, 161–62, 190–92, 207
International Communications Agency (ICA), 141
Interrogation of the hostages, 196–98, 346, 362
   in December 1979, 179–84, 194–200, 210
   in the first month of captivity, 108–9, 111–13, 126–28, 151, 152–59, 173–74
   on November 4, 1979, 92–93
Iran-America Society, 59, 71, 99, 114, 115, 116
Iranian air force, 183
Iranian army, 196, 401
Iranian Majlis. *See* Majlis, Iranian
Iranian National Bank, 6
Iranian parliament, 273n. *See also* Majlis, Iranian
Iranians in the United States, 291

Iran National Works, 389
Iraq-Iran war, 386–90, 391–93, 395,
    396–97, 398n, 400–402, 403,
    407, 412, 417, 428, 432
  death of Iranian guards in, 400–401
Isfahan, Iran, hostages held in, 313,
    321–22, 324–25, 326–27, 335–
    38, 340–41, 344–51

Jahrom, Iran, hostages held in, 339,
    342–44, 375
January to April 1980, 243–97
  April, 291–97
  closing down the Mushroom Inn,
    285–90
  the mock executions, 259–70, 271,
    272, 334
  the rescue mission and its aftermath,
    301–27
  rumors of release, 271–77
  surviving, 277–85
  waiting, 243–59
Javits, Jacob, 17
Johnson, Major Harold, 10
Johnson, Lillian, 114, 115, 116, 117,
    118
Johnson, Lyndon B., 5
Jones, Charles, 21, 27
  in the aftermath of the rescue mission,
    304–5, 311, 312, 317
  in the first months of captivity, 159–
    61, 163–64, 165
  Komiteh Prison period, 371, 372,
    373, 430
  in the last month of captivity, 409
  liberation, 430, 435, 451, 454
  on November 4, 1979, 33–34, 35–36,
    48, 59–60, 79, 81–82, 83, 89–90
  in the winter of 1980, 259, 260, 261,
    262, 267–68, 294–95
Jordan (Iranian working at the U.S. em-
    bassy), 11, 12
Jordan, Hamilton, 243

Kalp, Malcolm
  in the aftermath of the rescue mission,
    308, 332
  in December 1979, 200–201, 205
  in Evin Prison, 401
  Komiteh Prison period, 381–82

in the last month of captivity, 420,
    425
liberation, 430
in May to July 1980, 345–50, 351
on November 4, 1979, 55–56, 62–63,
    65–66, 85
in the winter of 1980, 263, 266–67
Kashani, Mashala, 199
Kaye, M. M., 224
Kean, Dr. Benjamin, 25
Keeping Faith: Memoirs of a President
    (Carter), 3n
Kennedy, Morehead, 170, 368, 408,
    410
Keough, Bill, 274, 286, 311, 342, 357,
    390, 391
Khalkhalli, Ayatollah, 212–13
Khameini, Ayatollah, 277
Khomeini, Ahmed, 121, 275, 276
Khomeini, Ayatollah Ruhollah, 4–5, 7,
    8, 10, 27, 34, 104, 134, 154,
    223, 278, 383–84, 394, 398n,
    399, 401, 444
  belief that U.S. wanted to overthrow,
    154, 158–59, 198
  events leading to release of the hos-
    tages and, 407
  in exile, 3–4, 5, 36
  in the first month of the hostage cri-
    sis, 119, 121, 122, 123–24, 133,
    134–35, 142
  hostages' political importance to, 229,
    396, 397
  illness of, 256–57
  Iraq-Iran war and, 396–97, 402
  order to release female and black hos-
    tages, 159–65
  son of, killing of, 3–4
  student militants' allegiance to, 179
  United Nations Commission and hos-
    tages' release, 273, 275–77
Khorramshahr, Iran, hostages held near,
    318–19, 327, 351–53
Kifner, John, 123n
Kirtley, Cpl. Steven
  in the aftermath of the rescue mission,
    302, 309, 313
  in December 1979, 190–91, 291
  in the first month of captivity, 122
  Komiteh Prison period, 358, 359,

360, 361–62, 363, 369, 373–74, 379–80, 392, 395–96
in the last month of captivity, 417–18, 419
liberation, 441
in May to July 1980, 351, 352–53
on November 4, 1979, 42, 44–45, 52, 57, 94
in the winter of 1980, 269, 289, 291, 292

Kissinger, Henry, 25, 224
Kitty Hawk, 168
Komiteh Prison, 357
camera in the bathroom at, 382–83
guards at, 368, 384–85, 398–99, 400–403, 407
hostages held in, 364–93, 395–403, 407–8, 409 n
hostages transferred to, 357–64
Iranian prisoners tortured in, 366–67, 371–73
TV videotapes at, 368–70
Koob, Katherine, 59, 144, 409 n
in the first month of the hostage crisis, 114, 115, 116, 117, 118
in May to December 1980, 327, 328, 357 n
Koran, 189–90
Krys, Sheldon, 237, 434
Kupke, Frederick L., 23, 35, 80, 368, 408, 442
Kurdistan, 154, 159, 324

Laingen, Bruce, 25–26, 128, 166, 188, 194
in April to December 1980, 301–2, 357 n, 386
change of status from diplomat to hostage, 221
knowledge of Americans protected by the Canadians, 219, 231, 239
in the last month of captivity, 409 n
liberation, 432, 434
on November 4, 1979, 36, 37, 43, 49, 50, 59, 60–61, 68, 78, 90
in the winter of 1979–80, 221–23, 224–25, 226, 239, 257, 273, 274–75, 277
Lambrikis, George, 93
Lauterbach, Steve, 146, 313, 381

LeCarré, John, 224
Lee, Gary, 51, 73, 85, 115
in the aftermath of the rescue mission, 308
in December 1979, 185, 187, 194
in the first month of captivity, 99–100, 120–21, 130, 139, 150, 166, 175–76
Komiteh Prison period, 368, 381, 388, 408
in the last month of captivity, 410–11, 414
in May to July 1980, 339
on November 4, 1979, 42–43, 45, 51, 52, 73, 75–76, 77, 85, 91–92
in the winter of 1980, 248–49, 252, 286, 288, 289
Lewis, Sgt. Paul, 19
in the aftermath of the rescue mission, 303, 313–15
in December 1979, 186–87, 188, 189, 190, 191, 204, 206–7, 208
in the first month of captivity, 101, 107–8, 109–10, 126–27, 136, 176
Komiteh Prison period, 369, 370–71, 378–79, 392, 397, 400–401
in the last month of captivity, 414–15, 422–23
liberation, 430, 434–35, 438, 439–40, 441, 443, 444–45
on November 4, 1979, 34, 57, 88–89, 92
in the winter of 1980, 245, 246–47, 292–93
Lijek, Cora
in hiding, 114, 118, 139–45
on November 4, 1979, 73–74, 75, 79
return to the U.S., 234–39
Lijek, Mark, 182
in hiding, 114, 115, 118, 139–45, 182
on November 4, 1979, 50, 52, 73–75, 79
return to the U.S., 234–39
Limbert, John
in the aftermath of the rescue mission, 320–21, 324–25
in December 1979, 187, 192–93, 206, 209–10, 211
in Evin Prison, 394

Limbert, John (*cont.*)
in the first month of captivity, 100,
102–3, 104, 107, 110, 121, 122–
24, 126, 151, 152–54, 155–56,
158–59, 169, 172–73
Komiteh Prison period, 367, 374–75,
378, 379–80, 381, 383–85, 386–
87, 389, 392–93
in the last month of captivity, 423–24,
425–26, 427
liberation, 428, 429, 436–37, 439,
447, 448
in May to July 1980, 337–38, 340–
41, 344–45
on November 4, 1979, 37, 40, 48–49,
66–67, 68, 87–88
in the winter of 1980, 252–54, 255,
262, 263–64, 272, 273, 274,
276–77, 283–84, 287, 290
Limbert, Parvaneh, 439, 447, 448
Lopez, Sgt. James, 23
in the aftermath of the rescue mission,
305, 314
in the first month of captivity, 167
Komiteh prison period, 368, 378,
396, 408
in the last month of captivity, 408
liberation, 438, 443
on November 4, 1979, 43, 45, 51–52,
73, 75, 77–78, 84
in the winter of 1980, 269–70, 284,
291–92
Los Angeles Times, 10
Lucy, Roger, 233

McKeel, J. D., 42, 204
in the aftermath of the rescue mission,
313, 314
in Komiteh Prison, 397
in the winter of 1980, 245, 246–47,
292–93
Mahalat, Iran, hostages held near, 321
Mail, 191, 211, 213, 265, 279, 280,
289–90, 328–29, 340, 380, 385–
86, 411, 413, 437–38
Majlis, Iranian, 398, 407
Manage (Gary Lee's secretary), 76
Mao Tse-tung, 136
Maples, Sgt. Ladell, 42, 44–45, 161–64,
165

Mary, Sister, 129, 130, 161, 180–81,
421–23, 425
"M*A*S*H," 368
May to July 1980, 301–53
aftermath of the rescue mission, 301–
27
five hostages remaining in the chancery, 327–35
life after the dispersal, 335–53
Media, 120–21, 139, 142, 170, 227,
410. *See also* News from outside
on American diplomats escaping with
Canadian assistance, 237–38
at Christmas 1979, 209, 210, 211
at Christmas 1980, 409, 410–11, 413
coverage of the release of the hostages, 433, 434–35, 437, 438,
445, 452–53
at Easter 1980, 294, 295–96
filming of hostages by militants, 148,
213n–14n
Hansen visit, 176
interviews before the release, 421–23,
425
press conferences, 99, 162–63
Richard Queen's release, 333
release of female and black hostages
and, 164, 165
videotapes of Father Rupiper, 369–71
Mehdi (Iranian student), 193, 398, 407–
8, 424
Mehrabad Airport, bombing of, 386
Meshed, Iran, hostages held in, 312,
317, 323–24, 342, 357
Metrinko, Michael, 49, 67, 400, 427
Mexico, 25, 28, 243
Middlemarch (Eliot), 290
Miele, Jerry, 151, 173
Miller, William, 134–35, 179
Mock executions, 259–60, 271, 272,
334
Moeller, Sgt. Mike, 63, 167, 318, 425
"Mohammadan System," 383–84
Mohammed (student guard), 337–38,
341
Montagne, Elizabeth, 61
Montazari, Ayatollah, 153, 211–12
Moore, Bert, 22, 34, 35, 185, 200–201,
302, 309, 352
Morefield, Dick, 171, 416–17

on November 4, 1979, 37, 72, 73, 75, 76
Morris, Joe Alex, 10
Mossadeq, Mohammed, 7, 154, 278
Mushroom Inn, 34, 146
closing down the, 285–90
hostages held in the, 146–49, 180, 182, 183, 184–94, 200, 206, 211–13, 243, 244, 247–51, 257–62, 265, 267–71, 273–74, 281–85
Muskie, Edmund, 334

Nass, Charlie, 15, 17
Nasser, Gamal, 27
National Council of the Churches of Christ, 206n, 209
Nationalism in Iran (Cottam), 153
National Medal of Honor, 214n
Needham, Capt. Paul
in the aftermath of the rescue mission, 307, 310–11
in December 1979, 179–80, 183, 190, 191–92, 209
in Evin Prison, 393–94, 407
in the first month of captivity, 103–4, 131, 146–47, 171
Komiteh Prison period, 385–86, 387
in the last month of captivity, 418, 425
on November 4, 1979, 71, 80
in the winter of 1980, 251, 257–58, 268–69
Newman Foundation, University of Illinois, 370
News from outside, 257, 324, 340, 341, 345, 380–81, 391. *See also* Media
of imminent freedom, 419–21, 423–24
on Iraq-Iran war, 386
learned through a stolen radio, 254–56, 262, 266, 272, 273, 276, 287
on 1980 Presidential election, 397
about possible release, 397–98
about the rescue mission, 301–2, 322–23, 380–81
about United Nations Commission, 272–77
Newsweek, 70, 227
New York Hospital, 25, 243

New York ticker tape parade, 451
Nimitz, USS, 301
1979
December, 179–215, 243
February 14, attack on the U.S. embassy, 8–15, 16, 19, 29, 104, 303, 315n
the first month of the hostage crisis, 99–176
November 4, 33–95
1980
August to December, 357–403
January to April, 243–96
May to July, 301–53
Presidential election, 385, 387, 397, 402, 403, 444
Nixon, Richard, 229
Niyavaran Palace, 409n
No Hiding Place (Kifner), 123n
Northern Tehran. *See also* Dispersal of the hostages
hostages held in houses in, 149, 168–74, 314, 315
hostages moved back to U.S. embassy from, 179
November 4, 1979, 33–95
abandoning the consulate, 73–78
at the Bijon Apartment Building, 41–42, 44–45, 46–49, 52, 56–59
captivity, 84–95
embassy employees in hiding, 78–79
the foreign ministry, 36, 37, 43, 44, 49, 50, 51, 58, 61, 78
inside the chancery, 38, 39, 45, 48–49, 52–56, 59–72
inside the consulate, 37, 43, 45, 50–52
on the periphery of the embassy, 45–47
surrendering the communications vault, 79–83
under siege, 33–45

Ode, Rita, 411, 447, 452
Ode, Robert, 75
in the aftermath of the rescue mission, 303, 305–6, 307–8
in December 1979, 208
in the first month of captivity, 110, 124–25, 146, 148–49

Ode, Robert (*cont.*)
  in the last month of captivity, 408,
    411
  liberation, 432, 447, 452
  in May to July 1980, 327–31, 334,
    335
  on November 4, 1979, 73, 75, 76,
    77, 84–85
  in the winter of 1980, 262, 264–65,
    287, 295–96
O'Neill, Tip, 174n

Pahlavi, Mohammed Reza, shah of Iran,
    3–4, 5, 85–86, 134, 138, 154,
    162, 190–91, 207, 223, 370, 394
  admitted to the U.S., 25–29, 107,
    137, 239
  death of, 341, 380, 391, 397
  demands for return of, to Iran, 99,
    119, 137, 142, 152
  leaves the U.S. for Panama, 243
  revolution and overthrowing of, 4–8,
    16, 190–91
  United Nations Commission of In-
    quiry and grievances against, 271,
    275
Pakistan, 198
  hostage from, 125n
Panama, 243
Paranoia, 416
Persinger, Greg, 120, 294
  in the aftermath of the rescue mission,
    305, 314, 315, 320, 326
  Komiteh Prison period, 358, 359,
    360, 361–62, 363, 369, 374,
    379–80, 392, 395–96
  in the last month of captivity, 417–18,
    419
  in May to July 1980, 351–52
Philippines, hostages from the, 125n
Physical examinations
  before release, 423–24
  in Germany, 440–42
PLO, 157, 197
Plotkin, Jerry, 125, 323
Plunkett, Jim, 449
Powell, Jody, 174n
Precht, Henry, 35
Press conferences, 99, 162–63
Prison cells, hostages taken to, 306–7,

    310–11, 316–18, 325–26, 357–
    403, 407–8
Provisional Government of Iran, 8, 15,
    16, 17, 18, 24, 26, 27, 28
  in the first month of the hostage cri-
    sis, 99, 100, 106, 119, 121, 123,
    124, 133, 134, 142, 152, 179,
    221
  on November 4, 1979, 44, 48, 64, 78
Psychiatrists, 436, 440–41, 442, 449
Pueblo, 71

Quarles, Sgt. William, 88–89
  in the first month of captivity, 121,
    122, 160, 161–63, 164–65
  on November 4, 1979, 41–42, 44–45,
    56–59, 88–89, 93–94
  release of, 164–65
Queen, Richard, 16
  in the aftermath of the rescue mission,
    302, 304–5
  in December 1979, 188, 193–94, 211
  illness leading to release of, 327–35
  on November 4, 1979, 37, 51, 52,
    72–73, 75, 76, 77, 85–86, 91
  in the winter of 1980, 249–50, 258–
    59, 260–61, 281–83, 285, 286,
    287–88, 296
Qöm, Iran, hostages held near, 313–14,
    319–20

Radford Observer, 214n
Ragan, Master Sgt. Regis, 82, 417
Reagan, Ronald, 397, 401, 402, 417,
    418, 428, 451
Red Cross, 374, 415
Red Lion Society, 129, 131
Rejavie, Masoud, 394
Releases of hostages
  blacks and female, 159–65
  interviews and physicals before, 419–
    24
  in January 1981, 418–55
  non-American, 125n
  Richard Queen, 333–34
  rumors of, 271–77
Religion, 189–90, 248–49, 261, 337–
    38, 365–66
  at Christmas 1979, 206–7, 208, 209
  at Easter 1980, 293, 294–95

Father Rupiper, 293n, 294–96, 369–71

Rescue mission, 301–2, 380–81, 391, 443–44
  aftermath of the, 301–27
  anticipated by the hostages, 148–49, 266–67, 269, 387–88
  anticipated by the Iranians, 168, 170, 357

Revolutionary Council, 66, 67, 105–6, 134, 301
  membership of the, 133–34
  takes over government functions, 133–34, 152
  United Nations Commission and, 273n, 275, 276

Revolutionary tribunals, 212n, 342

Revolution in Iran, 4–8, 136–37, 190–91, 401–2, 403

Reza, Gholam, 384–85

Rinker, Col., 183

Robinson, Capt. Neal, 68, 131

Rockefeller, David, 25

Roeder, Lt. Col. Dave, 158, 303, 321

Roman Catholic Archbishop of Algiers, 206n

Roman Catholic Archdiocese of Detroit, 206n

Roommate problems, 375–77, 378, 415

Roosevelt, Kermit, 154

Rosen, Barry, 6–7, 17–18, 26–27, 28
  in the aftermath of the rescue mission, 321
  on February 14, 1979, 10, 11, 12, 13, 14, 15
  in the first month of captivity, 147, 148, 169–70, 173–74
  Komiteh Prison period, 372–73, 389
  in the last month of captivity, 426
  liberation, 444
  in May to July 1980, 338–39
  on November 4, 1979, 39, 45–46, 47, 86–87
  in the winter of 1980, 262, 287

Royer, William
  in the aftermath of the rescue mission, 306, 307, 317, 323–24
  in December 1979, 207–8
  in the first month of the hostage crisis, 114, 115–16, 117–18, 175
  Komiteh Prison period, 357, 371
  in the last month of captivity, 417, 419
  liberation, 431
  in May to July 1980, 342
  in the winter of 1980, 243–44, 249, 274, 286–87

Rupiper, Father Darell, 293n, 294–96, 369–71, 411

Salinger, Pierre, 3n

Sam (Thai employee of ICA), 141, 143, 144

Saunders, Harold, 49

SAVAK (Iranian secret police), 3–4, 6, 8, 14, 93, 108, 155, 162, 191, 212, 223, 264, 271, 370

Schaefer, Anita, 439, 454

Schaefer, Col. Thomas, 7, 9, 10, 12–13, 14, 54, 106–7, 181, 182, 194
  in the aftermath of the rescue mission, 303–4, 313, 314–15
  in December 1979, 184, 194, 195, 197–99, 200
  in the first month of captivity, 166–67, 171
  Komiteh Prison period, 363–64, 382–83
  liberation, 439, 445–46, 453–54
  in May to July 1980, 338, 339, 340
  previous experience as a hostage, 315n
  in the winter of 1980, 267–68, 279–81

Schatz, Lee
  in hiding, 99, 101–2, 103, 106, 114, 116, 139, 141–42, 143, 145
  on November 4, 1979, 36, 37, 40, 41, 78–79
  return to the U.S., 234–39

Schellenberger, Jack, 10, 15

Scott, Col. Charles, 16–17, 28–29
  in Evin Prison, 394, 395, 396–97, 400
  in the first month of captivity, 111–13, 155, 157–58
  in the last month of captivity, 416–18
  liberation, 436, 450–51
  on November 4, 1979, 43, 44, 55, 63, 65, 68, 69–70, 92–93
  in the winter of 1980, 248, 268

Searches of the hostages, 261–62, 264, 266, 267, 272

Seyyed (Iranian student), 104, 109, 122, 135

Shah of Iran. *See* Pahlavi, Mohammed Reza, shah of Iran

Shahvastari (Iranian employee), 51

Sharer, Don, 103, 170, 260, 395, 417

Shariati, Dr. Ali, 104, 172

Sheardown, John, 144–45, 219, 220, 222, 223–24, 225–27, 231

Sheardown, Zena, 220, 225, 226, 231

Sheikholislam, Hossein, 92–93

Shiraz, Iran, hostages held in, 322–23

Shogun (Clavell), 225

Sickmann, Sgt. Rocky, 29
  in the aftermath of the rescue mission, 322–23
  in December 1979, 204, 207, 209
  in the first month of captivity, 100–101, 124, 138, 147, 167
  in the last month of captivity, 424, 427, 428
  liberation, 431, 434, 435, 441
  on November 4, 1979, 36, 39, 40, 53, 61, 64
  in the winter of 1980, 292

Sixth Fleet, 247, 321

Smoking, quitting, 364–65

Solzhenitsyn, Aleksandr, 169, 252

South Korean hostage, 125–26

Sporting News, 380

Staff houses (on the U.S. embassy compound), hostages held at, 90–91, 92, 93–94, 99, 101, 103, 104, 107–8, 109–10, 121–22, 125–27, 128–33, 135–38, 159–65

Stafford, Joe, 73–74, 75, 114, 115, 118
  in hiding, 114, 115, 118, 139–45
  on November 4, 1979, 73–74, 75
  return to the U.S., 234–39

Stafford, Kathy
  in hiding, 114, 115, 116, 139–45
  on November 4, 1979, 73–74, 75
  return to the U.S., 234–39

State Department. *See* U.S. State Department

Stewart Air Force Base, 446–47

Stone, Gen. Harold, 11

Subic, Sgt. Joseph, 88, 92, 213, 213n–14n, 268, 270
  in the aftermath of the rescue mission, 308, 310, 316, 325, 326, 327

in May to July 1980, 335, 336, 337, 345–50, 351

Suicide, 199, 266, 267, 352–53, 360, 362, 415–16

Sullivan, William, 6, 10, 11, 12, 16, 166

Super Bowl, 1981, 449

Swedish embassy, Tehran, 76

Swift, Elizabeth Ann, 36–37, 48, 49, 68, 69, 327, 328, 357n, 409n

Swiss ambassador to Iran, 150

Swiss embassy in Tehran, 201, 237

Syrians, 197

Tai-Pan (Clavell), 225

Taylor, Ken, 144–45, 219, 225, 227, 231, 232, 239

Tehran Hilton, 303

Tehran Times, 142, 228, 419, 428

Tehran University, 36, 37, 43

Television videotapes, 368–70, 415

Thompson, Rev. Nelson, 293n, 295, 296

"Three's Company," 369

Time magazine, 227, 322

Tom Jones (Fielding), 290

Tomseth, Victor, 16, 17
  from April to December 1980, 301–2, 357n, 386
  change in status from diplomat to hostage, 221
  in the first month of the hostage crisis, 99, 105–6, 114, 115, 116, 118, 119, 134–35, 139, 140–41, 144
  knowledge of the Americans protected by the Canadians, 219, 231, 239
  in the last month of captivity, 409n
  liberation, 431, 443
  on November 4, 1979, 36–37, 43–44, 49, 50, 78, 90
  in the winter of 1979–80, 221–23, 224–25, 226, 228–29, 239, 257, 272–73, 274–75, 277

Torrijos, Omar, 243

Turkey, 432

United Church of Christ, 206n

United Nations Commission of Inquiry, 271, 272–77, 301

United States Information Agency
(USIA), 26
University of Baluchistan, 394
Uris, Leon, 251
U.S. embassy in Cairo, 27, 48
U.S. embassy in Tehran, 29
ambassador's residence. *See* Ambassador's residence (at the U.S. embassy)
the chancery. *See* Chancery building (at U.S. embassy)
classified materials and equipment in, destroying, 48, 54, 60–61, 71–72, 79, 80, 89, 165
the consulate. *See* Consulate (at U.S. embassy)
February 14, 1979, attack on, 8–15, 16, 19, 29, 56, 62, 303, 305n
Mushroom Inn. *See* Mushroom Inn
new arrivals at, in summer of 1979, 18–24
November 4, 1979, events of, 33–95
return of some hostages to, in December 1979, 179, 180
security of, 9–11, 22–23, 24, 26, 27, 29, 33, 34, 36
staff houses. *See* Staff houses (on the

U.S. embassy compound), hostages held at
U.S. Senate, 17
Intelligence Committee, 134
U.S. State Department, 19, 25, 27, 211, 433
Americans returned with Canadian assistance and, 231, 237, 238
in the first month of the hostage crisis, 105, 114, 115, 119, 139
on November 4, 1979, 35, 69

Vance, Cyrus, 25, 238, 322, 334
Voice of America, 301, 397

Waldheim, Kurt, 271
Walker, Sgt., 89
War and Peace (Tolstoy), 262, 290
Ward, Phil, 60, 80
West Point, 447–51
When Hell Was in Session, 310
White, Danny, 214–15

Yaz, Iran, hostages held in, 326
Yazdi, Ibrahim, 14, 15, 50, 78, 90, 199n
resignation of, 123, 124, 221